Frommer's®

New Mexico

10th Edition

by Lesley S. King

Here's what the critics say about Frommer's:

"Amazingly easy to use. Very portable, very complete."
—BOOKLIST

"Detailed, accurate, and easy-to-read information for all price ranges."
—GLAMOUR MAGAZINE

"Hotel information is close to encyclopedic."
—DES MOINES SUNDAY REGISTER

"Frommer's Guides have a way of giving you a real feel for a place."
—KNIGHT RIDDER NEWSPAPERS

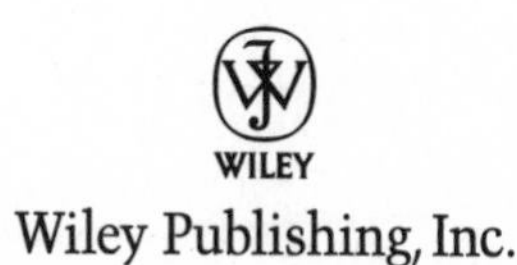

Wiley Publishing, Inc.

ABOUT THE AUTHOR

Lesley S. King grew up on a ranch in northern New Mexico. She's a freelance writer and photographer, and a columnist for *New Mexico* magazine. Formerly managing editor for *The Santa Fean,* she has written for *The New York Times,* United Airline's *Hemispheres* magazine, and *Audubon,* among other publications. She is the author of *Frommer's New Mexico, Frommer's Great Outdoor Guide to Arizona & New Mexico,* and *New Mexico For Dummies.* She's also the coauthor of *Frommer's American Southwest.* Her newest book, released in 2007, is *King of the Road,* and due for release in 2009 is *The Santa Fe Farmers' Market Cookbook.*

Published by:

WILEY PUBLISHING, INC.

111 River St.
Hoboken, NJ 07030-5774

ISBN: 978-0-470-37186-2

Editors: Cate Latting and Jennifer Moore
Production Editor: Michael Brumitt
Cartographer: Roberta Stockwell
Photo Editor: Richard Fox
Production by Wiley Indianapolis Composition Services

Front cover photo: Santa Fe: Dancer in ceremonial feathered dress
Back cover photo: Albuquerque International Balloon Festival: "The Alien Inflation" hot air balloon lifts off in a mass ascension of balloons

For information on our other products and services or to obtain technical support, please contact our Customer Care Department within the U.S. at 800/762-2974, outside the U.S. at 317/572-3993 or fax 317/572-4002.

Wiley also publishes its books in a variety of electronic formats. Some content that appears in print may not be available in electronic formats.

Manufactured in the United States of America

5 4 3 2

CONTENTS

4 SUGGESTED NEW MEXICO ITINERARIES 60

5 THE ACTIVE VACATION PLANNER 71

6 ALBUQUERQUE 78

7 SANTA FE 124

8 TAOS 200

9 NORTHWESTERN NEW MEXICO 244

10 NORTHEASTERN NEW MEXICO 281

11 SOUTHWESTERN NEW MEXICO 302

12 SOUTHEASTERN NEW MEXICO 342

APPENDIX: FAST FACTS, TOLL-FREE NUMBERS & WEBSITES 377

INDEX 387

LIST OF MAPS

ACKNOWLEDGEMENTS

Great thanks goes to Kathleen Raphael who helped research this book. As well, Andi Sutherland aided me in my travels. The assistance of the many tourism agencies, hotel and restaurant owners and managers, and attraction public relations people was invaluable, as was the support of my family, friends, and editor, Cate Latting.

AN INVITATION TO THE READER

In researching this book, we discovered many wonderful places—hotels, restaurants, shops, and more. We're sure you'll find others. Please tell us about them, so we can share the information with your fellow travelers in upcoming editions. If you were disappointed with a recommendation, we'd love to know that, too. Please write to:

Frommer's New Mexico, 10th Edition
Wiley Publishing, Inc. • 111 River St. • Hoboken, NJ 07030-5774

AN ADDITIONAL NOTE

Please be advised that travel information is subject to change at any time—and this is especially true of prices. We therefore suggest that you write or call ahead for confirmation when making your travel plans. The authors, editors, and publisher cannot be held responsible for the experiences of readers while traveling. Your safety is important to us, however, so we encourage you to stay alert and be aware of your surroundings. Keep a close eye on cameras, purses, and wallets, all favorite targets of thieves and pickpockets.

Other Great Guides for Your Trip:

Frommer's Santa Fe, Taos & Albuquerque
Frommer's American Southwest
Frommer's National Parks of the American West

FROMMER'S STAR RATINGS, ICONS & ABBREVIATIONS

Every hotel, restaurant, and attraction listing in this guide has been ranked for quality, value, service, amenities, and special features using a **star-rating system.** In country, state, and regional guides, we also rate towns and regions to help you narrow down your choices and budget your time accordingly. Hotels and restaurants are rated on a scale of zero (recommended) to three stars (exceptional). Attractions, shopping, nightlife, towns, and regions are rated according to the following scale: zero stars (recommended), one star (highly recommended), two stars (very highly recommended), and three stars (must-see).

In addition to the star-rating system, we also use **eight feature icons** that point you to the great deals, in-the-know advice, and unique experiences that separate travelers from tourists. Throughout the book, look for:

Finds	Special finds—those places only insiders know about
Fun Facts	Fun facts—details that make travelers more informed and their trips more fun
Kids	Best bets for kids, and advice for the whole family
Moments	Special moments—those experiences that memories are made of
Overrated	Places or experiences not worth your time or money
Tips	Insider tips—great ways to save time and money
Value	Great values—where to get the best deals
Warning!	Warning—traveler's advisories are usually in effect

The following **abbreviations** are used for credit cards:

AE	American Express	DISC	Discover	V	Visa
DC	Diners Club	MC	MasterCard		

FROMMERS.COM

Now that you have this guidebook to help you plan a great trip, visit our website at **www.frommers.com** for additional travel information on more than 4,000 destinations. We update features regularly to give you instant access to the most current trip-planning information available. At Frommers.com, you'll find scoops on the best airfares, lodging rates, and car rental bargains. You can even book your travel online through our reliable travel booking partners. Other popular features include:

- Online updates of our most popular guidebooks
- Vacation sweepstakes and contest giveaways
- Newsletters highlighting the hottest travel trends
- Podcasts, interactive maps, and up-to-the-minute events listings
- Opinionated blog entries by Arthur Frommer himself
- Online travel message boards with featured travel discussions

What's New in New Mexico

New Mexico has come by its *mañana* reputation honestly. Usually change happens . . . tomorrow. But some lively additions have occurred in the region that are well worth exploring.

A change that affects all here is a new area code. For years, this little-populated state operated with only one code, **505.** It has been retained for the northwestern quadrant, including Santa Fe and Albuquerque. In order to place calls to the remainder of the state, dial **575.**

WHERE TO STAY IN ALBUQUERQUE In recent years Albuquerque has gained some excellent new accommodations. Most notable among them is the **Sandia Resort & Casino,** 30 Rainbow Rd. NE, (✆ **877/272-9199** or 505/798-3930; www.sandiaresort.com). Set against the bold backdrop of the Sandia Mountains, this resort on the Sandia Reservation provides luxury rooms, an 18-hole golf course, spa, and casino. Meanwhile, near the heart of downtown, **Embassy Suites Albuquerque Hotel & Spa,** 1000 Woodward Place NE (✆ **800/EMBASSY** or 505/245-7100; www.embassysuites.com), with a new nine-floor building, caters to a lot of convention traffic, but also offers a comfortable stay to those who like having the space of a suite. See chapter 6.

WHERE TO DINE IN ALBUQUERQUE New Mexico's biggest city has a new hot district called EDo (East of Downtown), where restaurants and apartments have opened up. My favorite here is the **Grove Café & Market,** 600 Central Ave. SE (✆ **505/248-9800;** www.thegrovecafemarket.com). Locals love to hang out here eating soups, salads, and sandwiches made with organic produce and quality breads. Breakfast is a big hit, with the Croque Madame the showstopper.

Not new to the city, but in new digs is **Bien Shur,** 30 Rainbow Rd. NE, at Sandia Resort & Casino (✆ **800/526-9366;** www.sandiaresort.com). Serving New American cuisine, it offers stunning views of the Sandia Mountains and the Albuquerque skyline, while serving such savory dishes as chargrilled buffalo tenderloin and rack of lamb. See chapter 6.

WHAT TO SEE & DO IN ALBUQUERQUE Golfers will appreciate a team of courses that has combined efforts in **Golf on the Santa Fe Trail** (✆ **866/465-3660;** www.santafetrailgolf.com), which includes some of the region's most notable courses and a means of wrapping up packages to save money and time. See chapter 5.

GETTING TO KNOW SANTA FE The City Different now boasts the new 72,000-square-foot **Santa Fe Community Convention Center.** Set in the heart of downtown, it's a graceful Pueblo style structure with a large parking garage underneath. As well as hosting conventions, the site houses the Visitors Bureau and welcomes performances, festivals, and lectures.

Meanwhile, the new **Santa Fe Railyard** is springing to life. This downtown district of shops, galleries, and a park and performance space has given the city a whole new focal point. At the core of the space is a year-round home for the **Santa Fe Farmers' Market.** See chapter 7.

WHERE TO STAY IN SANTA FE One of Santa Fe's most notable historic inns has a new addition. **Bishop's Lodge Ranch Resort & Spa** (© **505/983-6377;** www.bishopslodge.com) has added elegant villas to its lineup north of town. These 2- and 3-bedroom town houses have luxury amenities, spectacular views, and their own pool and Jacuzzi. See chapter 7.

WHERE TO DINE IN SANTA FE Always a fountain of elegant high-end restaurants, Santa Fe has had fewer medium-priced ones. Fortunately, that's changed with the addition of some great informal spots. Most notable is **Clafoutis French Bakery & Restaurant,** 402 Guadalupe St. (© **505/988-1809**). This cafe fills up with locals eating elaborate salads and quiches. Usually they take home a pastry or two as well. See chapter 7.

WHERE TO DINE IN TAOS The Taos dining scene, always imaginative, has a few new notches on its hostess stand. First, **El Meze,** 1017 Paseo del Pueblo Norte (© **575/751-3337;** www.elmeze.com) serves Spanish/Mediterranean cuisine in an artfully decorated historic home. Try the Chilean sea bass with sweet potatoes. The locals' favorite new spot is **Graham's Grille,** 106 Paseo del Pueblo Norte (© **575/751-1350;** www.grahamsgrille.com), where they feast on comfort food such as mac & cheese with green chile and bacon or more elegant fare such as Moroccan chicken over cous cous. Another locals' spot is **Lula's,** 316 Paseo del Pueblo Sur (© **575/751-1280**), where gourmet soup, stews, salads, and sandwiches satisfy hungry appetites both in-house and to-go. See chapter 8.

WHAT TO SEE & DO IN TAOS For years, renegade snowboarders tromped out the motto "Free Taos" on hillsides around **Taos Ski Valley,** decrying the mountain's policy banning them. Finally in 2008, they won, and now Taos is open to boarders. More traditional-minded skiers are upset, but families with kids are overjoyed. See chapter 8.

NORTHWESTERN NEW MEXICO Just west of Grants, **Wow Diner,** 1300 Motel Dr., in Milan, (© **505/287-3801**), serves diner-style food in a Route 66 atmosphere. The pulled-pork carnitas may just be the reason for the cafe's name—"Wow."

South of there along NM 53, stop in at **Ancient Way Café,** near mile marker 46 (© **505/783-4612**). In a wood-paneled room with comfy booths, this place serves imaginative food using such treats as free-range chicken and eggs, hormone-free beef, and seasonal vegetables. Try one of their specials such as chicken and vegetable pesto over chile/tomato linguine.

Nearby, stay the night at **Cimarron Rose B&B,** on NM 53 (© **800/856-5776;** www.cimarronrose.com). An eco-friendly inn surrounded by ponderosas, it offers three suites, a great place for families exploring El Morro, El Malpais, and other outdoor sites.

Visitors to the **Farmington Museum and Gateway Center,** 3041 E. Main St. (© **505/599-1174;** www.farmingtonmuseum.org), will enjoy the new **Geovator,** which simulates a trip 7,285 feet into an oil well. After the trip, you might want to stop in at the new **Andrea Kristina's Bookstore & Kafé,** 218 W. Main St. (© **505/327-3313;** www.andreakristinas.com), for a cappuccino or sandwich.

Nearby Aztec has renovated its 19th-century **historic district** at the center of town, well worth a stroll. While doing so, stop in at **Feat of Clay,** 107 S. Main St. (© **505/334-4335**). A cooperative gallery, it holds the work of 14 local artists and has great prices. See chapter 9.

NORTHEASTERN NEW MEXICO Visitors to Cimarron will enjoy the shopping options there. Step into the **Cimarron Art**

Gallery, 337 E. 9th St. (✆ **575/376-2614**), which has a 1937 soda fountain and sells jewelry, sculptures, and Boy Scout badges. Another good stop is **Blue Moon Eclectics,** 333 E. 9th St. (✆ **575/376-9040**), with artful pottery, jewelry, books, and knives. Down the street, head to the studio of **L. Martin Pavletich,** 428 E. 9th St. (✆ **575/376-2871;** www.lmartinpavletich.com), to find colorful landscape paintings of the region.

Those cruising Route 66 through eastern New Mexico should sidetrack into the **Historic Districts of Tucumcari and Santa Rosa.** Both have been restored and have new galleries and restaurants opening up. You never know what sweet little morsel you'll find. See chapter 10 for details.

SOUTHWESTERN NEW MEXICO New to Socorro, the **Stage Door Grill,** Bernard and Abeyta streets (✆ **575/835-2403;** www.stagedoorgrill.net), offers tasty burgers, pasta dishes, and salads, but its Cajun food is a *real* treat. Try the etouffee.

Meanwhile, Truth or Consequences also has a new place to savor the flavors. **Café Bella Luca,** 303 Jones St. (✆ **575/894-9866**), serves Italian fare ranging from sandwiches to pizza to seafood in a sophisticated trattoria ambiance. Try the seafood puttanesca.

In Las Cruces, train buffs will enjoy the **Las Cruces Railroad Museum,** at the corner of Mesilla Street and Las Cruces Avenue (✆ **575/647-4480;** http://museums.las-cruces.org). Set in the historic Santa Fe Depot, this museum offers exhibits of Las Cruces railroad history from the train's arrival in 1881 to the present.

My new favorite place to stay in the City of Crosses is **Hotel Encanto de Las Cruces,** 705 S. Telshor Blvd. (✆ **866/383-0443** or 575/522-4300; www.hhandr.com). Previously the Hilton, it's been renovated utilizing elegant Spanish colonial-style furnishings throughout.

Las Cruces has a number of new dining options. My favorite is **Mix Pacific Rim Cuisine,** 1001 University Ave. D4 (✆ **575/532-2042;** www.mixpacificrim.com). An intimate cafe full of Asian knickknacks and a sushi bar, this place serves a broad range of dishes, from Polynesian spring rolls to delightful Asian-dressed steaks. Another fun ethnic experience, **Tiffany's Pizza & Greek American Cuisine,** Telshor Tower Plaza G-1 (✆ **575/532-5002**), serves huge portions of true Greek food. It's tough to choose, but today I'll recommend the mousaka. Tomorrow . . . maybe the roasted chicken. Meanwhile, fun-loving diners will enjoy **Farley's,** 3499 Foothills Rd. (✆ **575/522-0466**), a rowdy pub/restaurant with foosball and air hockey to play, and burgers and salads to eat.

Always interesting, Silver City has a few new dining/entertainment spots. **Isaac's Bar & Grill,** 200 N. Bullard (✆ **575/388-4090**), serves tasty buffalo burgers and salads in an atmospheric 1881 building at the center of town. On Saturday nights, live music plays. Meanwhile, **Silver City Brewing Co.** 101 E. College (✆ **575/534-2739;** www.swnmbeer.com), offers tasty beer and a brewpub menu including pizza, pasta, sandwiches, and salads. During warm months, live music plays on the patio on weekends.

The village of Reserve, on the edge of the Gila National Forest, has erected a statue of **Elfego Baca,** a Hispanic folk hero who stood up to some 80 cowboys back in 1884. On the main street through town, it's worth stopping to see. For details see chapter 11.

SOUTHEASTERN NEW MEXICO In the Tularosa/Alamogordo area, stop in at **Tulie Oasis,** 512 St. Francis (✆ **575/585-2102**). Owned by the folks from the Roslyn Café seen in the classic TV series *Northern Exposure,* the cute cafe has a broad menu highlighted by freshly baked breads and seasonal vegetables. The turkey, avocado, and Swiss cheese sandwich on sourdough is memorable.

Nearby, Ruidoso has had tough times in recent years. Flooding of the Rio Ruidoso devastated the town in 2008, but the new **Escape Resort,** 1016 Mechem Rd. (✆ **888/762-8551** or 575/258-1234; www.theescaperesort.com) came out unscathed. The town's finest lodging, it offers 1- and 2-bedroom casitas with contemporary furnishings, nestled among pines. Meanwhile, the new **Hotel Ruidoso,** 110 Chase St. (✆ **866/734-5197** or 575/257-2007; www.hotelruidos.net) offers reasonably priced rooms with comfortable beds and stylish furnishings in a pine-tree setting as well.

Ruidoso's newest restaurant, **Willmon's Prime Grille,** 2523 Sudderth Dr. (✆ **575/257-2954**), serves quality steaks and seafood right in the heart of town. At this writing, it was just getting its bearings, but it has potential to be one of the town's finest restaurants.

If you'd like to end the night with entertainment in Ruidoso, head to **Mountain Annie's Dinner Theater,** 2710 Sudderth Dr. (✆ **575/257-7982;** www.mountainannies.com). Along with dinner, this spot features performances, mostly music variety shows, with tunes ranging from rock to country. See chapter 12 for details.

1 The Best of New Mexico

I will never forget when I was in second grade, standing on the dusty playground at Alvarado Elementary School in Albuquerque, pointing west toward the volcanoes. "We went beyond those volcanoes," I bragged to my friend about what my family had done over the weekend. "No way," my friend replied. Actually, a number of times I'd been much farther than the 10 miles between us and the volcanoes, and I now know that the strong impact of the journey's distance had to do with culture rather than miles.

In a half-day drive, we traveled to the Intertribal Indian Ceremonial in Gallup, where I ate blue, crepe-paper-thin *piki* bread and gazed up at people dressed in dreamy rich velvet, their limbs draped in turquoise. I saw painted warriors twirl in the dust and felt drum rhythm pulse in my heart. In short, we had traveled to another world, and that otherworldliness is characteristic of New Mexico.

Never have I taken my strangely exotic home state for granted, nor has more traditional culture let me. When I was a kid, we used to travel to Illinois to visit my grandfather, and when people there heard we were from New Mexico, they would often cock their heads and say things like, "Do you have sidewalks there?" and "This bubble gum must be a real treat for you," as though such inventions hadn't yet arrived in the Southwest.

Our state magazine even dedicates a full page each month to the variety of ways in which New Mexico is forgotten. The most notable was when a New Mexico resident called the Atlanta Olympic committee to reserve tickets and the salesperson insisted that the person contact the international sales office. So, it seems people either don't know the state exists at all, or they believe it's a foreign country south of the border.

Ironically, those naive impressions hold some truth. New Mexico is definitely lost in some kind of time warp. Its history dates back far before Columbus set foot on the continent. The whole attitude here is often slower than that of the rest of the world. Like our neighbors down in Mexico, we use the word *mañana*—which doesn't so much mean "tomorrow" as it does "not today."

When you set foot here, you may find yourself a bit lost within the otherworldliness. You may be shocked at the way people so readily stop and converse with you, or you may find yourself in a landscape where there isn't a single landmark from which to negotiate.

In the chapters that follow, I give you some signposts to help you discover for yourself the many treasures of this otherworldly state. But first, here are my most cherished New Mexico experiences.

1 THE MOST MEMORABLE NEW MEXICO EXPERIENCES

- **New Mexican Enchiladas:** There are few things more New Mexican than the enchilada. You can order red or green chile, or "Christmas"—half and half. Sauces are rich, seasoned with *ajo* (garlic) and oregano. New Mexican cuisine isn't smothered in cheese and sour cream, so the flavors of the chiles, corn, and meats can really be savored. Enchiladas are often served with *frijoles* (beans), *posole*

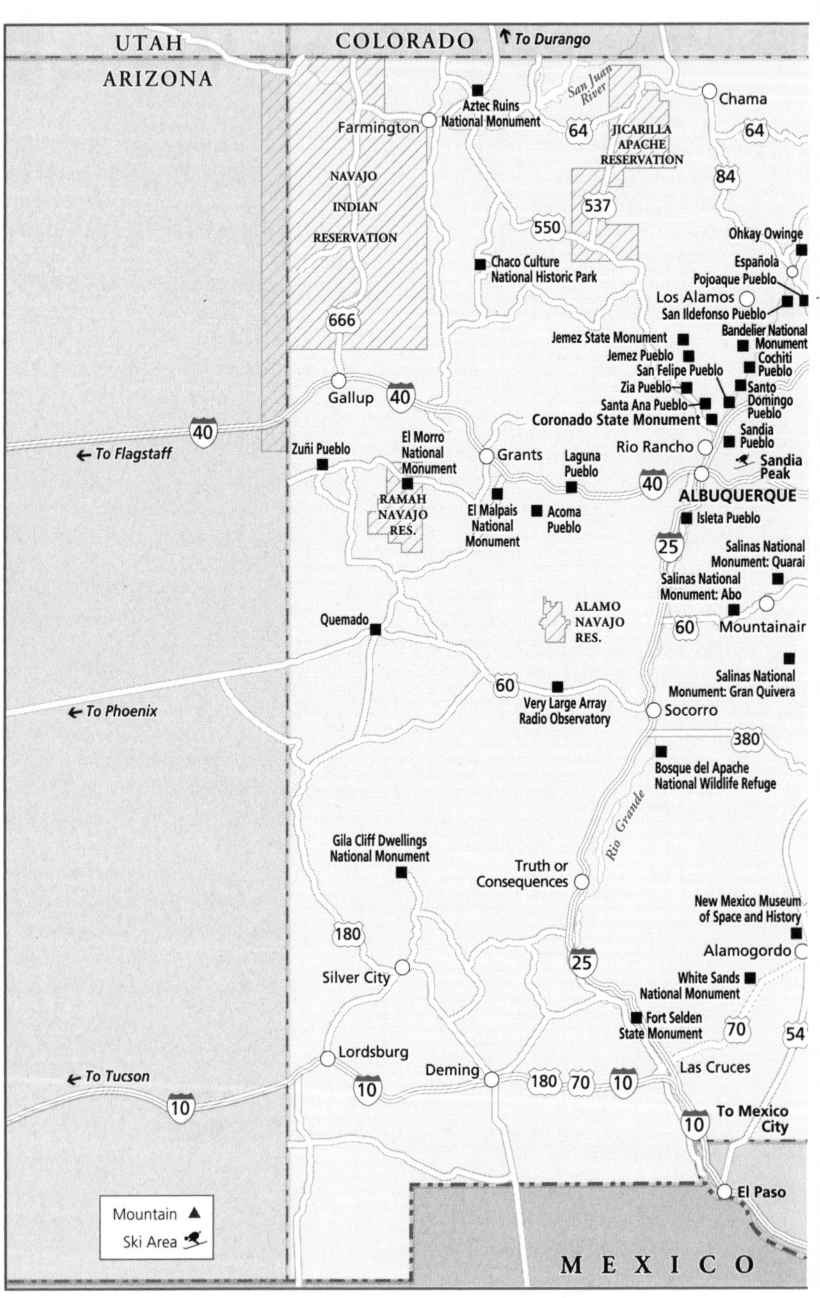
UTAH
COLORADO
To Durango
ARIZONA
Aztec Ruins National Monument
San Juan River
Chama
Farmington
64
JICARILLA APACHE RESERVATION
84
NAVAJO INDIAN RESERVATION
537
550
Ohkay Owinge
Chaco Culture National Historic Park
Española
Pojoaque Pueblo
Los Alamos
San Ildefonso Pueblo
666
Jemez State Monument
Bandelier National Monument
Jemez Pueblo
Cochiti Pueblo
San Felipe Pueblo
Santo Domingo Pueblo
Zia Pueblo
Santa Ana Pueblo
Gallup
40
Coronado State Monument
Sandia Pueblo
Rio Rancho
Zuñi Pueblo
El Morro National Monument
To Flagstaff
Grants
Laguna Pueblo
Sandia Peak
ALBUQUERQUE
RAMAH NAVAJO RES.
El Malpais National Monument
Acoma Pueblo
Isleta Pueblo
25
Salinas National Monument: Quarai
Salinas National Monument: Abo
ALAMO NAVAJO RES.
Quemado
60
Mountainair
Salinas National Monument: Gran Quivera
To Phoenix
Very Large Array Radio Observatory
Socorro
380
Bosque del Apache National Wildlife Refuge
Rio Grande
Gila Cliff Dwellings National Monument
Truth or Consequences
New Mexico Museum of Space and History
180
Alamogordo
Silver City
White Sands National Monument
Fort Selden State Monument
70
54
Lordsburg
Deming
Las Cruces
To Tucson
10
To Mexico City
El Paso
Mountain
Ski Area
MEXICO

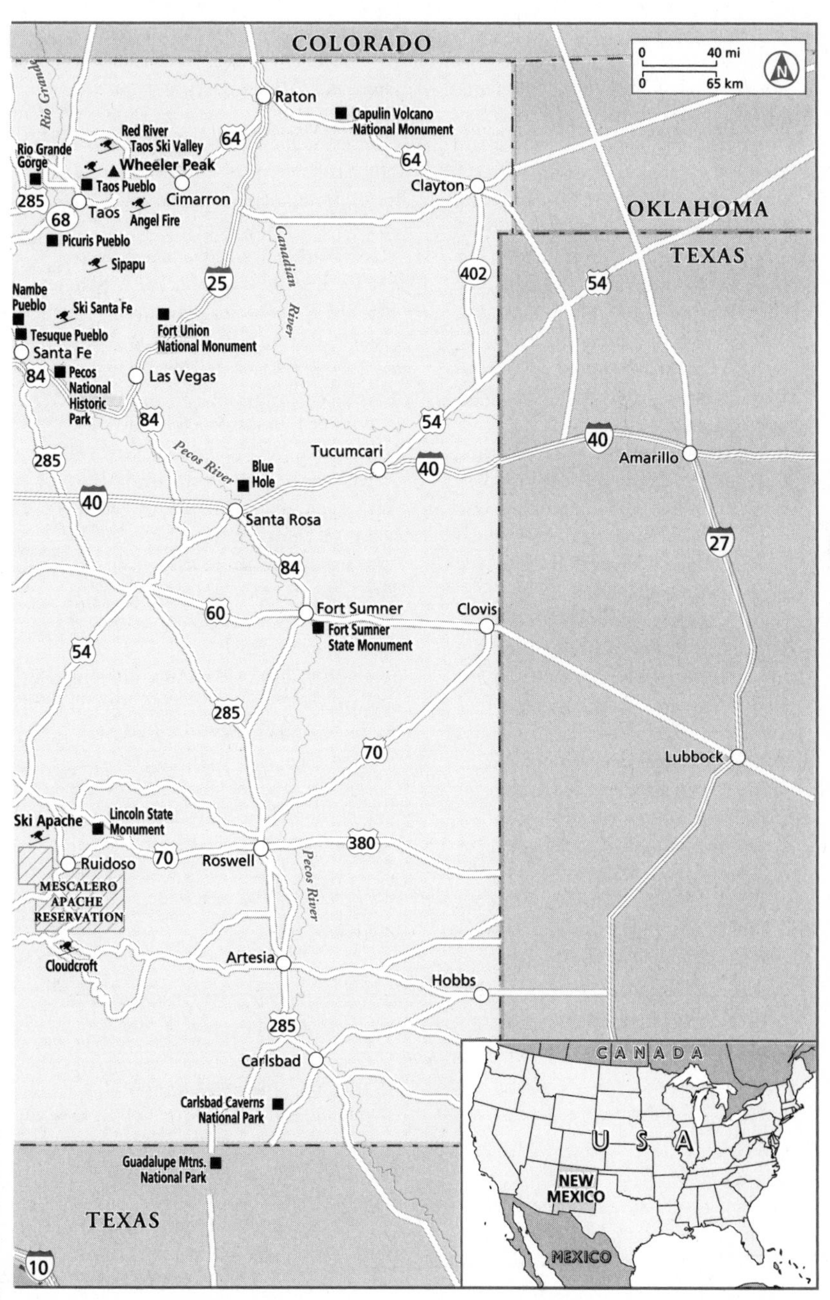

THE BEST OF NEW MEXICO

1

THE MOST MEMORABLE NEW MEXICO EXPERIENCES

(hominy), and *sopaipillas* (fried bread). See "Eating & Drinking in New Mexico," in chapter 2.

- **High Road to Taos:** This spectacular 80-mile route into the mountains between Santa Fe and Taos takes you through red painted deserts, villages bordered by apple and peach orchards, and the foothills of 13,000-foot peaks. You can stop in Cordova, known for its woodcarvers, or Chimayo, known for its weavers. At the fabled **Santuario de Chimayo,** you can rub healing dust between your fingers. See p. 193.
- **Chaco Culture National Historical Park** (Nageezi; © **505/786-7014;** www.nps.gov/chcu): A combination of a stunning setting and well-preserved ruins makes the long drive to Chaco Canyon an incredible adventure into ancestral Puebloan culture. Many good hikes and bike rides are in the area, and there's also a campground. See p. 264.
- **Santa Fe Opera** (© **800/280-4654** or 505/986-5900; www.santafeopera.org): One of the finest opera companies in the United States has called Santa Fe home for over 50 years. Performances are held during the summer months in a hilltop, open-air amphitheater. Highlights for 2009 include the world premiere of *The Letter,* composed by Paul Moravec, the first performance at the Santa Fe Opera of Gluck's *Alceste,* and new productions of Verdi's *La Traviata* and Donizetti's *The Elixir of Love.* See p. 179.
- **Albuquerque International Balloon Fiesta** (© **800/733-9918;** www.balloonfiesta.com): The world's largest balloon rally assembles some 750 colorful balloons and includes races and contests. Highlights are the mass ascension at sunrise and the special shapes rodeo, in which balloons in all sorts of whimsical forms, from liquor bottles to cows, rise into the sky. See p. 96.
- **María Benitez Teatro Flamenco** (Institute for Spanish Arts, Santa Fe; © **888/435-2636;** www.mariabenitez.com): Flamenco dancing originated in Spain, strongly influenced by the Moors. A native New Mexican, María Benitez was trained in Spain, to which she returns each year to find dancers and prepare her show. This world-class dancer and her troupe perform at the Lodge at Santa Fe from late June to early September. See p. 181.
- **Taos Pueblo** (Veterans Hwy., Taos Pueblo; © **575/758-1028;** www.taospueblo.com): Possibly the original home of pueblo-style architecture, this bold structure where 200 residents still live much as their ancestors did a thousand years ago is awe-inspiring. As you explore the pueblo, you can visit the residents' studios, munch on bread baked in an *horno* (a beehive-shaped oven), and wander past the fascinating ruins of the old church and cemetery. See p. 224.

2 THE BEST OUTDOOR EXPERIENCES

For a list of the best outdoor activities, see chapter 5. Here are a few specific sights:

- **Rio Grande Gorge** (Taos): A hike into this dramatic gorge is unforgettable. You'll first see it as you come over a rise heading toward Taos. It's a colossal slice in the earth, formed during the late Cretaceous period, 130 million years ago, and the early Tertiary period, about 70 million years ago. Drive about 35 miles north of Taos to the Wild Rivers Recreation Area. From the lip of the canyon, you descend through millions of years of geologic history If you're visiting during spring and early summer and enjoy an adrenaline rush, be sure to hook up with a professional guide and raft the Taos Box, a 17-mile stretch of class IV white water. See p. 229.

- **Blue Hole** (Santa Rosa): You'll find this odd natural wonder in Santa Rosa, "city of natural lakes." An 81-foot-deep artesian well, its waters are cool and completely clear. Often it appears like a fishbowl, full of scuba divers. See p. 298.
- **Capulin Volcano National Monument** (Capulin; © **575/278-2201;** www.nps.gov/cavo): Last active 60,000 years ago, the volcano is located about 27 miles east of Raton. A hike around its rim offers views into neighboring Oklahoma and Colorado, and another walk down into its lush mouth allows you to see the point from which the lava spewed. See p. 295.
- **Carlsbad Caverns National Park** (Carlsbad; © **800/967-CAVE;** www.nps.gov/ca): Truly one of the world's natural wonders, these caverns swallow visitors into what feels like a journey to the center of the earth, where nocturnal creatures thrive and water drips onto your body. Stalactites and stalagmites create another universe of seemingly alien life forms. Kids won't like the fact that they can't go climbing on the formations, but they'll be too fascinated to complain much. See p. 374.
- **White Sands National Monument** (Alamogordo; © **575/479-6124;** www.nps.gov/whsa): Like a bizarre, lost land of white, this place is a dream for kids. They can roll around in the fine sand or sled across it, all the while discovering the mysterious creatures that inhabit this truest of deserts. Bring extra clothing, sunglasses, and lots of sunscreen. See p. 350.

3 THE BEST NATIVE AMERICAN SIGHTS

- **Indian Pueblo Cultural Center** (2401 12th St. NW, Albuquerque; © **800/766-4405** or 505/843-7270; www.indianpueblo.org): Owned and operated as a nonprofit organization by the 19 pueblos of New Mexico, this is a fine place to begin an exploration of Native American culture. The museum is modeled after Pueblo Bonito, a spectacular 9th-century ruin in Chaco Culture National Historic Park, and it contains a wealth of art and artifacts. See p. 96.
- **Petroglyph National Monument** (6001 Unser Blvd. NW, Albuquerque; © **505/899-0205;** www.nps.gov/petr): This hunting and gathering area for prehistoric Native Americans has 25,000 petroglyphs (prehistoric rock carvings) and provides a variety of hiking trails in differing levels of difficulty, right on the outskirts of Albuquerque. See p. 98.
- **Bandelier National Monument** (Los Alamos; © **505/672-3861,** ext. 517; www.nps.gov/band): These ruins provide a spectacular peek into the lives of the Anasazi Pueblo culture, which flourished in the area between A.D. 1100 and 1550, a period later than the time when Chaco Canyon was a cultural center. The most dramatic site is a dwelling and *kiva* (a room used for religious activities) in a cave 140 feet above the canyon floor—reached by a climb up long pueblo-style ladders. A visitor center and museum offer self-guided and ranger-led tours. See p. 191.
- **Pecos National Historical Park** (Pecos; © **505/757-6414;** www.nps.gov/peco): It's hard to rank New Mexico's many ruins, but this one, sprawled on a plain about 25 miles east of Santa Fe, is one of the most impressive, resonating with the history of the Pueblo Revolt of 1680. You'll see evidence of where the Pecos people burned the mission church before joining in the attack on Santa Fe.

You'll also see where the Spanish conquistadors later compromised, allowing sacred kivas to be built next to the reconstructed mission. See p. 198.

- **Acoma Pueblo** (Acoma; ✆ **800/747-0181** or 505/552-6604; www.skycity.com): This spectacular adobe village sits high atop a sheer rock mesa. Known as "Sky City," it is home to 65 or so inhabitants who still live without electricity and running water. The sculpted mission church and the cemetery seem to be perched on the very edge of the world. Visitors can hike down through a rock cut, once the main entrance to the pueblo. See p. 247.
- **Gila Cliff Dwellings** (Gila; ✆ **575/536-9461;** www.nps.gov/gicl): Perched in deep caves within a narrow canyon outside Silver City, these ruins tell the mysterious tale of the Mogollon people who lived in the area from the late 1200s through the early 1300s. See p. 339.

4 THE BEST MUSEUMS

- **Albuquerque Museum of Art and History** (2000 Mountain Rd. NW, Albuquerque; ✆ **505/243-7255;** www.albuquerquemuseum.com): Take a journey into New Mexico's past and see highlights from the present day in this museum. Displays include Don Quixote–style armor, an 18th-century house compound, and modern art from some of the region's masters. See p. 95.
- **New Mexico Museum of Art** (107 W. Palace Ave., Santa Fe; ✆ **505/476-5072;** www.museumofnewmexico.org): This museum's permanent collection of more than 8,000 works emphasizes regional art and includes landscapes and portraits by all the Taos masters as well as contemporary artists, including R. C. Gorman, Amado Peña, Jr., and Georgia O'Keeffe. The museum also has a collection of photographic works by such masters as Ansel Adams, Edward Weston, and Elliot Porter. See p. 157.
- **Museum of International Folk Art** (706 Camino Lejo, Santa Fe; ✆ **505/476-1200;** www.moifa.org): Santa Fe's perpetually expanding collection of folk art is the largest in the world, with thousands of objects from more than 100 countries. You'll find an amazing array of imaginative works, ranging from Hispanic folk art *santos* (carved saints) to Indonesian textiles and African sculptures. See p. 161.
- **Georgia O'Keeffe Museum** (217 Johnson St., Santa Fe; ✆ **505/946-1000;** www.okeeffemuseum.org): This museum contains the largest collection of O'Keeffes in the world: currently 1,149 paintings, drawings, and sculptures, and 1,851 works by other artists of note. It offers visitors poetic views of Southwestern landscapes both vast and minute. See p. 157.
- **Taos Historic Museums** (Taos; ✆ **575/758-0505;** www.taoshistoricmuseums.org): What's nice about Taos is that you can see historic homes inside and out. You can wander through Taos Society artist **Ernest Blumenschein's home,** which is a museum. Built in 1797 and restored by Blumenschein in 1919, it represents another New Mexico architectural phenomenon: homes that were added on to year after year. Doorways are typically low, and floors rise and fall at the whim of the earth beneath them. The **Martinez Hacienda** is an example of a hacienda stronghold. Built without windows facing outward, it originally had 20 small rooms, many with doors opening out to the courtyard. The hacienda has been developed into a living museum featuring weavers, blacksmiths, and woodcarvers. See p. 223.

- **El Camino Real International Heritage Center** (30 miles south of Socorro off I-25, exit 115; ✆ **575/854-3600;** www.caminorealheritage.org): This museum traces the 1,500-mile historic route between Mexico City and the Española Valley north of Santa Fe. On view are artifacts, art, and devotional items used along the trail, along with state-of-the-art exhibits offering first-person stories of the trail. See p. 306.
- **The Lincoln Historic District** (37 miles northeast of Ruidoso on US 380; ✆ **575/653-4025;** www.nmmonuments.org): One of the last historic yet uncommercialized 19th-century towns remaining in the American West, Lincoln was the focal point of the Lincoln Country War of 1878–79. The town saw some of Billy the Kid's most renowned exploits. See p. 355.

5 THE BEST HISTORICAL SIGHTS

- **Old Town** (Albuquerque): Once the center of Albuquerque commerce, Old Town thrived until the early 1880s, when businesses relocated nearer to the railroad tracks. It has been a center of tourism since being rediscovered in the 1930s. Today you can visit shops, galleries, and restaurants in Old Town, as well as the Church of San Felipe de Neri, the first structure built when colonists established Albuquerque in 1706. See p. 98.
- **Georgia O'Keeffe's Home** (Abiquiu; ✆ **505/685-4539**): Hand-smoothed adobe walls, elk antlers, and a blue door—you'll encounter these images and many more that inspired the famous artist's work. When you view the landscape surrounding her residence in Abiquiu, you'll understand why she was so inspired. Be sure to make a reservation months in advance. See p. 197.
- **Palace of the Governors** (North Plaza, Santa Fe; ✆ **505/476-5100;** www.palaceofthegovernors.org): This is where, in 1680, the only successful Native American uprising took place. Before the uprising, this was the seat of power in the area, and after de Vargas reconquered the American Indians, it resumed that position. Built in 1610 as the original capitol of New Mexico, the palace has been in continuous public use longer than any other structure in the United States. Look for remnants of the history this building has seen through the years, such as a fireplace and chimney chiseled into the adobe wall, and storage pits where the Pueblo Indians kept corn, wheat, barley, and other goods during their reign at the palace. After the reconquest, the pits were used to dispose of trash. Most notable is the front of the palace, where Native Americans sell jewelry, pottery, and some weavings under the protection of the portal. See p. 157.
- **St. Francis Cathedral** (Cathedral Place at San Francisco St., Santa Fe; ✆ **505/982-5619**): Santa Fe's grandest religious structure was built between 1869 and 1886 by Archbishop Jean Baptiste Lamy, in the style of the great cathedrals of Europe. Inside the small adobe, Our Lady of the Rosary chapel is full of the romance of Spanish Catholicism. The chapel was built in 1807 and is the only portion that remains from Our Lady of the Assumption Church, founded along with Santa Fe in 1610. See p. 158.
- **San Francisco de Asis church** (Ranchos de Taos Plaza, Taos; ✆ **505/758-2754**): This is one the world's more

beautiful churches. Though some might not see how it could compete with elaborate structures such as Chartres or Notre Dame de Paris, it's like a Picasso sculpture: Simple and direct, it has massive, hand-smoothed adobe walls and a rising sense that nearly lifts the heavy structure off the ground. Maybe that's why such notables as Ansel Adams and Georgia O'Keeffe have recorded its presence in art. See p. 222.

- **El Morro National Monument** (Ramah; ✆ **505/783-4226;** www.nps.gov/elmo): In the Grants area, this sandstone monolith is known as "Inscription Rock," because travelers and explorers documented their journeys for centuries on its smooth face. See p. 253.
- **Cimarron:** Nestled against the eastern slope of the Sangre de Cristo mountain range, this town was a "wild and woolly" outpost on the Santa Fe Trail between the 1850s and 1880s and a gathering place for area ranchers, traders, gamblers, gunslingers, and other characters. See p. 290.
- **New Mexico Museum of Space History** (NM 2001, Alamogordo; ✆ **877/333-6589** outside NM, or 575/437-2840; www.spacefame.org): Tracing the story of space travel, this five-story museum recalls the accomplishments of America's Mercury, Gemini, and Apollo programs, including New Mexico's participation in space exploration, from ancient American Indians to rocketry pioneer Robert Goddard to astronauts. See p. 345.

6 THE BEST FAMILY EXPERIENCES

- **Albuquerque Aquarium** (2601 Central Ave. NW; ✆ **505/764-6200;** www.cabq.gov/biopark): Exhibits here focus on sea areas fed by the Rio Grande. You'll pass by many large tanks and within an eels' den; the star attraction is a 285,000-gallon shark tank, where many species of fish and 15 to 20 sand tiger, brown, and nurse sharks swim around, looking ominous. See p. 99.
- **Albuquerque Botanic Garden** (2601 Central Ave. NW; ✆ **505/764-6200;** www.cabq.gov/biopark): Within a state-of-the-art conservatory, a desert collection features plants from the lower Chihuahuan and Sonoran deserts, and a Mediterranean collection includes many exotic species native to the Mediterranean climates of Southern California, South Africa, Australia, and the Mediterranean Basin. See p. 99.
- **Rio Grande Zoo** (903 10th St. SW, Albuquerque; ✆ **505/764-6200;** www.cabq.gov/biopark/zoo): More than 250 species live on 64 acres of riverside bosque among ancient cottonwoods. Open-moat exhibits with animals in naturalized habitats are a treat for zoo-goers. Major exhibits include the polar bears, the giraffes, the sea lions (with underwater viewing), the cat walk, the bird show, and ape country, with its gorilla and orangutans. See p. 101.
- **Sandia Peak Tramway** (10 Tramway Loop NE, Albuquerque; ✆ **505/856-7325;** www.sandiapeak.com): The world's longest tramway ferries passengers about 3 miles from Albuquerque's city limits almost to the summit of the 10,678-foot Sandia Peak. On the way, you may see birds of prey and rare Rocky Mountain bighorn sheep. Go in the evening to watch the sun burn its way out of the western sky; then enjoy the glimmering city lights on your way down. See p. 99.
- **El Rancho de las Golondrinas** (334 Los Pinos Rd., Santa Fe; ✆ **505/471-2261;** www.golondrinas.org): This living museum re-creates an 18th- and

19th-century Spanish village. Kids like to visit the working molasses mill, the blacksmith shop, the shearing and weaving rooms, and the water mills, as well as the resident animals. See p. 164.

- **Santa Fe Children's Museum** (1050 Old Pecos Trail; © **505/989-8359;** www.santafechildrensmuseum.org): Designed for the whole family to experience, this museum offers interactive exhibits and hands-on activities in the arts, humanities, science, and technology. Most notable is a 16-foot climbing wall that kids can scale, outfitted with helmets and harnesses. A 1-acre Southwestern horticulture garden features animals, wetlands, and a greenhouse. *Family Life* magazine named this one of the 10 hottest children's museums in the nation. See p. 166.
- **New Mexico Mining Museum** (100 N. Iron Ave., Grants; © **800/748-2142** or 505/287-4802; www.grants.org): This museum takes you down into a spooky, low-lit replica mine. You begin in the station where uranium was loaded and unloaded, and travel back into the earth through places defined on wall plaques with such interesting names as "track drift" (where ore comes up in cars from the mine) and "stope" (a room stripped of all ore and off-limits in an actual mine). See p. 249.
- **Living Desert Zoo & Gardens State Park** (1504 Miehls Dr., Carlsbad; © **575/887-5516;** www.emnrd.state.nm.us/PRD/LivingDesert.htm): Spread across a vast plateau, this park offers visitors an hour-long trek through desert lands full of odd plants that survive on who-knows-what to zoo exhibits of hawks, cats, and bears. What's best about this zoo is that the animals aren't just captive, they're rehabilitating. See p. 370.

7 THE BEST SPLURGE HOTELS

- **Hyatt Regency Tamaya Resort and Spa** (1300 Tuyuna Trail, Santa Ana Pueblo; © **800/55-HYATT** or 505/867-1234; www.tamaya.hyatt.com): Situated on Santa Ana Pueblo land, this grand resort has all a person might need to get away from the world. Three swimming pools, a 16,000-square-foot full-service spa and fitness center, the 18-hole Twin Warriors Championship Golf Course designed by Gary Panks, and views of the Sandia Mountains make for plenty to do. It's only 25 minutes from Albuquerque and 45 minutes from Santa Fe. See p. 88.
- **Sandia Resort & Casino** (30 Rainbow Rd. NE, Albuquerque; © **877/272-9199;** www.sandiaresort.com), one of the state's newer luxury resort, offers spacious rooms, an 18-hole golf course, and gambling. With views toward the city and the Sandia Mountains, it's picturesque as well. See p. 84.
- **Bishop's Lodge** (Bishop's Lodge Rd., Santa Fe; © **505/983-6377;** www.bishopslodge.com): More than a century ago, Bishop Jean Baptiste Lamy often escaped clerical politics by hiking into a valley north of town called Little Tesuque. He built a retreat and chapel that years later have become the Bishop's Lodge. All rooms are spacious and feature handcrafted furniture and local artwork. Activities include horseback riding, hiking, tennis, swimming, and spa treatments. See p. 137.
- **La Posada de Santa Fe Resort and Spa** (330 E. Palace Ave., Santa Fe; © **800/727-5276** or 505/986-0000; www.laposadadesantafe.com): With the feel of a meandering adobe village but the service of a fine hotel, this has become

one of New Mexico's premier resorts. It has an elegant spa and pool and spacious spa rooms. Most rooms don't have views but have outdoor patios, and most are tucked back into the quiet compound. See p. 133.

- **Inn of the Five Graces** (150 E. de Vargas St., Santa Fe; ✆ **505/992-0957;** www.fivegraces.com) offers an exotic Southwest meets the Orient experience right in Santa Fe. Ornately carved beds, elaborate tile work, and cozy linens add up to an especially sumptuous stay. See p. 133.
- **Rancho de San Juan** (US 285 near Española; ✆ **505/753-6818;** www.ranchodesanjuan.com): Located in the enchanting country near Ojo Caliente, this award-winning inn offers complete luxury and the quiet of the country. Private casitas set among the hills are decorated with antiques and have spectacular views. See p. 198.
- **El Monte Sagrado** (317 Kit Carson Rd., Taos; ✆ **800/828-TAOS** or 575/758-3502; www.elmontesagrado.com): With guest rooms and casitas set around a grassy "Sacred Circle," this eco-resort is the quintessence of luxury. Every detail, from the waterfalls and chemical-free pool and hot tubs to the authentic theme decor in the rooms, has been created with conscious care. See p. 205.
- **Casa Blanca** (505 E. La Plata St., Farmington; ✆ **800/550-6503** or 505/327-6503; www.casablancanm.com): This inn offers patios, fountains, and lush gardens set on a ridge overlooking Farmington. The rooms have elegant furnishings rich in Native American and world folk art. The full breakfast included with the room is always gourmet. See p. 272.
- **Bear Mountain Lodge** (2251 Cottage San Rd., Silver City; ✆ **877/620-BEAR** or 575/538-2538; www.bearmountainlodge.com): This lodge, owned and managed by the Nature Conservancy, offers a nature-lover's paradise. The inn itself was built in 1928, but the grounds show evidence of visitors dating from 6000 B.C. Nature Conservancy staff members are on hand to guide visitors in their bird-, wildlife-, and plant-viewing pursuits. Rooms are large, with maple floors, high ceilings, and French windows. See p. 336.
- **Inn of the Mountain Gods Resort & Casino** (287 Carrizo Canyon Rd., Mescalero; ✆ **800/545-9011** or 575/464-7777; www.innofthemountaingods.com): Even though the architecture of this hotel on the Mescalero Apache Indian Reservation is a bit cold, the setting in the pines on the edge of a blue lake compensates, as do the spacious rooms, the lush bedding, and the many activity options, ranging from gambling to fishing to golf to skiing. See p. 357.
- **The Lodge at Cloudcroft** (1 Corona Place, Cloudcroft; ✆ **800/395-6343** or 575/682-2566; www.thelodgeresort.com): For those who enjoy the old-world style of a Victorian hotel, this lodge nestled on a pine-covered hilltop in southern New Mexico will certainly please. Rooms in the lodge are filled with antiques, from sideboards and lamps to mirrors and steam radiators. A high-elevation golf course and a new spa round out the experience. See p. 349.

8 THE BEST MODERATELY PRICED HOTELS

- **Nativo Lodge** (6000 Pan American Fwy. NE, Albuquerque; ✆ **888/628-4861** or 505/798-4300; www.nativolodge.com.): Utilizing a Native American theme, this hotel on the north end of town offers standard size rooms with a bit of designer flair and plenty of amenities, all at a reasonable price. See p. 86.

- **El Rey Inn** (1862 Cerrillos Rd., Santa Fe; ✆ **800/521-1349** or 505/982-1931; www.elreyinnsantafe.com): If old-style court motels awaken the road warrior in you, this is your place. Built in the 1930s and added onto over the years, this place provides a variety of types of rooms, all nicely appointed. See p. 139.
- **Santa Fe Motel and Inn** (510 Cerrillos Rd., Santa Fe; ✆ **800/930-5002** or 505/982-1039; www.santafemotel.com): Rooms at this inn are walking distance from the Plaza and provide ambience of the Southwest—bold colors and some handmade furniture—with a standard motel price tag. See p. 136.
- **Old Taos Guesthouse Bed & Breakfast** (1028 Witt Rd., Taos; ✆ **800/758-5448** or 575/758-5448; www.oldtaos.com): Set in a 190-year-old adobe dwelling, this inn offers acres of quiet within minutes of downtown Taos. Rooms range from atmospheric to very practical, all with comfortable beds. A family-run business, its owners take good care of their guests. See p. 211.
- **Step Back Inn** (103 W. Aztec Blvd., Aztec; ✆ **800/334-1255** or 505/334-1200): In a modern building, this hotel presents a good dose of Victorian charm. Rooms are spacious and quiet, with unique touches such as colorful wallpaper and antique armoire reproductions. Each is named after an early pioneer of the area. See p. 272.
- **Inn on the Santa Fe Trail** (1133 Grand Ave., Las Vegas; ✆ **888/448-8438** or 505/425-6791; www.innonthesantafetrail.com): This 1920s court motel set around a grassy courtyard has been restored to provide comfortable Southwestern style rooms with nice accents such as hand-crafted furniture and light fixtures. See p. 288.

9 THE BEST DINING EXPERIENCES

- **Bien Shur** (30 Rainbow Rd. NE., at Sandia Resort & Casino; ✆ **800/526-9366;** www.sandiaresort.com): Unforgettable views and finely prepared cuisine create an outstanding experience at this restaurant atop Sandia Resort. For entrees, the rack of lamb with a garlic mint au jus is excellent. See p. 93.
- **The Compound** (653 Canyon Rd., Santa Fe; ✆ **505/982-4353;** www.compoundrestaurant.com): This reincarnation of one of Santa Fe's classic restaurants serves daring contemporary American food in a soulful setting. Such delicacies as monkfish chorizo with watercress or grilled beef tenderloin with Italian potatoes will please sophisticated palates—and probably simpler ones, too. See p. 146.
- **Santacafé** (231 Washington Ave., Santa Fe; ✆ **505/984-1788;** www.santacafe.com): This restaurant, my all-time favorite, borrows from an international menu of preparations and offerings. The minimalist decor accentuates the beautiful architecture of the 18th-century Padre Gallegos House. One of the best dishes is the Alaskan halibut with English peas and saffron couscous. See p. 150.
- **Geronimo** (724 Canyon Rd., Santa Fe; ✆ **505/982-1500;** www.geronimorestaurant.com): Set in the 1756 Borrego House on Canyon Road, this restaurant offers brilliant flavors in a serene adobe atmosphere. The elk tenderloin here is Santa Fe's most prized entree. See p. 148.
- **The Shed** (113½ E. Palace Ave., Santa Fe; ✆ **505/982-9030;** www.sfshed.com): The Shed, a Santa Fe luncheon institution since 1953, occupies a rambling hacienda that was built in 1692.

The sauces here have been refined over the years, creating amazing flavors in basic dishes such as enchiladas, burritos, and stuffed *sopaipillas.* The mocha cake is renowned. See p. 155. Its sister restaurant, **La Choza,** is just as good, with a similar menu. See p. 154.

- **De La Tierra** (317 Kit Carson Rd., Taos; ✆ **800/828-TAOS** or 575/758-3502; www.elmontesagrado.com): Located at the ecoresort El Monte Sagrado, this elegant restaurant serves imaginative regional American food. The pan roasted east coast cod served with truffle Persian potatoes is delectable. An expansive wine list completes the experience. See p. 214.
- **Joseph's Table** (108-A S. Taos Plaza, Taos; ✆ **575/751-4512;** www.josephstable.com): Located on Taos Plaza, this font of creativity serves delightful dishes with plenty of flair. Try the steak au poivre over mashed potatoes with a Madeira mushroom sauce. See p. 216.
- **The Bluffs** (3450 E. Main St., Farmington; ✆ **505/325-8155**): Wooden partitions topped with glazed glass shaped like towering bluffs surround diners at this restaurant serving sandwiches and salads at lunch and steaks and seafood at dinner. The turkey bacon club is amazing, as are any of the angus beef steaks. See p. 273.
- **Blackjack's Grill** (1133 Grand Ave., Las Vegas; ✆ **888/448-8438** or 505/425-6791): One of the region's most sophisticated restaurants, Blackjack's serves tasty steaks and seafood in a festive atmosphere, especially on the patio, where diners sit under elm trees. My favorite dish is sautéed beef medallions with garlic mashed potatoes. See p. 289.
- **Double Eagle** (2355 Calle de Guadalupe, Las Cruces; ✆ **575/523-6700;** www.double-eagle-messilla.com): Continental cuisine is alive and well behind the walls of this historic hacienda located in Las Cruces. The decor is lush and dramatic—chandeliers hung with Baccarat crystals—and the food is richly traditional. Steaks are the way to go. See p. 325.
- **Diane's Bakery & Cafe** (510 N. Bullard St., Silver City; ✆ **575/538-8722**): Diane Barrett, who was once a pastry chef at La Traviata and Eldorado in Santa Fe, has brought refined flavors to the little mining town of Silver City. Come here to feast on sumptuous baked goods and sophisticated meals such as rack of lamb. See p. 337.

2 New Mexico in Depth

When I was a child in New Mexico, we'd sing a song while driving the dusty roads en route to such ruins as Chaco Canyon or Puye Cliff Dwellings. Sung to the tune of "Oh Christmas Tree," it went like this:

New Mexico, New Mexico
Don't know why we love you so.
It never rains
It never snows
The winds and sand
They always blow.
And how we live
God only knows
New Mexico, we love you so.

Although this song exaggerates the conditions here, the truth remains that in many ways New Mexico has an inhospitable environment. So why are so many people drawn here, and why do so many of us stay?

Ironically, the very extremes that this song presents are the reason. In this 121,666-square-mile state, you are met with wildly varied terrain, temperature, and temperament. On a single day you might experience temperatures from 25° to 75°F (–4° to 24°C). From the vast heat and dryness of White Sands in the summer to the 13,161-foot subzero, snow-encrusted Wheeler Peak in the winter, New Mexico's beauty is carved by extremes.

Culturally, this is also the case. Pueblo, Navajo, and Apache tribes occupy much of the state's lands, many of them still speaking their native languages and living within the traditions of their people. Some even live without running water and electricity. Meanwhile, the Hispanic culture remains deeply linked to its Spanish roots, practicing a devout Catholicism, and speaking a centuries-old Spanish dialect, some still living by subsistence farming in mountain villages.

New Mexico has its own sense of time and unique social mores. The pace is slower here, the objectives of life less defined. People rarely arrive on time for appointments, and businesses don't always hold to their posted hours. In most cases, people wear whatever they want here. You'll see men dressed for formal occasions wearing a buttoned collar with a bolo tie and women in cowboy boots and broomstick skirts.

All this leads to a certain lost-and-not-caring-to-be-found spell the place casts on visitors that's akin to some kind of voodoo magic. We find ourselves standing amid the dust or sparkling light, within the extreme heat or cold, not sure whether to speak Spanish or English. That's when we let go completely of society's common goals, its pace, and expectations. We slip into a kayak and let the river take us, or hike a peak and look at the world from a new perspective. Or we climb into a car and drive past ancient ruins being excavated at that instant, past ghost mining towns, and under hot-air balloons, by chile fields and around hand-smoothed *santuarios,* all on the road to nowhere, New Mexico's best destination. At some point in your travels, you'll likely find yourself on this road, and you'll realize that there's no destination so fine.

1 NEW MEXICO TODAY: FROM FLAMENCO TO CRAPS

GROWING PAINS

New Mexico is experiencing a reconquest of sorts, as the Anglo population soars and outside money and values again make their way in. The process continues to transform New Mexico's three distinct cultures and their unique ways of life, albeit in a less violent manner than during the Spanish conquest.

Certainly, the Anglos—many of them from large cities—add a cosmopolitan flavor to life here. The variety of restaurants has greatly improved, as have entertainment options. For their small size, towns such as Taos and Santa Fe offer a broad variety of restaurants and cultural events. Santa Fe has developed a strong dance and drama scene, with treats such as flamenco and opera that you'd expect to find in New York or Los Angeles. And Albuquerque has an exciting nightlife scene downtown; you can walk from club to club and hear a wealth of jazz, rock, country, and alternative music.

Transformation of the local way of life and landscape is also apparent in the stores continually springing up in the area. For some, these are a welcome relief from Western clothing stores and provincial dress shops. The downside is that city plazas, which once contained pharmacies and grocery stores frequented by residents, are now crowded with T-shirt shops and galleries appealing to tourists. Many locals now rarely visit their plazas except during special events.

Environmental threats are another regional reality. Nuclear-waste issues form part of an ongoing conflict affecting the entire Southwest, and a section of southern New Mexico has been designated a nuclear-waste site. Because much of the waste must pass through Santa Fe, the U.S. government, along with the New Mexico state government, constructed a bypass that directs some transit traffic around the west side of the city.

New ways of thinking have also brought positive changes to the life here, and many locals have benefited from New Mexico's influx of wealthy newcomers and popularity as a tourist destination. Businesses and industries large and small have come to the area. In Albuquerque, Intel Corporation now employs more than 3,300 workers, and in Santa Fe, the magazine *Outside* publishes monthly. Local artists and artisans also benefit from growth. Many craftspeople have expanded their businesses. The influx of people has broadened the sensibility of a fairly provincial state. The area has become a refuge for many gay and lesbian people, as well as for political exiles, such as Tibetans. With them has developed a level of creativity and tolerance you would generally find in very large cities but not in smaller communities such as the ones found in New Mexico.

CULTURAL QUESTIONS

Faced with new challenges to their ways of life, both Native Americans and Hispanics are marshaling forces to protect their cultural identities. A prime concern is language. Through the years, many Pueblo people have begun to speak more and more English, with their children getting little exposure to their native tongue. In a number of the pueblos, elders are working with schoolchildren in language classes. Some of the pueblos have even developed written dictionaries, the first time their languages have been systematized in this form.

Many pueblos have introduced programs to conserve the environment, preserve ancient seed strains, and protect religious rites. Because their religion is tied closely to nature, a loss of natural resources would threaten the entire culture. Certain activities have been closed to outsiders, the most notable being some of the rituals of Shalako at Zuni, a popular and elaborate series of year-end ceremonies.

Hispanics, through art and observance of cultural traditions, are also embracing their roots. In northern New Mexico, murals depicting important historic events, such as the Treaty of Guadalupe Hidalgo of 1848, adorn many walls. The **Spanish Market** in Santa Fe has expanded into a grand celebration of traditional arts—from tin working to *santo* carving. Public schools in the area have bilingual education programs, enabling students to embrace their Spanish-speaking roots.

Hispanics are also making their voices heard, insisting on more conscientious development of their neighborhoods and rising to positions of power in government. When she was in office, former Santa Fe Mayor Debbie Jaramillo made national news as an advocate of the Hispanic people, and Congressman Bill Richardson, Hispanic despite his Anglo surname, was appointed U.S. ambassador to the United Nations before becoming energy secretary in President Clinton's cabinet and later running for U.S. president. Currently, he is the governor of New Mexico.

GAMBLING WINS & LOSSES

Gambling, a fact of life and source of much-needed revenue for Native American populations across the country, has been a center of controversy in northern New Mexico for a number of years. In 1994, Gov. Gary Johnson signed a compact with tribes in New Mexico, ratified by the U.S. Department of the Interior, to allow full-scale gambling. **Tesuque Pueblo** was one of the first to begin a massive expansion, and many other pueblos followed suit.

Many New Mexicans are concerned about the tone gambling sets in the state. The casinos are for the most part large and unsightly buildings that stand out sorely on some of New Mexico's most picturesque land. Though most residents appreciate the boost that gambling can ultimately bring to the Native American economies, many critics wonder where gambling profits actually go—and if the casinos can possibly be a good thing for the pueblos and tribes. Some detractors suspect that profits go directly into the pockets of outside backers.

A number of pueblos and tribes, however, are showing signs of prosperity, and they are using newfound revenues to buy firefighting and medical equipment and to invest in local schools. Isleta Pueblo built a $3.5-million youth center, and the lieutenant governor says the money for it came from gambling revenues. Sandia Pueblo built a $2-million medical and dental clinic and, most recently, provided a computer for every tribal home. Its governor said these projects were "totally funded by gaming revenues." Some of the pueblos have built hotels on their property, most notably the Hyatt Regency Tamaya Resort at Santa Ana and the Sandia Resort & Casino at Sandia.

2 A LOOK AT THE PAST

IN THE BEGINNING

Archaeologists say that humans first migrated to the Southwest, moving southward from the Bering Land Bridge, around 12,000 B.C. Sites such as Sandia Cave and Folsom—where weapon points were discovered that, for the first time, clearly established that our prehistoric ancestors hunted now-extinct mammals such as woolly mammoths—are internationally known. When these large animals died off during the late Ice Age (about 8000 B.C.), people turned to hunting smaller game and gathering wild food.

Stable farming settlements, as evidenced by the remains of domestically grown maize, date from around 3000 B.C. As the nomadic peoples became more sedentary, they built permanent residences and pit houses and made pottery. Cultural differences began to emerge in their choice of architecture and decoration: The **Mogollon people,** in the southwestern part of modern New Mexico, created brown and red pottery and built large community lodges; the **ancestral Puebloans,** or **Anasazi,** in the north, made gray pottery and smaller lodges for extended families.

The Mogollon, whose pottery dates from around 100 B.C., were the first of the sophisticated village cultures. They lived primarily in modern-day Catron and Grant counties. The most important Mogollon ruins are in the Gila River Valley, including Gila Cliff Dwellings National Monument, north of Silver City.

By about A.D. 700, and perhaps a couple centuries earlier, the ancestral Puebloans of the northwest had absorbed village life and expanded through what is now known as the Four Corners region (where New Mexico, Arizona, Utah, and Colorado come together). Around A.D. 1000, their culture eclipsed that of the Mogollon. Chaco Culture National Historic Park, Aztec Ruins National Monument, and Salmon Ruins all exhibit architectural excellence and skill, as well as a scientific sensitivity to nature, that mark this as one of America's classic pre-Columbian civilizations.

Condominium-style communities of stone and mud adobe bricks, three and four stories high, were focused around central plazas. The villages incorporated circular spiritual chambers called kivas. The ancestral Puebloans also developed means to irrigate their fields of corn, beans, and squash by controlling the flow of water from the San Juan River and its tributaries. From Chaco Canyon, they built a complex system of well-engineered roads leading in four directions to other towns or ceremonial centers. Artifacts found during excavation, such as seashells and macaw feathers, indicate that they had a far-reaching trade network. The incorporation of solar alignments into some of their architecture has caused some to speculate on the importance of the equinoxes to their religion.

The diminishing of the Anasazi culture, and the emergence of the **Pueblo culture** in its place, is something of a mystery today. Historians disagree as to why the Anasazi left their villages around the 13th century. Some suggest drought or soil exhaustion; others posit invasion, epidemic, or social unrest. But by the time the first Spanish arrived in the 1500s, the ancestral Puebloans were long gone and the Pueblo culture was well established throughout northern and western New Mexico, from Taos to Zuni, near Gallup. Most of the people lived on the east side of the Continental Divide, in the Rio Grande Valley.

The Pueblos absorbed certain elements of the ancestral Puebloan civilization, including the apartmentlike adobe architecture, the creation of rather elaborate pottery, and the use of irrigation or flood farming in their fields. Agriculture, especially corn, was the economic mainstay.

Each pueblo, as the scattered villages and surrounding farmlands were known, fiercely guarded its independence. When the Spanish arrived, no alliances existed between pueblos. No more than a few hundred people lived in any one pueblo, an indication that the natives had learned to keep their population (which totaled 40,000–50,000) down in order to preserve their soil and other natural resources. But not all was peaceful: They alternately fought and traded with each other, as well as with nomadic Apaches. Even before the Spanish arrived, a pattern had been established.

THE ARRIVAL OF THE SPANISH

The Spanish controlled New Mexico for 300 years, from the mid-16th to the mid-19th century—twice as long as the United States has. The Hispanic legacy in language and culture is stronger today in New Mexico than anywhere else in the Southwest, no doubt a result of the prominence of the Rio Grande Valley as the oldest and most populous fringe province of the viceroyalty of New Spain.

The spark that sent the first European explorers into what is now New Mexico was a fabulous medieval myth that seven Spanish bishops had fled the Moorish invasion of the 8th century, sailed westward to the legendary isle of Antilia, and built themselves seven cities of gold. Hernán Cortés's 1519 discovery and conquest of the Aztecs' treasure-laden capital of Tenochtitlán, now Mexico City, fueled belief in the myth. When a Franciscan friar 20 years later claimed to have sighted, from a distance, "a very beautiful city" in a region known as Cíbola while on a reconnaissance mission for the viceroyalty, the gates were opened.

Francisco Vásquez de Coronado, the ambitious young governor of New Spain's western province of Nueva Galicia, was commissioned to lead an expedition to the "seven cities." Several hundred soldiers, accompanied by servants and missionaries, marched overland to Cíbola with him in 1540, along with a support fleet of three ships in the Gulf of California. What they discovered, after 6 hard months on the trail, was a bitter disappointment: Instead of a city of gold, they found a rock-and-mud pueblo at Hawikuh, the westernmost of the Zuni towns. The expedition wintered at Tiguex, on the Rio Grande near modern Santa Fe, before proceeding to the Great Plains, seeking more treasure at Quivira, in what is now Kansas. The grass houses of the Wichita Indians were all they found.

Coronado returned to New Spain in 1542, admitting failure. Historically, though, his expedition was a great success, contributing the first widespread knowledge of the Southwest and Great Plains, and encountering the Grand Canyon en route.

By the 1580s, after important silver discoveries in the mountains of Mexico, the Spanish began to wonder if the wealth of the Pueblo country might lie in its land rather than its cities. They were convinced that they had been divinely appointed to convert the natives of the New World to Christianity. And so a northward migration began, orchestrated and directed by the royal government. It was a mere trickle in the late 16th century. Juan de Oñate established a capital in 1598 at San Gabriel, near San Juan Pueblo, but a variety of factors led to its failure. In 1610, under **Don Pedro de Peralta,** the migration began in earnest.

It was not dissimilar to America's schoolbook stereotype. Bands of armored conquistadors did troop through the desert with humble robed friars striding by their sides. But most of the pioneers came up the Rio Grande Valley, with oxcarts and mule trains rather than armor, intent on transplanting their Hispanic traditions of government, religion, and material culture to this new world.

Peralta built his new capital at Santa Fe and named it La Villa Real de la Santa Fe de San Francisco de Asis, the Royal City of the Holy Faith of St. Francis of Assisi. His capitol building, the Palace of the Governors, has been continuously occupied as a public building ever since by Spanish, Mexicans, Americans, and, for 12 years (1680–92), the Pueblo Indians. Today, it's a museum.

RELIGION & REVOLT

The 17th century in New Mexico was essentially a missionary era, as Franciscan priests attempted to turn the Indians into model Hispanic peasants. Their churches became the focal point of every pueblo, with Catholic schools a mandatory adjunct. By 1625, the Rio Grande Valley was home to an estimated 50 churches.

But the Native Americans weren't enthused about doing "God's work"—building new adobe missions, tilling fields for the Spanish, and weaving garments for export to Mexico—so soldiers backed the padres in extracting labor, a system known as *repartimiento.* Simultaneously, the *encomienda* system provided that a yearly tribute in corn and blankets be levied upon each Indian. The Pueblos were amenable to taking part in Catholic religious ceremonies and proclaiming themselves converts. To them, spiritual forces were actively involved in the material world. If establishing harmony with the cosmos meant absorbing Jesus Christ and various saints into their hierarchy of katsinas and other spiritual beings, so much the better. But the Spanish friars demanded that they do away with their traditional singing, masked dancing, and other "pagan practices." When the Pueblo religion was violently crushed and driven literally underground, resentment toward the Spanish grew and festered. Rebellions at Taos and Jemez in the 1630s left village priests dead, but the Pueblos were savagely repressed.

A power struggle between church and state in Nuevo Mexico weakened the hand of the Spanish colonists, and a long drought in the 1660s and 1670s gave the Apaches reason to scourge the Spanish and Pueblo settlements for food. The Pueblos blamed the friars, and their ban on traditional rain dances, for the drought. The hanging of four medicine men as "sorcerers" and the imprisonment of 43 others was the last straw for the Rio Grande natives. In 1680, the Pueblo Revolt erupted.

Popé, a San Juan shaman, catalyzed the revolt. Assisted by other Pueblo leaders, he unified the far-flung Native Americans, who had never before confederated. They pillaged and burned the province's outlying settlements, and then turned their attention on Santa Fe, besieging the citizens who had fled to the Palace of the Governors. After 9 days, having reconquered Spain's northernmost American province, they let the refugees retreat south to Mexico.

Popé ordered that the Pueblos should return to the lifestyle they had before the arrival of the Spanish. All Hispanic items, from tools to fruit trees, were to be destroyed, and the blemish of baptism was to be washed away in the river. But the shaman misjudged the influence of the Spanish on the Pueblo people. They were not the people they had been a century earlier, and they *liked* much of the material culture they had absorbed from the Europeans. What's more, they had no intention of remaining confederated; their independent streaks were too strong.

In 1692, led by newly appointed **Gov. Don Diego de Vargas,** the Spanish recaptured Santa Fe without bloodshed. Popé had died, and without a leader to reunify them, the Pueblos were no match for the Spanish. Vargas pledged not to punish them but to pardon and convert. Still, when he returned the following year with

Impressions

"In New Mexico he always awoke a young man; not until he rose and began to shave did he realize that he was growing older."

—Archbishop Latour in Willa Cather's *Death Comes for the Archbishop,* 1927

70 families to recolonize the city, he did use force. And for the next several years, bloody battles persisted throughout the Pueblo country.

By the turn of the 18th century, Nuevo Mexico was firmly in Spanish hands. This time, however, the colonists seemed to have learned from some of their past errors. They were more tolerant in their religion and less ruthless in their demands and punishments.

THE ARRIVAL OF THE ANGLOS

By the 1700s, there were signals that new interlopers were about to arrive in New Mexico. The French had laid plans to begin colonizing the Mississippi River, and hostile Native American tribes were on the warpath. The Spanish viceroyalty fortified its position in Santa Fe as a defensive bastion and established a new villa at Albuquerque in 1706.

In 1739, the first French trade mission entered Santa Fe and was welcomed by the citizenry but not by the government. For 24 years, until 1763, a black-market trade thrived between Louisiana and New Mexico. It ended only when France lost its toehold on its North American claims during the French and Indian War.

The Native Americans were more fearsome foes. Apaches, Comanches, Utes, and Navajos launched raids against each other and the Rio Grande settlements for most of the 18th century, which led the Spanish and Pueblos to pull closer together for mutual protection. Pueblo and Hispanic militias fought side by side in campaigns against the invaders. But by the 1770s, the attacks had become so savage and destructive that the viceroy in Mexico City created a military jurisdiction in the province, and **Gov. Juan Bautista de Anza** led a force north to Colorado to defeat the most feared of the Comanche chiefs, **Cuerno Verde** ("Green Horn"), in 1779. Seven years later, the Comanches and Utes signed a lasting treaty with the Spanish and thereafter helped keep the Apaches in check.

France sold the Louisiana Territory to the young United States in 1803, and the Spanish suddenly had a new intruder to fear. The Lewis and Clark expedition of 1803 went unchallenged, much as the Spanish would have liked to challenge it; but in 1807, when **Lt. Zebulon Pike** built a stockade on a Rio Grande tributary in Colorado, he and his troops were taken prisoner by troops from Santa Fe. Pike was taken to the New Mexican capital, where he was interrogated extensively, and then to Chihuahua, Mexico. The report he wrote upon his return was the United States' first inside look at Spain's frontier province.

At first, pioneering American merchants—excited by Pike's observations of New Mexico's economy—were summarily expelled from Santa Fe or jailed, and their goods were confiscated. But after Mexico gained independence from Spain in 1821, traders were welcomed. The wagon ruts of the Santa Fe Trail soon extended from Missouri to New Mexico, and from there to Chihuahua. (Later, it became the primary southern highway to California.)

As the merchants hastened to Santa Fe, Anglo-American and French-Canadian fur trappers headed into the wilderness. Their commercial hub became Taos, a tiny village near a large pueblo a few days' ride north of Santa Fe. Many married into native or Hispanic families. Perhaps the best known was **Kit Carson,** a sometime federal agent, sometime scout, whose legend is inextricably interwoven with that of early Taos. He spent 40 years in Taos, until his death in 1868.

In 1846, the **U.S.–Mexican War** broke out, and New Mexico became a territory of the United States. There were several causes of the war, including the U.S. annexation of Texas in 1845, disagreement over the international boundary, and unpaid claims owed to American citizens by the Mexican government. But foremost was the prevailing U.S. sentiment of "manifest destiny," the belief that the Union should extend "from sea to shining sea." **Gen. Stephen Kearny** marched south from Colorado; on the Las Vegas plaza, he announced that he had come to take possession of New Mexico for the United States. His arrival in Santa Fe on August 18, 1846, went unopposed.

An 1847 revolt in Taos resulted in the slaying of the new governor of New Mexico, Charles Bent, but U.S. troops defeated the rebels and executed their leaders. That was the last threat to American sovereignty in the territory. In 1848, the **Treaty of Guadalupe Hidalgo** officially transferred the title of New Mexico, along with Texas, Arizona, and California, to the United States.

Kearney promised New Mexicans that the United States would respect their religion and property rights and would safeguard their homes and possessions from hostile Indians. His troops behaved with a rigid decorum. The United States upheld Spanish policy toward the Pueblos, assuring the survival of their ancestral lands, their traditional culture, and their old religion—which even 3 centuries of Hispanic Catholicism could not do away with.

THE CIVIL WAR

As conflict between the North and South flared east of the Mississippi, New Mexico found itself caught in the debate over **slavery.** Southerners wanted to expand slavery to the Western territories, but abolitionists bitterly opposed them. New Mexicans themselves voted against slavery twice, while their delegate to Congress engineered the adoption of a slavery code. In 1861, the Confederacy laid plans to make New Mexico theirs as a first step toward capturing the West.

In fact, southern New Mexicans, including those in Tucson (Arizona was then a part of the New Mexico Territory), were disenchanted with the attention paid them by Santa Fe and were already threatening to form their own state. So when Confederate Lt. Col. John Baylor captured Fort Fillmore, near Mesilla, and on August 1, 1861, proclaimed all of New Mexico south of the 34th parallel to be the new territory of Arizona, few complained.

The following year, **Confederate Gen. Henry Sibley** assembled three regiments of 2,600 Texans and moved up the Rio Grande. They defeated Union loyalists in a bloody battle at Valverde, near Socorro; easily took Albuquerque and Santa Fe; and proceeded toward the federal arsenal at Fort Union, 90 miles east of Santa Fe. Sibley planned to replenish his supplies there before continuing north to Colorado, and then west to California.

On March 27 and 28, 1862, the Confederates were met head-on in **Glorieta Pass,** about 16 miles outside Santa Fe, by regular troops from Fort Union, supported by a regiment of Colorado volunteers. By the second day, the rebels were in control, until a detachment of Coloradans circled behind the Confederate troops and destroyed their poorly defended supply train. Sibley was forced into a retreat down the Rio Grande. A few months later, Mesilla was reclaimed for the Union, ending the Confederate presence in New Mexico.

THE LAND WARS

The various tribes had not missed the fact that whites were fighting among themselves, and they took advantage of this weakness to step up their raids on border settlements. In 1864, the **Navajos,** in what is known in tribal history as the Long Walk, were relocated to the new Bosque Redondo Reservation on the Pecos River at Fort Sumner, in east-central New Mexico. Militia Col. Kit Carson led New Mexico troops in this venture, a position to which he acceded as a moderating influence between the Navajos and those who

Reflections

"I wasn't the leader of any gang. I was for Billy all the time."

—Billy the Kid

To a Las Vegas, New Mexico reporter, after his capture at Stinking Springs

called for their unconditional surrender or extermination.

Moving the Navajos was an ill-advised decision: The land could not support 9,000 people, the government failed to supply adequate provisions, and the Navajos were unable to live peacefully with the **Mescaleros.** By late 1868, the tribes retraced their routes to their homelands, where the Navajos gave up their warlike past. The Mescaleros' raids were squashed in the 1870s, and they were confined to a reservation southern New Mexico.

Corralling the rogue **Apaches** of southwestern New Mexico presented the territory with its biggest challenge. Led by chiefs Victorio, Nana, and Geronimo, these bands wreaked havoc on the mining region around Silver City. Eventually, however, they succumbed, and the capture of Geronimo in 1886 was the final chapter in New Mexico's long history of Indian wars.

As the Native American threat decreased, more and more livestock and sheep **ranchers** established themselves on the vast plains east of the Rio Grande, in the San Juan basin of the northwest, and in other equally inviting parts of the territory. Cattle drives up the Pecos Valley, on the Goodnight–Loving Trail, are the stuff of legend; so, too, was Roswell cattle baron John Chisum, whose 80,000 head of beef probably represented the largest herd in America in the late 1870s.

Mining grew as well. Albuquerque blossomed in the wake of a series of major gold strikes in the Madrid Valley, close to ancient turquoise mines; other gold and silver discoveries through the 1870s gave birth to boomtowns—now mostly ghost towns—such as Hillsboro, Mogollon, Pinos Altos, and White Oaks. The copper mines of Santa Rita del Cobre, near Silver City, are still thriving.

In 1879, the Atchison, Topeka, and Santa Fe Railway sent its main line through Las Vegas, Albuquerque, El Paso, and Deming, where it joined with the Southern Pacific line coming from California. (The Santa Fe station was, and is, at Lamy, 17 miles southeast of the capital.) Now linked by **railroad** to the great markets of America, New Mexico's economic boom period was assured.

But ranching invites cattle rustling and range wars, mining beckons feuds and land fraud, and the construction of railroads often brings political corruption and swindles. New Mexico had all of them, especially during the latter part of the 19th century. Best known of a great many conflicts was the **Lincoln County War** (1878–81), which began as a feud between rival factions of ranchers and merchants. It led to such utter lawlessness that President Rutherford B. Hayes ordered a federal investigation of the territorial government and the installation of Gen. Lew Wallace as governor (whose novel *Ben-Hur* was published in 1880).

One of the central figures of the Lincoln County War was **William "Billy the Kid" Bonney** (1858–81), a headstrong youth who became probably the best-known outlaw of the American West. He blazed a trail of bloodshed from Silver City to Mesilla, Santa Fe to Lincoln, and Artesia to Fort Sumner, where he was finally killed by Sheriff Pat Garrett in July 1881.

By the turn of the 20th century, most of the violence had been checked. The mineral lodes were drying up, and ranching was taking on increased importance. Economic and social stability were coming to New Mexico.

STATEHOOD, ART & ATOMS

Early in the 20th century, its Hispanic citizens having proved their loyalty to the U.S. by serving gallantly with Theodore Roosevelt's Rough Riders during the Spanish–American War, New Mexico's long-awaited dream of becoming an integral part of the Union was finally recognized. On January 6, 1912, President William Howard Taft signed a bill making New Mexico the **47th state.**

Within a few years, Taos began gaining fame as an artists' community. Two painters from the East Coast, **Ernest Blumenschein** and **Bert Phillips,** settled in Taos in 1898, lured others to join them, and in 1914 formed the **Taos Society of Artists,** one of the most influential schools of art in America. Writers and other intellectuals soon followed, including **Mabel Dodge Luhan,** novelists **D. H. Lawrence** and **Willa Cather,** and poet-activist **John Collier.** Other artists settled in Santa Fe and elsewhere in New Mexico; the best known was **Georgia O'Keeffe,** who lived miles from anywhere in tiny Abiquiu. Today, Santa Fe and Taos are world renowned for their contributions to art and culture.

The construction in 1916 of the Elephant Butte Dam near Hot Springs (now Truth or Consequences) brought irrigated farming back to a drought-ravaged southern New Mexico. Potash mining boomed in the southeast in the 1930s. Native Americans gained full citizenship in 1924, 2 years after the **All Pueblo Council** was formed to fight passage in Congress of a bill that would have given white squatters rights to Indian lands. And in 1934, tribes were accorded partial self-government. Hispanics, meanwhile, became the most powerful force in state politics and remain so today.

The most dramatic development in 20th-century New Mexico was induced by World War II. In 1943, the U.S. government sealed off a tract of land on the Pajarito Plateau, west of Santa Fe, that previously had been an exclusive boys' school. On this site, it built the Los Alamos National Laboratory, otherwise known as Project Y of the Manhattan Engineer District—the **"Manhattan Project."** Its goal: to split the atom and develop the first nuclear weapons.

Under the direction of **J. Robert Oppenheimer,** later succeeded by **Norris E. Bradbury,** a team of 30 to 100 scientists and hundreds of support staff lived and worked in almost complete seclusion for 2 years. Their work resulted in the atomic bomb, tested for the first time at

Reflections

"I am become death, the shatterer of worlds."

—Shortly after the successful detonation of the first atomic bomb, J. Robert Oppenheimer, who headed the Manhattan Project, said this, quoting from ancient Hindu texts the Trinity Site, north of White Sands, on July 16, 1945. The bombings of Hiroshima and Nagasaki, Japan, 3 weeks later, signaled to the world that the nuclear age had arrived.

Even before that time, New Mexico was gaining stature in America's scientific community. **Robert H. Goddard,** considered the founder of modern rocketry, conducted many of his experiments near Roswell in the 1930s, during which time he became the first person to shoot a liquid-fuel rocket faster than the speed of sound. **Clyde Tombaugh,** who discovered Pluto in 1930, helped establish the department of astronomy at New Mexico State University in Las Cruces. And former **Sen. Harrison (Jack) Schmitt,** an exogeologist and the first civilian to walk on the moon in 1972, is a native of the Silver City area.

Today, the **White Sands Missile Range** is one of America's most important astrophysics sites, and the **International Space Hall of Fame** in nearby Alamogordo honors men and women from around the world who have devoted their lives to space exploration. Aerospace research and defense contracts are economic mainstays in Albuquerque, and **Kirtland Air Force Base** is the home of the Air Force Special Weapons Center. **Los Alamos,** of course, continues to be a national leader in nuclear technology. Now in its embryonic stages, the **Southwest Regional Spaceport** near Las Cruces may launch privately funded space flights as early as 2010.

Despite the arrival of the 21st century in many parts of the state, other areas are still struggling to be a part of the 20th. Many Native Americans, be they Pueblo, Navajo, or Apache, and Hispanic farmers, who till small plots in isolated rural regions, hearken to a time when life was slower paced.

3 ART & ARCHITECTURE

A LAND OF ART

It's all in the light—or at least that's what many artists claim drew them to New Mexico. In truth, the light is only part of the attraction: Nature in this part of the country, with its awe-inspiring thunderheads, endless expanse of blue skies, and rugged desert, is itself a canvas. To record the wonders of earth and sky, the early natives of the area, the ancestral Puebloans, imprinted images (in the form of petroglyphs and pictographs) on the sides of caves and on stones, as well as on the sides of pots they shaped from clay dug in the hills.

Today's Native American tribes carry on that legacy, as do the other cultures that have settled here. Life in New Mexico is shaped by the arts. Everywhere you turn, you see pottery, paintings, jewelry, and weavings.

The area is full of little villages that maintain their own artistic specialties. Each Indian pueblo has a trademark design, such as **Santa Clara**'s and **San Ildefonso**'s black pottery and **Zuni**'s needlepoint silverwork. Bear in mind that the images used often have symbolic meaning. When purchasing art or an artifact, you may want to talk to its maker about what the symbols mean.

Hispanic villages are also distinguished by their artistic identities. **Chimayo** has become a center for Hispanic weaving, and the village of **Cordova** is known for its *santo* (icon) carving. *Santos, retablos* (paintings), and *bultos* (sculptures), as well as works in tin, are traditional devotional arts tied to the Roman Catholic faith. Often, these works are sold out of artists' homes in these villages, allowing you to glimpse the lives of the artists and the surroundings that inspire them.

Hispanic and Native American villagers take their goods to the cities, where for centuries people have bought and traded. Under the portals along the plazas of Santa

Impressions

[Sun-bleached bones] were most wonderful against the blue/that blue that will always be there as it is now after all man's destruction is finished.

—Georgia O'Keeffe, on the desert skies of New Mexico

Fe, Taos, and Albuquerque, you'll find a variety of works in silver, stone, and pottery for sale. In the cities, you'll find streets lined with galleries. At major markets, such as the **Spanish Market** and **Indian Market** in Santa Fe, some of the top artists from the area sell their works. Smaller shows at the pueblos also attract artists and artisans. The **Northern Pueblo Artists and Craftsman Show,** revolving each July to a different pueblo, continues to grow.

Drawn by the beauty of the local landscape and respect for indigenous art, artists from all over have flocked here, particularly during the 20th century. They have established locally important art societies; one of the most notable is the **Taos Society of Artists.** In 1898, the artists Bert Phillips and Ernest L. Blumenschein were traveling through the area from Colorado on a mission to sketch the Southwest when their wagon broke down north of Taos. The scenery so overwhelmed them that they abandoned their journey and stayed. Joseph Sharp joined them, and still later came Oscar Berninghaus, Walter Ufner, Herbert Dunton, and others. You can see a brilliant collection of some of their romantically lit portraits and landscapes at the Taos Art Museum.

A major player in the development of Taos as an artists' community was the arts patron **Mabel Dodge Luhan.** A writer who financed the work of many an artist, in the 1920s Luhan held court for many notables, including Georgia O'Keeffe, Willa Cather, and D. H. Lawrence. This illustrious history goes a long way to explaining how it is that Taos—a town of about 5,000 inhabitants—has more than 100 arts-and-crafts galleries and many resident painters.

Santa Fe has its own art society, begun in the 1920s by a nucleus of five painters who became known as **Los Cinco Pintores.** Jozef Bakos, Fremont Ellis, Walter Mruk, Willard Nash, and Will Shuster lived in the area of Canyon Road (now the arts center of Santa Fe). Despite its small size, Santa Fe is considered one of the top three art markets in the U.S.

Perhaps the most celebrated artist associated with New Mexico was **Georgia O'Keeffe** (1887–1986), a painter who worked and lived most of her later years in the region. O'Keeffe's first sojourn to New Mexico in 1929 inspired her sensuous paintings of the area's desert landscape and bleached animal skulls. The house where she lived in Abiquiu (42 miles northwest of Santa Fe on US 84) is now open for limited public tours (see chapter 7 for details). The **Georgia O'Keeffe Museum** in Santa Fe is the only museum in the United States entirely dedicated to an internationally known woman artist.

Santa Fe is also home to the **Institute of American Indian Arts,** where many of today's leading Native American artists have studied, including the Apache sculptor Allan Houser (whose works you can see near the state capitol building and in other public areas in Santa Fe). The best-known Native American painter is the late R. C. Gorman, an Arizona Navajo who made his home in Taos for more than 3 decades. Gorman is internationally acclaimed for his bright, somewhat surrealistic depictions of

Navajo women. Another artist who has achieved national fame is Dan Namingha, a Hopi painter and sculptor who weaves native symbology together with contemporary concerns.

If you look closely, you'll find notable works from a number of local artists. Tammy Garcia is a young Taos potter who year after year continues to sweep the awards at Indian Market with her intricately shaped and carved pots. Cippy Crazyhorse, a Cochiti, has acquired a steady following of patrons for his silver jewelry. All around the area you'll see the frescoes of Frederico Vigil, a noted muralist and Santa Fe native.

For the visitor interested in art, however, some caution should be exercised; a lot of schlock out there targets the tourist trade. But if you persist, you're likely to find some very inspiring work as well.

A RICH ARCHITECTURAL MELTING POT

Nowhere else in the United States are you likely to see such extremes of architectural style as in New Mexico. The state's distinctive architecture reflects the diversity of cultures that have left their imprint on the region. The first people in the area were the ancestral Puebloans, the Anasazi, who built stone and mud homes at the bottom of canyons and inside caves. **Pueblo–style adobe architecture** evolved and became the basis for traditional New Mexican homes: sun-dried clay bricks mixed with grass for strength, mud-mortared, and covered with additional protective layers of mud. Roofs are supported by a network of vigas—long beams whose ends protrude through the outer facades—and *latillas,* smaller stripped branches layered between the vigas. Other adapted Pueblo architectural elements include plastered adobe-brick kiva fireplaces, *bancos* (adobe benches that protrude from walls), and *nichos* (small indentations within a wall in which religious icons are placed). These adobe homes are characterized by flat roofs and soft, rounded contours.

Spaniards wedded many elements to Pueblo style, such as portals (porches held up with posts, often running the length of a home) and enclosed patios, as well as the simple, dramatic sculptural shapes of Spanish mission arches and bell towers. They also brought elements from the Moorish architecture found in southern Spain: heavy wooden doors and elaborate *corbels*—carved wooden supports for the vertical posts.

With the opening of the Santa Fe Trail in 1821 and later the 1860s gold boom, both of which brought more Anglo settlers, came the next wave of building. New arrivals contributed architectural elements such as neo-Grecian and Victorian influences popular in the middle part of the U.S. at the time. Distinguishing features of what came to be known as **Territorial-style** architecture can be seen today; they include brick facades and cornices as well as porches, often placed on the second story. You'll also note millwork on doors and wood trim around windows and doorways, double-hung windows, and Victorian bric-a-brac.

Santa Fe Plaza is an excellent example of the convergence of these early architectural styles. On the west side is a Territorial-style balcony, while the Palace of Governors is marked by Pueblo-style vigas and oversized Spanish/Moorish doors. Nearby, you'll see the Romanesque architecture of the **St. Francis Cathedral** and **Loretto chapel,** brought by Archbishop Lamy from France, as well as the railroad station built in the **Spanish Mission style**—popular in the early part of the 20th century.

Most notable architecturally in Taos is **Taos Pueblo,** the site of two structures emulated in homes and business buildings throughout the Southwest. Built to resemble Taos Mountain, which stands behind it, the two structures are pyramidal in form, with the different levels reached by ladders. Also quite prevalent is architecture echoing colonial hacienda style. What's nice about Taos is that you can see historic homes inside and out. You can wander through artist **Ernest Blumenschein's home.** Built in 1797 and restored by Blumenschein in 1919, it represents another New Mexico architectural phenomenon: homes that were added onto year after year. Doorways are typically low, and floors rise and fall at the whim of the earth beneath them. The **Martinez Hacienda** is an example of a hacienda stronghold. Built without windows facing outward, it originally had 20 small rooms, many with doors opening out to the courtyard. It is one of the few refurbished examples of colonial New Mexico architecture .

As you head into villages in the north, you'll see steep pitched roofs on most homes. This is because the common flat-roof style doesn't shed snow; the water builds up and causes roof problems. In just about any town in northern New Mexico, you may detect the strong smell of tar, a sure sign that another resident is laying out thousands to fix his enchanting but frustratingly flat roof.

Today, very few new homes are built of adobe. Instead, most are constructed with wood frames and plasterboard, and then stuccoed over. Several local architects are currently employing innovative architecture to create a Pueblo-style feel. They incorporate straw bales, pumice-crete, rammed earth, old tires, even aluminum cans in the construction of homes. Most of these elements are used in the same way bricks are used, stacked and layered, and then covered over with plaster and made to look like adobe. Often it's difficult to distinguish homes built with these materials from those built with wood-frame construction. West of Taos, a number of "earthships" have been built. Many of these homes are constructed with alternative materials, most bermed into the sides of hills, utilizing the earth as insulation and the sun as an energy source.

A visitor could spend an entire trip to New Mexico focusing on the architecture. As well as relishing the wealth of architectural styles, you'll find more subtle elements everywhere. You may encounter an ox-blood floor, for example. An old Spanish tradition, ox blood is spread in layers and left to dry, hardening into a glossy finish that's known to last centuries. You're also likely to see coyote fences—narrow cedar posts lined up side by side—a system early settlers devised to ensure safety of their animals. Winding around homes and buildings you'll see *acequias,* ancient irrigation canals still maintained by locals for watering crops and trees.

4 THE LAY OF THE LAND

It would be easy, and accurate, to call New Mexico "high and dry" and leave it at that. The lowest point in the state, in the southeastern corner, is still over 2,800 feet in elevation, higher than the highest point in at least a dozen other states. The southern **Rocky Mountains** extend well into New Mexico, rising above 13,000 feet in the **Sangre de Cristo range** and sending a final afterthought above 10,000 feet, just east of Alamogordo. Volcanic activity created the mountain range—and its aftereffects can be seen throughout the state, from Shiprock (the remaining core of a long-eroded volcano) to Capulin Volcano National Monument. Two fault lines, which created the Rio Grande Rift Valley, home to the **Rio Grande,** run through the center of the state, and seismic activity continues to change the face of New Mexico even today.

Although archaeologists have discovered fossils indicating that most of New Mexico was once covered by ancient seas,

Impressions

"New Mexico is old, stupendously old and dry and brown, and wind-worn by the ages. I went to New Mexico . . . to be overcome again by oldness."

—Charles Kuralt, *Charles Kuralt's America,* 1995

the surface area of the state is now quite dry. The greater portion of New Mexico receives fewer than 20 inches of precipitation annually, the bulk of that coming either as summer afternoon thunderstorms or winter snowfall. In an area of 121,666 square miles—the fifth-largest U.S. state—there are only 221 square miles of water. Rivers and lakes occupy less than 0.2% of the landscape. The most important source of water is the Rio Grande. It nourishes hundreds of small farms from the **Pueblo country** of the north to the bone-dry **Chihuahuan Desert** of the far south.

However, there's more water than meets the eye in New Mexico. Systems circulating beneath the earth's surface have created all sorts of beautiful and fascinating geologic formations, including the natural wonder known as **Carlsbad Caverns,** one of the greatest cave systems in the world. Other caves have formed throughout the state, many of which have collapsed over the centuries, creating large sinkholes. These sinkholes have since filled with water and formed beautiful lakes. **Bottomless Lakes State Park,** near the town of Roswell, is a good example of this type of geological activity.

Other natural wonders you'll encounter during a visit to New Mexico include red-, yellow-, and orange-hued high, flat **mesas,** and the 275-square-mile **White Sands National Monument** that contains more than 8 billion tons of pure white gypsum and is the largest field of sand dunes of this kind in the entire world. Here, mountains meet desert, and the sky is arguably bigger, bluer, and more fascinating than any other place in the country. Words can't do justice to the spectacular colors of the landscape, colors that have drawn contemporary artists from around the world for nearly a century, colors that have made Taos and Santa Fe synonymous with artists' communities. The blues, browns, greens, reds, oranges, and yellows in every imaginable variation make this land a living canvas. This is truly big sky country, where it seems you can see forever.

5 NEW MEXICO IN POPULAR CULTURE: BOOKS, FILMS & MUSIC

BOOKS

Many well-known writers made their homes in New Mexico in the 20th century. In the 1920s, the most celebrated were **D. H. Lawrence** and **Willa Cather,** both short-term Taos residents. Lawrence, the romantic and controversial English novelist, spent time here between 1922 and 1925; he reflected on his sojourn in *Mornings in Mexico* and *Etruscan Places.* Lawrence's Taos period is described in *Lorenzo in Taos,* which his patron, Mabel Dodge Luhan, wrote. Cather, a Pulitzer-prize winner famous for her depictions of the pioneer spirit, penned *Death Comes for the Archbishop,* among other works. This fictionalized account of the 19th-century

King of the Road

If you like road trip stories to small New Mexico towns, check out my book *King of the Road* (New Mexico Magazine Press, 2007). It's a compilation of articles from my monthly column in *New Mexico Magazine,* in which locals tell the stories of their hometowns. It's illustrated with my photos too. You can order the book online at www.nmmagazine.com and www.amazon.com.

Santa Fe bishop, Jean-Baptiste Lamy, grew out of her stay in the region.

Many contemporary authors also live in and write about New Mexico. John Nichols, of Taos, whose *Milagro Beanfield War* was made into a Robert Redford movie in 1987, writes insightfully about the problems of poor Hispanic farming communities. Albuquerque's Tony Hillerman has for decades woven mysteries around Navajo tribal police in books such as *Listening Woman* and *A Thief of Time.* In more recent years, Sarah Lovett has joined Hillerman's ranks with a series of gripping mysteries, most notably *Dangerous Attachments.* The Hispanic novelist Rudolfo Anaya's *Bless Me, Ultima,* and Pueblo writer Leslie Marmon Silko's *Ceremony* capture the lifestyles of their respective peoples. A coming-of-age story, Richard Bradford's *Red Sky at Morning* juxtaposes the various cultures of New Mexico. Edward Abbey wrote of the desert environment and politics; his *Fire on the Mountain,* set in New Mexico, was one of his most powerful works.

Excellent works about Native Americans of New Mexico include *The Pueblo Indians of North America* (Holt, Rinehart & Winston, 1970) by Edward P. Dozier and *Living the Sky: The Cosmos of the American Indian* (University of Oklahoma Press, 1987) by Ray A. Williamson. Also look for *American Indian Literature 1979–1994* (Ballantine, 1996), an anthology edited by Paula Gunn Allen.

For general histories of the state, try Myra Ellen Jenkins and Albert H. Schroeder's *A Brief History of New Mexico* (University of New Mexico Press, 1974) and Marc Simmons's *New Mexico: An Interpretive History* (University of New Mexico Press, 1988). In addition, Claire Morrill's *A Taos Mosaic: Portrait of a New Mexico Village* (University of New Mexico Press, 1973) does an excellent job of portraying the history of that small New Mexican town. I have also enjoyed Tony Hillerman's (ed.) *The Spell of New Mexico* (University of New Mexico Press, 1976) and John Nichols and William Davis's *If Mountains Die: A New Mexico Memoir* (Alfred A. Knopf, 1979). *Talking Ground* (University of New Mexico Press, 1996), by Santa Fe author Douglas Preston, tells of a contemporary horseback trip through Navajoland, exploring the native mythology. One of my favorite texts is *Enchantment and Exploitation* (University of New Mexico Press, 1985) by William deBuys. A very extensive book that attempts to capture the multiplicity of the region is *Legends of the American Southwest* (Alfred A. Knopf, 1997) by Alex Shoumatoff.

Enduring Visions: 1,000 Years of Southwestern Indian Art by the Aspen Center for the Visual Arts (Publishing Center for Cultural Resources, 1969) and Roland F. Dickey's *New Mexico Village Arts* (University of New Mexico Press, 1990) are both excellent resources for those interested in Native American art. If you become intrigued with Spanish art during your visit to New Mexico, you'll find E. Boyd's *Popular Arts of Spanish New Mexico* (Museum of New Mexico Press, 1974) to be quite informative.

If you like to cook, look for the *Santa Fe Farmer's Market Cookbook,* with recipes from vendors and chefs, to be released in spring 2009. And if you like to combine walking with literary history, pick up Barbara Harrelson's *Walks in Literary Santa Fe: A Guide to Landmarks, Legends, and Lore* (Gibbs-Smith, 2008).

FILMS

If you like to start traveling before you climb on the plane or into the car, you can do so easily by watching any number of movies filmed in the state. Over the years so many have been filmed that I won't list them all. Instead, I'll give the ones that provide a glimpse into the true nature of New Mexico. *Silverado* (1985), a lighthearted western, and the heartfelt miniseries *Lonesome Dove* (1989), based on a Larry McMurtry novel, start my list. Billy Bob Thorton's film adaptation (2000) of the novel *All the Pretty Horses,* Ron Howard's film version of *The Missing* (2003), and Billy Crystal in *City Slickers,* are also some of my favorite westerns.

Favorite classics include *Butch Cassidy and the Sundance Kid* (1969), filmed in Taos and Chama; *The Cowboys* (1972), with John Wayne; Clint Eastwood's *Every Which Way But Loose* (1978); and Dennis Hopper in the 1960s classic *Easy Rider* (1969).

More contemporary themes are explored in *Contact* (1997), which features the National Radio Astronomy Very Large Array in western New Mexico, as did *Independence Day* (1996). Also exploring alien themes, *The Man Who Fell to Earth* (1976), with David Bowie, was filmed in southern New Mexico.

MUSIC

Such musical legends as Bo Diddley, Buddy Holly, Roy Orbison, and the Fireballs basked in New Mexico's light for parts of their careers. More recent musicians whose music really reflects the state include Mansanares, two brothers who grew up in Abiquiu, known for their Spanish guitar and soulful vocals. Look for their album *Nuevo Latino.* Master flute player Robert Mirabal's music is informed by the ceremonial music he grew up with at Taos Pueblo. Check out his 2006 Grammy Award–winning album *Sacred Ground.* Using New Mexico as his creative retreat since the 1980s, Michael Martin Murphy often plays live here, where fans always cheer for his most notable song, "Wildfire." *The Best of Michael Martin Murphey* gives a good taste of his music. Country music superstar Randy Travis calls Santa Fe home. His newest release, *Around the Bend,* is a treasure, as are his classics. My favorite musician who resides in Santa Fe is Ottmar Liebert and his band the Luna Negra. All of their flamenco-inspired music is rich with New Mexico tones. Check out their CD *Leaning into the Night.*

6 EATING & DRINKING IN NEW MEXICO

You know you're in a food-conscious place when the local newspaper uses chiles (and onions) to rate movies, as does Santa Fe's *New Mexican.* A large part of that city's cachet as a chic destination derives from its famous cuisine, while Taos, Albuquerque, and Las Cruces are developing notable reputations themselves. The competition among restaurants is fierce, which means that visitors have plenty of options from which to choose. Aside from establishments serving the New Mexican and New Southwestern cuisine that the region is famed for, you can also find French, Italian, Asian, Indian, and interesting hybrids of those. Luckily, not all the top restaurants are high-end; several hidden gems satisfy your taste buds without emptying your wallet.

Fun Facts You Say Chili, We Say Chile

You'll never see "chili" on a menu in New Mexico. New Mexicans are adamant that *chile,* the Spanish spelling of the word, is the only way to spell it—no matter what your dictionary may say.

Virtually anything you order in a restaurant is likely to be topped with a chile sauce. If you're not accustomed to spicy foods, certain varieties will make your eyes water, your sinuses drain, and your palate feel as if it's on fire. ***Warning:*** No amount of water or beer will alleviate the sting. (Drink milk. A *sopaipilla* drizzled with honey is also helpful.)

But don't let these words of caution scare you away from genuine New Mexico chiles. The pleasure of eating them far outweighs the pain. Start slowly, with salsas and chile sauces first, perhaps rellenos (stuffed peppers) next. Before long, you'll be buying chile *ristras* (chiles strung on rope).

Reservations are always recommended at the higher-end restaurants and are essential during peak seasons. Only a few restaurants serve late, so be sure to plan dinner before 8pm. Most restaurants are casual, so almost any attire is fine, though for the more expensive ones, dressing up is a good idea.

At the beginning of each city's dining section I give more details about the dining scene there.

Food here isn't the same as Mexican cuisine or even those American variations of Tex-Mex and Cal-Mex. New Mexican cooking is a product of Southwestern history: Native Americans taught the Spanish conquerors about corn—how to roast it and how to make corn pudding, stewed corn, cornbread, cornmeal, and *posole* (hominy)—and they also taught the Spanish how to use chile peppers, a crop indigenous to the New World, having been first harvested in the Andean highlands as early as 4000 B.C. The Spaniards brought the practice of eating beef to the area.

Newcomers have introduced other elements to the food here. From Mexico came the interest in seafood. New Southwestern cuisine combines elements from various parts of Mexico, such as sauces from the Yucatán Peninsula, and fried bananas served with bean dishes, typical of Costa Rica and other Central American locales. You'll also find Asian elements mixed in.

The basic ingredients of New Mexico cooking are three indispensable, locally grown foods: **chile, beans,** and **corn.** Of these, perhaps the most crucial is the **chile,** whether brilliant red or green and with various levels of spicy bite. Chile forms the base for the red and green sauces that top most New Mexico dishes such as enchiladas and burritos. One is not necessarily hotter than the other; spiciness depends on the type, and where and during what kind of season (dry or wet) the chiles were grown.

Beans—spotted or painted pinto beans with a nutty taste—are simmered with garlic, onion, cumin, and red chile powder and served as a side dish. When mashed and refried in oil, they become *frijoles refritos.* **Corn** supplies the vital dough for tortillas and tamales called *masa.* New Mexican corn comes in six colors, of which yellow, white, and blue are the most common.

Even if you're familiar with Mexican cooking, the dishes you know and love are likely to be prepared differently here. The following is a rundown of some regional dishes, a number of which aren't widely known outside the Southwest:

biscochito A cookie made with anise.

carne adovada Tender pork marinated in red chile sauce, herbs, and spices, and then baked.

chile rellenos Peppers stuffed with cheese, deep-fried, and then covered with green chile sauce.

chorizo burrito (also called a "breakfast burrito") Mexican sausage, scrambled eggs, potatoes, and scallions wrapped in a flour tortilla with red or green chile sauce and melted Jack cheese.

empanada A fried pie with nuts and currants.

enchiladas Tortillas either rolled or layered with chicken, beef, or cheese, topped with chile sauce.

green chile stew Locally grown chiles cooked in a stew with chunks of meat, beans, and potatoes.

huevos rancheros Fried eggs on corn tortillas, topped with cheese and red or green chile, served with pinto beans.

pan dulce A sweet Native American bread.

posole A corn soup or stew (called hominy in other parts of the south), sometimes prepared with pork and chile.

sopaipilla A lightly fried puff pastry served with honey as a dessert or stuffed with meat and vegetables as a main dish. Sopaipillas with honey have a cooling effect on your palate after you've eaten a spicy dish.

tacos Spiced chicken or beef served either in soft tortillas or crispy shells.

tamales A dish made from cornmeal mush, wrapped in husks and steamed.

3

Planning Your Trip to New Mexico

As with any trip, a little preparation is essential before you start your journey to New Mexico. This chapter provides a variety of planning tools, including information on when to go and how to get there.

FROMMER'S PLANNING INFORMATION

Warning: A trip to New Mexico can give you an attitude problem. You may return home and find that your response to the world is completely different from the way it used to be. (That is, if you return at all.) When you enter the Land of Enchantment, you find few customary points of reference. Rather than sharp-cornered buildings, you find more rounded ones made of adobe bricks. Rather than hearing a single language on the street, you hear many, from Navajo and the Pueblo Tiwa and Tewa to Spanish and English. The pace here is slow and the objectives are less obvious than in most places.

And the northern part of the state has its own unique qualities as well. Travelers often think that since this is the desert, it should have saguaro cactus and always be warm. Think again. Much of the area lies upwards of 5,000 feet in elevation, which means that four full seasons act upon the land. So, when you're planning, be sure to take a look at the "When to Travel" sections so you can be prepared.

That said, preparation to come here is simple. Even though many people mistake New Mexico for our lovely neighbor to the south, really, traveling here is much like anywhere in the U.S. You can drink the water and eat all the food you care to eat, except you'll want to take care, as some of the chile can be very hot. The sun at these elevations can also be scorching, so come prepared with a hat and plenty of sunscreen. In fact, the elements here may present the greatest challenge, so be sure to review the section on health later.

Another point to be aware of are the distances between cities. Your best bet is to travel by car here, as many of the "must see" attractions are located off the main thoroughfares traversed by the few public transportation options available here. Besides, there are few enjoyments so great as driving in the sparkling light through crooked farming villages and past ancient ruins, around plazas and over mountain passes, finding your own road to nowhere, and then taking that attitude home.

For additional help in planning your trip and for more on-the-ground resources in New Mexico please turn to the "Fast Facts, Toll-Free Numbers & Websites" appendix on p. 377.

1 VISITOR INFORMATION

Numerous agencies can assist you with planning your trip. The Visitors Information Center for the **New Mexico Department of Tourism** is located at 491 Old Santa Fe Trail,

Santa Fe, NM 87501 (✆ **800/545-2070** or 505/827-7400; www.newmexico.org). Albuquerque, Santa Fe, and Taos each have their own information service for visitors (see the "Orientation" sections in chapters 6, 7, and 8, respectively).

A valuable resource for information on outdoor recreation is the **Public Lands Information Center,** on the south side of town at 1474 Rodeo Rd., Santa Fe, NM 87505 (✆ **877/276-9404** or 505/438-7542; www.publiclands.org). Here, adventurers can find out what's available on lands administered by the National Forest Service, the Bureau of Land Management, the Fish and Wildlife Service, the National Park Service, the New Mexico Department of Game and Fish (which sells hunting and fishing licenses), and the New Mexico State Parks Division. The Information Center collaborates with the New Mexico Department of Tourism. Log on to the website and you'll also be able to access links to hundreds of separate sites, which can be found by looking up either a particular activity or agency.

For Internet addresses of visitor centers in specific cities and towns, see chapters 6 to 12.

The New Mexico Department of Tourism will send you a free state map. Call **800/545-2070** or 505/827-7400. Or check out **www.maporama.com** or **www.mapquest.com**.

2 ENTRY REQUIREMENTS

PASSPORTS

New regulations issued by the Department of Homeland Security now require virtually every air traveler entering the U.S. to show a passport. As of January 23, 2007, all persons, including U.S. citizens, traveling by air between the United States and Canada, Mexico, Central and South America, the Caribbean, and Bermuda are required to present a valid passport. As of January 31, 2008, U.S. and Canadian citizens entering the U.S. at land and sea ports of entry from within the western hemisphere need to present government-issued proof of citizenship, such as a birth certificate, along with a government-issued photo ID, such as a driver's license. A passport is not required for U.S. or Canadian citizens entering by land or sea, but it is highly encouraged to carry one.

For information on how to obtain a passport, go to **"Passports"** in the **"Fast Facts"** section of the appendix (p. 381).

VISAS

The U.S. State Department has a **Visa Waiver Program (VWP)** allowing citizens of the following countries to enter the United States without a visa for stays of up to 90 days: Andorra, Australia, Austria, Belgium, Brunei, Denmark, Finland, France, Germany, Iceland, Ireland, Italy, Japan, Liechtenstein, Luxembourg, Monaco, the Netherlands, New Zealand, Norway, Portugal, San Marino, Singapore, Slovenia, Spain, Sweden, Switzerland, and the United Kingdom. (***Note:*** This list was accurate at press time; for the most up-to-date list of countries in the VWP, consult www.travel.state.gov/visa.) Even though a visa isn't necessary, in an effort to help U.S. officials check travelers against terror watch lists before they arrive at U.S. borders, as of January 12, 2009, visitors from VWP countries must register online before boarding a plane or a boat to the U.S. Travelers will complete an electronic application providing basic personal and travel eligibility information. The Department of Homeland Security recommends filling out the form at least 3 days before traveling. Authorizations will be valid for up to 2 years or until the traveler's passport expires, whichever comes first. Currently, there is no fee for the online application. Canadian citizens may enter the United

States without visas; they will need to show passports (if traveling by air) and proof of residence, however. ***Note:*** Any passport issued on or after October 26, 2006, by a VWP country must be an **e-Passport** for VWP travelers to be eligible to enter the U.S. without a visa. Citizens of these nations also need to present a round-trip air or cruise ticket upon arrival. E-Passports contain computer chips capable of storing biometric information, such as the required digital photograph of the holder. (You can identify an e-Passport by the symbol on the bottom center cover of your passport.) If your passport doesn't have this feature, you can still travel without a visa if it is a valid passport issued before October 26, 2005, and includes a machine-readable zone, or between October 26, 2005, and October 25, 2006, and includes a digital photograph. For more information, go to **www.travel.state.gov/visa.**

Citizens of all other countries must have (1) a valid passport that expires at least 6 months later than the scheduled end of their visit to the U.S., and (2) a tourist visa. To obtain a visa, applicants must schedule an appointment with a U.S. consulate or embassy, fill out the application forms (available from www.travel.state.gov/visa), and pay a $131 fee. Wait times can be lengthy, so it's best to initiate the process early.

As of January 2004, many international visitors traveling on visas to the United States will be photographed and fingerprinted on arrival at Customs in airports and on cruise ships in a program created by the Department of Homeland Security called **US-VISIT.** Exempt from the extra scrutiny are visitors entering by land or those (mostly in Europe; see p. 37) who don't require a visa for short-term visits. For more information, go to the Homeland Security website at **www.dhs.gov/dhspublic**.

For specifics on how to get a visa, go to **"Visas"** in the **"Fast Facts"** section of the appendix (p. 383).

MEDICAL REQUIREMENTS

Unless you're arriving from an area known to be suffering from an epidemic (particularly cholera or yellow fever), inoculations or vaccinations are not required for entry into the United States.

CUSTOMS

What You Can Bring into the U.S.

Every visitor more than 21 years of age may bring in, free of duty, the following: (1) 1 liter of wine or hard liquor; (2) 200 cigarettes, 100 cigars (but not from Cuba), or 3 pounds of smoking tobacco; and (3) $100 worth of gifts. These exemptions are offered to travelers who spend at least 72 hours in the United States and who have not claimed them within the preceding 6 months. It is forbidden to bring into the country almost any meat products (including canned, fresh, and dried meat products such as buillion, soup mixes, and so on). Generally, condiments including vinegars, oils, spices, coffee, tea, and some cheeses and baked goods are permitted. Avoid rice products, as rice can often harbor insects. Bringing fruits and vegetables is not advised, though not prohibited. Customs will allow produce depending on where you got it and where you're going after you arrive in the U.S. Foreign tourists may carry in or out up to $10,000 in U.S. or foreign currency with no formalities; larger sums must be declared to U.S. Customs on entering or leaving, which includes filing form CM 4790. For details regarding U.S. Customs and Border Protection, consult your nearest U.S. embassy or consulate, or **U.S. Customs** (www.customs.ustreas.gov).

What You Can Take Home from New Mexico

Canadian Citizens: For a clear summary of Canadian rules, write for the booklet *I Declare,* issued by the Canada Border Services

Agency (✆ **800/461-9999** in Canada, or 204/983-3500; www.cbsa-asfc.gc.ca).

U.K. Citizens: For information, contact **HM Customs & Excise** at ✆ **0845/010-9000** (from outside the U.K., 020/8929-0152), or consult the website at **www.hmce.gov.uk**.

Australian Citizens: A helpful brochure available from Australian consulates or Customs offices is *Know Before You Go.* For more information, call the **Australian Customs Service** at ✆ **1300/363-263,** or log on to **www.customs.gov.au**.

New Zealand Citizens: Most questions are answered in a free pamphlet available at New Zealand consulates and Customs offices: *New Zealand Customs Guide for Travellers, Notice no. 4.* For more information, contact **New Zealand Customs,** the Customhouse, 17–21 Whitmore St., Box 2218, Wellington (✆ **04/473-6099** or 0800/428-786; **www.customs.govt.nz**).

3 WHEN TO GO

Summers are hot throughout most of the state, though distinctly cooler at higher elevations. Winters are relatively mild in the south, harsher in the north and in the mountains. Spring and fall have pleasant temperatures, though in spring the wind blows throughout the state. Rainfall is sparse except in the higher mountains; summer afternoon thunderstorms and winter snows account for most precipitation.

Santa Fe and Taos, at 7,000 feet, have midsummer highs in the low 90s (about 32°C), overnight midwinter lows in the teens (between –12° and –7°C). Temperatures in Albuquerque, at 5,300 feet, often run about 10°F warmer than elsewhere in the northern region. Snowfall is common November through March, and sometimes as late as May, though it seldom lasts long. Santa Fe averages 32 inches total annual snowfall. At the high-mountain ski resorts, as much as 300 inches may fall—and stay—in a season. The plains and deserts of the southeast and south commonly have summer temperatures in excess of 100°F (38°C).

New Mexico Temperatures (High/Low) & Precipitation

		Jan	Apr	July	Oct	Annual Precipitation (inches)
Alamogordo	(°F)	57/28	78/40	95/65	79/42	7.5
	(°C)	14/–2	26/4	35/18	26/6	
Albuquerque	(°F)	47/28	70/41	92/66	74/45	8.5
	(°C)	8/–2	21/5	33/19	22/7	
Carlsbad	(°F)	60/28	81/46	96/67	80/49	12.6
	(°C)	16/–2	27/7	36/19	27/9	
Chama	(°F)	33/3	54/22	73/37	52/18	20.9
	(°C)	–1/–16	12/–6	23/3	11/–8	
Cloudcroft	(°F)	41/19	56/33	73/48	59/36	26.5
	(°C)	5/–7	13/–1	23/9	15/2	
Farmington	(°F)	44/16	70/36	92/58	70/37	8.2
	(°C)	7/–9	21/2	33/14	21/3	
Las Cruces	(°F)	56/29	79/48	96/68	78/50	8.6
	(°C)	13/–2	26/9	36/20	26/10	
Roswell	(°F)	56/24	78/42	91/65	79/46	12.7
	(°C)	13/–4	26/6	33/18	26/7	
Ruidoso	(°F)	50/17	65/28	82/48	68/31	21.4
	(°C)	10/–8	18/–2	28/9	20/–1	

		Jan	Apr	July	Oct	Annual Precipitation (inches)
Santa Fe	(°F)	47/18	64/33	85/56	67/38	11.4
	(°C)	8/–8	18/1	29/13	19/3	
Taos	(°F)	40/10°F	64/29°F	87/50°F	75/32°F	12.0
	(°C)	4/–12	18/–2	31/10	24/0	
Truth or	(°F)	54/27	75/44	92/66	75/47	9.9
Consequences	(°C)	12/–3	24/7	33/19	24/8	

NEW MEXICO CALENDAR OF EVENTS

New Mexico offers plenty of reasons to celebrate, ranging from a chile fest to an alien bash to a duck race. The most unique events, however, involve the culture here, such as Santa Fe's Indian and Spanish markets, Native American dances at the pueblos, and the many fiestas held on town plazas throughout the state. Of course, the region's most picturesque event, the Albuquerque International Balloon Fiesta, fills the sky with unforgettable beauty.

For an exhaustive list of events beyond those listed here, check http://events.frommers.com, where you'll find a searchable, up-to-the-minute roster of what's happening in cities all over the world.

January

New Year's Day. Transfer of canes to new officials and various dances at most pueblos. Turtle Dance at Taos Pueblo (no photography allowed). Call ✆ **575/758-1028** or go to www.taospueblo.com for more information. January 1.

Winter Wine Festival (✆ **575/776-2291;** www.skitaos.org). A variety of wine offerings and food tastings prepared by local chefs take place in the Taos Ski Valley. Mid-January.

February

Mt. Taylor Winter Quadrathlon (✆ **800/748-2142**). Hundreds of athletes come from all over the West to bicycle, run, cross-country ski, and snowshoe up and down this mountain. Mid-February.

Just Desserts Eat and Ski (✆ **505/754-2374;** www.enchantedforestxc.com). Cross-country skiers ski from point to point on the Enchanted Forest course near Red River, tasting decadent desserts supplied by area restaurants. Late February.

March

National Fiery Foods/Barbecue Show (✆ **505/873-8680;** www.fiery-foods.com). Here's your chance to taste the hottest of the hot and plenty of milder flavors, too. Some 10,000 people show up to taste sauces, salsas, candies, and more, and to see cooking demonstrations at the Sandia Resort and Convention Center. Early March.

Rio Grande Arts and Crafts Festival (✆ **505/292-7457;** www.riograndefestivals.com). A juried show featuring 200 artists and craftspeople from around the country takes place at the State Fairgrounds in Albuquerque. Second week of March.

Chimayo Pilgrimage (✆ **505/351-4889**). Thousands of pilgrims trek on foot to the Santuario de Chimayo, a small church north of Santa Fe that's believed to aid in miracles. Good Friday.

Rockhound Roundup, Deming (✆ **575/543-8915** or 575/267-4399; www.dgms.bravehost.com). Gems, jewelry, tools, and crafted items are displayed and sold at the Southwest New

Mexico State Fairgrounds. Second weekend in March.

April

Easter Weekend Celebration. Celebrations include Masses, parades, corn dances, and other dances, such as the bow and arrow dance at Nambe. Call ✆ **505/843-7270** for information.

American Indian Week, Indian Pueblo Cultural Center, Albuquerque. A celebration of Native American traditions and culture. For dates and information, contact ✆ **505/843-7270** or www.indianpueblo.org.

Gathering of Nations Powwow, University Arena, Albuquerque (✆ **505/836-2810;** www.gatheringofnations.com). Dance competitions, arts-and-crafts exhibitions, and Miss Indian World contest. Late April.

May

Cinco de Mayo Fiestas, statewide. The restoration of the Mexican republic (from French occupation during 1863–67) is celebrated in, among other places, Las Cruces at Old Mesilla Plaza. First weekend in May.

Taste of Santa Fe (✆ **505/982-6366,** ext. 112). Sample Santa Fe's best chefs' recipes, including appetizers, entrees, and desserts at Santa Fe's La Fonda Hotel. Held in May or June.

Taos Spring Arts Celebration. Contemporary visual, performing, and literary arts are highlighted during a month of gallery openings, studio tours, performances by visiting theatrical and dance troupes, live musical events, traditional ethnic entertainment, literary readings, and more. Events are held at venues throughout Taos and Taos County. For dates and ticket info contact the Taos County Chamber of Commerce, 108 F Kit Carson Rd., Taos, NM 87571 (✆ **800/732-TAOS** or 575/751-8800; www.taoschamber.com). All month.

June

Aztec Fiesta Days, Aztec (✆ **505/334-9551;** www.aztecchamber.com). Celebrate the arrival of summer with three parades, games, food, arts and crafts, and a carnival. First full weekend in June.

Rodeo de Santa Fe (✆ **505/471-4300;** www.rodeodesantafe.org). This 4-day event features a Western parade, a rodeo dance, and five rodeo performances. It attracts hundreds of cowboys and cowgirls from all over the Southwest who compete for sizable purses in such events as Brahma bull and bronco riding, calf roping, steer wrestling, barrel racing, trick riding, and clown and animal acts.

The rodeo grounds are at 3237 Rodeo Rd., off Cerrillos Road, 5½ miles south of the plaza. Performances are in the evening Wednesday to Saturday, and on Saturday afternoon. It takes place sometime around the third weekend in June.

Rodeo de Taos, County Fairgrounds, Taos. A fun event featuring local and regional participants. For information, call ✆ **575/758-5700** or, in mid- to late June, call ✆ 575/758-3974. Third or fourth weekend in June.

Taos Solar Music Festival, Kit Carson Municipal Park, Taos (✆ **575/758-9191;** www.solarmusicfest.com). Sit out on the grass, under the sun, and listen to major players at this event celebrating the summer solstice. A tribute to solar energy, the event has a stage powered by a solar generator and educational displays within a "Solar Village." Late June.

New Mexico Arts and Crafts Fair (✆ **505/884-9043;** www.nmartsandcraftsfair.org). A tradition for 47 years, this juried show held at the State Fairgrounds in Albuquerque offers works from more than 200 New Mexico artisans, accompanied by nonstop entertainment for the whole family. This can be a good place to find Hispanic arts and crafts. Last full weekend in June.

JULY

Apache Maidens' Puberty Rites, Mescalero. This 4-day ceremony concludes with a rodeo and the dance of the mountain spirits. Call ✆ **575/464-4494** for more information. July 1 to 4.

Fourth of July celebrations (including fireworks displays) are held all over New Mexico. Call the chambers of commerce in specific towns and cities for information. One of the best is the **Fiestas de Las Vegas,** at the plaza, which includes a parade, concerts, and food booths. Contact ✆ **800/832-5947** or 505/425-8631; www.lvsmchamber.org.

Pancake Breakfast on the Plaza, Santa Fe. Rub elbows with Santa Fe residents at this locals' event on the plaza. For information contact ✆ **505/982-2002** or www.santafe.org. July 4.

UFO Festival, Roswell (✆ **575/625-8607;** www.roswellufofestival.com). This festival celebrates all manner of extraterrestrial oddity that has sprung to life since the alleged 1947 alien crash in Roswell. More than 7,000 visitors fill the town to attend lectures and participate in a costume contest and parade. Early July.

Santa Fe International Folk Art Market (✆ **505/988-1234;** www.folkartmarket.org). This has fast become one of the city's most popular summer events. Artisans from all over the world come to display and sell works ranging from basketry to textiles outside the International Museum of Folk Art. Concerts, dance performances, and children's programs charge the air, while the scent of delectable food wafts about. Early July.

Santa Fe Opera (✆ **505/986-5955;** www.santafeopera.org). The world-class Santa Fe Opera season offers contemporary and traditional opera in a stunning indoor-outdoor theater in the hills outside the city. July through August.

Taos Pueblo Powwow (✆ **575/758-1028;** www.taospueblopowwow.com). An intertribal competition in traditional and contemporary dances. Second weekend in July.

Eight Northern Pueblos Artist and Craftsman Show. More than 600 Native American artists exhibit their work at the eight northern pueblos. Traditional dances and food booths; location varies. Contact ✆ **505/747-1593** or www.eightnorthern.org for location and exact dates. Third weekend in July.

Fiestas de Santiago y Santa Ana. The celebration begins with a Friday-night Mass at one of the three Taos-area parishes, where the fiesta queen is crowned. During the weekend there are candlelight processions, special Masses, music, dancing, parades, crafts, and food booths. Taos Plaza hosts many events and most are free. For information, contact the Taos Fiesta Council, P.O. Box 3300, Taos, NM 87571 (✆ **800/732-8267;** www.fiestasdetaos.com). Third weekend in July.

Spanish Market. More than 300 Hispanic artists from New Mexico and southern Colorado exhibit and sell their work in this lively community event. Artists are featured in special demonstrations, while an entertaining mix of traditional Hispanic music, dance, foods, and pageantry creates the ambience of a village celebration. Artwork for sale includes *santos* (painted and carved saints), textiles, tinwork, furniture, straw appliqué, and metalwork.

The markets are found at Santa Fe Plaza in Santa Fe. For information, contact the Spanish Colonial Arts Society, P.O. Box 5378, Santa Fe, NM 87502

(✆ **505/982-2226;** www.spanishmarket.org). Last full weekend in July.

Bat Flight Breakfast, Carlsbad Caverns National Park. An early morning buffet breakfast is served while participants watch the bats return to the cave. Contact ✆ **575/785-2232** for details and exact date or www.nps.gov/cave. Mid- to late-July or early August.

Old Lincoln Days and Billy the Kid Pageant, Lincoln. The main attraction is a reenactment of Billy the Kid's escape from the Lincoln jail. There are also a fiddling contest and living-history demonstrations (such as weaving and blacksmithing). Contact ✆ **575/653-4372** or www.nmmonuments.org for more information. Last weekend in July or first weekend in August.

August

Inter-tribal Indian Ceremonial, near Gallup Contact (✆ **800/242-4282** or http://gallup-ceremonial.org). Thirty tribes from the United States and Mexico participate in rodeos, parades, dances, athletic competitions, and an arts and crafts show at Red Rock Park, east of Gallup. Late July or early to mid-August.

Pueblo Independence Day, Jemez Pueblo. Participants from many of the Pueblos convene to celebrate the Pueblo Revolt of 1680. Food, art booths, dances, and live music fill the sunny plaza. Contact ✆ **575/834-7235** or go to www.jemezpueblo.org. Mid-August.

Zuni Arts & Cultural Expo. This 3-day event features arts-and-crafts sales and traditional food and dances. Contact ✆ **575/782-7238** or www.experiencezuni.com for more information. Second week in August.

Chama Days. A rodeo, parade, and arts-and-crafts fair highlight this mountain-town event. Second weekend of August.

The Indian Market. This is the largest all–Native American market in the country. About 1,000 artisans display their baskets and blankets, jewelry, pottery, woodcarvings, rugs, sand paintings, and sculptures at rows of booths around Santa Fe Plaza, surrounding streets, and de Vargas Mall. Sales are brisk. Costumed tribal dancing and crafts demonstrations are scheduled in the afternoon.

The market is free, but hotels are booked months in advance. For information, contact the **Southwestern Association for Indian Arts,** P.O. Box 969, Santa Fe, NM 87504-0969 (✆ **505/983-5220;** www.swaia.org). Third weekend in August.

Music from Angel Fire. World-class musicians gather in Angel Fire to perform classical and chamber music. For information and schedules, call ✆ **575/377-3233** or go to www.musicfromangelfire.org. Mid-August to the first week in September.

Great American Duck Race, Deming (✆ **888/345-1125;** www.demingduckrace.com). Devised in a bar in 1979, this event has grown to include a parade, a tortilla toss, an outhouse race, ballooning, dances, and, of course, the duck race. It takes place on the courthouse lawn ("Duck Downs"). Fourth weekend in August.

September

Artist Studio Tours take place all over northern New Mexico in the fall. For specific detail see "High on Art" in chapter 7.

The All American Futurity, Ruidoso Downs, Ruidoso. With a purse of $2 million, this is the world's richest quarter-horse race. Contact ✆ **575/378-4431** or www.ruidosodownsracing.com. Labor Day.

Chile Festival, Hatch (✆ **575/267-5050;** www.hatchchilefest.com). New

Mexicans celebrate their favorite fiery food item with a festival in the "Chile Capital of the World." Labor Day weekend.

New Mexico Wine Festival (✆ **505/867-3311;** www.newmexicowinefestival.com). New Mexico wines are showcased at this annual event in Bernalillo, near Albuquerque, which features wine tastings, an art show, and live entertainment. Labor Day weekend.

Las Fiestas de Santa Fe. An exuberant combination of spirit, history, and general merrymaking, Las Fiestas is the oldest community celebration in the United States. The first fiesta was celebrated in 1712, 20 years after the resettlement of New Mexico by Spanish conquistadors in 1692. The celebration includes Masses, parades, mariachi concerts, dances, food, and arts, as well as local entertainment on the plaza. Zozobra, "Old Man Gloom," a 40-foot-tall effigy made of wood, canvas, and paper, is burned at dusk on Thursday to revitalize the community. Zozobra kicks off Las Fiestas. For information, call ✆ **505/988-7575** or go to www.santafe.org. Weekend following Labor Day.

Enchanted Circle Century Bike Tour. About 500 cyclists turn out to ride 100 miles of scenic mountain roads, starting and ending in Red River. All levels of riders are welcome, though not everyone completes this test of endurance. Call ✆ **505/754-2366** or go to www.enchantedforestxc.com for details. Weekend following Labor Day.

New Mexico State Fair and Rodeo. This is one of America's top state fairs; it features parimutuel horse racing, a nationally acclaimed rodeo, entertainment by top country artists, Native American and Spanish villages, the requisite midway, livestock shows, and arts and crafts.

The fair and rodeo, which last 17 days, are held at the State Fairgrounds in Albuquerque. Advance tickets can be ordered by calling ✆ **505/265-1791** or visiting www.exponm.com. Early September.

Santa Fe Wine & Chile Fiesta. This lively celebration boasts 5 days of wine and food events, including seminars, guest chef demonstrations and luncheons, tours, a grand tasting and reserve tasting, an auction, and a golf tournament. It takes place at many venues in downtown Santa Fe with the big event on the last Saturday. Tickets go on sale in early July and sell out quickly. For tickets and information, call ✆ **505/438-8060** or visit www.santafewineandchile.org. Last Wednesday through Sunday in September.

Stone Lake Fiesta, Jicarilla Reservation, 19 miles south of Dulce. This Apache festival features a rodeo, ceremonial dances, and a foot race. For more information call ✆ **575/759-3242,** ext. 275 or 277, or go to www.jicarillaonline.com. September 15.

Mexican Independence Day. A parade and dances take place in Las Cruces at Old Mesilla Plaza (✆ **575/524-3262;** www.vivamesilla.org) and Carlsbad at San Jose Plaza (✆ **800/221-1224** or 575/887-6516; www.carlsbadchamber.com). Weekend closest to September 16.

Taos Trade Fair, La Hacienda de los Martinez, Lower Ranchitos Road, Taos (✆ **575/758-0505**). This 2-day affair reenacts Spanish colonial life of the mid-1820s and features Hispanic and Native American music, weaving and crafts demonstrations, traditional foods, dancing, and visits by mountain men. Last full weekend in September.

San Geronimo Vespers Sundown Dance and Trade Fair, Taos Pueblo. This event features a Mass and procession; traditional corn, buffalo, and

Comanche dances; an arts-and-crafts fair; foot races; and pole climbs by clowns. Contact © **575/758-0505** or go to www.taospueblo.com for details. Last weekend in September.

Taos Fall Arts Festival. Highlights include arts-and-crafts exhibitions and competitions, studio tours, gallery openings, lectures, concerts, dances, and stage plays. Simultaneous events include the **Old Taos Trade Fair,** the **Wool Festival,** and **San Geronimo Day** at Taos Pueblo.

The festival is held throughout Taos and Taos County. Events, schedules, and tickets (where required) can be obtained from the **Taos County Chamber of Commerce,** 108 F. Kit Carson Rd., Taos, NM 87571 (© **800/732-8267** or 575/751-8800; www.taoschamber.com). Mid-September (or the third weekend) to the first week in October.

The Whole Enchilada Fiesta, Las Cruces (© **575/524-1968;** www.enchilada fiesta.com). The world's biggest enchilada (sometimes over 7 ft. wide) is created and eaten. Late September or early October.

October

Shiprock Navajo Fair, Shiprock (© **800/448-1240**). The oldest and most traditional Navajo fair, it features a rodeo, dancing and singing, a parade, and arts-and-crafts exhibits. Early October.

Rio Grande Arts and Crafts Festival, Albuquerque (© **505/292-7457;** www. riograndefestivals.com). This event features artists and craftspeople from around the country. First and second weekends in October.

Albuquerque International Balloon Fiesta (© **800/733-9918;** www.balloon fiesta.com). The world's largest balloon rally, this 9-day festival brings together more than 700 colorful balloons and includes races and contests. There are mass ascensions at sunrise, "balloon glows" in the evening, and balloon rides for those desiring a little lift. Various special events are staged all week.

Balloons lift off at Balloon Fiesta Park (at I-25 and Alameda NE) on Albuquerque's northern city limits. Second week in October.

Taos Mountain Balloon Rally (© **800/732-8267**). The Albuquerque fiesta's "little brother" offers mass dawn ascensions, tethered balloon rides for the public, and a Saturday parade of balloon baskets (in pickup trucks) from Kit Carson Park around the plaza. Last weekend of October.

November

Weems Artfest (© **505/293-6133;** www.weemsgallery.com). Approximately 260 artisans, who work in a variety of media, come from throughout the world to attend this 3-day fair, held at the State Fairgrounds in Albuquerque. It's one of the top 100 arts-and-crafts fairs in the country. Early November.

Festival of the Cranes. People come from all over the world to attend this bird-watching event just an hour and a half south of Albuquerque at Bosque del Apache National Wildlife Refuge, near Socorro. For details call © **505/835-1828** or go to www.friendsoft hebosque.org. Weekend before Thanksgiving.

Yuletide in Taos. This holiday event emphasizes northern New Mexican traditions, cultures, and arts, with carols, festive classical music, Hispanic and Native American songs and dances, historic walking tours, art exhibitions, dance performances, candlelight dinners, and more.

Events are staged by the **Taos County Chamber of Commerce,** 108 F. Kit Carson Rd., Taos, NM 87571 (© **800/732-8267;** www.taoschamber.com). From Thanksgiving through New Year's Day.

Christmas on the Pecos, Carlsbad (✆ **800/221-1224** or 505/877-6516; www.christmasonthepecos.com). Pontoon-boat rides take place each evening, past a fascinating display of Christmas lights on riverside homes and businesses. Thanksgiving to New Year's Eve (except Christmas Eve).

Winter Spanish Market, Santa Fe Convention Center, Santa Fe. Approximately 150 artists show their wares at this little sister to July's major event. See the Spanish Market in July (see above) for more information. For details call ✆ **505/982-2226** or go to www.spanishcolonial.org. First full weekend in December.

Christmas in Madrid Open House. Even if you never get out of your car, it's worth going to see the spectacular lights display in this village between Albuquerque and Santa Fe on the Turquoise Trail. You'll also find entertainment, refreshments in shops, and Santa Claus. For additional information, contact ✆ **505/471-1054** or go to www.visitmadrid.com. First two weekends in December.

Canyon Road Farolito Walk, Santa Fe. Locals and visitors bundle up and stroll Canyon Road, where streets and rooftops are lined with *farolitos* (candle lamps). Musicians play and carolers sing around *luminarias* (little fires). Though it's not responsible for the event, the **Santa Fe Convention and Visitors Bureau** (✆ **505/955-6200;** www.santafe.org) can help direct you there; or ask your hotel concierge. Christmas Eve at dusk.

Christmas Native American Celebrations. Many of the pueblos have winter dances, including the Matachine and buffalo. For more information, contact the **Indian Pueblo Cultural Center** at ✆ **866/855-7902** or 505/843-7270; or go online to www.indianpueblo.org. December 24 and 25.

Our Lady of Guadalupe Fiesta, Tortugas, near Las Cruces. This pilgrimage to Tortugas Mountain and torchlight descent is followed by a Mass and traditional Native American and Hispanic dances. Call ✆ **575/526-8171** for more information. December 10 to 12.

Torchlight Procession, Taos Ski Valley. Bold skiers carve down a steep run named Snakedance in the dark while carrying golden fire. For information, call ✆ **800/992-7669** or 575/776-2291, or visit www.skitaos.org. December 31.

4 GETTING THERE & GETTING AROUND

GETTING TO NEW MEXICO

By Plane

The gateway to Santa Fe, Taos, and other New Mexico communities is the **Albuquerque International Sunport** (**ABQ;** ✆ **505/842-4366** for the administrative offices; www.cabq.gov/airport; call the individual airlines for flight information).

A secondary hub for southern New Mexico is **El Paso International Airport** (**ELP;** ✆ **915/780-4700;** www.elpasointernationalairport.com) in western Texas.

Both airports are served by **American** (✆ 800/433-7300; www.aa.com), **Continental** (✆ 800/523-3273; www.continental.com), **Delta** (✆ 800/221-1212; www.delta.com), **Express Jet** (✆ 888/958-9538; www.expressjet.com), **Frontier** (✆ 800/432-1359; www.frontierairlines.com), **Southwest** (✆ 800/435-9792; www.southwest.com), **United** (✆ 800/241-6522; www.united.com), and **US**

From	Distance	From	Distance
Atlanta	1,417	Minneapolis	1,199
Boston	2,190	New Orleans	1,181
Chicago	1,293	New York	1,971
Cleveland	1,558	Oklahoma City	533
Dallas	663	Phoenix	595
Denver	391	St. Louis	993
Detroit	1,514	Salt Lake City	634
Houston	900	San Francisco	1,149
Los Angeles	860	Seattle	1,477
Miami	2,011	Washington, D.C.	1,825

Airways (✆ 800/235-9292; www.usairways.com). An additional airline serving Albuquerque is **Northwest** (✆ 800/225-2525; www.nwa.com).

A few flights may be flying to the **Santa Fe Municipal Airport** (✆ **505/955-2900**), which would save time for those visiting the City Different, but will cost more than flying into Albuquerque. In conjunction with American Airlines, commuter flights are offered by **American Eagle** (✆ **800/433-7300;** www.aa.com); as well, Delta Airlines (✆ **800/221-1212;** www.delta.com) may begin service in 2009, though no date has been set.

Arriving at the Airport

IMMIGRATION & CUSTOMS CLEARANCE International visitors arriving by air, no matter what the port of entry, should cultivate patience and resignation before setting foot on U.S. soil. U.S. airports have considerably beefed up security clearances in the years since the terrorist attacks of September 11, and clearing Customs and Immigration can take as long as 2 hours.

Getting into Town from the Airport

Most hotels have courtesy vans to meet their guests and take them to their respective destinations. In addition, **Airport Shuttle of Albuquerque** (✆ **505/765-1234;** www.airportshuttleabq.com) in Albuquerque runs vans to and from city hotels. In Santa Fe, **Roadrunner Shuttle** (✆ **505/424-3367**) meets flights and takes visitors anywhere in Santa Fe. **Las Cruces Shuttle Service** (✆ **800/288-1784;** www.lascrucesshuttle.com) travels between the El Paso International Airport and Las Cruces. If you're flying into Albuquerque and need to get to Santa Fe, see the "By Bus" section below.

By Car

Three interstate highways cross New Mexico. The north-south I-25 bisects the state, passing through Albuquerque and Las Cruces. The east-west I-40 follows the path of the old Route 66 through Gallup, Albuquerque, and Tucumcari in the north; while I-10 from San Diego crosses southwestern New Mexico until intersecting I-25 at Las Cruces.

See "Getting Around New Mexico," below, for information about driving in New Mexico.

By Bus

Because Santa Fe is only about 58 miles northeast of Albuquerque via I-40, most visitors to Santa Fe take the bus directly from the Albuquerque airport, at a cost of about $20 to $25 one-way. **Sandia Shuttle**

Express buses (✆ **888/775-5696;** www.sandiashuttle.com) make the 70-minute run between the airport and Santa Fe hotels 10 times daily each way (from Albuquerque to Santa Fe 6:30am–6pm; from Santa Fe to Albuquerque 8:45am–8:20pm). Reservations are required, ideally 48 hours in advance. Two other bus services shuttle between Albuquerque and Taos (via Santa Fe) for $25 to $35 one-way: **Faust's Transportation** (✆ **888/830-3410** or 505/758-3410) and **Twin Heart Express & Transportation** (✆ **800/654-9456** or 505/751-1201).

The **public bus depot** in Albuquerque is located at 100 1st Street SW. Contact **Texas, New Mexico, and Oklahoma (TNM&O;** ✆ **505/242-4998;** www.tnmo.com) for information and schedules. Fares run about $15 to Santa Fe and $25 to Taos. However, the **bus stations** in Santa Fe (858 St. Michael's Dr.; ✆ **505/471-0008**) and Taos (5 miles south of the plaza at 710 Paseo del Pueblo Sur; ✆ **575/758-1144**) are several miles south of each city center. Because additional taxi or shuttle service is needed to reach most accommodations, travelers usually find it more convenient to pay a few extra dollars for an airport-to-hotel shuttle.

By Train

Amtrak (✆ **800/USA-RAIL** or 505/842-9650; www.amtrak.com) has two routes through the state. Greyhound/Trailways bus lines provide through-ticketing for Amtrak between Albuquerque and El Paso.

You can get a copy of Amtrak's National Timetable from any Amtrak station, from travel agents, or by writing Amtrak, 400 N. Capitol St. NW, Washington, DC 20001. You can also check Amtrak timetables online. A photo ID is required for check-in.

GETTING AROUND NEW MEXICO

By Plane

New Mexico doesn't have many carriers flying between its cities, which is just as well. The best parts of the region happen *between* the major destinations.

Overseas visitors can take advantage of the APEX (Advance Purchase Excursion) reductions offered by all major U.S. and European carriers. In addition, some large airlines offer transatlantic or transpacific passengers special discount tickets under the name **Visit USA,** which allows mostly one-way travel from one U.S. destination to another at very low prices. Unavailable in the U.S., these discount tickets must be purchased abroad in conjunction with your international fare. This system is the easiest, fastest, cheapest way to see the country.

If you don't have a car and don't want to rent one, there are a few flights. The principal carrier is **Great Lakes Airlines** (✆ **800/554-5111;** www.flygreatlakes.com), which flies from Albuquerque to Farmington and Grant County Airport near Silver City. As well, the **Roswell Airport,** at Roswell Industrial Air Center, is served commercially by **American Eagle Airlines** (✆ **800/433-7300;** www.aa.com), directly from Dallas, Texas, twice daily. And **New Mexico Airlines** (✆ **888/564-6119;** www.pacificwings.com/nma) provides daily flights between Albuquerque and **Cavern City Air Terminal** near Carlsbad.

By Car

If you plan to drive your own vehicle to and around New Mexico, give it a thorough road check before starting out. The state offers plenty of wide-open desert and wilderness spaces, and it's not fun to be stranded in the heat or cold with a vehicle that doesn't run. Check with your auto-insurance company to make sure you're covered when out of state or when driving a rental car.

Gasoline is readily available at service stations throughout the state. Prices are cheapest in Albuquerque and 10% to 15% more expensive in more isolated communities. All prices are subject to the same fluctuations as elsewhere in the United States.

Drive Carefully

US 491, formerly US 666, between Gallup and Shiprock, was at one time labeled America's "most dangerous highway" by *USA Today.* Though in recent years it has become safer, it still merits cautious driving. In addition, New Mexico has a high per-capita rate of traffic deaths. Drive carefully!

Indian reservations are considered sovereign nations, and they enforce their own laws. For instance, on the Navajo reservation (New Mexico's largest), it's prohibited to transport alcoholic beverages, to leave established roadways, or to travel without a seat belt. While there, abide by speed limits and follow traffic signs.

Drivers who need wheelchair-accessible transportation should call **Wheelchair Getaways of New Mexico,** 1015 Tramway Lane NE, Albuquerque (✆ **800/408-2626** or 505/247-2626; www.wheelchair-getaways.com); the company rents vans by the day, week, or month.

If you're visiting from abroad and plan to rent a car in the United States, keep in mind that foreign driver's licenses are usually recognized in the U.S., but you should get an international one if your home license is not in English.

Check out **Breezenet.com,** which offers domestic car-rental discounts with some of the most competitive rates around. Also worth visiting are Orbitz.com, Hotwire.com, Travelocity.com, and Priceline.com, all of which offer competitive online car-rental rates. For listings of the major car rental agencies in New Mexico, please see the "Toll-Free Numbers & Websites" section in the appendix, p. 383.

By Bus

For information about getting to the region's major cities by bus, see the "Getting to New Mexico," section above.

Bus travel is often the most economical form of public transit for short hops between U.S. cities, but it's certainly not an option for everyone (particularly when Amtrak, which is far more luxurious, offers similar rates). **Greyhound** (✆ **800/231-2222;** www.greyhound.com) is the sole nationwide bus line. International visitors can obtain information about the **Greyhound North American Discovery Pass.** The pass, which offers unlimited travel and stopovers in the U.S. and Canada, can be obtained from foreign travel agents or through www.discoverypass.com.

By Train

International visitors can buy a **USA Rail Pass,** good for 15 or 30 days of unlimited travel on **Amtrak** (✆ **800/USA-RAIL;** www.amtrak.com). The pass is available online or through many overseas travel agents. See Amtrak's website for the cost of travel within the western, eastern, or northwestern United States. Reservations are generally required and should be made as early as possible. Regional rail passes are also available.

Amtrak's northern New Mexico line, the *Southwest Chief,* runs west-east and east-west once daily, with stops in Gallup, Grants, Albuquerque, Lamy (for Santa Fe), Las Vegas, and Raton. The *Sunset Unlimited* connects Lordsburg and Deming with El Paso, Texas, three times weekly each direction. Greyhound/Trailways bus lines provide through-ticketing for Amtrak passengers between Albuquerque and El Paso. Railway routes are extremely limited around northern New Mexico. Contact **Amtrak** (✆ **800/USA-RAIL** or 505/842-9650; www.amtrak.com) for more information.

What Things Cost in Santa Fe	US$	Euro €	UK£
Double room in high season at La Posada de Santa Fe Resort & Spa	299.00	152.00	192.00
Double room in high season at Santa Fe Motel and Inn	130.00	66.00	84.00
Dinner for two at Geronimo, without drinks, tax, or tip	115.00	59.00	74.00
Dinner for two at La Choza, without drinks, tax, or tip	25.00	13.00	16.00
An imported Mexican beer at the Dragon Room	4.00	2.00	2.50
One-hour massage at Ten Thousand Waves Japanese Health Spa	92.00	47.00	59.00
Adult admission to the Museum of International Folk Art	8.00	4.00	5.00

5 MONEY & COSTS

If you come from a major city, such as New York or London, you may find New Mexico overall fairly inexpensive, although Santa Fe will be closer in price to what you're accustomed to. In Taos and Albuquerque, you can still get good accommodations and meals without wincing. Santa Fe, however, may hurt a bit, especially if you hit the hottest spots in town, which cater to sophisticated tastes.

The most common bills are the $1 (a "buck"), $5, $10, and $20 denominations. There are also $2 bills (seldom encountered), $50 bills, and $100 bills (the last two are usually not welcome as payment for small purchases).

Coins come in seven denominations: 1¢ (1 cent, or a penny); 5¢ (5 cents, or a nickel); 10¢ (10 cents, or a dime); 25¢ (25 cents, or a quarter); 50¢ (50 cents, or a half-dollar); the gold-colored Sacagawea coin, worth $1; and the rare silver dollar.

The easiest and best way to get cash away from home is from an ATM (automated teller machine), sometimes referred to as a "cash machine," or "cashpoint." They are available all over New Mexico.

6 HEALTH

STAYING HEALTHY

One thing that sets New Mexico apart from most other states is its elevation. Santa Fe and Taos are about 7,000 feet above sea level; Albuquerque is more than 5,000 feet above sea level. The reduced oxygen and humidity can precipitate some unique problems, as noted below. The desert environment can also present some challenges.

COMMON AILMENTS

HIGH DESERT CHALLENGES One of the most common ailments in New Mexico is acute mountain sickness. In its early stages, you might experience headaches, shortness of breath, loss of appetite and/or nausea, tingling in the fingers or toes, lethargy, and insomnia. The condition can usually be treated by taking aspirin as well

What Things Cost in Las Cruces	US$	Euro €	UK£
Double room in high season at the Hotel Encanto	150.00	95.00	75.00
Double room in high season at La Quinta	85.00	67.00	46.00
Dinner for two at the Double Eagle, without drinks, tax, or tip	80.00	63.00	43.00
Dinner for two at Chope's Bar & Café, without drinks, tax, or tip	25.00	16.00	13.00
An imported Mexican beer at La Posta de Mesilla	3.75	3.00	2.00
Hiking in the Organ Mountains	Free		
Adult admission to the New Mexico Farm and Ranch Heritage Museum	5.00	4.00	3.00

as getting plenty of rest, avoiding large meals, and drinking lots of nonalcoholic fluids (especially water). If the condition persists or worsens, you must return to a lower altitude. Other dangers of higher elevations include hypothermia and sun exposure, and these should be taken seriously. To avoid dehydration, drink water as often as possible.

Limit your exposure to the sun, especially during the first few days of your trip and, thereafter, between 11am and 2pm. Liberally apply sunscreen with a high protection factor. Remember that children need more protection than adults do. It's important to monitor your children's health while in New Mexico. They are just as susceptible to mountain sickness, hypothermia, sunburn, and dehydration as you are.

DIETARY RED FLAGS Though some places in New Mexico can have the feel of towns in our neighboring Mexico, the food and water here are safe. As well, a broad range of food is available, so that even vegetarians can usually find something to eat; small cafes often offer beans and rice. One of the few dietary concerns is the spicy chile, so be sure to ask how hot it is before ordering.

BUGS, BITES & OTHER WILDLIFE CONCERNS If you're an outdoorsperson, be on the lookout for snakes—particularly rattlers. Avoid them. Don't even get close enough to take a picture (unless you have a very good zoom lens). As well, watch for black widows, which have a bulbous body and an hourglass image on their belly; a bite from this spider can make you very sick. The same goes for scorpions, which are crablike spiders with a curled stinging tail. If you get bitten by a snake or spider, or stung by a scorpion, seek professional medical help immediately.

Visitors to the state should also be careful of contracting the plague and hantavirus, a few cases of each reported annually in the state. Both diseases can be fatal, and both are transmitted through exposure to infected rodent droppings. Though it's unlikely that you'll be exposed to such things while traveling, be careful anytime you note the presence of mice or other rodents.

WEATHER CONCERNS You'll also want to be wary of arroyos, or creek beds in the desert where flash floods can occur without warning. If water is flowing across a road, *do not* try to drive through it because chances are the water is deeper and flowing faster than you think. Just wait it out. Arroyo floods don't last long.

General Availability of Health Care

The most reliable hospitals in the area are **St. Vincent's Hospital,** 455 St. Michaels

Avoiding "Economy-Class Syndrome"

Deep vein thrombosis, or as it's know in the world of flying, "economy-class syndrome," is a blood clot that develops in a deep vein. It's a potentially deadly condition that can be caused by sitting in cramped conditions—such as an airplane cabin—for too long. During a flight (especially a long-haul flight), get up, walk around, and stretch your legs every 60 to 90 minutes to keep your blood flowing. Other preventative measures include frequent flexing of the legs while sitting, drinking lots of water, and avoiding alcohol and sleeping pills. If you have a history of deep vein thrombosis, heart disease, or another condition that puts you at high risk, some experts recommend wearing compression stockings or taking anticoagulants when you fly; always ask your physician about the best course for you. Symptoms of deep vein thrombosis include leg pain or swelling, or even shortness of breath.

Dr. in Santa Fe (✆ **505/820-5250**), **Presbyterian Hospital,** 1100 Central Ave. SE in Albuquerque (✆ **505/841-1234,** or 505/841-1111 for emergency service), and **Memorial Medical Center,** 2450 S. Telshor Blvd. in Las Cruces (✆ **575/522-8641**).

WHAT TO DO IF YOU GET SICK AWAY FROM HOME

We list **hospitals** and **emergency numbers** under "Fast Facts" for each city in chapters 6, 7, and 8.

If you suffer from a chronic illness, consult your doctor before your departure. Pack **prescription medications** in your carry-on luggage, and carry them in their original containers, with pharmacy labels—otherwise they won't make it through airport security. Visitors from outside the United States should carry generic names of prescription drugs. For U.S. travelers, most reliable health-care plans provide coverage if you get sick away from home. Foreign visitors may have to pay all medical costs upfront and be reimbursed later. See "Medical Insurance," under "Insurance," in the appendix.

We also list **additional emergency numbers** in the "Fast Facts" appendix, p. 378.

7 SAFETY

Tourist areas as a rule are safe, but, despite recent reports of decreases in violent crime in Santa Fe, it would be wise to check with the tourist offices in Santa Fe, Taos, and Albuquerque if you are in doubt about which neighborhoods are safe. (See the "Orientation" sections in chapters 6, 7, and 8 for the names and addresses of the specific tourist bureaus.)

Remember that hotels are open to the public, and in a large hotel, security may not be able to screen everyone who enters. Always lock your room door; don't assume that once inside your hotel you are automatically safe and no longer need to be aware of your surroundings.

Be aware that New Mexico has a higher-than-average reported incidence of rape. Women should not walk alone in isolated places, particularly at night.

8 SPECIALIZED TRAVEL RESOURCES

TRAVELERS WITH DISABILITIES

Most disabilities shouldn't stop anyone from traveling in the U.S. Thanks to provisions in the Americans with Disabilities Act, most public places are required to comply with disability-friendly regulations. Almost all public establishments (including hotels, restaurants, museums, and so on, but not including certain National Historic Landmarks), and at least some modes of public transportation provide accessible entrances and other facilities for those with disabilities.

Throughout the state of New Mexico, measures have been taken to provide access for travelers with disabilities. Several bed-and-breakfasts have made one or more of their rooms completely wheelchair accessible. The **Information Center for New Mexicans with Disabilities** (✆ **800/552-8195** in New Mexico, or 505/272-8549 outside the state) accesses a database with lists of services ranging from restaurants and hotels to wheelchair rentals. It's a service of the **Developmental Disabilities Planning Council** (✆ **800/311-2229**). The ***Access New Mexico*** guide lists accessible hotels, attractions, and restaurants throughout the state. For more information, contact the **Governor's Commission on Disabilities,** 491 Old Santa Fe Trail, Lamy Building Room 117, Santa Fe, NM 87503 (✆ **505/827-6465;** www.gcd.state.nm.us).

The chambers of commerce in Santa Fe and Taos will answer questions regarding accessibility in their areas. It is advisable to call hotels, restaurants, and attractions in advance to be sure that they are fully accessible.

The **America the Beautiful—National Park and Federal Recreational Lands Pass—Access Pass** (formerly the **Golden Access Passport**) gives visually impaired or those with permanent disabilities (regardless of age) free lifetime entrance to federal recreation sites administered by the National Park Service, including the Fish and Wildlife Service, the Forest Service, the Bureau of Land Management, and the Bureau of Reclamation. This may include national parks, monuments, historic sites, recreation areas, and national wildlife refuges.

The America the Beautiful Access Pass can be obtained only in person at any NPS facility that charges an entrance fee. You need to show proof of a medically determined disability. Besides free entry, the pass also offers a 50% discount on some federal-use fees charged for such facilities as camping, swimming, parking, boat launching, and tours. For more information, go to www.nps.gov/fees_passes.htm or call the United States Geological Survey (USGS), which issues the passes, at ✆ **888/275-8747.**

For more on organizations that offer resources to travelers with disabilities, go to www.frommers.com/planning.

GAY & LESBIAN TRAVELERS

New Mexico is a pretty gay-friendly place in general, especially Santa Fe, with its cosmopolitan attitude. Only in the smaller villages will locals look askance.

Common Bond (✆ **505/891-3647**) provides information and outreach services for Albuquerque's gay and lesbian community as well as referrals for other New Mexico cities. A recorded message on this phone line gives lists of bars and clubs, businesses, and publications, as well as health and crisis information and a calendar of events. Volunteers are on hand (generally in the evenings) to answer questions. Another good resource is **www.gaynm.com**, a website that provides news, resources, and lists of events.

For more gay and lesbian travel resources, visit www.frommers.com/planning.

SENIOR TRAVEL

Recommended publications offering travel resources and discounts for seniors include the Albuquerque-based monthly tabloid ***Prime Time*** (✆ **505/880-0470**), which publishes a variety of articles aimed at New Mexicans 50 years and older.

The U.S. National Park Service offers an **America the Beautiful—National Park and Federal Recreational Lands Pass—Senior Pass** (formerly the **Golden Age Passport**), which gives seniors 62 years or older lifetime entrance to all properties administered by the National Park Service—national parks, monuments, historic sites, recreation areas, and national wildlife refuges—for a one-time processing fee of $10. The pass must be purchased in person at any NPS facility that charges an entrance fee. Besides free entry, the American the Beautiful Senior Pass also offers a 50% discount on some federal-use fees charged for such facilities as camping, swimming, parking, boat launching, and tours. For more information, go to www.nps.gov/fees_passes.htm or call the United States Geological Survey (USGS), which issues the passes, at ✆ **888/275-8747.**

For more information and resources on travel for seniors, see www.frommers.com/planning.

FAMILY TRAVEL

If you have enough trouble getting your kids out of the house in the morning, dragging them thousands of miles away may seem like an insurmountable challenge. But family travel can be immensely rewarding, giving you new ways of seeing the world through smaller pairs of eyes.

Be aware that family travel in New Mexico may be a little different from what you're accustomed to. You'll find few huge Disney-like attractions here. Instead, the draws are culture and the outdoors. Rather than spending time in theme parks, you may go white-water rafting down the Rio Grande, skiing at one of the many family-friendly areas, climbing a wooden ladder up to a cliff dwelling, or trekking through the wilderness with a llama.

If your brood is not very adventurous, don't worry. Some of the hotels and resorts listed in this book have inviting pools to laze around or on-site activities planned especially for kids. Whatever your choice, New Mexico will definitely offer your children a new perspective on the United States by exposing them to ancient ruins, Southwestern cuisine, and Hispanic and Native American cultures that they may not experience elsewhere.

Recommended family travel reading includes:

- The Santa Fe quarterly ***Tumbleweeds*** (✆ **505/984-3171;** www.sftumbleweeds.com) offers useful articles on family-oriented subjects in the Santa Fe area, a quarterly day-by-day calendar of family events, and a seasonal directory of children's classes, camps, and programs. Free in locations all over Santa Fe or by mail for $15.
- Lynnell Diamond's ***New Mexico for Kids*** (Otter Be Reading Books), a learning activity guidebook for young people, is available online at **Amazon.com.**

To locate accommodations, restaurants, and attractions that are particularly kid-friendly, refer to the "Kids" icon throughout this guide. Another helpful resource is *Frommer's Family Vacations in the National Parks.* And, for a list of more family-friendly travel resources, visit www.frommers.com/planning.

9 SUSTAINABLE TOURISM

Sustainable tourism is conscientious travel. It means being careful with the environments you explore, and respecting the communities you visit. Two overlapping components of sustainable travel are **ecotourism** and **ethical tourism.** The **International Ecotourism Society** (TIES) defines ecotourism as responsible travel to natural areas that conserves the environment and improves the well-being of local people. TIES suggests that ecotourists follow these principles:

- Minimize environmental impact.
- Build environmental and cultural awareness and respect.
- Provide positive experiences for both visitors and hosts.
- Provide direct financial benefits for conservation and for local people.
- Raise sensitivity to host countries' political, environmental, and social climates.
- Support international human rights and labor agreements.

You can find some ecofriendly travel tips and statistics, as well as touring companies and associations—listed by destination under "Travel Choice"—at the **TIES** website, www.ecotourism.org. Also check out **Ecotravel.com,** which lets you search for sustainable touring companies in several categories (water-based, land-based, spiritually oriented, and so on).

While much of the focus of ecotourism is about reducing impacts on the natural environment, ethical tourism concentrates on ways to preserve and enhance local economies and communities, regardless of location. You can embrace ethical tourism by staying at a locally owned hotel or shopping at a store that employs local workers and sells locally produced goods.

New Mexico hasn't become a big ecotourism destination but there are a few options. In Taos, **El Monte Sagrado,** a resort near the center of town, offers luxurious surroundings totally in tune with nature, utilizing sustainable technologies throughout. Contact ✆ **800/828-TAOS;** www.elmontesagrado.com. Also, in Taos, the **Old Taos Guesthouse Bed & Breakfast** (✆ **800/758-5448;** www.oldtaos.com) employs many ecofriendly practices. See chapter 8 for more details.

In Santa Fe, **Bishop's Lodge Ranch Resort & Spa** (✆ **800/732-2240;** www.bishopslodge.com), north of town, recycles water in order to irrigate its lush landscape and employs other ecofriendly methods. Also in the City Different, **Santa Fe Mountain Adventures** (✆ **800/965-4010** or 505/988-4000; www.santafemountainadventures.com) leads programs that combine outdoor adventures with arts and cultural experiences, and spa treatments. A collaborative effort in conjunction with *Outside* magazine, the business is eco-conscious.

Responsible Travel (www.responsibletravel.com) is a great source of sustainable travel ideas; the site is run by a spokesperson for ethical tourism in the travel industry. **Sustainable Travel International** (www.sustainabletravelinternational.org) promotes ethical tourism practices and manages an extensive directory of sustainable properties and tour operators around the world.

Volunteer travel has become increasingly popular among those who want to venture beyond the standard group-tour experience to learn languages, interact with locals, and make a positive difference while on vacation. Volunteer travel usually doesn't require special skills—just a willingness to work hard—and programs vary in length from a few days to a number of weeks. Some programs provide free housing and food, but many require volunteers to pay for travel expenses, which can add up quickly.

Frommers.com: The Complete Travel Resource

Planning a trip or just returned? Head to **Frommers.com,** voted Best Travel Site by *PC Magazine.* We think you'll find our site indispensable before, during, and after your travels—with expert advice and tips; independent reviews of hotels, restaurants, attractions, and preferred shopping and nightlife venues; vacation giveaways; and an online booking tool. We publish the complete contents of over 135 travel guides in our **Destinations** section, covering over 4,000 places worldwide. Each weekday, we publish original articles that report on **Deals and News** via our free **Frommers.com Newsletters.** What's more, **Arthur Frommer** himself blogs 5 days a week, with cutting opinions about the state of travel in the modern world. We're betting you'll find our **Events** listings an invaluable resource; it's an up-to-the-minute roster of what's happening in cities everywhere—including concerts, festivals, lectures, and more. We've also added weekly **podcasts, interactive maps,** and hundreds of new images across the site. Finally, don't forget to visit our **Message Boards,** where you can join in conversations with thousands of fellow Frommer's travelers and post your trip report once you return.

For general info on volunteer travel, visit **www.volunteerabroad.org** and **www.idealist.org**. Specific volunteer options in New Mexico are listed under "Special-Interest Trips," below in this chapter.

Before you commit to a volunteer program, it's important to make sure any money you're giving is truly going back to the local community, and that the work you'll be doing will be a good fit for you. **Volunteer International** (www.volunteerinternational.org) has a helpful list of questions to ask to determine the intentions and the nature of a volunteer program.

10 PACKAGES FOR THE INDEPENDENT TRAVELER

Package tours are simply a way to buy the airfare, accommodations, and other elements of your trip (such as car rentals, airport transfers, and sometimes even activities) at the same time and often at discounted prices.

One good source of package deals is the airlines and train companies themselves. Most major airlines offer air/land packages, including **Southwest Airlines Vacations** (© 800/243-8372; www.swavacations.com), **American Airlines Vacations** (© 800/321-2121; www.aavacations.com), **Delta Vacations** (© 800/221-6666; www.deltavacations.com), **Continental Airlines Vacations** (© 800/301-3800; www.covacations.com), and **United Vacations** (© 888/854-3899; www.unitedvacations.com). Several big **online travel agencies**—Expedia, Travelocity, Orbitz, Site59, and Lastminute.com—also do a brisk business in packages. **Amtrak Vacations** (© 800/268-7252; www.amtrakvacations.com) offers train packages.

For more information on Package Tours and for tips on booking your trip, see www.frommers.com/planning.

11 ESCORTED GENERAL-INTEREST TOURS

Escorted tours are structured group tours, with a group leader. The price usually includes everything from airfare to hotels, meals, tours, admission costs, and local transportation.

Not many escorted tours are offered in New Mexico. The tour companies I spoke to said most visitors to New Mexico have such disparate interests it's difficult to create packages to please them. Still, a few tour companies can help you arrange a variety of day trips during your visit and can also secure lodging. **Tauck World Discovery,** 10 Norden Place, Norwalk, CT 06855 (✆ **800/788-7885;** www.tauck.com), offers weeklong cultural trips to New Mexico. **Destination Southwest, Inc.,** 20 First Plaza Galeria, Ste. 212, Albuquerque, NM 87102 (✆ **800/999-3109** or 505/766-9068; www.destinationsouthwest.com), offers an escorted tour to the Albuquerque International Balloon Fiesta. **Rojotours & Services,** P.O. Box 15744, Santa Fe, NM 87506-5744 (✆ **505/474-8333;** www.rojotours.com), can help with a variety of day trips during your visit.

For more information on escorted general-interest tours, including questions to ask before booking your trip, see www.frommers.com/planning.

12 SPECIAL-INTEREST TRIPS

New Mexico is in the process of developing a network of special-interest trips that I'm certain will expand even more in upcoming years.

One excellent operator is **Santa Fe Mountain Adventures** (✆ **800/965-4010** or 505/988-4000; www.santafemountainadventures.com), which combines outdoor adventures such as hiking and river running with cultural activities such as visits to pueblos or museums, with more relaxing ones such as spa treatments and meditation practices. A collaborative effort in conjunction with *Outside* magazine, the business is eco-conscious.

ACADEMIC TRIPS & LANGUAGE CLASSES

Some of the world's most outstanding photographers convene in Santa Fe at various times during the year for the **Santa Fe Workshops,** P.O. Box 9916, Santa Fe, NM 87504, at a delightful campus in the hills on the east side of town (✆ **505/983-1400;** www.santafeworkshops.com). Most courses are full time, lasting a week. Food and lodging packages are available.

Those who like a scholarly bent to their vacations can hook up with **Southwest Seminars** (✆ **505/466-2775;** www.southwestseminars.org) and their "Travels with a Scholar" program. This organization organizes tours throughout the Southwest, led by museum directors, historians, geologists, archaeologists, anthropologists, and authors. Southwest Seminars is able to arrange visits to sites that are not open to the general public, such as archaeological sites, petroglyph panels, volcanic calderas, contemporary Indian pueblos, and Native artists' homes and studios. Each Monday at 6pm, they offer a talk given by a regional scholar, well worth checking out.

ADVENTURE & ART TRIPS

Bicycle Adventures, P.O. Box 11219, Olympia, WA 98508 (✆ **800/443-6060** or 360/786-0989), offers tours to northern New Mexico. Riders get to experience some of the region's most lovely routes such as the High Road to Taos and the

Enchanted Circle. Participants visit major sights such as Santa Fe's Canyon Road and Taos Pueblo and can even opt for a river trip. In business for over 2 decades, this company knows how to put together a good tour.

If you'd like to pursue an artistic adventure, check out the week-long classes in such media as painting, Native American pottery making, and weaving offered by **Taos Art School** (✆ **505/758-0350;** www.taosartschool.org). This organization is especially known for its weaving and horseback-riding creative "odyssey." Open since 1989, the school is a virtual campus in which classes go where they need to be. For instance, a painting class on Georgia O'Keeffe is held in Abiquiu, a Pueblo pottery class at Taos Pueblo, and a class on the churches in New Mexico is held at five different churches in the region. The fees vary from class to class and include lodging and meals.

Great Expectations (✆ 800/663-3364; www.greatexpectations.com) offers an "Opera in Santa Fe" trip, which focuses on more than the opera, but also partakes of this world-class entertainment.

FOOD & WINE TRIPS

Jane Butel Cooking School, 2655 Pan American NE, Ste. F, Albuquerque, NM 87107 (✆ **800/473-8226** or 505/243-2622; www.janebutel.com), offers week-long and weekend packages with a hotel stay and full-participation classes. The weekend classes are held in noted chef and television personality Jane Butel's home kitchen in Corrales, a village along the Rio Grande on the edge of Albuquerque. The week-long classes are in Santa Fe.

VOLUNTEER & WORKING TRIPS

Sierra Club Outings (✆ **415/977-5522;** www.sierraclub.org/outings/national/service.asp) organizes working vacations all over the world, with some work to be done in New Mexico. **Global Citizens Network** offers volunteer vacations to worldwide destinations as well, including, at times, New Mexico. To check their schedule, contact (✆ **800/644-9292;** www.globalcitizens.org).

13 STAYING CONNECTED

TELEPHONES

Telephones work the same way here as they do in the rest of the U.S. For years, however, New Mexico had only one area code. That changed in 2007 when the state was split into two area codes. The northwest, including Albuquerque and Santa Fe, retained the 505 code, while the rest of the state changed to the 575 code. This change applies to wireline and wireless service as well as other communications services. Be aware that it may take businesses a while to make the changes in their promotional materials, so if you're having trouble getting through, you might check the area code.

To reach directory assistance, dial 1-411.

CELLPHONES

If you're not from the U.S., you'll be appalled at the poor reach of the **GSM (Global System for Mobile Communications) wireless network,** which is used by much of the rest of the world. Your phone will probably work in most major U.S. cities; it definitely won't work in many rural areas. To see where GSM phones work in the U.S., check out www.t-mobile.com/coverage. And you may or may not be able to send SMS (text messaging) home.

All the major cellphone companies have towers that serve the New Mexico region.

Be aware, though, that in areas far from major cities, reception will be spotty. Phones with both digital and analog service will have better reception in these areas.

VOICE-OVER INTERNET PROTOCOL (VOIP)

If you have Web access while traveling, consider a broadband-based telephone service (in technical terms, **Voice-over Internet protocol,** or **VoIP**) such as Skype (www.skype.com) or Vonage (www.vonage.com), which allow you to make free international calls from your laptop or in a cybercafe. Neither service requires the people you're calling to also have that service (though there are fees if they do not). Check the websites for details.

INTERNET & E-MAIL

With Your Own Computer

Wi-Fi and traditional Internet access are widely available in the cities in the region. For lists of places, see the orientation sections of chapters 6, 7, and 8. Currently there are 530 Wi-Fi hotspots in the state. In order to find one near you, log onto **www.jiwire.com**; its Hotspot Finder holds the world's largest directory of public wireless hotspots.

Without Your Own Computer

Most major airports have **Internet kiosks** that provide basic Web access for a per-minute fee that's usually higher than cybercafe prices. Check out copy shops like **Kinko's** (FedEx Office), which offers computer stations with fully loaded software (as well as Wi-Fi).

For help locating cybercafes and other establishments where you can go for Internet access, please see "Internet Access" under the "Fast Facts" section of the appendix (p. 380).

14 TIPS ON ACCOMMODATIONS

No two travelers are alike; fortunately, New Mexico has a broad enough range of accommodations to satisfy even the most eccentric adventurer. If you long to be pampered, you'll find a few swanky resorts within the region, with a variety of luxury options such as pool and exercise facilities, golf, tennis, horseback riding, and spa treatments. Of course, none of it comes cheap.

If you're looking to really savor the flavor of New Mexico, you may want to opt for one of its historic hotels. This may include a hacienda-style inn—an adobe one- or two-story structure often built around a courtyard. You'll also find some Victorian inns that have a frontier flavor. Within this variety of architecture, the amenities vary, from places with antique but workable plumbing and no television, to those with hot tubs and Wi-Fi in rooms.

In recent years, bed-and-breakfast inns (B&Bs) have proliferated in New Mexico. Though you can find traditional Victorian-style B&Bs here (and some lovely ones at that), complete with lacy bedding and elaborately carved accents, you can also choose from old hacienda-style homes or tiered adobe structures. All are comfortable and a few luxurious, with prices in the moderate to expensive range.

We all have those nights when only predictability will do. That's when a chain hotel comes in handy. You'll find all the major ones in New Mexico, though not quite everywhere. The small villages still shun such cookie-cutter establishments, but most everywhere else you can find them along the highways or in the town centers.

For tips on surfing for hotel deals online, visit www.frommers.com/planning.

4 Suggested New Mexico Itineraries

You may already have an idea of how you want to spend your time in New Mexico—power shopping, perhaps, or time-traveling through ancient cultures. But if you're not sure what to do, here are four suggested itineraries, outlined in 1-week and 2-week segments. For each one, I assume that you're starting in Albuquerque, either by driving in your own car or flying into the Albuquerque International Sunport, the air transportation hub of the state, and then renting a car.

New Mexico has a mix of museums and indoor activities, but the real attractions here are the living culture and spectacular scenery en route. With this in mind, I've combined scenic drives with city stays in these tours. In order to get a true sense of this place, take your time—linger at a cafe or wander a plaza for an hour. You might be surprised at how easily you get enveloped into the experience of being a New Mexican.

1 THE REGIONS IN BRIEF

NORTHCENTRAL NEW MEXICO The most highly populated and well-traveled area of the state, northcentral New Mexico roughly includes the cities of Albuquerque, Santa Fe, and Taos. It's also the economic center of New Mexico. In this portion of the state, lush mountains seem to rise directly out of the parched plateaus that have made New Mexico's landscape famous. Temperatures are generally lower in this area than they are in the rest of the state, and skiing is one of the most popular winter activities in both Santa Fe and Taos.

NORTHWESTERN NEW MEXICO Head to this region if you're interested in Native American culture. Sandstone bluffs here mark the homes of Pueblo, Navajo, and Apache Indians, in an area once inhabited by the ancestral Puebloans (also known as Anasazi) of the past. My favorite places to visit in this section of the state are Acoma Pueblo, Chaco Culture National Historical Park, and Aztec Ruins National Monument. A major portion of the northwestern region is part of a Navajo reservation, the largest in the country. This is also the gateway to the famous Four Corners region. The town of Grants, near Acoma, offers a glimpse into uranium mining. Railroad fanatics, hikers, hunters, and fishers should make a trip to Chama, home of the Cumbres & Toltec Railroad and a popular starting point for outdoor adventures.

NORTHEASTERN NEW MEXICO Covering the area north of I-40 and east of the Sangre de Cristo Mountains, northeastern New Mexico is prairie land once inhabited or visited by some of the West's most legendary gunslingers. Towns to visit for a bit of Wild West history are Cimarron and Las Vegas. The northeastern portion of the state also includes attractions such as Fort Union National Monument, a portion of the Santa Fe Trail, Kiowa and Rita Blanca National Grasslands, and Capulin Volcano National Monument. Due to its abundance of state parks and wildlife reserves, as well as the fact that it borders the ski resort towns of Angel Fire, Taos, Red River, and Santa Fe, this region is an excellent area for sports enthusiasts.

SOUTHWESTERN NEW MEXICO This region, like northeastern New Mexico, is another great place to visit if you're interested in the history of the Wild West and Native American culture, as it was once home to Billy the Kid and Geronimo. The Rio Grande, lifeline to this part of the state, acts as a border between the southwestern and southeastern portions of the state. Attractions west of the river include Gila National Forest, once home to the Mogollon Indians, whose past is preserved in the Gila Cliff Dwellings National Monument. The Chiricahua Apaches, a tribe once led by Geronimo, also lived in this area. The town of Silver City, which survives as an economic center of this area, was once a booming mining town. Surrounding ghost towns weren't as lucky. Las Cruces, at the foot of the Organ Mountains, is the state's second largest city, and Truth or Consequences, named for a television and radio game show, offers abundant hot springs.

SOUTHEASTERN NEW MEXICO Bounded on the west by the Rio Grande, to the north by I-40, and to the east by Texas, southeastern New Mexico is home to two of the most interesting natural wonders in this part of the country: Carlsbad Caverns and White Sands National Monument. The underground caverns, filled with stalactites and stalagmites, are infinitely interesting and hauntingly beautiful. Snow-white dunes at White Sands National Monument, which rise out of the desert landscape, are an extraordinary sight as you make the drive to Alamogordo. White Sands is a great place to camp out and watch the sunrise. This portion of the state is yet another former home of Billy the Kid. It's also where he died. Southeastern New Mexico has something of a controversial past as well: The world's first atomic bomb was detonated here.

2 NORTHERN NEW MEXICO IN A WEEK

New Mexico is a big state. Covering it all in 1 week would only wear a traveler out. That's why I've relegated this tour to the northern part, which has the highest concentration of sights. You can gaze at ancient petroglyphs etched on stone at the Petroglyph National Monument, shop one of the world's top art markets on Canyon Road in Santa Fe, marvel at the play of light on the Rio Grande Gorge in Taos—and even take a white-water rafting trip if you choose. Really, you can do this trip during any season, though the warmer months offer the mildest climate and the most options.

Days 1–2: Albuquerque

If you have some energy left after traveling, head to **Old Town** (p. 98), where you can wander through the **plaza** and peruse some shops. Be sure to tuck into some of the back alleyways and little nooks—you'll uncover some of the city's most inventive shops in these areas. Next, head over to the **Albuquerque Museum of Art and History** (p. 95) to get a good sense of this land's story. Finish the day with one of New Mexico's premier treats—an enchilada—at **Sadie's** (p. 90). Wash it down with one of their margaritas.

Start out your second day in Albuquerque at the **Indian Pueblo Cultural Center** (p. 96), where you'll get a sense of the cultures you'll encounter up north, and

Culture Cruising: Northern New Mexico in a Week

Taos
Santa Fe
Albuquerque
NEW MEXICO
25
40
10
Taos 6
Taos Pueblo
7
Chimayo
Bandelier National Monument
5
Santa Fe
4
Madrid
3
1–2
Albuquerque
40
25
1–2 Albuquerque
3 The Turquoise Trail & Santa Fe
4 Santa Fe Arts
5 Bandelier National Moument & North to Taos
6 Taos Pueblo
7 The High Road
0 50 mi
0 50 km
N

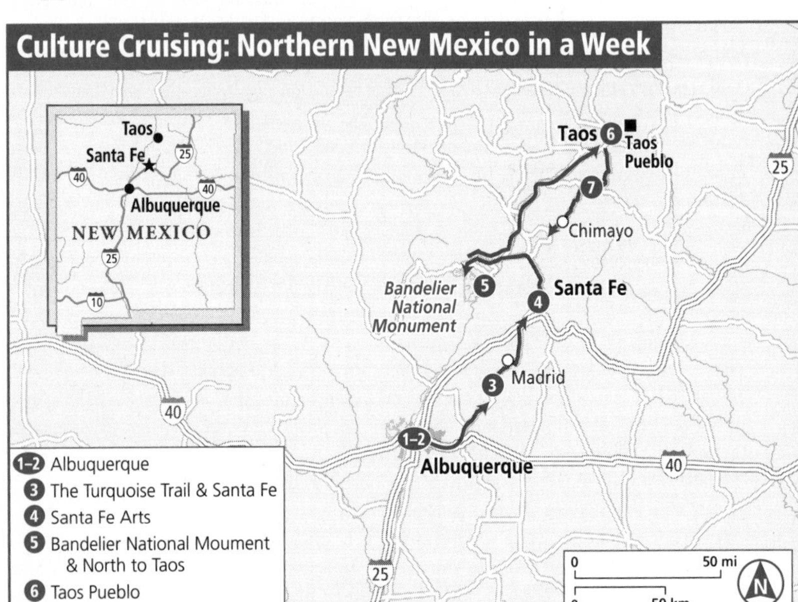

The Whole Enchillada: New Mexico in 2 Weeks

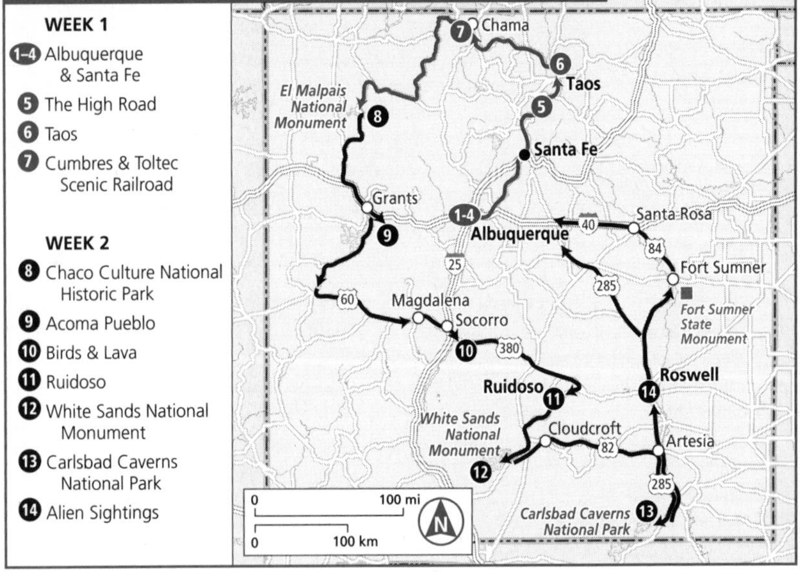
WEEK 1
1–4 Albuquerque & Santa Fe
5 The High Road
6 Taos
7 Cumbres & Toltec Scenic Railroad
WEEK 2
8 Chaco Culture National Historic Park
9 Acoma Pueblo
10 Birds & Lava
11 Ruidoso
12 White Sands National Monument
13 Carlsbad Caverns National Park
14 Alien Sightings
7 Chama
6
Taos
5
El Malpais National Monument
8
Santa Fe
Grants
9
1-4
Albuquerque
40
Santa Rosa
84
Fort Sumner
Fort Sumner State Monument
25
285
60
Magdalena
Socorro
10
380
Ruidoso
11
Roswell
14
White Sands National Monument
Cloudcroft
82
Artesia
12
285
Carlsbad Caverns National Park
13
0 100 mi
0 100 km
N

Family Time: New Mexico in a Week for Kids & the Young of Heart

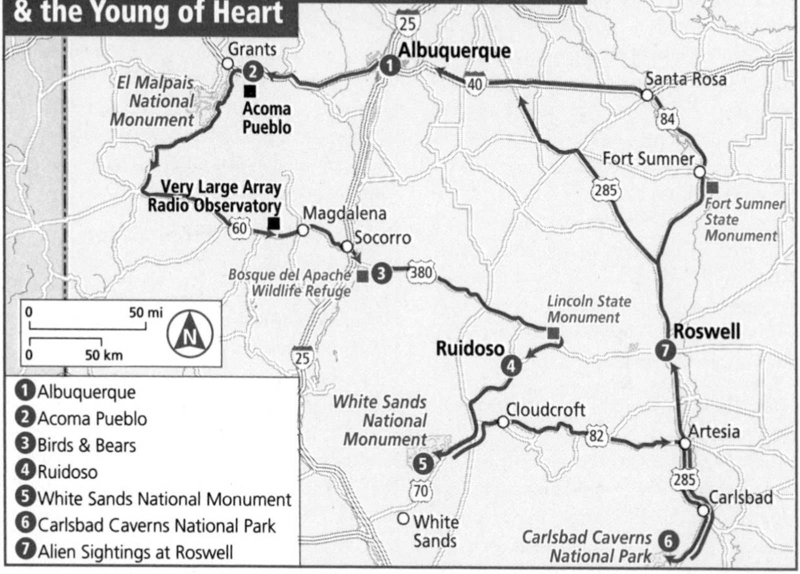
Grants
Albuquerque
El Malpais National Monument
Acoma Pueblo
Santa Rosa
Fort Sumner
Fort Sumner State Monument
Very Large Array Radio Observatory
Magdalena
Socorro
Bosque del Apache Wildlife Refuge
Lincoln State Monument
Roswell
Ruidoso
White Sands National Monument
Cloudcroft
Artesia
Carlsbad
White Sands
Carlsbad Caverns National Park
0 50 mi
0 50 km
N
1 Albuquerque
2 Acoma Pueblo
3 Birds & Bears
4 Ruidoso
5 White Sands National Monument
6 Carlsbad Caverns National Park
7 Alien Sightings at Roswell

Pack Your Gear: An Active Tour of New Mexico in 2 Weeks

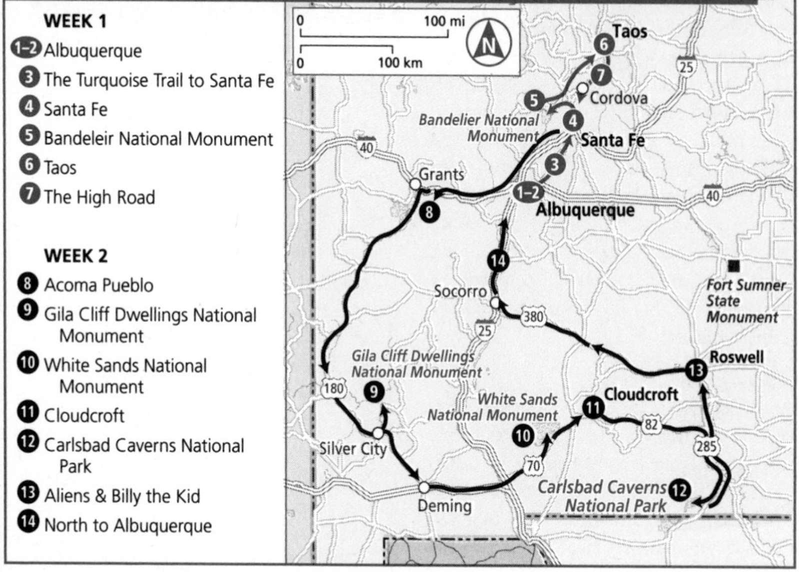
WEEK 1
1–2 Albuquerque
3 The Turquoise Trail to Santa Fe
4 Santa Fe
5 Bandeleir National Monument
6 Taos
7 The High Road
WEEK 2
8 Acoma Pueblo
9 Gila Cliff Dwellings National Monument
10 White Sands National Monument
11 Cloudcroft
12 Carlsbad Caverns National Park
13 Aliens & Billy the Kid
14 North to Albuquerque
0 100 mi
0 100 km
N
Taos
Cordova
Bandelier National Monument
Santa Fe
Grants
Albuquerque
Socorro
Fort Sumner State Monument
Roswell
Gila Cliff Dwellings National Monument
White Sands National Monument
Cloudcroft
Silver City
Deming
Carlsbad Caverns National Park

then head to the **Albuquerque Biological Park** (p. 99), both in the vicinity of **Old Town Plaza.** From here, go west of town to visit the **Petroglyph National Monument** (p. 98). (If it's summer, you may want to go during the cooler early morning.) In the late afternoon, find your way to Central Avenue, just south of Old Town, and drive east on **Route 66.** This takes you right through downtown, to the Nob Hill district and the Sandia Mountains foothills, respectively. Finish your day with a ride up the **Sandia Peak Tramway** (p. 99). Ideally, you should ride up during daylight and back down at night for a view of the city lights. You may even want to dine at the top.

Day ❸: The Turquoise Trail ★★ & Santa Fe

Today, strike out for the ghost towns and other sights along the **Turquoise Trail** (p. 121) to Santa Fe, stopping to peruse some of the galleries in **Madrid** (p. 121). This will put you in Santa Fe in time to do some sightseeing. Head straight to the **plaza** (p. 160), the **Palace of the Governors** (p. 157), and **St. Francis Cathedral** (p. 158). If you shop from the Native Americans selling under the portal, be sure to ask about the art you buy; the symbols on it may have interesting significance. Next, make your way over to the **Georgia O'Keeffe Museum** (p. 157). Finish your day with an enchilada at the **Shed** (p. 155). In the evening, depending on the season, you may want to check out Santa Fe's excellent arts scene; try the **Santa Fe Opera** (p. 179) or the **Santa Fe Chamber Music Festival** (p. 180).

Day ❹: Santa Fe Arts

In the morning, head up to Museum Hill, where you can take your pick from four unique museums: the **Museum of International Folk Art** (p. 161), the **Museum of Indian Arts & Culture** (p. 160), the **Wheelwright Museum of the American Indian** (p. 162), and the **Museum of Spanish Colonial Art** (p. 161). You can have lunch at the **Museum Hill Café** (p. 160). On your way back to the plaza, take a stroll and do some shopping on **Canyon Road** (p. 172). At sunset during the warmer months, you can enjoy a cocktail at the bell tower of the historic **La Fonda Hotel** (p. 133). Eat dinner at **Santacafé** (p. 150)—or if you lingered over your shopping, stop in at **Geronimo** (p. 148) or the **Compound** (p. 146) on Canyon Road.

Day ❺: Bandelier National Monument ★★★ & North to Taos

Head out of town today to **Bandelier National Monument** (p. 191). Explore the ruins and be sure to climb the ladders to see the kiva set high above the canyon floor. Then continue north to Taos. On your way into the city, stop at the **San Francisco de Asis church** (p. 222). And if you like music, head out to the **Sagebrush Inn** (p. 239) for some country-and-western tunes.

Day ❻: Taos Pueblo ★★★

Spend your morning exploring **Taos Pueblo** (p. 224), the **Millicent Rogers Museum** (p. 220), and the **Rio Grande Gorge Bridge** (p. 226). You can then ditch your car for the afternoon and step out on foot. Do some shopping around **Taos Plaza.** At cocktail hour, head to the **Adobe Bar** (p. 238) at the Historic Taos Inn or the **Anaconda Bar** (p. 239) at the new El Monte Sagrado.

Day ❼: The High Road ★★

On your last day, enjoy a leisurely morning and then head south on the **High Road to Taos** (p. 192). Be sure to spend some time at the **Santuario de Chimayo** (p. 193), where you can rub healing dust between your fingers. You may want to spend the night at a bed-and-breakfast in **Chimayo** (p. 193) or have lunch at **Rancho de Chimayo** (p. 194) along the way. Depending on your flight time the next morning, stay the night in Santa Fe or Albuquerque.

3 NEW MEXICO IN 2 WEEKS

If you've got 2 weeks to spend exploring the region, consider yourself fortunate. You'll not only be able to hit the highlights in the north, but you'll also be able to spend time getting to know such places as Chaco National Cultural Park, White Sands National Monument, and Carlsbad Caverns National Park. This trip is fun any time of year. In winter, the north will be cold and the south will be cool. In the warmer months, the north will be warm and the south very hot.

Days 1–4: Albuquerque & Santa Fe

For days 1 through 4, follow those days as outlined in the previous itinerary, "Culture Cruising: Northern New Mexico in a Week."

Day 5: The High Road ★★

Today, travel the **High Road to Taos** (p. 192), stopping at the little galleries and art studios along the way. Be sure to rub healing dust between your fingers at **Santuario de Chimayo** (p. 193). On the way into Taos, visit the **San Francisco de Asis church** (p. 222). If you like nightlife, head out to the **Sagebrush Inn** (p. 239) to dance to country-and-western music or to the **Anaconda Bar** (p. 239) to hear some jazz or other music.

Day 6: Taos

Spend the morning at **Taos Pueblo** (p. 224). Next head over to the **Millicent Rogers Museum** (p. 220) and the **Rio Grande Gorge Bridge** (p. 226). During the afternoon, do some shopping around the **Taos Plaza** (p. 234) and then visit the **Taos Art Museum** (p. 222). At cocktail hour, head to the **Adobe Bar** (p. 238) at the Historic Taos Inn.

Day 7: Cumbres & Toltec Scenic Railroad ★★

This morning, get up early and head west on a scenic drive to Chama, where you can spend the day riding the **Cumbres & Toltec Scenic Railroad** (p. 276). Be sure to check departure times for the train and make reservations in advance. Spend the night in Chama.

Day 8: Chaco Culture National Historic Park ★★★

From Chama, drive across the Jicarilla Apache Indian Reservation on NM 537 to **Chaco Culture National Historical Park** (p. 264). Though it's a long dusty drive, Chaco's combination of stunning setting and expansive ruins makes the day worthwhile. In fact, Chaco is the Holy Grail for Southwest history buffs. If you have camping equipment, spend the night at Chaco. If not, stay the night in Grants.

Day 9: Acoma Pueblo ★★★

Head east on Interstate 40 to **Acoma Pueblo** (p. 247). Upon arrival, spend some time in the pueblo's 40,000-square-foot museum to get a sense of the culture before taking the bus to the top of Sky City. Next, head south on NM 117, one of the state's prettiest drives, to **El Malpais** (p. 252), where you can stretch your legs on a short or long hike. Continue south through Quemado, then turn east ,and drive to Magdalena, where you can stop for a milkshake at **Evett's Cafe** (p. 307). (This is a long drive, so you'll need a refresher.) Spend the night in **Socorro** (p. 305), or continue south to San Antonio, where you can stay at the **Casa Blanca** B&B (p. 308).

Day 10: Birds & Lava

If it's wintertime, wake up before dawn today and head out to **Bosque del Apache**

National Wildlife Refuge (p. 103), where you can watch thousands of cranes and snow geese take flight. (Even if it's not winter—when thousands of cranes and geese fill the sky—you can still tour the refuge to see birds and wildlife.) From the refuge, head east on US 380 to the **Valley of Fires Recreation Area** (p. 362), an amazing lava field, where you can stretch your legs before lunch. Your next stop is Carrizozo to feast on a green chile cheeseburger at the **Outpost** (p. 362). Or, if you're not into burgers, continue on to Capitan to eat at the **Greenhouse Café** (p. 361). Either way, you'll want to make your way east along the **Lincoln Loop** (p. 361) through Capitan to Lincoln, where you can visit the **Lincoln State Monument** (p. 355) and walk in the footsteps of Billy the Kid. Spend the night in Ruidoso.

Day ⓫: Ruidoso

If you like to hike, stop at the Lincoln National Forest Ranger Station for directions to the many trails in the area. Otherwise, you may want to shop a little. If it's winter, you can ski at **Ski Apache** (p. 344). Or, if you have an interest in horses, head over to the **Hubbard Museum of the American West** (p. 353) and then take in some horse racing at **Ruidoso Downs** (p. 353). Spend the night in Ruidoso, and if you feel like splurging, stay at the **Inn of the Mountain Gods** (p. 357). Even if you don't stay there, you may want to drive to the inn for an evening stroll around the lake and a little dice throw in its casino.

Day ⓬: White Sands National Monument ★★★

This day takes you south out of Ruidoso through the **Mescalero Apache Indian Reservation** on US 70 and NM 244. Just outside the reservation, you arrive in **Cloudcroft** (p. 347), a darling mountain town with some good hiking and mountain biking. Next, head down a spectacularly scenic pass on US 82 into **Alamogordo** to visit the **New Mexico Museum of Space History** (p. 345) and one of the stars of this trip: **White Sands National Monument** (p. 350). Spend the night in Alamogordo.

Day ⓭: Carlsbad Caverns National Park ★★★

Spend the morning driving to **Carlsbad** (p. 369) and have lunch in the town itself. If you like zoos, you may want to visit the **Living Desert Zoo & Gardens State Park** (p. 370), but be sure to save energy for your afternoon. Head south to the most spectacular sight in New Mexico, **Carlsbad Caverns National Park** (p. 374), where you want to *walk* down into the cave, rather than ride the elevator (trust me). End your day by strolling along the water at the **riverwalk** (p. 369), or if it's summertime, by relaxing at your hotel pool.

Day ⓮: Alien Sightings

Spend your last day on a long cruise north to Albuquerque. Take US 285 to Roswell, where you can feed your *X-Files* fantasies at the **International UFO Museum and Research Center** (p. 364). History buffs may want to detour to Fort Sumner to see **Billy the Kid's grave** (p. 368), but more importantly to see the tragedy presented at **Fort Sumner State Monument** (p. 367). If you choose this option, stop for a bite afterward at **Joe's** (p. 301) in Santa Rosa. In Albuquerque, you can finish the trip with one last enchilada at **Sadie's** (p. 90).

4 NEW MEXICO FOR FAMILIES IN A WEEK

Although it's wonderful, northern New Mexico is not the most suitable vacationland for kids—unless they already have a credit card and a precocious interest in history and architecture. Some hearts are better suited to Wild West action and natural wonders than gourmet food and history, and those kinds of attractions mainly reside in the state's southern half. If you prefer a more active vacation, this 1-week trip is for you, whatever your age. The climate in this region is fairly mild, but summers in the south can be quite hot.

Day ➊: Albuquerque

On your first day, head to **Old Town** (p. 98), where you can wander the **plaza,** peruse some shops, and head over to the **¡Explora! Science Center** (p. 100). Next, visit the **Albuquerque Biological Park** (p. 99). Be sure to check out the Biological Park's butterfly exhibit. Or, you may want to visit the **Rio Grande Zoo** (p. 101). Don't miss the polar bears there. Finish the day with one of New Mexico's premier treats—an enchilada—at **Sadie's** (p. 90). If you have any energy left, ride the **Sandia Peak Tramway** (p. 99) in time to watch the sunset.

Day ➋: Acoma Pueblo ★★★

You'll cover a lot of ground this day, so head out early. Drive west about 70 miles to **Acoma Pueblo** (p. 247), taking time to see the new museum there before you ride the bus up to Sky City. Visit the **New Mexico Mining Museum** (p. 349) in Grants, where you can go underground in a simulated mine, and then have lunch at one of the restaurants nearby. Next, head south on NM 117 to **El Malpais and El Morro National Monuments** (p. 252), where you can stretch your legs on a short hike. Continue south through Quemado, then turn east, and drive to Magdalena, where the kids can enjoy a milkshake at **Evett's Cafe** (p. 307). Spend the night in Socorro or continue south to San Antonio, where you can stay at **Casa Blanca** B&B (p. 308).

Day ➌: Birds & Bears

On day 3, if it's wintertime, wake before dawn and head out to **Bosque del Apache National Wildlife Refuge** (p. 103). Even though it's early for kids, they're usually amazed to see thousands of cranes and snow geese take flight, and hear the air fill with their calls. (Even if it's not winter—when thousands of cranes and geese fill the sky—you can still tour the refuge to see birds and wildlife, and take a hike to a high point to view the scene from above.) From the refuge, head east on US 380 to the **Valley of Fires Recreation Area** (p. 362), an amazing lava field. Your next stop is Carrizozo to feast on a green chile cheeseburger at the **Outpost** (p. 362). Continue east to **Capitan** and **Smokey Bear Historical State Park** (p. 362). Farther east along the Lincoln Loop, stop at the **Lincoln State Monument** (p. 355). Spend the night in Ruidoso.

Day ➍: Ruidoso

This morning, if you like to hike, head to the Lincoln National Forest Ranger Station for directions to the many trails in the area. Otherwise, you may want to shop a little. If it's winter, you can ski at **Ski Apache** (p. 344). Or, if your kids have any interest in horses, head over to the **Hubbard Museum of the American West** (p. 353). In the evening, check out the **Flying J Ranch** (p. 354) for a chuck-wagon dinner and an Old-West show. Spend the night in Ruidoso.

Day ➎: White Sands National Monument ★★★

Today, head south out of Ruidoso through the **Mescalero Apache Indian Reservation** on US 70 and NM 244. Just outside the reservation, visit **Cloudcroft** (p. 347), a darling mountain town with some good hiking and mountain biking. Next, head down the spectacularly scenic pass on US 82 into **Alamogordo** to visit the **New Mexico Museum of Space History** (p. 345). Spend late afternoon exploring one of the stars of this trip: **White Sands**

National Monument (p. 350). Spend the night in Alamogordo.

Day 6: Carlsbad Caverns National Park ★★★

On day 6, head east to **Carlsbad** to visit the **Living Desert Zoo & Gardens State Park** (p. 370). Have lunch in Carlsbad and then drive out to the most spectacular sight in New Mexico, **Carlsbad Caverns National Park** (p. 374), where you want to *walk* down into the cave, rather than ride the elevator. If it's summer when you visit, end your hot day at your hotel pool, or alternatively, at the **riverwalk** (p. 369), where the kids can swim and pedal paddleboats.

Day 7: Alien Sightings at Roswell

Spend your last day on a long cruise north to Albuquerque. Take US 285 to Roswell, where your kids can stock up on little-green-men stickers and see the **International UFO Museum and Research Center** (p. 364). History buffs may want to detour to Fort Sumner to see **Billy the Kid's grave** (p. 368) and the tragedy presented at **Fort Sumner State Monument** (p. 367). If you take this option, stop for a bite afterward at **Joe's** (p. 301) in Santa Rosa.

Tip: Parents who are first-time visitors to New Mexico may want to trade the day 1 and day 2 schedules for a trip north to **Santa Fe** (see chapter 7) to take in the cultural sights there. You can then shoot down I-25 and resume the itinerary in Socorro on the evening of day 2.

5 AN ACTIVE TOUR OF NEW MEXICO IN 2 WEEKS

Anyone who skis, hikes, mountain bikes, or rafts knows that the Southwest is unsurpassed in its offerings for outdoor enthusiasts. New Mexico is no exception. This trip is for the road-warrior type of sportsperson. It takes in New Mexico's full sphere of terrain, from the Rocky Mountains in the north to the desert of White Sands in the South and the caves at Carlsbad. Be aware that the region is known for its mercurial weather conditions—always be prepared for extremes. Also, northern New Mexico is over 6,000 feet in elevation, so it may take you time to catch your breath. Be patient on those long upward hills. The sports you do will, of course, depend a lot on the season. For the full benefit of this trip, take it in late March or early April. With a little advance preparation, you might be able to ski and river raft on the same trip!

Days 1–2: Albuquerque

When you arrive in Albuquerque, you may want to get acclimated to the city by strolling through **Old Town** (p. 98). Next, visit the **Albuquerque Biological Park** (p. 99) to get a sense of the nature in the area and the **Pueblo Cultural Center** (p. 96) to get acquainted with the culture you'll encounter as you head north.

On day 2, for a truly unique experience, you may want to schedule a **balloon ride** (p. 168). ***Tip:*** Make reservations for this activity in advance, especially because you fly first thing in the morning. If you're a bike-rider or hiker, head to **Petroglyph National Monument** (p. 98) for a ride or hike to see thousands of symbols etched on stone. In the evening, ride the **Sandia Peak Tramway** (p. 99) and do a little hiking along the crest. If you'd like, you can have dinner at the top and view the city lights as you come down.

Day ❸: The Turquoise Trail ★★ to Santa Fe

On day 3, head for the ghost towns and other sights along the **Turquoise Trail** (p. 121) to Santa Fe. If you like to ride horses, schedule a ride in Cerrillos with **Broken Saddle Riding Company** (p. 112). This will put you in Santa Fe in time to do some late-afternoon sightseeing. Head straight to the **plaza** (p. 160), the **Palace of the Governors** (p. 157), and **St. Francis Cathedral** (p. 158). Have an enchilada at the **Shed** (p. 155).

Day ❹: Santa Fe

Either use your own bike or rent a cruiser in town to ride around the plaza and up **Canyon Road** (p. 172). Stop at the top of Canyon at the **Randall Davey Audubon Center** (p. 164) to do some bird-watching. Or, you may want to head to the mountains to do some hiking on the **Borrego Trail** (p. 170) or, if it's winter, some skiing at **Ski Santa Fe** (p. 171). Finish your day at one of the fun restaurants or cafes on **Canyon Road** (p. 145). In the evening, depending on the season, you may want to take in some of Santa Fe's excellent arts, such as the **Santa Fe Opera** (p. 179) or the **Santa Fe Chamber Music Festival** (p. 180).

Day ❺: Bandelier National Monument ★★

Head out from Santa Fe to **Bandelier National Monument** (p. 191) and hike among ancient ruins. Follow the Frijoles Trail as far up as you'd like, making sure you stop to climb the ladders to the kiva perched high on the canyon wall. Trail runners like to jog the Frijoles Trail, with its easy descent back to the start. Next, follow the Rio Grande River north and you'll come to Taos. On the way into town, stop at the **San Francisco de Asis church** (p. 222). Spend the evening strolling around the Taos **plaza** to get a feel of the city.

Day ❻: Taos

Sports lovers have many options in this town. If you like to ride horses, take a **ride on Taos Pueblo** (p. 232) land. Or, you may want to take a **llama trek** (p. 232) into the Rio Grande Gorge, or hike up to the top of **Wheeler Peak** (p. 232), New Mexico's highest, a full-day trek. If it's ski season, you'll definitely want to spend the day at **Taos Ski Valley** (p. 227). If it's spring and the rivers are running, either take the full-day, heart-throbbing romp through the **Taos Box** (p. 233), or a half-day trip at **Pilar** (p. 233).

Day ❼: The High Road ★★★

Take a leisurely drive south toward Santa Fe. You'll want to take the **High Road** (p. 192) through the art villages of Cordova and Chimayo. Stop at the **Santuario de Chimayo** (p. 193) and have lunch on the patio at **Rancho de Chimayo** (p. 194). Spend the night in Albuquerque.

Day ❽: Acoma Pueblo ★★★

Head east on Interstate 40 to **Acoma Pueblo** (p. 247) and spend some time in its 40,000-square-foot museum to get a sense of the area's culture before taking the bus to the top of Sky City. Have lunch in Grants, or, if you enjoy picnics, pick up goodies before leaving Albuquerque and eat at one of the beautiful stops I mention next. From Grants, head south on NM 117, one of the state's prettiest drives, to **El Malpais and El Morro National Monuments** (p. 252), where you'll see great views and some wonderful history. Continue south through Quemado and Reserve to the **Catwalk National Recreation Trail** (p. 341), where you'll stretch your legs on an easy hike. Then make your way to Silver City to spend the night. Wildlife lovers may want to stay at the **Bear Mountain Lodge** (p. 336), where you'll benefit from on-staff naturalists who can help you spot birds, deer, and other creatures. Have dinner at **Diane's Bakery & Cafe** (p. 337).

Day ❾: Gila Cliff Dwellings National Monument ★★★

Before you head out of town this morning, pick up supplies for a picnic, or, if you stay at Bear Mountain Lodge, have them pack you one. This day takes you deep into the Gila Wilderness to see the ruins at **Gila Cliff Dwellings National Monument** (p. 339). After you've toured the ruins, head up the Middle Fork Trail; the trail head is near the cliff dwellings. The trail follows the Gila River through the wilderness and offers some lovely picnic spots along the way. As you return to town, take a detour through Pinos Altos and stop for dinner at the **Buckhorn Saloon & Opera House** (p. 337). Return to Silver City, where you'll spend the night.

Day ❿: White Sands National Monument ★★★

This day takes you southeast, with a quick stop at **City of Rocks State Park** (p. 335) to see lovely rock formations. Have lunch in Las Cruces at one of the restaurants in the vicinity of **Old Mesilla** (p. 325), a lovely plaza where you can shop and stroll. In the afternoon, drive northeast on US 70 to **White Sands National Monument** (p. 350), where you'll want to spend the late afternoon and early evening. For the night, head to the **Lodge at Cloudcroft** (p. 349).

Day ⓫: Cloudcroft

Today, get ready to burn some calories as you hike or bike the Sacramento Mountains around **Cloudcroft** (p. 347). The **Rim Trail** (p. 342), which offers views out across White Sands, is considered one of the top bike trails in the United States. Or, choose one of the excellent hiking trails in the area. Spend the night in Cloudcroft.

Day ⓬: Carlsbad Caverns National Park ★★★

Head east to **Carlsbad** to visit the **Living Desert Zoo & Gardens State Park** (p. 370). Have lunch in Carlsbad and then drive out to the most spectacular sight in New Mexico, **Carlsbad Caverns National Park** (p. 374), where you want to *walk* down into the cave, rather than ride the elevator. If you're a serious spelunker, arrange in advance for one of the special tours. End your day at the **riverwalk** (p. 369), where you can swim and pedal paddleboats, or at your hotel pool.

Day ⓭: Aliens & Billy the Kid

Take US 285 to Roswell, where you can decide for yourself whether or not aliens landed there in the 1940s. Visit the **International UFO Museum and Research Center** (p. 364). From there, head west to **Lincoln State Monument** (p. 355). Spend the night there at **Ellis Store and Co. Country Inn** (p. 358) or at the nearby **Capitan Cabins** (p. 362). Have dinner at one of the cafes in Capitan, about 10 miles away.

Day ⓮: North to Albuquerque

Spend a leisurely morning enjoying the quiet village of Lincoln. Then go west to Capitan, where you can learn about the history of forest fire prevention at **Smokey Bear Historical State Park** (p. 362). Have lunch in Carrizozo, where you can feast on a green chile cheeseburger at the **Outpost** (p. 362). Continue west to see the **Valley of Fires Recreation Area** (p. 362), an amazing lava field. Then drive to San Antonio to the **Bosque del Apache National Wildlife Refuge** (p. 103), arriving in time to see the birds fly in to the lakes after a day in the fields. This takes place in winter at dusk, but there are still plenty of birds to see at other times of year. Finally, head north to Albuquerque, where you can cool down in the pool for the evening and have an enchilada before you catch your plane home.

5

The Active Vacation Planner

You may be pleasantly surprised at the range of outdoor fun available in this state. From the dry flatlands of the southern regions to the mountains and forests of the northcentral part of the state, diversity reigns here. Whether you're interested in a short day hike or an overnight horse trip, groomed ski trails or backcountry adventures, you won't be disappointed.

For more in-depth coverage of the activities that follow, contact some of the local outfitters or organizations that are listed in the "Outdoor Activities" and "Getting Outside" sections in the later chapters in this book.

For tips on staying healthy outdoors, see "Health," in chapter 3.

1 BALLOONING

New Mexico could just be *the* place to go **hot-air ballooning.** Its open spaces and relatively mild climate are ideal for the sport. In fact, one of the state's greatest attractions is the annual Albuquerque International Balloon Fiesta in early October (see "New Mexico Calendar of Events," in chapter 3), which draws thousands of people from all over the world. It is possible to charter hot-air balloon rides in most regions of the state. The outfitters offer a variety of packages, from a standard flight to a more elaborate all-day affair that includes meals. For more information, see the "Outdoor Activities" sections in chapters 6 and 7, and "Other Outdoor Activities," in chapter 8; for other cities, contact individual chambers of commerce.

2 BIRD-WATCHING

New Mexico is directly on the Central Flyway, which makes it a great spot for bird-watching all year long. Each region of the state offers refuge to a wide variety of birds, including doves, finches, bluebirds, and roadrunners (the state bird). The bald eagle is also frequently spotted during winter and spring migrations. A good place to pull out your binoculars is the **Gila National Forest** (✆ **575/388-8201;** www.fs.fed.us/r3/gila) near Silver City. Also check out the wildlife refuge centers in New Mexico, most notably the **Bosque del Apache National Wildlife Refuge,** 93 miles south of Albuquerque (✆ **575/835-1828;** www.fws.gov/southwest/refuges/newmex/bosque). Others include the **Rio Grande Nature Center State Park,** Albuquerque (✆ **505/344-7240;** www.nmparks.com), the **Las Vegas National Wildlife Refuge,** 5 miles southeast of Las Vegas (✆ **505/425-3581;** www.fws.gov/refuges), and **Bitter Lake National Wildlife Refuge,** 13 miles northeast of Roswell (✆ **575/622-6755;** www.fws.gov/refuges). Some common sightings at these areas include sandhill cranes, snow geese, a wide variety of ducks, and falcons. New Mexico is also home to an amazing variety of hummingbirds. The number of verified species in New Mexico is now 478. New Mexico ranks fourth (behind Texas, California, and Arizona) in the number of birds that live in or have passed through the state.

To find out about bird-watching activities in New Mexico, contact the state office of the **National Audubon Society,** 1800 Upper Canyon Rd., Santa Fe, NM 87504 (✆ **505/983-4609;** www.nm.audubon.org).

3 FISHING

You'll find scores of **fishing** opportunities in New Mexico. Warm-water lakes and streams are home to large- and small-mouth bass, walleye, stripers, catfish, crappie, and bluegill. In cold-water lakes and streams, look for the state fish, the Rio Grande cutthroat, as well as kokanee salmon and rainbow, brown, lake, and brook trout.

Two of the best places for fishing are the **San Juan River** near Farmington (see chapter 9) and **Elephant Butte Lake** (see chapter 11), not far from Truth or Consequences. The San Juan River offers excellent trout fishing and is extremely popular with fly fishers. Elephant Butte Lake is great for bass fishing; in fact, it's considered one of the top 10 bass-fishing locations in the United States.

All sorts of other possibilities are available, such as the Rio Grande, the Chama, Jemez, and Gila watershed areas, and the Pecos River. I recommend Ti Piper's *Fishing in New Mexico* (University of New Mexico Press). This excellent and wonderfully comprehensive book describes every waterway in New Mexico in great detail.

For information on obtaining fishing licensing, call the **New Mexico Game and Fish Department,** 1 Wildlife Way, Santa Fe, NM 87507 (✆ **505/476-8000;** www.wildlife.state.nm.us).

Although it is not necessary to have a fishing license in order to fish on Native American–reservation land, you must still receive written permission and an official tribal document before setting out on any fishing trips there. Phone numbers for tribes and pueblos are listed separately in the regional and city chapters in this book.

4 GOLF

New Mexico provides the clear air and oft-cool climates that draw many golfers. In northern New Mexico, golfers can find great packages for nine respected courses from **Golf on the Santa Fe Trail** (✆ **866/465-3660;** www.santafetrailgolf.com). The most challenging course in the state is the **University of New Mexico Championship Golf Course,** 3601 University Blvd. SE, Albuquerque (✆ **505/277-4546;** www.unmgolf.com), and one of the most scenic is the **Cochiti Lake Golf Course,** 5200 Cochiti Hwy., Cochiti Lake, NM (✆ **505/465-2239;** www.pueblodecochiti.org). If you're in the Farmington area, check out **Piñon Hills Golf Course,** 2101 Sunrise Pkwy. (✆ **505/326-6066;** www.fmtn.org), a few years ago rated by *Golf Digest* as the "best public golf course" in New Mexico. In the south, you can enjoy views, a challenging course, and cool climes even in summer at the **Links at Sierra Blanca,** in Ruidoso, 105 Sierra Blanca Dr. (✆ **800/854-6571** or 575/258-5330; www.thelinksatsierrablanca.com). See individual chapters for more suggestions.

5 HIKING

Everywhere you go in New Mexico you'll find opportunities for hiking adventures. The terrain and climate vary from the heat and flatness of the desert plains to the cold, forested alpine areas of the northern region of the state. You can visit both (going from 3,000–13,000 ft. in elevation) and anything in between in the same day without much trouble. You can go hiking virtually anywhere you please (except on private land or Native American land without permission); however, it's wise to stick to designated trails.

I mention some of the best hiking trails in each region of the state below. See later chapters for details about outfitters, guides, llama trekking services, and who to contact for maps and other information.

BEST HIKES

If you're around **Santa Fe,** I recommend hiking Santa Fe Baldy. It's a hike you can do in a day if you start out early; if you'd like a less strenuous walk, plan to spend a night camping. This is a good first hike for those who come from lower altitudes but are in good shape. Once you get to the top, you'll have panoramic views of the Sangre de Cristo and Jemez mountains, as well as the Rio Grande Valley.

If you're looking for something more challenging in the **northcentral region** of the state, head to Taos and give Wheeler Peak your best shot. The hike up New Mexico's highest peak is about 15 miles round-trip. If you're incredibly well conditioned, you may be able to do the hike in a day. Otherwise, plan to hike and camp for several days. The pain of getting to the top is worth it—at the top you'll find some of New Mexico's most spectacular views. See chapter 8 for details.

For a much easier hike in the Taos area, try hiking down into Rio Grande Gorge. It's beautiful and can be hiked year-round. See chapter 8 for details.

In the **northeastern region** of New Mexico, I recommend taking the 1-mile loop around Capulin Volcano. The crater rim offers stunning views, and you can look down into the dormant caldera. It's a nice, easy walk for those who'd rather not overexert themselves. Any time except winter is good for this hike. See chapter 10 for details.

If you're heading to the **northwestern region** of the state, try hiking the Bisti/De-Na-Zin Wilderness, 37 miles south of Farmington. Though there are no marked trails, the hiking is easy in this area of low, eroded hills and fanciful rock formations. You may see petrified wood or fossils from the dinosaurs that lived here millions of years ago. A walk to one of the more interesting areas is about 4 miles round-trip and is best taken in spring or fall. See chapter 9 for details.

The northwestern region is also home to El Malpais National Monument, where you can hike into great lava tubes. The hiking is easy, but it's also easy to get lost in this area,

Trail Closures

The drought that has spread across the Southwest in recent years has caused the U.S. Forest Service to close trails in many New Mexico mountains during the summer in order to reduce fire hazard. Before you head out in this area, contact the ranger district nearest your destination. The contact information is in the "Great Outdoors" section in chapters 9 through 12 of this book.

so be sure to carry a compass and a topographical map. Also in the area is El Morro National Monument, known as inscription rock, a stunning pinnacle offering a moderate hike to its summit, with stunning views. This hike is an especially good one to take in spring or fall. See chapter 9 for details.

In the **southwestern region** is the Gila National Forest, which has approximately 1,500 miles of trails, with varying ranges of length and difficulty. Your best bet is to purchase a guidebook devoted entirely to hiking the Gila Forest, but popular areas include the Crest Trail, the West Fork Trail, and the Aldo Leopold Wilderness. One favorite day hike in the forest is the Catwalk, a moderately strenuous hike along a series of steel bridges and walkways suspended over Whitewater Canyon. See chapter 11 for details.

In the **southeastern region,** you'll find one of my favorite places in all of New Mexico: White Sands National Monument. Hiking the white-sand dunes is easy, if sometimes awkward, and the magnificence of the views is unsurpassed. Be sure to take sunscreen and sunglasses, plenty of water, and a compass on this hike; there's no shade, and it's difficult to tell one dune from another here. See chapter 12 for more information.

Of course, you can choose from hundreds of other hikes. You can purchase a hiking book or contact the National Park Service, National Forest Service, Bureau of Land Management, or other appropriate agency directly. The best guides for the region are *50 Hikes in Northern New Mexico: From Chaco Canyon to the High Peaks of the Sangre de Cristos* (Countryman), by Kai Huschke, and *100 Hikes in New Mexico,* 2nd Edition, by Craig Martin (the Mountaineers). A popular guide with Santa Feans is *Day Hikes in the Santa Fe Area,* published by the local branch of the Sierra Club and available in most local bookstores.

6 HORSEBACK RIDING

What's unique about much of New Mexico's horseback riding is its variety. You'll find a broad range of riding terrain, from open plains to high mountain wilderness. In the Santa Fe area, you can ride across the plains of the spectacular Galisteo basin with **Santa Fe Detours,** 54½ E. San Francisco St. (✆ **800/338-6877** or 505/983-6565; www.sfdetours.com). In Taos, you can explore secluded Taos Pueblo land with the **Taos Indian Horse Ranch,** on Pueblo land off Ski Valley Road, just before Arroyo Seco (✆ **800/659-3210** or 505/758-3212; www.taosindianhorseranch.com). In the southeast, try **Inn of the Mountain Gods,** Carrizo Canyon Road (✆ **800/545-9011** or 575/464-4100; www.innofthemountaingods.com). If you're looking for a resort horseback riding experience, contact **Bishop's Lodge,** Bishop's Lodge Road, Santa Fe (✆ **800/732-2240** or 505/983-6377; www.bishopslodge.com). If you want an authentic cowpoke experience, I recommend the **Double E Guest Ranch,** 67 Double E Ranch Rd., Gila (✆ **866/242-3500** or 575/535-2048; www.doubleeranch.com), in the Silver City area.

7 MOUNTAIN BIKING

New Mexico offers not only fun and exciting biking terrain but also ancient history. Just about the entire state is conducive to the sport, making it one of the most popular places in the United States for avid mountain bikers.

Albuquerque has some excellent and very challenging trails in the Sandia Mountains, as well as less strenuous routes west of town, through Petroglyph National Monument (see chapter 6). In **Santa Fe,** you'll find some very rugged and steep mountain trails, most accessed off the road to Ski Santa Fe (see chapter 7). **Taos** is a rider's paradise, with lots of extreme mountain trails, as well as some that are purely scenic, such as the west rim of the Rio Grande Gorge (see chapter 8).

In northwestern New Mexico, you can ride around El Malpais National Monument in the **Grants** area. You can also take your bike with you to Chaco Culture National Historical Park and ride from Anasazi ruin to ruin. The **Farmington** area has its renowned Road Apple Trail within Lions Wilderness Park, which you can ride even through the winter. See chapter 9.

In the southwestern region, bikes are not allowed in the Gila Wilderness, but they are permitted in other parts of Gila National Forest; you'll find terrific trails that originate in **Silver City** (see chapter 11). In the southeastern region, the **Cloudcroft** area has some excellent trails; there are a few that explore history as well as natural terrain, most notably the 17-mile Rim Trail (see chapter 12).

Some books to check out are *Mountain Biking Northern New Mexico: A Guide to Taos, Santa Fe, and Albuquerque Areas' Greatest Off-Road Bicycle Rides* (Falcon) by Bob D'Antonio, which details 40 rides, and *Mountain Biking New Mexico* (Falcon) by Sarah Bennett, which covers the whole state.

Known World Guides, in Velarde (✆ **800/983-7756** or 505/983-7756; www.knownworldguides.com), offers single-day and multiday trips all over New Mexico, with options such as 3 days in the Jemez Mountains west of Santa Fe or 5 days in the Gila National Forest in Silver City. **Mellow Velo,** 636 Old Santa Fe Trail, Santa Fe (✆ **505/982-8986;** www.mellowvelo.com), runs bike tours to some of the most spectacular spots in northern New Mexico. Trips range from the easy Train Tour south of Santa Fe, to a challenging Borrego Bust ride in the Santa Fe National Forest.

8 SKIING & SNOWBOARDING

New Mexico has some of the best **downhill skiing** in the United States. With most alpine areas above 10,000 feet and many above 12,000 feet, several ski areas offer vertical drops of over 2,000 feet. Average annual snowfall at the nine major areas ranges from 100 to 300 inches. Many areas, aided by vigorous snow-making efforts, are able to open around Thanksgiving, and most open by mid-December, making New Mexico a popular vacation spot around the holidays. As a result, you'll see a definite rise in hotel room rates in or around ski areas during the holiday season. The ski season runs through March and often into the first week in April.

Some of the best skiing and snowboarding in the state is at Taos and the nearby resort towns of Angel Fire and Red River (see chapter 8). In addition, Taos Ski Valley is home to one of the best ski schools in the country. Ski areas in New Mexico offer runs for a variety of skill levels, and all-day adult lift tickets range from about $40 to $66. Also, some of the best **cross-country skiing** in the region can be found at the Enchanted Forest near Red River and in Chama.

Equipment for alpine, telemark, and cross-country skiing, as well as for snowboarding, can be rented at ski areas and nearby towns. Lessons are widely available.

For more information about individual ski areas, see regional and city chapters later in this book.

9 WATERSPORTS

Watersports in New Mexico? Absolutely! Here you'll find a variety of watersports activities, ranging from pleasure boating to white-water rafting and windsurfing.

New Mexico offers fantastic opportunities for **white-water rafting** and **kayaking.** The waters in the Chama River and the Rio Grande are generally at their best during the spring and summer (May–July). I've listed my favorite outfitters in chapters 8 and 9. If you're an experienced rafter or kayaker and intend to head out on your own, you still may want to contact one of the outfitters listed in order to get tips on how to negotiate New Mexico's waters. In addition to calling outfitters, you can also contact the **Bureau of Land Management,** 226 Cruz Alta Rd., Taos, NM 87571 (✆ **575/758-8851;** www.nm.blm.gov), for information.

Opportunities for **pleasure boating** are available on many of New Mexico's lakes and reservoirs, with boat ramps at more than 45 state parks, dams, and lakes. Elephant Butte Lake is one of the best and most beautiful spots for boating (see chapter 11). Unfortunately, the rules and regulations vary greatly from one body of water to another, so you'll have to contact the governing agencies for each place in which you intend to go boating.

The **U.S. Army Corps of Engineers,** 4101 Jefferson Plaza NE, Albuquerque (✆ **505/342-3100;** www.usace.army.mil), oversees the following lakes: Abiquiu, Cochiti, Conchas, Galisteo, Jemez, Santa Rosa, and Two Rivers. Most other boating areas are regulated by the **State Parks Division,** 1220 S. St. Francis, Santa Fe (✆ **888/NM-PARKS** or 505/476-3355; www.nmparks.com), or by the **New Mexico Game and Fish Department,** 1 Wildlife Way, Santa Fe (✆ **505/476-8000;** www.wildlife.state.nm.us). Some are, of course, overseen by tribes and pueblos, and in those cases, you'll have to contact them directly.

Another popular pastime, particularly at Cochiti and Storrie lakes in summer, is **windsurfing.** Elephant Butte is good for windsurfing all year.

10 OTHER OUTDOOR ACTIVITIES

In addition to the activities listed so far in this chapter, many other recreational opportunities are available in New Mexico. **Hot springs,** for example, are quite popular with locals and visitors. They take many different forms and offer a wide variety of facilities and amenities; some, which aren't owned and operated by anyone but Mother Nature, offer no amenities. You'll find hot springs in the Taos and Las Vegas areas as well as in the southwestern region of New Mexico. Many of them are listed later in this book.

ROCKHOUNDING

New Mexico abounds in rockhounding opportunities. Of course, you can't just go around picking up and taking rocks whenever it strikes your fancy—in many places it's illegal to take rocks—but a few places not only allow rockhounding, but also encourage it. **Rockhound State Park** (✆ **575/546-6182;** www.nmparks.com), about 14 miles from Deming, is one such place (see chapter 11 for information). Rockhounds from all over the country descend on this part of the state to find great rocks, such as agate, jasper, and opal. At Rockhound State Park, you're allowed to camp and take a handful or two of rocks home with you. For information on other popular rockhounding sites, contact the **New Mexico Bureau of Geology & Mineral Resources** (© **575/835-5410;** www.geoinfo.nmt.edu).

TENNIS

Although New Mexico's high and dry climate is ideal for tennis much of the year, the sport is somewhat underdeveloped in the state. Certainly each of the major cities has municipal courts, information about which you'll find in the city and regional chapters of this book. If you're looking for a tennis resort experience, try **Bishop's Lodge,** Bishop's Lodge Road, Santa Fe (© **800/732-2240** or 505/983-6377; www.bishopslodge.com).

6

Albuquerque

Albuquerque is the gateway to New Mexico, the portal through which most domestic and international visitors pass before traveling on to other towns. But it's worth stopping in Albuquerque for a day or two in order to get a feel for the history of this area.

From the rocky crest of Sandia Peak at sunset, one can see the lights of this city spread out across 16 miles of high desert grassland. As the sun drops beyond the western horizon, it reflects off the Rio Grande, flowing through Albuquerque more than a mile below. This waterway is the bloodline for the area, what allowed a city to spring up in this vast desert, and it continues to be at the center of the area's growth.

The railroad, which set up a major stop here in 1880, prompted much of Albuquerque's initial growth, but that economic explosion was nothing compared with what has happened since World War II. Designated a major national center for military research and production, Albuquerque became a trading center for New Mexico, whose populace is spread widely across the land. That's why the city may strike visitors as nothing more than one big strip mall. Look closely, and you'll see ranchers, Native Americans, and Hispanic villagers stocking up on goods to take home.

Mornings are always unique in this city, when the clear blue sky often fills with hot-air balloons. The Albuquerque International Balloon Fiesta celebrates the sport in October, but now visitors can partake of the city's airy legacy any time at the new Balloon Museum on the north end of town.

Climbing out of the valley is **Route 66,** well worth a drive, if only to see the rust that time has left. Old court motels still line the street, many with their funky '50s signage. One enclave on this route is the **University of New Mexico district,** with a number of hippie-ish cafes and shops.

Farther downhill, you'll come to **downtown Albuquerque.** During the day, this area is all suits and heels, but at night it boasts a hip nightlife scene. People from all over the state come to Albuquerque to check out the live music and dance clubs, most within walking distance from each other.

The section called **Old Town** is worth a visit. Though it's the most touristy part of town, it's also a unique Southwestern village with a beautiful and intact plaza. Also in this area are Albuquerque's aquarium and botanical gardens, as well as its zoo.

Indian pueblos in the area welcome tourists, and, along with other pueblos throughout New Mexico, have worked to create the Pueblo Cultural Center, a showplace of Indian crafts of both past and present. The country's longest aerial tramway takes visitors to the top of Sandia Peak, which protects the city's eastern flank. To the west run a series of volcanoes; the Petroglyph National Monument there is an amazing tribute to the area's ancient Native American past.

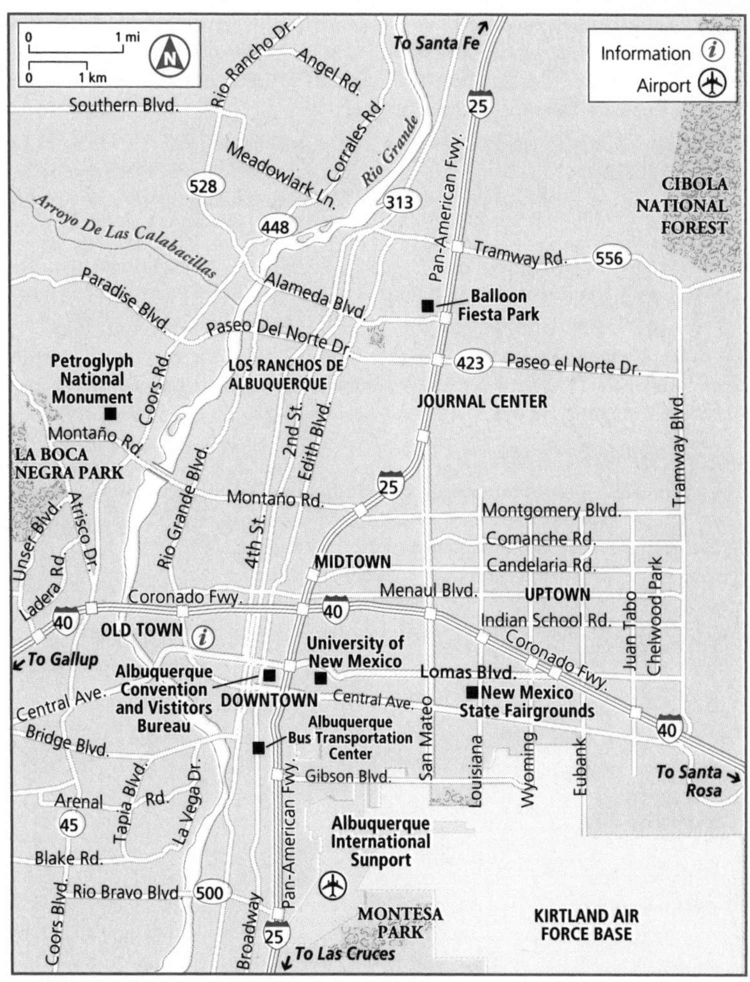

1 ORIENTATION

ARRIVING

Albuquerque is the transportation hub for New Mexico, so getting in and out of town is easy. For more detailed information, see "Getting There & Getting Around," in chapter 3.

BY PLANE The **Albuquerque International Sunport** (**© 505/842-4366;** www.cabq.gov/airport) is in the south-central part of the city, between I-25 on the west and Kirtland Air Force Base on the east, just south of Gibson Boulevard. Sleek and efficient, the airport is served by most national airlines and two local ones. It offers free Wi-Fi.

Most hotels have courtesy vans to meet their guests and take them to their respective destinations. In addition, **Airport Shuttle of Albuquerque** (ABQ; ✆ **505/765-1234;** www.airportshuttleabq.com) runs services to and from city hotels. **ABQ Ride** (✆ **505/243-7433;** www.cabq.gov/transit/index.html), Albuquerque's public bus system, also makes airport stops. There is efficient taxi service to and from the airport, and there are numerous car-rental agencies.

BY TRAIN **Amtrak's** "Southwest Chief" arrives and departs daily to and from Los Angeles and Chicago. The station is at the Alvarado Transportation Center, 300 Second St. SW (at the corner of Lead and Second; ✆ **800/USA-RAIL** or 505/842-9650; www.amtrak.com).

BY BUS **Greyhound/Trailways** (✆ **800/231-2222;** www.greyhound.com) and **TNM&O** (✆ **505/243-4435;** www.tnmo.com) arrive and depart from the Alvarado Transportation Center, 300 Second St. SW (at the corner of Lead and Second).

BY CAR If you're driving, you'll probably arrive via either the east–west I-40 or the north–south I-25. Exits are well marked. For information and advice on driving in New Mexico, see "Getting There & Getting Around," in chapter 3.

VISITOR INFORMATION

The main office of the **Albuquerque Convention and Visitors Bureau** is at 20 First Plaza NW (✆ **800/284-2282** or 505/842-9918; www.itsatrip.org). It's open Monday to Friday 8am to 5pm. There are information centers at the airport, on the lower level at the bottom of the escalator, open daily 9:30am to 8pm; and in Old Town at 303 Romero St. NW (Suite 107), open daily 10am to 5pm. Tape-recorded information about current local events is available from the bureau after 5pm weekdays and all day Saturday and Sunday. Call ✆ **800/284-2282.**

CITY LAYOUT

The city's sprawl takes awhile to get used to. A visitor's first impression is of a grid of arteries lined with shopping malls and fast-food eateries, with residences tucked behind on side streets.

If you look at a map of Albuquerque, you'll notice that it lies at the crossroads of I-25 north–south and I-40 east–west. Focus your attention on the southwest quadrant: Here, you'll find both downtown Albuquerque and Old Town, site of many tourist attractions. Lomas Boulevard and Central Avenue, the old Route 66 (US 66), flank downtown on the north and south. They come together 2 miles west of downtown near Old Town Plaza, the historical and spiritual heart of the city. Lomas and Central continue east across I-25, staying about half a mile apart as they pass by the University of New Mexico and the New Mexico State Fairgrounds. The airport is directly south of the UNM campus, about 3 miles via Yale Boulevard. Kirtland Air Force Base—site of Sandia National Laboratories—is an equal distance south of the fairgrounds, on Louisiana Boulevard.

Roughly paralleling I-40 to the north is Menaul Boulevard, the focus of midtown and uptown shopping, as well as the hotel districts. As Albuquerque expands northward, the Journal Center business park area, about 4½ miles north of the freeway interchange, is expanding. Near there is home to the Albuquerque International Balloon Fiesta and the new Balloon Museum. East of Eubank Boulevard lie the Sandia Foothills, where the alluvial plain slants a bit more steeply toward the mountains.

When looking for an address, it is helpful to know that Central Avenue divides the city into north and south, and the railroad tracks—which run just east of First Street downtown—comprise the dividing line between east and west. Street names are followed by a directional: NE, NW, SE, or SW.

MAPS The most comprehensive Albuquerque street map is distributed by the Convention and Visitors Bureau, 20 First Plaza NW (✆ **800/284-2282** or 505/842-9918).

2 GETTING AROUND

Albuquerque is easy to get around, thanks to its wide thoroughfares and grid layout, combined with its efficient transportation systems.

BY PUBLIC TRANSPORTATION **ABQ Ride** (✆ **505/243-7433**) cloaks the arterials with its city bus network. Call for information on routes and fares.

BY TAXI **Yellow Cab** (✆ **505/247-8888**) serves the city and surrounding area 24 hours a day.

BY CAR The Yellow Pages lists more than 30 car-rental agencies in Albuquerque. Among them are the following well-known national firms: **Alamo,** 3400 University Blvd. SE (✆ **505/842-4057;** www.alamo.com); **Avis,** at the airport (✆ **505/842-4080;** www.avis.com); **Budget,** at the airport (✆ **505/247-3443;** www.budget.com); **Dollar,** at the airport (✆ **505/842-4224;** www.dollar.com); **Hertz,** at the airport (✆ **505/842-4235;** www.hertz.com); **Rent-A-Wreck,** 2001 Ridegecrest Dr. SE (✆ **505/232-7552;** www.rentawreck.com/nm.htm); and **Thrifty,** 2039 Yale Blvd. SE (✆ **505/842-8733;** www.thrifty.com). Those not located at the airport itself are close by and can provide rapid airport pickup and delivery service.

Parking is generally not difficult in Albuquerque. Meters operate weekdays 8am to 6pm and are not monitored at other times. Only the large downtown hotels charge for parking. Traffic is a problem only at certain hours. Avoid I-25 and I-40 at the center of town around 8am and 5pm.

Fast Facts Albuquerque

Airport See "Orientation," above.

Area Code In 2007 New Mexico added a new area code. The northwestern section, including Santa Fe and Albuquerque, retained the **505** code, while the rest of the state changed to **575.**

ATMs You can find ATMs all over town, at supermarkets, banks, and drive-throughs.

Business Hours **Offices** and **stores** are generally open Monday to Friday, 9am to 5pm, with many stores also open Friday night, Saturday, and Sunday in the summer season. Most **banks** are also open Monday to Friday, 9am to 5pm. Some may be open Saturday morning. Most branches have ATMs available 24 hours. Call establishments for specific hours.

Car Rentals See "Getting Around New Mexico," in chapter 3, or "Getting Around," above.

Climate See "When to Go," in chapter 3.

Currency Exchange Foreign currency can be exchanged at any of the branches of **Bank of America** (its main office is at 303 Roma NW; ✆ **505/282-2450**).

Dentists Call the **Albuquerque District Dental Society,** at ✆ **505/237-1412,** for emergency service.

Doctors Call the **Greater Albuquerque Medical Association,** at ✆ **505/821-4583,** for information.

Emergencies For police, fire, or ambulance, dial ✆ **911.**

Hospitals The major hospital facilities are **Presbyterian Hospital,** 1100 Central Ave. SE (✆ **505/841-1234,** or 505/841-1111 for emergency services), and **University of New Mexico Hospital,** 2211 Lomas Blvd. NE (✆ **505/272-2111,** or 505/272-2411 for emergency services).

Hot Lines The following hot lines are available in Albuquerque: rape crisis (✆ **505/266-7711**), poison control (✆ **800/432-6866**), suicide (✆ **505/247-1121**), and Psychiatric Emergency Services (✆ **505/272-2920**).

Information See "Visitor Information," under "Orientation," above.

Internet Access **FedEx Office's** provides high-speed Internet access at five locations throughout the city. Two convenient ones are 6220 San Mateo Blvd. NE at Academy Boulevard (✆ **505/821-2222**) and 2706 Central Ave. SE at Princeton Boulevard (✆ **505/255-9673**).

Library The Albuquerque/Bernalillo County Public Library's **main branch** is at 501 Copper Ave. NW, between Fifth and Sixth streets (✆ **505/768-5140**). You can find the locations of the 17 other library facilities in the area by checking online at **www.cabq.gov/library**.

Liquor Laws The legal drinking age is 21 throughout New Mexico. Bars may remain open until 2am Monday to Saturday and until midnight on Sunday. Wine, beer, and spirits are sold at licensed supermarkets and liquor stores. It is illegal to transport liquor through most Native American reservations.

Lost Property Contact the city police at ✆ **505/768-2229** or 505/768-2278.

Newspapers & Magazines The daily newspaper is the ***Albuquerque Journal*** (✆ **505/823-7777;** www.abqjournal.com). You can pick up the ***Alibi*** (✆ **505/346-0660;** www.alibi.com), Albuquerque's alternative weekly, for free at newsstands all over town, especially around the University of New Mexico. It offers entertainment listings and alternative views on a variety of subjects.

Pharmacies **Walgreens** (www.walgreens.com) has many locations throughout Albuquerque. To find one near you, call ✆ **800-WALGREENS** (925-4733). Two centrally located ones that are open 24 hours are 8011 Harper Dr. NE at Wyoming Boulevard (✆ **505/858-3134**) and 5001 Montgomery Blvd. NE at San Mateo (✆ **505/881-5210**).

Police For emergencies, call ✆ **911.** For other business, contact the **Albuquerque City Police** (✆ **505/242-COPS** [2677]) or the **New Mexico State Police** (✆ **505/841-9256**).

Post Offices To find the nearest U.S. Post Office, dial ✆ **800/275-8777.** The service will ask for your zip code and give you the closest post office address and hours.

Radio The local AM station **KKOB** (770) broadcasts news and events. FM band stations include **KUNM** (89.9), the University of New Mexico station, which broadcasts Public Radio programming and a variety of music, **KPEK** (100.3), which plays adult contemporary music, and **KHFM** (95.5), which broadcasts classical music.

Taxes In Albuquerque, the sales tax is 6.875%. An additional hotel tax of 6% will be added to your bill.

Taxis See "Getting Around," above.

Television There are five Albuquerque network affiliates: **KOB-TV** (Channel 4, NBC), **KOAT-TV** (Channel 7, ABC), **KQRE-TV** (Channel 13, CBS), **KASA-TV** (Channel 2, FOX), and **KNME-TV** (Channel 5, PBS).

Time As is true throughout New Mexico, Albuquerque is on **Mountain Standard Time.** It's 2 hours earlier than New York, 1 hour earlier than Chicago, and 1 hour later than Los Angeles. Daylight saving time is in effect from mid-March to early November.

Transit Information **ABQ Ride** is the public bus system. Call ✆ **505/243-7433** for schedules and information.

Useful Telephone Numbers For **road information,** call ✆ **800/432-4269** and for **emergency road service** (AAA), call ✆ **505/291-6600.**

Weather For **time** and **temperature,** call ✆ **505/821-1111.** To get **weather forecasts** on the Internet, check **www.accuweather.com** and use the Albuquerque zip code, 87104.

3 WHERE TO STAY

Albuquerque's hotel glut is good news for travelers looking for quality rooms at a reasonable cost. Except during peak periods—specifically, the New Mexico Arts and Crafts Fair (late June), the New Mexico State Fair (Sept), and the Albuquerque International Balloon Fiesta (early Oct)—most of the city's hotels have vacant rooms, so guests can frequently request and get lower room rates than the ones posted.

A tax of approximately 12.875% is added to every hotel bill. All hotels and bed-and-breakfasts listed offer rooms for nonsmokers and travelers with disabilities.

HOTELS/MOTELS

Expensive

Albuquerque Marriott Pyramid North ★ About a 15-minute drive from Old Town and downtown, this Aztec pyramid–shaped structure provides well-appointed rooms in an interesting environment. The 10 guest floors are grouped around a skylit atrium. Vines drape from planter boxes on the balconies, and water falls five stories to a pool between the two glass elevators. The rooms are spacious, though not extraordinary, all with picture windows and ample views. The third stage of a $10-million renovation was completed in 2008. With lots of convention space at the hotel, you're likely to encounter name-tagged conventioneers here. Overall, the service seems to be good enough to handle the crowds, but there are only two elevators, so guests often must wait. Wireless Internet connection is offered in the lobby atrium.

5151 San Francisco Rd. NE, Albuquerque, NM 87109. ✆ **800/262-2043** or 505/821-3333. Fax 505/822-8115. www.marriott.com/abqmc. 310 units. $169–$199 double; $199 and up suite. Ask about special weekend and package rates. AE, DC, DISC, MC, V. Free parking. **Amenities:** Restaurant; lounge; indoor/outdoor pool; medium-size exercise room; Jacuzzi; concierge; business center; room service; valet laundry. *In room:* A/C, TV, high-speed Internet, coffeemaker, hair dryer, iron.

Embassy Suites Albuquerque Hotel & Spa ★★ This newer addition to Albuquerque's hotel scene, opened in 2005, boasts nine floors of suites set around a grand atrium. Its location between the university and downtown offers easy access to the freeway as well and is just 10 minutes from Old Town. It's an elegant place frequented by business people and conventioneers, but it can also prove a nice stay for travelers, especially families who enjoy the two-room suites. The elegant rooms, which are fairly large, have comfortable beds, large baths with granite counter tops, and many other amenities. A fold-out bed in the second room allows for plenty of space. The Spa Botanica offers a full range of treatments. Evenings bring a manager's reception, where hors d'oeuvres and drinks are served. Service here is friendly and efficient.

1000 Woodward Place NE, Albuquerque, NM 87102. ✆ **800/EMBASSY** (362-2779) or 505/245-7100. Fax 505/247-1083. www.embassysuites.com. 261 units. $179–$214 double. AE, DC, DISC, MC, V. Free parking. **Amenities:** 2 restaurants; lounge; indoor pool; Jacuzzi; large exercise room; concierge; business center; room service, valet laundry. *In room:* A/C, TV, Wi-Fi, fridge, microwave, coffeemaker, hair dryer, iron, in-room movies.

Hotel Albuquerque at Old Town ★★ This completely renovated hotel just 5 minutes from Old Town offers artfully decorated rooms with views and excellent service. No Albuquerque hotel is closer to top tourist attractions than the Hotel Albuquerque. Constructed in 1975, it existed for years under the Sheraton banner. Now a Heritage Hotel, it has received a $16-million makeover. The cathedral-style lobby has Spanish colonial furnishings and art, a theme that carries into the guest rooms. They're medium size, with comfortable beds and medium-size baths with outer vanities. Request a south-side room, and you'll get a balcony with a view over Old Town. A north-side room yields mountain views but no balconies (this is the side to request during the Balloon Fiesta). The lovely grounds have a long portal and a quaint chapel. The Q Bar is one of Albuquerque's chicest night spots, with a good tapas menu and billiards.

800 Rio Grande Blvd. NW, Albuquerque, NM 87104. ✆ **800/237-2133** (reservations only), or 505/843-6300. Fax 505/842-8426. www.hotelabq.com. 188 units. $99–$209 double; $149–$350 jr. suite double. Children stay free in parent's room. AE, DC, DISC, MC, V. Free parking. **Amenities:** 2 restaurants; lounge; outdoor pool (in summer); Jacuzzi; concierge; business center; room service; valet laundry; same-day dry cleaning; executive-level rooms. *In room:* A/C, TV w/pay movies, Wi-Fi, coffeemaker, hair dryer, iron.

Sandia Resort & Casino ★★★ On the Sandia Reservation at the north end of town in a grand nine-story pueblo-style structure, this resort offers plenty of fun activities in a scenic setting. The hotel has spectacular views of the Sandia Mountains and the Albuquerque skyline. The lobby, constructed in a majestic mission church style, offers space for lounging, and just off it, a casino, with 1,800 slots, Vegas-style gambling, and all the blinking lights that a gambler could want. The spacious rooms, decorated in an elegant Native American motif, have very comfortable beds, a lounge chair, desk, and louvered blackout blinds, as well as many amenities. The bathrooms are large, with Italian tile throughout, and robes. The suites are even more spacious, of course. The Green Reed Spa offers a full range of treatments, and the Scott Miller–designed 18-hole golf course wraps around the hotel, giving a sense of lush green to the desert. The Bien Shur restaurant on the ninth floor is one of the city's finest dining experiences. Be aware that

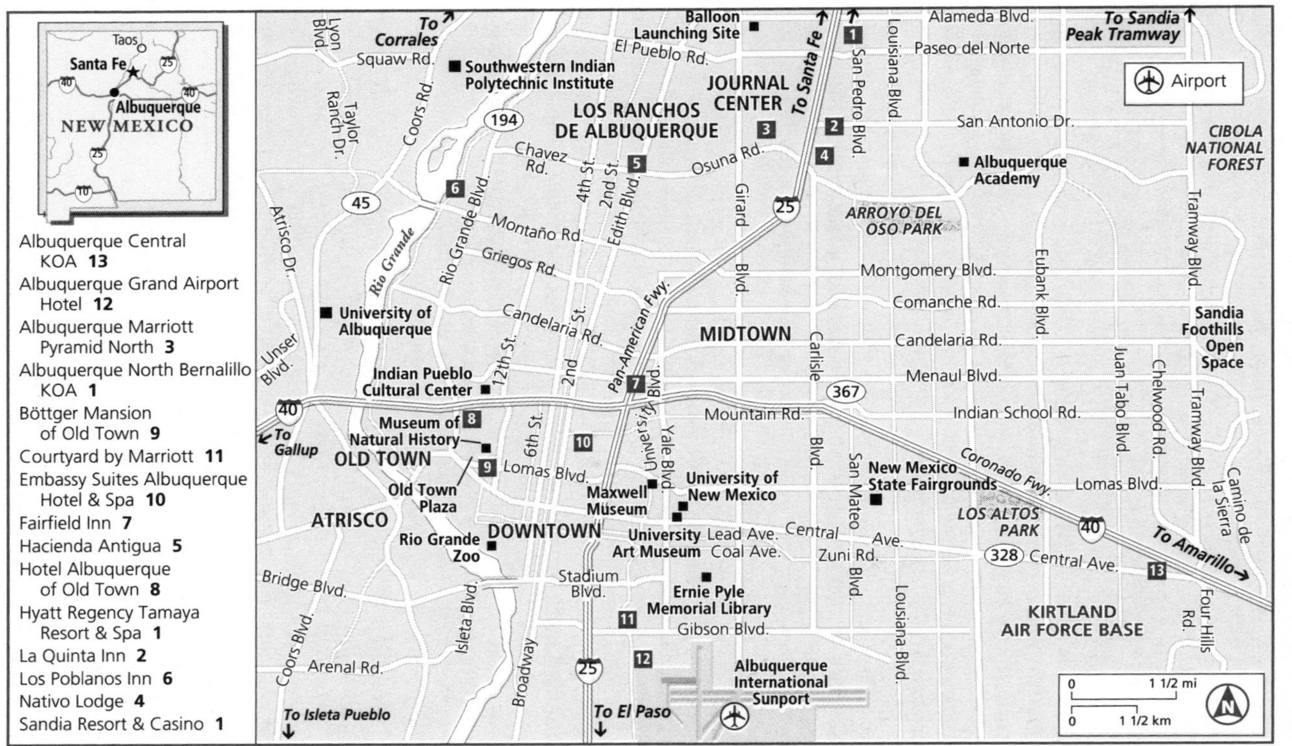
Taos
Santa Fe
Albuquerque
NEW MEXICO
Albuquerque Central KOA 13
Albuquerque Grand Airport Hotel 12
Albuquerque Marriott Pyramid North 3
Albuquerque North Bernalillo KOA 1
Böttger Mansion of Old Town 9
Courtyard by Marriott 11
Embassy Suites Albuquerque Hotel & Spa 10
Fairfield Inn 7
Hacienda Antigua 5
Hotel Albuquerque of Old Town 8
Hyatt Regency Tamaya Resort & Spa 1
La Quinta Inn 2
Los Poblanos Inn 6
Nativo Lodge 4
Sandia Resort & Casino 1
Lyon Blvd.
To Corrales
Squaw Rd.
Balloon Launching Site
El Pueblo Rd.
To Santa Fe
San Pedro Blvd.
Louisiana Blvd.
Alameda Blvd.
Paseo del Norte
To Sandia Peak Tramway
Airport
Southwestern Indian Polytechnic Institute
JOURNAL CENTER
LOS RANCHOS DE ALBUQUERQUE
Taylor Ranch Dr.
Coors Rd.
San Antonio Dr.
CIBOLA NATIONAL FOREST
Chavez Rd.
Osuna Rd.
Albuquerque Academy
4th St.
2nd St.
Edith Blvd.
Girard Blvd.
ARROYO DEL OSO PARK
Atrisco Dr.
Rio Grande
Rio Grande Blvd
Montaño Rd.
Griegos Rd.
Montgomery Blvd.
Eubank Blvd.
Tramway Blvd.
Comanche Rd.
University of Albuquerque
Candelaria Rd.
Pan-American Fwy.
MIDTOWN
Carlisle Blvd.
Candelaria Rd.
Sandia Foothills Open Space
Unser Blvd.
Indian Pueblo Cultural Center
12th St.
2nd St.
Menaul Blvd.
Juan Tabo Blvd.
Chelwood Rd.
Mountain Rd.
Indian School Rd.
To Gallup
Museum of Natural History
6th St.
University Blvd.
Yale Blvd.
OLD TOWN
Lomas Blvd.
San Mateo Blvd.
New Mexico State Fairgrounds
Coronado Fwy.
Old Town Plaza
Maxwell Museum
University of New Mexico
Camino de la Sierra
ATRISCO
LOS ALTOS PARK
DOWNTOWN
Rio Grande Zoo
University Art Museum
Lead Ave.
Coal Ave.
Central Ave.
Zuni Rd.
To Amarillo
Bridge Blvd.
Stadium Blvd.
Ernie Pyle Memorial Library
Gibson Blvd.
KIRTLAND AIR FORCE BASE
Four Hills Rd.
Coors Blvd.
Isleta Blvd.
Arenal Rd.
Broadway
Albuquerque International Sunport
To Isleta Pueblo
To El Paso
0 1 1/2 mi
0 1 1/2 km

this resort best serves active people who like to play into the night. If you're looking for a more relaxing stay, you might choose the Hyatt Tamaya.

30 Rainbow Rd. NE, Albuquerque, NM 87113. www.sandiaresort.com. ✆ **877/272-9199** (reservations only), 800/526-9366, or 505/798-3930. Fax 505/796-7606. 228 units. $139–$299 double; $319–$389 1-bedroom suite; $699 2-bedroom suite. AE, DC, DISC, MC, V. Free valet parking. **Amenities:** 3 restaurants; large outdoor pool, (weather permitting); Jacuzzi; exercise room; concierge; room service; business center; spa; salon; open-air amphitheater; golf course. *In room:* A/C, TV w/in-room movies, Wi-Fi, coffeemaker, hair dryer, iron.

Moderate

Albuquerque Grand Airport Hotel ★★ This 15-story hotel right at the airport provides spacious rooms with a touch of elegance. The lobby, grill, and lounge areas employ a lot of sandstone, wood, copper, and tile to lend an Anasazi feel, which carries into the rooms, each with a broad view from a balcony. A recent remodel brought new, comfortable mattresses and bright pine furnishings. Air travelers enjoy this hotel's location, but because it has good access to freeways and excellent views, it could also be a wise choice for a few days of browsing around Albuquerque. Of course, you will hear some jet noise. The Rojo Grill serves a variety of American and Southwestern dishes.

2910 Yale Blvd. SE, Albuquerque, NM 87106. ✆ **800/227-1117** or 505/843-7000. Fax 505/843-6307. www.albuquerquegrandairporthotel.com. 276 units. $79–$176 double. AE, DC, DISC, MC, V. Free parking. Small pets, 15 lb. or less, welcome with prior approval. **Amenities:** Restaurant; outdoor pool; access to golf club; 2 tennis courts; concierge; business center; coin-op laundry. *In room:* A/C, TV, Wi-Fi, dataport, coffeemaker, hair dryer, iron.

Courtyard by Marriott ★ If you don't like high-rises such as the Albuquerque Grand Airport Hotel (see above), this is the best selection of airport-area hotels. Opened in 1990, this four-story member of the Marriott family is built around an attractively landscaped courtyard. Families appreciate the security system—key cards must be used to access the hotel between 11pm and 6am—though most of the hotel's clients are business travelers. The units are roomy and comfortable, with walnut furniture and firm beds. Ask for a balcony room on the courtyard.

1920 Yale Blvd. SE, Albuquerque, NM 87106. ✆ **800/321-2211** or 505/843-6600. Fax 505/843-8740. www.marriott.com. 150 units. $159 double weekdays. Weekend rates $84–$99. AE, DC, DISC, MC, V. Free parking. **Amenities:** Restaurant; lounge; indoor pool; exercise room; Jacuzzi; valet and coin-op laundry. *In room:* A/C, TV, high-speed Internet, coffeemaker, hair dryer, iron.

Nativo Lodge ★ This full-service hotel provides comfortable rooms with a Native American theme, utilizing high-tech elements as well. It's part of the Heritage Hotels & Resorts group, which, in recent years, has renovated a number of New Mexico hotels such as the Hotel Encanto in Las Cruces and Hotel Albuquerque at Old Town. The five-story building, renovated in 2004, has tan walls throughout the two-tiered lobby and standard-size guest rooms. The rooms are tastefully decorated with Native American geometric patterns creating a cozy feel, with comfortable beds and good linens, a desk and small balcony. The bathrooms are small but functional. Be sure to request a room well away from the lounge area, which can be noisy on weekend nights. The service is thoughtful and efficient. This is a good home base for the Balloon Fiesta, as well as to explore the city. The property even has a tepee used for special events.

6000 Pan American Fwy. NE, Albuquerque, NM 87109. ✆ **888/628-4861** or 505/798-4300. Fax 505/798-4305. www.nativolodge.com. $79–$139 double. AE, DC, DISC, MC, V. Free parking. **Amenities:** Restaurant; lounge; indoor/outdoor pool; Jacuzzi; exercise room; room service; business center. *In room:* A/C, TV w/in-room movies, Wi-Fi, coffeemaker, hair dryer, iron.

Inexpensive

Fairfield Inn *Value* Owned by Marriott, this hotel has exceptionally clean rooms and easy access to freeways that can quickly get you to Old Town, downtown, or the heights. Ask for an east-facing room to avoid the noise and a view of the highway. Rooms are medium-size and have medium-size bathrooms. Each has a balcony or terrace. You probably couldn't get more for your money (in a chain hotel) anywhere else.

1760 Menaul Blvd. NE, Albuquerque, NM 87102. ✆ **800/228-2800** or 505/889-4000. Fax 505/872-3094. www.fairfieldinn.com. 188 units. $78 double. Additional person $10. Children 18 and under stay free in parent's room. Free continental breakfast. AE, DC, DISC, MC, V. Free parking. **Amenities:** Indoor/outdoor pool; health club; Jacuzzi; sauna; laundry service. *In room:* A/C, TV, Wi-Fi.

La Quinta Inn La Quinta offers reliable, clean rooms at a decent price. Rooms are tastefully decorated, fairly spacious, and comfortable, each with a table and chairs and a shower-only bathroom big enough to move around in. Each king room has a recliner, and two-room suites are available. If you're headed to the Balloon Fiesta, this is a good choice because it's not far from the launch site, though you'll have to reserve as much as a year in advance.

There's another La Quinta near the airport (La Quinta Airport Inn, 2116 Yale Blvd. SE); you can make reservations for either branch at the toll-free number.

5241 San Antonio Dr. NE, Albuquerque, NM 87109. ✆ **800/531-5900** or 505/821-9000. Fax 505/821-2399. www.lq.com. 130 units. $72–$79 double (higher during Balloon Fiesta). Children stay free in parent's room. AE, DC, DISC, MC, V. Free parking. Pets welcome. **Amenities:** Heated outdoor pool (May–Oct). *In room:* A/C, TV, Wi-Fi, coffeemaker, hair dryer, iron.

BED & BREAKFASTS

The Böttger Mansion of Old Town ★★ Decorated with antiques but not overdone with chintz, this Victorian inn situated right in Old Town is an excellent choice. It offers a sweet taste of a past era. My favorite room is the Carole Rose, with lots of sun; also lovely is the Rebecca Leah, with pink marble tile and a Jacuzzi tub. All rooms are medium-size and have excellent beds; most have small bathrooms. The rooms facing south let in the most sun but pick up a bit of street noise from nearby Central Avenue and a nearby elementary school (both quiet down at night). Breakfast (such as green-chile quiche) is elaborate enough to keep you going through the day, at the end of which you can enjoy treats from the guest snack bar (try the chocolate cookies with a little chile in them). During warm months, the patio is lovely.

110 San Felipe NW, Albuquerque, NM 87104. ✆ **800/758-3639** or 505/243-3639. www.bottger.com. 8 units. $99–$179 double. Rates include full breakfast and snack bar. AE, DISC, MC, V. *In room:* A/C, TV/VCR, Wi-Fi, hair dryer.

Hacienda Antigua ★★ *Finds* This adobe home built in 1790 was once the first stagecoach stop out of Old Town in Albuquerque. Now, it's one of Albuquerque's more elegant inns. The artistically landscaped courtyard, with its large cottonwood tree and abundance of greenery, offers a welcome respite for tired travelers. The rooms are gracefully and comfortably furnished with antiques. My favorites all open onto the Great Room. La Capilla, the home's former chapel, has a serene and holy feel, and is furnished with a queen-size bed, a fireplace, and a carving of St. Francis (the patron saint of the garden). All the rooms are equipped with fireplaces. Two more modern rooms built in 2000 aren't quite as atmospheric as those in the main house. A gourmet breakfast, such as pecan waffles, is served in the garden during warm weather and by the fire in winter.

The inn is a 15-minute drive from Old Town. High-speed Internet access is available in the lobby.

6708 Tierra Dr. NW, Albuquerque, NM 87107. ✆ **800/201-2986** or 505/345-5399. Fax 505/345-3855. www.haciendantigua.com. 8 units. $129–$209 double. Additional person $25. Rates include gourmet breakfast. AE, MC, V. Free parking. Pets welcome with $30 fee. **Amenities:** Outdoor pool; Jacuzzi; concierge; in-room massage and reflexology. *In room:* A/C, Wi-Fi, fridge, coffeemaker, hair dryer.

Los Poblanos Inn ★★ Lushness in the desert city of Albuquerque? It's no mirage. Nestled among century-old cottonwoods, this bed-and-breakfast sits on 25 acres of European-style gardens and peasant-like vegetable and lavender fields, providing one of the state's richest country living experiences. Notable architect John Gaw Meem built the structure, a 7-minute drive from Old Town, in the 1930s. Each of the six guest rooms, most arranged around a poetically planted courtyard with a fountain, has unique touches such as hand-carved doors, traditional tin fixtures, fireplaces, and views across the lushly landscaped grounds. The rooms vary in size. All are comfortable, tastefully decorated with good linens, and offer organic shampoo and soap scented with lavender from the inn's garden. At breakfast, you might feast on eggs Florentine made with eggs from the inn's chickens, spinach from the garden, and artisanal bread made locally, while watching peacocks preen outside the windows of the very Mexican-feeling, boldly decorated cantina. Light sleepers should be aware that the peacocks may caw at night. Fortunately, the inn provides earplugs. A copy of the *New York Times* arrives on each doorstep in the morning.

4803 Rio Grande Blvd. NW, Albuquerque, NM 87107. ✆ **866/344-9297** or 505/344-9297. Fax 505/342-1302. www.lospoblanos.com. 7 units. $150–$265 double. Rates include full breakfast. AE, MC, V. Free parking. **Amenities:** Swimming pool (in summer); walking trails; bike rentals. *In room:* A/C, Wi-Fi, hair dryer, iron.

NEAR ALBUQUERQUE

Hyatt Regency Tamaya Resort and Spa ★★★ This is the spot for a get-away-from-it-all luxury vacation. Set in the hills above the lush Rio Grande Valley on the Santa Ana Pueblo, this pueblo-style resort offers a 16,000-square-foot full-service spa and fitness center, an 18-hole Twin Warriors Championship Golf Course designed by Gary Panks, and views of the Sandia Mountains. Rooms are spacious, with large tile bathrooms. Request one that faces the mountains for one of the state's more spectacular vistas. Other rooms look out across a large courtyard, where the pools and hot tub are. Though the resort is surrounded by acres of quiet countryside, it's only 20 minutes from Albuquerque and 50 minutes from Santa Fe. The concierge offers trips to attractions daily, as well as on-site activities such as hot-air balloon rides, horseback rides, and nature/cultural walks or carriage rides by the river. Plan at least one dinner at the innovative Corn Maiden.

1300 Tuyuna Trail, Santa Ana Pueblo, NM 87004. ✆ **800/55-HYATT** (554-9288) or 505/867-1234. www.tamaya.hyatt.com. 350 units. May–Oct $245–$415; Nov–Apr $199–$305, depending on the type of room. Suite rates available upon request. Inquire about spa, horseback riding, golf, and family packages. AE, DC, DISC, MC, V. Free parking. From I-25 take exit 242, following US 550 west to Tamaya Blvd.; drive 1½ miles to the resort. **Amenities:** 2 restaurants; 2 snack bars; lounge; 3 pools (heated year-round); golf course; 2 tennis courts; health club and spa; children's programs; concierge; tour desk; elaborate business center; room service; laundry service; basketball court. *In room:* A/C, TV, high-speed Internet, Wi-Fi, fridge, coffeemaker, hair dryer, iron, safe.

RV PARKS

Albuquerque Central KOA This RV park in the foothills east of Albuquerque is a good choice for those who want to be close to town. It offers some shade trees, lots of amenities, and convenient freeway access. Cabins are available.

Finds Cruising Corrales

If you'd like to travel along meadows and apple orchards into a place where life is a little slower and sweeter, head 20 minutes north of Albuquerque to the village of Corrales. Home to farmers, artists, and affluent land owners, this is a fun place to roam through shops and galleries, and, in the fall, sample vegetables from roadside vendors. A good restaurant serving imaginative new American cuisine, sits on the main street. **Indigo Crow** ★, 4515 Corrales Rd. (✆ **505/898-7000**), serves lunch and dinner Tuesday to Saturday and brunch on Sunday. If you'd like to stay in the village, contact the **Sandhill Crane Bed-and-Breakfast,** 389 Camino Hermosa (✆ **800/375-2445** or 505/898-2445; www.sandhillcranebandb.com).

The town also has a nature preserve and a historic church. In September, the Harvest Festival is well worth the trip. For more information about Corrales, contact Corrales Village (✆ **505/897-0502;** www.corrales-nm.org).

To get to the village, head north on either I-25 or Rio Grande Boulevard, turn west on Alameda Boulevard, cross the Rio Grande, and turn north on Corrales Road (NM 448). The village is just a few minutes up the road.

12400 Skyline Rd. NE, Albuquerque, NM 87123. ✆ **800/562-7781** or 505/296-2729. www.koa.com. $30–$47 tent site; $35–$65 RV site, depending on hookup; $45–$85 1-room cabin; $48–$95 2-room cabin. All prices valid for up to 2 people. Additional adult $5, child $3. AE, DISC, MC, V. Free parking. Pets welcome. **Amenities:** Outdoor pool (summer only); Jacuzzi; bike rentals; store; coin-op laundry; bathhouse; miniature golf; playground; accessible restroom; Wi-Fi access throughout the park; fenced dog park.

Albuquerque North Bernalillo KOA ★ More than 1,000 cottonwood and pine trees shade this park, and you'll see many flowers in the warm months. At the foot of the mountains, 14 miles from Albuquerque, this campground has plenty of amenities. Guests enjoy a free pancake breakfast daily. Reservations are recommended. Six camping cabins are also available.

555 Hill Rd., Bernalillo, NM 87004. ✆ **800/562-3616** or 505/867-5227. www.koa.com. $21–$23 tent site; $30–$36 RV site, depending on hookup; $38 1-bedroom cabin; $48 2-bedroom cabin. Rates include pancake breakfast and are valid for up to 2 people. Additional person $4. Children 5 and under free with parent. AE, DISC, MC, V. Free parking. Pets welcome. **Amenities:** Restaurant; outdoor pool (summer only); store; coin-op laundry; playground; free outdoor movies; Wi-Fi access throughout the park.

4 WHERE TO DINE

IN OR NEAR OLD TOWN

Expensive

Seasons Grill ★★ AMERICAN Between sunshine-colored walls and under an arched ceiling, this restaurant serves sophisticated flavors just steps from Old Town. It's a sweet oasis at midday and a romantic spot in the evening. The upstairs cantina bustles at sundown, with folks drinking margaritas. Service is excellent. At lunch you can't go wrong with the Angus burger with lemon aioli and roasted poblano chiles and served with herb fries. For the lighter eater, a number of salads head the menu. Dinner brings more sophisticated offerings. The grilled pork chop with goat cheese and roasted potatoes is tasty, as is the hoisin-glazed Atlantic salmon with jasmine rice. A full bar and an imaginative wine and beer list accompany the menu. On Saturday and Sunday evenings in summer, live jazz plays.

2031 Mountain Rd. NW. ✆ **505/766-5100.** Reservations recommended at dinner. Main courses $7–$14 lunch, $16–$40 dinner. AE, DC, DISC, MC, V. Mon–Fri 11:30am–2:30pm; daily 5–10:30pm. Cantina daily 4pm–midnight.

Moderate

La Crêpe Michel ★★ FRENCH Locals love this small cafe tucked away in a secluded walkway not far from the plaza, where the food is fun and imaginatively prepared. Run by chef Claudie Zamet-Wilcox from France, it has a cozy, informal European feel, with checked table coverings and simple furnishings. Service is friendly and calm, which makes this a good place for a romantic meal. You can't miss with any of the crepes. The *crêpe aux fruits de mer* (blend of sea scallops, bay scallops, and shrimp in a velouté sauce with mushrooms) is especially nice, as is the *crêpe à la volaille* (chunks of chicken in a cream sauce with mushrooms and Madeira wine). For a heartier meal, try one of the specials listed on the board on the wall, such as the beef filet (tenderloin finished with either black peppercorn–brandy cream sauce or Roquefort-brandy cream sauce) or the *saumon au champagne* (filet of salmon with a white wine and cream sauce). Both are served with vegetables cooked just enough to leave them crisp and tasty. For dessert, don't leave without having a *crêpe aux fraises* (strawberry crepe). To accompany your meal, choose from a carefully planned beer and wine menu.

400 San Felipe C2. ✆ **505/242-1251.** www.lacrepemichel.com. Main courses $6–$24. AE, DISC, MC, V. Tues–Sun 11:30am–2pm; Tues–Sat 6–9pm.

Inexpensive

Duran Central Pharmacy ★ Finds NEW MEXICAN Sounds like an odd place to eat, I know. You could go to one of the touristy New Mexican restaurants in the middle of Old Town and have lots of atmosphere and mediocre food—or you could come here, where locals eat, and feast on better, more authentic fare. It's a few blocks up Central, east of Old Town. On your way through the pharmacy, you may want to stock up on specialty soaps; there's a pretty good variety here. The restaurant itself is plain, with a red tile floor and small tables, as well as a counter. For years, I used to come here for a bowl of green-chile stew and a homemade tortilla, which is still an excellent choice. Now I go for the full meals, such as the blue-corn enchilada plate or the huevos rancheros (eggs over corn tortillas, smothered with chile). The menu is short, but you can count on authentic northern New Mexican food.

1815 Central Ave. NW. ✆ **505/247-4141.** Menu items $6–$20. No credit cards. Mon–Fri 9am–6:30pm; Sat 9am–2pm.

Sadie's ★ Kids NEW MEXICAN Many New Mexicans lament the lost days when this restaurant was in a bowling alley. It's true that you can no longer hear the pins fall, and the main dining room is a little too big and the atmosphere a little too bright, but something is still drawing crowds: It's the food—simply some of the best in New Mexico, with tasty sauces and large portions. I recommend the enchilada, either chicken or beef. The stuffed *sopaipilla* dinner is also delicious and is one of the signature dishes. All meals come with chips and salsa, beans, and *sopaipillas.* There's a full bar, with excellent

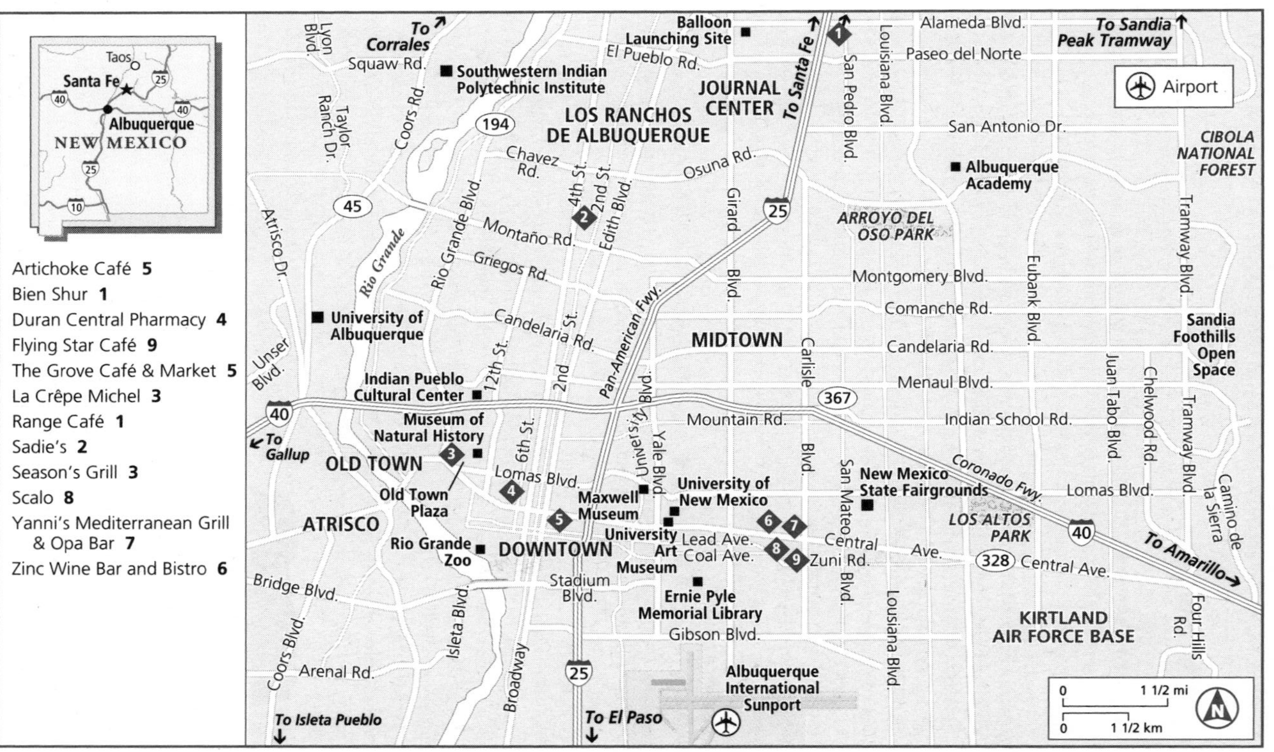
Taos
Santa Fe
Albuquerque
NEW MEXICO
Artichoke Café 5
Bien Shur 1
Duran Central Pharmacy 4
Flying Star Café 9
The Grove Café & Market 5
La Crêpe Michel 3
Range Café 1
Sadie's 2
Season's Grill 3
Scalo 8
Yanni's Mediterranean Grill & Opa Bar 7
Zinc Wine Bar and Bistro 6
Lyon Blvd.
To Corrales
Squaw Rd.
Balloon Launching Site
El Pueblo Rd.
Southwestern Indian Polytechnic Institute
JOURNAL CENTER
To Santa Fe
San Pedro Blvd.
Louisiana Blvd.
Alameda Blvd.
Paseo del Norte
To Sandia Peak Tramway
Airport
Taylor Ranch Dr.
Coors Rd.
LOS RANCHOS DE ALBUQUERQUE
San Antonio Dr.
CIBOLA NATIONAL FOREST
Chavez Rd.
4th St.
2nd St.
Edith Blvd.
Osuna Rd.
Albuquerque Academy
Girard Blvd.
ARROYO DEL OSO PARK
Tramway Blvd.
Atrisco Dr.
Rio Grande
Rio Grande Blvd.
Montaño Rd.
Griegos Rd.
Montgomery Blvd.
Eubank Blvd.
Comanche Rd.
University of Albuquerque
Candelaria Rd.
Pan-American Fwy.
MIDTOWN
Carlisle Blvd.
Candelaria Rd.
Sandia Foothills Open Space
Unser Blvd.
Indian Pueblo Cultural Center
12th St.
2nd St.
University Blvd.
Menaul Blvd.
Juan Tabo Blvd.
Chelwood Rd.
To Gallup
Museum of Natural History
6th St.
Yale Blvd.
Mountain Rd.
Indian School Rd.
OLD TOWN
Old Town Plaza
Lomas Blvd.
Maxwell Museum
University of New Mexico
San Mateo Blvd.
New Mexico State Fairgrounds
Coronado Fwy.
Lomas Blvd.
Camino de la Sierra
ATRISCO
University Art Museum
Lead Ave.
Coal Ave.
Central Ave.
Zuni Rd.
LOS ALTOS PARK
To Amarillo
Rio Grande Zoo
DOWNTOWN
Central Ave.
Bridge Blvd.
Stadium Blvd.
Ernie Pyle Memorial Library
Gibson Blvd.
KIRTLAND AIR FORCE BASE
Four Hills Rd.
Isleta Blvd.
Coors Blvd.
Arenal Rd.
Broadway
Albuquerque International Sunport
To Isleta Pueblo
To El Paso
0 1 1/2 mi
0 1 1/2 km

margaritas (and TV screens for you sports lovers). A casual atmosphere where kids can be themselves makes this a nice spot for families.

6230 4th St. NW. ✆ **505/345-5339.** Main courses $8–$17. AE, DC, DISC, MC, V. Mon–Sat 11am–10pm; Sun 10am–9pm.

DOWNTOWN

Expensive

Artichoke Cafe ★★ CONTINENTAL An art gallery as well as a restaurant, this popular spot has modern paintings and sculptures, offering bursts of color set against calm earth tones, a hint at the innovative dining experience offered here. Set in three rooms, this is a nice romantic place. The service is friendly and efficient. At lunch, a number of gourmet sandwiches top the menu along with salads. One of my favorites is the grilled Greek lamb salad, with tomatoes, capers, feta, and grilled eggplant. At dinner, you might start with roasted garlic with Montrachet goat cheese and then move onto the housemade pumpkin ravioli with hazelnut-sage butter sauce or sea scallops wrapped in proscuitto served with green beans and small potatoes. A carefully selected beer and wine (*Wine Spectator* award-winning) list accompanies the menu. Recently the Artichoke has opened a wine bar on the premises, a fun, cozy spot to sample their wine list.

424 Central Ave. SE. ✆ **505/243-0200.** www.artichokecafe.com. Reservations recommended. Main courses $9–$15 lunch, $18–$31 dinner. AE, DC, DISC, MC, V. Mon–Fri 11am–2:30pm; Mon 5:30–9pm; Tues–Sat 5:30–10pm; Sun 5–9 pm.

Moderate

The Grove Café & Market ★★ Finds CAFE/SANDWICHES Albuquerque's hippest new dining spot in the EDo district (east of downtown) offers fresh breakfasts and lunches utilizing organic and locally grown produce in a fun and open space. Colorful nature paintings hang on sky-blue walls, and a patio opens during warm months. Order at a counter and a very friendly server brings your food to the table. Breakfast, served all day, offers creative twists on standards, such as French-style pancakes with fruit and crème fraiche, but the real winner here is the croque madame—black forest ham, tomato, and gruyere cheese on rustic farm loaf, topped with a sunny-side-up egg. Lunch offers an array of salads and sandwiches. My favorites are the pressed ones such as the B.L.T., with applewood smoked bacon and guacamole on whole wheat, or the aged salami, with olive tapanade, arugula, and provolone on sourdough. The soup of the day is housemade, as are their delectable English Muffins. With cupcakes "in" these days, this place makes very special ones. My favorite is the strawberry cheesecake with marscapone frosting. Wash it

Welcome to EDo

Albuquerque's newest hotspot is east of downtown, thus termed EDo, around the area of Central Ave. SE. Renovation of some old buildings, including the brick Albuquerque High School campus into apartments, has brought new life to the area, and so some great restaurants have joined the all-time favorite, the Artichoke Cafe. Look for the Grove (see below) and the Standard Diner in EDo.

Family-Friendly Restaurants

Flying Star Café (p. 94) With a huge selection, a relaxed atmosphere, and a number of locations, the whole family can enjoy this place.

Range Café (p. 95) The fun and funky decor and Taos Cow Ice Cream make this a good spot for kids.

Sadie's (p. 90) Kids like the quesadillas, tacos, and *sopaipillas* drizzled with honey; parents like the casual atmosphere where kid noise isn't scorned.

all down with good coffees and teas. This is also an excellent place to stock a picnic basket and purchase specialty teas and cookies in the Market portion of the restaurant.

600 Central Ave. SE (just west of I-25). ✆ **505/248-9800.** www.thegrovecafemarket.com. All main courses under $10. AE, MC, V. Tues–Sat 7am–4pm; Sunday 8am–3pm.

THE NORTHEAST HEIGHTS

Expensive

Bien Shur ★★★ INTERNATIONAL Set on the top floor of the Sandia Resort & Casino, this fine dining restaurant offers impressive views and delicious food, with a hint of Native America. The best feature of this dining room is its openness. With big windows facing east and west, you can see the mountains and the city while eating—this, accented by high ceilings and elegant Native American motif decor. Plan your meal at sunset for the most stunning effect. Service is excellent. You might start with escargot bourguignon and/or a marinated heirloom tomato salad with toasted foccacia, Maytag blue cheese, and basil dressing. For entrees, the rack of lamb with a garlic mint au jus is excellent, served with green beans and a parmesan croquette. Some good fish dishes dress the menu as well. The wine list is eclectic, with Old and New World flavors—quite price-approachable. The lounge and patio bar carry the same elegance and views and offer a grill and taco bar menu.

30 Rainbow Rd. NE, at Sandia Resort & Casino. ✆ **800/526-9366.** www.sandiaresort.com. Reservations recommended. Main courses $23–$75. AE, DC, DISC, MC, V. Daily 5–9pm.

UNIVERSITY & NOB HILL

Expensive

Zinc Wine Bar and Bistro ★★ NEW AMERICAN In a moody, urban atmosphere with wood floors and a high ceiling, this Nob Hill in-place serves imaginative food, using meticulously prepared seasonal ingredients. The bi-level dining room with well-spaced tables can get crowded and noisy at peak hours (especially under the balcony, so avoid sitting there then). Service is congenial but inconsistent. The lunch menu offers a variety of salads and sandwiches, as well as other inventive dishes. One of my favorites is the mango glazed chicken breast stir-fry. At dinner, the baked crab stuffed sole is tasty. Sunday brunch is also offered, with items such as an Italian eggs Benedict, with pancetta and a sun-dried tomato hollandaise. An extensive wine list accompanies the menu, or you may simply opt for a martini from the full bar. In the lower level, a lounge serves less formally in a wine cellar atmosphere with live music playing 2 to 3 nights a week.

3009 Central Ave. NE. ✆ **505/254-ZINC** (9462). www.zincabq.com. Reservations recommended. Main courses $8–$14 lunch, $17–$27 dinner. AE, DC, DISC, MC, V. Mon–Fri 11am–2:30pm; Mon–Thurs 5–10pm; Fri–Sat 5–11pm; Sun 11am–2:30pm. Wine bar Mon–Sat 5pm–1am, with food served to midnight.

Moderate

Scalo ★★ INTERNATIONAL/ITALIAN This Nob Hill restaurant is a local favorite, so it's usually crowded, a good sign of the food's quality. The place has a simple, bistro-style elegance, with white-linen-clothed tables indoors, plus outdoor tables in a covered, temperature-controlled patio. Service is decent. The kitchen, which makes its own pasta and breads, offers an international menu with excellent selections for lunch and dinner. Seasonal menus focus on New Mexico–grown produce. At lunch you can select from salads, wood-fired pizzas, and paninis. Their panini con salsiccia has sausage, caramelized onions, and mozzarella. The varied dinner menu offers soups, salads, pizza, pasta, and meat and fish entrees. The *bianchi e neri al capesante* has black and white linguine, shrimp, salmon, and peas in a cream sauce. For dinner a standing favorite is the veal scallopine with sautéed mushrooms. The wine list won a *Wine Spectator* award; from it you can sample 30 wines by the glass; or you may order from the full bar.

3500 Central Ave. SE. ✆ **505/255-8781.** www.scalonobhill.com. Reservations recommended. Lunch $6–$10, dinner $8–$29. AE, DC, DISC, MC, V. Mon–Thurs 11:30am–10pm; Fri 11:30am–11pm; Sat 11:30am–11pm; Sun 11am–9pm.

Yanni's Mediterranean Grill and Opa Bar ★★ MEDITERRANEAN With bright blue and white decor, Athenian-style pillars, and Mediterranean paintings on the walls, this is a great place for a festive meal. Locals crowd the cafe any time they can, including the patio with big windows looking out on Central Avenue. Service is friendly, though overworked during peak hours. All food is made fresh, with specials daily. You might start with jumbo sea scallops seared and served with grilled tomato, and then move onto one of the excellent specials such as wild opa roasted with oranges or wild halibut seared crispy with lemon and thyme, or, my favorite, oven roasted lamb. The menu hosts a variety of pasta dishes and, of course, moussaka. Entrees come with a salad, bread, vegetable, and a potato or rice side. An international wine list featuring Greek offerings and a full bar accompany the menu. And the attached Opa! Bar provides live entertainment on weekends.

3109 Central Ave. NE. ✆ **505/268-9250.** www.yannisandopabar.com. Reservations recommended. Main courses $7–$14 lunch, $13–$27 dinner. AE, DISC, MC, V. Mon–Thurs 11am–10pm; Fri–Sat 11am–11pm; Sun noon–9pm.

Inexpensive

Flying Star Cafe ★ Kids CAFE/BAKERY The Flying Star Cafe makes good on its promise of uptown food with down-home ingredients. It's a fun and friendly place with excellent contemporary international food. But beware: During mealtime, the university location on Central Avenue gets packed and rowdy. The selections range broadly, all made with local and organic produce, when possible. You can choose from 16 different breakfast options ranging from homemade soups and salads to sandwiches and pasta (and pizza at the Juan Tabo and Rio Grande locations). Try the Rancher's melt (New Zealand sirloin sautéed with green chile, provolone, and horseradish on sourdough) or the Buddha's bowl (sautéed vegetables in ginger sauce with tofu over jasmine rice). Flying Star also has locations at 4501 Juan Tabo Blvd. NE (✆ **505/275-8311**); 8001 Menaul Blvd. NE (✆ **505/293-6911**); and 4026 Rio Grande Blvd. NW (✆ **505/344-6714**). They don't serve alcohol, but they do brew up plenty of espresso and cappuccino. Kids enjoy the relaxed atmosphere and their own selections from the menu. Though hours vary for each location, they are all open daily for breakfast, lunch, and dinner.

3416 Central Ave. SE. ✆ **505/255-6633.** www.flyingstarcafe.com. All menu items under $15. AE, DISC, MC, V. Daily 6am–11:30pm.

OUTSIDE ALBUQUERQUE

Range Café ★ Kids NEW MEXICAN/AMERICAN This cafe on the main drag of Bernalillo, about 20 minutes north of Albuquerque, is a perfect place to stop on your way out of town. Housed in what was once an old drugstore, the restaurant has a pressed tin ceiling and is decorated with western touches, such as cowboy boots and whimsical art. The food ranges from enchiladas and burritos to chicken-fried steak to more elegantly prepared meals. For lunch or dinner, I recommend Tom's meatloaf, served with roasted-garlic mashed potatoes, mushroom gravy, and sautéed vegetables. For dinner, you might try pan-seared trout with sun-dried tomato and caper butter sauce. Taos Cow ice cream is the order for dessert, or try the baked goods and specialty drinks from the full bar. In the same locale, the Range has opened the Lizard Rodeo Lounge, a hoppin' place with Wild West decor that offers live music many nights a week. There's also a retail space that sells local art and New Mexico wines. Two other branches of the restaurant in Albuquerque have similar food offerings (4200 Wyoming Blvd. NE, ✆ **505/293-2633,** and 2200 Menaul Blvd. NE ✆ **505/888-1660**).

925 Camino del Pueblo (P.O. Box 1780), Bernalillo. ✆ **505/867-1700.** www.rangecafe.com. Reservations accepted for 8 or more. Breakfast and lunch $7–$13; dinner $10–$27. AE, DISC, MC, V. Summer Sun–Thurs 7:30am–10pm; winter Sun–Thurs 7:30am–9:30pm; a half-hour later on Fri and Sat. Closed Thanksgiving and Christmas.

5 WHAT TO SEE & DO

Albuquerque's original town site, known today as Old Town, is the central point of interest for visitors. Here, grouped around the plaza, are the venerable Church of San Felipe de Neri and numerous restaurants, art galleries, and crafts shops. Several important museums are close by. Within a few blocks are the 25,000-square-foot Albuquerque Aquarium and the 50-acre Rio Grande Botanic Garden (near Central Ave. and Tingley Dr. NW), both well worth a visit.

But don't get stuck in Old Town. Elsewhere, you'll find the Sandia Peak Tramway, the new Balloon Museum, and a number of natural attractions. Within day-trip range are several pueblos and significant monuments (see "Touring the Pueblos Around Albuquerque," later in this chapter).

THE TOP ATTRACTIONS

Albuquerque Museum of Art and History ★ Kids Take an interesting journey into New Mexico's present and past in this museum on the outskirts of Old Town. An expansion has brought new gallery space, filled with impressive changing exhibits. Most notable for me are works from the museum's art collection, which includes canvases by Fritz Scholder, Peter Hurd, Ernest Blumenshein, and Georgia O'Keeffe, as well as contemporary woodwork by Luis Tapia. Downstairs take a trip through history, represented by an impressive collection of Spanish colonial artifacts. Displays include Don Quixote–style helmets, swords, and horse armor, a 19th-century house compound and chapel, and gear used by *vaqueros,* the original cowboys who came to the area in the 16th century. In an old-style theater, two films on Albuquerque history are shown. An Old Town walking tour originates here at 11am Tuesday to Sunday during spring, summer, and fall. A gift shop sells books and jewelry, and a cafe serves upscale sandwiches and soups. Plan to spend 1 to 2 hours here.

2000 Mountain Rd. NW. ✆ **505/243-7255.** www.albuquerquemuseum.com. Admission $4 adults, $2 seniors 65 and older, $1 children 4–12. Tues–Sun 9am–5pm. Closed major holidays.

Balloon Museum ★★ (Kids) The Anderson-Abruzzo Albuquerque International Balloon Museum holds special significance for me, as my parents owned part of the first hot-air balloon in Albuquerque over 30 years ago. Today, with the Albuquerque International Balloon Fiesta drawing hundreds of brilliantly colored and imaginatively shaped balloons to the city each October (p. 45), this museum's time has come. It tells the history of ballooning, from the first flight in France in 1783, with a rooster, sheep, and duck as passengers, to the use of balloons in military, science, and aerospace research. Most poignant are displays of Albuquerque balloonists Maxie Anderson and Ben Abruzzo, who, with Larry Newman, completed the first manned crossing of the Atlantic Ocean in 1978. Originals and replicas of various historic crafts dot the three-story-tall space, and windows look out at the Sandia Mountains and Rio Grande Valley. Kids will enjoy the flight simulator, which tests their ability to fly and land a balloon on target. Plan on spending at least an hour here.

9201 Balloon Museum Dr. NE. ✆ **505/768-6020.** www.cabq.gov/balloon.com. Admission $4 adults, $2 seniors 65 and older, $1 children 4–12, free for children 3 and under. Tues–Sun 9am–5pm. Closed New Year's Day, Thanksgiving, Christmas, and city holidays.

Indian Pueblo Cultural Center ★ (Kids) Owned and operated as a nonprofit organization by the 19 pueblos of New Mexico, this is a fine place to begin an exploration of Native American culture. About a mile northeast of Old Town, this museum—modeled after Pueblo Bonito, a spectacular 9th-century ruin in Chaco Culture National Historic Park—consists of several parts.

You'll want to spend 1 to 2 hours here. Begin above ground where you'll find changing shows of contemporary Puebloan arts and crafts. Next, head to the basement, where a permanent exhibit depicts the evolution of the various pueblos from prehistory to present, including displays of the distinctive handicrafts of each community. Note especially how pottery differs in concept and design from pueblo to pueblo. On the first floor is an enormous (10,000-sq.-ft.) **gift shop** featuring fine pottery, rugs, sand paintings, katsinas (kachinas), drums, and jewelry, among other things. Southwestern clothing and souvenirs are also available. Prices here are quite reasonable.

Throughout the year, **Native American dancers** perform in an outdoor arena surrounded by original murals. Dances are performed at noon in winter; and 11am and 2pm in spring. In summer, dances are scheduled at 2pm on Thursday and Friday and Saturday at 11am and 2pm. Often, artisans demonstrate their crafts there as well. During certain weeks of the year, such as the Balloon Fiesta, dances are performed daily.

The restaurant serves traditional Native American foods. It's a good place for some Indian fry bread and a bowl of *posole.*

2401 12th St. NW. ✆ **866/855-7902** or 505/843-7270. www.indianpueblo.org. Admission $6 adults, $5.50 seniors, $1 students, free for children 4 and under. AE, DISC, MC, V. Daily 9am–5:30pm; restaurant Mon–Fri 8am–3pm; Fri–Sat 8am–10pm. Closed New Year's Day, July 4, Labor Day, Thanksgiving, and Christmas.

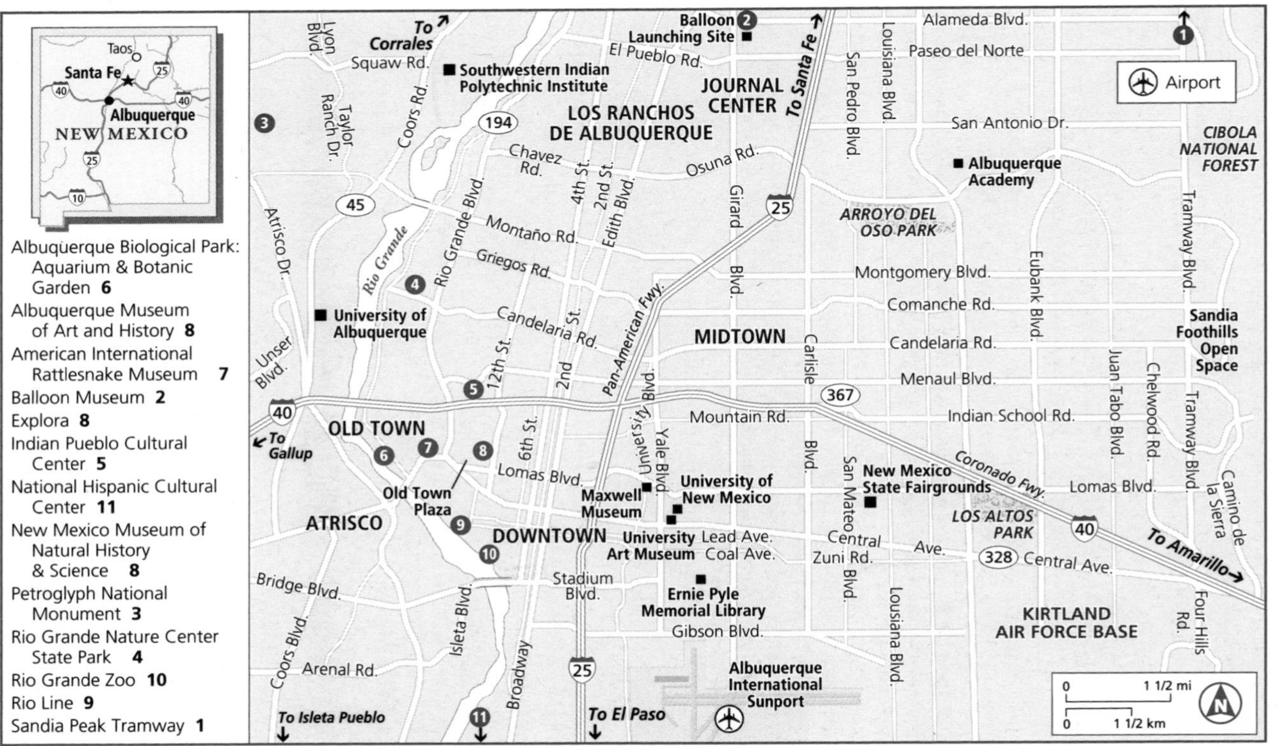
Taos
Santa Fe
Albuquerque
NEW MEXICO
Albuquerque Biological Park: Aquarium & Botanic Garden 6
Albuquerque Museum of Art and History 8
American International Rattlesnake Museum 7
Balloon Museum 2
Explora 8
Indian Pueblo Cultural Center 5
National Hispanic Cultural Center 11
New Mexico Museum of Natural History & Science 8
Petroglyph National Monument 3
Rio Grande Nature Center State Park 4
Rio Grande Zoo 10
Rio Line 9
Sandia Peak Tramway 1
Lyon Blvd.
To Corrales
Squaw Rd.
Southwestern Indian Polytechnic Institute
Balloon Launching Site
El Pueblo Rd.
JOURNAL CENTER
To Santa Fe
San Pedro Blvd.
Louisiana Blvd.
Alameda Blvd.
Paseo del Norte
Airport
Taylor Ranch Dr.
Coors Rd.
LOS RANCHOS DE ALBUQUERQUE
San Antonio Dr.
CIBOLA NATIONAL FOREST
Chavez Rd.
4th St.
2nd St.
Edith Blvd.
Osuna Rd.
Albuquerque Academy
Atrisco Dr.
Rio Grande Blvd.
Montaño Rd.
Girard Blvd.
ARROYO DEL OSO PARK
Tramway Blvd.
Rio Grande
Griegos Rd.
Montgomery Blvd.
Eubank Blvd.
University of Albuquerque
Candelaria Rd.
Pan-American Fwy.
MIDTOWN
Comanche Rd.
Candelaria Rd.
Sandia Foothills Open Space
Unser Blvd.
12th St.
2nd St.
Carlisle Blvd.
Juan Tabo Blvd.
Chelwood Rd.
Menaul Blvd.
To Gallup
OLD TOWN
6th St.
University Blvd.
Yale Blvd.
Mountain Rd.
Indian School Rd.
Lomas Blvd.
New Mexico State Fairgrounds
Coronado Fwy.
Lomas Blvd.
Camino de la Sierra
Old Town Plaza
Maxwell Museum
University of New Mexico
San Mateo Blvd.
LOS ALTOS PARK
ATRISCO
DOWNTOWN
University Art Museum
Lead Ave.
Coal Ave.
Central Ave.
Zuni Rd.
Central Ave.
To Amarillo
Bridge Blvd.
Stadium Blvd.
Ernie Pyle Memorial Library
Gibson Blvd.
KIRTLAND AIR FORCE BASE
Four Hills Rd.
Isleta Blvd.
Coors Blvd.
Arenal Rd.
Broadway
Albuquerque International Sunport
To Isleta Pueblo
To El Paso
0 1 1/2 mi
0 1 1/2 km
N

National Hispanic Cultural Center ★ In the historic Barelas neighborhood on the Camino Real, this gem of Albuquerque museums offers a rich cultural journey through hundreds of years of history and across the globe. It explores Hispanic arts and lifeways with visual arts, drama, music, dance, and other programs. I most enjoy the 11,000-square-foot gallery space, which exhibits exciting contemporary and traditional works, as well as changing exhibits. A restaurant offers New Mexican and American food for breakfast and lunch. It's a good spot to sample authentic regional dishes such as tacos, enchiladas, and the rich custard dessert called flan. The shop offers a broad range of fun gifts from Latin America and New Mexico. Plan to spend 1 to 2 hours here.

1701 4th St. SW (corner of 4th St. and Av. Cesar Chavez). ✆ **505/246-2261.** Fax 505/246-2613. www.nhccnm.org. Admission Tues–Sat $3 adults, $2 seniors 60 and over, free for children 16 and under; Sun free for adults and seniors. MC, V. Tues–Sun 10am–5pm; restaurant Tues–Fri 7:30am–3pm; Sat 8am–3pm; Sun 9am–3pm. Closed New Year's Day, Easter, Memorial Day, Labor Day, and Christmas.

Old Town ★★ A maze of cobbled courtyard walkways leads to hidden patios and gardens, where many of Old Town's 150 galleries and shops are located. Adobe buildings, many refurbished in the pueblo revival style of the 1950s, are grouped around the tree-shaded plaza, created in 1780. Pueblo and Navajo artisans often display their pottery, blankets, and silver jewelry on the sidewalks lining the plaza.

The buildings of Old Town once served as mercantile shops, grocery stores, and government offices, but the importance of Old Town as Albuquerque's commercial center declined after 1880, when the railroad came through 1¼ miles east of the plaza and businesses relocated to be closer to the trains. Old Town clung to its historical and sentimental roots, but the quarter fell into disrepair until the 1930s and 1940s, when artisans and other shop owners rediscovered it and the tourism industry burgeoned.

When Albuquerque was established in 1706, the first building erected by the settlers was the **Church of San Felipe de Neri,** which faces the plaza on its north side. It's a cozy church with wonderful stained-glass windows and vivid *retablos* (religious paintings). This house of worship has been in almost continuous use for nearly 300 years.

Though you'll wade through a few trinket and T-shirt shops on the plaza, don't be fooled: Old Town is an excellent place to shop. Look for good buys from the Native Americans selling jewelry on the plaza, especially silver bracelets and strung turquoise. If you want to take something fun home and spend very little, buy a dyed corn necklace. Your best bet when wandering around Old Town is to peek into shops, but there are a few places you'll definitely want to spend time. See "Shopping A to Z," later in this chapter, for a list of recommendations. An excellent Old Town historic walking tour originates at the Albuquerque Museum of Art and History (see above) at 11am Tuesday to Sunday during spring, summer, and fall. Plan to spend 2 to 3 hours strolling around.

Northeast of Central Ave. and Rio Grande Blvd. NW. Old Town Visitor Center: 303 Romero St. NW, Albuquerque, NM 87104 (across the street from the Church of San Felipe de Neri). ✆ **505/243-3215.** Visitor Center daily 10am–5pm summer; daily 10am–4:30pm rest of the year.

Petroglyph National Monument ★★ Kids These lava flows were once a hunting and gathering area for prehistoric Native Americans, who left a chronicle of their beliefs etched on the dark basalt boulders. Some 25,000 petroglyphs provide a nice outdoor adventure after a morning in a museum. You'll want to stop at the visitor center to get a map and check out the interactive computer. From there, you can drive north to the Boca Negra area, where you'll have a choice of three trails. Take the Mesa Point Trail (30 min.) that climbs quickly up the side of a hill, offering many petroglyph sightings as well as an outstanding view of the Sandia Mountains. If you're traveling with your dog, you can bring her along on the Rinconada Trail. Hikers can have fun searching the rocks for more petroglyphs; there are many yet to be found. This trail (a few miles south of the visitor center) runs for miles around a huge *rincon* (corner) at the base of the lava flow. Camping is not permitted in the park; it's strictly for day use, with picnic areas, drinking water, and restrooms provided.

6001 Unser Blvd. NW (3 miles north of I-40 at Unser and Western Trail). ✆ **505/899-0205.** Fax 505/899-0207. www.nps.gov/petr. Admission $1 per vehicle in spring, fall, and winter; $2 in summer. DISC, MC, V. Visitor Center and Boca Negra area daily 8am–5pm. Closed New Year's Day, Thanksgiving, and Christmas.

Sandia Peak Tramway ★★ Kids This fun and exciting half-day or evening outing allows incredible views of the Albuquerque landscape and wildlife. The Sandia Peak Tram is a "jigback"; in other words, as one car approaches the top, the other nears the bottom. The two pass halfway through the trip, in the midst of a 1½-mile "clear span" of unsupported cable between the second tower and the upper terminal.

Several hiking trails are available on Sandia Peak, and one of them—La Luz Trail—takes you on a steep and rigorous trek from the base to the summit. The views in all directions are extraordinary. ***Note:*** The trails on Sandia may not be suitable for children. If you'd like to enjoy a meal during your trip, you can eat lunch (salads, burgers, and pasta dishes) or dinner (steaks, seafood, and pasta) at the **High Finance Restaurant and Tavern** at the top of the tram. Special tram rates apply with dinner reservations. Be aware that the tram does not operate on very windy days.

10 Tramway Loop NE. ✆ **505/856-7325.** Fax 505/856-6335. www.sandiapeak.com. Admission $18 adults, $15 seniors and teens 13–20, $10 children 5–12, free for children 4 and under. Memorial Day to Labor Day daily 9am–9pm; spring and fall Wed–Mon 9am–8pm, Tues 5–8pm; ski season Wed–Mon 9am–8pm, Tues noon–8pm. Closed 2 weeks each spring and fall for maintenance; check the website for details. Parking $1 daily. AE, DISC, MC, V. To reach the base of the tram, take I-25 north to Tramway Rd. (exit 234), then proceed east about 5 miles on Tramway Rd. (NM 556); or take Tramway Blvd., exit 167 (NM 556), north of I-40 approximately 8½ miles.

6 ESPECIALLY FOR KIDS

Albuquerque Biological Park: Aquarium and Botanic Garden ★★ Kids For those of us born and raised in the desert, this attraction quenches years of soul thirst. The self-guided aquarium tour begins with a beautifully produced 9-minute film that describes the course of the Rio Grande from its origin to the Gulf Coast. Then, you'll move on to the touch pool, where at certain times of day you can gently touch hermit crabs and starfish. Next comes the eel tank, an arched aquarium you get to walk through and a colorful coral-reef exhibit. Finally, culminating the show, is a 285,000-gallon shark tank.

Within a state-of-the-art 10,000-square-foot conservatory, you'll find the botanical garden, split into two sections. The smaller one houses the desert collection and features plants from the lower Chihuahuan and Sonoran deserts, including unique species from Baja, California. The larger pavilion exhibits the Mediterranean collection and includes many exotic species native to the Mediterranean climates of southern California, South Africa, Australia, and the Mediterranean Basin. Allow at least 2 hours to see both parks. There is a restaurant on the premises. May to September, the PNM Butterfly Pavilion fills with the colors of several hundred North American butterflies.

In December, you can see the "River of Lights Holiday Light Display" Tuesday through Sunday; and June through August you can attend Thursday evening concerts.

2601 Central Ave. NW. ✆ **505/764-6200.** www.cabq.gov/biopark. Admission $7 adults ($12 with Rio Grande Zoo admission), $3 seniors 65 and over and children 12 and under ($5 with Rio Grande Zoo admission). Ticket sales stop a half-hour before closing. MC, V. Tues–Sun 9am–5pm (June–Aug Sat–Sun until 6pm). Closed New Year's Day, Thanksgiving, and Christmas.

American International Rattlesnake Museum ★ Finds Kids This unique museum, just off Old Town Plaza, has living specimens of common, uncommon, and very rare rattlesnakes of North, Central, and South America in naturally landscaped habitats. Oddities such as albino and patternless rattlesnakes are included, as is a display popular with youngsters: baby rattlesnakes. More than 30 species can be seen, followed by a 7-minute film on this contributor to the ecological balance of our hemisphere. Throughout the museum are rattlesnake artifacts from early American history, Native American culture, medicine, the arts, and advertising. You'll also find a gift shop that specializes in Native American jewelry, T-shirts, and other memorabilia related to the natural world and the Southwest, all with an emphasis on rattlesnakes.

202 San Felipe St. NW. ✆ **505/242-6569.** www.rattlesnakes.com. Admission $3.50 adults, $3 seniors, $2.50 children. AE, DISC, MC, V. Mon–Sat 10am–6pm, Sun 1–5pm in summer; Mon–Sat 11:30am–5:30pm, Sun 1–5pm in winter.

Explora ★ Kids As a center for lifelong learning, Explora houses more than 250 hands-on transactive exhibits in science, technology, and art. Visitors of all ages make their way through the maze-like museum exploring topics as diverse as water, the Rio Grande, light and optics, biological perception, and energy. The museum features exhibits utilizing technology that is creatively accessible to the public and exhibits that engage visitors in creating all kinds of art. My favorite is the Laminar Flow Fountain in which water leaps across spaces, seeming to come alive. Little kids especially enjoy the arts and crafts workshop where they can make art to take home. You could spend an hour and a half to a full day here.

1701 Mountain Rd. NW. ✆ **505/224-8300.** Fax 505/224-8325. www.explora.us. Admission $7 adults ages 12–64, $5 seniors 65 and over, $3 children 1–11, free for children under 1. Mon–Sat 10am–6pm; Sun noon–6pm.

New Mexico Museum of Natural History and Science ★★ Kids A trip through this museum will take you through 12 billion years of natural history, from the formation of the universe to the present day. Begin by looking at a display of stones and gems, and then stroll through the "Age Jurassic Super Giants" display, where you'll find dinosaur skeletons cast from the real bones. See the latest display "Triassic: Dawn of the Dinosaur." You can ride the Evolator (kids love this!), a simulated time-travel experience that moves and rumbles, taking you 1¹/₄ miles up (or down) and through 38 million years of history. Soon, you'll find yourself in the age of the mammoths and moving through the Ice Age. Be sure to check out the museum's Planetarium. That exhibit, as well as the DynaTheater, which surrounds you with images and sound, costs an additional fee. A gift shop on the ground floor sells imaginative nature games and other curios. Plan to spend 1 to 2 hours here, more if you take in extra attractions.

1801 Mountain Rd. NW. ✆ **505/841-2800.** www.nmnaturalhistory.org. Admission $7 adults, $6 seniors, $4 children 3–12, free for children 2 and under. DynaTheater, Planetarium, and Virtual Voyages cost extra, with prices in the $7 range for adults and $4 range for children. Buying ticket combinations qualifies you for discounts. Daily 9am–5pm. Jan and Sept closed Mon except major holidays, when it's open Mon; also closed New Year's Day, Thanksgiving, and Christmas.

In Search of Disneyland

If you want to occupy the kids for a day, there's a fun option, though don't expect Disneyland. **Cliff's Amusement Park,** 4800 Osuna Rd. NE (✆ **505/881-9373;** www.cliffs.net), has roller coasters, including the daring "Galaxy," and a waterpark with some fun get-wet rides. Gate entrance is $2.50; ride passes run $20 for kids 48 inches tall and under and $25 for those over 48 inches; individual ride tickets $2.

Rio Grande Nature Center State Park ★ Kids This center, just a few miles north of Old Town, spans 270 acres of riverside forest and meadows that include stands of 100-year-old cottonwoods and a 3-acre pond. On the Rio Grande Flyway, an important migratory route for many birds, it's an excellent place to see sandhill cranes, Canadian geese, and quail—more than 260 bird species have made this their temporary or permanent home. In a protected area where dogs aren't allowed (you can bring dogs on most of the 2 miles of trails), you'll find exhibits of native grasses, wildflowers, and herbs. Inside a building built half above and half below ground, you can sit next to the pond in a glassed-in viewing area and comfortably watch ducks and other birds in their avian antics. There are 21 self-guided interpretive exhibits as well as photo exhibits, a library, a small nature store, and a children's resource room. On Saturday mornings, you can join a guided bird walk. Other weekend programs are available for adults and children, including nature photography and bird- and wildflower-identification classes. Call for a schedule.

2901 Candelaria Rd. NW. ✆ **505/344-7240.** Fax 505/344-4505. www.nmparks.com. Admission $3 per vehicle. Cash and checks. Daily 10am–5pm; store Mon–Fri 11am–3pm, Sat–Sun 10am–4pm. Closed New Year's Day, Thanksgiving, and Christmas.

Rio Grande Zoo ★ Kids Some 250 species live on 64 acres of riverside bosque here among ancient cottonwoods. Open-moat exhibits with animals in naturalized habitats are a treat for zoo-goers. Major exhibits include polar bears, giraffes, sea lions (with underwater viewing), the cat walk, the bird show, and ape country, with gorillas and orangutans. The zoo has an especially fine collection of elephants, koalas, polar bears, reptiles, and native Southwestern species. The Thunderbird Express Train operates in a nonstop loop around the zoo, except on Mondays. As well, the Rio Line operates between the zoo and the Albuquerque Biological Park (p. 99). There are numerous snack bars on the zoo grounds, and La Ventana Gift Shop carries souvenirs. Check out the seal and sea lion feeding at 10:30am and 3:30pm daily and the summer Zoo Music Concert Series.

903 10th St. SW. ✆ **505/764-6200.** www.cabq.gov/biopark/zoo. Admission $7 adults ($10 with Aquarium and Botanic Garden admission), $3 seniors and children 3–12 ($5 with Aquarium and Botanic Garden admission), free for children 2 and under. MC, V. Daily 9am–5pm (6pm summer weekends). Closed New Year's Day, Thanksgiving, and Christmas.

The Rio Line ★ Kids This miniature train travels between the Tingley Train Station, the Albuquerque Biological Park, and the Rio Grande Zoo, stopping at each facility, with tickets available at each as well. Conductors give an interpretive tour and answer your questions as you ride. A round-trip journey lasts approximately 1 hour. This is a fun trip for families.

903 10th St. SW. (station at Tingley Beach on Tingley Dr.) ✆ **505/768-2000.** www.cabq.gov/biopark/trains.html. Train ride $2 adult, $1 children 3–12. MC, V. The train operates Tues–Sun from approximately 10am–3:45pm. The last trains leave the Aquarium/Garden Station and the Asia Station at the zoo at 3:45pm. The last train leaves the Tingley Station at 3pm. ***Note:*** If you purchase a "combo ticket" for the Biological Park and Rio Grande Zoo, you get free access to all trains. Also, during summer weekends, because of the high volume of visitors, only those with "combo tickets" can ride the Rio Line.

7 OUTDOOR ACTIVITIES

BALLOONING

Visitors have a choice of several hot-air balloon operators; rates start at about $160 per person per hour. Call **Rainbow Ryders,** 5601 Eagle Rock Ave. NE (✆ **505/823-1111;** www.rainbowryders.com), or **World Balloon Corporation,** 1103 La Poblana NW (✆ **505/293-6800;** www.worldballoon.com).

If you'd rather just watch, go to the annual **Albuquerque International Balloon Fiesta ★★**, which is held the first through second weekends of October (see "The Most Memorable New Mexico Experiences," in chapter 1, and "New Mexico Calendar of Events," in chapter 3, for details).

BIKING

Albuquerque is a major bicycling hub in the summer, for both road racers and mountain bikers. For an excellent map of Albuquerque bicycle routes, call the **Albuquerque Parks & Recreation Department** at ✆ **505/768-3550.** You can also find links to many recreation opportunities for adults and kids at **www.cabq.gov/visiting.html**. A great place to bike is **Sandia Peak** (✆ **505/242-9133;** www.sandiapeak.com) in Cíbola National Forest. You can't take your bike on the tram, but chairlift no. 1 is available for up- or downhill transportation with a bike. Bike rentals are available at the top and bottom of the chairlift. They cost $40 for adult bikes and $30 for junior ones. The lift costs $16 and runs on Saturday and Sunday, with Friday added in July and August, though you'll want

Getting Pampered: The Spa Scene

Albuquerque's top two luxurious spa experiences are at the **Hyatt Regency Tamaya Resort & Spa,** 1300 Tuyuna Trail, Santa Ana Pueblo (✆ **505/771-6134;** www.tamaya.hyatt.com) and the **Sandia Resort & Casino,** 30 Rainbow Rd. NE (✆ **800/526-9366** or 505/798-3930; www.sandiacasino.com). Each offers a broad array of treatments, as well as a sauna and a steam room, in refined atmospheres. The Tamaya is 15 minutes north of Albuquerque, near the village of Bernalillo, while the Sandia is on the north end of town, off Tramway Boulevard.

to call to be sure. Helmets are mandatory. Bike maps are available; the clearly marked trails range from easy to very difficult.

Down in the valley, there's a **bosque trail** that runs along the Rio Grande, accessed through the Rio Grande Nature Center (see "Especially for Kids," above). To the east, the **Foothills Trail** runs along the base of the mountains. It's a fun 7-mile-long trail that offers excellent views. Access it by driving east from downtown on Montgomery Boulevard, past the intersection with Tramway Boulevard. Go left on Glenwood Hills Drive and head north about a half mile before turning right onto a short road that leads to the Embudito trail head.

Northeast Cyclery, 8305 Menaul Blvd. NE (✆ **505/299-1210**) rents bikes at the rate of $25 per day for front-suspension mountain bikes and $35 per day for road bikes. Multiday discounts are available. Unfortunately, the shop doesn't rent children's bikes. Rentals come with helmets.

BIRD-WATCHING

Bosque del Apache National Wildlife Refuge ★★ (✆ **505/835-1828;** www.fws.gov/southwest/refuges/newmex/bosque/index.html) is a haven for migratory waterfowl such as snow geese and cranes. It's 90 miles south of Albuquerque on I-25, and it's well worth the drive. See chapter 11 for more details. Closer to town, check out the **Rio Grande Nature Center State Park** (see "Especially for Kids," above).

FISHING

Albuquerque's most notable fishing spot is **Tingley Beach,** (✆ **505/768-2000;** www.cabq.gov/biopark/tingley), stocked weekly with trout, bass, and catfish. It's open daily and is free. To access Tingley from Rio Grande Boulevard, head west to Tingley Drive (Parkway) and turn south. Another option is **Shady Lakes** (✆ **505/898-2568**). Nestled among cottonwood trees, it's near I-25 on Albuquerque's north side. The most common catches are rainbow trout, black bass, bluegill, and channel catfish. To reach Shady Lakes, take I-25 north to the Tramway exit. Follow Tramway Road west for a mile and then go right on NM 313 for a 1/2 mile. **Sandia Lakes Recreational Area** (✆ **505/897-3971;** www.sandiapueblo.nsn.us), also on NM 313, is another popular fishing spot. There is a bait and tackle shop there.

GOLF

There are quite a few public courses in the Albuquerque area. The **Championship Golf Course at the University of New Mexico,** 3601 University Blvd. SE (✆ **505/277-4546;** www.unmgolf.com), is one of the best in the Southwest and was rated one of the country's top 25 public links by *Golf Digest.* **Desert Greens Golf Course,** 10035 Country Club Lane NW (✆ **505/898-7001;** www.desertgreens.com), is a popular 18-hole golf course on the west side of town.

Other Albuquerque courses to check with for tee times are **Ladera,** 3401 Ladera Dr. NW (✆ **505/836-4449**); **Los Altos,** 9717 Copper Ave. NE (✆ **505/298-1897;** www.cabq.gov/golf/los-altos); **Puerto del Sol,** 1800 Girard Blvd. SE (✆ **505/265-5636;** www.cabq.gov/golf/puerto-del-sol); **Arroyo del Oso,** 7001 Osuna Rd. NE (✆ **505/884-7505;** www.cabq.gov/golf/arroyo-del-oso); and **Sandia Golf Club** (✆ **505/798-3990;** www.sandiagolf.com), located at Sandia Resort and Casino on the north end of town.

If you're willing to drive a short distance just outside Albuquerque, you can play at the **Santa Ana Golf Club at Santa Ana Pueblo,** 288 Prairie Star Rd., Bernalillo, NM 87004 (✆ **505/867-9464;** www.santaanagolf.com), which was rated by the *New York Times* as one of the best public golf courses in the country. Club rentals are available (call for information). In addition, **Isleta Pueblo,** 4001 Hwy. 47 (✆ **505/869-0950;** www.isleta pueblo.com), south of Albuquerque, has an 18-hole course.

HIKING

The 1½-million-acre **Cíbola National Forest** offers ample hiking opportunities. Within town, the best hike is the **Embudito Trail,** which heads up into the foothills, with spectacular views down across Albuquerque. The 5.5-mile one-way hike is moderate to difficult. Allow 1 to 8 hours, depending on how far you want to go. Access it by driving east from downtown on Montgomery Boulevard past the intersection with Tramway Boulevard. Go left on Glenwood Hills Drive and head north about a half mile before turning right onto a short road that leads to the trail head. The premier Sandia Mountain hike is **La Luz Trail,** a very strenuous journey from the Sandia foothills to the top of the Crest. It's a 15-mile round-trip jaunt, and it's half that if you take the Sandia Peak Tramway (see "The Top Attractions," earlier in this chapter) either up or down. Allow a full day for this hike. Access is off Tramway Boulevard and Forest Service Road 333. For more details contact **Sandia Ranger Station,** Highway 337 south toward Tijeras (✆ **505/281-3304;** www.fs.fed.us/r3/cibola).

HORSEBACK RIDING

Sometimes I just have to get in a saddle and eat some trail dust. If you get similar hankerings, call the **Hyatt Regency Tamaya Resort and Spa,** 1300 Tuyuna Trail, Santa Ana Pueblo (✆ **505/771-6037;** www.tamaya.hyatt.com). The resort offers 2½-hour-long rides near the Rio Grande for $75 per person. Children must be over 7 years of age and over 4 feet tall. The resort is about 15 miles north of Albuquerque. From I-25 take exit 242, following US 550 west to Tamaya Boulevard, and drive 1½ miles to the resort.

SKIING

The **Sandia Peak Ski Area** is a good place for family skiing. There are plenty of beginner and intermediate runs. (However, if you're looking for more challenge or more variety, you'd better head north to Santa Fe or Taos.) The ski area has twin base-to-summit chairlifts to its upper slopes at 10,360 feet and a 1,700-foot vertical drop. There are 30 runs (35% beginner, 55% intermediate, 10% advanced) above the day lodge and ski-rental shop. Four chairs and two pomas accommodate 3,400 skiers an hour. All-day lift tickets are $48 for adults, $38 for teens ages 13 to 20, $35 for children ages 6 to 12 and seniors (ages 62–71), and free for children 46 inches tall or less in ski boots and seniors ages 72 and over; rental packages are available. The season runs mid-December to mid-March. Contact the ski area, 10 Tramway Loop NE (✆ **505/242-9052;** www.sandiapeak.com), for more information, or call the hot line for ski conditions (✆ **505/857-8977**).

Cross-country skiers can enjoy the trails of the Sandia Wilderness from the ski area, or they can go an hour north to the remote Jemez Wilderness and its hot springs.

TENNIS

Albuquerque has 29 public parks with tennis courts. Because of the city's size, your best bet is to call the **Albuquerque Convention and Visitors Bureau** (✆ **800/284-2282;** www.itsatrip.org) to find out which park is closest to your hotel.

8 SPECTATOR SPORTS

BASEBALL

The **Albuquerque Isotopes** play 72 home games as part of the Pacific Coast League in their stadium, Isotopes Park. Tickets range in price from $6 to $24. For information, contact ✆ **505/924-2255;** www.albuquerquebaseball.com. Isotopes Park is at 1601 Av. Cesar Chavez SE. Take I-25 south of town to Avenida Cesar Chavez and go east; the stadium is at the intersection of Avenida Cesar Chavez and University Boulevard.

BASKETBALL

The University of New Mexico team, the **Lobos,** plays an average of 16 home games from late November to early March. Capacity crowds cheer the team at the 17,121-seat University Arena (fondly called "the Pit") at University and Stadium boulevards. For tickets and information, call ✆ **505/925-LOBO** or visit www.golobos.com.

FOOTBALL

The **UNM Lobos** football team plays a September-to-November season, usually with five home games, at the 30,000-seat University of New Mexico Stadium, opposite both Albuquerque Sports Stadium and University Arena at University and Stadium boulevards. For tickets and information, call ✆ **505/925-LOBO** or visit www.golobos.com.

HOCKEY

The **New Mexico Scorpions** play in the Western Professional Hockey League. Their home is at the **Rio Rancho Events Center,** 3001 Civic Center, Rio Rancho (✆ **505/881-7825;** www.scorpionshockey.com).

HORSE RACING

The **Downs at Albuquerque Racetrack and Casino,** New Mexico State Fairgrounds (✆ **505/266-5555** for post times; www.abqdowns.com) is near Lomas and Louisiana boulevards NE. Racing and betting—on thoroughbreds and quarter horses—take place August 16 through November 16 (including the New Mexico State Fair in Sept). The Downs has a glass-enclosed grandstand and exclusive club seating. General admission is free. Simulcast racing happens year-round daily, except Christmas. The 340-slot casino is open daily 10am to 2am, with drinks and dining in the Jockey Club. ***Note:*** The Downs is planning to move east of Albuquerque, so call before setting out.

9 SHOPPING A TO Z

Visitors seeking regional specialties will find many **local artists** and **galleries** of interest in Albuquerque, although not as many as in Santa Fe and Taos. The galleries and regional fashion designers around the plaza in Old Town comprise a kind of a shopping center for travelers, with more than 40 merchants represented. The Sandia Pueblo runs its own **crafts market** at the reservation, off I-25 at Tramway Road, just beyond Albuquerque's northern city limits.

Albuquerque has three of the largest **shopping malls** in New Mexico, two within 2 blocks of each other on Louisiana Boulevard just north of I-40—Coronado Center and Winrock Center. The other is the Cottonwood Mall on the west mesa, at 10,000 Coors

A Taste of the Grape

In addition to everything else New Mexico has to offer, wineries seem to be springing up all over the state. Call to find out about their wine-tasting hours. Wineries in Albuquerque or within a short driving distance of the city include **Anderson Valley Vineyards,** 4920 Rio Grande Blvd. NW, Albuquerque, NM 87107 (✆ **505/344-7266;** www.avwines.com); **Sandia Shadows Vineyard and Winery,** 11704 Coronado NE, Albuquerque 87122 (✆ **505/856-1006;** www.vivanewmexico.com/nm/wines.central.sandia.html); and **Gruet Winery,** 8400 Pan-American Hwy. NE, Albuquerque, NM 87113 (✆ **505/821-0055;** www.gruetwinery.com).

Blvd. NW (✆ **505/899-SHOP** [7467]). But the city's best mall is the new **ABQ Uptown** ★★ at Louisiana Boulevard NE and Indian School Road NE (✆ **505/883-7676;** www.abquptown.com), an outdoor mall with such anchors as Williams Sonoma, Pottery Barn, Sharper Image, Chicos, and Ann Taylor.

Business hours vary, but shops are generally open Monday to Saturday 10am to 6pm; many have extended hours; some have reduced hours; and a few, especially in shopping malls or during the high tourist season, are open on Sunday.

In Albuquerque the sales tax is 6.875%.

BEST BUYS

The best buys in Albuquerque are Southwestern regional items, including **arts and crafts** of all kinds—traditional Native American and Hispanic as well as contemporary works. In local Native American art, look for silver and turquoise jewelry, pottery, weavings, baskets, sand paintings, and Hopi katsina (kachina) dolls. Hispanic folk art—handcrafted furniture, tinwork, and *retablos*—is worth seeking out. The best contemporary art is in paintings, sculpture, jewelry, ceramics, and fiber art, including weaving.

Other items of potential interest are Southwestern fashions, gourmet foods, and unique local Native American and Hispanic creations.

By far, the most **galleries** are in Old Town; others are spread around the city, with smaller groupings in the university district and the northeast heights. Consult the brochure published by the **Albuquerque Gallery Association,** *A Select Guide to Albuquerque Galleries,* or Wingspread Communications's annual *The Collector's Guide to Albuquerque,* widely distributed at shops. Once a month, usually from 5 to 9pm on the third Friday, the **Albuquerque Art Business Association** (✆ **505/244-0362** for information) sponsors an ArtsCrawl to dozens of galleries and studios. It's a great way to meet the artists.

You'll find some interesting shops in the Nob Hill area, which is just west of the University of New Mexico and has an Art Deco feel.

Following are some shopping recommendations for the greater Albuquerque area.

ARTS & CRAFTS

Amapola Gallery ★ Fifty artists and craftspeople show their talents at this lovely cooperative gallery upstairs in the historic 1849 Romero House. You'll find pottery, paintings, textiles, carvings, baskets, jewelry, and other items. 205 Romero St. ✆ **505/242-4311.**

Andrews Pueblo Pottery ★ Carrying Pueblo pottery ranging from the black firings of San Ildefonso to the sand-colored Acoma, this gallery is a place for rich perusing as well as serious buying. Also of note here are Zuni stone fetishes and Hopi katsinas (kachinas). 303 N. Romero NW, Old Town. ✆ **877/606-0543** or 505/243-0414. www.andrewspueblopottery.com.

Bien Mur Indian Market Center ★ Sandia Pueblo's crafts market, on the reservation, sells turquoise and silver jewelry, pottery, baskets, katsina (kachina) dolls, handwoven rugs, sand paintings, and other arts and crafts. The market is open Monday through Saturday from 9:30am to 5:30pm and Sunday from 11am to 5pm. I-25 at Tramway Road NE. ✆ **800/365-5400** or 505/821-5400.

Gallery One This gallery features folk art, jewelry, contemporary crafts, cards and paper, and natural-fiber clothing. In the Nob Hill Shopping Center, 3500 Central Ave. SE. ✆ **505/268-7449.**

Hispaniae in Old Town ★ (Finds) Day of the Dead people and Frida Kahlo faces greet you at this wild shop with everything from kitschy Mexican tableware to fine Oaxacan woodcarvings. 410 Romero St. NW, Old Town. ✆ **505/244-1533.** www.hispaniae.com.

Mariposa Gallery ★★ (Value) Eclectic contemporary art, jewelry, blown glass, and sculpture fill this Nob Hill shop, with prices that even a travel writer can afford. In the Nob Hill Shopping Center, 3500 Central Ave. SE. ✆ **505/268-6828.** www.mariposa-gallery.com.

Ortega's Indian Arts and Crafts An institution in Gallup, adjacent to the Navajo Reservation, Ortega's now has this Albuquerque store. It sells, repairs, and appraises silver and turquoise jewelry. 6600 Menaul Blvd. NE, no. 359. ✆ **505/881-1231.**

R. C. Gorman Nizhoni Gallery Old Town ★ The painting and sculpture of the late Navajo artist Gorman, who was a resident of Taos, are shown here. Most works are available in limited-edition lithographs. 323 Romero St. NW, Suite 1, and another shop at 400 Romero St. NW, Suite 3, Old Town. ✆ **505/843-7666.** www.rcgorman-nizhoni.com.

Skip Maisel's (Value) If you want a real bargain in Native American arts and crafts, this is the place to shop. You'll find a broad range of quality and price here in goods such as pottery, weavings, and katsinas (kachinas). ***Take note:*** Adorning the outside of the store are murals painted in 1933 by notable Navajo painter Harrison Begay and Pueblo painter Pablita Velarde. 510 Central Ave. SW. ✆ **505/242-6526.**

Tanner Chaney Galleries ★ In business since 1875, this gallery has fine jewelry, pottery, rugs, and more. 323 Romero St. NW, no. 4, Old Town. ✆ **800/444-2242** or 505/247-2242. www.tannerchaney.com.

Wright's Collection of Indian Art This gallery, first opened in 1907, features a free private museum and carries fine handmade Native American arts and crafts, both contemporary and traditional. 1100 San Mateo Blvd. NE. ✆ **505/266-0120.** www.wrightsgallery.com.

BOOKS

Barnes & Noble On the west side, just north of Cottonwood Mall, this huge bookstore offers plenty of browsing room and a Starbucks Cafe for lounging. The store is known for its large children's section and weekly story-time readings. 3701 Ellison Dr. NW #A. ✆ **505/792-4234.** Or at the Coronado Center, 6600 Menaul Blvd. NE. ✆ **505/883-8200.** www.barnesandnoble.com.

Bookworks ★ Selling both new and used books, Bookworks has one of the most complete Southwestern nonfiction and fiction sections in the region. A good place to linger, the store has a coffee bar and an area for readings. It also carries CDs, cassettes, and books on tape. 4022 Rio Grande Blvd. NW. ✆ **505/344-8139.** www.bkwrks.com.

Borders This branch of the popular chain provides a broad range of books, music, and videos, and hosts in-store appearances by authors, musicians, and artists. Uptown Center, 2240 Q St. NE. ✆ **505/884-7711.** www.borders.com.

FOOD

The Candy Lady Having made chocolate for over 30 years, the Candy Lady is especially known for 21 varieties of fudge, including jalapeño flavor. 524 Romero St. NW, Old Town. ✆ **800/214-7731** or 505/243-6239. www.thecandylady.com.

FASHIONS

Albuquerque Pendleton Cuddle up in a large selection of blankets and shawls, and haul them away in a handbag. 1100 San Mateo NE Blvd., Suite 2 and 4. ✆ **505/255-6444.**

Gertrude Zachary ★★ This large well of imagination has beaded velvet scarves and elaborate antique furniture, but the real buy here is jewelry, ranging from traditional Native American bracelets and necklaces to wildly kitschy butterfly concho belts. Purses, beaded lamps, this place has anything that a contemporary gal could want. 3300 Central Ave. SE (in the Nob Hill area at Wellsley). ✆ **505/766-4700.** www.gertrudezachary.com.

GIFTS/SOUVENIRS

Jackalope International ★★ Wandering through this vast shopping area is like an adventure to another land—to many lands, really. You'll find Mexican *trasteros* (armoires) next to Balinese puppets. The store sells sculpture, pottery, and Christmas ornaments as well. 834 US 550, Bernalillo. ✆ **505/867-9813.** www.jackalope.com.

HOME FURNISHINGS

A ★ Offering contemporary furnishings and colorful kitchenware, this shop is a fun place to browse and buy. As well as home furnishings, it offers eclectic soaps and even men's ties. 3500 Central SE, in the Nob Hill Shopping Center. ✆ **505/266-2222.**

El Paso Import Company ★ Advertising "unique furnishings from around the world," this place in the Nob Hill Shopping Center is packed with all manner of tables, trasteros, and chairs, most with aged and chipped paint for those who love the worn look.

Moments **All That Glitters Is on Gold**

For years, downtown Albuquerque has been reinventing itself and nowhere is the luster more brilliant than on Gold Avenue. A funky boutique street, it's the home of many unique shops and restaurants, well worth a morning or afternoon perusal. Look for "fine, fun, and funky" functional art at **Patrician Design,** 216 Gold Ave. SW (✆ **505/242-7646**). Down the street, step into **Ooh! Aah! Jewelry,** 311 Gold Ave. SW (✆ **505/242-7101**), to find a wide selection of contemporary jewelry and handbags. If you work up an appetite, head to **Gold Street Caffè,** or for a creamy snack try **Cold Stone Creamery,** 101 Gold Ave. SW (✆ **505/843-9456**), for a serious selection of ice cream flavors made in-house.

It's a fun place to browse even if you don't buy. 3500 Central SE, Nob Hill. ✆ **505/265-1160.** www.elpasoimportco.com.

Strictly Southwestern You'll find nice, solid pine and oak Southwestern-style furniture here. Lighting, art, pottery, and other interior items are also available. 1321 Eubank Blvd. NE. ✆ **505/292-7337.** www.strictlysouthwestern.com.

MARKETS

Flea Market Every Saturday and Sunday, year-round, the fairgrounds hosts this market from 8am to 5pm. It's a great place to browse for turquoise and silver jewelry and locally made crafts, as well as newly manufactured inexpensive goods such as socks and T-shirts. The place takes on a fair atmosphere, with the smell of cotton candy filling the air. There's no admission charge. New Mexico State Fairgrounds. For information, call the Albuquerque Convention and Visitors Bureau, ✆ **800/284-2282.** www.abqfleamarket.com.

10 ALBUQUERQUE AFTER DARK

Albuquerque has an active performing-arts and nightlife scene, as befits a city of half a million people. As also befits this area, the performing arts are multicultural, with Hispanic and (to a lesser extent) Native American productions sharing stage space with Anglo works, including theater, opera, symphony, and dance. Albuquerque also attracts many national touring companies. Nightclubs cover the gamut, with rock, jazz, and country predominant.

Complete information on all major cultural events can be obtained from the **Albuquerque Convention and Visitors Bureau** (✆ **800/284-2282** for recorded information after 5pm). Current listings appear in the two daily newspapers; detailed weekend arts calendars can be found in Friday's *Journal.* The monthly *On the Scene* also carries entertainment listings.

Tickets for nearly all major entertainment and sporting events can be obtained from **Ticketmaster,** 4004 Carlisle Blvd. NE (✆ **505/883-7800**). Discount tickets are often available for midweek and matinee performances; check with individual theater or concert hall box offices.

THE PERFORMING ARTS

Classical Music

New Mexico Ballet Company Founded in 1972, the state's oldest ballet company holds most of its performances at Popejoy Hall. Typically there's a fall production such as *Dracula,* a holiday one such as *The Nutcracker* or *A Christmas Carol,* and a contemporary spring production. 4200 Wyoming Blvd. NE, Suite B2 Albuquerque, NM 87154-1518. ✆ **505/292-4245.** www.nmballet.org. Tickets $15–$40 adults, depending on the performance and venue.

New Mexico Symphony Orchestra ★ The NMSO first played in 1932 and has continued as a strong cultural force throughout the state. The symphony performs classics and pops, as well as family and neighborhood concerts. It plays for more than 20,000 grade-school students and visits communities throughout the state in its annual tour program. Concert venues are generally Popejoy Hall on the University of New Mexico campus, the National Hispanic Cultural Center, and the Rio Grande Zoo, all of which

The Major Concert & Performance Halls

- **Journal Pavilion,** 5601 University Blvd. NE (✆ **505/452-5100**).
- **Keller Hall,** University of New Mexico, Cornell Street at Redondo Drive South NE (✆ **505/277-4569**).
- **KiMo Theatre,** 423 Central Ave. NW (✆ **505/768-3544**).
- **Popejoy Hall,** University of New Mexico, Cornell Street at Redondo Drive South NE (✆ **505/277-3824**).
- **South Broadway Cultural Center,** 1025 Broadway Blvd. SE (✆ **505/848-1320**).

are accessible to people with disabilities. Guillermo Figueroa is the music director and conductor. I recommend going to one of the outdoor concerts at the band shell at the Rio Grande Zoo. 4407 Menaul Blvd. NE. ✆ **800/251-6676** for tickets and information, or 505/881-9590. www.nmso.org. Ticket prices vary with concert; call for details.

THEATER

Albuquerque Little Theatre The Albuquerque Little Theatre has been offering a variety of productions ranging from comedies to dramas to musicals since 1930. Eight plays are presented here annually during a July-to-June season. Located across from Old Town, the theater offers plenty of free parking. Box office Mon–Fri 9am–6pm. 224 San Pasquale Ave. SW. ✆ **505/242-4750.** www.albuquerquelittletheatre.org. Tickets $22; $10 for student rush-tickets purchased 30 min. before showtime, $18 seniors.

Musical Theatre Southwest From February to January, this theater presents six major Broadway musicals, in addition to several smaller productions, at either Popejoy Hall or the MTS's own 890-seat Hiland Theater. Most productions are staged for 3 consecutive weekends, including some Sunday matinees. 2401 Ross. SE. ✆ **505/265-9119.** www.musicaltheatresw.com. Tickets $15–$30 adults; students and seniors receive a $2 discount.

Vortex Theatre ★ A 35-year-old community theater known for its innovative productions, the Vortex is Albuquerque's "Off-Broadway" theater, presenting a range of plays from classic to original. You'll see such plays as *I Hate Hamlet* by Paul Rudnik and *Death & the Maiden* by Ariel Dorfman. Performances take place on Friday and Saturday at 8pm and on Sunday at 6pm. The black-box theater seats 90. 2004½ Central Ave. SE. ✆ **505/247-8600.** www.vortexabq.org. All tickets $12.

THE CLUB & MUSIC SCENE

Comedy Clubs/Dinner Theater

Laffs Comedy Cafe This club offers top acts from each coast, including comedians who have appeared on *The Late Show with David Letterman* and HBO. Shows Wed–Sun nights. San Mateo Blvd. and Osuna Rd., in the Fiesta del Norte Shopping Center. ✆ **505/296-5653.** www.laffscomedy.com. $8 per person, with a two-item minimum purchase. Call for showtimes.

Mystery Cafe ★ (Finds) If you're in the mood for a little interactive dinner theater, the Mystery Cafe might be just the ticket. You'll help the characters in this ever-popular, delightfully funny show solve the mystery as they serve you a four-course meal. Reservations are a must. Performances Fri and Sat evenings at 7:30pm; doors open at 7pm. P.O. Box 11433. Performances held at Sheraton Uptown (at Menaul Blvd. and Louisiana Blvd.). ✆ **505/237-1385.** www.abqmystery.com. Approximately $38 plus tip.

Rock/Jazz

Burt's Tiki Lounge This club won the weekly paper *Alibi's* award for the best variety of drinks. The club offers live music Thursday to Sunday and charges no cover. 313 Gold Ave. ✆ **505/247-2878.** www.burtstikilounge.com.

Kelly's BYOB Near the university, Kelly's is a local brewpub, set in a renovated autobody shop. The place has tasty pub fare, excellent brew specials, and live music for special events. 3222 Central SE. ✆ **505/262-2739.** www.kellysbrewpub.com.

Martini Grille ★ On the eastern side of the Nob Hill district, this is the place for young professionals and the gay crowd, who lush out on more than 30 flavors of martinis within a seductive Batman cave atmosphere. Live entertainment plays most weekends and some weeknights. 4200 Central SE. ✆ **505/255-4111.**

O'Niell's Pub A favorite club in the University of New Mexico area, this Irish bar serves up good pub fare as well as live local music on Saturday nights and Celtic and bluegrass on Sunday evenings. 3211 Central NE. ✆ **505/256-0564.** www.oniells.com.

Q Bar ★ With sophisticated decor—lots of plush couches and comfy chairs in muted tones—this lounge in the Hotel Albuquerque at Old Town offers innovative cuisine, jazz piano entertainment, and media and billiards rooms. 800 Rio Grande Blvd. NW. ✆ **505/843-6300.**

MORE ENTERTAINMENT

Albuquerque's best nighttime attraction is the **Sandia Peak Tramway,** from which you can enjoy a view nonpareil of the Rio Grande Valley and the city lights.

The best place to catch foreign films, art films, and limited-release productions is the **Guild Cinema,** 3405 Central Ave. NE (✆ **505/255-1848**). For film classics, check out the **Southwest Film Center,** on the UNM campus (✆ **505/277-5608**), which has double features, changing nightly (when classes are in session). In addition, Albuquerque has a number of first-run movie theaters whose numbers you can find in the local telephone directory.

Many travelers like to include a little dice-throw and slot-machine play in their trip to New Mexico. Those who do are in luck, with the expansive **Sandia Resort & Casino,** north of I-25 and a quarter mile east on Tramway Boulevard (✆ **800/526-9366;** www.sandiacasino.com). The $80-million structure sits on Sandia Pueblo land and has outstanding views of the Sandia Mountains. Built in pueblo architectural style, the graceful casino has a 3,650-seat outdoor amphitheater, three restaurants (one, **Bien Shur,** has excellent food), a lounge, more than 1,800 slot and video poker machines, the largest poker room in the state, and blackjack, roulette, and craps tables. It's open from 8am to 4am Sunday to Wednesday and 24 hours Thursday to Saturday. The **Isleta Gaming Palace,** 11000 Broadway SE (✆ **877/ISLETA** or 505/724-3800; www.isletacasinoresort.com), is a luxurious, air-conditioned casino (featuring blackjack, poker, slots, bingo, and keno) with a full-service restaurant, nonsmoking section, and free bus transportation on request. Open Monday to Wednesday 8am to 4am, Thursday to Sunday 24 hours a day.

11 TOURING THE PUEBLOS AROUND ALBUQUERQUE

Ten Native American pueblos are located within an hour's drive of central Albuquerque. Two of them, Acoma and Laguna, are discussed in chapter 9, "Northwestern New Mexico." The others, from south to north, are discussed here, followed by Coronado and Jemez state monuments, which preserve ancient pueblo ruins. If you'd like to combine a tour of the archaeological sites and inhabited pueblos, consider driving the **Jemez Mountain Trail** ★. Head north on Interstate 25 to Bernalillo, where you can visit the Coronado State Monument. Continue west on US 550 to Zia Pueblo. Six miles farther on US 550 takes you to NM 4, where you'll turn north and drive through orchards and along narrow cornfields of Jemez Pueblo. Farther north on NM 4, you'll find another archaeological site, the Jemez State Monument. You'll also find Jemez Springs, where you can stop for a hot soak. The road continues to the Los Alamos area, where you can see the spectacular ruins at Bandelier National Monument. From there you have the option of returning the way you came or via Santa Fe.

AREA PUEBLOS

Isleta Pueblo

Located just 14 miles south of Albuquerque, off I-25 or US 85, **Isleta Pueblo,** P.O. Box 1270, Isleta, NM 87022 (✆ **505/869-3111;** www.isletapueblo.com), is the largest of the Tiwa-speaking pueblos, comprising several settlements on the west side of the Rio Grande. The largest village, Shiaw-iba, contains the Mission of San Agustin de Isleta, built in 1613, partially destroyed during the Pueblo Revolt, and then rebuilt in 1716. On the quiet plaza is Isleta's church, St. Augustine, built in 1629, with thick adobe walls and vigas adorning the ceiling. It is one of the oldest churches in New Mexico.

Isleta women potters make red wares distinctive for their red-and-black designs on white backgrounds. The tribe operates the **Isleta Casino and Resort** (✆ **877/747-5382** or 505/724-3800; www.isletacasinoresort.com) and fishing and camping areas at Isleta Lakes. An RV site costs $30. No tent sites are available. A fishing permit is $15 and can be purchased at the recreation area.

The Isleta hold an evergreen dance sometime in late February. The big day of the year is the feast day honoring St. Augustine, August 28, when a morning Mass and procession are followed by an afternoon harvest dance.

The pueblo is open to visitors daily during daylight hours. Admission is free. Photography is limited to the church.

Sandia Pueblo

Established about 1300, **Sandia Pueblo,** 481 Sandia Loop, Bernalillo, NM 87004 (✆ **505/867-3317**), is one of the few pueblos visited by Coronado's contingent in 1540. Remains of that village, known as Nafiat, or "sandy," are still visible near the present church. The Sandia people temporarily fled to Hopi country after the Pueblo rebellion of 1680, but they returned to the Rio Grande in 1742. Many of today's 4,000 Tiwa-speaking (Tanoan) inhabitants work in Albuquerque or at Pueblo Enterprises. They also run the **Bien Mur Indian Market Center** on Tramway Road (✆ **800/365-5400** or 505/821-5400) and **Sandia Casino** (✆ **800/526-9366;** www.sandiacasino.com). It's about 5 miles north of Albuquerque off I-25.

Chama
San Juan R.
Aztec Ruins National Monument
JICARILLA APACHE RESERVATION
Rio Grande
Red River
Taos Ski Valley
Taos Pueblo
Wheeler Peak
Taos
Angel Fire
Ohkay Owinge
Picuris Pueblo
Chaco Culture National Historic Park
Española
Sipapu
Los Alamos
Nambé Pueblo
Ski Santa Fe
Bandelier National Monument
Tesuque Pueblo
Fort Union National Monument
Jemez State Monument
Jemez Pueblo
Santa Fe
Cochiti Pueblo
Pecos National Monument
Zia Pueblo
Los Cerrillos
Las Vegas
Coronado State Monument
Madrid
Turquoise Trail
Grants
Laguna Pueblo
Rio Rancho
Golden
Pecos River
ALBUQUERQUE
El Malpais National Monument
Acoma Pueblo
Isleta Pueblo
Santa Rosa
Salinas National Monument: Quarai
ALAMO NAVAJO RESERVATION
Mountainair
Salinas National Monument: Abo
Salinas National Monument: Gran Quivera
Very Large Array Radio Observatory
Socorro
Bosque del Apache National Wildlife Refuge
Lincoln State Monument
Ski Apache
Rio Grande
Ruidoso
Roswell
Truth or Consequences
MESCALERO APACHE RESERVATION
Alamogordo
Cloudcroft
White Sands National Monument
Taos
Santa Fe
Albuquerque
NEW MEXICO
Mountain
Pueblos
Ski Area
Fort Selden State Monument
Rio Grande
Las Cruces
Deming
Carlsbad Caverns National Park
0 40 mi
0 40 km
N
NEW MEXICO
El Paso
TEXAS

64 64 285 64 84 550 68 25 4 84 14 84 40 40 337 60 25 54 60 285 380 25 70 54 70 180 10 70 180 10 40 25 40 25 10

Pueblo Etiquette: Do's & Don'ts

Those who are not Native American are welcome to visit Indian pueblos and reservations; however, there are some guidelines you should follow as a guest on tribal land.

Native American reservations and pueblos have their own systems of government and, therefore, their own laws and regulations. If you don't follow their laws, you will be subject to punishment as outlined by the American Indian government. The best thing that could happen is that you'd simply be asked to leave.

Stay out of cemeteries and ceremonial rooms, such as kivas, as these are sacred grounds. Remember, these are not museums or tourist attractions in their own right; they are people's homes. Don't peek into doors and windows, and don't climb on top of buildings.

Most pueblos require a permit to carry a camera or to sketch or paint on location, and many prohibit photography at any time. If you want to take pictures, make a video, or sketch anything on pueblo or reservation land, find out about permits and fees in advance.

Do not wander around on your own if the residents have asked that you visit the pueblo only by guided tour. If, on a guided tour, you are asked not to take pictures of something, or are asked to stay out of a certain area, please follow the guidelines. If you don't have to visit by guided tour, don't go into private buildings without being escorted by someone who lives there or who has the authority to take you inside.

Be respectful of ceremonial dances. Do not speak during dances or ceremonies and don't applaud at the end of the dance—they aren't dancing for your amusement; they are dancing as part of their ceremony.

In short, be courteous and don't do anything you wouldn't do in your own mother's house.

The pueblo celebrates its St. Anthony feast day on June 13, with a midmorning Mass, procession, and afternoon corn dance. Another dance honors newly elected governors in January.

The pueblo is open to visitors weekdays during daylight hours, and admission is free. No photographing, video recording, or sketching is allowed.

Santa Ana Pueblo

Though partially abandoned, **Santa Ana Pueblo,** 2 Dove Rd., Santa Ana Pueblo, NM 87004 (✆ **505/867-3301;** www.santaana.org), on the lower Jemez River, claims a population of about 500. Many "residents" who maintain family homes at the pueblo actually live nearer the stream's confluence with the Rio Grande, in Ranchos de Santa Ana, near Bernalillo, where farming is more productive. A handful of craftspeople in the old village produce pottery, woodcarvings, ceremonial bands, red-cloth belts, and unique wooden crosses with straw inlay.

Guests are normally welcomed only on ceremonial days. Pueblo members perform the turtle and corn dances on New Year's Day; the eagle, elk, buffalo, and deer dances on January 6; and several days of dances at Christmastime. Feast Day celebrations honoring Saint Ann take place on July 26.

The pueblo is about 15 to 20 miles north of Albuquerque, reached via I-25 to Bernalillo, and then 8 miles northwest on US 550. Admission is free and allowed only on dance days; photography is prohibited. Visitors can stay on Santa Ana Pueblo land at the **Hyatt Regency Tamaya Resort** (✆ **505/867-1234;** see "Where to Stay," earlier in this chapter). The **Santa Ana Star Casino** (✆ **505/867-0000;** www.santaanastar.com) offers all manner of gambling.

Zia Pueblo

Zia Pueblo, 135 Capitol Square Dr., Zia Pueblo, NM, 87053 (✆ **505/867-3304**), which has 720 inhabitants, blends in so perfectly with the soft tans of the stone and sand of the desertlike land around it that it's very hard to see—it's like a chameleon on a tree trunk. The pueblo is best known for its famous sun symbol—now the official symbol of the state of New Mexico—adapted from a pottery design showing three rays going in each of the four directions from a sun, or circle. It is hailed in the pledge to the state flag as "a symbol of perfect friendship among united cultures."

Zia has a reputation for excellence in pottery making. Its pottery is identified by its unglazed terra-cotta coloring, traditional geometric designs, and plant and animal motifs painted on a white slip. Paintings, weaving, and sculptures are also prized products of the artists of the Zia community. Their work can be viewed at the **Zia Cultural Center** located at the pueblo. Our Lady of the Assumption, the patron saint, is given a celebratory corn dance on her day, August 15.

The pueblo is about 17 miles northwest of Bernalillo, just off of US 550. It's open to visitors daily during daylight hours, and admission is free. Photography is not permitted.

Jemez Pueblo

The more than 2,500 **Jemez Pueblo** natives—including descendants of the Pecos Pueblo, east of Santa Fe, abandoned in 1838—are the only remaining people to speak the Towa dialect of the Tanoan group. The Jemez are famous for their excellent dancing and feast-making; their feast days attract residents from other pueblos, turning the celebrations into multitribal fairs. Two rectangular kivas are central points for groups of dancers. However, in recent years the pueblo has been closed to visitors. Though they are allowed to visit on dance days, the pueblo has become close-mouthed about when dances occur. However, visitors can partake of the crafts at local shops along NM 4 and at the Walatowa Visitor Center (see box below). The primary craft is Jemez pottery.

On weekends April through mid-October, weather permitting, arts and crafts and traditional foods are sold across the street from the visitor center at the **Jemez Red Rocks Open-Air Market.**

You can enjoy fishing and picnicking along the Jemez River on government forestlands and camping at the Dragonfly Recreation Area. Call about getting permits. The pueblo, P.O. Box 100, Jemez Pueblo, NM 87024 (✆ **575/834-7235;** www.jemezpueblo.org), is 55 miles northwest of Albuquerque via I-25 to Bernalillo, US 550 to San Ysidro, and NM 4 for 6 final miles.

San Felipe Pueblo

San Felipe Pueblo, a conservative pueblo of 3,500 people, located on a mesa on the west bank of the Rio Grande, is known for its beautiful ritual ceremonies. The plaza has been worn into the shape of a bowl by the feet of San Felipe's dancers over the centuries. In the grandest of these dances, hundreds of men, women, and children move through their rhythmic steps all day long in the spring corn dance on May 1, performed in honor of the pueblo's patron, St. Philip (San Felipe). The dancing is done to a great chorus of male singers intoning music that reaches back into prehistory and evokes strong emotions in participants and in visitors, too. Another notable event here is a corn dance on January 6.

San Felipe Pueblo, P.O. Box 4339, San Felipe, NM 87001 (✆ **505/867-3381**), is 30 miles northeast of Albuquerque via I-25 and an access road. Admission is free. Photography and sketching are not permitted. The pueblo is open to visitors during daylight hours. **Casino Hollywood,** exit 252 off I-25 north of Albuquerque (✆ **505/867-6700;** www.sanfelipecasino.com), offers most types of gambling.

Santo Domingo Pueblo

One of New Mexico's largest pueblos, with 3,500 residents, this farming community on the east bank of the Rio Grande is also one of the state's most traditional. Craftspeople are known for their beautiful silver jewelry, unique necklaces of heishi (shell fragments), innovative pottery, and fine weaving.

At the dramatic **Santo Domingo Pueblo** feast day, August 4, the corn dance is performed as it is done nowhere else. It is a lavish production involving clowns, scores of singers and drummers, and 500 tireless and skilled dancers in imaginative traditional costumes. Other festive occasions during the year include the Easter spring corn dance and basket dance and an arts-and-crafts festival on Labor Day weekend, with more than 300 artisans in attendance.

Santo Domingo Pueblo, P.O. Box 99, Santo Domingo, NM 87052 (✆ **505/465-2214**), is 40 miles northeast of Albuquerque via I-25 north to NM 22. The pueblo is open daily to visitors during daylight hours. Admission is free, but no photography or sketching is permitted.

Cochiti Pueblo

Occupied continuously since about the 13th century, **Cochiti Pueblo,** P.O. Box 70, Cochiti Pueblo, NM 87072 (✆ **505/465-2244;** www.pueblodecochiti.org), the northernmost of the Keresan-speaking pueblos, stretches along the Rio Grande. Its Church of San Buenaventura, though rebuilt and remodeled since, still contains sections of its original 1628 structure.

Cochiti (pop. 1,500) is well known for its pottery, especially the famous "storyteller" figures created by Helen Cordero. Beadwork and soft leather moccasins are other craft specialties. The pueblo's double-headed dance drums, made from hollowed-out cottonwood logs and covered with leather, are used in ceremonies throughout the Rio Grande area.

San Buenaventura Feast Day is July 14, when the corn and rain dances are performed. Other events include a buffalo dance December 25, and other dances December 26 to 29.

The pueblo is about 40 miles north of Albuquerque, via I-25, and then north on NM 22. It is open to visitors daily during daylight hours; admission is free. Photography, sketching, and tape recording are not permitted. Cochiti Lake, though fairly silty, is popular for watersports, especially windsurfing. Tent Rocks National Monument, on Cochiti Pueblo land, is a fun place to hike.

An Eerie Land of Tents

A visit to the **Kasha-Katuwe Tent Rocks National Monument** ★★, north of Albuquerque (✆ **505/761-8700;** www.nm.blm.gov/recreation/albuquerque/kasha_katuwe.htm), offers a lunar landscape pocked by white cone-shaped rocks. Hikers follow a wash through the formations, ending above them. It's a good hike for kids, since the round-trip distance is only 2 miles—about 1½ hours—and it's the kind of place to wander. No supplies are available, so it's best to get them in Albuquerque or Santa Fe. To reach the monument from Albuquerque, take I-25 north to the exit for Santo Domingo/Cochiti Lake Recreation Area (exit 259) onto NM 22. Follow the signs. Admission is $5 per vehicle. April to October the monument is open daily 7am to 7pm; November to March, daily 8am to 5pm.

A STATE MONUMENT IN THE AREA

Coronado State Monument ★ When the Spanish explorer Coronado traveled through this region in 1540–41 while searching for the Seven Cities of Cíbola, he wintered at a village on the west bank of the Rio Grande—probably one on the ruins of the ancient Anasazi Pueblo known as Kuaua. Those excavated ruins have been preserved in this state monument.

Hundreds of rooms can be seen, and a kiva has been restored so that visitors can descend a ladder into the enclosed space, once the site of sacred rites. Unique multicolored murals, depicting human and animal forms, were found on successive layers of wall plaster in this and other kivas here; some examples are displayed in the monument's small archaeological museum.

485 Kuaua Rd., Bernalillo. ✆ **505/867-5351.** Admission $3 adults, free for children 16 and under. Wed–Mon 8:30am–5pm. Closed Easter, Thanksgiving, Christmas, New Year's. To get to the site (20 miles north of Albuquerque), take I-25 to Bernalillo and US 550 west for 1.7 mile.

JEMEZ SPRINGS

Getting to this village along the Jemez River is half the fun. You'll drive the **Jemez Mountain Trail** ★ into the Jemez Mountains, a trip that can provide a relaxing retreat and/or an exhilarating adventure. In the area are historic sites and relaxing hot springs, as well as excellent stream fishing, hiking, and cross-country skiing. You may want to combine a drive through this area with a visit to Los Alamos and Bandelier National Monument (see chapter 7).

North of town you'll come to the **Soda Dam,** a strange and beautiful mineral mass formed by travertine deposits—minerals that precipitate out of geothermal springs. Considered a sacred site by Native Americans, it has a gushing waterfall and caves. During the warm months, it's a popular swimming hole.

Jemez State Monument ★ A stop at this small monument takes you on a journey through the history of the Jemez people. The journey begins in the museum, which tells the tale of Giusewa, "place of boiling waters," the original Tewa name of the area. Then it moves out into the mission ruins, whose story is told on small plaques that juxtapose the first impressions of the missionaries against the reality of the Jemez life. The missionaries saw the Jemez people as barbaric and set out to settle them. Part of the process involved hauling up river stones and erecting 6-foot-thick walls of the Mission of San José de los Jemez (founded in 1621) in the early 17th century. Excavations in 1921–22 and 1935–37 unearthed this massive complex through which you may wander. You enter through a broad doorway to a room that once held elaborate fresco paintings, the room tapering back to the nave, with a giant bell tower above. The setting is startling next to a creek, with steep mountains rising behind.

18160 NM 4 (P.O. Box 143), Jemez Springs. ✆ **505/829-3530.** www.nmmonuments.org. Admission $3 adults, free for children 17 and under. Wed–Mon 8:30am–5pm. Closed Tues, New Year's Day, Easter, Thanksgiving, and Christmas. From Albuquerque, take NM 550 (NM 44) to NM 4 and then continue on NM 4 for about 18 miles.

Where to Stay & Dine

Cañon del Rio–Riverside Inn ★ "Eventually the watcher joined the river, and there was only one of us. I believe it was the river," wrote Norman Maclean in *A River Runs Through It.* That was my experience while sitting on a cottonwood-shaded bench at Cañon del Rio, on a long bow of the Jemez River, a small, fast-flowing stream lined with cottonwoods. Built in 1994, the inn has clean lines and comfortable rooms, each named after a Native American tribe. Each has a sliding glass door that opens out to a patio where there's a fountain. Located on the river there are decks for enjoying nature and a heated pool. The beds are comfortable, with good reading lights. The Great Room has a cozy, welcoming feel, with a big-screen TV, as well as a large table where breakfast is served family style. Smoking is not allowed.

16445 (Scenic) NM 4, Jemez Springs, NM 87025. ✆ **505/829-4377.** www.canondelrio.com. 7 units. $119–$200 double, depending on the season; house $125–$150. Rates include full breakfast with inn room. AE, DISC, MC, V. **Amenities:** Jacuzzi; outdoor pool. *In room:* A/C, Wi-Fi, hair dryer.

The Laughing Lizard Inn & Cafe ★ AMERICAN This is the kind of small-town cafe that doesn't have to try to have a personality. It already has thick adobe walls, wood floors, and a wood-burning stove for its innate charm. Added touches are the brightly painted walls and funky old tables. If there were a Western version of the Whistle Stop Cafe, this would be it. The menu is somewhat eclectic—most dishes have a bit of an imaginative flair. The burritos come in a variety of types, such as fresh spinach with black beans, mushrooms, jack cheese, salsa, and guacamole. The homemade pizzas, made with blue-corn crusts, feature ingredients such as pesto, sun-dried tomatoes, and feta, or more basic ones with red sauce as well. Beer and wine are served, and there are daily dessert

Historic Culture with a Hint of Honey

Jemez Pueblo, home to more than 3,000, no longer welcomes visitors except on selected days. However, visitors can get a taste of the Jemez culture at the **Walatowa Visitor Center,** on NM 4, 8 miles north of the junction with US 550 (✆ **877/733-5687** or 505/834-7235; www.jemezpueblo.org). A museum and shop highlight the center, which also offers information about hiking and scenic tour routes. While in the area, you may encounter Jemez people sitting under ramadas (thatch-roofed lean-tos) selling home-baked bread, cookies, and pies. If you're lucky, they may also be making fry bread, which you can smother with honey for one of New Mexico's more delectable treats.

Moments Sampling Nature's Nectars

If you like to soak in warm springs, head to Jemez. The waters running through the area are high in mineral content. In fact, the owner of **Jemez Springs Bath House,** 62 NM 4, on the Jemez Springs Plaza (✆ **505/829-3303;** www.jemezspringsbathhouse.com) says they are so healing, more than once she's had to run after visitors who walked off without their canes. This bathhouse was one of the first structures to be built in what is now Jemez Springs. Built in 1870 and 1878 of river rock and mud, it has thick walls and a richly herbal scent. You soak in individual tubs in either the men's side or the women's side. In back are a series of massage rooms, and outside is a hot tub within a wooden fence—not the most romantic setting. In front is a gift shop packed with interesting soaps and soulful gifts. Jemez Springs Bath House is open daily 10am to 8pm.

Another option in town is the **Giggling Springs** ★ (✆ **505/829-9175;** www.gigglingsprings.com), across the street from the Laughing Lizard. A small outdoor pool, surrounded by sandstone and funky art, highlights this place. The Jemez River acts as a cold plunge. It's open Wednesday to Sunday 11am to 8pm, with an abbreviated schedule in winter. Reservations recommended.

At **Ponderosa Valley Vineyard & Winery,** 3171 Hwy. 290, Ponderosa, NM 87044 (✆ **800/WINE-MAKER** [946-3625] or 575/834-7487; www.ponderosawinery.com), 3 miles off NM 4 south of Jemez Springs, you'll find a quaint country store with some of New Mexico's best wines. If you're lucky, the vintners will pour you delectable tastes while telling stories of the history of wine in New Mexico and of the Jemez area, where they have lived and grown grapes for over 3 decades. This is the oldest wine-growing region in the United States, and the product definitely has its own spirit. A 10- to 15-minute tour will take you through the cellar and vineyards. You'll likely want to take a bottle with you. They range in price from $10 to $30.

treats such as piñon pie, chocolate mousse, and berry cobbler. The staff is friendly and accommodating. A small inn attached to the cafe provides inexpensive rooms that are clean but a bit timeworn.

17526 NM 4, Jemez Springs, NM 87025. ✆ **505/829-3108.** www.thelaughinglizard.com. Main courses lunch $5–$10, dinner $6–$13. DISC, MC, V. May–Nov Tues–Sat 11am–8pm, Sun 11am–6pm; Dec–Apr Thurs–Sat 11am–8pm, Sun 11am–6pm.

12 THREE HISTORIC MISSIONS

These rarely visited ruins provide a unique glimpse into history. The Spanish conquistadors' Salinas Jurisdiction, on the east side of the Manzano Mountains (southeast of Albuquerque), was an important 17th-century trade center because of the salt extracted by the Native Americans from the salt lakes. Franciscan priests, utilizing native labor,

A Renovated Relic

In Mountainair, the **Shaffer Hotel and Restaurant ★**, 103 W. Main St. (✆ **505/847-2888;** www.shafferhotel.com), offers a fun glimpse into the past. Renovated by Joel Marks, who stumbled on the place while riding his Harley through the Manzano Mountains, it has a stone fireplace and molded tin ceiling, as well as original Tiffany stained glass windows. The attached restaurant is even more remarkable, with bright Southwest Art Deco murals on the ceiling, and chandeliers sporting Native American symbols. Diners enjoy huevos rancheros and breakfast burritos. Built in the 1920s by blacksmith Clem "Pop" Shaffer, it also has a curios shop named after the founder, selling turquoise jewelry, dreamcatchers, and katsinas (kachinas). The hotel includes 19 rooms, some with shared bath. The rooms are fairly basic, but will serve those who like frontier-style antique hotels. Prices range from $79 to $225.

constructed missions of Abo red sandstone and blue-gray limestone for the native converts. The ruins of some of the most durable missions—along with evidence of preexisting Anasazi and Mogollon cultures—are the highlights of a visit to Salinas Pueblo Missions National Monument. The monument consists of three separate units: the ruins of Abo, Quarai, and Gran Quivira. They are situated around the quiet town of Mountainair, 75 miles southeast of Albuquerque at the junction of US 60 and NM 55.

Abo (✆ **505/847-2400**) boasts the 40-foot-high ruins of the **Mission of San Gregorio de Abo,** a rare example of medieval architecture in the United States. **Quarai** (✆ **505/847-2290**) preserves the largely intact remains of the **Mission of La Purísima Concepción de Cuarac** (1630). Its vast size, 100 feet long and 40 feet high, contrasts with the modest size of the pueblo mounds. A small museum in the visitor center has a scale model of the original church, along with a selection of artifacts found at the site. **Gran Quivira** (✆ **505/847-2770**) once had a population of 1,500. The pueblo has 300 rooms and seven kivas. Rooms dating back to 1300 can be seen. There are indications that an older village, dating to 800, may have previously stood here. Ruins of two churches (one almost 140 ft. long) and a *convento* (convent) have been preserved. The visitor center includes a museum with many artifacts from the site and shows a 40-minute movie about the excavation of some 200 rooms, plus a short history video of the pueblo.

All three pueblos and the churches that were constructed above them are believed to have been abandoned in the 1670s. Self-guided tour pamphlets can be obtained at the units' respective visitor centers and at the **Salinas Pueblo Missions National Monument Visitor Center** in Mountainair, on US 60, 1 block west of the intersection of US 60 and NM 55. The visitor center offers an audiovisual presentation on the region's history, a bookstore, and an art exhibit.

P.O. Box 517, Mountainair. ✆ **505/847-2585.** www.nps.gov/sapu. Free admission. Sites summer daily 9am–6pm; rest of year 9am–5pm. Visitor center in Mountainair daily 8am–5pm. Closed New Year's Day, Thanksgiving, and Christmas. Abo is 9 miles west of Mountainair on US 60. Quarai is 8 miles north of Mountainair on NM 55. Gran Quivira is 25 miles south of Mountainair on NM 55. All roads are paved.

13 EN ROUTE TO SANTA FE: THE TURQUOISE TRAIL

THE TURQUOISE TRAIL ★★

Known as "the Turquoise Trail," NM 14 begins about 16 miles east of downtown Albuquerque, at I-40's Cedar Crest exit, and winds some 46 miles to Santa Fe along the east side of the Sandia Mountains. This state-designated scenic and historic route traverses the revived ghost towns of Golden, Madrid, and Cerrillos, where gold, silver, coal, and turquoise were once mined in great quantities. Modern-day settlers, mostly artists and craftspeople, have brought a renewed frontier spirit to the old mining towns.

SANDIA CREST As you start along the Turquoise Trail, you may want to turn left onto Sandia Crest Road and drive about 5 minutes to the **Tinkertown Museum,** ★ 121 Sandia Crest Rd. (✆ **505/284-5233;** www.tinkertown.com). The creation of Ross Ward, who took 40 years to carve, collect, and construct the place, it is mostly a miniatures museum, featuring dollhouse-type exhibits of a mining town, a circus, and other venues, with push buttons to make the little characters move. The building itself is constructed of glass bottles, wagon wheels, and horseshoes, among other ingredients. Great fun for the kids here. It's open daily from April 1 to November 1 from 9am to 6pm. Adults $3, children ages 4 to 16, $1.

GOLDEN Golden is approximately 10 miles north of the Sandia Park junction on NM 14. Its sagging houses, with their missing boards and the wind whistling through the broken eaves, make it a purist's ghost town. There's a general store widely known for its large selection of well-priced jewelry, as well as, across the street, a bottle seller's "glass garden." Be sure to slow down and look for the village church, a great photo opportunity, on the east side of the road. Nearby are the ruins of a pueblo called **Paako,** abandoned around 1670.

MADRID Madrid (pronounced *mah*-drid) is about 12 miles north of Golden. This town and neighboring Cerrillos were in a fabled turquoise-mining area dating back to prehistory. Gold and silver mines followed, and when they faltered, there was coal. The Turquoise Trail towns supplied fuel for the locomotives of the Santa Fe Railroad until the 1950s, when the railroad converted to diesel fuel. Madrid used to produce 100,000 tons of coal a year and was a true "company town" but the mine closed in 1956. Today, this is a village of artists and craftspeople seemingly stuck in the 1960s: Its funky, ramshackle houses have many counterculture residents who operate several crafts stores and import shops.

The **Old Coal Mine Museum and Old West Photography** (✆ **505/438-3780**) invites visitors to peek into a mine that was saved when the town was abandoned. You can see the old mine's offices, steam engines, machines, and tools. It's open daily; admission is $5 for adults, $3 for seniors, and free for children age 5 and under. You might want to have a picture taken in one of the 1,000 costumes at Old West Photography, $3 per person, $25 for one 8x10 or two 5x7s.

Next door, the **Mine Shaft Tavern** (✆ **505/473-0743**) continues its colorful career by offering a variety of burgers (try the green chile cheeseburger) and presenting live music Saturday nights and Sunday afternoons; it's open for meals in summer Monday to Thursday 11am to 6pm and Friday to Sunday 11am to 8pm. In winter, meals are served

Turquoise & Much More

Once a fabled mining town, now Madrid has become a notable arts village, a great place to wander on a sunny day. Start on the south end of town at **Al Leedom Studio,** 2485 NM 14 (✆ 505/473-2054), where the studio's namesake sells inventive glassware, made in New Mexico from recycled glass. Around the corner, step into the **Painted Horse Gallery,** 2850 NM 14 (✆ 505/473-5900), an intimate place showing modern landscape paintings by Dean Dovey, as well as jewelry and gifts. **Jezebel,** 2860 NM 14 (✆ 505/471-3795), just down the street, has lamps with dazzling slumped-glass shades. Next door, **Indigo Gallery ★**, 2584 NM 14 (✆ 505/438-6202), represents 20 artists who live in New Mexico, their colorful work ranging from realism to abstract. On the north end of town, check out **Seppanen & Daughters Fine Textiles ★**, 2879 NM 14 (✆ 505/242-7470), a quaint house draped floor to ceiling with weavings from lands as near as Navajo and as distant as Tibet.

Monday to Thursday from noon to 4pm and Friday to Sunday noon to 8pm. The bar is open in summer Sunday to Thursday 11am to 11pm and Friday to Saturday 11am to 1am. In winter the bar is open from Sunday to Thursday noon to 10pm and Friday to Saturday noon to 1am. Next door is the **Madrid Engine House Theater** (✆ **505/438-3780**), offering melodrama during the summer. Its back doors open out so a steam locomotive can take center stage. The place to eat is **Mama Lisa's Café ★**, 2859 NM 14 (✆ **505/471-5769**). You'll find salads, sandwiches, and New Mexican specialties, all prepared with fresh ingredients. During the summer, it's open Wednesday to Monday, from 11am to 4:30pm. In winter, it's open intermittently, so call ahead.

CERRILLOS AND GALISTEO Cerrillos, about 3 miles north of Madrid, is a village of dirt roads that sprawls along Galisteo Creek. It appears to have changed very little since it was founded during a lead strike in 1879; the old hotel, the saloon, and even the sheriff's office look very much like parts of an Old West movie set. You may want to stop in at **Casa Grande Trading Post,** 17 Waldo St. (✆ **505/438-3008**), a shop that was featured on PBS's *Antiques Roadshow.* You'll find lots of jewelry and rocks, as well as the **Cerrillos Turquoise Mining Museum,** full of artifacts from this region's mining era.

It's another 15 miles to Santa Fe and I-25. If, like me, you're enchanted by the Galisteo Basin, you might want to stay a night or two in nearby Galisteo at the **Galisteo Inn ★★** (✆ **866/404-8200** or 505/466-4000; www.galisteoinn.com). Set on grassy grounds under towering cottonwood trees, this 300-year-old hacienda has thick adobe walls and all the quiet a person could want. Rooms, all remodeled in 2004, are decorated with brightly painted walls and fun, bold-colored art. In their award-winning **La Mancha** restaurant, the inn serves dinner Wednesday to Saturday, and Sunday brunch; some nights live music plays on the lovely patio; in winter, hours are more limited. There's a lovely pool large enough to swim laps, a hot tub, and guided horseback riding with **Linda Vista Stables** (✆ **505/466-8930**). The inn is on NM 41, 15 miles from Cerrillos via the dirt County Road 42. For another good horseback-riding outfitter in this beautiful area, try **Broken Saddle Riding Company.** A 1¼-hour ride is $55 a person, 2-hour ride is $75, 3-hour ride is $95, and riders are grouped according to skill level. For more information, call © **505/424-7774** and listen to the recorded message, or go to www.brokensaddle.com.

If you're getting hungry on the way back to Santa Fe, stop by the **San Marcos Café** ★, 3877 NM 14, near Lone Butte (© **505/471-9298**). Set next to a feed store in a curvaceous old adobe with wood plank floors and lots of Southwest ambience, this cafe serves creative fare such as cinnamon rolls and their special eggs San Marcos—tortillas stuffed with scrambled eggs and topped with guacamole, pinto beans, jack cheese, and red chile. Open daily 8am to 2pm (cafe stops serving at 1:50pm).

7

Santa Fe

A city of 70,000 people living 7,000 feet above sea level, Santa Fe is an exotic and sophisticated place. The Native Americans enlighten the area with viewpoints and lifestyles deeply tied to nature and completely contrary to the American norm. Many of the Hispanics here still live within extended families and practice a devout Catholicism; they bring a slower pace to the city and an appreciation for deep-rooted ties. Meanwhile, a strong cosmopolitan element contributes cutting-edge cuisine, world-class opera, first-run art films, and some of the finest artwork in the world, seen easily while wandering on foot from gallery to gallery, museum to museum.

The city's history is told through its architecture. For its first 2 centuries, it was constructed mainly of adobe bricks. When the U.S. took over the territory from Mexico in 1846 and trade began flowing from the eastern states, new tools and materials began to change the face of the city. The old adobe took on brick facades and roof decoration in what became known as the Territorial style. But the flat roofs were retained so that the city never lost its unique, low profile, creating a sense of serenity found in no other U.S. city.

Bishop Jean Baptiste Lamy, the inspiration for the character of Bishop Latour in Willa Cather's *Death Comes for the Archbishop,* built the French Romanesque St. Francis Cathedral shortly after he was appointed to head the diocese in 1851. Other structures still standing include what is claimed to be the oldest house in the United States. The San Miguel Mission is the oldest mission church in the country, while the state capitol, built in the circular form of a ceremonial Indian kiva, is among the newest in the U.S.

The city was originally named La Villa Real de la Santa Fe de San Francisco de Asis (the Royal City of the Holy Faith of St. Francis of Assisi) by its founder, Spanish governor Don Pedro de Peralta. He built the Palace of the Governors as his capitol on the central plaza; today it's an excellent museum of the city's 4 centuries of history. It is one of the major attractions in the Southwest, and under its portico, Native Americans sell their crafts to eager travelers, as they have done for decades.

The plaza is the focus of numerous bustling art markets and Santa Fe's early September fiesta, celebrated annually since 1770. The fiesta commemorates the time following the years of the Pueblo revolt, when Spanish governor Don Diego de Vargas reconquered the city in 1692. The plaza was also the terminus of the Santa Fe Trail from Missouri, and of the earlier Camino Real (Royal Rd.) from Mexico, when the city thrived on the wool and fur of the Chihuahua trade. Today, a central **gazebo** makes a fun venue for summer concerts.

What captures the eye most, though, is the city's setting, backed by the rolling hills and the blue peaks of the Sangre de Cristo Mountains. In the summer, thunderheads build into giant swirling structures above those peaks and move over the city, dropping cool rain. In the winter, snow often covers the many flat-roofed adobe homes, creating a poetic abstraction that at every glance convinces you that the place itself is exotic art.

1 ORIENTATION

Part of the charm of Santa Fe is that it's so easy to get around. Like most cities of Hispanic origin, it was built around a parklike central plaza. Centuries-old adobe buildings and churches still line the narrow streets; many of them house shops, restaurants, art galleries, and museums.

Santa Fe sits high and dry at the foot of the Sangre de Cristo range. Santa Fe Baldy rises to more than 12,600 feet, a mere 12 miles northeast of the plaza. The city's downtown straddles the Santa Fe River, a tiny tributary of the Rio Grande that is little more than a trickle for much of the year. North is the Española Valley and, about 70 miles beyond that, the village of Taos (see chapter 8). South are ancient Indian turquoise mines in the Cerrillos Hills; southwest is metropolitan Albuquerque, 58 miles away (see chapter 6). To the west, across the Caja del Rio Plateau, is the Rio Grande, and beyond that, the 11,000-foot Jemez Mountains and Valle Grande, an ancient and massive volcanic caldera. Native American pueblos dot the entire Rio Grande valley; they're an hour's drive in any direction.

ARRIVING

BY PLANE Many people choose to fly into the Albuquerque International Sunport. However, if you want to save time and don't mind paying a bit more, you may be able to fly into the **Santa Fe Municipal Airport** (✆ **505/955-2900;** www.santafenm.gov), just outside the southwestern city limits on Airport Road. In conjunction with American Airlines, commuter flights will likely be offered by **American Eagle** (✆ **800/433-7300;** www.aa.com); as well, Delta Airlines (✆ **800/221-1212;** www.delta.com) is planning to begin service in late 2009

If you do fly into Albuquerque, you can rent a car or take one of the bus services. See "Getting There & Getting Around," in chapter 3, for details.

From the Santa Fe Municipal Airport, **Roadrunner Shuttle** (✆ **505/424-3367**) meets every commercial flight and takes visitors anywhere in Santa Fe. From the Albuquerque Sunport to Santa Fe, **Sandia Shuttle Express** (✆ **888/775-5696** or 505/474-5696; www.sandiashuttle.com) runs shuttles from 8:45am to 10:45pm.

BY TRAIN & BUS For detailed information about train and bus service to Santa Fe, see "Getting There & Getting Around," in chapter 3.

BY CAR I-25 skims past Santa Fe's southern city limits, connecting it along one continuous highway from Billings, Montana, to El Paso, Texas. I-40, the state's major east–west thoroughfare, which bisects Albuquerque, affords coast-to-coast access to Santa Fe. (From the west, motorists leave I-40 in Albuquerque and take I-25 north; from the east, travelers exit I-40 at Clines Corners and continue 52 miles to Santa Fe on US 285. ***Note:*** Diesel is scarce on US 285, so be sure to fill up before you leave Clines Corners.) For those coming from the northwest, the most direct route is via Durango, Colorado, on US 160, entering Santa Fe on US 84.

For information on car rentals in Albuquerque, see "Getting Around New Mexico," in chapter 3; for agencies in Santa Fe, see "Getting Around," below.

VISITOR INFORMATION

The **Santa Fe Community Convention Center and Visitors Bureau** is located downtown at 201 W. Marcy St. (P.O. Box 909), Santa Fe, NM 87504-0909 (✆ **800/777-CITY** [2489] or 505/955-6200). You can also log on to the bureau's website, at **www.santafe.org**.

CITY LAYOUT

MAIN ARTERIES & STREETS The limits of downtown Santa Fe are demarcated on three sides by the horseshoe-shaped Paseo de Peralta and on the west by St. Francis Drive, otherwise known as US 84/285. Alameda Street follows the north side of the Santa Fe River through downtown, with the State Capitol and other government buildings on the south side of the river, and most buildings of historic and tourist interest on the north, east of Guadalupe Street.

The plaza is Santa Fe's universally accepted point of orientation. Its four diagonal walkways meet at a central monument, around which a strange and wonderful assortment of people of all ages, nationalities, and lifestyles can be found at nearly any hour of the day or night.

If you stand in the center of the plaza looking north, you'll be gazing directly at the Palace of the Governors. In front of you is Palace Avenue; behind you, San Francisco Street. To your left is Lincoln Avenue, and to your right is Washington Avenue, which divides the downtown avenues into east and west. St. Francis Cathedral is the massive Romanesque structure a block east, down San Francisco Street. Alameda Street is 2 full blocks behind you.

Near the intersection of Alameda Street and Paseo de Peralta, you'll find Canyon Road running east toward the mountains. Much of this street is one-way. The best way to see it is to walk up or down, taking time to explore shops and galleries and even have lunch or dinner.

Running to the southwest from the downtown area, beginning opposite the state office buildings on Galisteo Avenue, is Cerrillos Road. Once the main north–south highway connecting New Mexico's state capital with its largest city, Albuquerque, it is now a 6-mile-long motel and fast-food strip. St. Francis Drive, which crosses Cerrillos Road 3 blocks south of Guadalupe Street, is a far less tawdry byway, linking Santa Fe with I-25, 4 miles southwest of downtown. The Old Pecos Trail, on the east side of the city, also joins downtown and the freeway. St. Michael's Drive connects the three arteries.

FINDING AN ADDRESS The city's layout makes it difficult to know exactly where to look for a particular address. It's best to call ahead for directions.

MAPS Free city and state maps can be obtained at tourist information offices. An excellent state highway map is published by the **New Mexico Department of Tourism,** 491 Old Santa Fe Trail, Lamy Building, Santa Fe, NM 87503 (✆ **800/733-6396** or 505/827-7400; www.newmexico.org; to receive a tourism guide call ✆ **800/777-CITY** [2489]). There's also a Santa Fe visitor center in the same building. More specific county and city maps are available from the **State Highway and Transportation Department,** 1120 Cerrillos Rd., Santa Fe, NM 87504 (✆ **505/827-5100**). Members of the **American Automobile Association (AAA),** 1644 St. Michael's Dr. (✆ **505/471-6620;** www.aaa.com), can obtain free maps from the AAA office. Other good regional maps can be purchased at area bookstores.

2 GETTING AROUND

The best way to see downtown Santa Fe is on foot. Free **walking-tour maps** are available at the **tourist information center,** 201 W. Marcy St. (✆ **800/777-CITY** [2489] or 505/955-6200), and several guided walking tours, as well as two self-guided tours, are included later in this chapter.

BY BUS

In 1993, Santa Fe opened **Santa Fe Trails** (✆ **505/955-2001;** www.santafenm.gov), its first public bus system. There are seven routes, and visitors can pick up a map from the Community Convention Center and Visitors Bureau. Most buses operate Monday to Friday 6am to 11pm and Saturday 8am to 8pm. There is some service on Sunday and holidays. Call for a current schedule and fare information.

BY CAR

Cars can be rented from any of the following firms in Santa Fe: **Avis,** Santa Fe Airport (✆ **505/471-5892**); **Budget,** 1946 Cerrillos Rd. (✆ **505/984-1596**); **Enterprise,** 2641A Cerrillos Rd., and 4450 Cerrillos Rd. (at the Auto Park; ✆ **505/473-3600**); and **Hertz,** Santa Fe Airport (✆ **505/471-7189**).

Note: In 2002, the Santa Fe City Council imposed a law prohibiting use of cellphones while driving within the city limits, with strict fines imposed. If you need to make a call, be sure to pull off the road.

Street parking is difficult to find during summer months. There's a metered parking lot near the federal courthouse, 2 blocks north of the plaza; a city lot behind Santa Fe Village, a block south of the plaza; and another city lot at Water and Sandoval streets. If you stop by the Santa Fe Community Convention Center and Visitors Bureau, at 201 W. Marcy St., you can pick up a wallet-size guide to Santa Fe parking areas. The map shows both street and lot parking.

BY TAXI

Cabs are difficult to flag from the street, but you can call for one. Expect to pay a standard fee of $4 for the service and an average of about $2.75 per mile. **Capital City Cab** (✆ **505/438-0000**) is the main company in Santa Fe.

BY BICYCLE

Riding a bicycle is a good way to get around town, though you'll have to ride cautiously because there are few designated bike paths. Check with **Mellow Velo,** 638 Old Santa Fe Trail (✆ **505/982-8986;** www.mellowvelo.com); **Bike-N-Sport,** 524 Cordova Rd. (✆ **505/820-0809;** www.nmbikensport.com), or **Santa Fe Mountain Sports,** 607 Cerrillos Rd. (✆ **505/988-3337;** www.santafemountainsports.com), for rentals.

Fast Facts Santa Fe

Airport See "Orientation," p. 125.

Area Code In 2007 New Mexico added a new area code. The northwestern section, including Santa Fe and Albuquerque, retained the **505** code, while the rest of the state changed to 575.

ATM Networks As in most U.S. destinations, ATMs are ubiquitous in the cities of northern New Mexico. However, in the small mountain towns, they're scarce. ATMs are linked to a network that most likely includes your bank at home. **Cirrus** (✆ **800/424-7787;** www.mastercard.com) and **PLUS** (✆ **800/843-7587;** www.visa.com) are the two most popular networks in the United States and in this region.

Babysitters Most hotels can arrange for sitters on request. Alternatively, call the professional, licensed sitter **Linda Iverson** (✆ **505/982-9327**).

Business Hours **Offices** and **stores** are generally open Monday to Friday, 9am to 5pm, with many stores also open Friday night, Saturday, and Sunday in the summer season. Most **banks** are open Monday to Thursday, 9am to 5pm, and Friday, 9am to 6pm. Some may also be open Saturday morning. Most branches have ATMs available 24 hours. Call establishments for specific hours.

Car Rentals See "Getting Around New Mexico" in chapter 3, or "Getting Around," above.

Climate See "When to Go," in chapter 3.

Currency Exchange You can exchange foreign currency at **Bank of America,** 1234 St. Michaels Dr. (✆ **505/473-8211**).

Dentists **Dr. Gilman Stenzhorn** (✆ **505/982-4317** or 505/983-4491) offers emergency service. He's located at 1496 St. Francis Dr., in the St. Francis Professional Center.

Doctors **ABQ Health Partners,** 465 St. Michaels Dr. (✆ **505/995-2400**), is open Monday to Thursday 8am to 6pm and Friday 8am to 5pm. For physician and surgeon referral and information services, call the **American Board of Medical Specialties** (✆ **866/275-2267**).

Emergencies For police, fire, or ambulance emergencies, dial ✆ **911.**

Etiquette & Customs Certain rules of etiquette should be observed when visiting the pueblos. See "Pueblo Etiquette" later in this chapter for details.

Hospitals **St. Vincent Hospital,** 455 St. Michaels Dr. (✆ **505/983-3361,** or 505/995-3934 for emergency services), is a 248-bed regional health center. Patient services include urgent and emergency-room care and ambulatory surgery. Health services are also available at the **Women's Health Services Family Care and Counseling Center** (✆ **505/988-8869**). **Ultimed,** 707 Paseo de Peralta (✆ **505/989-8707**), a new urgent-care facility near the plaza, offers comprehensive health care.

Hot Lines The following hot lines are available in Santa Fe: **battered families** (✆ **505/473-5200**), **poison control** (✆ **800/432-6866**), **psychiatric emergencies** (✆ **888/920-6333** or 505/820-6333), and **sexual assault** (✆ **505/986-9111**).

Information See "Visitor Information," under "Orientation," above.

Internet Access Head to the **Santa Fe Public Library** at 145 Washington Ave. (✆ **505/955-6780**), or retrieve your e-mail at **FedEx Office,** 301 N. Guadalupe (✆ **505/982-6311**).

Libraries The **Santa Fe Public Library** is half a block from the plaza, at 145 Washington Ave. (✆ **505/955-6780**). The Oliver La Farge Branch library is at 1730 Llano St., just off St. Michaels Drive, and the new Southside Library at 6599 Jaguar Dr., at the intersection with Country Club Road. The **New Mexico State Library** is at 1209 Camino Carlos Rey (✆ **505/476-9700**).

Liquor Laws The legal drinking age is 21 throughout New Mexico. Bars may remain open until 2am Monday to Saturday and until midnight on Sunday. Wine, beer, and spirits are sold at licensed supermarkets and liquor stores, but there are no package sales on election days until after 7pm, or on Sundays before noon. It is illegal to transport liquor through most Native American reservations.

Lost Property Contact the **city police** at ✆ **505/955-5030.**

Newspapers & Magazines The ***New Mexican***—Santa Fe's daily paper—is the oldest newspaper in the West. Its offices are at 202 E. Marcy St. (✆ **505/983-3303;** www.santafenewmexican.com). The weekly ***Santa Fe Reporter,*** 132 E. Marcy St. (✆ **505/988-5541;** www.sfreporter.com), published on Wednesdays and available free at stands all over town, is often more willing to be controversial, and its entertainment listings are excellent. Regional magazines published locally are ***New Mexico*** magazine (monthly, statewide interest; www.nmmagazine.com) and the ***Santa Fean*** magazine (six times a year, Southwestern lifestyles; www.santa fean.com).

Pharmacies **Del Norte Pharmacy,** at 1691 Galisteo St. (✆ **505/988-9797**), is open Monday to Friday, 8am to 6pm, and Saturday, 9am to 1pm. Delivery service is available.

Police In case of emergency, dial ✆ **911.** For all other inquiries, call the **Santa Fe Police Department,** 2515 Camino Entrada (✆ **505/428-3710**). The **Santa Fe County Sheriff,** with jurisdiction outside the city limits, is at 35 Camino Justicia (✆ **505/986-2400**).

Post Offices The **main post office** is at 120 S. Federal Place (✆ **505/988-2239**), 2 blocks north and 1 block west of the plaza. It's open from 8am to 5:30pm. The **Coronado Station branch** is at 2071 S. Pacheco St. (✆ **800/275-8777**) and is open Monday to Friday 8am to 6pm, and Saturday 9am to 4pm. Some of the major hotels have stamp machines and mailboxes with twice-daily pickup. The zip code for central Santa Fe is 87501.

Radio Local radio stations are **BLU** (102.9), which plays contemporary jazz, and **KBAC** (98.1), which plays alternative rock and folk music.

Safety Although the tourist district appears very safe, Santa Fe is not on the whole a safe city; theft and the number of reported rapes have risen. The good news is that Santa Fe's overall crime statistics do appear to be falling. Still, when walking the city streets, guard your purse carefully because there are many bag-grab thefts, particularly during the summer tourist months. Also, be as aware of your surroundings as you would in any other major city.

Taxes A tax of 7.937% is added to all purchases, with an additional 5% added to lodging bills.

Taxis See "Getting Around," above.

Television There are five network affiliates out of Albuquerque: **KOB-TV** (Channel 4, NBC), **KOAT-TV** (Channel 7, ABC), **KQRE-TV** (Channel 13, CBS), **KASA-TV** (Channel 2, FOX), and **KNME-TV** (Channel 5, PBS).

Time Zone New Mexico is on **Mountain Standard Time,** 1 hour ahead of the West Coast and 2 hours behind the East Coast. When it's 10am in Santa Fe, it's noon in New York, 11am in Chicago, and 9am in San Francisco. Daylight saving time is in effect from early March to early November.

Useful Telephone Numbers Information on **road conditions** in the Santa Fe area can be obtained by calling the State Highway and Transportation Department (✆ **800/432-4269**). For **time and temperature,** call ✆ **505/473-2211.**

Weather For weather forecasts, call ✆ **505/988-5151.**

3 WHERE TO STAY

The City Different offers a broad range of accommodations. From downtown hotels to Cerrillos Road motels, ranch-style resorts to quaint bed-and-breakfasts, the standard is almost universally high.

You should be aware of the seasonal nature of the tourist industry in Santa Fe. Accommodations are often booked solid through the summer months, and most places raise their prices accordingly. Rates increase even more during Indian Market, the third weekend of August. During these periods, it's essential to make reservations well in advance.

Still, there seems to be little agreement on what constitutes the tourist season; one hotel may raise its rates July 1 and lower them again in mid-September, while another may raise its rates from May to November. Some hotels recognize a shoulder season, so it pays to shop around during the in-between seasons of May through June and September through October.

No matter the season, discounts are often available to seniors, affiliated groups, corporate employees, and others. If you have any questions about your eligibility for these lower rates, be sure to ask.

A combined city-state tax of about 14.89% is added to every hotel bill in Santa Fe. And unless otherwise indicated, all recommended accommodations come with a private bathroom.

RESERVATIONS SERVICES Year-round reservation assistance is available from **Santa Fe Hotels.com** (✆ 800/745-9910), the **Accommodation Hot Line** (✆ 800/338-6877), **All Santa Fe Reservations** (✆ 877/737-7366), and **Santa Fe Stay,** which specializes in casitas (✆ 800/995-2272). **Emergency Lodging Assistance** is available free after 4pm daily (✆ 505/986-0038). All of the above are private companies and may have biases toward certain properties. Do your own research before calling.

HOTELS/MOTELS

Downtown

Everything within the horseshoe-shaped Paseo de Peralta and east a few blocks along either side of the Santa Fe River is considered downtown Santa Fe. All these accommodations are within walking distance of the plaza.

Very Expensive

Eldorado Hotel & Spa ★★ Since its opening in 1986, the Eldorado has been a model hotel for the city. In a large structure, the architects managed to meld pueblo revival style with an interesting cathedral feel, inside and out. The lobby has a high ceiling that continues into the court area and the cafe, all adorned with well over a million dollars' worth of Southwestern art. The spacious, quiet rooms received a makeover in 2006, maintaining an artistic motif, with a warm feel created by custom-made furniture in all and kiva fireplaces in many. You'll find families, businesspeople, and conference-goers staying here.

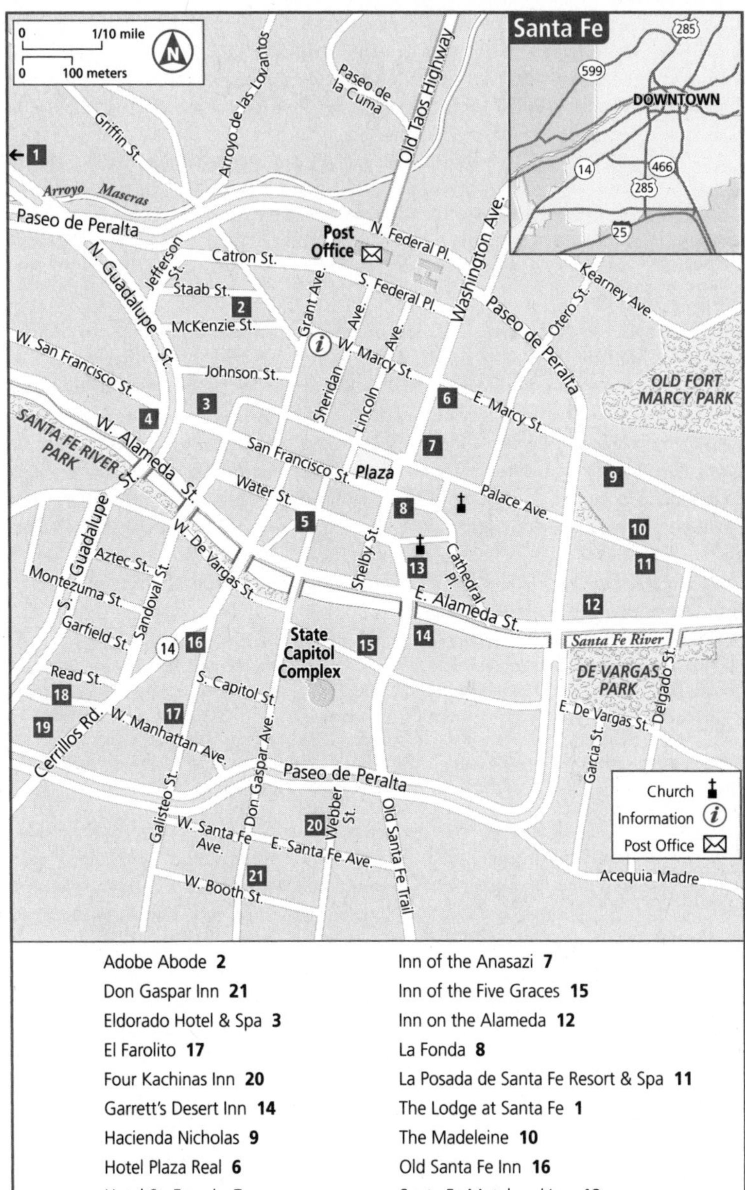

Adobe Abode **2**
Don Gaspar Inn **21**
Eldorado Hotel & Spa **3**
El Farolito **17**
Four Kachinas Inn **20**
Garrett's Desert Inn **14**
Hacienda Nicholas **9**
Hotel Plaza Real **6**
Hotel St. Francis **5**
Hotel Santa Fe **19**
Inn & Spa at Loretto **13**
Inn of the Anasazi **7**
Inn of the Five Graces **15**
Inn on the Alameda **12**
La Fonda **8**
La Posada de Santa Fe Resort & Spa **11**
The Lodge at Santa Fe **1**
The Madeleine **10**
Old Santa Fe Inn **16**
Santa Fe Motel and Inn **18**
Water Street Inn **4**

Most of the rooms have views of downtown Santa Fe, many from balconies. If you're really indulging, join the ranks of Mick Jagger, Geena Davis, and King Juan Carlos of Spain and try the penthouse five-room presidential suite for $1,500 per night. The Nidah Spa offers a full range of treatments, including a turquoise gemstone therapy, worth sampling. The Eldorado also manages the nearby Zona Rosa condominiums, which are two-, three-, and four-bedroom suites with full kitchens. The hotel's innovative and elegant restaurant, the Old House, serves creative American cuisine.

309 W. San Francisco St., Santa Fe, NM 87501. ✆ **800/955-4455** or 505/988-4455. Fax 505/995-4544. www.eldoradohotel.com. 219 units. $139–$389 double. Seasonal package rates are available. AE, DC, DISC, MC, V. Valet parking $18 per night. Pets accepted. **Amenities:** 2 restaurants; bar; heated rooftop pool; medium-size health club (w/view); Jacuzzi; his-and-hers saunas and steam baths; spa; concierge; business center; salon; room service; massage; laundry service; dry cleaning. *In room:* A/C, TV, high-speed Internet, minibar, coffeemaker, hair dryer, iron, safe.

Inn & Spa at Loretto ★★ This much-photographed hotel, just 2 blocks from the plaza, was built in 1975 to resemble Taos Pueblo. Light and shadow dance upon the five-level structure as the sun crosses the sky. With a multi-million-dollar renovation in 2008, this has become a comfortable and elegant place to stay. The medium-size rooms employ a Navajo motif, with comfortable beds and fine linens, while the medium-size baths have fine tiling and robes. Be aware that the Loretto likes convention traffic, so sometimes service lags for travelers. Overall, it is fairly quiet and has nice views—especially on the northeast side, where you'll see both the historic St. Francis Cathedral and the Loretto Chapel (with its "miraculous" spiral staircase; see "More Attractions," later in the chapter). The Spa Terre offers a range of treatments, from facials to massages, in intimate, Southwest-meets-Asia rooms.

211 Old Santa Fe Trail (P.O. Box 1417), Santa Fe, NM 87501. ✆ **800/727-5531** or 505/988-5531. Fax 505/984-7968. www.innatloretto.com. 134 units. Jan–Mar $179–$279 double; Apr–June $189–$349 double; July–Oct $199–$499 double; Nov–Dec $179–$299 double. Additional person $30. Children 17 and under stay free in parent's room. Resort fee of $10 per night. AE, DC, DISC, MC, V. Valet parking $16 per night. AE, DC, DISC, MC, V. **Amenities:** Restaurant; lounge; outdoor pool (heated year-round); spa; exercise room; concierge; business center w/audiovisual conferencing equipment; room service; valet laundry. *In room:* A/C, TV, Wi-Fi, coffeemaker, hair dryer, iron.

Inn of the Anasazi ★★★ The designers of this fine luxury hotel have crafted a feeling of grandness in a very limited space. A 2006 remodel added even finer touches, including new bedding and decor in the rooms, with bold splashes of color from artwork and weavings. Flagstone floors and vigas create a warm and welcoming ambience that evokes the feeling of an Anasazi cliff dwelling. Oversize cacti complete the look. Accents are appropriately Navajo, in a nod to the fact that the Navajo live in the area the Anasazi once inhabited. A half-block off the plaza, this hotel was built in 1991 to cater to travelers who know their hotels. On the ground floor are a living room and library with oversize furniture and replicas of Anasazi pottery and Navajo rugs. The rooms range from medium-size to spacious, with pearl-finished walls, comfortable four-poster beds, and novelties such as iron candle sconces, gaslit kiva fireplaces (in some), and humidifiers. All the rooms are quiet and comfortable, though none have dramatic views. Though this is still a great hotel, a recent visit left me asking if it was worth the price. The Anasazi Restaurant (p. 145) serves creative Southwestern cuisine.

113 Washington Ave., Santa Fe, NM 87501. ✆ **800/688-8100** or 505/988-3030. Fax 505/988-3277. www.innoftheanasazi.com. 57 units. Jan 5–Feb 26 $269–$469; Feb 27–Apr 28 $325–$525; Apr 29–Jan 4 $325–$525 double. AE, DC, DISC, MC, V. Valet parking $15 per day. **Amenities:** Restaurant (p. 145); concierge;

room service; in-room massage; laundry service; library/boardroom. *In room:* A/C, TV/DVD, Wi-Fi, coffeemaker, hair dryer, iron, safe.

Inn of the Five Graces ★★ *Finds* In the historic Barrio de Analco, just a few blocks from the Plaza, this inn holds true to its stated theme: "Here the Orient and the Old West meet, surprisingly at home in each other's arms." With floral-decked courtyards, elaborately decorated suites with kilim rugs, ornately carved beds, and often beautiful mosaic tile work in the bathrooms, this is truly a "sheik" place. All but a few suites are medium size, most with small bathrooms, and some with fireplaces. The lower-priced rooms are smaller. Request one of the suites in the buildings on the north side of East de Vargas Street; they're more spacious and substantially built. Travelers seeking an exotic stay will like this place; it's of the same caliber as Inn of the Anasazi, but with more flair. The inn's biggest news is the purchase of the **Pink Adobe** (p. 150) next door, which they've turned into their restaurant. All rooms have robes, stocked fridges, patios, and CD players; some have kitchenettes. Wine and cheese hour is offered every other day. This is a non-tipping property and all amenities are included with the room rate. Wi-Fi access is available in the lobby.

150 E. de Vargas St., Santa Fe, NM 87501. ✆ **505/992-0957.** www.fivegraces.com. 23 units. $400–$900 double, depending on the season and type of room. Price includes full breakfast with specialty items and afternoon treats. AE, MC, V. Free parking. Pets welcome with fee and deposit. **Amenities:** Restaurant; lounge; concierge. *In room:* A/C, TV, CD player, fridge, coffeemaker, hair dryer, iron, microwave.

La Fonda ★ Whether you stay in this hotel or not, it's worth strolling through just to get a sense of how Santa Fe once was—and in some ways still is. Located right on the plaza, this was the inn at the end of the Santa Fe Trail; it saw trappers, traders, and merchants, as well as notables such as President Rutherford B. Hayes and General Ulysses S. Grant. The original inn was dying of old age in 1920 when it was razed and replaced by the current La Fonda. Its architecture is pueblo revival: imitation adobe with wooden balconies and beam ends protruding over the tops of windows. Inside, the lobby is rich and slightly dark, with people bustling about, sitting in the cafe, and buying jewelry from Native Americans.

The hotel has seen some renovation through the years, as well as a whole new wing to the east, where you'll find deluxe suites and new meeting spaces. If you want a feel of the real Santa Fe, this is the place to stay. Overall, however, this hotel isn't the model of refinement. For that, you'd best go to the Hotel Santa Fe or other newer places. No two rooms are the same here, and while each has its own funky touch, some are more kitsch than quaint. Some have refrigerators, fireplaces, and private balconies. A recently added spa offers a variety of treatments ranging from massages to salt glows, as well as a sauna and Jacuzzi. The Bell Tower Bar is the highest point in downtown Santa Fe—a great place for a cocktail and a view of the city.

100 E. San Francisco St. (P.O. Box 1209), Santa Fe, NM 87501. ✆ **800/523-5002** or 505/982-5511. Fax 505/988-2952. www.lafondasantafe.com. 167 units. $219–$319 standard double; $239–$319 deluxe double; $349–$549 suite. Additional person $15. Children 11 and under stay free in parent's room. AE, DC, DISC, MC, V. Parking $10 per day in a covered garage. **Amenities:** Restaurant; 2 bars; outdoor pool; spa; exercise room; Jacuzzi; concierge; tour desk; business center; room service; babysitting; laundry service; dry cleaning. *In room:* A/C, TV, Wi-Fi, coffeemaker, hair dryer, iron, safe.

La Posada de Santa Fe Resort and Spa ★★ If you're in the mood to stay in a little New Mexico adobe village, you'll enjoy this luxury hotel just 3 blocks from the plaza. It's especially nice in the summer, when surrounded by acres of green grass. Here, you get to experience squeaky maple floors, vigas and *latillas,* and, in many rooms, kiva fireplaces. Be aware that unless you've secured a suite, most rooms tend to be fairly small. Fortunately, the hotel benefited from major remodels in recent years, including a $6-million one in 2008, so all the bathrooms are modern and the rooms have fine linens and comfortable beds. Most notable are the Zen-Southwestern–style spa rooms, as well as a few "gallery suites," appointed with original artwork from some of the region's most prestigious artists. Travelers who are reluctant to trust the whims of older adobe construction should reserve one of the spa rooms or any of the other 40 newer rooms. Most rooms don't have views but have outdoor patios, and most are tucked back into the quiet compound. The top-notch onsite restaurant, Fuego (p. 148), serves artfully prepared international cuisine in a romantic, Spanish-colonial dining room. The Rockresorts Spa offers a full range of treatments.

330 E. Palace Ave., Santa Fe, NM 87501. ✆ **800/727-5276** or 505/986-0000. Fax 505/982-6850. www.rockresorts.com. 157 units. $239–$359 double; suites $449 and way up, depending on the season. Various spa packages available. AE, DC, DISC, MC, V. $30 resort fee per day includes parking. **Amenities:** 2 restaurants; bar; outdoor pool; exercise room; spa w/full treatments; Jacuzzi; conference center; concierge; salon; room service; in-room massage; babysitting; dry cleaning. *In room:* A/C, TV, DVD, Wi-Fi, CD player, minibar, coffeemaker, hair dryer, iron, safe.

Expensive

Don Gaspar Inn ★★ Finds If you'd like to pretend that you live in Santa Fe during your vacation, that you're blessed with your very own Southwestern-style home, in a historic neighborhood, full of artful touches such as Native American tapestries and a kiva fireplace, this is your inn. A 10-minute walk from the plaza, the Don Gaspar occupies three homes, connected by brilliant gardens and brick walkways. Rooms vary in size, though all are plenty spacious, most with patios, some with kitchenettes, and there's even a full house for rent. Travelers looking for an adventure beyond a hotel stay, but without the close interaction of a B&B, enjoy this place. Though the rooms don't have views, all are quiet. The Courtyard Casita, with a kitchenette and a sleeper couch in its own room, is nice for a small family. The Territorial Suite, with carpet throughout and Italian marble in the bath, is perfect for a romantic getaway. All rooms have bathrobes and fireplaces. The friendly and dedicated staff serves a full breakfast such as green-chile stew with fresh baked items on the patio under a peach tree (the fruit from which they make cobbler) in the warm months and in the atrium in winter.

623 Don Gaspar Ave., Santa Fe, NM 87505. ✆ **888/986-8664** or 505/986-8664. Fax 505/986-0696. www.dongaspar.com. 12 units. $118–$165 double; $165–$205 suite; $185–$245 casita; $295–$355 house. Rates include full breakfast. AE, MC, V. Free parking. **Amenities:** Babysitting; same-day laundry service. *In room:* A/C, TV/DVD, high-speed Internet, hair dryer, iron.

Hotel Plaza Real ★ Value This New Orleans–meets–Santa Fe Territorial–style hotel built in 1990 provides comfortable rooms near the plaza. The construction and decor of the lobby are rustically elegant, built around a fireplace with balconies perched above. Clean and attractively decorated rooms have Southwestern-style furniture, many with French doors opening onto balconies or terraces that surround a quiet courtyard decorated with *ristras* (strung chiles). Beds are comfortably soft and baths small but with an outer sink vanity. The junior suites have an especially nice layout, with a sitting area near a fireplace and good light from the north and south. In recent years, the hotel has been receiving some needed upgrades.

125 Washington Ave., Santa Fe, NM 87501. ✆ **877/901-7666** or 505/988-4900. Fax 505/983-9322. www.hhandr.com. 56 units. $119–$149 double; $149–$289 suite, depending on time of year and type of room.

Additional person $20. Children 11 and under stay free in parent's room. AE, DC, DISC, MC, V. Parking $12 per day. Pets $50 per stay. **Amenities:** Lounge; laundry service; dry cleaning. *In room:* A/C, TV, Wi-Fi, coffeemaker, hair dryer, iron.

Hotel St. Francis ★ If you long for the rich fabrics, fine antiques, and slow pace of a European hotel, this is your place. The building was first constructed in the 1880s; it became fairly dilapidated but was renovated in 1986. Now elegantly redecorated, the lobby is crowned by a Victorian fireplace with hovering cherubs, a theme repeated throughout the hotel. The small rooms continue the European decor, each with its own unique bent. You'll find a fishing room, a golf room, a garden room, and a music room, with each motif evoked by the furnishings: a vintage set of golf clubs here, a sheet of music in a dry-flower arrangement there. The hotel, which attracts individual travelers as well as families and many Europeans, is well cared for by a concierge who speaks six languages. Enjoy high tea in the lobby from 3 to 5:30pm daily. Request a room facing east, and you'll wake each day to a view of the mountains, seen through lovely lace. Larger rooms have coffeemakers and hair dryers.

210 Don Gaspar Ave., Santa Fe, NM 87501. ✆ **800/529-5700** or 505/983-5700. Fax 505/989-7690. www.hotelstfrancis.com. 82 units. $99–$349 all rooms, depending on the season. Children 11 and under stay free in parent's room. AE, DC, DISC, MC, V. Parking $5 per day. **Amenities:** Restaurant; bar; exercise room; access to nearby spa; concierge; room service; laundry service; dry cleaning; library and gaming tables. *In room:* A/C, TV, Wi-Fi, fridge, iron, safe.

Hotel Santa Fe ★ (Finds About a 10-minute walk south of the plaza you'll find this newer three-story establishment, the only Native American–owned hotel in Santa Fe. It is a good choice for consistent, well-planned lodgings. Picuris Pueblo is the majority stockholder here, and part of the pleasure of staying here is the culture the Picuris bring to your visit. This is not to say that you'll get any sense of the rusticity of a pueblo in your accommodations—this sophisticated hotel, built in the late 1980s, is decorated in Southwestern style, with a few novel aspects such as an Allan Houser bronze buffalo dancer watching over the front desk and a fireplace surrounded by comfortable furniture in the lobby. The rooms are medium size, with clean lines and comfortable beds, the decor accented with pine Taos-style furniture. Rooms on the north side get less street noise from Cerrillos Road and have better views of the mountains, but they don't have the sun shining onto their balconies. You will get a strong sense of the Native American presence on the patio during the summer, when Picuris dancers come to perform and bread bakers uncover the *horno* (oven) and prepare loaves for sale. Wireless Internet access is available in the lobby.

1501 Paseo de Peralta, Santa Fe, NM 87501. ✆ **800/825-9876** or 505/982-1200. Fax 505/984-2211. www.hotelsantafe.com. 163 units. $129–$199 double; $239–$459 suite, depending on the season. Hacienda rooms and suites $199–$459. Additional person $20. Children 17 and under stay free in parent's room. AE, DC, DISC, MC, V. Free parking. Pets accepted with $20 fee. **Amenities:** Restaurant; outdoor pool; Jacuzzi; concierge; car-rental desk; room service; in-room massage; babysitting; dry cleaning. *In room:* A/C, TV, high-speed Internet, minibar, iron, safe.

Inn on the Alameda ★★ Just across the street from the bosque-shaded Santa Fe River sits the Inn on the Alameda, a cozy stop for those who like the services of a hotel with the intimacy of an inn. Built in 1986, with additions over the years, it's now a little like a village, with a number of buildings and casitas. All are pueblo-style adobe, ranging in age, but most were built in the late 1980s. The owner, Joe Schepps, appreciates traditional Southwestern style; he's used red brick in the dining area and Mexican *equipae* (wicker) furniture in the lobby, as well as thick vigas and shiny *latillas* in a sitting area set around a grand fireplace. The rooms follow a similar good taste, some with refrigerators, CD players, safes, and kiva fireplaces. All rooms have comfortable beds, good linens, robes, and well planned bathrooms with tile. The trees surrounding the inn—cottonwoods and aspens—add a bit of a rural feel to the property. If you're an art shopper, this is an ideal spot because it's a quick walk to Canyon Road. A full-service bar is open nightly. Breakfast is delicious, with bakery items and always a hot dish.

303 E. Alameda, Santa Fe, NM 87501. ✆ **800/289-2122** or 505/984-2121. Fax 505/986-8325. www.innonthealameda.com. 71 units. $125–$240 queen; $140–$245 king; $255–$390 suites; additional adult $25; reduced off-season rates are available. Rates include breakfast and afternoon wine and cheese reception. AE, DC, DISC, MC, V. Free parking. Small pets under 30 pounds welcome with $30 fee. **Amenities:** Bar; medium-size fitness facility; 2 open-air Jacuzzis; concierge; massage; child care by arrangement; coin-op laundry; same-day dry cleaning; pet amenities and a pet-walking map. *In room:* A/C, TV, high-speed Internet, hair dryer, iron.

Moderate

Garrett's Desert Inn (Value) Completion of this hotel in 1957 prompted the Historic Design Review Board to implement zoning restrictions throughout downtown. Apparently, residents were appalled by the huge air conditioners adorning the roof. Though they're still unsightly, the hotel offers decent accommodations just 3 blocks from the plaza. It's a clean, two-story, concrete-block building around a broad parking lot. The hotel underwent a complete remodel in 1994, with touch-ups through the years, though new carpet and updated furnishings are now needed. It has managed to maintain some '50s touches, such as Art Deco tile in the bathrooms and plenty of space in the rooms. If you're traveling in winter, ask for a south-facing room and you might be able to sunbathe under the portal. Minisuites have refrigerators and microwaves. The outdoor pool here is one of the nicest in town.

311 Old Santa Fe Trail, Santa Fe, NM 87501. ✆ **800/888-2145** or 505/982-1851. Fax 505/989-1647. www.garrettsdesertinn.com. 83 units. $89–$169, depending on season and type of room. AE, DISC, MC, V. **Amenities:** Restaurant; outdoor pool heated year-round. *In room:* A/C, TV, Wi-Fi, coffeemaker, hair dryer.

Old Santa Fe Inn ★ (Finds) Want to stay downtown and savor Santa Fe–style ambience without wearing out your plastic? This is your hotel. A multi-million-dollar renovation to this 1930s court motel has created a comfortable, quiet inn just a few blocks from the plaza. Rooms verge on small but are decorated with such lovely handcrafted colonial-style furniture that you probably won't mind. All have small Mexican-tiled bathrooms, and some have gas fireplaces and DVD players. You have a choice of king, queen, or twin bedrooms as well as suites. Breakfast is served in an atmospheric dining room next to a comfortable library. This inn jacks prices *way* up during special event times such as the Indian Market.

320 Galisteo St., Santa Fe, NM 87501. ✆ **800/745-9910** or 505/995-0800. Fax 505/995-0400. www.oldsantafeinn.com. 43 units. $90–$450 depending on season. Rates include continental breakfast. AE, DC, DISC, MC, V. *In room:* A/C, TV, Wi-Fi, coffeemaker.

Santa Fe Motel and Inn ★ If you like walking to the plaza and restaurants but don't want to pay big bucks, this little compound is a good choice. Rooms here are larger than at the Old Santa Fe Inn and have more personality than those at Garrett's Desert Inn. Ask for one of the casitas in back—you'll pay more but get a little turn-of-the-20th-century charm, plus more quiet and privacy. Some have vigas; others have skylights, fireplaces, and patios. The main part of the motel, built in 1955, is two-story Territorial style, with upstairs rooms that open onto a portal with a bit of a view. All guest rooms are decorated with a Southwest motif and some have antique furnishings. All have

Kids Family-Friendly Hotels

Bishop's Lodge Ranch Resort & Spa (p. 137) Riding lessons, tennis courts with instruction, a pool with a lifeguard, a stocked trout pond just for kids, a summer daytime program, horseback trail trips, and more make this a veritable day camp for all ages.

El Rey Inn (p. 139) A picnic area and playground in a courtyard set back away from the street make this a nice place for families to commune in summer.

The Lodge at Santa Fe (p. 138) Built above the city, with a bit of a country-club feel, this place offers a nice outdoor pool and condo units that serve family needs well.

Residence Inn (p. 138) Spacious suites house families comfortably. An outdoor pool, fully equipped kitchens, patio grills, and a grocery-shopping service add to the appeal.

Santa Fe Sage Inn (p. 137) With its fenced-in pool and reasonable prices, this is a good spot for families.

medium-size baths and comfortable beds. Some rooms have kitchenettes, with refrigerators, microwaves, stoves, coffeemakers, and toasters. A full breakfast, including Sage Bakehouse bread, is served each morning in the Southwest-style dining room or on a quaint patio.

510 Cerrillos Rd., Santa Fe, NM 87501. ✆ **800/930-5002** or 505/982-1039. Fax 505/986-1275. www.santafemotel.com. 23 units. $80–$149, depending on the season and type of room. Additional person $10. Rates include full breakfast. AE, DC, MC, V. Free parking. *In room:* A/C, TV, high-speed Internet, hair dryer, iron.

Inexpensive

Santa Fe Sage Inn Value Kids If you're looking for a convenient, almost-downtown location at a reasonable price, this is one of your best bets. This two-story stucco adobe motel with portals is spread through three buildings and is about a 10-minute walk from the plaza. Built in 1985, it was remodeled in 2005. The smallish rooms have Southwestern furnishings, with comfortable beds and small baths. There's a park in the back and an outdoor pool set in a secluded fenced area, a good place for kids. To avoid street noise, ask for a room at the back of the property.

725 Cerrillos Rd., Santa Fe, NM 87501. ✆ **866/433-0335** or 505/982-5952. Fax 505/984-8879. www.santafesageinn.com. 160 units. $58–$95 double. Rates include continental breakfast. Additional person $10. AE, DC, DISC, MC, V. Free parking. **Amenities:** Outdoor pool. *In room:* A/C, TV, Wi-Fi, coffeemaker, hairdryer, iron.

The North Side

Within easy reach of the plaza, the north side encompasses the area that lies north of the loop of Paseo de Peralta.

Very Expensive

Bishop's Lodge Ranch Resort & Spa ★★★ Moments This resort holds special significance for me because my parents met in the lodge and were later married in the chapel. It's a place rich with history. More than a century ago, when Bishop Jean-Baptiste

Lamy was the spiritual leader of northern New Mexico's Roman Catholic population, he often escaped clerical politics by hiking into this valley called Little Tesuque. He built a retreat and a humble chapel (now on the National Register of Historic Places) with high-vaulted ceilings and a hand-built altar. Today, Lamy's 450-acre getaway has become Bishop's Lodge.

In recent years, a $17-million renovation spruced up the place and added a spa and 8,000 square feet of meeting space. The guest rooms, spread through many buildings, feature handcrafted furniture and regional artwork. The traditional rooms are medium size with the rustic feel of the historic buildings they occupy; many have balconies or patios. The newer Ridge Rooms are spacious, with high ceilings, vigas, gas fireplaces, patios or balconies, and most with views. All rooms have comfortable beds with fine linens and tile baths with the hotel's own signature bath products. The newest addition are villas: spectacular two- and three-bedroom town houses, filled with amenities, including full kitchens, fireplaces, patios, and views, a great option for families or couples who travel together. The Bishop's Lodge is an active resort three seasons of the year, with activities such as horseback riding, nature walks, and cookouts; in the winter, it takes on the character of a romantic country retreat. A children's program keeps kids busy for much of the day. Wireless Internet is available in the lobby and conference areas. As well as the tranquility and peace of an Old World resort, this place offers excellent service.

Bishop's Lodge Rd. (P.O. Box 2367), Santa Fe, NM 87504. ✆ **505/983-6377.** Fax 505/989-8939. www.bishopslodge.com. 111 units. Summer $399–$489 double; fall and spring $299–$399 double; midwinter $189–$269 double. Villas $550–$1,500. Resort fee $15 per person per day. Additional person $15. Children 3 and under stay free in parent's room. Ask about packages that include meals. AE, DC, DISC, MC, V. Free parking. **Amenities:** Restaurant; outdoor pool; tennis courts; spa; Jacuzzi; concierge; courtesy shuttle; room service; in-room massage; babysitting; laundry service. *In room:* A/C, TV, high-speed Internet, fridge, coffeemaker, hair dryer, iron, safe.

Expensive

The Lodge at Santa Fe ★ Kids Set on a hill as you head north toward the Santa Fe Opera, this three-story hotel is a convenient and relaxing place to stay. The new theme here is Native American, with Anasazi-style stacked sandstone throughout the lobby and dining room, a theme that carries into the guest rooms. They are medium size, decorated in earth tones with bold prints, some with views of the mountains, others overlooking the pool. Premium rooms are more spacious, some with large living rooms and private balconies. Each parlor suite has a Murphy bed and kiva fireplace in the living room, a big dining area, a wet bar and refrigerator, and a jetted bathtub. The condo units nearby come with fully equipped kitchens, fireplaces, and private decks.

750 N. St. Francis Dr., Santa Fe, NM 87501. ✆ **800/LODGESF** (563-4373) or 505/992-5800. Fax 505/992-5856. www.lodgeatsantafe.com. 135 units. $89–$179 double; $129–$199 suite; $200–$300 condo. AE, DC, DISC, MC, V. Free parking. **Amenities:** Outdoor pool; free shuttle service to downtown. *In room:* A/C, TV, high-speed Internet, Wi-Fi, hair dryer, iron.

The South Side

Santa Fe's major strip, Cerrillos Road, is US 85, the main route to and from Albuquerque and the I-25 freeway. It's about 5¼ miles from the plaza to the Santa Fe Place, which marks the southern boundary of the city. Most motels are on this strip, although several of them are to the east, closer to St. Francis Drive (US 84) or the Las Vegas Highway.

Expensive

Residence Inn by Marriott ★ Kids Designed to look like a neighborhood, this inn provides the efficient stay you'd expect from a Marriott, and a renovation in 2006 brought freshness to the rooms and some common areas. It's a 10-minute drive away from the plaza, through a few quiet neighborhoods. The lobby and breakfast area are warmly decorated in tile, with a fireplace and Southwestern accents such as *bancos* and drums. There are three sizes of suites, each roomy, each with a fully equipped kitchen. All rooms have fireplaces and balconies and are decorated with Southwestern furnishings. Outside, there are plenty of amenities to keep family members happy, including barbecue grills on the patio. Most who stay here are leisure travelers, but you'll also encounter some government workers and business travelers, all of whom benefit from free high-speed Internet access. Guests gather for complimentary hors d'oeuvres Monday through Wednesday from 5 to 6:30pm.

1698 Galisteo St., Santa Fe, NM 87505. ✆ **800/331-3131** or 505/988-7300. Fax 505/988-3243. www.marriott.com. 120 units. $109–$199 studio suite; $149–$259 studio double suite; $159–$279 penthouse suite. Rates vary according to season and include hot breakfast buffet and Mon–Wed evening hors d'oeuvres. AE, DC, DISC, MC, V. Free parking. **Amenities:** Outdoor pool; sports court; exercise room; 3 Jacuzzis; coin-op laundry; laundry service; dry cleaning; jogging trail. *In room:* A/C, TV, kitchen, high-speed Internet.

Moderate

El Rey Inn ★ (Finds) (Kids) Staying at "the King" makes you feel like you're traveling the old Route 66 through the Southwest. The white stucco buildings of this court motel are decorated with bright trim around the doors and hand-painted Mexican tiles on the walls. Opened in the 1930s, it received additions in the 1950s, and remodeling is ongoing. No two rooms are alike. The oldest section, nearest the lobby, feels a bit cramped, though the rooms have style, with Art Deco tile in the bathrooms and vigas on the ceilings. Some have little patios. Be sure to request a room as far back as possible from Cerrillos Road. The two stories of suites around the Spanish colonial courtyard are sweet deals. These rooms make you feel like you're at a Spanish inn, with carved furniture and cozy couches. Some rooms have kitchenettes. To the north sit 10 deluxe units around the courtyard. These rooms offer more upscale amenities and gas log fireplaces, as well as distinctive furnishings and artwork. A complimentary continental breakfast is served in a sunny room or on a terrace in the warmer months. There's also a sitting room with a library and games tables, as well as a picnic area, a playground, and an exercise room. Wireless Internet access is available in the lobby.

1862 Cerrillos Rd. (P.O. Box 4759), Santa Fe, NM 87502. ✆ **800/521-1349** or 505/982-1931. Fax 505/989-9249. www.elreyinnsantafe.com. 86 units. $99–$165 double; $125–$225 suite. Rates include continental breakfast. AE, DC, DISC, MC, V. Free parking. **Amenities:** Outdoor pool; exercise room; 2 Jacuzzis; sauna; coin-op laundry. *In room:* A/C, TV, fridge, coffeemaker, hair dryer, iron, safe.

Inexpensive

La Quinta Inn (Value) Though it's a good 15-minute drive from the plaza, this is my choice of economical Cerrillos Road chain hotels. Built in 1986, it has had ongoing remodeling to keep the rooms comfortable and tasteful. The rooms within the three-story building have an unexpectedly elegant feel, with lots of deep colors and Art Deco tile in the bathrooms. There's plenty of space in these rooms, and they're lit for mood as well as for reading. A complimentary continental breakfast is served in the intimate lobby. The outdoor kidney-shaped pool has a nice lounging area and is open and heated May to October. The hotel is just across a parking lot from the Santa Fe Place mall, which shoppers and moviegoers will appreciate. The Flying Tortilla coffee shop is adjacent.

4298 Cerrillos Rd., Santa Fe, NM 87507. ✆ **800/531-5900** or 505/471-1142. Fax 505/438-7219. www.lq.com. 130 units. June to mid-Oct $92–$115 double; late Oct to May $79–$89 double. Children 18 and under stay free in parent's room. Discount for AAA members. Rates include continental breakfast. AE, DC,

Greater Santa Fe

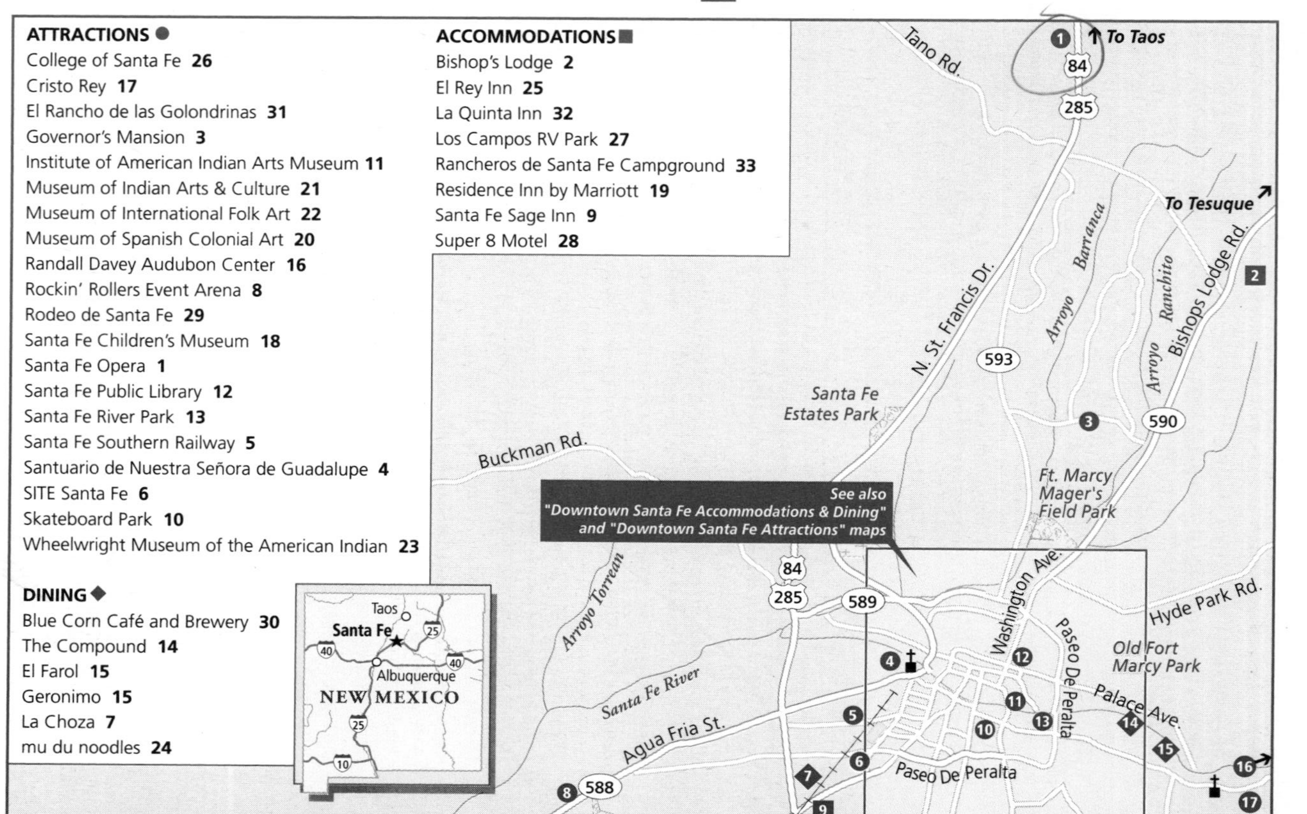

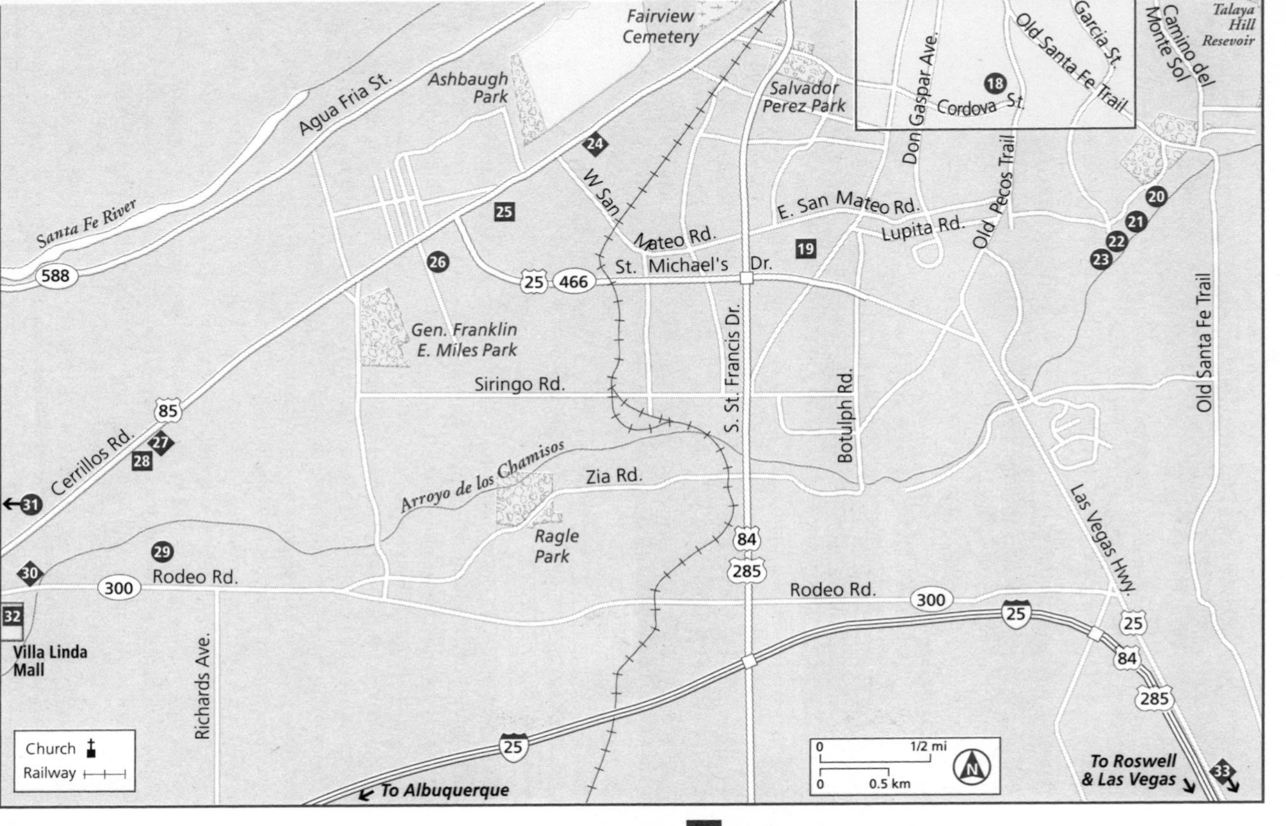
Fairview Cemetery
Ashbaugh Park
Agua Fria St.
Santa Fe River
Salvador Perez Park
Don Gaspar Ave.
Cordova St.
Old Santa Fe Trail
Garcia St.
Camino del Monte Sol
Talaya Hill Resevoir
W San Mateo Rd.
E. San Mateo Rd.
Lupita Rd.
Old Pecos Trail
St. Michael's Dr.
Gen. Franklin E. Miles Park
Siringo Rd.
S. St. Francis Dr.
Botulph Rd.
Old Santa Fe Trail
Cerrillos Rd.
Arroyo de los Chamisos
Zia Rd.
Ragle Park
Las Vegas Hwy.
Rodeo Rd.
Rodeo Rd.
Villa Linda Mall
Richards Ave.
Church
Railway
To Albuquerque
0 1/2 mi
0 0.5 km
N
To Roswell & Las Vegas

DISC, MC, V. Free parking. Maximum 2 pets stay free. **Amenities:** Outdoor heated pool; coin-op laundry; executive-level rooms. *In room:* A/C, TV, Wi-Fi, coffeemaker, hair dryer, iron.

Super 8 Motel (Value) It's nothing flashy, but this pink-stucco, boxy motel, which has received the Pride of Super 8 award, attracts regulars who know precisely what to expect. You'll get a clean room with a comfortable bed or beds and a few other amenities at a great price.

3358 Cerrillos Rd., Santa Fe, NM 87507. ✆ **800/800-8000** or 505/471-8811. Fax 505/471-3239. www.super8.com. 96 units. $47–$80 double, depending on the season. Rates include continental breakfast. AE, DC, DISC, MC, V. Free parking. **Amenities:** Coin-op laundry. *In room:* A/C, TV, Wi-Fi, coffeemaker, safe.

BED & BREAKFASTS

If you prefer a homey, intimate setting to the sometimes-impersonal ambience of a large hotel, one of Santa Fe's bed-and-breakfast inns may be right for you. All those listed here are in or close to the downtown area and offer comfortable accommodations at expensive to moderate prices.

Adobe Abode ★ A short walk from the plaza, in the same quiet residential neighborhood as the Georgia O'Keeffe Museum, Adobe Abode is one of Santa Fe's most imaginative B&Bs. The living room is cozy, decorated with folk art. The creativity shines in each of the guest rooms as well, some in the main house, which was built in 1907. Others, in back, are newer. The Galisteo Suite is decorated with Spanish colonial furniture and artwork, while the Bronco Room is filled with cowboy paraphernalia: hats, Pendleton blankets, pioneer chests, and an entire shelf lined with children's cowboy boots. Two rooms have fireplaces, and several have private patios. Complimentary sherry, fruit, and cookies are served daily in the living room. Every morning, a full breakfast of fresh fruit and a hot dish such as green-chile corn soufflé is served in the country-style kitchen.

202 Chapelle St., Santa Fe, NM 87501. ✆ **505/983-3133.** Fax 505/983-3132. www.adobeabode.com. 6 units. $165–$205 double. Rates include breakfast and afternoon snacks. DISC, MC, V. Limited free parking. *In room:* A/C, TV, Wi-Fi, coffeemaker, hair dryer, iron.

El Farolito ★★ The owners of this inn, which is within walking distance of the plaza, have created an authentic theme experience for guests in each room. The themes include the Native American Room, decorated with rugs and pottery; the South-of-the-Border Room, with Mexican folk art with a full-size sleeper sofa; and the elegant Santa Fe–style Opera Room, with hand-carved, lavishly upholstered furniture. A two-room suite has been added in the main building, with a queen-size iron bed and Southwestern decor. The walls of most of the rooms are rubbed with beeswax during plastering to give them a smooth, golden finish. All rooms have kiva fireplaces and private patios. The common area displays works by notable New Mexico artists. Part of the inn was built before 1912, and the rest is new, but the old-world elegance carries through. For breakfast, the focus is on healthy food with a little decadence thrown in. You'll enjoy fresh fruit and home-baked breads and pastries. Under the same stellar ownership (but a little less expensive) is the nearby **Four Kachinas Inn** ★ (✆ **888/634-8782;** www.fourkachinas.com), where Southwestern-style rooms sit around a sunny courtyard. A little less lavish than those at El Farolito, these rooms are sparkly clean, all with patios.

514 Galisteo St., Santa Fe, NM 87501. ✆ **888/634-8782** or 505/988-1631. Fax 505/988-4589. www.farolito.com. 8 units. $150–$280 casita. Rates include hot entree breakfast buffet. AE, DISC, MC, V. Free parking. **Amenities:** Babysitting by appointment; valet laundry. *In room:* A/C, TV, coffeemaker, fridge, hair dryer, iron.

Hacienda Nicholas ★★ This inn, a few blocks from the plaza, has a delightful Southwest hacienda feel. Rooms surround a sunny patio; my favorite is the bright Cottonwood, with a serene feel created by the sunshine-colored walls, wood floors, and a kiva fireplace. Even more luxurious, the Sunflower has French doors, plenty of space, and also a fireplace. The rooms off the sitting room in the house are more modest but also have a warm "Southwest meets Provence" feel. All beds are comfortable and baths range from small (with showers only) to larger (with tub/showers). A full breakfast—including such delicacies as homemade granola and red-and-green chile breakfast burritos—and afternoon wine and cheese are served in the lovely Great Room or on the patio, both with fireplaces. Service in this inn is excellent. Under the same ownership, **Alexander's Inn** (✆ **888/321-5123** or 505/986-1431; www.alexanders-inn.com) has long been one of the city's finest B&Bs. In recent years, the inn itself has closed, but the same managers rent four casitas in the older district of Santa Fe. Each is a fully equipped home, with a kitchen, including fridge, range, and microwave. All have unique Southwestern furnishings and plenty of charm.

320 E. Marcy St., Santa Fe, NM 87501. ✆ **888/284-3170** or 505/992-8385; www.haciendanicholas.com. Fax 505/982-8572. 7 units. $120–$240 double. Additional person $25. Rates include breakfast and afternoon wine and cheese. AE, DISC, MC, V. Free parking. Pets accepted with $20 fee. **Amenities:** Concierge; activities desk. *In room:* A/C, TV, Wi-Fi, hair dryer.

The Madeleine ★★ Lace, flowery upholstery, and stained glass surround you at this 1886 Queen Anne–style inn just 5 blocks east of the plaza. All rooms have terry robes and some offer fireplaces. One of my favorites is the Morning Glory, with a king-size bed, a corner fireplace, and lots of sun. All rooms have comfortable beds and those in the main house have small baths. An adjacent cottage built in 1987 received an award for compatible architecture from the Santa Fe Historical Association. The two rooms in the cottage are larger than the other rooms, with king-size beds and bay windows, some of the nicest rooms in the city. In winter, a full breakfast is served family style at the adjacent Hacienda Nicholas, which is under the same excellent management. In the Victorian-cum-Asian lobby and out on a flagstone patio surrounded by flowers and fruit trees, guests enjoy chai from the **Absolute Nirvana Spa & Gardens** (✆ **505/983-7942;** www.absolutenirvana.com). This creation, voted one of the three best spas in town by the *Santa Fe Reporter,* offers imaginative Indo-Asian spa treatments and facials. For more details about Nirvana, see p. 171.

106 E. Faithway St., Santa Fe, NM 87501. ✆ **888/877-7622** or 505/982-3465. Fax 505/982-8572. www.madeleineinn.com. 7 units. $125–$240 double. Additional person $25. Rates include full breakfast and afternoon wine and cheese. AE, DISC, MC, V. Free parking. **Amenities:** Spa w/steam showers and soaking tubs; concierge. *In room:* A/C, TV/DVD, Wi-Fi, hair dryer.

Water Street Inn ★★ An award-winning adobe restoration 4 blocks from the plaza, this friendly inn features elegant Southwestern-style rooms, with antique furnishings, and several with kiva fireplaces. Rooms are medium size to large, some with four-poster beds, all comfortable with fine linens, and well-planned Mexican-tiled baths. Four suites have elegant contemporary Southwestern furnishings and outdoor private patios with fountains. Most rooms have balconies or patios. In the afternoons, a happy hour, with quesadillas and margaritas (on Friday), is offered in the living room or on the upstairs portal, where an extended continental breakfast is also served.

427 W. Water St., Santa Fe, NM 87501. ✆ **800/646-6752** or 505/984-1193. Fax 505/984-6235. www.waterstreetinn.com. 12 units. $150–$250 double. Rates include continental breakfast and afternoon hors d'oeuvres and refreshments. AE, DISC, MC, V. Free parking. Children and pets welcome with prior approval. **Amenities:** Jacuzzi; concierge; room service. *In room:* A/C, TV/VCR/DVD, Wi-Fi, hair dryer.

RV Parks

At least four private camping areas, mainly for recreational vehicles, are located within a few minutes' drive of downtown Santa Fe. Typical rates are $30 for full RV hookups, $20 for tents. Be sure to book ahead at busy times.

Los Campos RV Resort The resort has 95 spaces with full hookups, picnic tables, and covered pavilion for use with reservation at no charge. It's just 5 miles south of the plaza, so it's plenty convenient, but keep in mind that it is surrounded by the city. The campground honors a variety of discounts. Wireless Internet access is available in half the park.

3574 Cerrillos Rd., Santa Fe, NM 87507. ✆ **800/852-8160.** Fax 505/471-9220. $28–$33 daily; $172–$212 weekly; $450 monthly/winter; $500 monthly/summer. MC, V. Pets welcome. **Amenities:** Outdoor pool; concierge; coin-op laundry; restrooms; showers; grills; vending machines; free cable TV.

Rancheros de Santa Fe Campground ★ Tents, motor homes, and trailers requiring full hookups are welcome here. The park's 127 sites are situated on 22 acres of piñon and juniper forest. Cabins are also available. It's about 6 miles southeast of Santa Fe and is open March 15 to October 31. Wireless Internet access is available throughout the park and high-speed Internet access is available in the lobby.

736 Old Las Vegas Hwy. (exit 290 off I-25), Santa Fe, NM 87505. ✆ **800/426-9259** or 505/466-3482. www.rancheros.com. Tent site $20–$22; RV hookup $24–$36. AE, DISC, MC, V. **Amenities:** Outdoor pool; coin-op laundry; restrooms; showers; grills; cable TV hookups; grocery store; recreation room; tables; fireplaces; nature trails; playground; free nightly movies May–Sept; public telephones; propane.

Santa Fe KOA This campground, about 11 miles northeast of Santa Fe, sits among the foothills of the Sangre de Cristo Mountains, an excellent place to enjoy northern New Mexico's pine-filled high desert. It offers full hookups, pull-through sites, and tent sites. Wireless Internet access is available throughout the park.

934 Old Las Vegas Hwy. (exit 290 or 294 off I-25), Santa Fe, NM 87505. ✆ **800/KOA-1514** or 505/466-1419 for reservations. www.koa.com. Tent site $22–$25; RV hookup $29–$40. MC, V. **Amenities:** Coin-op laundry; restrooms; showers; store/gift shop; recreation room; playground; picnic tables; propane; dumping station.

Campgrounds

There are three forested sites along NM 475 on the way to Ski Santa Fe. All are open from May to October. Overnight rates start at about $12.

Hyde Memorial State Park ★ About 8 miles from the city, this pine-surrounded park offers a quiet retreat. Seven RV pads with electrical pedestals and an RV dumping station are available. There are nature and hiking trails and a playground as well as a small winter skating pond.

740 Hyde Park Rd., Santa Fe, NM 87501. ✆ **505/983-7175.** www.nmparks.com. **Amenities:** Shelters; water; tables; vault toilets.

Santa Fe National Forest ★★ You'll reach Black Canyon campground, with 44 sites, before you arrive at Hyde State Park. It's one of the only campgrounds in the state for which you can make a reservation (✆ **877/444-6777;** www.reserveusa.com). The sites sit within thick forest, with hiking trails nearby. Big Tesuque, a first-come, first-served campground with 10 newly rehabilitated sites, is about 12 miles from town. The sites here are closer to the road and sit at the edge of aspen forests. Both Black Canyon and Big Tesuque campgrounds, along the Santa Fe Scenic Byway, NM 475, are equipped with vault toilets.

1474 Rodeo Rd., Santa Fe, NM 87505. ✆ **505/438-7840** or 505/753-7331 (Espanola District). www.fs.fed.us/r3/sfe. **Amenities:** Water; vault toilets.

4 WHERE TO DINE

Santa Fe abounds in dining options, with hundreds of restaurants in all categories. Competition among them is steep, and spots are continually opening and closing. Locals watch closely to see which ones will survive. Some chefs create dishes that incorporate traditional Southwestern foods with ingredients not indigenous to the region; their restaurants are referred to in the listings as "creative Southwestern." There is also standard regional New Mexican cuisine, and beyond that, diners can opt for excellent steak and seafood, as well as Continental, European, Asian, and, of course, Mexican menus. On the south end of town, Santa Fe has the requisite chain establishments such as **Outback Steakhouse,** 2574 Camino Entrada (✆ **505/424-6800**), **Olive Garden,** 3781 Cerrillos Rd. (✆ **505/438-7109**), and **Red Lobster,** 4450 Rodeo Rd. (✆ **505/473-1610**).

Especially during peak tourist seasons, dinner reservations may be essential. Reservations are always recommended at better restaurants.

DOWNTOWN

This area includes the circle defined by the Paseo de Peralta and St. Francis Drive, as well as Canyon Road.

Expensive

Anasazi Restaurant ★★ CREATIVE SOUTHWESTERN This ranks as one of Santa Fe's more interesting dining experiences. It's part of the Inn of the Anasazi (p. 132), but it's a fine restaurant in its own right. You'll dine surrounded by diamond-finished walls and stacked flagstone, which create an Anasazi feel to this restaurant, named for the ancient people who once inhabited the area. There's no pretension here; the waitstaff is friendly but not overbearing, and tables are spaced nicely, making it a good place for a romantic dinner. A new chef has brought new flavors to what has always been an imaginative menu. All the food is inventive, utilizing regional and seasonal ingredients. For breakfast, you might try the egg and bacon quesadilla. At lunch I recommend the ruby trout with jalapeno lime glaze and sautéed bok choi, and at dinner the New York strip with crushed fingerling potatoes and local oyster mushrooms. There are daily specials, as well as a nice list of wines by the glass and special wines of the day. The Anasazi's new patio dining is a great way to sample these flavors from a variety of "small plates."

At the Inn of the Anasazi, 113 Washington Ave. ✆ **505/988-3236.** www.innoftheanasazi.com. Reservations recommended. Main courses $7.50–$12 breakfast, $9.50–$15 lunch, $25–$36 dinner. AE, DISC, MC, V. Daily 7–10:30am, 11:30am–2:30pm, and 5:30–10pm.

Aqua Santa ★★★ *Finds* NEW AMERICAN This is one of my favorite Santa Fe restaurants. Tucked into a little nook along the Santa Fe River, it could easily go unnoticed, but it already has a strong following of locals who enjoy the serene environment and fresh artesanal food. The atmosphere is like a quaint country hacienda with a touch of elegance created by hardwood floors, a kiva fireplace, cream-colored walls, and fine art. Service is excellent, though cooking times run a little long. The chef employs organic meats and seasonal vegetables. At lunch, I've enjoyed the local lamb braised with rapini greens and pistachios. At dinner, a great start is the escarole salad with feta and grapefruit, and one of many exquisite entrees is the sautéed sea scallops in duck fat with shitake mushrooms and lemon. For dessert, try the buttermilk panna cotta or espresso mascarpone parfait. A carefully chosen beer and wine list compliments the menu. In warmer months, you might want to request a table on the patio where you can sit under a cherry tree. If you want a peaceful and delectable meal out, this is the spot to have it.

451 W. Alameda St. ✆ **505/982-6297.** Reservations recommended. Main courses $10–$15 lunch, $11–$29 dinner. AE, MC, V. Wed–Fri noon–2pm; Tues–Sat 5:30–9pm.

Cafe Pasqual's ★★ CREATIVE SOUTHWESTERN/MEXICAN "You have to become the food, erase the line between it as an object and you," says Pasqual's owner Katharine Kagel, who uses mostly organic ingredients in her dishes. Her attitude is apparent in this restaurant, where the walls are lined with murals depicting voluptuous villagers playing guitars, drinking, and even flying. Needless to say, it's a festive place, though it's also excellent for a romantic dinner. Service is jovial and professional. My favorite dish for breakfast or lunch is the *huevos motuleños* (two eggs over easy on blue-corn tortillas and black beans topped with sautéed bananas, feta cheese, salsa, and green chile). Soups and salads are also served for lunch, and there's a delectable grilled-salmon burrito with herbed goat cheese and cucumber salsa. The frequently changing dinner menu offers grilled meats and seafood, plus vegetarian specials. Start with the Mexican prawn cocktail with lime, tomato, and avocado, and move on to the chicken mole enchiladas with cilantro rice and orange-jicama salad or "flame-kissed" ahi tuna with caramelized onions and sautéed spinach. There's a communal table for those who would like to meet new people over a meal. Pasqual's offers imported beers and wine by the bottle or glass. Try to go at an odd hour—late morning or afternoon—or make a reservation for dinner; otherwise, you'll have to wait.

121 Don Gaspar Ave. ✆ **505/983-9340.** www.pasquals.com. Reservations recommended for dinner. Main courses $8–$15 breakfast, $9–$17 lunch, $19–$39 dinner. AE, MC, V. Mon–Sat 7am–3pm; Sun–Thurs 5:30–9:30pm; Fri–Sat 5:30–10pm; summer daily 5:30–10:30pm. Brunch Sun 8am–2pm.

The Compound ★★★ NEW AMERICAN This reincarnation of one of Santa Fe's classic restaurants serves some of the most flavorful and daring food in the Southwest. Inside, it's an elegant old adobe with white walls often offset by bold splashes of flowers. Outside, during warm months, a broad patio shelters diners from the city bustle. With friendly, efficient service, this is an excellent place for a romantic dinner or a relaxing lunch. Chef and owner Mark Kiffin (a James Beard award winner and the former chef at Coyote Café [see below]), lets his creativity soar. For lunch, monkfish chorizo with watercress is outrageously tasty. At dinner, you might start off with tuna tartare topped with Osetra caviar. For an entree, a signature dish is the grilled beef tenderloin with Italian potatoes and foie gras hollandaise, the beef so tender you won't quite believe it. Finish with a warm bittersweet liquid chocolate cake. A carefully selected beer and wine list accompanies the menu.

653 Canyon Rd. ✆ **505/982-4353.** www.compoundrestaurant.com. Reservations recommended. Main courses $12–$20 lunch, $25–$44 dinner. AE, DC, DISC, MC, V. Mon–Sat noon–2pm; daily 6–9pm; bar opens nightly at 5pm.

Coyote Café ★★ CREATIVE SOUTHWESTERN World-renowned chef and cookbook author Mark Miller put this place on the map decades ago. Now under new ownership, it has gained new popularity as a place for innovative food in a festive environment. The atmosphere blends warm colors and creative lighting to make for a memorable meal. The waitstaff is efficient and friendly. The menu changes seasonally, so the specific dishes I mention may not be available. Past favorites have included sautéed Italian porcinis or prawns over corn cakes with chipotle butter and guacamole. For a main course look for delights such as pan seared white miso halibut with roasted lobster

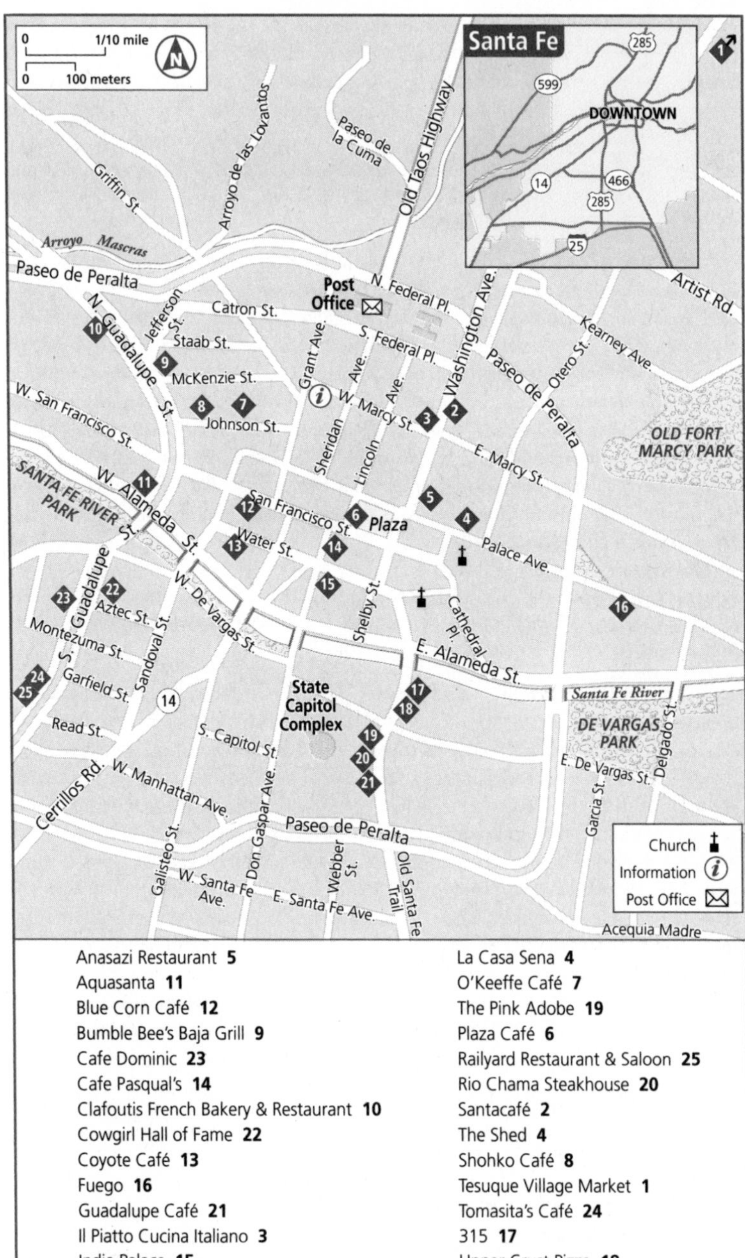

Anasazi Restaurant **5**
Aquasanta **11**
Blue Corn Café **12**
Bumble Bee's Baja Grill **9**
Cafe Dominic **23**
Cafe Pasqual's **14**
Clafoutis French Bakery & Restaurant **10**
Cowgirl Hall of Fame **22**
Coyote Café **13**
Fuego **16**
Guadalupe Café **21**
Il Piatto Cucina Italiano **3**
India Palace **15**
La Casa Sena **4**
O'Keeffe Café **7**
The Pink Adobe **19**
Plaza Café **6**
Railyard Restaurant & Saloon **25**
Rio Chama Steakhouse **20**
Santacafé **2**
The Shed **4**
Shohko Café **8**
Tesuque Village Market **1**
Tomasita's Café **24**
315 **17**
Upper Crust Pizza **18**

jus, wasabi mashed potatoes, and braised baby bok choy, or the "Cowboy Cut," a rib-eye with "borracho" beans, red chile onion rings, and roasted fingerling potatoes. You can order drinks from the full bar or wine by the glass.

Coyote Café has an adjunct establishment. In summer, the place to be seen is **La Nueva Cantina,** where light Mexican fare and cocktails are served on a festively painted terrace. Try the guacamole and chips, the crispy calamari strips, or the jalapeno rellenos with buttermilk roasted garlic sauce.

132 Water St. ✆ **505/983-1615.** www.coyotecafe.com. Reservations highly recommended. Main courses $6–$16 (Rooftop Cantina), $19–$36 (Coyote Café). AE, DC, DISC, MC, V. Rooftop Cantina: daily 11:30am–9:30pm. Dining room: daily 5:30–10pm.

El Farol ★★ SPANISH This is the place to head for local ambience and flavors of Spain, Santa Fe, and Mexico. El Farol (the Lantern), set in an 1835 adobe building, is the Canyon Road artists' quarter's original neighborhood bar. The restaurant has cozy low ceilings and hand-smoothed adobe walls. Thirty-five varieties of tapas are offered, including such delicacies as *gambas al ajillo* (shrimp with chile, garlic, Madeira, and lime) and *pinchos morunos* (grilled pork skewers with harissa sauce). You can make a meal out of two or three tapas shared with your friends or order a full dinner such as the paella or the mixed grill, with lamb, chorizo, and shrimp over delectable potatoes. There is live entertainment 7 nights a week—including jazz/swing, folk, and Latin guitar music—starting at 9:30pm. In summer, two outdoor patios are open to diners. Call ahead to find out about their flamenco dinner shows. The restaurant offers some of the finest wines and sherries in the world.

808 Canyon Rd. ✆ **505/983-9912.** www.elfarolsf.com. Reservations recommended. Tapas $8; main courses $8.75–$18 lunch, $26–$33 dinner. AE, DC, DISC, MC, V. Daily 11:30am–3pm and 5:30–10pm. Bar until 2am Mon–Sat; until midnight Sun.

Fuego ★★★ Moments INTERNATIONAL This is one of Santa Fe's most stylish and sophisticated dining experiences. The restaurant offers the ambience of a traditional Southwestern hacienda, accented with colorful paintings from local galleries, grand iron chandeliers hanging from high ceilings, and comfortable couches, along with a broad dining patio that's one of Santa Fe's best. Service is excellent. Some locals consider the "Rancher's Brunch" one of the town's finest. It includes favorites such as eggs Benedict, along with inventive items such as a shellfish and brie omelet. Lunch might start with a seafood platter or Caesar salad and move onto duck leg confit, cooked for 10 hours and served with sautéed potatoes. Dinner might start with lobster medallions, followed by a Kobe New York strip steak with truffles and braised potatoes. For dessert, try selections from a world-class artisanal farmhouse cheese cart or variety of sweets. An excellent wine list accompanies the menu. Bring your heaviest plastic; this is one of the most expensive spots in Santa Fe, but a well-worth-it, memorable choice for special occasions.

330 E. Palace Ave. (at La Posada de Santa Fe Resort and Spa). ✆ **800/727-5276** or 505/954-9670. www.rockresorts.com. Reservations recommended. Main courses $45 adult, $25 children 12 and under brunch; $15–$28 lunch; $25–$45 dinner. Prix-fixe tasting menus at dinner $75–$125. AE, DC, DISC, MC, V. Breakfast daily 6:30–11am; lunch Mon–Sat 11:30am–1:30pm; brunch Sun 11:30am–2pm; dinner daily 6–9:30pm.

Geronimo ★★★ CONTINENTAL This elegant restaurant offers one of Santa's Fe's most delectable and atmospheric dining experiences. Occupying an old adobe structure known as the Borrego House—which was built by Geronimo Lopez in 1756 but has since been completely restored—it retains the feel of an old Santa Fe home. And now, with Chef Martin Rios at the helm, its food is simply fantastic, always utilizing seasonal produce. If you enjoy dining outside, reserve a spot on the porch and watch the action on Canyon Road. You might start with Hawaiian tuna, smoked salmon and avocado tartare, served with chive buttermilk pancakes, and then move onto Alaskan halibut with red and yellow peppers, baby fennel, and saffron risotto. If you want to try one of Santa Fe's most renowned entrees, order the peppery elk tenderloin with applewood smoked bacon served with fork-mashed Yukon gold potatoes. For dessert try the Jivara chocolate Palet d'Or, a flourless cake with apricot cream and caramelized Rice Krispies. The menu changes seasonally, and there's an excellent wine list.

724 Canyon Rd. ✆ **505/982-1500.** www.geronimorestaurant.com. Reservations recommended. Main courses $30–$50 dinner. AE, MC, V. Daily 5:45–9:30pm.

La Casa Sena ★★ CREATIVE SOUTHWESTERN Combining alluring ambience and tasty food, this is one of Santa Fe's favorite restaurants, though the food here isn't as precise and flavorful as at Santacafé or Geronimo. It sits within the Sena compound, a prime example of a Spanish hacienda, in a Territorial-style adobe house built in 1867 by Civil War–hero Major José Sena. The house, which surrounds a garden courtyard, is today a veritable art gallery, with museum-quality landscapes on the walls and Taos-style handcrafted furniture. During the warm months, this restaurant has the best patio in town. The cuisine might be described as northern New Mexican with a continental flair. One of my favorite lunches is the fish tacos with achiote-corn rice. In the evening, diners might start with a salad of garden greens and grilled mushrooms, and then move onto a pork loin with roasted sweet potatoes and a peach prickly pear sauce.

In the adjacent **La Cantina,** waitstaff sing Broadway show tunes as they carry platters from the kitchen to the table. The more moderately priced Cantina menu offers the likes of enchiladas with black beans and Mexican rice. Both restaurants have exquisite desserts; try the black-and-white bittersweet chocolate terrine with raspberry sauce. The award-winning wine list features more than 850 selections.

125 E. Palace Ave. ✆ **505/988-9232.** www.lacasasena.com. Reservations recommended. La Casa Sena main courses $11–$23 lunch, $24–$42 dinner; 5-course chef's tasting menu $58, with wine $82; La Cantina main courses $13–$28. AE, DC, DISC, MC, V. Mon–Sat 11:30am–3pm; Sun brunch 11am–3pm; daily 5:30–10pm.

O'Keeffe Café ★★ NEW AMERICAN Following Georgia O'Keeffe's appreciation for sparse interiors, this restaurant has refined minimalist decor, with much more elaborate food. It's a place of clean lines and innovative color use. Large black-and-white photographs of O'Keeffe stirring stew and serving tea adorn the walls. This is a good place to stop in between museums or, in the warm months, to sit on the open patio and watch the summer scene pass by. The food is excellent, but for a nice dinner (in winter), the atmosphere lags behind that of places in a similar price range, such as Santacafé and Geronimo. The menu is eclectic, with a good balance of chicken, lamb, fish, and vegetarian dishes, some in salad and sandwich form (at lunch), along with more elaborate entree offerings. Most recently for lunch I had the crab cakes with chipotle aioli. Dinner might start with a crispy shrimp and watercress salad and move onto fennel-crusted halibut with Parissienne potatoes. Finish with a coconut crème brûlée. There's also a children's menu. The restaurant has a notable wine list and offers periodic wine tasting menus.

217 Johnson St. ✆ **505/946-1065.** www.okeeffecafe.com. Lunch $11–$27, dinner $9–$35. AE, MC, V. Mon–Sat 11am–3pm and 5:30–9:30pm (wine bar 3–5:30pm); Sun brunch 11am–3pm.

The Pink Adobe ★ CONTINENTAL/SOUTHWESTERN This restaurant, a few blocks off the plaza, offers a swirl of local old-timer gaiety and food that has remained popular since the restaurant opened in 1944. I remember eating my first lamb curry here, and my mother ate her first blue-corn enchilada, back in the '50s, and was taken aback by the odd colors. Under new ownership now, the restaurant has updated its look and menu. The restaurant occupies an adobe home believed to be at least 350 years old. Guests enter through a narrow side door into a series of quaint, informal dining rooms with tile or hardwood floors. Adobe colored walls, ceiling vigas, and kiva fireplaces complete the Santa Fe feel. For lunch, a favorite is the gypsy stew (chicken, green chile, tomatoes, onions, and mozzarella in a sherry broth). At dinner, steak Dunigan, a New York strip with sautéed mushrooms and green chile, is their signature dish, though the cut of meat isn't as good as you'd find next door at the Rio Chama (below). Lighter eaters will like the half-order portions available for some entrees. You can't leave without trying the hot French apple pie.

Under the same ownership, the charming bar (a real local scene) has its own menu, offering traditional New Mexican food. Locals come to eat hearty green-chile stew.

406 Old Santa Fe Trail. ✆ **505/983-7712.** www.thepinkadobe.com. Reservations recommended. Main courses $8–$34 lunch, $20–$38 dinner. AE, DC, DISC, MC, V. Mon–Fri 11:30am–2pm; daily 5:30pm–closing. Bar Mon–Fri 11:30am–midnight; Sat–Sun 5pm–midnight.

Rio Chama Steakhouse ★★ STEAK/SEAFOOD Serving up tasty steaks in a refined ranch atmosphere, this is one of Santa Fe's most popular restaurants. It's a good spot for a business lunch or a fun-filled evening, and the patio is a bright spot during warm months. Service is efficient, and there's a full bar. I suggest sticking to the meat dishes here, though the fish and pasta dishes can be quite good too. At lunch or dinner you might start with the Capitol salad, with lots of fresh greens, piñon nuts, and blue cheese crumbles. My favorite for lunch is the ½ BLT with soup or salad, best when ordered with their green chile stew. Lunch also brings more formal dishes such as a lumpy crab over angel hair pasta. At dinner, the prime rib is a big hit, as is the filet mignon, both served with a potato and vegetable. For dessert, try chocolate cake. The bar here romps during happy hour, when the booths fill up, martinis nearly overflow, and reasonably priced menu items sate post-work appetites.

414 Old Santa Fe Trail. ✆ **505/955-0765.** www.riochamasteakhouse.com. Reservations recommended on weekend nights. Main courses $8.50–$24 lunch, $18–$39 dinner. AE, DC, DISC, MC, V. Daily 11am–3pm and 5–10pm; patio bar 5pm–closing.

Santacafé ★★★ (Moments) NEW AMERICAN/CREATIVE SOUTHWESTERN This is where my mother and I go to celebrate birthdays and other special occasions because the place exudes unique charm, both in its food and ambiance. The food combines the best of many cuisines, from Asian to Southwestern, served in an elegant setting with minimalist decor that accentuates the graceful architecture of the 18th-century Padre Gallegos House, 2 blocks from the plaza. The white walls are decorated only with deer antlers, and each room contains a fireplace. In warm months you can sit under elm trees in the charming courtyard. Beware that on busy nights the rooms are noisy. The dishes change to take advantage of local and seasonal specialties, each served with precision. Their Sunday brunch menu offers such delights as a mascarpone-stuffed French toast and poached eggs with corned beef. For a lunch or dinner starter, try the shiitake and cactus spring rolls with Southwestern ponzu. One of my favorite main courses at lunch is the baby spinach niçoise salad with tuna seared to perfection. At dinner I've enjoyed the grilled rack of lamb with

 **Family-Friendly Restaurants**

Blue Corn Café (p. 153) A relaxed atmosphere and their own menu pleases kids, while excellent brewpub beer pleases parents.

Bumble Bee's Baja Grill (p. 153) A casual atmosphere allows parents to relax while their kids chow down on quesadillas and burritos.

Upper Crust Pizza (p. 156) Many people feel it has the best pizza in town, and it'll deliver it to tired tots and their families at downtown hotels.

potato-leek gratin. A lighter eater might try the sautéed Diver scallops with kalamata olive linguine and wild mushrooms. There's an extensive wine list, with wine by the glass as well. Desserts, as elegant as the rest of the food, are made in-house; try the warm chocolate upside-down cake with vanilla ice cream.

231 Washington Ave. ✆ **505/984-1788.** www.santacafe.com. Reservations recommended. Main courses $9–$15 lunch, $22–$40 dinner. AE, DISC, MC, V. Mon–Sat 11:30am–2pm; daily 5:30–10pm. Sun brunch served in summer, Easter Sunday, and Mother's Day.

315 ★★ FRENCH This classy French bistro enjoyed instant success when it opened in 1995 because the food is simply excellent. The elegant atmosphere provides a perfect setting for a romantic meal, and during warm months the patio is a popular place to people-watch, with little white lights setting the whole place aglow. Service is excellent. The menu changes seasonally; on one of my visits, I started with a smooth and flavorful lobster bisque and moved on to lamb chops served with a tart mustard sauce and mashed potatoes. My favorite dessert here is the flourless chocolate cake: not too sweet, and luscious. Because the restaurant is so popular, reservations are an absolute must. The wine list includes over 250 offerings from France to California to Australia.

315 Old Santa Fe Trail. ✆ **505/986-9190.** www.315santafe.com. Reservations highly recommended. Main courses $9–$17 lunch, $20–$29 dinner. AE, DISC, MC, V. Summer Mon–Sat 11:30am–2pm, Sun–Thurs 5:30–9pm, Fri–Sat 5:30–9:30pm; winter 5:30–9pm daily.

Moderate

Cowgirl Hall of Fame ★ REGIONAL AMERICAN/BARBECUE/CAJUN This raucous bar/restaurant serves decent food in a festive atmosphere. The main room is a bar—a hip hangout spot, and a good place to eat as well. The back room is quieter, with wood floors and tables and plenty of cowgirl memorabilia. Best of all is sitting out on a brick patio lit with strings of white lights during the warm season. The service is at times brusque, and the food varies. In winter, my favorite is a big bowl of gumbo or crawfish étoufée, and the rest of the time, I order Jamaican jerk chicken or pork tenderloin when it's a special. Careful, both can be hot. The daily blue-plate special is a real buy, especially on Tuesday nights, when it's chile rellenos. There's even a special "kid's corral" that has horseshoes, a rocking horse, a horse-shaped rubber tire swing, hay bales, and a beanbag toss. Happy hour is from 3 to 6pm. There is also live music almost every night, a pool hall, and a deli.

319 S. Guadalupe St. ✆ **505/982-2565.** www.santafestation.com/cowgirl. Reservations recommended. Main courses $7–$13 lunch, $8–$23 dinner. AE, DISC, MC, V. Mon–Fri 11am–midnight; Sat 8:30am–midnight; Sun 8:30am–11pm. Bar Mon–Sat until 2am; Sun until midnight.

Il Piatto Cucina Italiano ★★ (Value) NORTHERN ITALIAN This simple Italian cafe brings innovative flavors to thinner wallets. It's simple and elegant, with contemporary art on the walls—nice for a romantic evening. Service is efficient, though on a busy night, overworked. The menu changes seasonally, complemented by a few perennial standards. For a starter, try the grilled calamari with shaved fennel and aioli. Among entrees, my favorite is the pancetta-wrapped trout with grilled polenta and wild mushrooms, though you can't go wrong with the jumbo scampi risotto with sweet peppers. The Gorgonzola-walnut ravioli is a favorite of many, though not quite enough food to fill me up, so I order an appetizer. A full wine and beer menu is available.

95 W. Marcy St. ✆ **505/984-1091.** Reservations recommended. Main courses $15–$22. AE, DISC, MC, V. Mon–Fri 11:30am–2pm; daily 5:30–9pm. Closed July 4.

India Palace ★ (Value) INDIAN Once every few weeks, I get a craving for the lamb vindaloo served at this restaurant in the center of downtown. A festive ambience, with pink walls painted with mosque shadows, makes this a nice place for a romantic meal. The service is efficient, and most of the waitstaff are from India, as is chef Amarjit Behal. The tandoori chicken, fish, lamb, and shrimp are rich and flavorful, as is the *baingan bhartha* (eggplant in a flavorful sauce). A lunch buffet provides an excellent selection of vegetarian and nonvegetarian dishes at a reasonable price. Beer and wine are available, or you might want some chai tea.

227 Don Gaspar Ave. (inside the Water St. parking compound). ✆ **505/986-5859.** www.indiapalace.com. Reservations recommended. Main courses $11–$26; luncheon buffet $9.50. AE, DC, DISC, MC, V. Daily 11:30am–2:30pm and 5–10pm. Closed Super Bowl Sunday.

Railyard Restaurant & Saloon ★★ (Finds) NEW AMERICAN Santa Fe locals' most talked-about newer spot, the Railyard, is a fun and thoughtful addition to the restaurant scene. Set in one of the city's old railroad buildings, the place offers a comfortable ambience and imaginative food at not-too-steep prices. The space has clean lines, with maroon walls and spacious booths and tables set under an industrial ceiling with visible ductwork. Service is friendly and knowledgeable. This is the creation of Louis Moskow, who put 315 (see above) on the map. Here, he's offering a slice of Americana, with creative twists. At lunch you might try shrimp tacos with black beans and rice or one of the excellent burgers or salads. Dinner might start with crispy calamari and move onto dishes such as an outstanding rib-eye and tasty pan-fried pork chop, but also some less American fare such as, my favorite, sesame-and-panko-crusted tuna. All menu items are a la carte, but the side portions you'll order separately are large enough to share. Select from a carefully considered wine list or from the full bar. An excellent but more limited selection of food is available all day at the bar. The patio is a lively place to hang in the warm months.

530 S. Guadalupe St. (1/4 block north of Paseo de Peralta). ✆ **505/989-3300.** www.railyardrestaurantandsaloon.com. Reservations recommended on weekend nights. Main courses $7.50–$23 lunch, $9–$25 dinner. Mon–Sat 11:30am–2:30pm; Mon–Thurs 5:30–9:30pm; Fri–Sat 5:30–10pm; Sun 5–9:30pm. Bar Mon–Sat 11:30am–close; Sun 5pm–close.

Shohko Cafe ★★ JAPANESE/SUSHI Santa Fe's favorite sushi restaurant serves fresh fish in a 150-year-old adobe building that was once a bordello. The atmosphere is sparse and comfortable, a blending of New Mexican decor (such as ceiling vigas and Mexican tile floors) with traditional Japanese decorative touches (rice-paper screens, for instance). Up to 30 fresh varieties of raw seafood, including sushi and sashimi, are served at plain pine tables in various rooms or at the sushi bar. Request the sushi bar, where the atmosphere is coziest, and you can watch the chefs at work. My mother likes the tempura combination with veggies, shrimp, and scallops. On an odd night, I'll order the salmon teriyaki, but most nights I have sushi, particularly the *anago* and spicy tuna roll—though if you're daring, you might try the Santa Fe Roll (with green chile, shrimp tempura, and *masago*). My new favorite is a caterpillar, with eel and lots of avocado, shaped like its crawling namesake. Wine, imported beers, and hot sake are available.

321 Johnson St. ✆ **505/982-9708.** Reservations recommended. Main courses $5–$19 lunch, $8.50–$25 dinner. AE, DISC, MC, V. Mon–Fri 11:30am–2pm; Sun–Thurs 5:30–9pm; Fri–Sat 5:30–9:30pm.

Inexpensive

Blue Corn Café ★ Kids NEW MEXICAN/MICROBREWERY If you're ready for a fun and inexpensive night out to eat decent New Mexican food, this is your place. Within a clean and breezy decor—wooden tables and abstract art—you'll find a raucous and buoyant atmosphere; it's a good place to bring kids. The overworked waitstaff may be slow, but they're friendly. I recommend sampling dishes from the combination menu. You can get two to five items served with your choice of rice, beans, or one of the best *posoles* (hominy and chile) that I've tasted. I had the chicken enchilada, which I recommend, and the chalupa, which I don't because it was soggy. You can have tacos, tamales, and rellenos, too. Kids have their own menu and crayons to keep them occupied. Nightly specials include the tasty shrimp fajitas, served with a nice guacamole and the usual toppings. Because this is also a brewery, you might want to sample the High Altitude Pale Ale or Sleeping Dog Stout. My beverage choice is the prickly-pear iced tea (black tea with enough cactus juice to give it a zing). The Spanish flan is tasty and large enough to share. The **Blue Corn Cafe & Brewery** (4056 Cerrillos Rd., Suite G; ✆ **505/438-1800**), on the south side at the corner of Cerrillos and Rodeo roads, has similar fare and atmosphere.

133 W. Water St. ✆ **505/984-1800.** Reservations accepted for parties of 6 or more. www.bluecorncafe.com. Main courses $10–$12. AE, DC, DISC, MC, V. Daily 11am–10pm.

Bumble Bee's Baja Grill ★ Finds Kids MEXICAN This new "beestro" offers a refreshing twist on fast food: It's actually healthy! The secret? Tacos are made Mexican style, with a tortilla folded around quality meat, fish, and poultry grilled with veggies. You pick from an array of salsas. Waist watchers can sample from a selection of salads, including one with grilled chicken and avocado. Rotisserie chicken and various burritos round out the main menu, while kids have their own options, such as the quesadillas. Diners order at a counter, and a waiter brings the food. The decor is a bit Formica-esque for my tastes, though the primary colors are fun. During warm months, I try to nab a patio table. Evenings often offer live jazz music, when folks sit back and sip beer and wine. There's also a drive-through window. There's another **Bumble Bee's Baja Grill** (3777 Cerrillos Rd.; ✆ **505/988-3278**), with similar decor and offerings, on the south side of town.

301 Jefferson St. (from W. San Francisco St., take Guadalupe 2 blocks north). ✆ **505/820-2862.** www.bumblebeesbajagrill.com. Main courses $7–$12. AE, MC, V. Daily 11am–9pm.

Cafe Dominic ★ AMERICAN/DELI This cafe offers sophisticated flavors with casual ease in a comfortable urban environment. Diners order at a counter, and a waiter brings the food. The restaurant serves a variety of breakfasts as well as soups, salads, sandwiches, New Mexican food, grilled fish and meat, and pasta. Breakfast is served all day, and it's delicious. Their huevos rancheros (eggs over corn tortillas smothered in chile) is my dad's new favorite. My best choice for lunch or dinner is the cobb salad, which comes with crisp bacon, grilled chicken, Gorgonzola cheese, avocado, and egg wedges.

For a real City Different bargain, try the grilled salmon, served with beans, rice, salad, and grilled foccacia. When dessert rolls around, you can feast on a caramel turtle cheesecake or four-layer chocolate cake.

320 S. Guadalupe St. ✆ **505/982-4743.** Main courses $7–$15. AE, MC, V. Daily 7am–9pm.

Clafoutis French Bakery & Restaurant ★★ COUNTRY FRENCH Set in a cozy building on the north end of town, this new restaurant serves delectable meals in a country kitchen environment. Immediately upon opening, it became so popular that there's always a wait during mealtime, though it's usually not long. The ambiance is simple, with wooden utensils and jars of herbs adorning the walls and wooden chairs and a padded banco for seating. At lunch, the place can get noisy, with excited diners remarking on the food. All of it is prepared fresh with seasonal ingredients. Breakfast might include an egg croissant with bacon or ham and cheese, or a crepe (served all day). A number of varieties are available, including my favorite with ham and cheese. For lunch, you can select from a number of quiches, served with a mixed green salad. My favorite lunch, though, is the chicken-mango salad, with lots of fresh vegetables and a tasty but simple vinaigrette. The sandwiches made on homemade organic bread are also popular. Order dessert from the pastry counter (strawberry tart!) and even take home some croissants. A selection of good coffees and teas accompanies the menu.

402 Guadalupe St. ✆ **505/988-1809.** Reservations for 5 or more. All menu items under $11. AE, DISC, MC, V. Mon–Sat 7am–4pm.

Guadalupe Cafe ★★ NEW MEXICAN When I want New Mexican food, I go to this restaurant, and like many Santa Feans, I go there often. This casually elegant cafe is in a white stucco building that's warm and friendly and has a nice-size patio for dining in warmer months. Service is friendly and conscientious. For breakfast, try the spinach-mushroom burritos or huevos rancheros, and for lunch, the chalupas or stuffed *sopaipillas.* Any other time, I'd start with fresh roasted ancho chiles (filled with a combination of Montrachet and Monterey Jack cheeses and piñon nuts, and topped with your choice of chile) and move on to the sour-cream chicken enchilada or any of the other Southwestern dishes. Order both red and green chile ("Christmas") so that you can sample some of the best sauces in town. Beware, though: The chile here can be hot, and the chef won't put it on the side. Diners can order from a choice of delicious salads, such as a Caesar with chicken. Daily specials are available, and don't miss the famous chocolate-amaretto adobe pie for dessert. Beer and wine are served.

422 Old Santa Fe Trail. ✆ **505/982-9762.** Breakfast $5.50–$9.75; lunch $6–$12; dinner $8–$17. DISC, MC, V. Tues–Fri 7am–2pm; Sat–Sun 8am–2pm; Tues–Sat 5:30–9pm.

La Choza ★★ NEW MEXICAN This sister restaurant of the Shed (p. 155) offers some of the best New Mexican food in town at a convenient location near the intersection of Cerrillos Road and St. Francis Drive. When other restaurants are packed, you'll only wait a little while here. It's a warm, casual eatery with vividly painted walls; it's especially popular on cold days, when diners gather around the wood-burning stove and fireplace. The patio is delightful in summer. Service is friendly and efficient. The menu offers enchiladas, tacos, and burritos, as well as green-chile stew, chile con carne, and carne adovada. The portions are medium size, so if you're hungry, start with guacamole or nachos. For years, I've ordered the cheese or chicken enchilada, two dishes I will always recommend, served with *posole.* For dessert, you can't leave without trying the mocha cake (chocolate cake with a mocha pudding filling, served with whipped cream). Vegetarians and children have their own menus. Beer and wine are available.

905 Alarid St. ✆ **505/982-0909.** Lunch or dinner $8.95–$12. AE, DISC, MC, V. Summer Mon–Sat 11am–9pm; winter Mon–Thurs 11am–8pm, Fri–Sat 11am–9pm.

Plaza Cafe ★ AMERICAN/DELI/NEW MEXICAN/GREEK Santa Fe's best example of diner-style eating, this cafe has excellent food in a bright and friendly atmosphere right on the plaza. A restaurant since the turn of the 20th century, it's been owned by the Razatos family since 1947. The decor has changed only enough to stay comfortable and clean, with red upholstered banquettes, Art Deco tile, and a soda fountain–style service counter. Service is always quick and conscientious, and only during the heavy tourist seasons will you have to wait long for a table. Breakfasts are excellent and large, and the hamburgers and sandwiches at lunch and dinner are good. I also like the soups and New Mexican dishes, such as the bowl of green-chile stew, or, if you're more adventurous, the pumpkin *posole.* Check out the Greek dishes, such as vegetable moussaka or beef and lamb gyros. Wash it down with an Italian soda, in flavors from vanilla to Amaretto. Alternatively, you can have a shake, a piece of coconut cream pie, or Plaza Cafe's signature dessert, *cajeta* (apple and pecan pie with Mexican caramel). Beer and wine are available.

54 Lincoln Ave. (on the plaza). ✆ **505/982-1664.** www.thefamousplazacafe.com. No reservations. Main courses $8–$17. AE, DISC, MC, V. Daily 7am–9pm.

The Shed ★★ NEW MEXICAN This longtime locals' favorite is so popular that during lunch lines often form outside. Half a block east of the plaza, a luncheon institution since 1953, it occupies several rooms and the patio of a rambling hacienda that was built in 1692. Festive folk art adorns the doorways and walls. The food is delicious, some of the best in the state, and a compliment to traditional Hispanic and Pueblo cooking. The red chile cheese enchilada is renowned in Santa Fe. Tacos, and burritos are good, too. The green-chile stew is a local favorite. The Shed's Joshua Carswell has added vegetarian and low-fat Mexican foods to the menu, as well as a variety of soups and salads and grilled chicken and steak. Don't leave without trying the mocha cake, possibly the best dessert you'll ever eat. In addition to wine and a number of beers, there's full bar service. The cantina style bar is a fun place to schmooze, and the brick patio is well shaded.

113½ E. Palace Ave. ✆ **505/982-9030.** www.sfshed.com. Reservations accepted at dinner. Lunch $5.75–$9.50, dinner $8–$17. AE, DC, DISC, MC, V. Mon–Sat 11am–2:30pm and 5:30–9pm.

Tomasita's Cafe ★ NEW MEXICAN When I was in high school, I used to eat at Tomasita's, a little dive on a back street. I always ordered a burrito, and I think people used to bring liquor in bags. It's now in a modern building near the train station, and its food has become renowned. The atmosphere is simple—hanging plants and wood accents—with lots of families sitting at booths or tables and a festive spillover from the bar, where many come to drink margaritas. Service is quick, even a little rushed, which is my biggest gripe about Tomasita's. Sure, the food is still tasty, but unless you go at some totally odd hour, you'll wait for a table, and once you're seated, you may eat and be out again in less than an hour. The burritos are still excellent, though you may want to try the chile rellenos, a house specialty. Vegetarian dishes, burgers, steaks, and daily specials are also offered. There's full bar service.

500 S. Guadalupe St. ✆ **505/983-5721.** No reservations; large parties call ahead. Lunch $6–$15, dinner $6.25–$16. AE, DISC, MC, V. Mon–Sat 11am–10pm.

Upper Crust Pizza ★ Kids PIZZA/ITALIAN Upper Crust serves some of Santa Fe's best pizzas, in an adobe house near the old San Miguel Mission. The atmosphere is plain, with wooden tables; in summer, the outdoor patio overlooking Old Santa Fe Trail is more inviting. Meals-in-a-dish include the Grecian gourmet pizza (feta and olives) and the whole-wheat vegetarian pizza (topped with sesame seeds). You can either eat here or request free delivery (it takes about 30 min.) to your downtown hotel. Beer and wine are available, as are salads, calzones, sandwiches, and stromboli.

329 Old Santa Fe Trail. ✆ **505/982-0000.** www.uppercrustpizza.com. Pizzas $7.95–$18. DISC, MC, V. Summer daily 11am–midnight; winter Sun–Thurs 11am–10pm, Fri–Sat 11am–11pm.

THE NORTH SIDE

Moderate

Tesuque Village Market ★ AMERICAN/SOUTHWESTERN You'll see shiny Range Rovers parked alongside beat-up ranch trucks in front of this charming market and restaurant, an indication that the food here has broad appeal. Located under a canopy of cottonwoods at the center of this quaint village, the restaurant doesn't have the greatest food but makes for a nice adventure 15 minutes north of town. During warmer months, you can sit on the porch; in other seasons, the interior is comfortable, with plain wooden tables next to a deli counter and upscale market. For me, this is a breakfast place, where blue-corn pancakes rule. Friends of mine like the breakfast burritos and huevos rancheros. Lunch and dinner are also popular, and there's always a crowd (though, if you have to wait for a table, the wait is usually brief). For lunch, I recommend the burgers, and for dinner, one of the hearty specials, such as lasagna. For dessert, there's a variety of house-made pastries and cakes at the deli counter, as well as fancy granola bars and oversize cookies in the market. A kids' menu is available.

At the junction of Bishop's Lodge Rd. and NM 591, in Tesuque Village. ✆ **505/988-8848.** Reservations recommended for holidays. Main courses $5–$10 breakfast, $6–$12 lunch, $8–$20 dinner. MC, V. Daily 7am–9pm.

SOUTHSIDE

Santa Fe's motel strip and other streets south of Paseo de Peralta have their share of good, reasonably priced restaurants. Note that the Blue Corn Café and Bumble Bee's Baja Grill have southside locations (see above).

Moderate

mu du noodles ★★ PACIFIC RIM If you're ready for a light, healthy meal with lots of flavor, head to this small restaurant about an 8-minute drive from downtown. There are two rooms, with plain pine tables and chairs and sparse Asian prints on the walls. The carpeted back room is cozier, and a woodsy-feeling patio is definitely worth requesting during the warmer months. The waitstaff is friendly and unimposing. I almost always order the Malaysian *laksa,* thick rice noodles in a blend of coconut milk, hazelnuts, onions, and red curry, stir-fried with chicken or tofu and julienned vegetables and sprouts. If you're eating with others, you may each want to order a different dish and share. The pad thai is lighter and spicier than most, served with a chile-vinegar sauce. A list of beers, wines, and sakes is available, tailored to the menu. I'm especially fond of the ginseng ginger ale. Menu items change seasonally.

1494 Cerrillos Rd. ✆ **505/983-1411.** www.mudunoodles.com. Reservations for parties of 3 or larger only. Main courses $9–$18. AE, DC, DISC, MC, V. Tues–Sat 5:30–9pm (sometimes 10pm in summer).

5 WHAT TO SEE & DO

One of the oldest cities in the United States, Santa Fe has long been a center for the creative and performing arts, so it's not surprising that most of the city's major sights are related to local history and the arts. The city's Museum of New Mexico, art galleries and studios, historic churches, and cultural sights associated with local Native American and Hispanic communities all merit a visit. It would be easy to spend a full week sightseeing in the city, without ever heading out to any nearby attractions.

THE TOP ATTRACTIONS

Georgia O'Keeffe Museum ★★ The Georgia O'Keeffe Museum, inaugurated in July 1997, contains the largest collection of O'Keeffes in the world: currently 1,149 paintings, drawings, and sculptures, and 1,851 works by other artists of note. It's the largest museum in the United States dedicated solely to an internationally known woman artist. You can see such remarkable O'Keeffes as *Jimson Weed,* painted in 1932, and *Evening Star No. VII,* from 1917. The museum presents special exhibitions that are either devoted entirely to O'Keeffe's work or combine examples of her art with works by her American modernist contemporaries. My favorite in recent years brought together works of O'Keeffe and photographer Ansel Adams. The rich and varied collection adorns the walls of a cathedral-like, 13,000-square-foot space—a former Baptist church with adobe walls. O'Keeffe's images are tied inextricably to local desert landscapes. She first visited New Mexico in 1929 and returned for extended periods from the '20s through the '40s. In 1949 she moved here permanently. An excellent film at the museum depicts her life.

217 Johnson St. ✆ **505/946-1000.** www.okeeffemuseum.org. Admission $8, free for students and youth 18 and under, free for all Fri 5–8pm. June–Oct daily 10am–5pm (Fri until 8pm); Nov–May closed Tues.

New Mexico Museum of Art ★ Opposite the Palace of the Governors, this was one of the first pueblo revival–style buildings constructed in Santa Fe (in 1917). The museum's permanent collection of more than 20,000 works emphasizes regional art and includes landscapes and portraits by all the Taos masters, *los Cincos Pintores* (a 1920s organization of Santa Fe artists), and contemporary artists. The museum also has a collection of photographic works by such masters as Ansel Adams and Elliot Porter. Modern artists are featured in temporary exhibits throughout the year. Two sculpture gardens present a range of three-dimensional art, from the traditional to the abstract.

Graceful **St. Francis Auditorium,** patterned after the interiors of traditional Hispanic mission churches, adjoins the art museum. A museum shop sells gifts, art books, prints, and postcards of the collection.

107 W. Palace (at Lincoln Ave.). ✆ **505/476-5072.** www.museumofnewmexico.org. Admission $8 adults, free for seniors Wed, free for children 16 and under, free for all Fri 5–8pm. 4-day passes (good at all 4 branches of the Museum of New Mexico and the Museum of Spanish Colonial Art) $18 for adults. Tues–Sun 10am–5pm; Fri 10am–8pm. Closed New Year's Day, Easter, Thanksgiving, Christmas.

Palace of the Governors ★★ In order to fully appreciate this structure, it's important to know that this is where the only successful Native American uprising took place in 1680. Prior to the uprising, this was the local seat of power, and after de Vargas reconquered the natives, it resumed that position. Built in 1610 as the original capitol of New Mexico, the palace has been in continuous public use longer than any other structure in the United States. A watchful eye can find remnants of the conflicts this building has seen through the years. Begin out front, where Native Americans sell jewelry, pottery, and

Value Museum Bingeing

If you're a museum buff, pick up one of **Museum of New Mexico's 4-day passes.** It's good at all five branches of the Museum of New Mexico: the Palace of the Governors, the Museum of Fine Arts, the Museum of International Folk Art, and the Museum of Indian Arts & Culture, with the Museum of Spanish Colonial Art thrown in for good measure. The cost is $18 for adults. Also ask about the new **Culture Pass,** good for 1 year, to visit museums all over the state for $25.

some weavings under the protection of the portal. This is a good place to buy, and it's a fun place to shop, especially if you take the time to visit with the artisans about their work. When you buy a piece, you may learn its history, a treasure as valuable as the piece itself.

Inside, a map illustrates 400 years of New Mexico history, from the 16th-century Spanish explorations through the frontier era and modern times. Two shops are of particular interest. One is the bookstore/gift shop, which has an excellent selection of art, history, and anthropology books. The other is the print shop and bindery, where limited-edition works are produced on hand-operated presses.

North plaza. ✆ **505/476-5100.** www.palaceofthegovernors.org. Admission $8 adults, free for children 16 and under, free for all Fri 5–8pm. 4-day passes (good at all 4 branches of the Museum of New Mexico and the Museum of Spanish Colonial Art) $18 for adults. Tues–Sun 10am–5pm. Closed New Year's Day, Thanksgiving, Christmas.

St. Francis Cathedral ★ Santa Fe's grandest religious structure is an architectural anomaly in Santa Fe because its design is French. Just a block east of the plaza, it was built between 1869 and 1886 by Archbishop Jean-Baptiste Lamy in the style of the great cathedrals of Europe. French architects designed the Romanesque building—named after Santa Fe's patron saint—and Italian masons assisted with its construction. The small adobe Our Lady of the Rosary chapel on the northeast side of the cathedral has a Spanish look. Built in 1807, it's the only portion that remains from Our Lady of the Assumption Church, founded along with Santa Fe in 1610. The new cathedral was built over and around the old church.

A wooden icon set in a niche in the wall of the north chapel, Our Lady of Peace, is the oldest representation of the Madonna in the United States. Rescued from the old church during the 1680 Pueblo Rebellion, it was brought back by Don Diego de Vargas on his (mostly peaceful) reconquest 12 years later—thus, the name. Today, Our Lady of Peace plays an important part in the annual Feast of Corpus Christi in June and July.

The cathedral's front doors feature 16 carved panels of historic note and a plaque memorializing the 38 Franciscan friars who were martyred during New Mexico's early years. There's also a large bronze statue of Archbishop Lamy himself; his grave is under the main altar of the cathedral.

Cathedral Place at San Francisco St. ✆ **505/982-5619.** Donations appreciated. Daily. Visitors may attend Mass Mon–Sat 7am and 5:15pm; Sun 8, 10am, noon, and 5:15pm. Free parking in city lot next to the cathedral to attend church services.

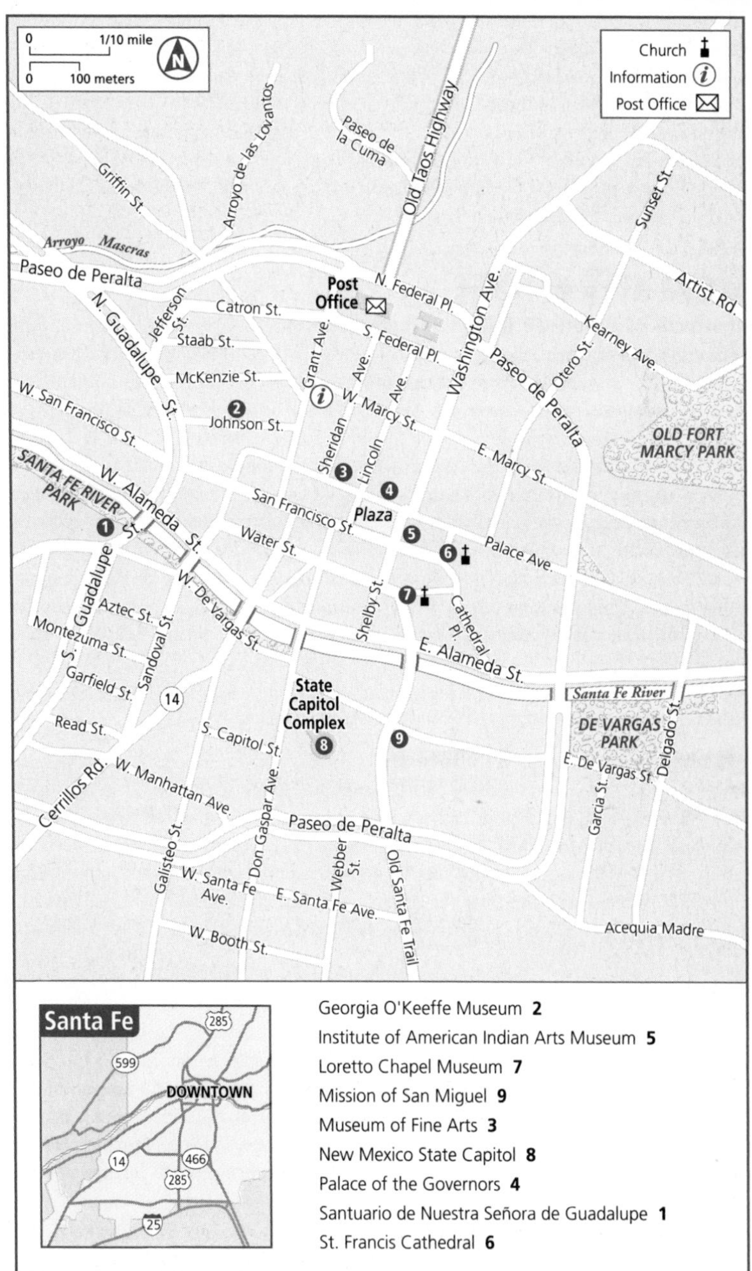
0 1/10 mile
0 100 meters
N
Church
Information
Post Office
Paseo de la Cuma
Old Taos Highway
Arroyo de las Lovantos
Griffin St.
Arroyo Mascras
Paseo de Peralta
Post Office
N. Federal Pl.
Sunset St.
Artist Rd.
N. Guadalupe St.
Jefferson St.
Catron St.
Staab St.
McKenzie St.
Grant Ave.
S. Federal Pl.
Washington Ave.
Kearney Ave.
Otero St.
W. San Francisco St.
Johnson St.
Sheridan Ave.
Lincoln Ave.
W. Marcy St.
E. Marcy St.
OLD FORT MARCY PARK
SANTA FE RIVER PARK
W. Alameda St.
San Francisco St.
Plaza
Water St.
Palace Ave.
S. Guadalupe St.
Aztec St.
Montezuma St.
Garfield St.
Sandoval St.
W. De Vargas St.
Shelby St.
Cathedral Pl.
E. Alameda St.
Santa Fe River
State Capitol Complex
DE VARGAS PARK
Delgado St.
14
Read St.
S. Capitol St.
E. De Vargas St.
Cerrillos Rd.
W. Manhattan Ave.
Don Gaspar Ave.
Paseo de Peralta
Garcia St.
Galisteo St.
Webber St.
Old Santa Fe Trail
W. Santa Fe Ave.
E. Santa Fe Ave.
W. Booth St.
Acequia Madre
Santa Fe
285
599
DOWNTOWN
14
466
285
25
Georgia O'Keeffe Museum 2
Institute of American Indian Arts Museum 5
Loretto Chapel Museum 7
Mission of San Miguel 9
Museum of Fine Arts 3
New Mexico State Capitol 8
Palace of the Governors 4
Santuario de Nuestra Señora de Guadalupe 1
St. Francis Cathedral 6

Santa Fe Plaza ★★ (Moments) This square has been the heart and soul of Santa Fe, as well as its literal center, since its concurrent establishment with the city in 1610. Originally designed as a meeting place, it has been the site of innumerable festivals and other historical, cultural, and social events. Long ago the plaza was a dusty hive of activity as the staging ground and terminus of the Santa Fe Trail. Today, those who congregate around the central monument enjoy the best people-watching in New Mexico. Live music and dancing are often staged on the gazebo/bandstand in summer. At Christmastime the plaza is decked out with lights. Santa Feans understandably feel nostalgic for the days when the plaza, now the hub of the tourist trade, still belonged to locals rather than outside commercial interests.

At the corner of San Francisco St. and Lincoln Ave. Daily 24 hr.

MORE ATTRACTIONS

Institute of American Indian Arts Museum ★ A visit to this museum (with over 7,000 works, often called the "national collection of contemporary Native American art") offers a profound look into the lives of a people negotiating two worlds: traditional and contemporary. Here, you'll see cutting-edge art that pushes the limits of many media, from creative writing to textile manufacturing to painting. Much of the work originates from artists from the Institute of American Indian Arts (IAIA), the nation's only congressionally chartered institute of higher education devoted solely to the study and practice of the artistic and cultural traditions of all American Indian and Alaskan native peoples.

Exhibits change periodically, while a more permanent collection of Allan Houser's monumental sculpture is on display in the museum's Art Park. The museum store offers a broad collection of contemporary jewelry, pottery, and other crafts, as well as books and music.

108 Cathedral Place. ✆ **505/983-8900.** www.iaia.edu. Admission $5 adults, $2.50 seniors and students, free for children 16 and under. Mon–Sat 10am–5pm; Sun noon–5pm.

Museum of Indian Arts & Culture ★★ An interactive permanent exhibit here has made this one of the most exciting Native American museum experiences in the Southwest. "Here, Now and Always" takes visitors through thousands of years of Native American history. More than 70,000 pieces of basketry, pottery, clothing, carpets, and jewelry—much of it quite old—are on continual rotating display. You begin by entering through a tunnel that symbolizes the *sipapu,* the ancestral Puebloan (Anasazi) entrance into the upper worlds; you're greeted by the sounds of trickling water, drums, and Native

Cultural Chow

If you get hungry while visiting the Museum of Indian Arts & Culture, the Museum of International Folk Art, the Wheelwright Museum of the American Indian, and the Museum of Spanish Colonial Art (all located together, southeast of the plaza), you can now feast on more than your fingernails. The **Museum Hill Café** ★ (✆ **505/820-1776**) opens Tuesday through Saturday for beverages and snacks at 10am, and a tasty lunch from 11am to 3pm; it serves brunch on Sunday from 11am to 3pm.

American music. Videos show Native Americans telling creation stories. Visitors can reflect on the lives of modern-day Native Americans by juxtaposing a traditional Pueblo kitchen with a modern kitchen. You can step into a Navajo hogan (log and mud hut) and stroll through a trading post. The rest of the museum houses a lovely pottery collection as well as changing exhibits. There's always a contemporary show.

710 Camino Lejo. ✆ **505/476-1250.** www.miaclab.org. Admission $8 adults, free for kids 16 and under. 4-day passes (good at all 4 branches of the Museum of New Mexico and the Museum of Spanish Colonial Art) $18 for adults. Tues–Sun 10am–5pm. Drive southeast on Old Santa Fe Trail (beware: Old Santa Fe Trail takes a left turn; if you find yourself on Old Pecos Trail, you missed the turn). Look for signs pointing right onto Camino Lejo.

Museum of International Folk Art ★★★ Kids This branch of the Museum of New Mexico may not seem quite as typically Southwestern as other Santa Fe museums, but it's the largest of its kind in the world. With a collection of some 130,000 objects from more than 100 countries, it's my favorite city museum, well worth an hour or two of perusing. It was founded in 1953 by the Chicago collector Florence Dibell Bartlett, who said, "If peoples of different countries could have the opportunity to study each other's cultures, it would be one avenue for a closer understanding between men." That's the basis on which the museum operates today.

The special collections include Spanish colonial silver, traditional and contemporary New Mexican religious art, Mexican tribal costumes and majolica ceramics, Brazilian folk art, European glass, African sculptures, and East Indian textiles. Particularly delightful are numerous dioramas of people around the world at work and play in typical town, village, and home settings, which kids love.

The Hispanic Heritage Wing houses a fine collection of Spanish colonial and contemporary Hispanic folk art. Folk-art demonstrations, performances, and workshops are often presented here. The 80,000-sq.-ft. museum also has a lecture room, a research library, and two gift shops, where a variety of folk art is available for purchase.

706 Camino Lejo. ✆ **505/476-1200.** www.moifa.org. Admission $8 adults, free for kids 16 and under. 4-day passes (good at all 4 branches of the Museum of New Mexico and at the Museum of Spanish Colonial Art) $18 for adults. Daily 10am–5pm Memorial Day to Labor Day; Tues–Sun the rest of the year 10am–5pm. The museum is about 2 miles southeast of the plaza. Drive southeast on Old Santa Fe Trail (beware: Old Santa Fe Trail takes a left turn; if you find yourself on Old Pecos Trail, you missed the turn). Look for signs pointing right onto Camino Lejo.

Museum of Spanish Colonial Art ★ Beauty often follows in the wake of imperialism. A good example of this point is Spanish colonial art, which has flourished from Europe across the Americas and even in the Philippines. This newer museum, located in the same compound as the Museum of International Folk Art, the Museum of Indian Arts & Culture, and the Wheelwright Museum of the American Indian, celebrates this art with a collection of 3,000 devotional and decorative works and utilitarian artifacts. Housed in a home built by noted architect John Gaw Meem, the museum displays *retablos* (religious paintings on wood), *bultos* (free-standing religious sculptures), furniture, metalwork, and textiles and, outside, an 18th-century wooden colonial house from Mexico.

750 Camino Lejo. ✆ **505/982-2226.** www.spanishcolonial.org. Admission $8 adults, free for kids 16 and under. 4-day passes (good at all 4 branches of the Museum of New Mexico and this one) $18 for adults. Tues–Sun 10am–5pm. The museum is located about 2 miles southeast of the plaza. Drive southeast on Old Santa Fe Trail (beware: Old Santa Fe Trail takes a left turn; if you find yourself on Old Pecos Trail, you missed the turn). Look for signs pointing right onto Camino Lejo.

SITE Santa Fe ★ This not-for-profit, 18,000-square-foot contemporary art space without a permanent collection has made a place for itself in the City Different, as well as in the international art scene. It's no wonder, with shows by some of the world's most noted contemporary artists. As well as bringing cutting-edge visual art to Santa Fe, SITE sponsors an art and culture series of lectures, multidisciplinary programs, and artist dialogues. SITE sponsors other events; in 2010, it celebrates International Biennial starting in midsummer and running through the end of the year.

1606 Paseo de Peralta. ✆ **505/989-1199.** www.sitesantafe.org. $10 adults, $5 students and seniors, free for SITE Santa Fe members, free for all Fri. Wed–Sat 10am–5pm (Fri until 7pm); Sun noon–5pm. Closed Thanksgiving, Christmas Eve, Christmas, New Year's Eve, New Year's Day. Call for information about docent tours and tours in Spanish.

Wheelwright Museum of the American Indian ★ Kids Next door to the folk art museum, this museum resembles a Navajo hogan, with its doorway facing east (toward the rising sun) and its ceiling formed in the interlocking "whirling log" style. It was founded in 1937 by Boston scholar Mary Cabot Wheelwright, in collaboration with a Navajo medicine man, Hastiin Klah, to preserve and document Navajo ritual beliefs and practices. In 1976, the museum's focus was altered to include the living arts of all Native American cultures. The museum offers three or four exhibits per year. You may see a basketry exhibit, mixed-media Navajo toys, or amazing contemporary Navajo rugs. An added treat here is the Case Trading Post, an arts-and-crafts shop built to resemble the typical turn-of-the-20th-century trading post found on the Navajo reservation. Best of all here are the storytelling sessions ★★ given by **Joe Hayes,** scheduled in July and August on Saturday and Sunday evenings at 7pm. Check the Web schedule for more details.

704 Camino Lejo. ✆ **800/607-4636** or 505/982-4636. Fax 505/989-7386. www.wheelwright.org. Donations appreciated. Mon–Sat 10am–5pm; Sun 1–5pm. Closed New Year's Day, Thanksgiving, Christmas. Drive southeast on Old Santa Fe Trail (beware: Old Santa Fe Trail takes a left turn; if you find yourself on Old Pecos Trail, you missed the turn). Look for signs pointing right onto Camino Lejo.

CHURCHES

Cristo Rey This Catholic church ("Christ the King," in Spanish), a huge adobe structure, was built in 1940 to commemorate the 400th anniversary of Coronado's exploration of the Southwest. Parishioners did most of the construction work, even making adobe bricks from the earth where the church stands. The local architect John Gaw Meem designed the building, in missionary style, as a place to keep some magnificent stone *reredos* (altar screens) created by the Spanish during the colonial era and recovered and restored in the 20th century.

1120 Canyon Rd. ✆ **505/983-8528.** Free admission. Mon–Fri 8am–5pm.

Loretto Chapel Museum ★★ Though no longer consecrated for worship, the Loretto Chapel is an important site in Santa Fe. Patterned after the famous Sainte-Chapelle church in Paris, it was constructed in 1873—by the same French architects and Italian masons who were building Archbishop Lamy's cathedral—as a chapel for the Sisters of Loretto, who had established a school for young women in Santa Fe in 1852.

The chapel is especially notable for its remarkable spiral staircase: It makes two complete 360-degree turns, with no central or other visible support. The structure is steeped in legend. The building was nearly finished in 1878, when workers realized the stairs to the choir loft wouldn't fit. Hoping for a solution more attractive than a ladder, the sisters made a novena (9-day prayer) to St. Joseph—and were rewarded when a mysterious carpenter appeared astride a donkey and offered to build a staircase. Armed with only a saw, a hammer, and a T-square, the master constructed this work of genius by soaking slats of wood in tubs of water to curve them and holding them together with wooden pegs. Then he disappeared without bothering to collect his fee.

207 Old Santa Fe Trail (btw. Alameda and Water sts.). ✆ **505/982-0092.** www.lorettochapel.com. Admission $2.50 adults, $2 children 7–12 and seniors 65 and over, free for children 6 and under. Mon–Sat 9am–5pm; Sun 10:30am–5pm.

Mission of San Miguel If you really want to get the feel of colonial Catholicism, visit this church. Better yet, attend Mass here. You won't be disappointed. Built in 1610, the church has massive adobe walls, high windows, an elegant altar screen (erected in 1798), and a 780-pound San José bell (now found inside), which was cast in Spain in 1356. If that doesn't impress you, perhaps the buffalo-hide and deerskin Bible paintings used in 1630 by Franciscan missionaries to teach the Native Americans will. Anthropologists have excavated near the altar, down to the original floor that some claim to be part of a 12th-century pueblo. A small store just off the sanctuary sells religious articles.

401 Old Santa Fe Trail (at E. de Vargas St.). ✆ **505/983-3974.** Admission $1 adults, free for children 6 and under. Mon–Sat 9am–5pm; Sun 9am–4pm. Summer hours start earlier. Mass Sun 5pm.

Santuario de Nuestra Señora de Guadalupe ★ This church, built between 1776 and 1796 at the end of El Camino Real by Franciscan missionaries, is believed to be the oldest shrine in the United States honoring the Virgin of Guadalupe, the patron saint of Mexico. Better known as Santuario de Guadalupe, the shrine's adobe walls are almost 3-feet thick, and the deep-red plaster wall behind the altar was dyed with oxblood in traditional fashion when the church was restored early in the 20th century.

It is well worth a visit to see photographs of the transformation of the building over time; its styles have ranged from flat-topped pueblo to New England town meeting and today's northern New Mexico style. On one wall is a famous oil painting, *Our Lady of Guadalupe,* created in 1783 by the renowned Mexican artist José de Alzibar. Painted expressly for this church, it was brought from Mexico City by mule caravan.

100 S. Guadalupe St. ✆ **505/983-8868.** Donations appreciated. Mon–Sat 9am–4pm. Labor Day–Memorial Day 9am–6pm. Masses: Mon–Fri 6:30am, Sat 8am, Sun noon.

PARKS & REFUGES

Arroyo de los Chamisos Trail This trail, which meanders through the southwestern part of town, is of special interest to those staying in hotels along Cerrillos Road. The 2.5-mile paved path follows a chamisa-lined arroyo (stream) and has mountain views. It's great for walking or bicycling; dogs must be leashed.

Begin at Santa Fe High School on Yucca St. or on Rodeo Rd. near Sam's Club. ✆ **505/955-6977.**

Old Fort Marcy Park Marking the 1846 site of the first U.S. military reservation in the Southwest, this park overlooks the northeast corner of downtown. Only a few mounds remain from the fort, but the Cross of the Martyrs, at the top of a winding brick walkway from Paseo de Peralta near Otero Street, is a popular spot for bird's-eye photographs. The cross was erected in 1920 by the Knights of Columbus and the Historical Society of New Mexico to commemorate the Franciscans killed during the Pueblo Rebellion of 1680. It has since played a role in numerous religious processions. The park's open daily 24 hours, though it's dark and not likely safe at night.

617 Paseo de Peralta (or travel 3 blocks up Artist Rd. and turn right).

Randall Davey Audubon Center ★ Named for the late Santa Fe artist who willed his home to the National Audubon Society, this wildlife refuge occupies 135 acres at the mouth of Santa Fe Canyon. Just a few minutes' drive from the plaza, it's an excellent escape. More than 100 species of birds and 120 types of plants live here, and varied mammals have been spotted—including black bears, mule deer, mountain lions, bobcats, raccoons, and coyotes. Trails winding through more than 100 acres of the nature sanctuary are open to day hikers, but not to dogs. There's also a natural history bookstore on site.

1800 Upper Canyon Rd. ✆ **505/983-4609.** http://nm.audubon.org. Trail admission $2 adults, $1 children. Daily 9am–5pm. House tours conducted Mon and Fri at 2pm, $5 per person. Gift shop daily 10am–4pm (call for winter hours). Free 1-hr. guided bird walk every Sat at 8:30am.

Santa Fe River Park This is a lovely spot for an early morning jog, a midday walk beneath the trees, or perhaps a sack lunch at a picnic table. The green strip follows the midtown stream for about 4 miles as it meanders along Alameda from St. Francis Drive upstream beyond Camino Cabra, near its source. It's open daily 24 hours, but it's not a safe place to linger at night.

Alameda St. ✆ **505/955-6977.**

OTHER ATTRACTIONS

El Rancho de las Golondrinas ★★ (Kids) This 200-acre ranch, about 15 miles south of the plaza via I-25, was once the last stopping place on the 1,000-mile El Camino Real from Mexico City to Santa Fe. Today, it's a living 18th- and 19th-century Spanish village, comprising a hacienda, a village store, a schoolhouse, and several chapels and kitchens. There's also a working molasses mill, wheelwright and blacksmith shops, shearing and weaving rooms, a threshing ground, a winery and vineyard, and four water mills, as well as dozens of farm animals. A walk around the entire property is 1³/₄ miles in length, with amazing scenery and plenty of room for the kids to romp.

334 Los Pinos Rd. ✆ **505/471-2261.** www.golondrinas.org. Admission $5 adults, $4 seniors and teens, $2 children 5–12, free for children 4 and under. Festival weekends $7 adults, $5 seniors and teens, $3 children 5–12. June–Sept Wed–Sun 10am–4pm; Apr–May and Oct by advance arrangement. Closed Nov–Mar. From Santa Fe, drive south on I-25, taking exit 276; this will lead to NM 599 going north; turn left on W. Frontage Rd.; drive ¹/₂ mile; turn right on Los Pinos Rd.; travel 3 miles to the museum.

New Mexico State Capitol (Roundhouse) Some are surprised to learn that this is the only round capitol building in the U.S. Built in 1966, it's designed in the shape of a Zia Pueblo emblem (or sun sign, which is also the state symbol). It symbolizes the Circle of Life: four winds, four seasons, four directions, and four sacred obligations. Surrounding the capitol is a lush 6¹/₂-acre garden boasting more than 100 varieties of plants, including roses, plums, almonds, nectarines, Russian olive trees, and sequoias. Inside you'll find standard functional offices, with New Mexican art hanging on the walls. Check out the Governor's Gallery and the Capitol Art Collection. Self-guided tours are available 8am to 5pm Monday through Friday year-round; Memorial Day to Labor Day guided tours are available Monday through Saturday at 10am and 2pm. All tours and self-guided brochures are free to the public.

Paseo de Peralta and Old Santa Fe Trail. ✆ **505/986-4589.** www.legis.state.nm.us. Free admission. Mon–Sat 8am–5pm. Free parking.

Santa Fe Southern Railway ★ "Riding the old Santa Fe" always referred to riding the Atchison, Topeka & Santa Fe railroad. Ironically, the main route of the AT&SF bypassed Santa Fe, which probably forestalled some development for the capital city. A spur was run off the main line to Santa Fe in 1880, and today, an 18-mile ride along that spur offers views of some of New Mexico's most spectacular scenery.

Inside the restored coach, passengers are surrounded by aged mahogany and faded velvet seats. The train snakes through Santa Fe and into the Galisteo Basin, broad landscapes spotted with piñon and chamisa, with views of the Sandia and Ortiz mountains. Arriving in the small track town of Lamy, you get another glimpse of a Mission-style station, this one surrounded by spacious lawns where passengers picnic. Check out the sunset rides on weekends and specialty trains throughout the year.

410 S. Guadalupe St. ✆ **888/989-8600** or 505/989-8600. Fax 505/983-7620. www.thetraininsantafe.com. Tickets range from $18 (children) to $30 (adults), $30–$80 Fri–Sat evening rides (May–Oct). Discounts available. Depending on the season, trains depart the Santa Fe Depot (call to check schedule) 9:30am–1pm Mon–Sat. Rides also available Fri–Sat evening and Sun afternoon.

COOKING, ART & PHOTOGRAPHY CLASSES

If you're looking for something to do that's a little off the beaten tourist path, you might consider taking a class.

You can master the flavors of Santa Fe with an entertaining 3-hour demonstration cooking class at the **Santa Fe School of Cooking and Market** ★, on the upper level of the Plaza Mercado, 116 W. San Francisco St. (✆ **505/983-4511;** fax 505/983-7540; www.santafeschoolofcooking.com). The class teaches about the flavors and history of traditional New Mexican and contemporary Southwestern cuisines. "Cooking Light" classes are available as well. Prices range from $40 to $150 and include a meal; call for a class schedule. The adjoining market offers a variety of regional foods and cookbooks, with gift baskets available.

If Southwestern art has you hooked, you can take a drawing and painting class led by Santa Fe artist Jane Shoenfeld. Students sketch such outdoor subjects as the Santa Fe landscape and adobe architecture. In case of inclement weather, classes are held in the studio. Each class lasts for 3 hours, and art materials are included in the fee, which is $125. Private lessons can also be arranged. All levels of experience are welcome. Children's classes can be arranged, and discounts are available for families. You can create your own personal art adventure with one of Shoenfeld's 1-day classes at Ghost Ranch in Abiquiu. Contact Jane at **Sketching Santa Fe** ★ P.O. Box 5912, Santa Fe, NM 87502 (✆ **505/986-1108;** www.skyfields.net).

WINE TASTINGS

If you enjoy sampling regional wines, consider visiting the wineries within easy driving distance of Santa Fe: **Santa Fe Vineyards,** with a retail outlet at 235 Don Gaspar Ave., in Santa Fe (✆ **505/982-3474**), or the vineyard itself about 20 miles north of Santa Fe on US 84/285 (✆ **505/753-8100**); **Madison Vineyards & Winery,** in Ribera (✆ **505/421-8028**), about 45 miles east of Santa Fe on I-25 North; and the **Black Mesa Winery,** 1502 Hwy. 68, in Velarde (✆ **800/852-6372**), north on US 84/285 to NM 68 (about 1-hr. drive). Be sure to call in advance to find out when the wineries are open for tastings and to get specific directions.

ESPECIALLY FOR KIDS

Don't miss taking the kids to the **Museum of International Folk Art** (p. 161), where they'll love the international dioramas and the toys. Also visit the tepee at the **Wheelwright Museum of the American Indian** (p. 162), where storyteller Joe Hayes spins traditional Spanish *cuentos,* Native American folk tales, and Wild West tall tales on weekend evenings. **The Bishop's Lodge Ranch Resort and Spa** has extensive children's programs during the summer. These include horseback riding, swimming, arts-and-crafts programs, and special activities, such as archery and tennis. Kids are sure to enjoy **El Rancho de las Golondrinas** (p. 164), a living 18th- and 19th-century Spanish village comprising a hacienda, a village store, a schoolhouse, and several chapels and kitchens.

The **Genoveva Chavez Community Center** is a full-service family recreation center on the south side of Santa Fe (3221 Rodeo Rd.). The complex includes a 50m pool, a leisure pool, a therapy pool, an ice-skating rink, three gyms, a workout room, racquetball courts, and an indoor running track, as well as a spa and sauna. For hours and more information, call ✆ **505/955-4001.** www.gccommunitycenter.com.

Rockin' Rollers Event Arena This roller rink offers public-skating sessions—what the owners call family nights—on Fridays, as well as lessons and rentals. There's also a concession area to buy snacks. In-line skates are allowed.

2915 Agua Fria St. ✆ **505/473-7755.** $5. Fri 7–9pm.

Santa Fe Children's Museum ★ This museum offers interactive exhibits and hands-on activities in the arts, humanities, and science. The most notable features include a 16-foot climbing wall that kids—outfitted with helmets and harnesses—can scale, and a 1-acre Southwestern horticulture garden, complete with animals, wetlands, and a greenhouse. This fascinating area serves as an outdoor classroom for ongoing environmental educational programs. Special performances and hands-on sessions with artists and scientists are regularly scheduled. *Family Life* magazine named this as one of the 10 hottest children's museums in the nation.

1050 Old Pecos Trail. ✆ **505/989-8359.** www.santafechildrensmuseum.org. Admission $8 for nonresidents; $4 New Mexico residents; $4 children 12 and under, must be accompanied by an adult. Wed–Sat 10am–5pm; Sun noon–5pm.

Santa Fe Public Library Special programs, such as storytelling and magic shows, can be found here weekly throughout the summer. The library is in the center of town, 1 block from the plaza.

145 Washington Ave. ✆ **505/955-6780.** www.santafelibrary.org. Mon–Thurs 10am–9pm; Fri–Sat 10am–6pm; Sun 1–5pm. Call for additional information.

Skateboard Park Split-level ramps for daredevils, park benches for onlookers, and climbing structures for youngsters are located at this park near downtown.

At the intersection of de Vargas and Sandoval sts. ✆ **505/955-2100.** Free admission. 24 hr.

6 ORGANIZED TOURS

BUS, CAR & TRAM TOURS

LorettoLine ★ For an open-air tour of the city covering history and sights, contact this company that has been running tours for 17 years. Tours last 1¼ hours and are offered daily from April to October. They depart at 10am, noon, and 2pm—and sometimes more frequently in high summer.

At the Hotel Loretto, 211 Old Santa Fe Trail. Tours depart from the Loretto Chapel. ✆ **505/983-3701.** www.toursofsantafe.com. Tours $14 adults, $10 children 12 and under.

WALKING TOURS

As with the independent strolls described above, the following are the best way to get an appreciable feel for Santa Fe's history and culture.

Storytellers and the Southwest: A Literary Walking Tour ★ Barbara Harrelson, a former Smithsonian museum docent and local writer, takes you on a 2-hour literary walking tour of downtown, exploring the history, legends, characters, and authors of the region through its landmarks and historic sites. It's a great way to absorb the unique character of Santa Fe. Tours take place by appointment. Harrelson's book, *Walks in Literary Santa Fe: A Guide to Landmarks, Legends, and Lore* ($12.95, Gibbs Smith) allows for self-guided tours and is available in local bookstores and online.

924 Old Taos Hwy. ✆ **505/989-4561.** barabarah@newmexico.com. Apr–Oct. Tours $20 per adult, $10 for children 16 and under, with a $40 minimum.

Walking Tour of Santa Fe ★ One of Santa Fe's best walking tours begins under the T-shirt tree at Tees & Skis, 107 Washington Ave., near the northeast corner of the plaza (at 9:30am and 1:30pm). It lasts about 2½ hours. From November through March, the tour runs by reservation only.

54½ E. San Francisco St. (tour meets at 107 Washington Ave.). ✆ **800/338-6877** or 505/983-6565. Tours $10 adults, free for children 12 and under.

MISCELLANEOUS TOURS

Pathways Customized Tours ★ Don Dietz offers several planned tours, including a downtown Santa Fe walking tour, a full city tour, a trip to the cliff dwellings and native pueblos, a "Taos adventure," and a trip to Georgia O'Keeffe country (with a focus on the landscape that inspired the art now viewable in the O'Keeffe Museum). He will try to accommodate any special requests you might have. These tours last anywhere from 2 to 9 hours, depending on the one you choose. Don has extensive knowledge of the area's culture, history, geology, and flora and fauna, and will help you make the most of your precious vacation time.

161-F Calle Ojo Feliz. ✆ **505/982-5382.** www.santafepathways.com. Tours $60–$200+ per day, covers up to 2 people. No credit cards.

Rain Parrish ★ A Navajo (or *Diné*) anthropologist, artist, and curator, Rain Parrish offers custom guide services focusing on cultural anthropology, Native American arts, and the history of the Native Americans of the Southwest. Some of these are true adventures to insider locations. Parrish includes visits to local Pueblo villages.

704 Kathryn St. ✆ **505/984-8236.** Tours $135 for up to 2 people for 4 hr.

Recursos de Santa Fe/Royal Road Tours ★ This organization is a full-service destination management company, emphasizing custom-designed itineraries to meet the interests of any group. They specialize in the archaeology, art, literature, spirituality, architecture, environment, food, and history of the Southwest. Call or visit the website for a calendar and information about their annual writers' conferences.

826 Camino de Monte Rey. ✆ **505/982-9301.** www.recursos.org.

Rojo Tours & Services Customized and private tours are arranged to pueblos, cliff dwellings, ruins, hot-air ballooning, backpacking, or white-water rafting. Rojo also provides planning services for groups.

P.O. Box 15744. ✆ **505/474-8333.** Fax 505/474-2992. www.rojotours.com.

Santa Fe Detours ★ Santa Fe's most extensive tour-booking agency accommodates almost all travelers' tastes, from bus and rail tours to river rafting, backpacking, and cross-country skiing. The agency can also facilitate hotel reservations, from budget to high end.

54½ E. San Francisco St. (summer tour desk, 107 Washington Ave.). ✆ **800/338-6877** or 505/983-6565. www.sfdetours.com.

Southwest Safaris ★★ This tour is one of the most interesting Southwestern experiences available. You'll fly in a small plane 1,000 feet off the ground to various destinations while pilot Bruce Adams explains millions of years of geologic history. En route to the Grand Canyon, for instance, you may pass by the ancient ruins of Chaco Canyon, over the vivid colors of the Painted Desert, and then, of course, over the spectacular Grand Canyon itself. Trips to many Southwestern destinations are available.

P.O. Box 945. ✆ **800/842-4246** or 505/988-4246. www.southwestsafaris.com. Tours $89–$699 per person.

7 OUTDOOR ACTIVITIES

Set between the granite peaks of the Sangre de Cristo Mountains and the subtler volcanic Jemez Mountains, and with the Rio Grande flowing through, the Santa Fe area offers outdoor enthusiasts many opportunities to play. This is the land of high desert, where temperatures vary with the elevation, allowing for a full range of activities throughout the year.

BALLOONING

New Mexico is renowned for its spectacular Balloon Fiesta, which takes place annually in Albuquerque (p. 45). If you want to take a ride, you'll probably have to go to Albuquerque or Taos, but you can book your trip in Santa Fe through **Santa Fe Detours,** 54½ E. San Francisco St. (tour desk for summer, 107 Washington Ave.; ✆ **800/338-6877** or 505/983-6565; www.sfdetours.com). Flights take place early in the day. Rates begin at around $175 a flight. If you have your heart set on a balloon flight, I suggest that you reserve a time early in your trip because flights are sometimes canceled due to bad weather. That way, if you have to reschedule, you'll have enough time to do so.

BIKING

You can cycle along main roadways and paved country roads year-round in Santa Fe, but be aware that traffic is particularly heavy around the plaza—and all over town, motorists are not particularly attentive to bicyclists, so you need to be especially alert. Mountain-biking interest has exploded here and is especially popular in the spring, summer, and fall; the high-desert terrain is rugged and challenging, but mountain bikers of all levels can find exhilarating rides. The Santa Fe Community Convention Center and Visitors Bureau can supply you with bike maps.

I recommend the following trails: The **railroad tracks south of Santa Fe** provide wide-open biking on beginner-to-intermediate technical trails; and the **Borrego Trail** up toward the Santa Fe Ski Area is a challenging technical ride that links in with the **Windsor Trail,** a nationally renowned technical romp with plenty of verticality.

In Santa Fe bookstores, or online at sites like Amazon.com, look for *Mountain Biking Northern New Mexico: A Guide to Taos, Santa Fe, and Albuquerque Areas' Greatest Off-Road Bicycle Rides* by Bob D'Antonio. The book details 40 rides ranging in difficulty from beginner to advanced. **Santa Fe Mountain Sports,** 606 Cerrillos Rd. (✆ **505/988-3337;**

www.santafemountainsports.com), rents hard-tail mountain bikes for $20/half-day and $25/full day, or full-suspension bikes for $35/full day. **Mellow Velo Bikes,** 638 Old Santa Fe Trail (✆ **505/982-8986;** www.mellowvelo.com), rents front-suspension mountain bikes for $23/half-day and $30/full day. Town cruisers run $23/half-day and $30/ full day. Full-suspension bikes run $43 per day. Add $7, and Mellow Velo will deliver to and pick up from your hotel (in the Santa Fe area). Multiday rentals can be arranged. Both shops supply accessories such as helmets, locks, maps, and trail information, usually at an additional cost. **Mellow Velo** also runs a private guided tour service, which includes back-country guided adventures starting from $60 to $95 per person. On their guided train tour, clients cycle to Lamy and take a train back.

BIRD-WATCHING

Bird-watchers flock to the **Randall Davey Audubon Center** ★ (see "Parks & Refuges," earlier in this chapter), 1800 Upper Canyon Rd. (✆ **505/983-4609**), to see more than 100 species of birds and many other animals. For guided bird-watching tours all over the region, contact **Wings West** at ✆ **800/583-6928;** http://home.earthlink.net/~wings westnm. Bill West guides half-day tours to local spots such as the Santa Fe Mountains and Cochiti Lake ($105 for 1–2 people) and full-day ones farther afield ($195 for 1–2 people).

FISHING

In the lakes and waterways around Santa Fe, anglers typically catch trout (there are five varieties in the area). Other local fish include bass, perch, and kokanee salmon. The most popular fishing holes are Cochiti and Abiquiu lakes as well as the Rio Chama, Pecos River, and the Rio Grande. A world-renowned fly-fishing destination, the **San Juan River,** near Farmington, is worth a visit and can make for an exciting 2-day trip in combination with a tour around **Chaco Culture National Historic Park** (see chapter 9). Check with the **New Mexico Game and Fish Department** (✆ **505/476-8000;** www.wildlife.state.nm.us) for information (including maps of area waters), licenses, and fishing proclamations. **High Desert Angler,** 453 Cerrillos Rd. (✆ **505/988-7688;** www.highdesertangler.com), specializes in fly-fishing gear and guide services.

GOLF

There are three courses in the Santa Fe area: the 18-hole **Santa Fe Country Club,** on Airport Road (✆ **505/471-2626;** www.santafecountryclub.com); the often-praised 18-hole **Cochiti Lake Golf Course,** 5200 Cochiti Hwy., Cochiti Lake, about 35 miles southwest of Santa Fe via I-25 and NM 16 and 22 (✆ **505/465-2239;** www.pueblodecochiti.org); and Santa Fe's newest 18-hole course, **Marty Sanchez Links de Santa Fe,** 205 Caja del Rio (✆ **505/955-4400;** www.linksdesantafe.com). Both the Santa Fe Country Club and the Marty Sanchez Links offer driving ranges as well. North of Santa Fe on Pojoaque Pueblo land, the **Towa Golf Resort** (Buffalo Thunder Resort, 12 miles north of Santa Fe on US 285/84; ✆ **877/465-3489** or 505/455-9000; www.towagolf.com), offers 36 holes, 27 of them designed by Hale Irwin and William Phillips, set with views of the Jemez and Sangre de Cristo mountains.

HIKING

It's hard to decide which of the 1,000 miles of nearby national forest trails to tackle. Four wilderness areas are nearby, most notably **Pecos Wilderness,** with 223,000 acres east of Santa Fe. Also visit the 58,000-acre **Jemez Mountain National Recreation Area.** Information on these and other wilderness areas is available from the **Santa Fe National Forest,** P.O. Box 1689 (1474 Rodeo Rd.), Santa Fe, NM 87504 (© **505/438-7840;** www.fs.fed.us). If you're looking for company on your trek, contact the Santa Fe branch of the **Sierra Club,** 1807 Second St. (© **505/983-2703;** www.riogrande.sierraclub.org). A hiking schedule can be found in the local newsletter; you can pick one up outside the office. Some people enjoy taking a chairlift ride to the summit of the **Santa Fe Ski Area** (© **505/982-4429;** www.skisantafe.com) and hiking around up there during the summer. A popular guide with Santa Feans is *Day Hikes in the Santa Fe Area,* put out by the local branch of the Sierra Club. The most popular hiking trails are the **Borrego Trail,** a moderate 4-mile jaunt through aspens and ponderosa pines, ending at a creek, and **Aspen Vista,** an easy 1- to 5-mile hike through aspen forest with views to the east. Both are easy to find; simply head up Hyde Park Road toward Ski Santa Fe. The Borrego Trail is 8¼ miles up, while Aspen Vista is 10 miles. In recent years an energetic crew has cut the **Dale Ball Trails** (© **505/955-6977**), miles of hiking/biking trails throughout the Santa Fe foothills. The easiest access is off Hyde Park Road toward Ski Santa Fe. Drive 2 miles from Bishop's Lodge Road and watch for the trail head on the left. If you're looking for "outspiration" (versus inspiration) on a guided day-hiking experience, call **Outspire** (© **505/660-0394;** www.outspire.com). They'll set you up with a guide and design just the hike for your ability level and interest. A 3- to 4-hour hike runs at a flat rate of $150, with prices going up from there. Outspire also guides snowshoeing trips.

HORSEBACK RIDING

Trips ranging in length from a few hours to overnight can be arranged by **Santa Fe Detours,** 54½ E. San Francisco St. (summer tour desk, 107 Washington Ave.; © **800/338-6877** or 505/983-6565; www.sfdetours.com). You'll ride with "experienced wranglers," and they can even arrange a trip that includes a cookout or brunch. Rides are also major activities at the **Bishop's Lodge** (see earlier). The **Broken Saddle Riding Company** (© **505/424-7774**) offers rides through the stunning Galisteo Basin south of Santa Fe.

HUNTING

Elk and mule deer are taken by hunters in the Pecos Wilderness and Jemez Mountains, as are occasional black bears and bighorn sheep. Wild turkeys and grouse are frequently bagged in the uplands, geese and ducks at lower elevations. Check with the **New Mexico Game and Fish Department** (© **505/476-8000;** www.wildlife.state.nm.us) for information and licenses.

RIVER RAFTING & KAYAKING

Although Taos is the real rafting center of New Mexico, several companies serve Santa Fe during the April-to-October white-water season. They include **New Wave Rafting,** 70 County Rd. 84B, Santa Fe, NM 87506 (© **800/984-1444** or 505/984-1444; www.newwaverafting.com), and **Santa Fe Rafting Co.,** 1000 Cerrillos Rd., Santa Fe, NM 87505 (© **888/988-4914** or 505/988-4914; www.santaferafting.com). You can expect the cost of a full-day trip to range from about $110 to $125 per person before tax and the 3% federal land use fee. The day of the week (weekdays are less expensive) and group size may also affect the price.

RUNNING

Despite its elevation, Santa Fe is popular with runners and hosts numerous competitions, including the annual **Old Santa Fe Trail Run** on Labor Day. The website **Santa Fe Striders**

Getting Pampered: The Spa Scene

If traveling, skiing, or other activities have left you weary, Santa Fe has a number of relaxation options. Newest to the city is the **Absolute Nirvana Spa & Gardens** ★★ (✆ **505/983-7942;** www.absolutenirvana.com). This creation, voted one of the best three spas in town by the *Santa Fe Reporter,* offers imaginative Indo-Asian spa "experiences" as well as massages and facials. The spa is open Sunday to Thursday 10am to 6pm, and Friday and Saturday 10am to 8pm. Prices range from $105 to $240. Another option with a more Japanese bent is **Ten Thousand Waves** ★★, a spa about 3 miles northeast of Santa Fe on Hyde Park Road (✆ **505/982-9304;** www.tenthousandwaves.com). This serene retreat, nestled in a grove of piñons, offers hot tubs, saunas, and cold plunges, plus a variety of massage and other bodywork techniques. If you call far enough in advance, you may be able to find lodging at Ten Thousand Waves as well. The spa is open Monday, Wednesday, and Thursday from 10:30am to 10:30pm; Tuesday from 2 to 10:30pm; and Friday through Sunday from 9am to 10:30pm (winter hours are shorter, so be sure to call). Reservations are recommended, especially on weekends.

The City Different's newest retreat, **Shánah Spa and Wellness Center** ★★ (✆ **800/732-2240;** www.bishopslodge.com), at Bishop's Lodge Resort & Spa, offers a full range of treatments in a serene Native America–style ambiance surrounded by lush grounds 10 minutes north of Santa Fe. Their signature Natural Stone Massage features warmed river-smoothed rocks from northern New Mexico. A hot tub and outdoor treatments—even one in a tepee—add to the allure. Plan a trip there to include a meal at **Las Fuentes** ★★, where you'll sample some of the region's best New American fare. Another luxurious option is **Rockresorts Spa** ★★ at La Posada de Santa Fe Resort and Spa (✆ **505/986-0000;** www.rockresorts.com). Offering a range of treatments from massage to salt glows, this spot offers free use of a steam room, hot tub, and grass-surrounded pool.

Also within town is the new **Body** ★, 333 Cordova Rd. (✆ **505/986-0362;** www.bodyofsantafe.com). This spa/studio/restaurant offers a full range of massage treatments, yoga, Nia, and Pilates classes, and organic food. Moms enjoy the childcare available. A south-of-town option, **Sunrise Springs Inn and Retreat** ★, at 242 Los Pinos Rd. (✆ **505/471-3600**), offers treatments in a lovely pond-side setting. Along with your treatment, plan a meal at the inn's **Blue Heron Restaurant** ★★, where you'll feast on delectable New American cuisine with a healthy flair.

(www.santafestriders.org) lists various runs during the year, as well as weekly runs. This is a great opportunity for travelers to find their way and to meet some locals.

SKIING

There's something available for every ability level at **Ski Santa Fe,** about 16 miles northeast of Santa Fe via Hyde Park (Ski Basin) Road. Lots of locals ski here, particularly on weekends; if you can, go on weekdays. It's a good family area and fairly small, so it's easy to split off from and later reconnect with your party. Built on the upper reaches of 12,000-foot Tesuque Peak, the area has an average annual snowfall of 225 inches and a vertical drop of 1,725 feet. Seven lifts, including a 5,000-foot triple chair and a quad chair, serve 69 runs and 660 acres of terrain, with a total capacity of 7,800 riders an hour. Base facilities, at 10,350 feet, center around **La Casa Mall,** with a cafeteria, lounge, ski shop, and boutique. A restaurant, **Totemoff's,** has a midmountain patio.

The ski area is open daily from 9am to 4pm; the season often runs from Thanksgiving to early April, depending on snow conditions. Rates for all lifts are $58 for adults, $46 for teens (13–20 years), $40 for children and seniors; half-day tickets run $42. Tickets are free for kids less than 46 inches tall (in their ski boots), and for seniors 72 and older. For more information, contact **Ski Santa Fe,** 2209 Brothers Rd., Ste. 220 (**✆ 505/982-4429;** www.skisantafe.com). For 24-hour reports on snow conditions, call **✆ 505/983-9155. Ski New Mexico** (**✆ 505/585-2422**) gives statewide reports. Ski packages are available through **SantaFeHotels.com** (**✆ 800/745-9910**).

Cross-country skiers find seemingly endless miles of snow to track in the **Santa Fe National Forest** (**✆ 505/438-7840;** www.fs.fed.us). A favorite place to start is at the Black Canyon campground, about 9 miles from downtown en route to the Ski Santa Fe. In the same area are the **Borrego Trail** (high intermediate), **Aspen Vista Trail,** and the **Norski Trail,** all en route to Ski Santa Fe as well. Other popular activities at the ski area in winter include snowshoeing, snowboarding, sledding, and inner tubing. Ski, snowboard, and snowshoe rentals are available at a number of downtown shops and the ski area.

SWIMMING

There's a public pool at the **Fort Marcy Complex** (**✆ 505/955-2500;** www.santafenm.gov) on Camino Santiago, off Bishop's Lodge Road. In summer, the public **Bicentennial Pool,** 1121 Alto St. (**✆ 505/955-4778**) offers outdoor swimming. Admission to both is less than $2 for all ages.

TENNIS

Santa Fe has 44 public tennis courts and four major private facilities. The **City Recreation Department** (**✆ 505/955-2100;** www.santafenm.gov) can help you locate indoor, outdoor, and lighted public courts.

8 SHOPPING

Santa Fe offers a broad range of art, from very traditional Native American crafts and Hispanic folk art to extremely innovative contemporary work. Some locals call Santa Fe one of the top art markets in the world. Galleries speckle the downtown area, and as an artists' thoroughfare, Canyon Road is preeminent. The greatest concentration of Native American crafts is displayed beneath the portal of the Palace of the Governors.

Any serious arts aficionado should try to attend one or more of the city's great arts festivals—the Spring Festival of the Arts in May, the Spanish Market in July, the Indian Market in August, and the Fall Festival of the Arts in October.

Few visitors to Santa Fe leave the city without acquiring at least one item from the Native American artisans at the Palace of the Governors. You can also peruse one of the outstanding **gallery catalogs** for an introduction to local dealers. They're available for free in many galleries and hotels. They include *The Collector's Guide to Art in Santa Fe* *and Taos* by Wingspread Incorporated (www.collectorsguide.com), *The Essential Guide* by Essential Guides, LLC (www.essentialguide.com), and others. For a current listing of gallery openings, with recommendations on which ones to attend, purchase a copy of the monthly magazine the *Santa Fean* by Santa Fean, LLC (466 W. San Francisco St., Santa Fe, NM 87501; www.santafean.com). Also check in the "Pasatiempo" section of the local newspaper, the *New Mexican* (www.santafenewmexican.com), every Friday.

Business hours vary quite a bit among establishments, but most are open at least Monday through Friday from 10am to 5pm, with mall stores open until 8 or 9pm. Most shops are open similar hours on Saturday, and many also open on Sunday afternoon during the summer. Winter hours tend to be more limited.

After the high-rolling 1980s, during which art markets around the country prospered, came the penny-pinching 1990s and the fearful 2000s. Many galleries in Santa Fe have been forced to shut their doors. Those that remain tend to specialize in particular types of art, a refinement process that has improved the gallery scene here. Some locals worry that the lack of serious art buyers in the area leads to fewer good galleries and more T-shirt and trinket stores. The plaza has its share of those but still has a good number of serious galleries, appealing to those buyers whose interests run to accessible art—Southwestern landscapes and the like. On Canyon Road, the art is often more experimental and diverse.

THE TOP GALLERIES

Contemporary Art

Canyon Road Contemporary Art This gallery represents some of the finest emerging U.S. contemporary artists as well as internationally known artists. You'll find figurative, landscape, and abstract paintings, as well as raku pottery. 403 Canyon Rd. ✆ **505/983-0433.**

Hahn Ross Gallery Owners Tom Ross and Elizabeth Hahn, a children's book illustrator and surrealist painter, respectively, specialize in representing artists who create colorful, fantasy-oriented works. Check out the sculpture garden here. 409 Canyon Rd. ✆ **505/984-8434.** www.hahnross.com.

La Mesa of Santa Fe ★ Finds Step into this gallery and let your senses dance. Dramatically colored ceramic plates, bowls, and other kitchen items fill one room. Contemporary katsinas by Gregory Lomayesva—a real buy—line the walls, accented by steel lamps and rag rugs. 225 Canyon Rd. ✆ **505/984-1688.** www.lamesaofsantafe.com.

LewAllen Contemporary ★★ Finds This is one of Santa Fe's most prized galleries. You'll find bizarre and beautiful contemporary works in a range of media, from granite to clay to twigs. There are always exciting works on canvas. 129 W. Palace Ave. ✆ **505/988-8997.** www.lewallencontemporary.com.

Linda Durham Contemporary Art ★ The opening of this broad and bright art space in summer 2004 marks the return of one of Santa Fe's best galleries. Longtime gallery owner Linda Durham had moved her gallery 25 miles south of town, but has now returned, with a strong roster of talent including Greg Erf and Judy Tuwaletstiwa. 1101 Paseo de Peralta. ✆ **505/466-6600.** www.lindadurham.com.

Patina Gallery Finds Selling functional objects and sculptural art, including jewelry, fiber, clay and wood pieces, this gallery exhibits the work of more than 100 leading American and European artists. Look for silver work by Harold O'Connor. 131 W. Palace Ave. ✆ **877/877-0827.** www.patina-gallery.com.

Peyton Wright Gallery ★ Housed within the Historic Spiegelberg House (a refurbished Victorian adobe), this excellent gallery offers contemporary, American Modernism, Spanish Colonial, Russian, and 18th-century New Mexico *bultos* and *santos.* In addition to representing such artists as Orlando Leyba, Roni Stretch, and Tim Murphy, the gallery features monthly exhibitions—including contemporary paintings, sculptures, and works on paper. 237 E. Palace Ave. ✆ **800/879-8898** or 505/989-9888. www.peytonwright.com.

Shidoni Foundry, Gallery, and Sculpture Gardens ★★ Moments Shidoni Foundry is one of the area's most exciting spots for sculptors and sculpture enthusiasts. At the foundry, visitors may take a tour through the facilities to view casting processes. In addition, Shidoni Foundry includes a 5,000-square-foot contemporary gallery, a bronze gallery, and a wonderful sculpture garden—a great place for a picnic. Bishop's Lodge Rd., Tesuque. ✆ **505/988-8001.** www.shidoni.com.

Waxlander Gallery Primarily featuring the whimsical acrylics and occasional watercolors of Phyllis Kapp, this is the place to browse if you like bold color. 622 Canyon Rd. ✆ **800/342-2202** or 505/984-2202. www.waxlander.com.

Native American & Other Indigenous Art

Andrea Fisher Fine Pottery ★ This expansive gallery is a wonderland of authentic Southwestern Indian pottery. You'll find real showpieces here, including the work of renowned San Ildefonso Pueblo potter Maria Martinez. 100 W. San Francisco St. ✆ **505/986-1234.** www.andreafisherpottery.com.

Frank Howell Gallery If you've never seen the wonderful illustrative hand of the late Frank Howell, you'll want to visit this gallery. You'll find a variety of works by contemporary American Indian artists. The gallery also features sculpture, jewelry, and graphics. 103 Washington Ave. ✆ **505/984-1074.** www.frankhowellgallery.com.

Morning Star Gallery ★★ Finds This is one of my favorite places to browse. Throughout the rambling gallery are American Indian art masterpieces, all elegantly displayed. You'll see a broad range of works, from late-19th-century Navajo blankets to 1920s Zuni needlepoint jewelry. 513 Canyon Rd. ✆ **505/982-8187.** www.morningstargallery.com.

Ortega's on the Plaza A hearty shopper could spend hours here, perusing inventive turquoise and silver jewelry and especially fine strung beadwork, as well as rugs and pottery. An adjacent room showcases a wide array of clothing, all with a hip Southwestern flair. 101 W. San Francisco St. ✆ **505/988-1866.**

Sherwoods ★ Set in the historic Bandelier House, this gallery features museum-quality Plains Indians antiquities such as an 1870 Nez Perce beaded dress and a Crow warshirt. Some paintings hang here as well, including works by Santa Fe masters such as J. H. Sharp and Gene Kloss. Firearm buffs will go ballistic over the gun room here. 1005 Paseo de Peralta. ✆ **505/988-1776.** www.sherwoodsspirit.com.

Photography

Andrew Smith Gallery ★ I'm always amazed when I enter this gallery and notice works I've seen reprinted in major magazines for years. There they are, photographic prints, large and beautiful, hanging on the wall. Here, you'll see famous works by Edward Curtis, Henri Cartier-Bresson, Ansel Adams, Annie Leibovitz, and others. A new gallery at the corner of Grant and Johnson streets extends this collection. 203 W. San Francisco St. ✆ **505/984-1234.** www.andrewsmithgallery.com.

Lisa Kristine Gallery ★★ With galleries here in Santa Fe and in Sausalito, Sonoma, and Mendocino, Lisa Kristine's work gets around, and it's no wonder. These richly colored portraits and landscapes of Asian and African culture will have you gaping in wonderment. 204 W. San Francisco St. ✆ **505/820-6330.** www.lisakristine.com.

Photo-Eye Gallery You're bound to be surprised each time you step into this gallery a few blocks off Canyon Road. Dealing in contemporary photography, the gallery represents both internationally renowned and emerging artists. 370 Garcia St. ✆ **505/988-5152.** www.photoeye.com.

Traditional Art

Altermann Galleries This is a well of interesting traditional art, mostly 19th-, 20th-, and 21st-century American paintings and sculpture. The gallery represents Remington and Russell, in addition to Taos founders, Santa Fe artists, and members of the Cowboy Artists of America and the National Academy of Western Art. Stroll through the sculpture garden among whimsical bronzes of children and dogs. 225 Canyon Rd. ✆ **505/983-1590.** www.altermann.com.

Gerald Peters Gallery ★★ Displayed throughout a graceful pueblo-style building, the works here are so fine you'll feel as though you're in a museum. You'll find 19th-, 20th-, and 21st-century American painting and sculpture, featuring the art of Georgia O'Keeffe, William Wegman, and the founders of the Santa Fe and Taos artist colonies, as well as more contemporary works. 1011 Paseo de Peralta. ✆ **505/954-5700.** www.gpgallery.com.

The Mayans Gallery Ltd. Established in 1977, this is one of the oldest galleries in Santa Fe. You'll find 20th-century American and Latin American paintings, photography, prints, and sculpture. 601 Canyon Rd. ✆ **505/983-8068.**

Nedra Matteucci Galleries ★★ As you approach this gallery, note the elaborately crafted stone and adobe wall that surrounds it, merely a taste of what's to come. The gallery specializes in 19th-, 20th-, and 21st-century American art. Inside, you'll find a lot of high-ticket works such as those of early Taos and Santa Fe painters, as well as classic American Impressionism, historical Western modernism, and contemporary Southwestern landscapes and sculpture. Another excellent gallery, Nedra Matteucci Fine Art, is located at 555 Canyon Rd. There look for the fabulous impressionist works by Evelyne Boren. 1075 Paseo de Peralta. ✆ **505/982-4631.** www.matteucci.com.

Owings-Dewey Fine Art ★ These are treasure-filled rooms. You'll find 19th-, 20th-, and 21st-century American painting and sculpture, including works by Georgia O'Keeffe, Robert Henri, Maynard Dixon, Fremont Ellis, and Andrew Dasburg, as well as antique works such as Spanish colonial *retablos, bultos,* and tin works. Look for the exciting bird sculptures by Peter Woytuk. 76 E. San Francisco St., upstairs, and a second shop at 120 E. Marcy St. ✆ **505/982-6244.**

Zaplin Lampert Gallery ★★ Art aficionados as well as those who just like a nice landscape will enjoy this gallery, one of Santa Fe's classics. Hanging on old adobe walls are works by some of the region's early masters, including Bert Phillips, Gene Kloss, and Gustauve Baumann. 651 Canyon Rd. ✆ **505/982-6100.** www.zaplinlampert.com.

MORE SHOPPING A TO Z

Antiques

El Paso Import Company ★ Whenever I'm in the vicinity of this shop, I always stop in. It's packed—and I mean packed—with colorful, weathered colonial and ranchero

Arcade Shopping on the Plaza

Opened in 2004, the **Santa Fe Arcade,** 60 E. San Francisco St. (✆ **505/988-5792**), on the south side of the plaza, offers three stories of shops in a sleek, glassy European-style space. It's a far cry from the Woolworth's that once lived there. Showy Western wear, fine Indian jewelry, and hip clothing fill the display windows of some 60 spaces in the mall. If you like to pamper yourself with natural products, many made in northern New Mexico, step into **Sombria** (ste. 222; ✆ **888/480-5554** or 505/982-7383). Look for their margarita salt glow, made with salt from Utah's Great Salt Lake. Prima Fine Jewelry's **Oro Fino** (ste. 218; ✆ **505/983-9699**) sells contemporary and Southwestern inlaid jewelry in silver, gold, and platinum.

furniture. The affordable home furnishings and folk art here are imported from Mexico, India, and Romania. 418 Sandoval St. ✆ **505/982-5698.** www.elpasoimportco.com.

Jackalope ★ Kids Value Spread over 7 acres of land, this is a wild place to spend a morning or an afternoon browsing through exotic furnishings from India and Mexico, as well as imported textiles, pottery, jewelry, and clothing. It's a great place to find gifts. Kids will love the prairie-dog village. 2820 Cerrillos Rd. ✆ **505/471-8539.** www.jackalope.com.

Books

Borders With close to 200 stores nationwide, this chain provides a broad range of books, music, and videos, and it hosts in-store appearances by authors, musicians, and artists. 500 Montezuma Ave. ✆ **505/954-4707.** www.borders.com.

Collected Works Bookstore This is a good downtown book source, with carefully recommended books up front, in case you're not sure what you want, and shelves of Southwest, travel, nature, and other books. 208–B W. San Francisco St. ✆ **505/988-4226.** www.collectedworksbookstore.com.

Garcia Street Books One of Santa Fe's best shops for perusing, this gem stocks a broad range of titles on the Southwest and collectibles. Not sure what to read? The knowledgeable staff here will help you decide. 376 Garcia St. ✆ **866/986-0151** or 505/986-0151. www.garciastreetbooks.com.

Children

Gypsy Baby This shop sells bright clothes, beaded slippers, and mustang rocking horses, all mindful of the slogan "Born to be spoiled." 318 S. Guadalupe St. ✆ **505/820-1898.** www.gypsybabies.com.

Crafts

Nambe ★ Finds The cooking, serving, and decorating pieces here are fashioned from an exquisite sand-cast and handcrafted alloy. These items are also available at the Nambe stores at 104 W. San Francisco St. (✆ **505/988-3574**) and in Taos at 113A Paseo del Pueblo Norte (✆ **575/758-8221**). 924 Paseo de Peralta. ✆ **505/988-5528.** www.nambe.com.

Fashions

Back at the Ranch ★ This shop has chic western wear and what it calls the "largest selection of handmade cowboy boots in the country." 209 E. Marcy St. ✆ **888/962-6687** or 505/989-8110; www.backattheranch.com.

Origins ★ (Moments) A little like a Guatemalan or Turkish marketplace, this store is packed with wearable art, folk art, and the work of local designers. Look for good buys on ethnic jewelry. Throughout the summer there are trunk shows, which offer opportunities to meet the artists. 135 W. San Francisco St. ✆ **505/988-2323.** www.originssantafe.com.

Overland Sheepskin Company The rich smell of leather will draw you in the door and possibly hold onto you until you purchase a coat, blazer, hat, or other finely made leather item. 74 E. San Francisco St. ✆ **505/983-4727.** www.overland.com.

Food

The Chile Shop This store has too many cheap trinket-like items for me, but many people find some novelty items to take back home. You'll find everything from salsas to cornmeal and tortilla chips. The shop also stocks cookbooks and pottery items. 109 E. Water St. ✆ **505/983-6080.** www.thechileshop.com.

Señor Murphy Candy Maker Unlike any candy store you'll find in other parts of the country—everything here is made with local ingredients. The chile piñon-nut brittle is a taste sensation! Señor Murphy has another shop in the Santa Fe Place mall (✆ **505/471-8899**). 100 E. San Francisco St. (La Fonda Hotel). ✆ **505/982-0461.** www.senormurphy.com.

Furniture

Southwest Spanish Craftsmen The Spanish colonial and Spanish provincial furniture, doors, and home accessories in this store are a bit too elaborate for my tastes, but if you find yourself dreaming of carved wood, this is your place. 314 S. Guadalupe St. ✆ **505/982-1767.** www.nussbaumerfineart.com.

Taos Furniture Here you'll find classic Southwestern furnishings handcrafted in solid ponderosa pine—both contemporary and traditional. Prices are a little better here than in downtown shops. 217 Galisteo St. ✆ **800/443-3448** or 505/988-1229. www.taosfurniture.com.

Gifts & Souvenirs

El Nicho (Value) If you want to take a little piece of Santa Fe home with you, you'll likely find it at this shop. You'll find handcrafted Navajo folk art as well as jewelry and other items by local artisans, including woodcarvings (watch for the *santos!*) by the renowned Ortega family. 227 Don Gaspar Ave. ✆ **505/984-2830.**

Hats

Montecristi Custom Hat Works ★ This fun shop hand-makes fine Panama and felt hats in a range of styles, from Australian outback to Mexican bolero. 322 McKenzie St. ✆ **505/983-9598.** www.montecristihats.com.

Jewelry

Packards ★ Opened by a notable trader, Al Packard, and later sold to new owners, this store on the plaza is worth checking out to see some of the best jewelry available. You'll also find exquisite rugs and pottery. 61 Old Santa Fe Trail. ✆ **505/983-9241.** www.packards-santafe.com.

Tresa Vorenberg Goldsmiths You'll find some wildly imaginative designs in this jewelry store, where more than 40 artisans are represented. All items are handcrafted, and custom commissions are welcomed. 656 Canyon Rd. ✆ **505/988-7215.** www.tvgoldsmiths.com.

Malls & Shopping Centers

de Vargas Center There are approximately 50 merchants and restaurants in this mall just northwest of downtown. This is Santa Fe's small, more intimate mall, with anchors Ross and Office Depot. Open Monday to Friday 10am to 7pm, Saturday 10am to 6pm, and Sunday noon to 5pm. N. Guadalupe St. and Paseo de Peralta. ✆ **505/982-2655.** www.devargascenter.com.

Fashion Outlets of Santa Fe Outlet shopping fans will enjoy this open-air mall on the south end of town. Anchors include Brooks Brothers, Jones New York, and Coach. 8380 Cerrillos Rd. ✆ **505/474-4000.** www.fashionoutletssantafe.com.

Sanbusco Market Center ★ Unique shops and restaurants occupy this remodeled warehouse near the old Santa Fe Railyard. Many of the shops are overpriced, but it's a fun place to window-shop. Borders is here as well. Open Monday to Saturday 10am to 6pm, Sunday noon to 5pm. 500 Montezuma St. ✆ **505/989-9390.** www.sanbusco.com.

Santa Fe Place Santa Fe's largest mall is near the southwestern city limits, not far from the I-25 on-ramp. If you're from a major city, you'll probably find shopping here very provincial. Anchors include JCPenney, Sears, Dillard's, and Mervyn's. Open Monday to Saturday 10am to 9pm, Sunday noon to 6pm. 4250 Cerrillos Rd. (at Rodeo Rd.). ✆ **505/473-4253.** www.shopsantafeplace.com.

Markets

Santa Fe Farmers' Market ★★ Finds This farmers' market has everything from fruits, vegetables, and flowers to cheeses, cider, and salsas. Great local treats! If you're an early riser, stroll through and enjoy good coffee, excellent breakfast burritos, and music ranging from flute to fiddle. In 2008, the market moved into a beautiful new building in the railyard district. Open April to mid-November, Tuesday and Saturday 7am to noon. In winter, an abbreviated version takes place indoors. Look for the *Santa Fe Farmers' Market Cookbook,* a compilation of vendor and chef recipes from the region, with vivid photography. In the Santa Fe Railyard, off Paseo de Peralta. ✆ **505/983-4098.** www.santafefarmersmarket.com.

Tesuque Flea Market ★ Moments If you're a flea-market hound, you'll be happy to discover this one. More than 500 vendors sell everything from used cowboy boots (you might find some real beauties) to clothing, jewelry, books, and furniture, all against a big northern New Mexico view. Open March to late November, Friday to Sunday. Vendors start selling at about 7:30am and stay open until about 6:30pm, weather permitting. US 84/285 (about 8 miles north of Santa Fe). No phone. www.tesuquepueblofleamarket.com.

Natural Art

Mineral & Fossil Gallery of Santa Fe ★ You'll find ancient artwork here, from fossils to geodes in all sizes and shapes. Natural mineral jewelry and decorative items for the home, including lamps, wall clocks, furniture, art glass, and carvings are also on hand. Mineral & Fossil also has galleries in Taos, and in Scottsdale and Sedona, Arizona. 127 W. San Francisco St. ✆ **800/762-9777** or 505/984-1682. www.mineralgallery.com.

Stone Forest ★★ Finds Proprietor Michael Zimber travels to China and other Asian countries every year to collaborate with the stone carvers who create the fountains, sculptures, and bath fixtures that fill this inventive shop and garden not far from the plaza. 213 St. Francis Dr. ✆ **505/986-8883.** www.stoneforest.com.

Pottery & Tiles

Artesanos Imports Company ★ (Moments) Coming here is like taking a trip south of the border, with all the scents and colors you'd expect on such a journey. You'll find a wide selection of Talavera tile and pottery, as well as light fixtures and many other accessories for the home. 1414 Maclovia St. ✆ **505/471-8020.** www.artesanos.com.

Santa Fe Pottery at Double Take The work of more than 120 master potters from New Mexico and the Southwest is on display here; you'll find everything from mugs and lamps to home furnishings. 323 S. Guadalupe St. ✆ **505/989-3363.** www.santafepottery.com.

Rugs

Seret & Sons Rugs, Furnishings, and Architectural Pieces ★ If you're like me and find Middle Eastern decor irresistible, you'll want to wander through this shop. You'll find kilims and Persian and Turkish rugs, as well as some of the Moorish-style ancient doors and furnishings that you see around Santa Fe. 224 Galisteo St. ✆ **505/988-9151** or 505/983-5008. www.seretandsons.com.

9 SANTA FE AFTER DARK

Santa Fe is a city committed to the arts, so it's no surprise that the Santa Fe night scene is dominated by highbrow cultural events, beginning with the world-famous Santa Fe Opera. The club and popular music scene runs a distant second.

Information on all major cultural events can be obtained from the **Santa Fe Community Convention Center and Visitors Bureau** (✆ **800/777-CITY** [2489] or 505/955-6200) or from the **City of Santa Fe Arts Commission** (✆ **505/955-6707**). Current listings are published each Friday in the "Pasatiempo" section of the *New Mexican* (www.santafenewmexican.com), the city's daily newspaper, and in the *Santa Fe Reporter* (www.sfreporter.com), published every Wednesday.

You can also order tickets to events by phone from **Ticketmaster** (✆ **505/883-7800**). Discount tickets may be available on the night of a performance; for example, the opera offers standing-room tickets on the day of the performance. Sales start at 10am.

A variety of free concerts, lectures, and other events are presented in the summer, cosponsored by the City of Santa Fe and the Chamber of Commerce. Many of these musical and cultural events take place on the plaza; check in the "Pasatiempo" section for current listings and information.

Many performing-arts groups flourish in this city of 65,000. Many of them perform year-round, but others are seasonal. The acclaimed Santa Fe Opera, for instance, has just a 2-month summer season: late June to August.

Note: Many companies noted here perform at locations other than their listed addresses, so check the site of the performance you plan to attend.

MAJOR PERFORMING ARTS COMPANIES

Opera & Classical Music

Santa Fe Opera ★★★ Many rank the Santa Fe Opera second only to the Metropolitan Opera of New York in the United States. Established in 1957, it consistently attracts famed conductors, directors, and singers. At the height of the season, the company is 500 strong. It's noted for its performances of the classics, little-known works by classical European composers, and American premieres of 21st-century works. The theater, completed for the 1998 season, sits on a wooded hilltop 7 miles north of the city, off US 84/285. It's partially open-air, with open sides. A controversial structure, this new theater replaced the original, built in 1968, but preserved the sweeping curves attuned to the contour of the surrounding terrain. At night, the lights of Los Alamos can still be seen in the distance under clear skies.

The 8-week, 40-performance opera season runs from late June through late August. Highlights for 2009 include the world premiere of *The Letter,* composed by Paul Moravec, the first performance at the Santa Fe Opera of Gluck's *Alceste,* and new productions of Verdi's *La Traviata* and Donizetti's *The Elixir of Love.* All performances begin at 9pm, until the end of July, when performances start at 8:30pm, and the last week of the season, when performances begin at 8pm. A small screen in front of each seat shows the libretto during the performance. A gift shop has been added, as has additional parking. The entire theater is wheelchair accessible. P.O. Box 2408. ✆ **800/280-4654** or 505/986-5900. www.santafeopera.org. Tickets $28–$180; standing room $10; Opening Night Gala $1,750–$3,000. Backstage tours June–Aug Mon–Sat at 9am; $5 adults, free for children ages 5–17.

Orchestral & Chamber Music

Santa Fe Pro Musica Chamber Orchestra & Ensemble ★ Recently nominated for a Grammy Award, this chamber ensemble performs everything from Bach to Vivaldi to contemporary masters. During Holy Week, the Santa Fe Pro Musica presents its annual Mozart and Hayden Concert at the St. Francis Cathedral. Christmas brings candlelight chamber ensemble concerts. Pro Musica's season runs September to May. 430 Manhattan, Suite 10. ✆ **505/988-4640.** www.santafepromusica.com. Tickets $15–$50.

Santa Fe Symphony Orchestra and Chorus ★ This 60-piece professional symphony orchestra has grown rapidly in stature since its founding in 1984. Matinee and evening performances of classical and popular works are presented in a subscription series at the Lensic Performing Arts Center from August to May. There's a preconcert lecture before each performance. During the spring, the orchestra presents music festivals (call for details). P.O. Box 9692. ✆ **800/480-1319** or 505/983-1414. www.sf-symphony.org. Tickets $18–$65.

MUSIC FESTIVALS & CONCERT SERIES

Santa Fe Chamber Music Festival ★★ An extraordinary group of international artists comes to Santa Fe every summer for this festival. Its 6-week season runs mid-July to mid-August and is held in the St. Francis Auditorium and the Lensic Performing Arts Center. Each festival features chamber-music masterpieces, new music by a composer in residence, jazz, free youth concerts, preconcert lectures, and open rehearsals. Performances are Monday, Tuesday, Thursday, and Friday at 8pm; Saturday at various evening times; and Sunday at 6pm. Open rehearsals, youth concerts, and preconcert lectures are free to the public. 239 Johnson St., Suite B (P.O. Box 2227). ✆ **505/983-2075** or 505/982-1890 for box office (after June 22). www.sfchambermusic.com. Tickets $16–$125.

Santa Fe Concert Association Founded in 1937, this oldest musical organization in northern New Mexico has a September-to-May season that includes a 6-performance series. Among them are a "Great Performances" series and an "Adventures" series, which feature renowned instrumental and vocal soloists and chamber ensembles. The association also hosts special holiday concerts around Christmas and New Year's. Performances are held at the Lensic Performing Arts Center; tickets are available at the Lensic box office (✆ **505/988-1234**) and at ✆ 800/905-3315 (www.tickets.com), or ✆ 505/984-8759; www.santafeconcerts.org. 210 E. Marcy St., Suite 15. Tickets $20–$85.

THEATER COMPANIES

Greer Garson Theater Center In this graceful, intimate theater, the College of Santa Fe's Performing Arts Department produces four plays annually, with six presentations of each, given between October and May. Usually, the season consists of a comedy, a drama, a musical, and a classic. The college also sponsors studio productions and various contemporary music concerts. College of Santa Fe, 1600 St. Michaels Dr. ✆ **505/473-6511.** www.csf.edu. Tickets $10–$20 adults, $5 students.

Santa Fe Playhouse ★ Founded in the 1920s, this is the oldest extant theater group in New Mexico. Still performing in a historic adobe theater in the Barrio de Analco, it attracts thousands for its dramas, avant-garde theater, and musical comedy. Its popular one-act melodramas call on the public to boo the sneering villain and swoon for the damsel in distress. 142 E. de Vargas St. ✆ **505/988-4262.** www.santafeplayhouse.org. Tickets "Pay What You Wish"–$20, depending on the show.

Theater Grottesco ★★ Finds This troupe combines the best of comedy, drama, and dance in its original productions performed each spring, summer, or fall, at whatever venue suits the performance. Expect to be romanced, shocked, intellectually stimulated, and, above all, struck silly with laughter. Look for upcoming winter shows as well. 551 W. Cordova Rd., #8400. ✆ **505/474-8400.** www.theatergrottesco.org. Tickets $10–$25.

Theaterwork Studio ★ This community theater goes out of its way to present refreshing, at times risky, plays. In an intimate space on the south end of town, Theaterwork offers seven main-stage productions a year, a broad variety including new plays and classics by regional and national playwrights. Expect to see works by such names as Brecht, Shakespeare, and Victor Hugo. 1336 Rufina Circle (mail: P.O. Box 842). ✆ **505/471-1799.** www.theaterwork.org. Tickets $10–$18. Call for performance times.

DANCE COMPANIES

Aspen Santa Fe Ballet ★ In its second decade, the Aspen Santa Fe Ballet brings classically trained dancers to Santa Fe and Aspen. Performances are an eclectic repertoire by some of the world's foremost choreographers. The season is year-round, with performances at the Lensic Performing Arts Center. 550-B St. Michaels Dr. ✆ **505/983-5591;** www.aspensantafeballet.com. Purchase tickets at the Lensic ✆ **505/988-1234.** Tickets $20–$58.

María Benitez Teatro Flamenco ★★ Finds You won't want to miss this cultural treat. True flamenco is one of the most thrilling of dance forms, displaying the inner spirit and verve of the gypsies of Spanish Andalusia, and María Benitez, trained in Spain, is a fabulous performer. The Benitez Company's "Estampa Flamenca" summer series is performed nightly except Monday from late June to early September. The María Benitez Theater at the Lodge at Santa Fe is modern and showy, and yet it's intimate enough so you're immersed in the art. Institute for Spanish Arts, P.O. Box 8418. For tickets call ✆ **888/435-2636,** or the box office (June 16–Sept 3; ✆ **505/982-1237**). www.mariabenitez.com. Tickets $30–$50.

MAJOR CONCERT HALLS & ALL-PURPOSE AUDITORIUMS

Center for Contemporary Arts and Cinematheque ★ CCA presents the work of internationally, nationally, and regionally known contemporary artists in art exhibitions, dance, music concerts, poetry readings, performance-art events, theater, and video screenings. The Cinematheque screens films from around the world nightly, with special series presented regularly. CCA's galleries are open daily noon to 7pm. 1050 Old Pecos Trail. ✆ **505/982-1338.** www.ccasantafe.org. Film tickets $8. Art exhibitions are free; performances range broadly in price.

Lensic Performing Arts Center ★★ The Santa Fe arts scene's best venue, the Lensic hosts many of the city's major performances, including the Santa Fe Chamber Music Festival and the Santa Fe Symphony Orchestra and Chorus, among others. The setting is wonderfully atmospheric; a multimillion-dollar face-lift brought out the 1931 movie palace's Arabian Nights charm. 211 W. San Francisco St. ✆ **505/988-7050.** www.lensic.com.

St. Francis Auditorium This atmospheric music hall, patterned after the interiors of traditional Hispanic mission churches, is noted for its excellent acoustics. The hall hosts a wide variety of musical events, including the Santa Fe Chamber Music Festival in July and August. Museum of Fine Arts, Lincoln and Palace aves. ✆ **505/476-5072.** Ticket prices vary; see above for specific performing-arts companies.

THE CLUB & MUSIC SCENE

In addition to the clubs and bars listed below, there are a number of hotels whose bars and lounges feature some type of entertainment (see "Where to Stay," earlier in this chapter).

Country, Jazz & Latin

Chispa! ★ A tapas bar with the *chispa* or "spark" of fun entertainment and dancing, this hot spot next to the dining room at El Meson draws locals of all types. Music ranges from guitar duos to jazz combos and Brazilian music, with flamenco dancers performing on some Saturday nights. On tango Tuesdays, locals turn out in their tightest dance clothes to party. The tapas are excellent. Open Tuesday to Saturday. 213 Washington Ave. ✆ **505/983-6756.** www.elmeson-santafe.com. Cover charge for select performances.

Cowgirl Hall of Fame ★ It's difficult to categorize what goes on in this bar and restaurant, but there's live entertainment nightly. Some nights there's blues guitar, others folk music; you might also find "progressive rock," comedy, or cowboy poetry. In the summer, this is a great place to sit under the stars and listen to music. 319 S. Guadalupe St. ✆ **505/982-2565.** No cover for music Sun, Mon, and Wed. Tues and Thurs–Sat $3–$4 cover. Special performances $10.

Eldorado Hotel ★ In a grand lobby-lounge full of fine art, classical guitarists and pianists perform nightly. 309 W. San Francisco St. ✆ **505/988-4455.** www.eldoradohotel.com.

El Farol ★ This original neighborhood bar of the Canyon Road artists' quarter (its name means "the lantern") is the place to head for local ambience. Its low ceilings and

Snub Out the Smokes

In 2006, smoking in Santa Fe bars and restaurants, including outdoor-dining areas, became illegal. The law was instituted mainly to protect entertainment and hospitality workers from secondhand smoke, but it will likely protect many others as well.

brown walls are home to Santa Fe's largest and most unusual selection of tapas (bar snacks and appetizers). Jazz, swing, folk, and most notably, salsa and flamenco musicians (and dancers)—some of national note—perform most nights. 808 Canyon Rd. ✆ **505/983-9912.** www.elfarolsf.com. Cover $7.

La Fiesta Lounge ★ Set in the notable La Fonda hotel on the plaza, this nightclub offers excellent country bands on weekends, with old- and new-timers two-stepping across the floor. This lively lobby bar offers cocktails, an appetizer menu, and live entertainment nightly. It's a great authentic Santa Fe spot. La Fonda Hotel, 110 E. San Francisco St. ✆ **505/982-5511.** www.lafondasantafe.com.

Rock & Disco

Catamount Bar and Grille The postcollege crowd hangs out at this bar, where live rock and blues music play on weekends. Food is served until 11pm, and there is also a billiards room. 125 E. Water St. ✆ **505/988-7222.**

THE BAR SCENE

The Dragon Room ★ A number of years ago, *International Newsweek* named the Dragon Room at the Pink Adobe (p. 150) one of the top 20 bars in the world. The reason is its spirited but comfortable ambience, which draws students, artists, politicians, and even an occasional celebrity. The decor theme is dragons, which you'll find carved on the front doors as well as depicted on the walls, all within low-lit, aged elegance akin to the Pink Adobe's interior. Live trees also grow through the roof. In addition to the tempting lunch and bar menu, there's always a complimentary bowl of popcorn close at hand. 406 Old Santa Fe Trail. ✆ **505/983-7712.**

El Paseo Bar and Grill You can almost always catch live music at this casual, unpretentious place (yet it's not a "sports bar"). The crowd here is somewhat younger than at most other downtown establishments, and on certain nights, the bar is completely packed. In addition to the open mic night on Tuesdays, a variety of local bands play here regularly—cranking out many types of music, from blues to rock to jazz to bluegrass. 208 Galisteo St. ✆ **505/992-2848.** www.elpaseobar.com. Cover $3–$5 weekends.

Evangelo's A popular downtown hangout, with tropical decor and a mahogany bar, this place can get raucous at times. It's a bit seedy, but more than 200 varieties of imported beer are available, and pool tables are an added attraction. On Friday and Saturday nights starting at 9pm and Wednesdays at 7:30pm, live bands play (jazz, rock, or reggae). Evangelo's is extremely popular with the local crowd. You'll find your share of business people, artists, and even bikers here. Open Monday to Saturday noon to 1:30am and Sundays until midnight. 200 W. San Francisco St. ✆ **505/982-9014.** Cover for special performances only.

Vanessie of Santa Fe ★ This is unquestionably Santa Fe's most popular piano bar. The talented Doug Montgomery and Charles Tichenor have a loyal local following. Their repertoire ranges from Bach to Billy Joel, Gershwin to Barry Manilow. They play nightly from 8pm until closing, which could be anywhere from midnight to 2am. There's an extra microphone, so if you're daring (or drunk), you can stand up and accompany the piano and vocals (though this is *not* a karaoke scene). National celebrities have even joined in—including Harry Connick, Jr. Vanessie's offers a great bar menu. 434 W. San Francisco St. ✆ **505/982-9966.** www.vanessiesantafe.com.

10 TOURING THE PUEBLOS AROUND SANTA FE

Of the eight northern pueblos, Tesuque, Pojoaque, Nambe, San Ildefonso, San Juan, and Santa Clara are within about 30 miles of Santa Fe. Picuris (San Lorenzo) is on the High Road to Taos (see "Taking the High Road to Taos," later in this chapter), and Taos Pueblo is just outside the town of Taos (p. 224).

The six pueblos described in this section can easily be visited in a single day's round-trip from Santa Fe, though I suggest visiting just the two that really give a feel of the ancient lifestyle: San Ildefonso, with its broad plaza, and Ohkay Owinge, with its setting along the Rio Grande. In an easy day trip from Santa Fe you can take in both, with some delicious New Mexican food in Española en route. If you're in the area at a time when you can catch certain rituals, that's when you should see some of the other pueblos.

TESUQUE PUEBLO

Tesuque (te-*soo*-keh) Pueblo is about 9 miles north of Santa Fe on US 84/285. You'll know that you're approaching the pueblo when you see a large store near the highway. If you're driving north and you get to the unusual Camel Rock and a large roadside casino, you've missed the pueblo entrance.

The 800 pueblo dwellers at Tesuque are faithful to their traditional religion, rituals, and ceremonies. Excavations confirm that a pueblo has existed here at least since the year A.D. 1200; accordingly, this pueblo is now on the National Register of Historic Places. When you come to the welcome sign at the pueblo, turn right, go a block, and park on the right. You'll see the plaza off to the left. There's not a lot to see; in recent years renovation has brought a new look to some of the homes around it. There's a big open area where dances are held and the **San Diego Church,** completed in 2004 on the site of an 1888 structure that burned down recently. It's the fifth church on the pueblo's plaza since 1641. Visitors are asked to remain in this area.

Some Tesuque women are skilled potters; Ignacia Duran's black-and-white and red micaceous pottery and Teresa Tapia's miniatures and pots with animal figures are especially noteworthy. You'll find many crafts at a gallery on the plaza's southeast corner. The **San Diego Feast Day,** which may feature harvest, buffalo, deer, flag, or Comanche dances, is November 12.

The Tesuque Pueblo's address is Route 5, Box 360-T, Santa Fe, NM 87501 (© **505/983-2667**). Admission to the pueblo is free; however, there is a $20 charge for use of still cameras; special permission is required for filming, sketching, and painting. The pueblo is open daily from 9am to 5pm. **Camel Rock Casino** (© **505/984-8414;** www.camelrockcasino.com) is open Sunday to Wednesday from 8am to 4am, and Thursday to Saturday for 24 hours; it has a snack bar on the premises.

POJOAQUE PUEBLO

About 6 miles farther north of Tesuque Pueblo on US 84/285, at the junction of NM 502, Pojoaque (Po-*hwa*-keh) Pueblo provides a roadside peek into Pueblo arts. Though small (pop. 2,712) and without a definable village (more modern dwellings exist now), Pojoaque is important as a center for traveler services; in fact, Pojoaque, in its Tewa form, means "water-drinking place." The historical accounts of the Pojoaque people are sketchy, but we do know that in 1890 smallpox took its toll on the Pojoaque population, forcing most of the pueblo residents to abandon their village. Since the 1930s, the population

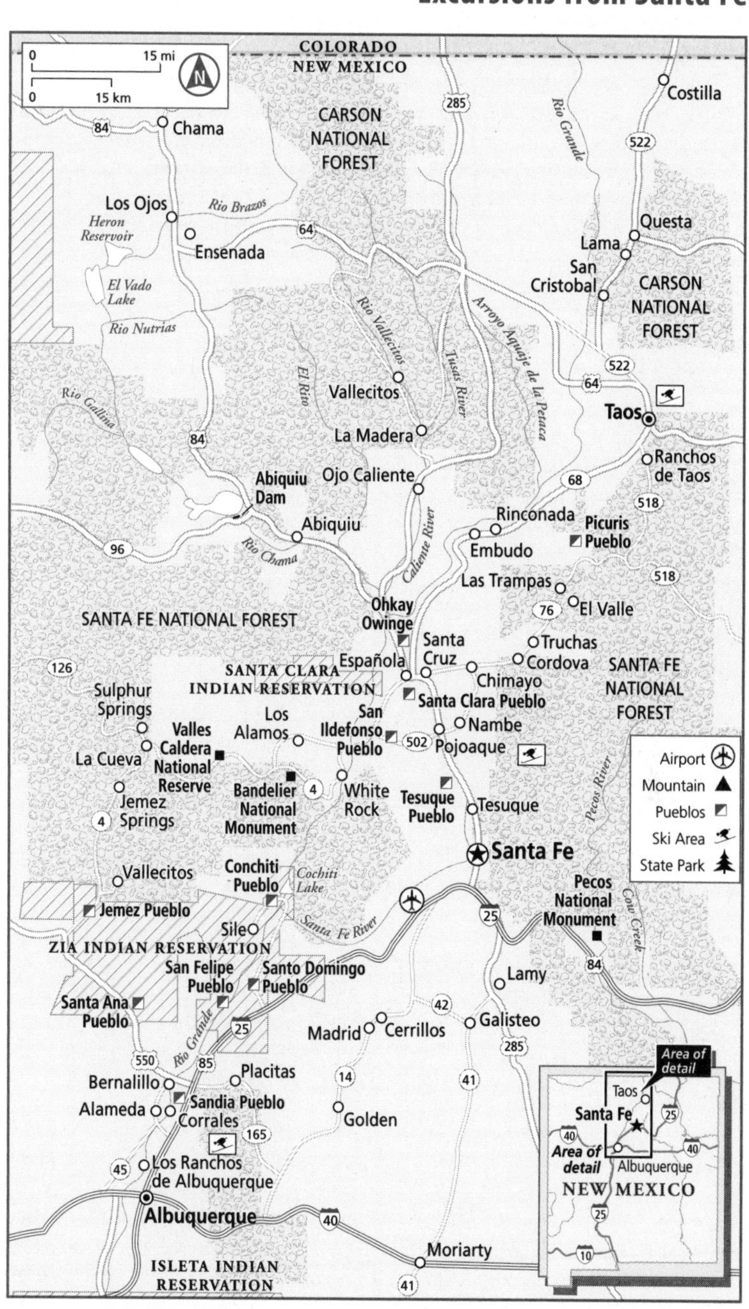
COLORADO
NEW MEXICO
0 15 mi
0 15 km
N
Chama
CARSON NATIONAL FOREST
Costilla
Rio Grande
Los Ojos
Rio Brazos
Heron Reservoir
Ensenada
Questa
Lama
San Cristobal
El Vado Lake
Rio Nutrias
Rio Vallecitos
Arroyo Aguaje de la Petaca
Tusas River
El Rito
Vallecitos
Rio Gallina
La Madera
Taos
Ranchos de Taos
Abiquiu Dam
Ojo Caliente
Rinconada
Picuris Pueblo
Abiquiu
Embudo
Rio Chama
Caliente River
Las Trampas
El Valle
Ohkay Owinge
SANTA FE NATIONAL FOREST
Santa Cruz
Truchas
Española
Cordova
SANTA CLARA INDIAN RESERVATION
Chimayo
Santa Clara Pueblo
Sulphur Springs
Los Alamos
San Ildefonso Pueblo
Nambe
Valles Caldera National Reserve
Pojoaque
La Cueva
Bandelier National Monument
White Rock
Tesuque Pueblo
Tesuque
Pecos River
Jemez Springs
Santa Fe
Airport
Mountain
Pueblos
Ski Area
State Park
Vallecitos
Conchiti Pueblo
Cochiti Lake
Pecos National Monument
Jemez Pueblo
Santa Fe River
Cow Creek
Sile
ZIA INDIAN RESERVATION
San Felipe Pueblo
Santo Domingo Pueblo
Lamy
Santa Ana Pueblo
Madrid
Cerrillos
Galisteo
Rio Grande
Placitas
Bernalillo
Alameda
Sandia Pueblo
Corrales
Golden
Los Ranchos de Albuquerque
Albuquerque
Moriarty
ISLETA INDIAN RESERVATION
Area of detail
Taos
Santa Fe
Albuquerque
NEW MEXICO
84
285
522
64
522
64
84
68
518
96
518
76
126
502
4
4
25
84
42
25
285
550
85
14
41
165
45
40
41
40
40
25
10

Pueblo Etiquette

When you visit pueblos, it is important to observe certain rules of etiquette. These are personal dwellings and/or important historic sites and must be respected as such. Don't climb on the buildings or peek into doors or windows. Don't enter sacred grounds, such as cemeteries and kivas. If you attend a dance or ceremony, remain silent while it is taking place and refrain from applause when it's over. Many pueblos prohibit photography or sketches; others require you to pay a fee for a permit. If you don't respect the privacy of the Native Americans who live at the pueblo, you'll be asked to leave.

has gradually increased, and in 1990, a war chief and two war captains were appointed. Today, visitors won't find much to look at, but the **Poeh Cultural Center and Museum,** on US 84/285, operated by the pueblo, features a museum, a cultural center, and artists' studios. It's situated within a complex of adobe buildings, including the three-story Sun Tower. There are frequent artist demonstrations, exhibitions, and, in the warmer months, traditional ceremonial dances. Indigenous pottery, embroidery, silverwork, and beadwork are available for sale at the Pojoaque Pueblo Visitor Center nearby.

If you leave US 84/285 and travel on the frontage road back to where the pueblo actually was, you'll encounter lovely orchards and alfalfa fields backed by desert and mountains. There's a modern community center near the site of the old pueblo and church. On December 12, the annual feast day of **Our Lady of Guadalupe** features a buffalo dance.

The pueblo's address is Route 11, Box 71, Santa Fe, NM 87506 (✆ **505/455-2278**). The pueblo is open every day during daylight hours. The Poeh Center is at 78 Cities of Gold Rd. (✆ **505/455-3334;** www.poehcenter.com). Admission is free. Open daily 8am to 5pm. Sketching, photography, and filming are prohibited.

Owned by the pueblo, the new **Hilton Santa Fe Buffalo Thunder Resort** (✆ **800/HILTONS** [445-8667]; www.hiltonworldresorts.com/resorts/SantaFe/index.html) opened in 2008. Located on Pojoaque Pueblo, the luxury resort has the 36-hole Towa golf course (p. 169), a casino, horseback riding, and many other amenities.

NAMBE PUEBLO

If you're still on US 84/285, continue north from Pojoaque about 3 miles until you come to NM 503; turn right, and travel until you see the Bureau of Reclamation sign for Nambe Falls; turn right on NP 101. Approximately 2 miles farther is Nambe ("mound of earth in the corner"), a 700-year-old Tewa-speaking pueblo (pop. 500), with a solar-powered tribal headquarters, at the foot of the Sangre de Cristo range. Only a few original pueblo buildings remain, including a large round kiva, used today in ceremonies. Pueblo artisans make woven belts, beadwork, and brown micaceous pottery. One of my favorite reasons for visiting this pueblo is to see the small herd of bison that roam on 179 acres set aside for them.

Nambe Falls make a stunning three-tier drop through a cleft in a rock face about 4 miles beyond the pueblo. You can reach the falls via a 15-minute hike on a rocky, clearly marked path that leaves from the picnic area. A recreational site at the reservoir offers fishing, boating (non-motor boats only), hiking, camping, and picnicking. The **Waterfall Dances** on July 4 and the **Saint Francis of Assisi Feast Day** on October 4, which has buffalo and deer dances, are observed at the pueblo. Recent dry weather has caused cancellations; before setting out, call the pueblo.

The address is Route 1, Box 117-BB, Santa Fe, NM 87506 (© **505/455-2036,** or 505/455-2304 for the Ranger Station). Admission to the pueblo is free, but there is a $10 charge for taking photographs. Filming and sketching are prohibited. The pueblo is open daily 8am to 5pm. The recreational site is open 8am to 8pm April 1 through October 1.

SAN ILDEFONSO PUEBLO ★★

Pox Oge, as San Ildefonso Pueblo is called in its own Tewa language, means "place where the water cuts down through," possibly named such because of the way the Rio Grande cuts through the mountains nearby. Turn left on NM 502 at Pojoaque, and drive about 6 miles to the turnoff. This pueblo has a broad, dusty plaza, with a kiva on one side, ancient dwellings on the other, and a church at the far end. It's nationally famous for its matte-finish, black-on-black pottery, developed by tribeswoman María Martinez in the 1920s. One of the most visited pueblos in northern New Mexico (pop. 1,524), San Ildefonso attracts more than 20,000 visitors a year.

The San Ildefonsos could best be described as rebellious because this was one of the last pueblos to succumb to the reconquest spearheaded by Don Diego de Vargas in 1692. Within view of the pueblo is the volcanic Black Mesa, a symbol of the San Ildefonso people's strength. Through the years, each time San Ildefonso felt itself threatened by enemy forces, the residents, along with members of other pueblos, would hide out up on the butte, returning to the valley only when starvation set in. Today, a visit to the pueblo is valuable mainly in order to see or buy rich black pottery. A few shops surround the plaza, and there's the **San Ildefonso Pueblo Museum** tucked away in the governor's office beyond the plaza. I especially recommend visiting during ceremonial days. **San Ildefonso Feast Day,** on January 23, features the buffalo and Comanche dances in alternate years. **Corn dances,** held in late August or early September, commemorate a basic element in pueblo life, the importance of fertility in all creatures—humans as well as animals—and plants.

The pueblo has a 4½-acre fishing lake that is surrounded by *bosque* (Spanish for "forest"), open April to October. Picnicking is encouraged, though you may want to look at the sites before you decide to stay; some are nicer than others. Camping is not allowed.

The pueblo's address is Route 5, Box 315A, Santa Fe, NM 87506 (© **505/455-3549**). The admission charge is $5 per car. The charge for taking photographs is $10; you'll pay $20 to film and $25 to sketch. If you plan to fish, the charge is $10 for adults and $5 for seniors and children 11 and under, but you'll want to call to be sure the lake is open. The pueblo is open in the summer, daily, from 8am to 5pm; call for weekend hours. In the winter, it's open Monday to Friday from 8am to 4:30pm. It's closed for major holidays and tribal events.

OHKAY OWINGE (SAN JUAN PUEBLO) ★

If you continue north on US 84/285, you will reach San Juan Pueblo, now renamed in Tewa language Ohkay Owinge, via NM 74, a mile off NM 68, about 4 miles north of Española.

The largest (pop. 6,748) and northernmost of the Tewa-speaking pueblos and headquarters of the Eight Northern Indian Pueblos Council, San Juan is on the east side of the Rio Grande—opposite the 1598 site of San Gabriel, the first Spanish settlement west of the Mississippi River and the first capital of New Spain. In 1598, the Spanish, impressed with the openness and helpfulness of the people of San Juan, decided to establish a capital there (it was moved to Santa Fe 10 years later), making San Juan Pueblo the first to be subjected to Spanish colonization. The Indians were generous, providing food, clothing, shelter, and fuel—they even helped sustain the settlement when its leader, Conquistador Juan de Oñate, became preoccupied with his search for gold and neglected the needs of his people.

The past and present cohabit here. Though many of the tribe members are Catholics, most of the San Juan tribe still practice traditional religious rituals. Thus, two rectangular kivas flank the church in the main plaza, and *caciques* (pueblo priests) share power with civil authorities. The annual **San Juan Fiesta** is held June 23 and 24; it features buffalo and Comanche dances. Another annual ceremony is the **turtle dance** on December 26. The **Matachine dance,** performed here Christmas Day, vividly depicts the subjugation of the Native Americans by the Catholic Spaniards (p. 46).

The address of the pueblo is P.O. Box 1099, San Juan Pueblo, NM 87566 (© **505/852-4400** or 505/852-4210). Admission is free. Photography or sketching may be allowed for a fee with prior permission from the governor's office. For information, call the number above. The charge for fishing is $8 for adults and $5 for children and seniors. The pueblo is open every day during daylight hours.

The **Eight Northern Indian Pueblos Council** (© **505/747-1593**) is a sort of chamber of commerce and social-service agency.

Fishing and picnicking are encouraged at the **San Juan Tribal Lakes,** open year-round. **Ohkay Casino** (© **505/747-1668;** www.ohkay.com) offers table games and slot machines, as well as live music nightly Tuesday through Saturday. It's open 24 hours on weekends.

SANTA CLARA PUEBLO

Close to Española (on NM 5), Santa Clara, with a population of about 1,944, is one of the largest pueblos. You'll see the village sprawling across the river basin near the beautiful Black Mesa, rows of tract homes surrounding an adobe central area. Although it's in an incredible setting, the pueblo itself is not much to see; however, a trip through it will give a real feel for the contemporary lives of these people. Though stories vary, the Santa Clarans teach their children that their ancestors once lived in cliffside dwellings named Puye and migrated down to the river bottom in the 13th century. This pueblo is noted for its language program. Artisan elders work with children to teach them their native Tewa language, on the brink of extinction because so many now speak English. This pueblo is also the home of noted potter Nancy Youngblood, who comes from a long line of famous potters and now does alluring contemporary work.

Follow the main route to the old village, where you come to the visitor center, also known as the neighborhood center. There you can get directions to small shops that sell distinctive black incised Santa Clara pottery, red burnished pottery, baskets, and other crafts. One stunning sight here is the cemetery. Stop on the west side of the church and look over the 4-foot wall. It's a primitive site, with plain wooden crosses and some graves adorned with plastic flowers.

There are corn and harvest dances on **Santa Clara Feast Day** (Aug 12); information on other special days (including the corn or harvest dances, as well as children's dances) can be obtained from the pueblo office.

The famed **Puye Cliff Dwellings** are on the Santa Clara reservation, though they are currently closed to visitors.

The pueblo's address is P.O. Box 580, Española, NM 87532 (✆ **505/753-7326**). Admission is free. The charge for taking photographs is $5; filming and sketching are not allowed. The pueblo is open every day from 9am to 4pm.

11 PECOS NATIONAL HISTORICAL PARK ★★

About 15 miles east of Santa Fe, I-25 meanders through **Glorieta Pass,** site of an important Civil War skirmish. In March 1862, volunteers from Colorado and New Mexico, along with Fort Union regulars, defeated a Confederate force marching on Santa Fe, thereby turning the tide of Southern encroachment in the West.

Follow NM 50 east to **Pecos** for about 7 miles. This quaint town, well off the beaten track since the interstate was constructed, is the site of a noted **Benedictine monastery.** About 26 miles north of here on NM 63 is the village of **Cowles,** gateway to the natural wonderland of the **Pecos Wilderness.** There are many camping, picnicking, and fishing locales en route.

Pecos National Historical Park ★★ (✆ **505/757-6414;** www.nps.gov/peco), about 2 miles south of the town of Pecos off NM 63, contains the ruins of a 15th-century pueblo and 17th- and 18th-century missions that jut up spectacularly from a high meadow. Coronado mentioned Pecos Pueblo in 1540: "It is feared through the land," he wrote. The approximately 2,000 Native Americans here farmed in irrigated fields and hunted wild game. Their pueblo had 660 rooms and many kivas. By 1620, Franciscan monks had established a church and convent. Military and natural disasters took their toll on the pueblo, and in 1838, the 20 surviving Pecos went to live with relatives at the Jemez Pueblo.

The **E. E. Fogelson Visitor Center** tells the history of the Pecos people in a well-done, chronologically organized exhibit, complete with dioramas. A 1.5-mile loop trail begins at the center and continues through Pecos Pueblo and the **Misión de Nuestra Señora de Los Angeles de Porciuncula** (as the church was formerly called). This excavated structure—170 feet long and 90 feet wide at the transept—was once the most magnificent church north of Mexico City.

Pecos National Historical Park is open Memorial Day to Labor Day, daily 8am to 6pm; the rest of the year, daily 8am to 5pm. It's closed January 1 and December 25. Admission is $3 per person over age 16.

12 LOS ALAMOS & BANDELIER NATIONAL MONUMENT

Pueblo tribes lived in the rugged Los Alamos area for well over 1,000 years, and an exclusive boys' school operated atop the 7,300-foot plateau from 1918 to 1943. Then, the **Los Alamos National Laboratory** was established here in secrecy, code-named Site Y of the Manhattan Project, the hush-hush wartime program that developed the world's first atomic bombs.

Project director J. Robert Oppenheimer, later succeeded by Norris E. Bradbury, worked along with thousands of scientists, engineers, and technicians in research, development, and production of those early weapons. Today, more than 10,000 people work at the Los Alamos National Laboratory, making it the largest employer in northern New Mexico. Operated by Los Alamos National Security, currently under a contract through the U.S. Department of Energy, its 2,800 individual facilities and 42 separate technical areas occupy 36 square miles of mesa-top land.

The laboratory is one of the world's foremost scientific institutions. It primarily focuses on nuclear weapons research—the Trident and Minuteman strategic warheads were designed here, for example—and has many other interdisciplinary research programs, including international nuclear safeguards and nonproliferation, space, and atmospheric studies; supercomputing; theoretical physics; biomedical and materials science; and environmental restoration.

Currently Los Alamos National Laboratory is building a limited number of replacement plutonium pits for use in the enduring U.S. nuclear weapons stockpile. The lab has the only plutonium-processing facility in the United States that is capable of producing those components.

ORIENTATION/USEFUL INFORMATION

Los Alamos is about 35 miles west of Santa Fe and about 65 miles southwest of Taos. From Santa Fe, take US 84/285 north approximately 16 miles to the Pojoaque junction, and then turn west on NM 502. Driving time is only about 50 minutes.

Los Alamos is a town of 18,000, spread over the colorful, finger-like mesas of the Pajarito Plateau, between the Jemez Mountains and the Rio Grande Valley. As NM 502 enters Los Alamos from Santa Fe, it follows Trinity Drive, where accommodations, restaurants, and other services are located. Central Avenue parallels Trinity Drive and has restaurants, galleries, and shops, as well as the **Los Alamos Historical Museum** (1921 Juniper St.; ✆ **505/662-4493;** free admission) and the **Bradbury Science Museum** (15th St. and Central Ave.; ✆ **505/667-4444;** free admission).

The **Los Alamos Chamber of Commerce,** P.O. Box 460, Los Alamos, NM 87544 (✆ **505/662-8105;** fax 505/662-8399; www.losalamoschamber.com), runs a visitor center that is open Monday to Saturday 9am to 5pm and Sunday 10am to 3pm. It's at 109 Central Park Sq. (across from the Bradbury Science Museum).

WHAT TO SEE & DO

Aside from the sights described below, Los Alamos offers the **Pajarito Mountain ski area,** Camp May Road (P.O. Box 155), Los Alamos, NM 87544 (✆ **505/662-5725;** www.skipajarito.com), with five chairlifts—it's only open on Friday through Sunday and federal holidays. It's an outstanding ski area that rarely gets crowded; many trails are steep and have moguls. Los Alamos also offers the **Los Alamos Golf Course,** 4250 Diamond Dr. (✆ **505/662-8139**), at the edge of town, where greens fees are around $25, and the **Larry R. Walkup Aquatic Center,** 2760 Canyon Rd. (✆ **505/662-8170**), the highest-altitude indoor Olympic-size swimming pool in the United States. Not far from downtown is an outdoor ice-skating rink, with a snack bar and skate rentals, open Thanksgiving to late February (✆ **505/662-4500**). It's at 4475 West Rd. (take Trinity Dr. to Diamond St., turn left, and watch for the sign on your right). There are no outstanding restaurants in Los Alamos, but if you get hungry, you can stop at the **Blue Window Bistro,** 813 Central Ave. (✆ **505/662-6305**), a country-style restaurant serving pasta, sandwiches, and salads, with a view of the Sangre de Cristo Mountains. The

Chamber of Commerce has maps for self-guided historical walking tours, and you can find self-guided driving-tour tapes at stores and hotels around town.

The Art Center at Fuller Lodge This is a public showcase for work by visual artists from northern New Mexico and the surrounding region. Two annual arts-and-crafts fairs are also held here—in August and October. The gallery shop sells local crafts at good prices.

In the same building is the **Los Alamos Arts Council** (✆ **505/663-0477**), a multidisciplinary organization that sponsors an art fair in May, as well as evening and noontime cultural programs.

2132 Central Ave., Los Alamos. ✆ **505/662-9331.** www.artfulnm.org. Free admission. Mon–Sat 10am–4pm.

Bradbury Science Museum ★ This is a great place to get acquainted with what goes on at a weapons production facility after nuclear proliferation. Although the museum is run by Los Alamos National Laboratory, which definitely puts a positive spin on the business of producing weapons, it's a fascinating place to explore and it includes more than 35 hands-on exhibits.

Begin in the History Gallery, where you'll learn about the evolution of the site from the Los Alamos Ranch School days through the Manhattan Project to the present. Meanwhile, listen for announcement of the film *The Town That Never Was,* a 16-minute presentation on this community that grew up shrouded in secrecy (shown in the auditorium). Further exploration will take you to the Defense Gallery, where you can test the heaviness of plutonium against that of other substances, see an actual 5-ton Little Boy nuclear bomb (like the one dropped on Hiroshima), and see firsthand how Los Alamos conducts worldwide surveillance of nuclear explosions.

15th St. and Central Ave., Los Alamos. ✆ **505/667-4444.** www.lanl.gov/museum. Free admission. Tues–Sat 10am–5pm; Sun–Mon 1–5pm. Closed Thanksgiving, Christmas, New Year's Day.

Los Alamos Historical Museum ★ Fuller Lodge, a massive vertical-log building built by John Gaw Meem in 1928, is well worth the visit. The log work is intricate and artistic, and the feel of the old place is warm and majestic. It once housed the dining and recreation hall for the Los Alamos Ranch School for boys and is now a National Historic Landmark. Its current occupants include the museum office and research archives and the Art Center at Fuller Lodge (see above). The museum, located in the small log-and-stone building to the north of Fuller Lodge, depicts area history from prehistoric cliff dwellers to the present. Exhibits range from Native American artifacts to school memorabilia and an excellent Manhattan Project exhibit that offers a more realistic view of the devastation resulting from use of atomic bombs than is offered at the Bradbury Science Museum.

1921 Juniper St., Los Alamos. ✆ **505/662-4493.** www.losalamoshistory.org. Free admission. Summer Mon–Sat 9:30am–4:30pm, Sun 1–4pm; winter Mon–Sat 10am–4pm, Sun 1–4pm. Closed New Year's Day, Thanksgiving, Christmas, Easter.

Nearby

Bandelier National Monument ★★★ Less than 15 miles south of Los Alamos along NM 4, this National Park Service area contains stunningly preserved ruins of the ancient cliff-dwelling ancestral Puebloan (Anasazi) culture within 46 square miles of canyon-and-mesa wilderness. The national monument is named after the Swiss-American archaeologist Adolph Bandelier, who explored here in the 1880s. During busy summer months, head out early; there can be a waiting line for cars to park.

Inside a Volcano

While you're in the area, check out the **Valles Caldera National Preserve,** past Bandelier National Monument on NM 4, beginning about 15 miles from Los Alamos. The reserve is all that remains of a volcanic caldera created by a collapse after eruptions nearly a million years ago. When the mountain spewed ashes and dust as far away as Kansas and Nebraska, its underground magma chambers collapsed, forming this great valley—one of the largest volcanic calderas in the world. Lava domes that pushed up after the collapse obstruct a full view across the expanse, but the beauty of the place is still within grasp. Visitors have many guided options for exploring the preserve, from sleigh rides in winter to fly-fishing in summer. For more information, contact ✆ **866-382-5537;** www.vallescaldera.gov.

After an orientation stop at the visitor center and museum to learn about the culture that flourished here between 1100 and 1550, most visitors follow a trail along Frijoles Creek to the principal ruins. The pueblo site, including an underground kiva, has been stabilized. The biggest thrill for most folks is climbing hardy ponderosa pine ladders to visit an alcove—140 feet above the canyon floor—that was once home to prehistoric people. Tours are self-guided or led by a National Park Service ranger. Be aware that dogs are not allowed on trails.

On summer nights, rangers offer campfire talks about the history, culture, and geology of the area. During the day, nature programs are sometimes offered for adults and children. The small museum at the visitor center displays artifacts found in the area.

The separate **Tsankawi** section, reached by an ancient 2-mile trail close to **White Rock,** has a large unexcavated ruin on a high mesa overlooking the Rio Grande Valley. The town of White Rock, about 10 miles southeast of Los Alamos on NM 4, offers spectacular panoramas of the river valley in the direction of Santa Fe; the **White Rock Overlook** is a great picnic spot. Within Bandelier, areas have been set aside for picnicking and camping.

NM 4 (HCR 1, Box 1, Suite 15, Los Alamos). ✆ **505/672-3861,** ext 517. www.nps.gov/band. Admission $12 per vehicle. Daily during daylight hours. No pets allowed on trails. Closed Jan 1 and Dec 25.

13 TAKING THE HIGH ROAD TO TAOS ★★

Unless you're in a hurry to get from Santa Fe to Taos, the High Road—also called the Mountain Road or the King's Road—is by far the most fascinating route between the two cities. It begins in lowlands of mystically formed pink and yellow stone, passing by apple and peach orchards and chile farms in the weaving village of **Chimayo.** Then it climbs toward the highlands to the village of **Cordova,** known for its woodcarvers, and higher still to **Truchas,** a renegade arts town where Hispanic traditions and ways of life continue much as they did a century ago. Though I've described this tour from south to north, the most scenic way to see it is from north to south, when you travel down off the mountains rather than up into them. This way, you see more expansive views.

CHIMAYO

About 28 miles north of Santa Fe on NM 76/285 is the historic weaving center of Chimayo. It's approximately 16 miles past the Pojoaque junction, at the junction of NM 520 and NM 76 via NM 503. In this small village, families still maintain the tradition of crafting hand-woven textiles initiated by their ancestors seven generations ago, in the early 1800s. One such family is the Ortegas, and **Ortega's Weaving Shop** (✆ **505/351-4215;** www.ortegasweaving.com) and **Galeria Ortega** ★ (✆ **505/351-2288;** www.galeriaortega.com), both at the corner of NM 520 and NM 76, are fine places to take a close look at this ancient craft. A more humble spot is **Trujillo Weaving Shop** (✆ **505/351-4457**) on NM 76. If you're lucky enough to find the proprietors in, you might get a weaving history lesson. You can see a 100-year-old loom and an even older shuttle carved from apricot wood. The weavings you'll find are some of the best of the Rio Grande style, with rich patterns, many made from naturally dyed wool. Also on display are some fine Cordova woodcarvings. Also check out **Centinela Traditional Arts,** 946 NM 76 (✆ **877/351-2180** or 505/351-2180; www.chimayoweavers.com), for a good selection of rugs made by weavers from up and down the Rio Grande Valley. Watch for the chenille shawls by Scarlet Rose.

One of the best places to shop in Chimayo, **Chimayo Trading and Mercantile** ★ (✆ **505/351-4566**), on Highway 76, is a richly cluttered store carrying local arts and crafts as well as select imports. It has a good selection of katsinas and Hopi corn maidens, as well as specialty items such as elaborately beaded cow skulls. Look for George Zarolinski's "smoked porcelain."

Many people come to Chimayo to visit **El Santuario de Nuestro Señor de Esquipulas (the Shrine of Our Lord of Esquipulas)** ★★ (✆ **505/351-4360;** holyfamily@cybermesa.com), better known simply as "El Santuario de Chimayo." Ascribed with miraculous powers of healing, this church has attracted thousands of pilgrims since its construction in 1814 to 1816. Up to 30,000 people participate in the annual Good Friday pilgrimage, many of them walking from as far away as Albuquerque.

Although only the earth in the anteroom beside the altar is presumed to have the gift of healing powers, the entire shrine radiates true serenity. A National Historic Landmark, the church has five beautiful *reredos* (panels of sacred paintings)—one behind the main altar and two on each side of the nave. The Santuario is open daily March to September 9am to 6pm, and October to February 9am to 5pm. Please remember that this is a place of worship, so quiet is always appreciated.

A good place to stop for a quick bite, **Leona's Restaurante de Chimayo** (✆ **505/351-4569**) is right next door to the Santuario de Chimayo. Leona herself presides over this little taco and burrito stand with plastic tables inside and, during warm months, out. Burritos and soft tacos made with chicken, beef, or veggie-style with beans will definitely tide you over en route to Taos or Santa Fe. Open Thursday through Monday 11am to 5pm.

Where to Stay

Casa Escondida ★ On the outskirts of Chimayo, this inn offers a lovely retreat and a good home base for exploring the Sangre de Cristo Mountains and their many soulful farming villages. This hacienda-feeling place has a cozy living room with a large kiva fireplace. Decor is simple and classic, with Mission-style furniture lending a colonial feel. The breakfast room is a sunny atrium with French doors that open out in summer to a grassy yard spotted with apricot trees. The rooms are varied; all of my favorites are within the main house. The Sun Room catches all that passionate northern New Mexico sun

Fun Facts High on Art

If you really like art and want to meet artists, check out one of the **Art Studio Tours** held in the fall in the region. Artists spend months preparing their best work, and then open their doors to visitors. Wares range from pottery and paintings to furniture and woodcarvings to ristras and dried-flower arrangements. The most notable tour is the **High Road Studio Art Tour** (www.highroadnewmexico.com) in mid- to late September. If you're not in the region during that time, watch the newspapers (such as the *Santa Fe New Mexican's* Friday edition "Pasatiempo") for notices of other art-studio tours. Good ones are held in **Galisteo** (in mid-Oct; www.galisteostudiotour.com); **Abiquiu** (early Sept; www.abiquiustudiotour.org); **El Rito** (mid-Oct; www.elritolibrary.org/studiotour.html); and **Dixon** (early Nov; www.dixonarts.org). If you're not here during those times, you can still visit many of the galleries listed on the websites.

upon its red brick floors and on its private flagstone patio as well. It has an elegant feel and connects with a smaller room, so it's a good choice for families. The Vista is on the second story. Its dormer windows give it an uniquely shaped roofline. It has a wrought-iron queen-size bed as well a twin, and it opens out onto a large deck offering spectacular sunset views. The casita adjacent to the main house has a kiva fireplace, a stove, and a minirefrigerator, as well as nice meadow views.

P.O. Box 142, Chimayo, NM 87522. ✆ **800/643-7201** or 505/351-4805. Fax 505/351-2575. www.casaescondida.com. 8 units. $95–$155 double. Rates include full breakfast. MC, V. Pets welcome in four rooms for a small fee; prearrangement required. **Amenities:** Jacuzzi; in-room massage.

Where to Dine

Restaurante Rancho de Chimayo ★ NEW MEXICAN For as long as I can remember, my family and many of my friends' families have scheduled trips into northern New Mexico to coincide with lunch or dinner at this fun restaurant. In an adobe home built by Hermenegildo Jaramillo in the 1880s, it's now run as a restaurant by his descendants. Unfortunately, over the years the restaurant has become so famous that tour buses now stop here. However, the food has suffered only a little. In the warmer months, request to dine on the terraced patio. During winter, you'll be seated in one of a number of cozy rooms with thick viga ceilings. The food is native New Mexican, prepared from generations-old Jaramillo family recipes. You can't go wrong with the enchiladas, served layered, northern New Mexico style, rather than rolled. For variety you might want to try the *combinación picante* (carne adovada, tamale, enchilada, beans, and posole). Each plate comes with a *sopaipilla.* With a little honey, who needs dessert? The full bar serves delicious margaritas.

300 County Rd. 98 (1/4 mile west of the Santuario), Chimayo, NM 87522. ✆ **505/351-4444.** www.ranchodechimayo.com. Reservations recommended. Lunch $7.50–$13; dinner $11–$21. AE, DC, DISC, MC, V. Daily May–Oct 11:30am–9pm; Sat–Sun breakfast 8:30–10:30am. Nov 1–Apr 30 closed Mon.

CORDOVA

Just as Chimayo is famous for its weaving, the village of Cordova, about 7 miles east on NM 76, is noted for its woodcarving. It's easy to whiz by this village, nestled below the

High Road, but don't. Just a short way through this truly traditional northern New Mexico town is a gem: The **Castillo Gallery ★** (✆ **505/351-4067**), a mile into the village of Cordova, carries moody and colorful acrylic paintings by Paula Castillo, as well as her metal welded sculptures. It also carries the work of Terry Enseñat Mulert, whose contemporary woodcarvings are treasures of the high country. En route to the Castillo, you may want to stop in at two other local carvers' galleries. The first you'll come to is that of **Sabinita Lopez Ortiz;** the second belongs to her cousin, **Gloria Ortiz.** Both are descendants of the well-noted José Dolores Lopez. Carved from cedar wood and aspen, their works range from simple statues of saints *(santos)* to elaborate scenes of birds.

TRUCHAS

Robert Redford's 1988 movie *The Milagro Beanfield War* featured the town of Truchas (which means "trout"). A former Spanish colonial outpost built on top of an 8,000-foot mesa, 4 miles east of Cordova, it was chosen as the site for the film in part because traditional Hispanic culture is still very much in evidence. Subsistence farming is prevalent here. The scenery is spectacular: 13,101-foot Truchas Peak dominates one side of the mesa, and the broad Rio Grande Valley dominates the other.

Look for the **High Road Marketplace ★** (✆ **866/343-5381** or 505/351-1078), an artists' co-op gallery with a variety of offerings ranging from jewelry to landscape paintings to a broad range of crosses made from tin, rusted metal, and nails. Be sure to find your way into the **Cordovas' Handweaving Workshop** (✆ **505/689-1124**). In the center of town, this tiny shop is run by Harry Cordova, a fourth-generation weaver with a unique style. His works tend to be simpler than many Rio Grande weavings, utilizing mainly stripes in the designs.

Just down the road from Cordovas' is **Hand Artes Gallery** (✆ **800/689-2441** or 505/689-2443), a definite surprise in this remote region. Here you'll find an array of contemporary as well as representational art from noted regional artists. Look for Sheila Keeffe's worldly painted panels, and Norbert Voelkel's colorful paintings and monoprints.

About 6 miles east of Truchas on NM 76 is the small town of **Las Trampas,** noted for its 1780 **San José de Gracia Church,** which, with its thick walls and elegant lines, might possibly be the most beautiful of all New Mexico churches built during the Spanish colonial period.

PICURIS (SAN LORENZO) PUEBLO

Not far from the regional education center of Peñasco, about 24 miles from Chimayo, near the intersection of NM 75 and NM 76, is the Picuris (San Lorenzo) Pueblo (✆ **505/587-2519;** www.picurispueblo.net). The 375 citizens of this 15,000-acre mountain pueblo, native Tewa speakers, consider themselves a sovereign nation: Their forebears never made a treaty with any foreign country, including the United States. Thus, they observe a traditional form of tribal council government. A few of the original mud-and-stone houses still stand, as does a lovely church. A striking aboveground ceremonial kiva called "the Roundhouse," built at least 700 years ago, and some historic excavated kivas and storerooms are on a hill above the pueblo and are open to visitors. The **annual feast days** at San Lorenzo Church are August 9 and 10.

The people here are modern enough to have fully computerized their public showcase operations as Picuris Tribal Enterprises. Besides running the Hotel Santa Fe in the state capital, they own the **Picuris Pueblo Museum and Visitor's Center,** where weaving, beadwork, and distinctive reddish-brown clay cooking pottery are exhibited daily 8am to

5pm. Self-guided tours through the old village ruins begin at the museum and cost $5; the camera fee is $6; sketching and video camera fees are $25. There's also an information center, crafts shop, and restaurant. Fishing permits ($11 for all ages) are available, as are permits to camp ($8) at Tu-Tah Lake, which is regularly stocked with trout.

You might want to plan your High Road trip to include a visit to **Sugar Nymphs Bistro ★★**, 15046 NM 75 (✆ **505/587-0311**) for some inventive food. Inside a vintage theater in the little farming village of Peñasco, Kai Harper, former executive chef at Greens in San Francisco, prepares contemporary bistro cuisine, using local and seasonal ingredients. Lunch brings imaginative pizza, salads, and burgers, while dinner includes a full range of entrees. Yaki Udon is a favorite at lunch and dinner: Grilled chicken is combined with red bell peppers, poblano chiles, carrots, and snap peas in a soy-ginger sauce. In summer, the cafe is open Tuesday to Saturday 11:30am to 3pm, and Thursday to Saturday 5:30 to 7:30 or 8pm, with Sunday brunch 11am to 2pm. In winter, spring, and fall, the schedule is abbreviated. Call ahead to be sure it's open.

DIXON & EMBUDO

Taos is about 24 miles north of Peñasco via NM 518, but day-trippers from Santa Fe can loop back to the capital by taking NM 75 west from Picuris Pueblo. Dixon, approximately 12 miles west of Picuris, and its twin village Embudo, a mile farther on NM 68 at the Rio Grande, are home to many artists and craftspeople who exhibit their works during the annual **autumn show** sponsored by the Dixon Arts Association.

To taste the local grape, follow signs to **La Chiripada Winery** (✆ **505/579-4437;** www.lachiripada.com), whose product is surprisingly good, especially to those who don't know that New Mexico has a long winemaking history. Local pottery is also sold in the tasting room. The winery is open Monday to Saturday 10am to 6pm, Sunday noon to 6pm.

Two more small villages lie in the Rio Grande Valley at 6-mile intervals south of Embudo on NM 68. Along NM 68 is **Velarde,** a fruit-growing center; in season, the road here is lined with stands selling fresh fruit or crimson chile ristras and wreaths of native plants.

ESPAÑOLA

The commercial center of Española (pop. 9,688) no longer has the railroad that led to its establishment in the 1880s, but it may have New Mexico's greatest concentration of **low riders.** These are late-model customized cars, so called because their suspension leaves them sitting quite close to the ground. Watch for them as you pass through town.

Sights of interest in Española include the **Bond House Museum** (✆ **505/747-8535**), a Victorian-era adobe home that exhibits local history and art, and the **Santa Cruz Church,** built in 1733 and renovated in 1979, which houses many fine examples of Spanish colonial religious art. The **Convento,** built to resemble a colonial cathedral, on the Española Plaza (at the junction of NM 30 and US 84), houses a variety of shops, including a trading post and an antiques gallery, as well as a display room for the Historical Society.

Complete information on Española and the vicinity can be obtained from the **Española Valley Chamber of Commerce,** #1 Calle de Las Espanolas, NM 87532 (✆ **505/753-2831;** www.espanolanmchamber.com).

If you admire the work of Georgia O'Keeffe, try to plan a short trip to **Abiquiu,** a tiny town at a bend of the Rio Chama, 14 miles south of Ghost Ranch and 22 miles north of Española on US 84. When you see the surrounding terrain, it will be clear that this

Georgia O'Keeffe & New Mexico: A Desert Romance

In June 1917, during a short visit to the Southwest, the painter Georgia O'Keeffe (born 1887) visited New Mexico for the first time. She was immediately enchanted by the stark scenery; even after her return to the energy and chaos of New York City, her mind wandered frequently to New Mexico's arid land and undulating mesas. However, not until coaxed by the arts patron and "collector of people" Mabel Dodge Luhan 12 years later did O'Keeffe return to the multihued desert of her daydreams.

O'Keeffe was reportedly ill, both physically and emotionally, when she arrived in Santa Fe in April 1929. New Mexico seemed to soothe her spirit and heal her physical ailments almost magically. Two days after her arrival, Mabel Dodge Luhan persuaded O'Keeffe to move into her home in Taos. There, she would be free to paint and socialize as she liked.

In Taos, O'Keeffe began painting what would become some of her best-known canvases—close-ups of desert flowers and objects such as cow and horse skulls. "The color up there is different . . . the blue-green of the sage and the mountains, the wildflowers in bloom," O'Keeffe once said of Taos. "It's a different kind of color from any I've ever seen—there's nothing like that in north Texas or even in Colorado." Taos transformed not only her art, but her personality as well. She bought a car and learned to drive. Sometimes, on warm days, she ran naked through the sage fields. That August, a new, rejuvenated O'Keeffe rejoined her husband, photographer Alfred Stieglitz, in New York.

The artist returned to New Mexico year after year, spending time with Mabel Dodge Luhan as well as staying at the isolated Ghost Ranch. She drove through the countryside in her snappy Ford, stopping to paint in her favorite spots along the way. Until 1949, O'Keeffe always returned to New York in the fall. Three years after Stieglitz's death, though, she relocated permanently to New Mexico, spending each winter and spring in Abiquiu and each summer and fall at Ghost Ranch. Georgia O'Keeffe died in Santa Fe in 1986.

A great way to see Ghost Ranch is on a hike that climbs above the mystical area. Take US 84 north from Española about 36 miles to Ghost Ranch and follow the road to the Ghost Ranch office. The ranch is owned by the Presbyterian Church, and the staff will supply you with a primitive map for the **Kitchen Mesa** and **Chimney Rock** hikes. If you hike there, be sure to check in at the front desk, which is open Monday to Saturday from 8am to 5pm. For more information, contact **Ghost Ranch,** 401 Old Taos Hwy., Santa Fe (✆ **505/685-4333;** www.ghostranch.org).

was the inspiration for many of her startling landscapes. **O'Keeffe's adobe home** ★ (where she lived and painted) is open for public tours. However, a reservation must be made in advance; the fee for adults is $30 (some discounts apply) for a 1-hour tour. A number of tours are given each week—on Tuesday, Thursday, and Friday (mid-Mar–late

Nov only)—and a limited number of people are accepted per tour. Visitors are not permitted to take pictures. Fortunately, O'Keeffe's home remains as it was when she lived there (until 1986). Call several months in advance for reservations (✆ **505/685-4539**).

Where to Stay & Dine

El Paragua ★ NORTHERN NEW MEXICAN This Española restaurant is a great place to stop en route to Taos, though some Santa Feans make a special trip here. Every time I enter El Paragua (which means "the umbrella"), with its red-tile floors and colorful Saltillo-tile trimmings, I feel as though I've stepped into Mexico. The restaurant opened in 1958 as a small taco stand owned by two brothers, and through the years it has flourished. It has received praise from many sources, including *Gourmet Magazine* and N. Scott Momaday, writing for the *New York Times*. You can't go wrong ordering the enchilada suprema, a chicken and cheese enchilada with onion and sour cream. Also on the menu are fajitas and a variety of seafood dishes and steaks, including the *churrasco Argentino*. Served at your table in a hot brazier, it's cooked in a green herb *salsa chimichurri*. There's a full bar from which you may want to try Don Luis's Italian coffee, made with a coffee-flavored liquor called Tuaca. For equally excellent but faster food, skip next door to the kin restaurant **El Parasol** ★ and order a chicken taco—the best ever.

603 Santa Cruz Rd., Española (off the main drag; turn east at Long John Silver's). ✆ **505/753-3211.** www.elparagua.com. Reservations recommended. Main courses $11–$22. AE, DISC, MC, V. Daily 11am–8:30pm.

Rancho de San Juan ★★★ Moments Just 38 miles from Santa Fe, set between Española and Ojo Caliente, this inn provides an authentic northern New Mexico desert experience with the comforts of a luxury hotel and the ease of staying with friends. In 2006, this place received some serious recognition; it was listed on the *Conde Nast Traveler* Gold List and named as one of the top six inns in the United States by *Executive Traveler*. It's the passion of architect and chef John Johnson, responsible for the design and cuisine, and interior designer David Heath, responsible for the elegant interiors. The original part of the inn comprises four recently renovated and enlarged rooms around a central courtyard. Additional casitas with kitchens are in the outlying hills. Rooms here are open, bright, and very elegant—stylishly decorated with a creative mix from the owners' personal art collections including contemporary paintings, tribal masks, and European antiques. From private patios, you'll have spectacular views of desert landscapes and distant, snow-capped peaks. The Kiva suite is the most innovative, with a round bedroom and a skylight just above the bed, perfect for stargazing.

Meals here are some of the best in the state. The weekly seasonal menus are original, flavorful, and beautifully presented. The selection of appetizers, entrees ($38), and desserts often take a French-inspired twist on local Southwest ingredients.

US 285 (en route to Ojo Caliente), P.O. Box 4140, Fairview Station, Española, NM 87533. ✆ **505/753-6818.** www.ranchodesanjuan.com. 13 units. $285–$685 double. AE, MC, V. **Amenities:** Restaurant; concierge; in-room massage and other spa treatments; laundry service. *In room:* A/C, CD player, fridge w/ stocked beverages, coffeemaker, hair dryer.

OJO CALIENTE

Many locals from the area like to rejuvenate at **Ojo Caliente Mineral Springs,** Ojo Caliente, NM 87549 (✆ **800/222-9162** or 505/583-2233; http://ojocalientesprings.com); it's on US 285, 50 miles (a 1-hr. drive) northwest of Santa Fe and 50 miles southwest of Taos. This National Historic Site was considered sacred by prehistoric tribes.

When Spanish explorer Cabeza de Vaca discovered and named the springs in the 16th century, he called them "the greatest treasure that I found these strange people to possess." No other hot spring in the world has Ojo Caliente's combination of iron, soda, lithium, sodium, and arsenic. If the weather is warm enough, the outdoor mud bath is a treat. The dressing rooms are in fairly good shape; however, the whole place has an earthy feel. If you're a fastidious type, you won't be comfortable here. The resort offers herbal wraps and massages, lodging, and meals. It's open daily 8am to 10pm.

8

Taos

New Mexico's favorite arts town sits in a masterpiece setting. It's wedged between the towering peaks of the Rocky Mountains and the plunging chasm of the Rio Grande Gorge.

About 70 miles north of Santa Fe, this town of 5,000 residents combines 1960s hippiedom (thanks to communes set up in the hills back then) with the ancient culture of Taos Pueblo (some people still live without electricity and running water, as their ancestors did 1,000 years ago). It can be an odd place, where some completely eschew materialism and live "off the grid" in half-underground houses called earthships. But there are plenty of more mainstream attractions as well—Taos boasts some of the best restaurants in the state, a hot and funky arts scene, and incredible outdoors action, including world-class skiing.

Its history is rich. Throughout the Taos valley, ruins and artifacts attest to a Native American presence dating back 5,000 years. The Spanish first visited this area in 1540, colonizing it in 1598. In the last 2 decades of the 17th century, they put down three rebellions at Taos Pueblo. During the 18th and 19th centuries, Taos was an important trade center: New Mexico's annual caravan to Chihuahua, Mexico, couldn't leave until after the annual midsummer **Taos Fair.** French trappers began attending the fair in 1739. Even though the Plains tribes often attacked the pueblos at other times, they would attend the market festival under a temporary annual truce. By the early 1800s, Taos had become a meeting place for American mountain men, the most famous of whom, Kit Carson, made his home in Taos from 1826 to 1868.

Taos remained loyal to Mexico during the U.S.–Mexican War of 1846. The town rebelled against its new U.S. landlord in 1847, even killing newly appointed Governor Charles Bent in his Taos home. Nevertheless, the town was eventually incorporated into the Territory of New Mexico in 1850. During the Civil War, Taos fell into Confederate hands for 6 weeks; afterward, Carson and two other men raised the Union flag over Taos Plaza and guarded it day and night. Since that time, Taos has had the honor of flying the flag 24 hours a day.

Taos's population declined when the railroad bypassed it in favor of Santa Fe. In 1898, two East Coast artists—Ernest Blumenschein and Bert Phillips—discovered the dramatic, varied effects of sunlight on the natural environment of the Taos valley and depicted them on canvas. By 1912, thanks to the growing influence of the **Taos Society of Artists,** the town had gained a worldwide reputation as a cultural center. Today, it's estimated that more than 15% of the population are painters, sculptors, writers, or musicians, or in some other way earn their income from artistic pursuits.

The town of Taos is merely the focal point of the rugged 2,200-square-mile Taos County. Two features dominate this sparsely populated region: the high desert mesa, split in two by the 650-foot-deep chasm of the **Rio Grande;** and the **Sangre de Cristo** range, which tops out at 13,161-foot Wheeler Peak, New Mexico's highest mountain. From the forested uplands to the sage-carpeted mesa, the county is home to a large variety of wildlife.

Taos is also inhabited by many people who have chosen to retreat from, or altogether drop out of, mainstream society. Most Taoseños live here to play here—and that means outdoors. Many work at the ski area all winter (skiing whenever they can) and work for raft companies in the summer (to get on the river as much as they can). Others are into rock climbing, mountain biking, and backpacking. That's not to say that Taos is just a resort town. With the Hispanic and Native American populations' histories in the area, there's a richness and depth here that most resort towns lack.

1 ORIENTATION

BY PLANE The **Taos Regional Airport** (✆ **575/758-4995**) is about 8 miles northwest of town on US 64. Most people opt to fly into Albuquerque International Sunport, rent a car, and drive up to Taos from there. The drive takes approximately 2½ hours. If you'd rather be picked up at Albuquerque International Sunport, call **Faust's Transportation, Inc.** (✆ **575/758-3410**), which offers daily service, as well as taxi service between Taos and Taos Ski Valley.

BY BUS The **Taos Bus Center** is 5 miles south of the plaza at 710 Paseo del Pueblo Sur (✆ **575/758-1144**). **TNM&O** arrives and departs from this depot several times a day. For more information on this and other bus services to and from Albuquerque and Santa Fe, see "Getting There & Getting Around," in chapter 3.

BY CAR Most visitors arrive in Taos via either NM 68 or US 64. Northbound travelers should exit I-25 at Santa Fe, follow US 285 as far as Española, and then continue on the divided highway when it becomes NM 68. Taos is about 79 miles from the I-25 junction. Southbound travelers from Denver on I-25 should exit about 6 miles south of Raton at US 64 and then follow it about 95 miles to Taos. Another major route is US 64 from the west (214 miles from Farmington).

VISITOR INFORMATION

The **Taos County Chamber of Commerce,** at 108 F Kit Carson Rd., Taos, NM 87571 (✆ **575/751-8800;** www.taoschamber.com), is open in summer, daily 9am to 5pm. It's closed on major holidays.

CITY LAYOUT

The **plaza** is a short block west of Taos's major intersection—where US 64 (Kit Carson Rd.) from the east joins NM 68, **Paseo del Pueblo Sur.** US 64 proceeds north from the intersection as **Paseo del Pueblo Norte. Camino de la Placita (Placita Rd.)** circles the west side of downtown, passing within a block of the other side of the plaza. Many of the streets that join these thoroughfares are winding lanes lined by traditional adobe homes, many of them over 100 years old.

Most of the art galleries are located on or near the plaza, which was paved over with bricks several years ago, and along neighboring streets. Others are in the **Ranchos de Taos** area, a few miles south of the plaza.

MAPS To find your way around town, pick up a free Taos map from the **Town of Taos Visitor Center,** 1139 Paseo del Pueblo Sur (✆ **800/732-TAOS** [8267] or 575/758-3873). Good, detailed city maps can be found at area bookstores as well. **Carson National Forest** information and maps are available in the same building.

2 GETTING AROUND

BY CAR

With offices at the Taos airport, **Enterprise** (✆ **575/751-7490**) is reliable and efficient. Other car-rental agencies are available out of Albuquerque. See "Getting Around," in chapter 6, for details.

PARKING Parking can be difficult during the summer rush, when the stream of tourists' cars moving north and south through town never ceases. If you can't find parking on the street or in the plaza, check out some of the nearby roads (Kit Carson Rd., for instance); there are plenty of metered and unmetered lots in Taos.

ROAD CONDITIONS Information on highway conditions throughout the state can be obtained from the **State Highway Department** (✆ **800/432-4269**).

BY BUS & TAXI

If you're in Taos without a car, you're in luck because there's local bus service, provided by **Chile Line Town of Taos Transit** (✆ **575/751-4459**). It operates every half-hour Monday to Saturday 7am to 7pm in summer, 7am to 6pm in winter, and on the hour Sunday 8am to 5pm. Two simultaneous routes run southbound from Taos Pueblo and northbound from the Ranchos de Taos Post Office. Each route makes stops at the casino and various hotels in town, as well as at Taos RV Park. Bus fares are 50¢ one-way, $1 round-trip, $5 for a 7-day pass, and $20 for a 31-day pass.

In addition, **Faust's Transportation** (✆ **575/758-3410**) has a taxi service linking town hotels and Taos Ski Valley. Faust's Transportation also offers shuttle service and on-call taxi service daily from 8am to 5pm (special arrangements made for after hours; Sun by appointment only), with fares of about $10 anywhere within the city limits for up to two people.

BY BICYCLE

Bicycle rentals are available from **Gearing Up Bicycle Shop,** 129 Paseo del Pueblo Sur (✆ **575/751-0365**); daily rentals run $35 for a full day and $25 for a half-day for a mountain bike with front suspension. From April to October, **Native Sons Adventures,** 1334 Paseo del Pueblo Sur (✆ **800/753-7559** or 575/758-9342; www.nativesonsadventures.com), rents front-suspension bikes for $25/half-day and $35/full day. It also rents car racks for $5. Each shop supplies helmets and water bottles with rentals.

Warning for Drivers

En route to many recreation sites, reliable paved roads often give way to poorer forest roads. When you get off the main roads, you don't find gas stations or cafes. Four-wheel-drive vehicles are recommended on snow and much of the unpaved terrain of the region. If you're doing some off-road adventuring, it's wise to go with a full gas tank, extra food and water, and warm clothing—just in case. At the higher-than-10,000-foot elevations of northern New Mexico, sudden summer snowstorms are not unheard of.

Fast Facts Taos

Airport See "Orientation," above.

Area Code The telephone area code for Taos area is **575.**

ATMs You can find ATMs all over town, at supermarkets, banks, and drive-throughs.

Business Hours Most **businesses** are open at least Monday to Friday 10am to 5pm, though some may open an hour earlier and close an hour later. Many **tourist-oriented shops** are also open on Saturday morning, and some **art galleries** are open all day Saturday and Sunday, especially during peak tourist seasons. **Banks** are generally open Monday to Thursday 9am to 5pm and often for longer hours on Friday. Some may be open Saturday morning. Most branches have cash machines available 24 hours. Call establishments for specific hours.

Car Rentals See "Getting Around New Mexico," in chapter 3, or "Getting Around," above.

Climate Taos's climate is similar to that of Santa Fe. Summer days are dry and sunny, except for frequent afternoon thunderstorms. Winter days are often bracing, with snowfalls common but rarely lasting too long. Average **summer temperatures** range from 50° to 87°F (10°–31°C). **Winter temperatures** vary between 9° and 40°F (–13° to 4°C). **Annual rainfall** is 12 inches; annual snowfall is 35 inches in town and 300 inches at Taos Ski Valley, where the elevation is 9,207 feet. (A foot of snow is equal to an inch of rain.)

Currency Exchange Foreign currency can be exchanged at the **Centinel Bank of Taos,** 512 Paseo del Pueblo Sur (© **575/758-6700**).

Dentists If you need dental work, try **Dr. Walter Jakiela,** 1392 Weimer Rd. (© **575/758-8654**); **Dr. Michael Rivera,** 107 Plaza Garcia, Suite. E (© **575/758-0531**); or **Dr. Tom Simms,** 1392 Weimer Rd. (© **575/758-8303**).

Doctors Members of the **Taos Medical Group,** on Weimer Road (© **575/758-2224**), are highly respected. Also recommended are **Family Practice Associates of Taos,** 630 Paseo del Pueblo Sur, Suite. 150 (© **575/758-3005**).

Emergencies Dial © **911** for police, fire, and ambulance.

Hospital **Holy Cross Hospital,** 1397 Weimer Rd., off Paseo del Canyon (© **575/758-8883**), has 24-hour emergency service. Serious cases are transferred to Santa Fe or Albuquerque.

Hot Lines The **crisis hot line** (© **575/758-9888**) is available for emergency counseling.

Information See "Visitor Information," under "Orientation," above.

Internet Access You can retrieve your e-mail via Wi-Fi or the cafe's computers at **Sustaining Cultures,** 114 Doña Luz (© **575/751-0959**). It's located 1 block west of the plaza. And the Taos County Chamber of Commerce, 108 F Kit Carson Rd. (© **575/751-8800**), just off the Plaza, offers free access. As well, the **Taos Public Library** offers free access (see below).

Library The **Taos Public Library,** 402 Camino de la Placita (✆ **575/758-3063** or 575/737-2590), has a general collection for Taos residents, a children's library, and special collections on the Southwest and Taos art.

Lost Property Check with the **Taos police** at ✆ **575/758-2216.**

Newspapers & Magazines The ***Taos News*** (✆ **575/758-2241;** www.taosnews.com) and the ***Sangre de Cristo Chronicle*** (✆ **575/377-2358;** www.sangrechronicle.com) are published every Thursday. ***Taos Magazine*** is also a good source of local information. The ***Albuquerque Journal*** (www.abqjournal.com) and the ***New Mexican*** (from Santa Fe; www.santafenewmexican.com) are easily obtained at book and convenience stores.

Pharmacies There are several full-service pharmacies in Taos. **Sav-on Drug** (✆ **575/758-1203**), **Smith's Pharmacy** (✆ **575/758-4824**), and **Wal-Mart Pharm acy** (✆ **575/758-2743**) are all on Pueblo Sur and are easily seen from the road.

Police In case of emergency, dial ✆ **911.** All other inquiries should be directed to the **Taos police,** Civic Plaza Drive (✆ **575/758-2216**). The **Taos County Sheriff,** with jurisdiction outside the city limits, is in the county courthouse on Paseo del Pueblo Sur (✆ **575/758-3361**).

Post Offices The main **Taos post office** is at 318 Paseo del Pueblo Norte (✆ **575/758-2081**), a few blocks north of the plaza traffic light. There are smaller offices in **Ranchos de Taos** (✆ **575/758-3944**) and at **El Prado** (✆ **575/758-4810**). The zip code for Taos is 87571.

Radio A local station is **KTAOS-FM** (101.9), which broadcasts an entertainment calendar daily (✆ **575/758-5826**); National Public Radio can be found on **KUNM-FM** (98.5) from Albuquerque.

Taxes Gross receipts tax for the city of Taos is 7.5%, and for Taos County it's 6.3%. There is an additional lodgers' tax of 5% in both the city of Taos and in Taos County.

Taxis See "Getting Around," above.

Television **Channel 2,** the local access station, is available in most hotels. For a few hours a day it shows local programming. Cable networks carry Santa Fe and Albuquerque stations.

Time As is true throughout New Mexico, Taos is on **Mountain Standard Time.** It's 2 hours earlier than New York, 1 hour earlier than Chicago, and 1 hour later than Los Angeles. Clocks change the second Sunday in March and the first Sunday in November.

Useful Telephone Numbers For **emergency road service** in the Taos area, call the state police at ✆ **575/758-8878;** for **road conditions** dial ✆ **800/432-4269** (within New Mexico) for the state highway department. **Taos County offices** are at ✆ **575/737-6300.**

Weather Taos has no number to call for weather forecasts, but if you're hooked up, log on to www.taoschamber.com.

3 WHERE TO STAY

A tiny town with a big tourist market, Taos has thousands of rooms in hotels, motels, condominiums, and bed-and-breakfasts. Many new properties have recently opened, turning this into a buyer's market. In the slower seasons—January through early February and April through early May—when competition for travelers is steep, you may even want to try bargaining your room rate down. Most of the hotels and motels are on Paseo del Pueblo Sur and Norte, with a few scattered just east of the town center, along Kit Carson Road. The condos and bed-and-breakfasts are generally scattered throughout Taos's back streets.

During peak seasons, visitors without reservations may have difficulty finding vacant rooms. **Taos Chamber of Commerce,** 108 F Kit Carson Rd. (✆ **575/751-8800**), might be able to help. If you're looking to hook up to the Internet in this town, head for the plaza, which offers wireless access anywhere you sit.

Southern Rockies Reservations (✆ **866/250-7313;** www.taosskitrips.com) will help you find accommodations ranging from bed-and-breakfasts to home rentals, hotels, and cabins throughout Taos, Taos Ski Valley, and the rest of northern New Mexico. It'll also help you arrange package trips for outdoor activities such as skiing, horseback riding, hot-air ballooning, and snowmobiling.

There are two high seasons in Taos: winter (the Christmas-to-Easter ski season, except for January, which is notoriously slow) and summer. Spring and fall are shoulder seasons, often with lower rates. The period between Easter and Memorial Day is also slow in the tourist industry here, and many proprietors of restaurants and other businesses take their annual vacations at this time. Book well ahead for ski holiday periods (especially Christmas) and for the annual arts festivals (late May to mid-June and late Sept to early Oct).

TAOS

Hotels/Motels

Expensive

El Monte Sagrado ★★★ (Moments) New to Taos in 2003, this resort near the center of town offers a feast for the senses. Water running over falls, lush landscaping, and delicious food and drink lull guests into a sweet *samadhi,* or state of relaxation, while the eyes luxuriate in the beauty of rooms impeccably decorated. These range in theme from the Caribbean casita, a medium-size room with a medium-size bathroom, which evokes the feel of an African jungle, to the Argentina global suite, a huge two-bedroom decorated in cowboy-contemporary style with wood floors, leather furniture, iron and copper accents, and two large bathrooms featuring stone and glass mosaic-decorated shower and bath, not to mention its own patio and outdoor hot tub. In 2007, the inn nearly doubled in size with a series of new, more reasonably priced rooms and an elegant meeting center. All rooms are quiet and lovely, with patios or balconies and views. In line with the resort owner Tom Worrell's plan to preserve the earth's environment through responsible development and sustainable technologies, the resort recycles its water, using it to irrigate the grassy, cottonwood-shaded "Sacred Circle," at the resort's center. The intimate spa, with a waiting area that resembles a greenhouse filled with plants, offers a full range of excellent treatments, and the Living Spa Program offers classes such as yoga and T'ai Chi free for guests. The **Anaconda Bar** and **De La Tierra** restaurant (see later) combine a contemporary feel with elegant Asian touches.

317 Kit Carson Rd., Taos, NM 87571. ✆ **800/828-TAOS** (8267) or 575/758-3502. www.elmontesagrado.com. 84 units. $159–$369 historic 1-bedroom casita; $179–$399 Taos Mountain Room; $199–$439 Native American suite; $219–$479 Bali and Tibet premier suite; $419–$839 2-bedroom global suite. AE, DC, DISC, MC, V. Valet parking $12. **Amenities:** Restaurant (p. 214); bar (p. 239); indoor pool; well-equipped health club and spa; Jacuzzi; concierge; laundry service. *In room:* A/C, TV, CD player, high-speed Internet, Wi-Fi, minibar, coffeemaker, hair dryer, safe.

The Historic Taos Inn ★ It's rare to see a hotel that has withstood the years with grace, but the Historic Taos Inn has done just that. Here, you'll be surrounded by 21st-century luxury without ever forgetting that you're within the thick walls of a number of 19th-century Southwestern homes once owned by Dr. Thomas Paul Martin, the town's first physician, who purchased the complex in 1895. It's now listed on both the State and National Registers of Historic Places.

The lobby doubles as the **Adobe Bar,** a popular local gathering place, with adobe *bancos* (benches) and a sunken fireplace, all surrounding a wishing well that was once the old town well. A number of rooms open onto a balcony that overlooks this area. I don't recommend these rooms, as they can be noisy. All the other rooms sit among a number of "houses" separated by walkways and grass. Some have more modest style, with lower ceilings and Spanish Colonial furnishings, while others are more chic. My favorites are #204 in the Sandoval House, decorated with antiques, and any room in the recently built Helen House ★★. These rooms, with saltillo tile floors, kiva fireplaces and stylish furnishings made from interesting things such as saguaro cactus, in one, will appeal to travelers who don't appreciate the whims of an older building, but still enjoy character. When reserving here, be sure to discuss your needs with the reservation service. Wireless Internet is available in the lobby.

Doc Martin's (p. 214), serving nouveau Southwestern and international cuisine, some of it organic, is a good bet for any meal.

125 Paseo del Pueblo Norte, Taos, NM 87571. ✆ **800/TAOS-INN** (826-7466) or 575/758-2233. Fax 575/758-5776. www.taosinn.com. 44 units. $85–$275, depending on the type of room and season. AE, DISC, MC, V. **Amenities:** Restaurant (p. 214); lounge; Jacuzzi; room service; coffee or refreshments in lobby. *In room:* A/C, TV, hair dryer, iron, DVD on request.

Hotel La Fonda de Taos ★ Finally, Taos has a recommendable hotel on the plaza. A $3-million renovation to this historic property built in 1880 has turned it into a comfortable, fun spot with a stellar location. The charismatic Taos figure Saki Kavaras put this hotel on the society map in the 1930s, when, most notably, British author D. H. Lawrence frequented it. His legacy is preserved in a unique D. H. Lawrence Forbidden Art Museum, where some of his risqué paintings hang—a must-see even if you don't stay here (free for guests; $3 for nonguests). Rooms are set off broad hallways, each styled in earth tones, Southwestern furnishings, and tile bathrooms. Standards are small, each with a queen-size bed. Your better bet is to reserve a plaza or deluxe plaza room, or a suite. These are larger, with king beds. My favorite rooms are nos. 201 and 301, which overlook the plaza. Groups can rent the whole top floor (or the whole hotel), which includes a full kitchen suite. **Joseph's Table** (p. 216), one of Taos' finest restaurants, is off the lobby.

108 South Plaza, Taos, NM 87571. ✆ **800/833-2211** or 575/758-2211. Fax 575/758-8508. www.lafondataos.com. 24 units. $109–$149 standard double; $139–$209 plaza and deluxe plaza double; $199–$239 suite. AE, DC, DISC, MC, V. Free parking. **Amenities:** Restaurant; coffee shop; bar. *In room:* A/C, TV, high-speed Internet, hair dryer, iron.

Inger Jirby's Guest Houses ★★ Two blocks from the plaza, between the R.C. Gorman Gallery and the Ernest L. Blumenschein Museum, this inn provides a stay in an

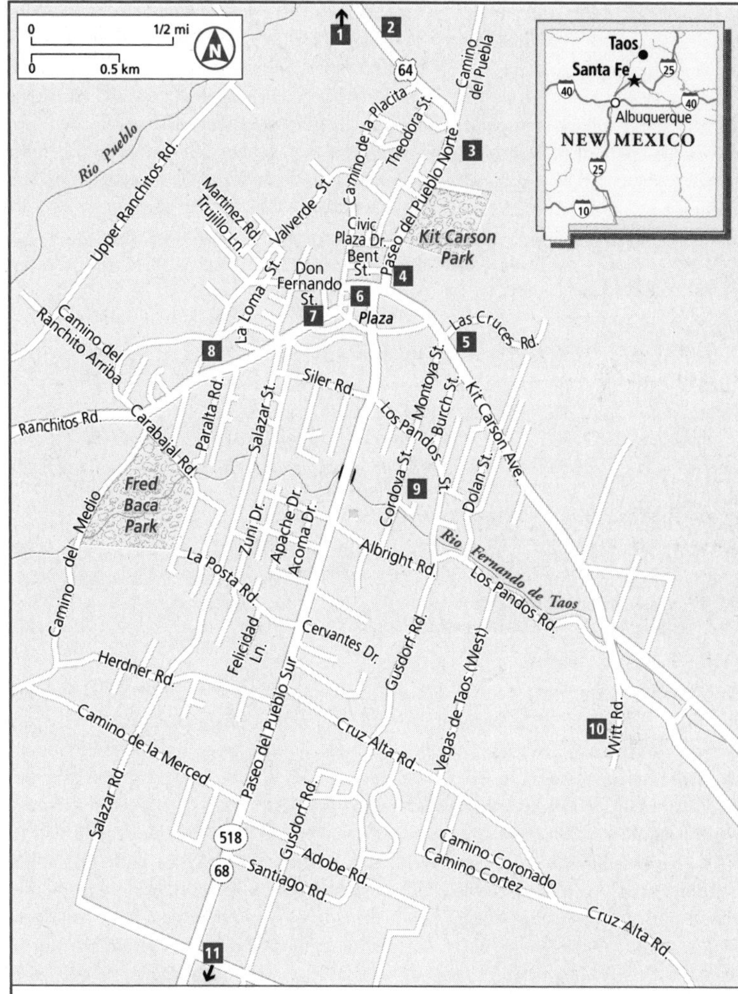

Adobe & Pines Inn **11**

Adobe & Stars Bed & Breakfast Inn **1**

Best Western Kachina Lodge **3**

Carson National Forest **1**

Casa del las Chimeneas **9**

El Monte Sagrado **5**

Hacienda del Sol **2**

The Historic Taos Inn **4**

Hotel La Fonda de Taos **6**

Inger Jirby's Guest Houses **7**

Inn on La Loma Plaza **8**

Little Tree Bed & Breakfast **1**

Old Taos Guesthouse Bed & Breakfast **10**

Taos Hampton Inn **11**

Taos Valley RV Park & Campground **11**

artistic ancient adobe. Painter Inger Jirby has chosen this for her gallery space as well as a home for travelers. From the remains of a 400-year-old adobe, she's carved and added these lively dwellings and adorned them with her unique style. Full of rich Mexican and Balinese art, and then accented by her own vivid landscapes of the Southwest and beyond, the casitas are artsy as well as comfortable. Both have a full kitchen, flagstone floors, large windows, and sleeping lofts. (Very big people might have trouble maneuvering the spiral staircases in these.) They also have fold-out couches, so they're a great option for families. Both are equipped with stereos and robes. More than anywhere else in town, these casitas provide a real home away from home. The attached Inger Jirby Gallery provides Internet access for guests.

207 Ledoux St., Taos, NM 87571. ✆ **575/758-7333.** www.jirby.com. 2 units. $175–$225 double; up to $325 during holidays. Additional person $25–$35. *In room:* TV/DVD, hair dryer, stove, microwave, dishwasher, washer/dryer.

Moderate

Taos Hampton Inn ★ Kids The most reliable moderately priced hotel in town, the Hampton was built in the mid-1990s and is about 5 minutes (by car) from the plaza. Rooms are medium-size with either two queens or one king bed, a few with Jacuzzis and mountain views. All have nice pine furnishings, quality bedding, and a hint of Southwestern decor, some with desks, others with a table and chair. The beds are comfortable and the medium-size bathrooms very clean and functional. The medium-size indoor pool keeps kids entertained year-round.

1515 Paseo del Pueblo Sur, Taos, NM 87571. **800/HAMPTON** (426-7866) or 575/737-5700. Fax 575/737-5701. www.hampton.com. 71 units. $109–$149. Rates include full hot breakfast and afternoon snack. AE, DC, DISC, MC, V. **Amenities:** Indoor pool; Jacuzzi; business center; guest laundry. *In room:* A/C, TV, high-speed Internet, Wi-Fi, coffeemaker, hair dryer, iron.

Inexpensive

Best Western Kachina Lodge & Meeting Center Kids Built in the early 1960s, this lodge on the north end of town, in walking distance of the plaza, has a lot of charm despite the fact that it's a motor hotel. Unfortunately, with an aged owner who's looking to sell the property, it's in dire need of remodeling right now, so only stay here if you don't mind crumbling sidewalks and frayed carpeting and furnishings. The Southwestern-style rooms—some have couches and most have Taos-style *trasteros* (armoires) that hold the TVs—have comfortable beds and small but functional and clean baths. Rooms sit around a grassy courtyard studded with huge blue spruce trees, allowing kids room to run. In the center is a stage where a family from Taos Pueblo builds a bonfire and dances nightly in the summer and explains the significance of the dances—a real treat for anyone baffled by the Pueblo rituals. A full, hot breakfast is served in a retro kiva-shaped cafe.

413 Paseo del Pueblo Norte (P.O. Box NM), Taos, NM 87571. ✆ **800/522-4462** or 575/758-2275. Fax 575/758-9207. www.kachinalodge.com. 118 units. $59–$159 double; includes full breakfast. Additional person $10. Children 11 and under stay free in parent's room. AE, DISC, MC, V. **Amenities:** 2 restaurants; lounge; outdoor pool; courtesy shuttle; salon; coin-op laundry. *In room:* A/C, TV, Wi-Fi, coffeemaker, hair dryer, iron.

Bed & Breakfasts

Expensive

Adobe & Pines Inn ★★ The Adobe & Pines Inn seeks to create a magical escape, and it succeeds. Much of it's in a 150-year-old adobe directly off NM 68, less than half a mile south of St. Francis Plaza (about a 10-min. drive from Taos Plaza). The inn is set around a courtyard marked by an 80-foot-long grand portal and surrounded by pine and fruit trees. Each room has a private entrance and fireplace (three even have fireplaces in their bathrooms), and each is uniquely decorated. The theme here is the use of colors, which are richly displayed on the walls and in the furnishings. There's Puerta Azul, a cozy blue room with thick adobe walls, and Puerta Turquese, a separate whimsically painted guest cottage with a full kitchen. The two rooms, completed in 1996, have bold maroon and copper-yellow themes. Because this inn is near the highway, at times cars can be heard on the grounds, but the rooms themselves are quiet. Morning brings a delicious full gourmet breakfast in the glassed-in breakfast room. A courtesy computer with Internet is available for guest use.

NM 68, Ranchos de Taos, NM 87557. ✆ **800/723-8267** or 575/751-0947. Fax 575/758-8423. www.adobepines.com. 8 units. $98–$225 double; $215–$250 suite for up to 6 people. Rates include full gourmet breakfast. MC, V. Pets accepted with prior arrangement. **Amenities:** In-room massage; complimentary laundry facility available evenings. *In room:* TV, Wi-Fi, no phone.

Adobe and Stars Bed and Breakfast Inn ★★ This inn sitting on the mesa between Taos town and Taos Ski Valley offers chic Southwestern-style rooms with a focus on fine detail in a quiet country setting. The breakfast area and common room are sunny, with large windows facing the mountains. A few rooms are upstairs, such as La Luna, my favorite, with views in every direction and a heart-shaped Jacuzzi tub for two. All rooms have kiva fireplaces and private decks or patios. Most of the downstairs rooms open onto a portal. All are decorated with hand-crafted Southwestern-style furniture, and many have Jacuzzi tubs. As well, guests enjoy an outdoor hot tub under the stars, reserved by the half-hour. The full breakfast may vary from New Mexican dishes such as breakfast burritos with green chile to gingerbread waffles with whipped cream. In the afternoons, a glass of New Mexico wine is served with a snack. A courtesy computer with Internet is available for guest use.

At the corner of State Hwy. 150 and Valdez Rim Rd. (P.O. Box 2285), Taos, NM 87571. ✆ **800/211-7076** or 575/776-2776. Fax 575/776-2872. www.taosadobe.com. 8 units. $95–$190 double. Rates include full breakfast and hors d'oeuvres. AE, MC, V. Pets accepted with $20 per-pet fee and $50 damage deposit. **Amenities:** Jacuzzi. *In room:* Wi-Fi, hair dryer.

Casa de las Chimeneas ★★★ This 82-year-old adobe home set on spacious grounds has, since its opening as a luxury inn in 1988, been a model of Southwestern elegance. Adding to its appeal is a spa with a small fitness room and sauna, as well as complete massage and facial treatments for an additional charge. I recommend the Rio Grande and Territorial rooms, which are spacious and air-conditioned. Both of these rooms have heated Saltillo-tile floors, gas kiva fireplaces, and Jacuzzi tubs. If you prefer a more antique-feeling room, try the delightful older section, especially the Library Suite. Each room in the inn is decorated with original works of art and has elegant bedding, a private entrance, and robes. All rooms have kiva fireplaces, and most look out on flower and herb gardens. Breakfasts are delicious. Specialties include an artichoke-heart and mushroom omelet or ricotta cream-cheese blintz. In the evenings the inn offers a full dinner, which may include corn-crusted tilapia or roasted chicken served with vegetables from a local organic farm. End the day at the large hot tub in the courtyard. Smoking is not permitted. Ask about the spa specials. A courtesy computer with Internet is available for guest use.

405 Cordoba Rd., at Los Pandos Rd. (5303 NDCBU), Taos, NM 87571. ✆ **877/758-4777** or 575/758-4777. Fax 575/758-3976. www.visittaos.com. 8 units. $180–$320 double; $325 suite. Rates include breakfast and light evening supper. AE, DC, DISC, MC, V. **Amenities:** Small exercise room; spa; Jacuzzi; sauna; concierge; car-rental desk; in-room massage; coin-op laundry. *In room:* TV/VCR, Wi-Fi, free stocked nonalcoholic minibar, coffeemaker, hair dryer, iron.

Hacienda del Sol ★★ What's unique about this bed-and-breakfast is its spectacular view of Taos Mountain. Because the 1¼-acre property borders Taos Pueblo, the land is pristine. The inn also has a rich history. It was once owned by arts patron Mabel Dodge Luhan, and it was here that author Frank Waters wrote *The People of the Valley.* You'll find bold splashes of color from the gardens—where in summer tulips, pansies, and flax bloom—to the rooms themselves—where woven bedspreads and original art lend a Mexican feel. The main house is 204 years old, so it has the wonderful curves of adobe as well as thick vigas. Some guest rooms are in this section. Others range from 9 to 27 years in age. The newer rooms are finely constructed, and I almost recommend them over the others because they're a little more private and the bathrooms are more refined. All rooms have robes and CD players, most have fireplaces, three have private Jacuzzis, and four have private steam showers. Some have minirefrigerators. A full and delicious breakfast is served in the Spanish-hacienda-style dining area. The outdoor hot tub has a mountain view and is available for private guest use in half-hour segments. A courtesy computer with Internet is available for guest use.

109 Mabel Dodge Lane (P.O. Box 177), Taos, NM 87571. ✆ **575/758-0287.** Fax 575/758-5895. www.taoshaciendadelsol.com. 11 units. $135–$325 double. Rates include full breakfast and evening sweets. AE, DISC, MC, V. **Amenities:** Jacuzzi; concierge; in-room massage. *In room:* CD player, Wi-Fi, minibar, hair dryer.

Inn on La Loma Plaza ★★ Named by *American Historic Inns* as one of the 10 most romantic inns in America, the Inn on La Loma Plaza provides the comfortable intimacy of a B&B with the service and amenities of an inn. It's on a historic neighborhood plaza, complete with dirt streets and a tiny central park, which was once a 1796 neighborhood stronghold—adobe homes built around a square, with thick outer walls to fend off marauders. The building, a 10-minute walk from Taos Plaza, is a 200-year-old home, complete with aged vigas and maple floors, decorated tastefully with comfortable furniture and Middle Eastern rugs. Each room is unique, most with sponge-painted walls and Talavera tile in the bathrooms to provide an eclectic ambience. All have robes, slippers, lighted makeup mirrors, bottled water, and fireplaces, and most have balconies or terraces and views. Some have special touches, such as the Happy Trails Room, with knotty pine paneling, a brass bed, old chaps, and decorative hanging spurs. Some rooms have kitchenettes. Guests dine in a plant-filled sunroom or on the patio. Internet connection is available on a courtesy computer.

315 Ranchitos Rd., Taos, NM 87571. ✆ **800/530-3040** or 575/758-1717. Fax 575/751-0155. www.vacationtaos.com. 10 units. $155–$240 double; $265–$325 artist's studios; $480–$540 suite. Additional person $25. Children 12 and under stay free in parent's room. Discounts available. Rates include full breakfast. AE, DISC, MC, V. **Amenities:** Pool and spa privileges at nearby Taos Spa; Jacuzzi. *In room:* TV/VCR/DVD, WiFi, hair dryer, iron.

Little Tree Bed & Breakfast ★★ Finds Little Tree is one of my favorite Taos bed-and-breakfasts, partly because it's in a beautiful, secluded setting, and partly because it's constructed with real adobe that's been left in its raw state, lending the place an authentic hacienda feel. Two miles down a country road, about midway between Taos and the ski area, it's surrounded by sage and piñon. The charming and cozy rooms have radiant heat under the floors, queen-size beds (one with a king-size), nice medium-size baths, and access to the portal and courtyard garden, at the center of which is the little tree for which the inn is named. The Piñon (my favorite) and Juniper rooms are equipped with fireplaces and private entrances. The Piñon and Aspen rooms offer sunset views. The Spruce Room has a private patio and outdoor hot tub. Visiting hummingbirds enchant guests as they enjoy a scrumptious breakfast on the portal during warmer months. On arrival, guests are treated to refreshments. A courtesy computer with Internet is available for guest use.

County Road B-143 (P.O. Box 509), Arroyo Hondo, NM 87513. ✆ **800/334-8467** or 575/776-8467. www.littletreebandb.com. 4 units. $135–$195 double. Rates include breakfast and afternoon snack. MC, V. *In room:* TV/VCR.

Moderate

Old Taos Guesthouse Bed & Breakfast ★ Kids Once a farmer's home and later an artist's estate, this 190-year-old adobe hacienda has been restored by owners and incorrigible ski bums Tim and Leslie Reeves, who, for more than 18 years, have carefully maintained the country charm: Mexican tile in the bathrooms, vigas on the ceilings, and kiva-style fireplaces in most of the rooms. Each room has an entrance from the outside, some off the broad portal that shades the front of the hacienda, some from a grassy lawn in the back, with a view toward the mountains. Some rooms are more utilitarian, some quainter, so make a request depending on your needs. One of my favorites is the Taos Suite, with a king-size bed, a big picture window, and a full kitchen that includes an oven, a stove, a minirefrigerator, and a microwave. Less than 2 miles from the plaza, this inn sits on 7½ acres and provides a cozy northern New Mexico rural experience, complete with an *acequia* (irrigation system), birds galore, and healthy breakfast. Kids enjoy the inn's dogs and plenty of space to run free. Wireless Internet access is available in much of the inn.

1028 Witt Rd., Taos, NM 87571. ✆ **800/758-5448** or 575/758-5448. www.oldtaos.com. 10 units. $90–$175 double. Rates include a full breakfast. Ask about seasonal rates. DISC, MC, V. Pets accepted in some rooms with $25 flat fee. **Amenities:** Jacuzzi; concierge; tour desk; in-room massage; babysitting. *In room:* Hair dryer, iron.

TAOS SKI VALLEY

For information on the skiing and the facilities offered at Taos Ski Valley, see "Skiing," later in this chapter.

Lodges

Expensive

Powderhorn Suites and Condominiums ★ Value A cozy, homelike feel and Euro-Southwestern ambience make this condo-inn one of the best buys in Taos Ski Valley, just a 2-minute walk from the lift. You'll find consistency and quality here, with clean medium-size rooms, mountain views, vaulted ceilings, well-planned bathrooms, and comfortable beds. The larger suites have stoves, balconies, and fireplaces. Adjoining rooms are good for families. As with almost all of the accommodations in Taos Ski Valley, this one has been condo-ized so each suite has a distinct owner; thus the service isn't what you would find at a full-service hotel, though it is still conscientious. There's no elevator, so if stairs are a problem for you, make sure to ask for a room on the ground floor.

5 Ernie Blake Rd. (P.O. Box 69), Taos Ski Valley, NM 87525. ✆ **800/776-2346** or 575/776-2341. Fax 575/776-2341, ext. 103. www.taoswebb.com/powderhorn. 17 units. Ski season $99–$165 double, $130–$200 suite, $195–$400 condo; summer $69–$129. 2- to 6-person occupancy. MC, V. Valet parking. **Amenities:** 2 Jacuzzis; massage. *In room:* TV, Wi-Fi, kitchenette.

Moderate

Alpine Village Suites ★★ Alpine Village is a small village within Taos Ski Valley, a few steps from the lift. Owned by John and Barbara Cottam, the complex also houses a ski shop and bar/restaurant. The Cottams began with seven rooms, still nice rentals, above their ski shop. Each has a sleeping loft for the agile who care to climb a ladder, as well as sunny windows. The newer section has elegantly decorated rooms, with attractive touches such as Mexican furniture and inventive tile work done by locals. Like most other accommodations at Taos Ski Valley, the rooms are not especially soundproof. Fortunately, most skiers go to bed early. All rooms have VCRs and small kitchenettes equipped with stoves, microwaves, and minirefrigerators. In the newer building, rooms have fireplaces and private balconies. Request a south-facing room for a view of the slopes. The Jacuzzi sits below a lovely mural and has a fireplace and a view of the slopes. High-speed and wireless Internet access is available in all but two rooms.

100 Thunderbird Rd. (P.O. Box 98), Taos Ski Valley, NM 87525. ✆ **800/576-2666** or 575/776-8540. Fax 575/776-8542. www.alpine-suites.com. 29 units. Ski season $150–$215 suite for 2, $216–$347 suite for 4, $216–$391 suite for up to 6; summer $66–$172 suite for 2 (includes continental breakfast). AE, DISC, MC, V. Covered valet parking $10 per night. **Amenities:** Jacuzzi; sauna; massage; business center. *In room:* TV/VCR, kitchenette.

Condominiums

Expensive

Edelweiss Lodge & Spa ★★ Opened in 2005, this lodge at the base of the mountain took the place of a 1960s classic chalet. Now, it's a brand new condo-hotel. The condominiums are upscale, each with a flagstone fireplace and full kitchen with marble countertops, stainless steel appliances, and many with nice views of the slopes. All have luxury furnishings decorated in earth tones. For those looking for an upscale stay, this is your choice. Hotel rooms follow with the same luxury as the condos. Rooms are medium size with comfortable beds and medium-size baths. Check the website for a glimpse of the rooms and other facilities. Underground parking, a full spa, an excellent restaurant, and valet service for your skis, add to the appeal. Wireless Internet access is available in the lobby.

106 Sutton Place, Taos Ski Valley, NM 87525. ✆ **800/I-LUV-SKI** (458-8754) or 575/737-6900. Fax 575/737-6995. www.edelweisslodgeandspa.com. 31 units. Hotel room winter $220–$440 double; summer $125 double; condo winter $275–$1,156, summer $198–$375 (ranges cover 1 bedroom/1 bath–3 bedrooms/3 baths). AE, DISC, MC, V. Free parking. **Amenities:** Restaurant; bar; health club and full spa; 2 Jacuzzis; sauna; concierge; massage; ski shop. *In room:* TV, high-speed Internet, coffeemaker, hair dryer.

Sierra del Sol Condominiums ★ I have wonderful memories of these condominiums, which are just a 2-minute walk from the lift; family friends used to invite me to stay with them when I was young. I'm happy to say that the units, built in the 1960s, with additions through the years, have been well maintained. Though they're privately owned, and therefore decorated at the whim of the owners, management does inspect them every year and make suggestions. They're smartly built and come in a few sizes: studio, one-bedroom, and two-bedroom. The one- and two-bedroom units have big living rooms with fireplaces and porches that look out on the ski runs. The bedrooms are spacious, and some have sleeping lofts. Each has a full kitchen, with a dishwasher, stove, oven, microwave, and refrigerator. Two-bedroom units sleep up to six. Grills and picnic tables on the grounds sit near a mountain river. High-speed and wireless Internet access is available in a guest computer room.

13 Thunderbird Rd. (P.O. Box 84), Taos Ski Valley, NM 87525. ✆ **800/523-3954** or 575/776-2981. Fax 575/776-2347. www.sierrataos.com. 32 units. Prices range from $79 for studio in summer to $414 for 2-bedroom condo in high season. DISC, MC, V. Free parking. **Amenities:** 2 Jacuzzis; 2 saunas; massage; babysitting; coin-op laundry. *In room:* TV/DVD, Wi-Fi, kitchen, microwave, hair dryer upon request, iron upon request, safe.

Snakedance Condominiums and Spa ★★ A $3.5-million renovation has transformed the rooms of this once-hotel into elegant condominiums. Skiers appreciate the inn's location, just steps from the lift, as well as amenities such as ski storage and boot dryers. The original structure that stood on this site was known as the Hondo Lodge. Before there was a Taos Ski Valley, Hondo Lodge served as a refuge for fishermen, hunters, and artists. The Snakedance Condominiums today are privately owned units, so each may differ some, though they are consistent in quality. All are bright comfortable spaces with balconies with French doors and kitchens with granite counters and a range, fridge, dishwasher, and microwave. All have gas fireplaces. The hotel also offers shuttle service to and from nearby shops and restaurants, and, at certain times, to Albuquerque and Santa Fe.

110 Sutton Place (P.O. Box 89), Taos Ski Valley, NM 87525. ✆ **800/322-9815** or 575/776-2277. Fax 575/776-1410. www.snakedancecondos.com. 33 units. 1-bedroom condo $225–$400 double in winter, in summer $95; 2-bedroom condo $285–$600 for 4 people in winter, $120 in summer; 2-bedroom loft condo $345–$725 for 6 people in winter, $150 in summer. Extra person $30 in winter, $10 in summer. Rates include a complimentary continental breakfast. AE, DC, DISC, MC, V. Free parking at Taos Ski Valley parking lot. Closed mid-Apr to Memorial Day and mid-Oct to mid-Nov. **Amenities:** Restaurant; bar; exercise room; spa; Jacuzzi; sauna; massage; convenience store (w/food, sundries, DVD rental, and alcoholic beverages). *In room:* Satellite TV, Wi-Fi, kitchen, coffeemaker, hair dryer, safe.

Moderate

Taos Mountain Lodge (Value) These loft suites (which can each accommodate up to six) provide airy, comfortable lodging for a good price. Built in 1990, about a mile west of Taos Ski Valley on the road from Taos, the place has undergone some renovation over the years. Don't expect a lot of privacy in these condominiums, but they're good for a romping ski vacation. The beds are comfortable and the baths are small but functional. Each unit has a small bedroom downstairs and a loft bedroom upstairs, as well as a foldout or futon couch in the living room. Regular rooms have kitchenettes, with minirefrigerators and stoves, and deluxe rooms have full kitchens, with full refrigerators, stoves, and ovens.

Taos Ski Valley Rd. (P.O. Box 202), Taos Ski Valley, NM 87525. ✆ **866/320-8267** or 575/776-2229. Fax 575/776-3982. www.taosmountainlodge.com. 10 units. Ski season $119–$280 suite; May–Oct $80–$100 suite. AE, DISC, MC, V. *In room:* Satellite TV, kitchen or kitchenette, hair dryer.

RV Parks & Campgrounds

Carson National Forest There are nine national forest camping areas within 20 miles of Taos; these developed areas are open from Memorial Day to Labor Day. They range from woodsy, streamside sites on the road to Taos Ski Valley to open lowlands with lots of sage. Call the Forest Service to discuss the best location for your needs.

208 Cruz Alta Rd., Taos, NM 87571. ✆ **575/758-6200.** www.fs.fed.us/r3/carson. Fees range from $7–$15 per night. No credit cards.

Taos Valley RV Park and Campground ★ Just 2½ miles south of the plaza, this lovely, well-maintained campground is surrounded by sage and offers views of the surrounding mountains. Each site has a picnic table and grill. The place has a small store, a laundry room, a playground, and tent shelters, as well as a dump station and very clean restrooms. Pets are welcome. Wireless Internet access is available throughout the park.

120 Este Rd., off NM 68 (7204 NDCBU), Taos, NM 87571. ✆ **800/999-7571** or 575/758-4469. Fax 575/758-4469. www.camptaos.com/rv. 95 spaces. $22 without RV hookup; $30–$39 with RV hookup. AE, DISC, MC, V.

4 WHERE TO DINE

Taos has some of the region's most inventive and fun restaurants. The creativity of the town flourishes in the flavors here. It's also a comfortable place to dine. Informality reigns; at a number of restaurants you can eat world-class food while wearing jeans or even ski pants. Nowhere is a jacket and tie mandatory. This informality doesn't extend to reservations, however; especially during the peak season, it's important to make reservations well in advance and keep them or else cancel. Also, be aware that Taos is not a late-night place; most restaurants finish serving at about 9pm.

TAOS

Expensive

De La Tierra ★★★ REGIONAL AMERICAN Located in the eco-resort El Monte Sagrado (p. 205), this restaurant offers delectably inventive American cuisine in an old-world Orient ambience, with a high ceiling, comfortable black silk chairs, and elegant contemporary art on the walls. Service is excellent. The chef utilizes seasonal and local ingredients, including organic ones when he can. For starters, you might have winter squash raviolis in a caramel orange broth or a Caesar salad with tamale croutons. For a main course, the beef tenderloin is very juicy, served with potato enchiladas and swiss chard. The pan roasted East Coast cod served with truffle Persian potatoes is delectable. Kids have their own menu here. Excellent food, including Sunday brunch, is served during the day at the Gardens, a more casual spot, with lots of exotic plants and a lovely patio. Meals are also served at the Anaconda Bar (p. 239).

In the El Monte Sagrado Hotel, 317 Kit Carson Rd. ✆ **800/828-TAOS** (8267) or 575/758-3502. www.elmontesagrado.com/dining/de_la_tierra.asp. Reservations recommended. The Gardens breakfast $7–$12; lunch $8–$16; De La Tierra dinner $19–$39. AE, DC, DISC, MC, V. The Gardens daily 7am–3pm; De La Tierra Sun–Thurs 6–9pm, Fri–Sat 6–10pm.

Doc Martin's ★ NEW AMERICAN Doc Martin's serves innovative food in a historic setting. The chef uses local and organic ingredients, and wild game, when available. In the rich atmosphere of a thick-walled adobe home with a kiva fireplace, diners feast on Southwestern breakfast fare such as a grilled organic buffalo patty and eggs, with wild mushroom gravy and home fries or blue corn and blueberry hotcakes. Lunch might include the house specialty, Doc's Chile relleno or a turkey, avocado, bacon, and green chile sandwich. For dinner, a good bet is the almond dusted ruby trout with posole (hominy) or the rack of red deer with roasted potatoes. If you still have room, there's always a nice selection of desserts—try the chocolate mousse cake or the *capirotada* (New Mexican bread pudding). The Adobe bar has live jazz with no cover charge. Brunch is served on Saturdays and Sundays from 7:30am to 2:30pm.

In the Historic Taos Inn, 125 Paseo del Pueblo Norte. ✆ **575/758-1977.** www.taosinn.com. Reservations recommended. Breakfast $5–$10; lunch $7–$15; dinner $18–$30. AE, DISC, MC, V. Daily 7:30–11am, 11:30am–2:30pm, and 5:30–9pm.

El Meze ★★ (Finds) SPANISH/MEDITERRANEAN Meaning "table" in Arabic, El Meze offers delicious Spanish/Mediterranean food with Moorish influences. The creation of Fred Muller, who for years ran the popular Fred's Place, this new restaurant is set in El Torreon, an 1847 hacienda with the vigas (wooden beams), walls painted orange and green, a gold fireplace, and bright contemporary art on the walls. A classically trained chef, Muller puts much thought into his food and its preparation. Service is helpful and

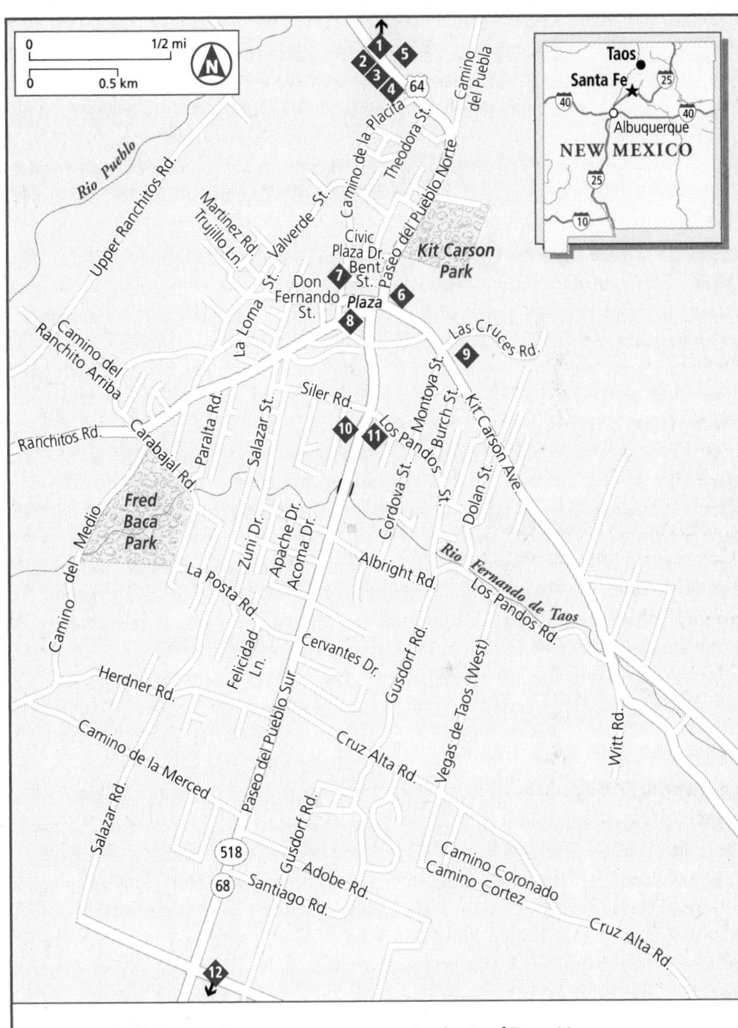

Caffé Renato **6**	Lambert's of Taos **11**
De La Tierra **9**	Lula's **10**
Doc Martin's **6**	Old Blinking Light **1**
El Meze **5**	Orlando's New Mexican Café **2**
Graham's Grill **7**	Taos Pizza Out Back **4**
Guadalajara Grill **3**, **12**	Stakeout Grill & Bar **12**
Gutiz **3**	Trading Post Café **12**
Joseph's Table **8**	Taos Cow **1**

efficient. Dinner might begin with grilled prawns with lemon and Moroccan spices, and move onto a butternut squash and chick pea soup with smoked ham hock. For an entree I've enjoyed a terrific Chilean sea bass with sweet potatoes, fennel, and andouille sausage in a rich broth. Another excellent offering is the grilled double cut lamb chops cooked with lavender and served with vegetable jus and fried garlic chips. For dessert, the chocolate truffle soufflé is as good as it sounds. A thoughtful beer and wine list accompanies the menu.

1017 Paseo del Pueblo Norte. ✆ **575/751-3337.** www.elmeze.com. AE, DISC, MC, V. Reservations recommended. Main courses $18–$32. AE, DISC, MC, V. Mon–Sat 5:30–9:30pm in summer; winter hours vary, call ahead.

Joseph's Table ★★★ Finds NEW AMERICAN/MEDITERRANEAN This notable eatery, in the Hotel La Fonda de Taos on the plaza, serves some of the most imaginative and precisely prepared food in northern New Mexico. The ambience is something like old-west saloon meets sophisticated artist's home. Hand-painted pastel flowers decorate the walls and pussy-willow-and-iron chandeliers hang between hand-hewn vigas on the ceiling. There are hardwood floors and some Asian-style tables with pillow seating along the back. Chef/owner Joseph Wrede (once selected as one of the 10 "Best New Chefs" in America by *Food & Wine Magazine*) creates such delicacies as a juicy green chile buffalo cheeseburger served with a mixed green salad for lunch. Dinner is equally inventive. It might start with mussels and move on to pepper-crusted beef tenderloin over butter mashed potatoes or a soy-cured duck breast with a sweet potato tamal. There's typically a vegetarian option as well. Be aware that Wrede likes complex flavors, so those who prefer more conservative food might opt for the Stakeout. The friendly and attentive servers can help guide you through the menu, so be sure to ask. An eclectic selection of beers and wines by the bottle and glass is available.

In the Hotel La Fonda de Taos, 108-A S. Taos Plaza. ✆ **575/751-4512.** www.josephstable.com. Reservations recommended. Main courses $8–$18 lunch, $18–$35 dinner. AE, DISC, MC, V. May–Aug Mon–Sat 11:30am–2:30pm and daily 5:30–10pm; Sun brunch 10:30am–2:30pm. Hours are abbreviated in winter; call first.

Lambert's of Taos ★★ CONTEMPORARY AMERICAN Zeke Lambert opened this fine dining establishment in late 1989 in the historic Randall Home near Los Pandos Road. It's a sparsely decorated hacienda with wood floors and lacy curtains—a nice spot for a romantic evening. The service ranges from good to begrudging. The food is well prepared and imaginative, though not quite of the caliber of Joseph's Table (see above). You might start with roasted rock shrimp dusted with red chile, or the spinach salad with sautéed mushrooms and bacon in a walnut raspberry dressing, which is excellent. For an entree, the pepper-crusted lamb—very peppery—served with garlic pasta is a signature dish, but you might opt for one of the fresh fish specials, such as seared ahi tuna, or a game special such as buffalo tenderloin. A full bar, with an interesting wine and beer list and espresso coffee, is available. The restaurant also has a cozy lounge with its own menu.

309 Paseo del Pueblo Sur. ✆ **575/758-1009.** www.lambertsoftaos.com. Reservations recommended. Main courses $15–$35. AE, DC, DISC, MC, V. Daily 5pm–closing, usually 9pm or so.

Stakeout Grill & Bar ★★ CONTINENTAL/STEAKS/SEAFOOD This is one of northern New Mexico's most adventurous dining experiences. You drive about a mile up a dirt road toward the base of the Sangre de Cristo Mountains to reach the restaurant, and dine looking down on the Taos gorge while the sun sets over the Jemez Range. The warm, rustic decor of this sprawling hacienda with a broad patio (a great place to sit in summer) includes creaking hardwood floors—and a crackling fireplace in the winter. The fare, which focuses on steak and seafood, is fresh and thoughtfully prepared. Start with baked brie with sliced almonds and apples, or green chile crab cakes with citrus aioli. Move on to a filet mignon served with béarnaise sauce, or sample one of the chef's excellent pasta specials. Recently, I had shrimp over linguini with goat cheese that was a bowl of pure joy. This is also the place to come if you have a craving for lobster. Try to time your reservation so you can see the sunset. A full bar, an extensive wine list, and cigars are available.

101 Stakeout Dr. (9 miles south of Taos, just off Hwy. 68). ✆ **575/758-2042.** www.stakeoutrestaurant.com. Reservations recommended. Main courses $20–$70. AE, DC, DISC, MC, V. Daily 5–9:30pm.

Moderate

Caffé Renato ★★ (Moments) AMERICAN/ITALIAN You can't miss this cafe decked out with bright red umbrellas on its patio. Diners enjoy the cool Taos air while feasting on tasty food prepared with fine ingredients. A back patio is quieter, and inside, sun-porch- and kitchen-side dining rooms provide a comfortable ambience decorated with art—the restaurant shares space with the Farnsworth Gallery, fun to stroll through while you await your food. Service is friendly but may be understaffed. The lunch menu holds a variety of sandwiches (including create-your-own panini options) and salads. The angus burger is stellar, as is the turkey bacon ranch salad. For dinner, the old classic spaghetti with meatballs is easy on the wallet, while the grilled salmon with a lemon tarragon aioli is equally delicious. Finish with a chocolate truffle torte. A selection of beers and wines accompanies the menu.

133 Paseo del Pueblo North. ✆ **575/758-0244.** Reservations recommended on weekend nights. Main courses lunch $7–$15; dinner $10–$29. Daily 11am–9pm.

Graham's Grille ★★ NEW AMERICAN Opened in 2007, this restaurant offers comfort food with a Southwestern flair. It's set in a long, narrow space just off the plaza, a cozy urban atmosphere with hanging halogen lamps and a long banco along one wall. Meals start with delectable flour tortilla crisps. The must-have appetizer is the baked mac and cheese with green chile and bacon, but if that sounds too rich, the grilled artichokes served with lemon aioli will also please. Lunches offer soup, salad, and sandwich combinations, if you'd like. The town is buzzing about the salmon BLT, which is just what it sounds, salmon with good bacon, lettuce, and tomato. Burritos, tamale pie, and burgers—even veggie, buffalo, and lamb ones—come on house-made buns. For dinner, the spice crusted grilled salmon with Israeli cous cous is the most popular dish here; the Moroccan chicken, also served with cous cous, runs a close second. For dessert, the chocolate nachos are a real novelty, but my favorite is the mango coconut cake. A select beer and wine list accompanies the menu.

106 Paseo del Pueblo Norte. ✆ **575/751-1350.** www.grahamsgrille.com. AE, MC, V. Reservations recommended at dinner. Main courses $7–$11 lunch; $14–$20 dinner. Mon–Sat 11am–2pm and 5–9pm.

Old Blinking Light ★ AMERICAN This restaurant on the Ski Valley Road provides tasty American food in a casual atmosphere. It's named for the blinking yellow light that was once the marker Taoseños used to give directions ("turn left at the blinking light," and so on), now replaced by a stoplight. Decorated with Spanish colonial furniture and an excellent art collection, this restaurant is a good place to stop after skiing or for a romping night of music. The service is friendly and efficient. To accompany the free chips and homemade salsa, order a margarita—preferably their standard, made with Sauza Gold Tequila—and sip it next to the patio bonfire, open evenings year-round. The

Kids Family-Friendly Restaurants

Lula's (p. 219) A relaxed atmosphere and lots of sandwich choices, as well as soups, are sure to please here.

Orlando's New Mexican Café (p. 220) The relaxed atmosphere and playfully colorful walls will please the kids almost as much as the tacos and quesadillas made especially for them.

Taos Cow (p. 220) Pot pies and sandwiches will fill kids up before they dive into the all-natural ice cream at this cafe north of town.

Taos Pizza Out Back (p. 218) The pizza will please both parents and kids, and so will all the odd decorations, such as the chain with foot-long links hanging over the front counter.

menu is broad, ranging from salads and burgers to steaks, seafood, and Mexican food. I say head straight for the fajitas, especially the jumbo shrimp wrapped in bacon and stuffed with poblano peppers and jack cheese. Leave room for the Old Blinking Light mud pie, made with local Taos Cow ice cream. Live music plays on Monday and Friday nights.

US 150, mile marker 1. ✆ **575/776-8787.** Reservations recommended weekends and Mon nights. Main courses $9–$26. AE, MC, V. Wine shop daily noon–10pm. Restaurant daily 5–10pm.

Taos Pizza Out Back ★ Kids PASTA/PIZZA My kayaking buddies always go here after a day on the river. That will give you an idea of the level of informality (very), as well as the quality of the food and beer (great), and the size of the portions (large). It's a raucous old hippie-decorated adobe restaurant, with a friendly and eager waitstaff. What to order? I have one big word here: PIZZA. Sure the spicy Greek pasta is good, as is the Veggie Zone (a calzone filled with stir-fried veggies and two cheeses)—but, why? The pizzas are incredible. All come with a delicious thin crust (no sogginess here) that's folded over on the edges and sprinkled with sesame seeds. The sauce is unthinkably tasty, and the variations are broad. There's the Killer, with sun-dried tomatoes, Gorgonzola, green chile, and black olives; and my favorite, pizza Florentine (spinach, basil, sun-dried tomatoes, chicken breast, mushrooms, capers, and garlic, sautéed in white wine). Check out the small selection of wines and large selection of microbrews.

712 Paseo del Pueblo Norte (just north of Allsup's). ✆ **575/758-3112.** Reservations recommended weekends and holidays. Pizzas $13–$28; pastas and calzones $10–$13. MC, V. Summer daily 11am–10pm; winter Sun–Thurs 11am–9pm, Fri–Sat 11am–10pm.

Trading Post Café ★★ Finds NORTHERN ITALIAN/INTERNATIONAL One of my tastiest writing assignments was when I did a profile of this restaurant for the *New York Times.* Chef/owner René Mettler spent 3 hours serving course after course of dishes prepared especially for us. If you think this gastronomical orgy might color my opinion, just ask anyone in town where he or she most likes to eat. Even notables such as Dennis Hopper and Gene Hackman will likely name the Trading Post. What draws the crowds here is a gallery atmosphere, where rough plastered walls washed with an orange hue are set off by sculptures, paintings, and photographs. If you show up without reservations, be prepared to wait for a table, and don't expect quiet romance here: The place bustles.

A bar encloses an open-exhibition kitchen. If you're dining alone or just don't feel like waiting for a table, the bar is a fun place to sit. Although the focus is on the fine food, diners can feel comfortable here, even if trying three appetizers and skipping the main course. The outstanding Caesar salad has an interesting twist—garlic chips. If you like pasta, you'll find a nice variety on the menu. The fettuccine alla carbonara is tasty, as is the seafood pasta. Heartier appetites might like the New Zealand lamb chops with tomato-mint sauce. A good list of beers and wines rounds out the experience.

4179 Paseo del Pueblo Sur, Ranchos de Taos. ✆ **575/758-5089.** Reservations accepted. Menu items $8–$30. AE, DC, DISC, MC, V. Tues–Sat 11:30am–9:30pm; Sun 4–9:30pm.

Inexpensive

Guadalajara Grill ★ MEXICAN My organic-lettuce-farmer friend Joe introduced me to this authentic Mexican restaurant; then he disappeared into Mexico, only communicating occasionally by e-mail. Did the incredible food lure him south? I wonder. The restaurant is in a plain building on the south side, but don't let that put you off; the food here is excellent. It's Mexican rather than New Mexican, a refreshing treat. I recommend the tacos, particularly pork or chicken, served in soft homemade corn tortillas, the meat artfully seasoned and grilled. The burritos are large and smothered in chile. *Platos* are served with rice and beans, and half orders are available for smaller appetites. There are also some seafood dishes available—try the *mojo de ajo* (shrimp cooked with garlic), served with rice, beans, and guacamole. Beer and wine are served. Equally popular, and casual, is their north side location.

1384 Paseo del Pueblo Sur. ✆ **575/751-0063.** Main courses $5–$15. MC, V. Mon–Sat 10:30am–9pm; Sun 11am–9pm. Second location, 1822 Paseo del Pueblo Norte (✆ **575/737-0816**), Mon–Sat 10:30am–9pm; Sun 11am–8:30pm.

Gutiz ★★ **Finds** FRENCH/LATIN FUSION Between azure walls hung with bright contemporary art, this restaurant, the creation of chef Eduardo Gutiz, serves some of Taos's most unique and flavorful cuisine. Born in Spain, raised in France, he traveled in Peru and Bolivia. From these locales, he's combined flavors using organic greens and fresh meats and fish, and a broad variety of chile peppers. Service is friendly and efficient. Breakfast brings delicacies such as my favorite the Taoseño (some mornings I wake up in Santa Fe and want to drive to Taos just to eat this!)—rice, potatoes, chile, cheese, and fresh herbs baked in a ceramic dish and then topped with scrambled eggs. The French toast is thick, made with home-baked bread. Lunch might begin with a Nicoise salad made with fresh tuna, French beans, veggies, potatoes, and nicoise olives. Another favorite is the tilapia, cooked with white wine. The many varied sandwiches come on homemade bread. Alongside the great food, sip from a variety of coffees and chai tea.

812-B Paseo del Pueblo Norte. ✆ **575/758-1226.** Main courses $6.50–$15. No credit cards. Tues–Sun 7am–4pm (3pm in winter). In summer, call to see if the chef is serving dinner.

Lula's ★★ **Kids** COMFORT FOOD/SANDWICHES/SOUPS A few blocks south of the plaza, this new deli run by the same folks as the excellent Out Back Pizza offers gourmet soups and sandwiches and a select few diner-style meals between sun-colored walls or to go. The tables here, tall and glass, with stools, don't quite match the comfort level of the food, so diners tend to grab the few regular wooden ones, which you should try to do too. Everything else works well. You order at a counter and the food is served at your table relatively quickly. Paninis are a big draw here, the one with roasted eggplant, roasted red bell peppers, zucchini, spinach, provolone, and pesto a real favorite, as is the Wellington sandwich, which has sliced roast beef, caramelized onions, and sharp Cheddar on a ciabatta roll. The nightly blue plate specials served after 4pm on weekdays and all day Saturday may include all-American meat loaf with a twice-baked potato or veggie lasagna, to name a few. A kids menu pleases the tots, and lots of good teas and coffees wash it all down.

316 Paseo del Pueblo Sur. ✆ **575/751-1280.** Main courses lunch and dinner $5–$13. MC. V. Mon–Sat in summer 11am–9pm; in winter Mon–Fri 11am––8pm, Sat 11am–6pm.

Orlando's New Mexican Café ★ Kids NEW MEXICAN Festivity reigns in this spicy little cafe on the north end of town. Serving some of northern New Mexico's best chile, this place has colorful tables set around a bustling open kitchen and airy patio dining during warmer months. Service is friendly but minimal. Try the Los Colores, their most popular dish, with three enchiladas (chicken, beef, and cheese) smothered in chile and served with beans and *posole* (a Mexican stew). The taco salad is another favorite. Portions are big here, and you can order a Mexican or microbrew beer, or a New Mexican or California wine.

114 Don Juan Valdez Lane. (1¾ miles north of the plaza, off Paseo del Pueblo Norte). ✆ **575/751-1450.** Reservations not accepted. Main courses under $12. MC, V. Daily 10:30am–3pm and 5–9pm.

NORTH OF TOWN

Taos Cow ★ Kids DELI/ICE CREAM Set in one of my favorite villages, Taos Cow offers fun breakfast and lunch fare in a relaxed atmosphere—and, of course, ice cream! Diners order and pick up at a counter. A variety of sandwiches and soups are made with fresh ingredients ranging from black forest ham to portobello mushrooms. All that said, the real reason to come here is the hormone-free ice cream in a variety of flavors. My favorite this week is the Cherry Ristra, with piñon nuts and chocolate chunks. Kids love their shakes. On chillier afternoons, there's espresso, cappuccino, and hot chocolate to warm you after a day on the slopes.

485 Hwy. 150, Arroyo Seco. ✆ **575/776-5640.** All menu items under $12. AE, DISC, MC, V. Daily 7am–7pm in summer; 7am–6pm in winter.

5 WHAT TO SEE & DO

With a history shaped by pre-Columbian civilization, Spanish colonialism, and the Wild West; outdoor activities that range from ballooning to world-class skiing; and a clustering of artists, writers, and musicians, Taos has something to offer almost everybody. Its pueblo is the most accessible in New Mexico, and its museums represent a world-class display of regional history and culture.

THE TOP ATTRACTIONS

Millicent Rogers Museum of Northern New Mexico ★ This museum will give you a glimpse of some of the finest Southwestern arts and crafts anywhere, but it's small enough to avoid being overwhelming. It was founded in 1953 by Millicent Rogers's family members after her death. Rogers was a wealthy Taos émigré who in 1947 began acquiring a magnificent collection of beautiful Native American arts and crafts. Included are Navajo and Pueblo jewelry, Navajo textiles, Pueblo pottery, Hopi and Zuni katsina (kachina) dolls, paintings from the Rio Grande Pueblo people, and basketry from a wide variety of Southwestern tribes. The museum also presents exhibitions of Southwestern art, crafts, and design.

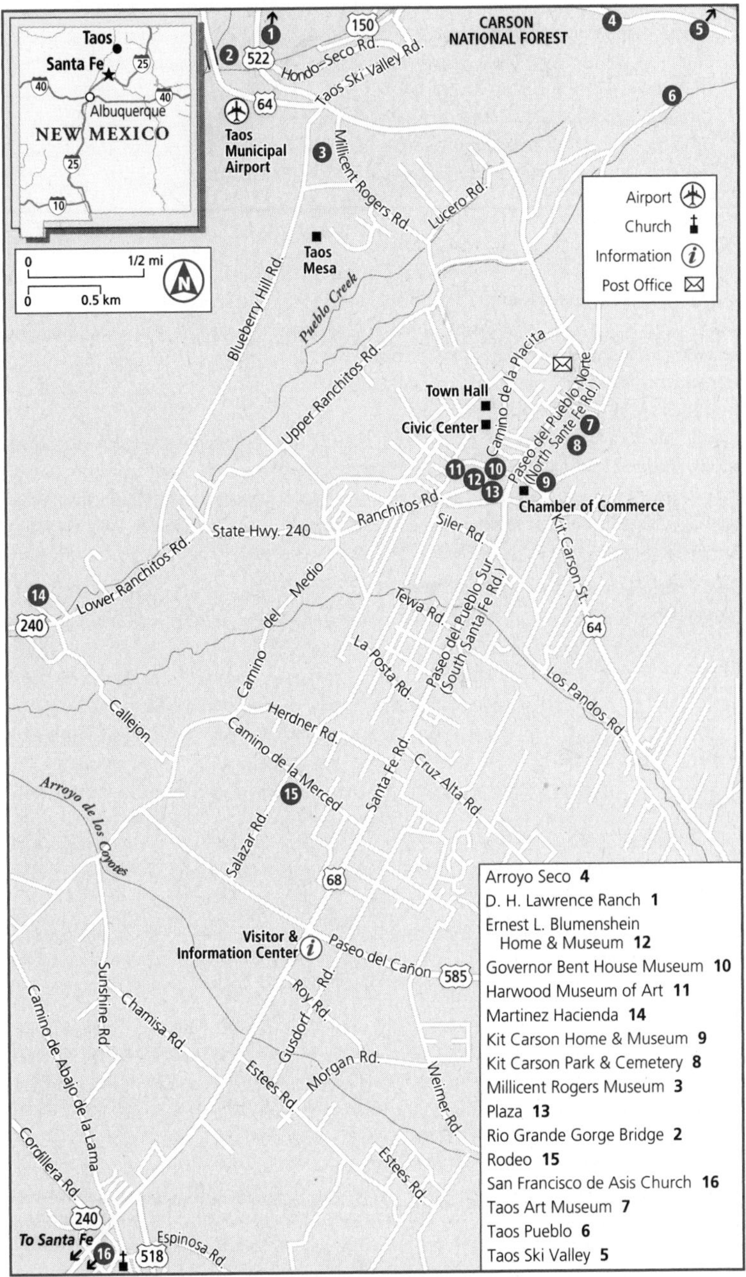

Taos
Santa Fe
Albuquerque
NEW MEXICO
0 1/2 mi
0 0.5 km
CARSON NATIONAL FOREST
Hondo-Seco Rd.
Taos Ski Valley Rd.
Taos Municipal Airport
Millicent Rogers Rd.
Lucero Rd.
Taos Mesa
Blueberry Hill Rd.
Pueblo Creek
Upper Ranchitos Rd.
Airport
Church
Information
Post Office
Camino de la Placita
Paseo del Pueblo Norte (North Sante Fe Rd.)
Town Hall
Civic Center
Chamber of Commerce
Ranchitos Rd.
State Hwy. 240
Siler Rd.
Kit Carson St.
Lower Ranchitos Rd.
Camino del Medio
Tewa Rd.
Paseo del Pueblo Sur (South Santa Fe Rd.)
La Posta Rd.
Los Pandos Rd.
Callejon
Herdner Rd.
Camino de la Merced
Santa Fe Rd.
Cruz Alta Rd.
Arroyo de los Coyotes
Salazar Rd.
Visitor & Information Center
Paseo del Cañon
Sunshine Rd.
Chamisa Rd.
Roy Rd.
Gusdorf Rd.
Morgan Rd.
Weimer Rd.
Estees Rd.
Camino de Abajo de la Lama
Cordillera Rd.
To Santa Fe
Espinosa Rd.
Arroyo Seco 4
D. H. Lawrence Ranch 1
Ernest L. Blumenshein Home & Museum 12
Governor Bent House Museum 10
Harwood Museum of Art 11
Martinez Hacienda 14
Kit Carson Home & Museum 9
Kit Carson Park & Cemetery 8
Millicent Rogers Museum 3
Plaza 13
Rio Grande Gorge Bridge 2
Rodeo 15
San Francisco de Asis Church 16
Taos Art Museum 7
Taos Pueblo 6
Taos Ski Valley 5

Tips A Tip for Museumgoers

If you'd like to visit five museums that comprise the Museum Association of Taos—Blumenschein Home, Martinez Hacienda, Harwood Museum, Millicent Rogers Museum, and Taos Art Museum—you'll save money by purchasing a combination ticket for $25. The ticket allows one-time entry to each museum during a 1-year period and is fully transferable. You may purchase the pass at any of the five museums. For more information, call ✆ **575/758-0505.**

Since the 1970s, the scope of the museum's permanent collection has been expanded to include Anglo arts and crafts and Hispanic religious and secular arts and crafts, from Spanish and Mexican colonial to contemporary times. Included are *santos* (religious images), furniture, weavings, *colcha* embroideries, and decorative tinwork. Agricultural implements, domestic utensils, and craftspeople's tools dating from the 17th and 18th centuries are also displayed.

The museum gift shop has a fine collection of superior regional art. Classes, workshops, lectures, and field trips are held throughout the year.

Off US 64, 4 miles north of Taos Plaza, on Millicent Rogers Rd. ✆ **575/758-2462.** www.millicentrogers.org. Admission $10 adults, $8 students and seniors, $2 children 6–16, $18 family rate. Daily 10am–5pm. Closed Mon Nov–Mar, Easter, Thanksgiving, Christmas, New Year's Day.

San Francisco de Asis church ★★ On NM 68, about 4 miles south of Taos, this famous church appears as a modern adobe sculpture with no doors or windows, an image that has often been photographed and painted, most notably by Ansel Adams and Georgia O'Keeffe. Visitors must walk through the garden on the east side to enter the two-story church and get a full perspective of its massive walls, authentic adobe plaster, and beauty.

A video presentation is given in the church office every hour on the half-hour. Also, displayed on the wall is an unusual painting, *The Shadow of the Cross,* by Henri Ault (1896). Under ordinary light, it portrays a barefoot Christ at the Sea of Galilee; in darkness, however, the portrait becomes luminescent, and the perfect shadow of a cross forms over the left shoulder of Jesus's silhouette. The artist reportedly was as shocked as everyone else to see this. The reason for the illusion remains a mystery. A few crafts shops surround the square.

Ranchos de Taos Plaza. ✆ **575/758-2754.** Admission $3 for video and mystery painting. Mon–Sat 9am–4pm. Visitors may attend Mass Mon–Fri 5pm, Sat 6pm (Mass rotates from this church to the 3 mission chapels), Sun 7 (Spanish), 9, and 11:30am. Closed to the public 1st 2 weeks in June, when repairs are done; however, services still take place.

Taos Art Museum ★ Finds Set in the home of Russian artist Nicolai Fechin (*Feh-shin*), this collection displays works of the Taos Society of Artists, which give a sense of what Taos was like in the late 19th and early 20th centuries. The works are rich and varied, including panoramas and images of the Native American and Hispanic villagers. The setting in what was Fechin's home from 1927 until 1933 is truly unique. The historic building commemorates his career. Born in Russia in 1881, Fechin came to the United States in 1923, already acclaimed as a master of painting, drawing, sculpture, architecture, and woodwork. In Taos, he renovated the home and embellished it with hand-carved doors, windows, gates, posts, fireplaces, and other features of a Russian country home. Fechin died in 1955. Though the collection and home are interesting, some visitors balk at the price. If you're one of those, you can at least see Fechin's studio, which is attached to the gift shop, for free. Also, bear in mind that this museum is privately funded, so your dollars are a real help.

227 Paseo del Pueblo Norte. ✆ **575/758-2690.** www.taosmuseums.org. Admission $8 adults, $7 seniors, $4 children 6–12, free for children 5 and under. Summer Thurs–Sun 10am–5pm; call for winter hours.

Taos Historic Museums ★★ Two historical homes are operated as museums, affording visitors a glimpse of early Taos lifestyles. The Martinez Hacienda and Ernest Blumenschein home each has unique appeal.

The **Martinez Hacienda,** Lower Ranchitos Road, Highway 240 (✆ **575/758-1000**), is one of the only Spanish colonial haciendas in the United States that's open to the public year-round. This was the home of the merchant, trader, and *alcalde* (mayor) Don Antonio Severino Martinez, who bought it in 1804 and lived here until his death in 1827. His eldest son was Padre Antonio José Martinez, northern New Mexico's controversial spiritual leader from 1826 to 1867. Located on the west bank of the Rio Pueblo de Taos, about 2 miles southwest of the plaza, the museum is remarkably beautiful, with thick, raw adobe walls. The hacienda has no exterior windows—this was to protect against raids by Plains tribes.

Twenty-one rooms were built around two *placitas,* or interior courtyards. They give you a glimpse of the austerity of frontier lives, with only a few pieces of modest period furniture in each. You'll see bedrooms, stables, a kitchen, and a large fiesta room. Exhibits tell the story of the Martinez family and life in Spanish Taos between 1598 and 1821, when Mexico gained control.

Taos Historic Museums has developed the Martinez Hacienda into a living museum with weavers, blacksmiths, and wood carvers. Demonstrations are scheduled daily, and during the **Taos Trade Fair** (held in late Sept) they run virtually nonstop. The Trade Fair commemorates the era when Native Americans, Spanish settlers, and mountain men met here to trade with each other.

The **Ernest L. Blumenschein Home & Museum,** 222 Ledoux St. (✆ **575/758-0505**), 1½ blocks southwest of the plaza, re-creates the lifestyle of one of the founders of the Taos Society of Artists (founded 1915). An adobe home with garden walls and a courtyard, parts of which date from the 1790s, it became the home and studio of Blumenschein (1874–1960) and his family in 1919. Period furnishings include European antiques and handmade Taos furniture in Spanish colonial style.

Blumenschein was born and raised in Cincinnati. In 1898, after training in New York and Paris, he and fellow painter Bert Phillips were on assignment for *Harper's* and *McClure's* magazines of New York when a wheel of their wagon broke 30 miles north of Taos. Blumenschein drew the short straw and thus was obliged to bring the wheel by horseback to Taos for repair. He later recounted his initial reaction to the valley he entered: "No artist had ever recorded the New Mexico I was now seeing. No writer had ever written down the smell of this air or the feel of that morning sky. I was receiving . . . the first great unforgettable inspiration of my life. My destiny was being decided."

That spark later led to the foundation of Taos as an art colony. An extensive collection of works by early-20th-century Taos artists, including some by Blumenschein's wife, Mary, and daughter, Helen, are on display in several rooms of the home.

222 Ledoux St. ✆ **575/758-0505** (information for both museums can be obtained at this number). www.taoshistoricmuseums.org. Admission for each museum $8 adults, $4 children ages 6–16, free for children 5 and under. Summer daily 9am–5pm; call for winter hours.

Taos Pueblo ★★★ It's amazing that in our frenetic world more than 100 Taos Pueblo residents still live much as their ancestors did 1,000 years ago. When you enter the pueblo, you'll see two large buildings, both with rooms piled on top of each other, forming structures that echo the shape of Taos Mountain (which sits to the northeast). Here, a portion of Taos residents lives without electricity and running water. The remaining 2,000 residents of Taos Pueblo live in conventional homes on the pueblo's 95,000 acres.

The main buildings' distinctive flowing lines of shaped mud, with a straw-and-mud exterior plaster, are typical of Pueblo architecture throughout the Southwest. It's architecture that blends in with the surrounding land. Bright blue doors are the same shade as the sky that frames the brown buildings.

The northernmost of New Mexico's 19 pueblos, Taos Pueblo has been home to the Tiwa tribes for more than 900 years. Many residents here still practice ancestral rituals. The center of their world is still nature; women use hornos to bake bread, and most still drink water that flows down from the sacred Blue Lake. Meanwhile, arts and crafts and other tourism-related businesses support the economy, along with government services, ranching, and farming.

The village looks much the same today as it did when a regiment from Coronado's expedition first came upon it in 1540. Though the Tiwa were essentially a peaceful agrarian people, they are perhaps best remembered for spearheading the only successful revolt by Native Americans in history. Launched by Pope (poh-*pay*) in 1680, the uprising drove the Spanish from Santa Fe until 1692 and from Taos until 1698.

As you explore the pueblo, you can visit the residents' studios, sample homemade bread, look into the **San Geronimo Chapel,** and wander past the fascinating ruins of the old church and cemetery. You're expected to ask permission from individuals before taking their photos; some will ask for a small payment. Do not trespass into kivas (ceremonial rooms) and other areas marked as restricted.

The **Feast of San Geronimo** (the patron saint of Taos Pueblo), on September 29 and 30, marks the end of the harvest season. The feast day is reminiscent of an ancient trade fair for the Taos Indians, when tribes from as far south as South America and as far north as the Arctic would come and trade for wares, hides, clothing, and harvested crops. The day is filled with foot races, pole climbing done by traditional Indian clowns, and artists and craftspeople mimicking the early traders. Dances are performed the evening of September 29. Other annual events include a **turtle dance** on New Year's Day, **deer or buffalo dances** on Three Kings Day (Jan 6), and **corn dances** on Santa Cruz Day (May 3), San Antonio Day (June 13), San Juan Day (June 24), Santiago Day (July 25), and Santa Ana Day (July 26). The annual **Taos Pueblo Powwow,** a dance competition and parade that brings together tribes from throughout North America, is held the second weekend of July on tribal lands off NM 522 (see "New Mexico Calendar of Events," in chapter 3). The pueblo Christmas celebration begins on Christmas Eve, with bonfires and a procession with children's dances. On Christmas day, the deer or **Matachine dances** take place (p. 46).

During your visit to the pueblo you will have the opportunity to purchase traditional fried and oven-baked bread as well as a variety of arts and crafts. If you would like to try traditional feast-day meals, the **Tiwa Kitchen,** near the entrance to the pueblo, is a good place to stop. Close to Tiwa Kitchen is the **Oo-oonah Children's Art Center,** where you can see the creative works of pueblo children.

As with many of the other pueblos in New Mexico, Taos Pueblo has opened a casino. **Taos Mountain Casino** (✆ **888/WIN-TAOS** [946-8267]; www.taosmountaincasino.com) is on the main road to Taos Pueblo and features slot machines, blackjack, and poker.

Note: To learn more about the pueblo and its people, I highly recommend taking a 30-minute guided tour. Ask upon arrival when the next one will be given and where you should meet your guide.

Veterans Hwy. (P.O. Box 1846), Taos Pueblo. (From Paseo del Pueblo Norte, travel north 2 miles on Veterans Hwy.) ✆ **575/758-1028.** www.taospueblo.com. Admission cost, as well as camera, video, and sketching fees, subject to change on a yearly basis; be sure to ask about telephoto lenses and digital cameras; photography not permitted on feast days. Daily 8am–4:30pm, with a few exceptions. Guided tours available. Closed for 45 consecutive days every year late winter or early spring (call ahead). Also, because this is a living community, you can expect periodic closures.

MORE ATTRACTIONS

D. H. Lawrence Ranch A trip to this ranch north of Taos leads you into odd realms of devotion for the controversial early-20th-century author who lived and wrote in the area in the early '20s. A short uphill walk from the ranch home (not open to visitors) is the D. H. Lawrence Memorial, a shedlike structure that's a bit of a forgotten place, where people have left a few mementos such as juniper berries and sticks of gum. The guest book is also interesting: One couple wrote of trying for 24 years to get here from England.

NM 522, San Cristobal. ✆ **575/776-2245.** Free admission. Daily 8am–5pm. To reach the site, head north from Taos about 15 miles on NM 522, and then another 6 miles east into the forested Sangre de Cristo Range via a well-marked dirt road.

Governor Bent House Museum (Kids) This residence of Charles Bent, New Mexico Territory's first American governor, offers an interesting peek into the region's at-times brutal history. Bent, a former trader who established Fort Bent, Colorado, was murdered during the 1847 Native American and Hispanic rebellion, while his wife and children escaped by digging through an adobe wall into the house next door. The hole is still visible. Period art and artifacts are on display at the museum, just a short block north of the plaza. Owned by the same family since the 1950s, the museum also has a charming gift shop with historic memorabilia.

117 Bent St. ✆ **575/758-2376.** Admission $3 adults, $1 children 8–15, free for children 7 and under. MC, V. Summer daily 9:30am–5pm; winter daily 10am–5pm. Closed Easter, Thanksgiving, Christmas, New Year's Day. Street parking.

Harwood Museum of Art of the University of New Mexico ★ With its high ceilings and broad wood floors, this museum is a lovely place to wander among New Mexico–inspired images. A cultural and community center since 1923, the museum displays paintings, drawings, prints, sculpture, and photographs by Taos-area artists from 1800 to the present. Featured are paintings from the early days of the art colony by members of the Taos Society of Artists, including Oscar Berninghaus, Ernest Blumenschein, Herbert Dunton, Victor Higgins, Bert Phillips, and Walter Ufer. Also included are works by Emil Bisttram, Andrew Dasburg, Agnes Martin, Larry Bell, and Thomas Benrimo.

Upstairs are 19th-century pounded-tin pieces and *retablos,* religious paintings of saints that have traditionally been used for decoration and inspiration in the homes and churches of New Mexico. The permanent collection includes sculptures by Patrociño Barela, one of the leading Hispanic artists of 20th-century New Mexico. It's well worth seeing, especially his 3-foot-tall *Death Cart,* a rendition of Doña Sebastiána, the bringer of death.

The museum also schedules more than eight changing exhibitions a year, many of which feature works by celebrated artists currently living in Taos.

238 Ledoux St. ✆ **575/758-9826.** www.harwoodmuseum.org. Admission $7, $6 seniors, free for children 11 and under. Tues–Sat 10am–5pm; Sun noon–5pm.

Kit Carson Home and Museum If you want a glimpse into the modest lifestyle of Taos's frontiersmen, head to this 3-room adobe home, a block east of the plaza. Built in 1825 and purchased in 1843 by Carson—the famous mountain man, Indian agent, and scout—it was a wedding gift for his young bride, Josefa Jaramillo. It remained their home for 25 years, until both died (exactly a month apart) in 1868. Rooms have sparse displays such as buffalo hide and sheepskin bedding, a wooden chest, basic kitchen utensils, and a cooking fireplace. The treasure of the museum is interpreter Natívídad Mascarenas-Gallegos, a distant relative of Carson, who can tell you plenty about the family. The museum also includes a film on Carson produced by the History Channel. The price of a visit here is a bit steep for what you see, but if you decide to come, plan on spending about a half-hour. If you'd like to see more of Carson's possessions, visit the Martinez Hacienda (see above).

113 Kit Carson Rd. ✆ **575/758-4613.** www.kitcarsonhome.com. Admission $5 adult, $4 seniors 65 years and older, $3 teens 13–18, $2 children 6–12. Daily 9am–6pm.

Kit Carson Park and Cemetery Major community events are held in the park in summer. The cemetery, established in 1847, contains the graves of Carson, his wife, Governor Charles Bent, the Don Antonio Martinez family, Mabel Dodge Luhan, and many other noted historical figures and artists. Their lives are described briefly on plaques.

Paseo del Pueblo Norte. ✆ **575/758-8234.** Free admission. Daily 24 hr.

Rio Grande Gorge Bridge ★ Kids This impressive bridge, west of the Taos airport, spans the Southwest's greatest river. At 650 feet above the canyon floor, it's one of America's highest bridges. If you can withstand the vertigo, it's interesting to come more than once, at different times of day, to observe how the changing light plays tricks with the colors of the cliff walls. A curious aside is that the wedding scene in the movie *Natural Born Killers* was filmed here.

US 64, 10 miles west of Taos. Free admission. Daily 24 hr.

ORGANIZED TOURS

An excellent opportunity to explore the historic downtown area of Taos is offered by **Taos Historic Walking Tours** (✆ **575/758-4020**). Tours cost $12 and take 1½ to 2 hours, leaving from the Kit Carson Cemetery at 10am Monday to Saturday (June–Aug). Closed Sundays and holidays. Call to make an appointment during the off season.

If you'd really like a taste of Taos history and drama, call **Enchantment Dreams Walking Tours ★** (✆ **575/776-2562**). Roberta Courtney Meyers, a theater artist, dramatist, and composer, will tour you through Taos's history while performing a number of characters, such as Georgia O'Keeffe and Kit Carson. Walking tours cost $25 per person.

6 SKIING ★★★

DOWNHILL SKIING

Five alpine resorts are within an hour's drive of Taos; all offer complete facilities, including equipment rentals. Although exact opening and closing dates vary according to snow conditions, the season usually begins around Thanksgiving and continues into early April.

Ski clothing can be purchased, and ski equipment can be rented or bought, from several Taos outlets. Among them are **Cottam's Ski & Outdoor Shops,** with four locations (call ✆ **800/322-8267** or 575/758-2822 for the one nearest you; www.cottams outdoor.com), and **Taos Ski Valley Sportswear, Ski & Boot Co.,** in Taos Ski Valley (✆ **575/776-2291**).

Taos Ski Valley ★★★, P.O. Box 90, Taos Ski Valley, NM 87525 (✆ **575/776-2291;** www.skitaos.org), is the preeminent ski resort in the southern Rocky Mountains. It was founded in 1955 by a Swiss-German immigrant, Ernie Blake. According to local legend, Blake searched for 2 years in a small plane for the perfect location for a ski resort comparable to what he was accustomed to in the Alps. He found it at the abandoned mining site of Twining, high above Taos. Today, under the management of two younger generations of Blakes, the resort has become internationally renowned for its light, dry powder (as much as 320 in. annually), its superb ski school, and its personal, friendly service.

Taos Ski Valley can best be appreciated by the more experienced skier and snowboarder. It offers steep, high-alpine, high-adventure skiing. The mountain is more intricate than it might seem at first glance, and it holds many surprises and challenges—even for the expert. The *London Times* called the valley "without any argument the best ski resort in the world. Small, intimate, and endlessly challenging, Taos simply has no equal." The quality of the snow here (light and dry) is believed to be due to the dry Southwestern air and abundant sunshine. ***Note:*** In 2008, Taos Ski Valley began allowing snowboarders onto its slopes.

Between the 11,819-foot summit and the 9,207-foot base, there are 72 trails and bowls, more than half of them designated for expert and advanced skiers. Most of the remaining trails are suitable for advanced intermediates; there is little flat terrain for novices to gain experience and mileage. However, many beginning skiers find that after spending time in lessons they can enjoy the **Kachina Bowl,** which offers spectacular views as well as wide-open slopes.

The area has an uphill capacity of 15,000 skiers per hour on its five double chairs, one triple, four quads, and one surface tow. Full-day lift tickets, depending on the season, cost $40 to $66 for adults, $30 to $55 for teens ages 13 to 17, $25 to $40 for children 12 and under, $40 to $50 for seniors ages 65 to 79, and are free for seniors 80 and over and for children 6 and under with an adult ticket purchase. Full rental packages are $29 for adults and $20 for children. Taos Ski Valley is open daily 9am to 4pm from Thanksgiving to around the second week of April. ***Note:*** Taos Ski Valley has one of the best ski schools in the country, specializing in teaching people how to negotiate steep and challenging runs.

Taos Ski Valley has many lodges and condominiums, with nearly 1,500 beds. (See "Taos Ski Valley," earlier, for details on accommodations.) All offer ski-week packages; three of them have restaurants. There are three restaurants on the mountain in addition to the many facilities of Village Center at the base. Call the **Taos Ski Valley** (✆ **800/776-1111** or 505/776-2233).

Kids Skiing with Kids

With its children's ski school, Taos Ski Valley has always been an excellent choice for skiing families, but with the 1994 addition of an 18,000-square-foot children's center (Kinderkäfig Center), skiing with your children in Taos is even better. Kinderkäfig offers many services, from equipment rental for children to babysitting services. Call ahead for more information.

Not far from Taos Ski Valley is **Red River Ski & Snowboard Area,** P.O. Box 900, Red River, NM 87558 (✆ **800/331-7669** for reservations; 505/754-2223 for information; www.redriverskiarea.com). One of the bonuses of this ski area is that lodgers at Red River can walk out their doors and be on the slopes. Two other factors make this almost 50-year-old, family-oriented area special: First, most of its 58 trails are geared toward the intermediate skier, though beginners and experts also have some trails, and second, good snow is guaranteed early and late in the year by snowmaking equipment that can work on 87% of the runs, more than any other in New Mexico. However, be aware that this human-made snow tends to be icy, and the mountain is full of inexperienced skiers, so you really have to watch your back. Locals in the area refer to this as "Little Texas" because it's so popular with Texans and other Southerners. A very friendly atmosphere, with a touch of redneck attitude, prevails.

There's a 1,600-foot vertical drop here to a base elevation of 8,750 feet. Lifts include four double chairs, two triple chairs, and a surface tow, with a capacity of 7,920 skiers per hour. The cost of a lift ticket for all lifts is $55 for adults for a full day, $40 half-day; $48 for teens 13 to 19 for a full day, $35 half-day; and $39 for children ages 4 to 12 and seniors 60 through 69 for a full day, $28 half-day. Free for seniors 70 and over. All rental packages start at $20 for adults, $13 for children. Lifts run daily 9am to 4pm Thanksgiving to about March 28. Ask about their lesson packages.

Also quite close to Taos (approx. 20 miles) is **Angel Fire Resort** ★, P.O. Drawer B, Angel Fire, NM 87710 (✆ **800/633-7463** or 505/377-6401; www.angelfireresort.com). If you (or your kids) don't feel up to skiing steeper Taos Mountain, Angel Fire is a good choice. The 73 trails are heavily oriented to beginner and intermediate skiers and snowboarders, with a few runs for more advanced skiers and snowboarders. The mountain has received over $7 million in improvements in past years. This is not an old village like you'll find at Taos and Red River. Instead, it's a Vail-style resort, built in 1960, with a variety of activities other than skiing (see "A Scenic Drive Around the Enchanted Circle," later in this chapter). The snowmaking capabilities here are excellent, and the ski school is good, though I hear it's so crowded that it's difficult to get in during spring break. Two high-speed quad lifts whisk you to the top quickly. There are also three double lifts and one surface lift. A large snowboard park contains a banked slalom course, rails, jumps, and other obstacles. Cross-country skiing, snowshoeing, and snowbiking are also available. All-day lift tickets cost $59 for adults, $49 for teens (ages 13–17), and $39 for children (ages 7–12). Kids 6 and under and seniors 70 and over ski free. Open from approximately mid-December to March 29 (depending on the weather) daily 9am to 4pm.

The oldest ski area in the Taos region, founded in 1952, **Sipapu Ski and Summer Resort,** HC 65, Rte. Box 29, Vadito, NM 87579 (✆ **505/587-2240;** www.sipapunm.com), is 25 miles southeast of Taos, on NM 518 in Tres Ritos Canyon. It prides itself on being a small local ski area, especially popular with schoolchildren. It has two triple chairs and two surface lifts, with a vertical drop of 1,025 feet to the 8,200-foot base elevation. There are 31 trails, half classified as intermediate, and two terrain park trails have been added. It's a nice little area, tucked way back in the mountains, with excellent lodging rates. Be aware that because the elevation is fairly low, runs can be icy. Lift tickets are $40 for adults for a full day, $26 half-day; $26 for children 12 and under for a full day, $22 half-day; $22 for seniors (ages 60–69) for a half- or full day; and free for seniors age 70 and over, as well as children 5 and under. A package including lift tickets, equipment rental, and a lesson costs $53 for adults and $42 for children. Sipapu is open from about the end of November to April 1, and lifts run daily from 9am to 4pm.

CROSS-COUNTRY

Just east of Red River, with 16 miles of groomed trails (in addition to 6 miles of trails strictly for snowshoers) in 400 acres of forestlands atop Bobcat Pass, is the **Enchanted Forest Cross Country Ski Area ★** (✆ **505/754-6112;** www.enchantedforestxc.com). Full-day trail passes, good from 9am to 4:30pm, are $14 for adults, $10 for teens 13 to 17 and seniors 62 to 69, $6 for children age 7 to 12, and free for seniors age 70 and over, as well as for children 6 and under. In addition to cross-country ski and snowshoe rentals, the ski area also rents pulk sleds—high-tech devices in which children are pulled by their skiing parents. The ski area offers a full snack bar. Equipment rentals and lessons can be arranged either at Enchanted Forest or at **Miller's Crossing** ski shop at 417 W. Main St. in Red River (✆ **505/754-2374**). Nordic skiers can get instruction in cross-country classic as well as freestyle skating. **Taos Mountain Outfitters,** 114 S. Plaza (✆ **505/758-9292;** www.taosmountainoutfitters.com), offers telemark and cross-country sales, and rentals.

7 OTHER OUTDOOR ACTIVITIES

Taos County's 2,200 square miles embrace a great diversity of scenic beauty, from New Mexico's highest mountain, 13,161-foot **Wheeler Peak,** to the 650-foot-deep chasm of the **Rio Grande Gorge ★★**. Carson National Forest, which extends to the eastern city limits of Taos and cloaks a large part of the county, contains several major ski facilities as well as hundreds of miles of hiking trails through the Sangre de Cristo range.

Recreation areas are mainly in the national forest, where pine and aspen provide refuge for abundant wildlife. Forty-eight areas are accessible by road, including 38 with campsites. There are also areas on the high desert mesa, carpeted by sagebrush, cactus, and, frequently, wildflowers. Two beautiful areas within a short drive of Taos are the **Valle Vidal Recreation Area,** north of Red River, and the **Wild Rivers Recreation Area,** near Questa. For complete information, contact **Carson National Forest,** 208 Cruz Alta Rd. (✆ **575/758-6200;** www.fs.fed.us/r3/carson), or the **Bureau of Land Management,** 226 Cruz Alta Rd. (✆ **575/758-8851;** www.blm.gov.nm/st/en.html).

BALLOONING

As in many other towns throughout New Mexico, hot-air ballooning is a top attraction. Recreational trips over the Taos Valley and Rio Grande Gorge are offered by **Paradise Hot Air Balloon Adventure** (✆ **505/751-6098;** www.taosballooning.com). The company also offers ultra-light rides.

Along a Green Shore

A sweet spot en route to Taos from Santa Fe, the **Orilla Verde** (green shore) **Recreation Area,** offers just what its name implies: lovely green shores along the Rio Grande. It's an excellent place to camp or to simply have a picnic. If you're adventurous, the flat water in this section of the river makes for scenic canoeing, kayaking, rafting, and fishing. Hiking trails thread through the area as well. Along them, you may come across ancient cultural artifacts, but be sure to leave them as you find them.

While traveling to the area, you'll encounter two places of note. The village of **Pilar** ★ is a charming farming village, home to apple orchards, corn fields, and artists. The **Rio Grande Gorge Visitor Center** (at the intersection of NM 570 and NM 68; © **575/751-4899**) provides information about the gorge and has very clean restrooms. It's open daily during business hours from Memorial Day to Labor Day.

The day-use fee for Orilla Verde is $3 per day, camping is $7 per night, and RV camping is $15 per night. All campsites have picnic tables, grills, and restrooms. For information contact the **Orilla Verde Visitor Station** (© **575/751-4899;** www.blm.gov.nm/st/en.html), at the campground. To reach the recreation area, travel north from Santa Fe 50 miles or southwest from Taos 15 miles on NM 68; turn north on NM 570 and travel 1 mile.

The **Taos Mountain Balloon Rally,** P.O. Box 3096 (© **505/751-1000;** www.taosballoonrally.com), is held each year in late October. (See "New Mexico Calendar of Events," in chapter 3.)

BIKING

Even if you're not an avid cyclist, it won't take long for you to realize that getting around Taos by bike is preferable to driving. You won't have the usual parking problems, and you won't have to sit in the line of traffic as it snakes through the center of town. If you feel like exploring the surrounding area, Carson National Forest rangers recommend several biking trails in the greater Taos area. Head to the **West Rim Trail** for a scenic and easy ride. To reach the trail, travel US 64 to the Taos Gorge Bridge, cross it and find the trail head on your left, or head south on NM 68 for 17 miles to Pilar; turn west onto NM 570. Travel along the river for 6¼ miles, cross the bridge, and drive to the top of the ridge. Watch for the trail marker on your right. For a more technical and challenging ride, go to **Devisadero Loop:** From Taos drive out of town on US 64 to your first pull-out on the right, just as you enter the canyon at El Nogal Picnic Area. The **U.S. Forest Service** office, 208 Cruz Alta Rd. (© **505/758-6200**), has excellent trail information. Also look for the *Taos Trails* map (created jointly by Carson National Forest, Native Sons Adventures, and Trails Illustrated) at area bookstores.

Bicycle rentals are available from the **Gearing Up Bicycle Shop,** 129 Paseo del Pueblo Sur (© **505/751-0365;** www.gearingupbikes.com); daily rentals run $35 for a mountain bike with front suspension.

Annual touring events include Red River's **Enchanted Circle Century Bike Tour** (✆ **505/754-2366**) on the weekend following Labor Day.

FISHING

In many of New Mexico's waters, fishing is possible year-round, though, due to conditions, many high lakes and streams are fishable only during the warmer months. Overall, the best fishing is in the spring and fall. Naturally, the Rio Grande is a favorite fishing spot, but there is also excellent fishing in the streams around Taos. Taoseños favor the Rio Hondo, Rio Pueblo (near Tres Ritos), Rio Fernando (in Taos Canyon), Pot Creek, and Rio Chiquito. Rainbow, cutthroat, German brown trout, and kokanee (a freshwater salmon) are commonly stocked and caught. Pike and catfish have been caught in the Rio Grande as well. Jiggs, spinners, or woolly worms are recommended as lure, or worms, corn, or salmon eggs as bait; many experienced anglers prefer fly-fishing.

Licenses are required, of course, and are sold, along with tackle, at several Taos sporting-goods shops. For backcountry guides, try **Deep Creek Wilderness Outfitters and Guides,** P.O. Box 721, El Prado, NM 87529 (✆ **575/776-8423** or 575/776-5901), or **Taylor Streit Flyfishing Service,** 405 Camino de la Placita (✆ **575/751-1312;** www.streitflyfishing.com).

FITNESS FACILITIES

The **Taos Spa and Tennis Club,** 111 Dona Ana Dr. (across from Sagebrush Inn; ✆ **575/758-1980;** www.taosspa.com), is a fully equipped fitness center that rivals any you'd find in a big city. It has a variety of cardiovascular machines, bikes, and weight-training machines, as well as saunas, indoor and outdoor Jacuzzis, a steam room, and indoor and outdoor pools. Classes range from yoga to Pilates to water fitness. In addition, it has tennis and racquetball courts. Therapeutic massage, facials, and physical therapy are available daily by appointment. Children's programs include a tennis camp and swimming lessons, and babysitting programs are available in the morning and evening. The spa is open Monday to Friday 4am to 9pm; Saturday and Sunday 7am to 8pm. Monthly memberships are available for individuals and families, as are summer memberships and punchcards. For visitors, there's a daily rate of $12.

The **Northside Health and Fitness Center,** at 1307 Paseo del Pueblo Norte (✆ **575/751-1242**), is also a full-service facility, featuring top-of-the-line Cybex equipment, free weights, and cardiovascular equipment. Aerobics classes are scheduled daily (Jazzercise classes weekly), and there are indoor/outdoor pools and four tennis courts, as well as children's and seniors' programs. Open weekdays 6am to 9pm, weekends 8am to 8pm. The daily visitors' rate is $11. Also of note, with classes daily, is **Taos Pilates Studio,** 1103 Paseo del Pueblo Norte (✆ **575/758-7604;** www.taospilates.net).

GOLF

Since the summer of 1993, the 18-hole golf course at the **Taos Country Club,** 54 Golf Course Dr., Ranchos de Taos (✆ **800/758-7375** or 575/758-7300), has been open to the public. Located on Country Road 110, just 6 miles south of the plaza, it's a first-rate championship golf course designed for all levels of play. It has open fairways and no hidden greens. The club also features a driving range, practice putting and chipping greens, and instruction by PGA professionals. Greens fees are seasonal and start at $49; cart and club rentals are available.

The par-72, 18-hole course at the **Angel Fire Resort Golf Course** (✆ **800/633-7463** or 575/377-3055) is PGA endorsed. Surrounded by stands of ponderosa pine, spruce, and aspen, at 8,500 feet, it's one of the highest regulation golf courses in the world. It also has a driving range and putting green. Carts and clubs can be rented at the course, and the club pro provides instruction. Greens fees range from $47 to $99.

HIKING

There are hundreds of miles of hiking trails in Taos County's mountain and high-mesa country. The trails are especially well traveled in the summer and fall, although nights turn chilly and mountain weather may be fickle by September.

Free materials and advice on all **Carson National Forest** trails and recreation areas can be obtained from the **Forest Service Building,** 208 Cruz Alta Rd. (✆ **575/758-6200**), open Monday to Friday 8am to 4:30pm. Detailed USGS topographical maps of backcountry areas can be purchased from **Taos Mountain Outfitters,** South Plaza (✆ **575/758-9292**).

One of the easiest hikes to access is the **West Rim Trail,** aptly named because it runs along the rim of the Rio Grande Gorge. Access this 9-mile-long trail by driving west from Taos on U.S. 64, crossing the Rio Grande Gorge Bridge and turning left into the picnic area. The 19,663-acre **Wheeler Peak Wilderness** is a wonderland of alpine tundra, encompassing New Mexico's highest peak (13,161 ft.). A favorite (though rigorous) hike to Wheeler Peak's summit (15 miles round-trip with a 3,700-ft. elevation gain) makes for a long but fun day. The trail head is at Taos Ski Valley. For year-round hiking, head to the **Wild Rivers Recreation Area** ★ (✆ **575/770-1600**), near Questa (see "A Scenic Drive Around the Enchanted Circle," later in this chapter).

The sage meadows and pine-covered mountains around Taos make it one of the West's most romantic places to ride. **Taos Indian Horse Ranch** ★★, on Pueblo land off Ski Valley Road, just before **Arroyo Seco** (✆ **505/758-3212;** www.taosindianhorseranch.com), offers a variety of guided rides. Open by appointment, the ranch provides horses for all types of riders (English, Western, Australian, and bareback) and ability levels. Call ahead to reserve and for prices, which will likely run about $100 for a 2-hour trail ride.

Horseback riding is also offered by **Rio Grande Stables,** P.O. Box 2122, El Prado (✆ **505/776-5913;** www.lajitasstables.com/taos.htm), with rides taking place during the summer months at Taos Ski Valley. Most riding outfitters offer lunch trips and overnight trips. Call for prices and further details.

HUNTING

Hunters in **Carson National Forest** bag deer, turkey, grouse, band-tailed pigeons, and elk by special permit. Hunting seasons vary year to year, so it's important to inquire ahead with the New Mexico **Game and Fish Department** in Santa Fe (✆ **505/476-8000;** www.wildlife.state.nm.us).

JOGGING

The paved paths and grass of Kit Carson Park (see "More Attractions," earlier in this chapter) provide a quiet place to stretch your legs.

LLAMA TREKKING

For a taste of the unusual, you might want to try letting a llama carry your gear and food while you walk and explore, free of any heavy burdens. They're friendly, gentle animals that have keen senses of sight and smell. Often, other animals, such as elk, deer, and mountain sheep, are attracted to the scent of the llamas and will venture closer to hikers if the llamas are present.

Wild Earth Llama Adventures ★★ (✆ 800/758-LAMA [5262] or 575/586-0174; www.llamaadventures.com) offers a "Take a Llama to Llunch" day hike—a full day of hiking into the Sangre de Cristo Mountains, complete with a gourmet lunch for $89. Wild Earth also offers a variety of custom multiday wilderness adventures tailored to trekkers' needs and fitness levels for $125 per person per day. Children under 12 receive discounts. **El Paseo Llama Expeditions** ★ (✆ **800/455-2627** or 575/758-3111; www.elpaseollama.com) utilizes U.S. Forest Service–maintained trails that wind through canyons and over mountain ridges. The llama expeditions are scheduled March to November, and day hikes are scheduled year-round. The rides are for all ages and kids can ride, too. Gourmet meals are provided. Half-day hikes cost $74 and $84, day hikes $94, and 2- to 8-day hikes run $299 to $1,199.

RIVER RAFTING

Half- or full-day white-water rafting trips down the Rio Grande and Rio Chama originate in Taos and can be booked through a variety of outfitters in the area. The wild **Taos Box** ★★★, a steep-sided canyon south of the Wild Rivers Recreation Area, offers a series of class IV rapids that rarely let up for some 17 miles. The water drops up to 90 feet per mile, providing one of the most exciting 1-day white-water tours in the West. May and June, when the water is rising, is a good time to go. Experience is not required, but you will be required to wear a life jacket (provided), and you should be willing to get wet.

Most of the companies listed run the **Taos Box** ($104–$115 per person) and **Pilar Racecourse** ($45–$56 per person for a half-day) on a daily basis.

I highly recommend **Los Rios River Runners** ★ in Taos, P.O. Box 2734 (✆ **800/544-1181** or 505/776-8854; www.losriosriverrunners.com). Other safe bets are **Native Sons Adventures,** 1033-A Paseo del Pueblo Sur (✆ **800/753-7559** or 505/758-9342; www.nativesonsadventures.com), and **Far Flung Adventures,** P.O. Box 707, El Prado (✆ **800/359-2627** or 575/758-2628; www.farflung.com).

Safety warning: Taos is not the place to experiment if you're not an experienced rafter. Do yourself a favor and check with the **Bureau of Land Management** (✆ **575/758-8851**) to make sure that you're fully equipped to go white-water rafting without a guide. Have them check your gear to make sure that it's sturdy enough—this is serious rafting!

ROCK CLIMBING

Mountain Skills, P.O. Box 206, Arroyo Seco, NM 87514 (✆ **575/776-2222;** www.climbingschoolusa.com), offers rock-climbing instruction for all skill levels, from beginners to more advanced climbers who would like to fine-tune their skills or just find out about the best area climbs.

SKATEBOARDING

Try your board at **Taos Youth Family Center,** 406 Paseo del Cañon, 2 miles south of the plaza and about 3/4 mile off Paseo del Pueblo Sur (✆ **505/758-4160**), where there is an in-line-skate and skateboarding park, open when there's no snow or ice. Admission is free.

SNOWMOBILING & ATV RIDING

Native Sons Adventures, 1335 Paseo del Pueblo Sur (✆ **800/753-7559** or 575/758-9342; www.nativesonsadventures.com), runs fully guided tours in the Sangre de Cristo Mountains. Rates run $67 to $150. Advance reservations required.

Getting Pampered: The Spa Scene

Taos doesn't have the spa scene that Tucson and Phoenix do, but you can get pampered with treatments ranging from body polishes to mud wraps to massages at **Estrella Massage & Day Spa,** 601 Callejon Rd. (✆ **575/751-7307;** www.estrellamassage.com). **Taos Spa and Tennis Club** (see "Fitness Facilities," above) also offers massages.

If you'd like to stay at a spa, **El Monte Sagrado,** 317 Kit Carson Rd. (✆ **800/828-TAOS** [8267] or 505/758-3502; www.elmontesagrado.com), and **Casa de las Chimeneas,** 405 Cordoba Rd. (✆ **877/758-4777** or 505/758-4777; www.visittaos.com), offer a variety of treatments to their guests (see earlier).

SWIMMING

The **Taos Swimming Pool,** Civic Plaza Drive at Camino de la Placita, opposite the Convention Center (✆ **575/758-4160**), admits swimmers 8 and over without adult supervision.

TENNIS

Taos Spa and Tennis Club (see "Fitness Facilities," above) has four courts, and the **Northside Health and Fitness Center** (see "Fitness Facilities," above) has three tennis courts. In addition, there are four free public courts in Taos, two at **Kit Carson Park,** on Paseo del Pueblo Norte, and two at **Fred Baca Memorial Park,** on Camino del Medio, south of Ranchitos Road.

8 SHOPPING

Given the town's historical associations with the arts, it isn't surprising that many visitors come to Taos to buy fine art. Some 50-odd galleries are within walking distance of the plaza, and a couple dozen more are just a short drive from downtown. Galleries and shops are generally open 7 days a week during summer and closed Sundays during winter. Hours vary but generally run from 10am to 5 or 6pm. Some artists show their work by appointment only.

The best-known artist in modern Taos is the late R. C. Gorman, a Navajo from Arizona who made his home in Taos for more than 2 decades. He was internationally acclaimed for his bright, somewhat surrealistic depictions of Navajo women. His **Navajo Gallery,** at 210 Ledoux St. (✆ **575/758-3250;** www.rcgormangallery.com), is a showcase for his widely varied work: acrylics, lithographs, silk screens, bronzes, tapestries, hand-cast ceramic vases, etched glass, and more.

My favorite new spot to shop is the village of **Arroyo Seco** ★ on NM 150, about 5 miles north of Taos en route to Taos Ski Valley. Not only is there a lovely 1834 church, La Santísima Trinidad, but there also are a few cute little shops lining the winding lane through town. My favorites are the **Taos Sunflower** ★ (✆ **575/776-5644;** www.taossunflower.com), selling specialty yarns and fibers, and **Arroyo Seco Mercantile** ★ (✆ **575/776-8806**) at 488 NM 150, which is full of cowboy hats, antiques, and country home items.

ART

Act I Gallery This gallery has a broad range of works in a variety of media. You'll find watercolors, *retablos,* furniture, paintings, Hispanic folk art, pottery, jewelry, and sculpture. 218 Paseo del Pueblo Norte. ✆ **800/666-2933** or 575/758-7831. www.actonegallery.com.

Fenix Gallery The Fenix Gallery focuses on Taos artists with national and/or international collections and reputations who live and work in Taos. The work is primarily nonobjective and very contemporary. Some "historic" artists are represented as well. 208A Ranchitos Rd. ✆ **575/758-9120.** www.fenixgallery.com.

Inger Jirby Gallery ★ Finds The word *expressionist* could have been created to define the work of internationally known artist Inger Jirby. Full of bold color and passionate brush strokes, Jirby's oils record the lives and landscapes of villages from the southwestern U.S. to Guatemala to Bali. This gallery, which meanders back through a 400-year-old adobe house, is a feast for the eyes and soul. 207 Ledoux St. ✆ **575/758-7333.**

Lumina Contemporary Art ★★ Finds North of Taos (about 8 min.) outside the village of Arroyo Seco, this gallery, a new version of the notable gallery that was in Taos, offers a tranquil museum-quality experience. Set within a 3-acre Japanese garden, it has a water cascade and Buddhist teahouse accented with large stone sculptures. Inside, works offer a refreshing look at the world. Open in summer Thursday to Monday 11am to 6:30pm; winter Friday to Monday 11am to 5pm. 11 NM 230, Arroyo Seco. ✆ **877/5LUMINA** (558-6462) or 575/758-7282. www.luminagallery.com.

Michael McCormick Gallery ★ Finds Nationally renowned artists dynamically play with Southwestern themes in the works hanging at this gallery, steps from the plaza. Especially notable are the bright portraits by Miguel Martinez. If the gallery's namesake is in, strike up a conversation about art or poetry. 106C Paseo del Pueblo Norte. ✆ **800/279-0879** or 575/758-1372. www.mccormickgallery.com.

Nichols Taos Fine Art Gallery Here you will find traditional works in all media, including Western and cowboy art. 403 Paseo del Pueblo Norte. ✆ **575/758-2475.** www.nicholsgallery.com.

Parks Gallery ★ Some of the region's finest contemporary art decks the walls of this gallery just off the plaza. Some of the top artists here include Melissa Zink, Jim Wagner, Susan Contreres, and Erin Currier. 127 Bent St. ✆ **575/751-0343.** www.parksgallery.com.

Philip Bareiss Gallery The works of some 30 leading Taos artists, including sculptor and painter Ron Davis, painter Norbert Voelkel, and watercolorist Patricia Sanford, are exhibited here, along with early Taos modernists. 15 Rt. 150. ✆ **575/776-2284.** www.taosartappraisal.com.

R. B. Ravens A trader for many years, including 25 on the Ranchos Plaza, R. B. Ravens is skilled at finding incredible period artwork. Here, you'll see (and have the chance to buy) Navajo rugs and pottery, all in the setting of an old home with raw pine floors and hand-sculpted adobe walls. 4146 NM 68 (across from the St. Francis Church Plaza), Ranchos de Taos. ✆ **575/758-7322.** www.rbravens.com.

BOOKS

Moby Dickens Bookshop ★ This is Taos's best bookstore, with comfortable places to sit and read. You'll find children's and adults' collections of Southwest, Native American, and out-of-print books. 124A Bent St. ✆ **888/442-9980** or 575/758-3050. www.mobydickens.com.

CRAFTS

Taos Artisans Cooperative Gallery *Value* This seven-member cooperative gallery, owned and operated by local artists, sells local handmade jewelry, wearables, clay work, glass, leather work, and garden sculpture. You'll always find an artist in the shop. 107C Bent St. ✆ **575/758-1558.** www.taosartisanscooperative.com.

Taos Blue This gallery has fine Native American and contemporary handcrafts. 101A Bent St. ✆ **575/758-3561.** www.taosblue.com.

Weaving Southwest Contemporary tapestries by New Mexico artists, as well as one-of-a-kind rugs, blankets, and pillows, are the woven specialties found here. 216B Paseo del Pueblo Norte. ✆ **575/758-0433.** www.weavingsouthwest.com.

FASHIONS

Artemisia ★ Advertising "one-of-a-kind artwear and accessories," this shop delivers, with wearable art in bold colors, all hand-woven or hand-sewn, all for women. 115 Bent St. ✆ **575/737-9800.** www.artemisiataos.com.

Overland Sheepskin Company ★ *Finds* You can't miss the romantically weathered barn sitting on a meadow north of town. Inside, you'll find anything you can imagine in leather: coats, gloves, hats, slippers. The coats here are exquisite, from oversize ranch styles to tailored blazers in a variety of leathers from sheepskin to buffalo hide. NM 522 (a few miles north of town). ✆ **575/758-8820.** www.overland.com.

FOOD

Cid's Food Market This store has the best selection of natural and gourmet foods in Taos. It's a great place to stock your picnic basket with such items as roasted chicken and barbecued brisket, or with lighter fare, such as sushi, Purple Onion–brand sandwiches, black-bean salad, and fresh hummus and tabbouleh. 623 Paseo del Pueblo Norte. ✆ **575/758-1148.** www.cidsfoodmarket.com.

FURNITURE

Country Furnishings of Taos Here, you'll find unique hand-painted folk-art furniture. The pieces are as individual as the styles of the local folk artists who make them. There are also home accessories, unusual gifts, clothing, and jewelry. 534 Paseo del Pueblo Norte. ✆ **575/758-4633.**

The Taos Company This interior-design showroom specializes in unique Southwestern and contemporary furniture and decorative accessories. Especially look for graceful stone fountains, iron-and-wood furniture, and custom jewelry. 124K John Dunn Plaza, Bent St. ✆ **800/548-1141** or 575/758-1141. www.thetaoscompany.com.

GIFTS & SOUVENIRS

Chimayo Trading del Norte Specializing in Navajo weavings, pueblo pottery, and other types of pottery, this is a fun spot to peruse on the Ranchos de Taos Plaza. Look especially for the Casas Grandes pottery from Mexico. #1 Ranchos de Taos Plaza. ✆ **575/758-0504.**

El Rincón Trading Post *Finds* This shop has a real trading-post feel. It's a wonderful place to find turquoise jewelry, whether you're looking for contemporary or antique. In the back of the store is a museum full of Native American and Western artifacts. 114 Kit Carson Rd. ✆ **575/758-9188.**

San Francisco de Asis Gift Shop Local devotional art fills this funky little shop behind the San Francisco de Asis church. *Retablos* (altar paintings), rosary beads, and hand-carved wooden crosses appeal to a range of visitors, from the deeply religious to the pagan power shopper. Ranchos de Taos Plaza. ✆ **575/758-2754.**

JEWELRY

Artwares Contemporary Jewelry The gallery owners here call their contemporary jewelry "a departure from the traditional." True to this slogan, each piece here offers a new twist on traditional Southwestern and Native American design, by artists such as Roberto Coin, John Hardy, Diane Malouf, Judith Ripka, and Alex Sepkus. 129 N. Plaza. ✆ **800/527-8850** or 575/758-8850. www.artwaresjewelry.com.

Taos Gems & Minerals In business for over 30 years, Taos Gems & Minerals is a fine lapidary showroom. This is a great place to explore; you can buy jewelry, carvings, and antique pieces at reasonable prices. 637 Paseo del Pueblo Sur. ✆ **575/758-3910.**

MUSICAL INSTRUMENTS

Taos Drum Company ★ Taos Drums has one of the largest selections of Native American log and hand drums in the world. In addition to drums, the showroom displays Southwestern and wrought-iron furniture, cowboy art, and more than 60 styles of rawhide lampshades. To find Taos Drum Company, look for the tepees and drums off NM 68. Ask about the tour that demonstrates the drum-making process. 5 miles south of Taos Plaza (off NM 68). ✆ **575/758-3796.** www.taosdrums.com.

POTTERY

Stephen Kilborn Pottery Visiting this shop in town is a treat, but for a real adventure, go 17 miles south of Taos toward Santa Fe to Stephen Kilborn's studio in Pilar, open Monday to Saturday 11am to 5pm and noon to 4pm on Sunday. There, you'll see where the pottery is made. 136A Paseo del Pueblo Norte. ✆ **800/758-0136** or 575/758-5760. www.kilbornpottery.com.

9 TAOS AFTER DARK

For a small town, Taos has its share of top entertainment. The resort atmosphere and the arts community attract performers, and the city enjoys annual programs in music and literary arts. State troupes, such as the New Mexico Repertory Theater and New Mexico Symphony Orchestra, make regular visits.

Many events are scheduled by the **Taos Center for the Arts (TCA),** 133 Paseo del Pueblo Norte (✆ **575/758-2052;** www.taoscenterforthearts.org), at the Taos Community Auditorium. The TCA imports local, regional, and national performers in theater, dance, and concerts (Robert Mirabal, among others, has performed here). Also, look for a weekly film series offered year-round.

You can obtain information on current events in the *Taos News,* published every Thursday. The **Taos County Chamber of Commerce** (✆ **800/732-TAOS** [8267] or 575/758-3873; www.taoschamber.com) publishes semiannual listings of *Taos County Events,* as well as the annual *Taos Country Vacation Guide* that also lists events and happenings around town.

The Major Concert & Performance Halls

Taos Convention Center, 121 Civic Plaza Dr. (✆ **575/758-5792**). This convention space has an exhibit center where presentations, lectures, and concerts are held.

Taos Community Auditorium, Kit Carson Memorial State Park (✆ **575/758-4677**). A comfortable, small-town space, this community auditorium makes a nice venue for films, concerts, and lectures.

THE PERFORMING ARTS

Fort Burgwin This historic site (of the 1,000-year-old Pot Creek Pueblo), located about 10 miles south of Taos, is a summer campus of Dallas's Southern Methodist University. From mid-May through mid-August, the SMU-in-Taos curriculum (including studio arts, humanities, and sciences) includes courses in music and theater. There are regularly scheduled orchestral concerts, guitar and harpsichord recitals, and theater performances available to the community, without charge, throughout the summer. 6580 NM 518, Ranchos de Taos. ✆ **575/758-8322.**

Music from Angel Fire This acclaimed program of chamber music begins in mid-August, with weekend concerts, and continues up to Labor Day. Based in the small resort community of Angel Fire (located about 21 miles east of Taos, off US 64), it also presents numerous concerts in Taos, Las Vegas, and Raton. P.O. Box 502, Angel Fire. ✆ **575/377-3233** or 888/377-3300. www.musicfromangelfire.org.

Taos School of Music ★ Founded in 1963, this music summer school located at the Hotel St. Bernard in Taos Ski Valley offers excellent concerts by notable artists. From mid-June to mid-August there is an intensive 8-week study and performance program for advanced students of violin, viola, cello, and piano. The 8-week **Chamber Music Festival,** an important adjunct of the school, offers 16 concerts and seminars for the public; performances are given by pianist Robert McDonald, the Borromeo, St. Lawrence, and Brentano String Quartets, and the international young student artists. Performances are held at the Taos Community Auditorium and the Hotel St. Bernard. P.O. Box 1879. ✆ **575/776-2388.** www.taosschoolofmusic.com. Tickets for chamber music concerts $15 for adults, $10 for children 16 and under.

THE CLUB & MUSIC SCENE

Adobe Bar ★ A favorite gathering place for locals and visitors, the Adobe Bar is known for its live music series (nights vary) devoted to the eclectic talents of Taos musicians. The schedule offers a little of everything—classical, jazz, folk, flamenco, and world music. The Adobe Bar features a wide selection of international beers, wines by the glass, light New Mexican dining, desserts, and an espresso menu. Their margarita consistently wins the "Best of Taos" competition in *Taos News.* In the Historic Taos Inn, 125 Paseo del Pueblo Norte. ✆ **575/758-2233.**

Alley Cantina ★ (Moments) This bar that touts its location as the oldest house in Taos has become the hot late-night spot. The focus is on interaction, as well as TV sports, but there's also a cozy outdoor patio. Patrons playing shuffleboard, pool, chess, and backgammon listen to live music 4 to 5 nights a week. Burgers, fish and chips, and other informal dishes are served until 11pm. 121 Teresina Lane. ✆ **575/758-2121.** Cover for live music only.

Anaconda Bar ★★ Set in the eco-resort El Monte Sagrado, this is Taos's most happening nightspot, with live entertainment—jazz, blues, Native American flute, or country—playing Thursday through Saturday. An anaconda sculpture snaking across the ceiling and an 11,000-gallon fish tank set the contemporary tone of the place, where a variety of the hotel's signature dishes are served. In the El Monte Sagrado hotel, 317 Kit Carson Rd. ✆ **575/758-3502.** www.elmontesagrado.com.

Caffe Tazza ★ This cozy three-room cafe, with a summer patio, attracts local community groups, artists, performers, and poets. Plays, films, comedy, and musical performances are given here on weekends (and some weeknights in summer). You can read one of the assorted periodicals available (including the *New York Times*) while sipping a cappuccino or *cafe Mexicano* (espresso with steamed milk and Mexican chocolate), made from organic coffee beans. The food—soups and sandwiches—is quite good. Pastries, which are imported from many bakeries around the region, are almost as big a draw here as the Taos Cow ice cream. Choose from 15 flavors. 122 Kit Carson Rd. ✆ **575/758-8706.**

Eske's Brew Pub and Eatery ★ I have a fondness for this place that one might have for an oasis in the desert. The first time I ate here, I'd been on assignment ice climbing and just spent 8 hours in the shadow of a canyon, hacking my way up an 80-foot frozen waterfall. I sat down at one of the high tables in the main room, dipped into a big bowl of Wanda's green chile turkey stew, and felt the blood return to my extremities. Owner, Steve "Eske" Eskeback, designs all the beers here, which are excellent. At times this can be a rowdy place, but mostly it's just fun, with lots of ski patrollers and mountain guides showing up to swap stories. In summer, you can eat on picnic tables outside. March to September and peak times such as spring and winter breaks it's open daily 11:30am to 10pm; rest of winter Friday to Sunday 11:30am to 10pm. 106 Des Georges Lane. ✆ **575/758-1517.**

Sagebrush Inn ★ This is a real hot spot for locals. The atmosphere is Old West, with a rustic wooden dance floor and plenty of rowdiness. Dancers generally two-step to country music nightly, year-round, starting at 9pm. Paseo del Pueblo Sur (P.O. Box 557). ✆ **575/758-2254.**

10 A SCENIC DRIVE: THE ENCHANTED CIRCLE

If you're in the mood to explore, take this 90-mile loop north of Taos, through the old Hispanic villages of Arroyo Hondo and Questa, into a pass that the Apaches, Kiowas, and Comanches once used to cross the mountains to trade with the Taos Indians. You'll come to the Wild West mining town of Red River, pass through the expansive Moreno Valley, and travel along the base of some of New Mexico's tallest peaks. Then, you'll skim the shores of a high mountain lake at Eagle Nest, pass through the resort village of Angel Fire, and head back to Taos along the meandering Rio Fernando de Taos. Although one can drive the entire loop in 2 hours from Taos, most folks prefer to take a full day, and many take several days.

ARROYO HONDO

Traveling north from Taos via NM 522, it's a 9-mile drive to this village, the remains of an 1815 land grant along the Rio Hondo. Along the dirt roads that lead off NM 522, you may find a windowless *morada* or two, marked by plain crosses in front—places of worship for the still-active Penitentes, a religious order known for self-flagellation. This is also the turnoff point for trips to the Rio Grande Box, an awesome 1-day, 17-mile white-water run for which you can book trips in Santa Fe, Taos, Red River, and Angel Fire. (See the "Outdoor Activities" section in chapter 7 and "Other Outdoor Activities," earlier in this chapter for booking agents in Santa Fe and Taos, respectively.)

Arroyo Hondo was also the site of the New Buffalo commune in the 1960s. Hippies flocked here, looking to escape the mores of modern society. Over the years, the commune members have dispersed throughout northern New Mexico, bringing an interesting creative element to the food, architecture, and philosophy of the state. En route north, the highway passes near **San Cristobal,** where a side road turns off to the **D. H. Lawrence Ranch** (see "More Attractions," earlier in this chapter) and **Lama,** site of an isolated spiritual retreat.

QUESTA

Next, NM 522 passes through Questa, most of whose residents are employed at a molybdenum mine about 5 miles east of town. Mining molybdenum (an ingredient in lightbulbs, television tubes, and missile systems) in the area has not been without controversy. The process has raked across hillsides along the Red River, and though Chevron Mining Inc., the mine's owner, treats the water it uses before returning it to the river, studies show that it has adversely affected the fish life. Still, the mine is a major employer in the area, and locals are grateful for the income it generates. Stop in at **Paloma Blanca Coffee House,** a new bright spot at 2322 NM 522 (✆ **575/586-2261**). You'll find a variety of coffees and teas as well as homemade pies, cookies, and ice cream. Also for sale are weavings, earrings, and paintings.

If you turn west off NM 522 onto NM 378 about 3 miles north of Questa, you'll travel 8 miles on a paved road to the Bureau of Land Management–administered **Wild Rivers Recreation Area** ★ (✆ **575/770-1600**). Here, where the Red River enters the gorge, you'll find 22 miles of trails, some suited for biking and some for hiking, a few trails traveling 800 feet down into the gorge to the banks of the Rio Grande. Forty-eight miles of the Rio Grande, which extend south from the Colorado border, are protected under the national Wild and Scenic River Act of 1968. Information on geology and wildlife, as well as hikers' trail maps, can be obtained at the visitor center here.

RED RIVER

To continue on the Enchanted Circle loop, turn east at Questa onto NM 38 for a 12-mile climb to Red River, a rough-and-ready 1890s gold-mining town that has parlayed its Wild West ambience into a pleasant resort village that's especially popular with families from Texas and Oklahoma.

This community, at 8,750 feet, is a center for skiing, snowmobiling, fishing, hiking, off-road driving, horseback riding, mountain biking, river rafting, and other outdoor pursuits. Frontier-style celebrations, honky-tonk entertainment, and even staged shootouts on Main Street are held throughout the year.

Though it can be a charming and fun town, Red River's food and accommodations are mediocre at best. Its patrons are down-home folks, happy with a bed and a diner-style

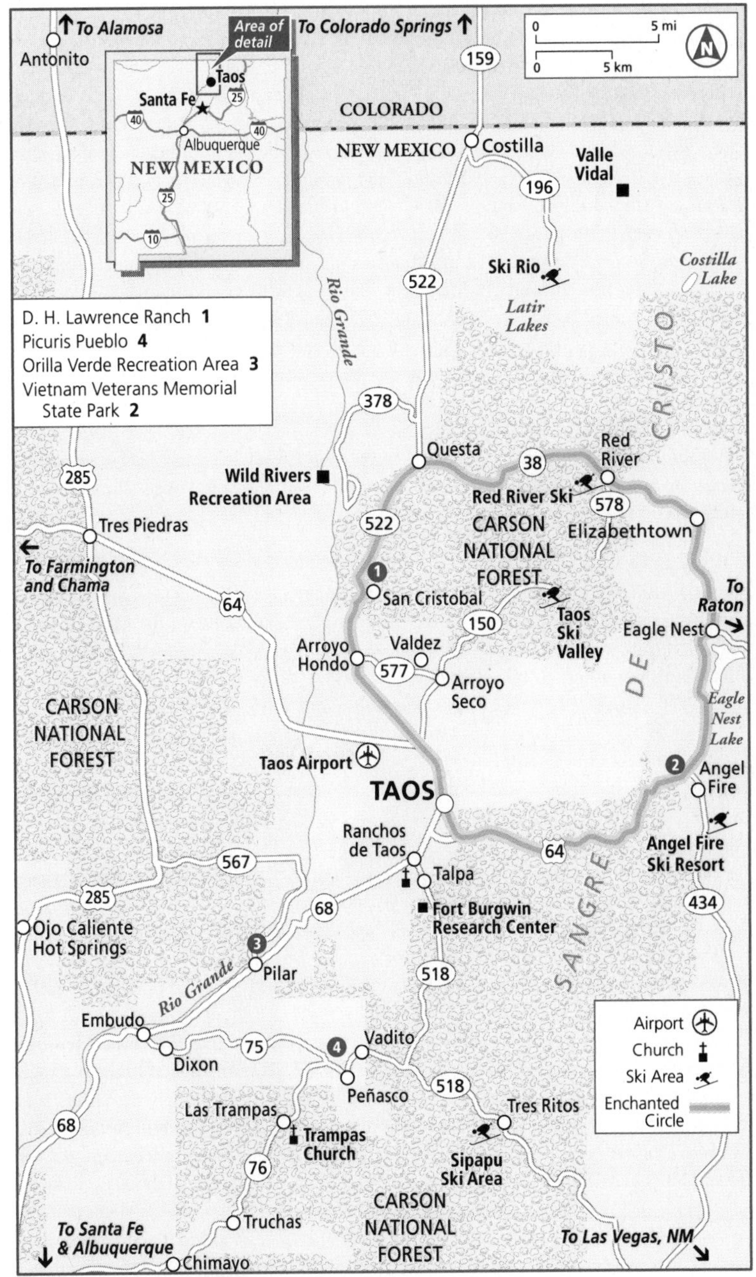

To Alamosa
Antonito
Area of detail
Taos
Santa Fe
Albuquerque
NEW MEXICO
To Colorado Springs
159
COLORADO
NEW MEXICO
Costilla
Valle Vidal
196
0 5 mi
0 5 km
N
Ski Rio
Costilla Lake
522
Latir Lakes
Rio Grande
D. H. Lawrence Ranch 1
Picuris Pueblo 4
Orilla Verde Recreation Area 3
Vietnam Veterans Memorial State Park 2
378
Questa
38
Red River
Wild Rivers Recreation Area
Red River Ski
578
285
Tres Piedras
522
CARSON NATIONAL FOREST
Elizabethtown
SANGRE DE CRISTO
To Farmington and Chama
San Cristobal
64
150
Taos Ski Valley
To Raton
Eagle Nest
Arroyo Hondo
Valdez
577
Arroyo Seco
Eagle Nest Lake
CARSON NATIONAL FOREST
Taos Airport
Angel Fire
TAOS
Ranchos de Taos
64
Angel Fire Ski Resort
567
Talpa
285
68
Fort Burgwin Research Center
434
Ojo Caliente Hot Springs
Pilar
Rio Grande
518
Embudo
Airport
Church
Ski Area
Enchanted Circle
75
Vadito
Dixon
Peñasco
518
Las Trampas
Tres Ritos
68
Trampas Church
Sipapu Ski Area
76
CARSON NATIONAL FOREST
Truchas
To Santa Fe & Albuquerque
To Las Vegas, NM
Chimayo
TAOS
8
A SCENIC DRIVE: THE ENCHANTED CIRCLE

meal. If you decide to stay, try the **Lodge at Red River,** P.O. Box 189, Red River, NM 87558 (✆ **800/91-LODGE** [915-6343] or 575/754-6280; www.lodgeatredriver.com), in the center of town. It offers hotel rooms ranging in price from $84 to $225. Knotty pine throughout, the accommodations are clean and comfortable. Downstairs, the restaurant serves three home-style meals daily.

If you're passing through and want a quick meal, **Mountain Treasures** (212 W. Main St., Red River, NM 87558; ✆ **575/754-2700**), a gallery, bistro, and espresso coffee bar, offers excellent sandwiches. Go straight for the muffulettas or "muffys," Italian sandwiches made popular in New Orleans. Salami, turkey, provolone, cheddar, and olive spread are set within homemade Sicilian round bread and heated until the outside is crusty, the inside gooey rich. For dessert try the Czech pastry *kolache* in a variety of fruits ranging from peach to cherry. Summer and winter ski season the cafe is open daily 6am to 6pm. Other times Monday to Saturday 7am to 2pm. A good bet for dinner is **Texas Reds Steak House** ★, 111 E. Main St. (✆ **575/754-2964**), where you can order steaks, burgers, and chicken dishes in a rustic Old West atmosphere. It's open in summer and winter daily from 4:30 to 10pm. During the shoulder seasons in spring and fall, it's open on weekends only.

The **Red River Chamber of Commerce,** P.O. Box 870, Red River, NM 87558 (✆ **800/348-6444** or 575/754-2366; www.redrivernewmexico.com), lists more than 40 accommodations, including lodges and condominiums. Some are open winters or summers only.

EAGLE NEST

About 16 miles southeast of Red River, on the other side of 9,850-foot Bobcat Pass, is the village of Eagle Nest, resting on the shore of Eagle Nest Lake in the Moreno Valley. Gold was mined in this area as early as 1866, starting in what is now the ghost town of **Elizabethtown** about 5 miles north; Eagle Nest itself (pop. 200) wasn't incorporated until 1976. The 4-square-mile **Eagle Nest Lake State Park** (✆ **888-NM-PARKS** [667-2757] or 575/377-1594; www.nmparks.com) stretches out below the village. Currently facilities include restrooms, a boat ramp, and visitor center. The lake is considered one of the top trout producers in the United States and attracts ice fishermen in winter as well as summer anglers. It's too cold for swimming, but sailboaters and windsurfers ply the waters.

One of New Mexico's more atmospheric country bars, the **Laguna Vista Saloon,** resides here, with an attached **Texas Reds Steakhouse,** on U.S. 64 at the center of Eagle Nest (✆ **505/377-6522** or 505/377-2755; www.lagunavistalodge.com).

If you're heading to Cimarron or Denver, proceed east on US 64 from Eagle Nest. But if you're circling back to Taos, continue southwest on NM 38 and US 64 to Agua Fría and Angel Fire.

Shortly before the Agua Fría junction, you'll see the **Vietnam Veterans Memorial State Park** (County Rd., B-4, Angel Fire; ✆ **575/377-6900**). It's a stunning structure with curved white walls soaring high against the backdrop of the Sangre de Cristo range. Consisting of a chapel and an underground visitor center, it was built by Dr. Victor Westphall in memory of his son, David, a marine lieutenant killed in Vietnam in 1968. The 6,000-square-foot memorial houses exhibits, videos, and memorabilia.

ANGEL FIRE

If you like the clean efficiency of a resort complex, you may want to plan a night or two here—at any time of year. Angel Fire is approximately 150 miles north of Albuquerque and 21 miles east of Taos. Opened in the late 1960s, this resort offers a hotel, condominiums, and cabins. Winter is the biggest season. This medium-size beginner and intermediate mountain is an excellent place for families to roam about (see "Skiing," earlier in this chapter).

During spring, summer, and fall, **Angel Fire Resort** offers golf, tennis, hiking, mountain biking (you can take your bike up on the quad lift), fly-fishing, river rafting, and horseback riding. There are other fun family activities, such as video arcade, a miniature golf course, theater performances, and, throughout the year, a variety of festivals, including a hot-air balloon festival, Winterfest, and concerts of both classical and popular music.

The unofficial community center is the **Angel Fire Resort,** 10 Miller Lane (P.O. Box 130), Angel Fire, NM 87710 (✆ **800/633-7463** or 575/377-6401; www.angelfireresort.com), a 155-unit hotel with spacious, comfortable rooms, some with fireplaces and some with balconies. Rates range from $90 to $200.

For more information on the Moreno Valley, including full accommodations listings, contact the **Angel Fire Chamber of Commerce,** P.O. Box 547, Angel Fire, NM 87710 (✆ **800/446-8117** or 575/377-6661; fax 575/377-3034; www.angelfirechamber.org).

A fascinating adventure you may want to try here is a 1-hour, 1-day, or overnight horseback trip with **Roadrunner Tours,** P.O. Box 274, Angel Fire, NM 87710 (✆ **575/377-6416;** www.rtours.com). One-and-a-half-hour rides run year-round for $70, but if you'd like a little more adventure, try an overnight. Call for prices.

9

Northwestern New Mexico

Exotic adventure awaits you in New Mexico's "Indian Country." At **Acoma,** you may peek through a hole in the wall of an ancient cemetery on a mesa hundreds of feet above the ground. It's there so that the spirits of some children who were taken from the pueblo can return. In **Grants** (pop. 9,043), a former uranium-mining boomtown, travel deep into a mine. In **Gallup** (pop. 20,000), self-proclaimed "Indian capital of the world" and a mecca for silver jewelry shoppers, you can cruise along Route 66 and pick up some authentic "pawn." In **Farmington** (pop. 42,000), center of the fertile San Juan valley and gateway to the Four Corners region, you might sleep in a cave. And in **Chama** (pop. 1,250), ride on the Cumbres & Toltec Railroad—the longest and highest narrow-gauge steam railroad in the country.

Each is an adventure in its own right, but what really makes them special is the people you'll encounter along the way. The biggest presence here is the Native American culture, old and new. Each time I travel to this area, I'm pleasantly surprised by the number of Pueblos, Navajos, and Apaches who inhabit it. Truly, they are the majority, and they set the pace and tone of the place. The Zuni, Acoma, and Laguna pueblos are each within a short distance of I-40. Acoma's "Sky City" has been continually occupied for more than 9 centuries. A huge chunk of the northwest is taken up by a part of the Navajo Reservation, the largest in America; and the Jicarilla Apache Reservation stretches 65 miles south from the Colorado border. All share their arts and crafts as well as their distinctive cultures with visitors, but they ask that their personal privacy and religious traditions be respected.

The past lives here, too. The Pueblo people believe that their ancestors' spirits still inhabit the ruins. **Chaco Culture National Historical Park,** with 12 major ruins and hundreds of smaller ones, represents the development of ancient Puebloan civilization, which reached its peak in the 11th century. **Aztec Ruins National Monument** and the nearby **Salmon Ruins** are similarly spectacular Pueblo preservations.

Two other national monuments in northwestern New Mexico also speak of the region's history. **El Morro** is a sandstone monolith known as Inscription Rock, where travelers and explorers documented their journeys for centuries; **El Malpais** is a volcanic badland with spectacular cinder cones, ice caves, and lava tubes.

1 NORTHWESTERN NEW MEXICO'S OUTDOORS

Like the rest of New Mexico, the northwestern region offers much in the way of outdoor recreation. If you're an outdoor enthusiast, you could spend months here.

BIKING Mountain biking is permitted in parts of **Cíbola National Forest** (✆ **505/ 346-2650;** www.fs.fed.us/r3/cibola), which, in this region, is on both sides of I-40 in the

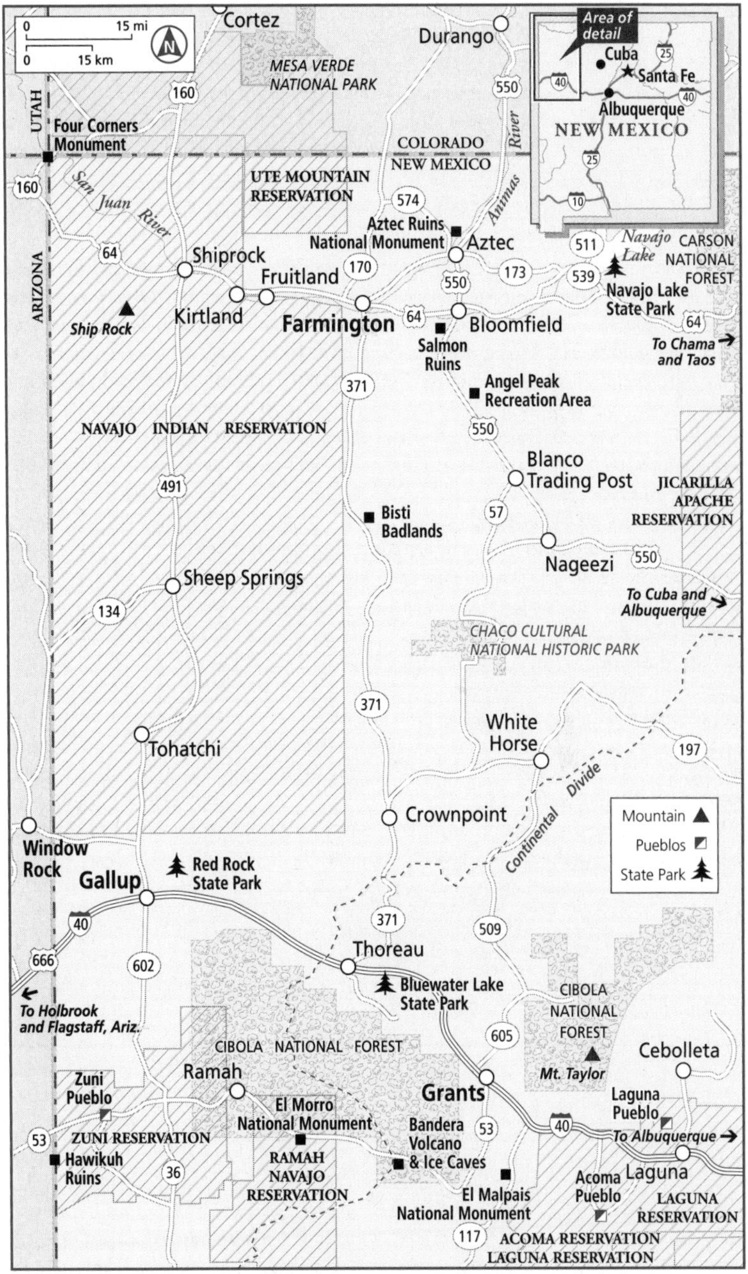

0 15 mi
0 15 km
N

Area of detail
Cuba
Santa Fe
Albuquerque
NEW MEXICO
25
40
10

Cortez
MESA VERDE NATIONAL PARK
Durango
160
550
UTAH
Four Corners Monument
COLORADO
NEW MEXICO
Animas River
160
San Juan River
UTE MOUNTAIN RESERVATION
574
Aztec Ruins National Monument
Aztec
511
Navajo Lake
CARSON NATIONAL FOREST
64
ARIZONA
Shiprock
Fruitland
170
550
173
539
Navajo Lake State Park
Ship Rock
Kirtland
Farmington
64
Bloomfield
Salmon Ruins
64
To Chama and Taos
371
Angel Peak Recreation Area
NAVAJO INDIAN RESERVATION
550
Blanco Trading Post
JICARILLA APACHE RESERVATION
491
57
Bisti Badlands
Nageezi
550
Sheep Springs
To Cuba and Albuquerque
134
CHACO CULTURAL NATIONAL HISTORIC PARK
371
White Horse
197
Tohatchi
Continental Divide
Crownpoint
Mountain
Pueblos
State Park
Window Rock
Red Rock State Park
Gallup
40
371
509
666
602
Thoreau
Bluewater Lake State Park
To Holbrook and Flagstaff, Ariz.
CIBOLA NATIONAL FOREST
CIBOLA NATIONAL FOREST
605
Cebolleta
Zuni Pueblo
Ramah
Mt. Taylor
Grants
El Morro National Monument
Laguna Pueblo
53
ZUNI RESERVATION
Bandera Volcano & Ice Caves
53
40
To Albuquerque
Hawikuh Ruins
36
RAMAH NAVAJO RESERVATION
El Malpais National Monument
Acoma Pueblo
Laguna
LAGUNA RESERVATION
117
ACOMA RESERVATION
LAGUNA RESERVATION

 Grants to Gallup area. The national forest has six districts; call the number above for a referral to the district you want to visit. Some of the best biking is in Farmington, which is where the "Durangatangs" come during the winter to train and ride (Durango is a mountain-biking mecca). **Bicycle Express,** 103 N. Main Ave. (✆ **505/334-4354**), in Aztec will give trail directions, as will **Cottonwood Cycles,** 4370 E. Main (✆ **505/326-0429;** www.cottonwoodcycles.com), in Farmington. Cottonwood also rents bikes. Be sure to check out the **Lions Wilderness Park,** where you'll find its renowned **Road Apple Trail** on the north end of town. Bikers are also welcome at the **Bureau of Land Management Conservation Area** just off NM 117 near **El Malpais National Monument** (see "Acoma & Laguna Pueblos & Grants," below). At Chaco Canyon, check out the Wijiji Ruin trail, nice and easy but through beautiful country leading to an Anasazi ruin.

BOATING If you're towing a boat, good places to stop are **Bluewater Lake State Park** (✆ **505/876-2391**), a reservoir between Gallup and Grants, and **Navajo Lake State Park** (✆ **505/632-2278**), about 25 miles east of Bloomfield. Both of these state parks have boat ramps, and Navajo Lake has several marinas (from which visitors can rent boats), picnic areas, a visitor center, and groceries for those who plan to make a day of it. To find information on New Mexico state parks, go to **www.nmparks.com**. **Zuni Lakes,** six bodies of water operated by the Zuni tribe, also offers opportunities for boating, although you're not allowed to use gasoline motors and you must receive a permit (✆ **505/782-5851**) before setting out.

FISHING **Bluewater Lake State Park** (mentioned above for boating) is one of the best places to fish in the area. In fact, some people believe it has the highest catch rate of all New Mexico lakes. Look to catch trout here. A world-renowned fishing destination, the **San Juan River ★★**, just below Navajo Dam, was named the best fishing spot in the United States by *Field & Stream.* The scenery is outstanding and excellent guides in the area can help you find the choicest spots. **Navajo Lake State Park** (see "Boating," above) features about 150 miles of shoreline where fishers go to catch trout, bass, catfish, and pike. Navajo Lake is one of the largest lakes in New Mexico, and the park is very heavily trafficked, so if crowds aren't your thing, look for another fishing hole. Just 4 miles south of Kirtland is **Morgan Lake,** a quiet spot for largemouth bass and catfish. If you need fishing gear or want to hire a guide while in the area, contact **Abe's Motel and Fly Shop,** 1791 US 173, Navajo Dam (✆ **505/632-2194**). In Farmington, contact **Dad's Boat Parts and Backyard Boutique,** 210 E. Piñon St. (✆ **505/326-1870**), or **Zia Sporting Goods,** 500 E. Main (✆ **505/327-6004;** www.ziasportinggoods.com).

GOLF In 2002, *Golf Digest* rated **Piñon Hills Golf Course,** 2101 Sunrise Pkwy., in Farmington (✆ **505/326-6066;** www.fmtn.org), the "best municipal course" in the United States. Also in Farmington is the **Civitan Golf Course,** 2100 N. Dustin (✆ **505/599-1194**). In Kirtland (approximately 7 miles west of Farmington), your golf option is **Riverview Golf Course,** on US 64 (✆ **505/598-0140**). In Grants, tee off at the 18-hole Coyote del Malpais Golf Course, at the base of Mount Taylor (✆ **505/285-5544;** http://coyotedelmalpaisgolfcourse.com).

HIKING This part of the state has some great hiking trails. You'll get to see ancient archaeological ruins in places such as Aztec Ruins and Chaco Canyon. In **Cíbola National Forest** (✆ **505/287-8833;** www.fs.fed.us/r3/cibola), the hike to the summit of Mount Taylor is excellent. In cooler months, but not winter, try hiking around **El Malpais National Monument** (✆ **505/285-4641;** www.nps.gov/elma). Two good hikes to try in El Malpais are the Zuni–Acoma Trail (this one is extremely taxing, so if you're not in shape, don't expect to make the 15-mile round-trip hike) and the Big Lava Tubes Trail (1 mile round-trip). My favorite hike in the region is to the top of **El Morro National Monument** ★★ (✆ **505/285-4641;** www.nps.gov/elma), which takes you to some Anasazi ruins. For quiet hiking on fairly level ground, head to **Bluewater Lake State Park** (✆ **505/876-2391**), **Red Rock Park** (✆ **505/722-3839**), or **Angel Peak Recreation Area** (✆ **505/599-8900**).

Sporting goods stores where you can get hiking gear include **REI-Albuquerque,** 1550 Mercantile Ave. NE, in Albuquerque (✆ **505/247-1191;** www.rei.com), **Frontier Sports,** 300 NE Aztec Blvd., in Aztec (✆ **505/334-0009**), and **Zia Sporting Goods,** 500 E. Main, in Farmington (✆ **505/327-6004;** www.ziasportinggoods.com).

RAFTING & KAYAKING The Chama River Canyon Wilderness begins just below El Vado Dam and runs past the Monastery of Christ in the Desert, usually an overnight trip, though some last up to 3 nights. The river snakes through one of the most spectacular canyons I've ever seen, at one point rising 1,500 feet above your head. Rapids are mostly Class II (on a scale from I to VI), but there are some big waves. Water is released on most weekends throughout the summer, so you can count on enough to make the trip exciting. Half-day trips are $60 for adults, $50 for kids. Full-day trips are $100 to $110 for adults; $105 for kids. Contact **Far Flung Adventures,** P.O. Box 707, El Prado, NM 87529 (✆ **800/359-2627** or 505/758-2628; www.farflung.com).

SKIING Some of the best cross-country skiing in the state is in the Chama area. Lots of broad bowls make the area a favorite of backcountry skiers as well as day-touring skiers. If you're up for an overnight adventure, contact **Southwest Nordic Center** (✆ **575/758-4761;** www.southwestnordiccenter.com), a company that rents yurts (Russian-style huts). Skiers trek into them, carrying their clothing and food in backpacks. Guide service is provided, or you can go in on your own, following directions on a map. The yurts are rented by the night and range from $65 to $125 per group. Call for reservations as much in advance as possible as they do book up. The season is from mid-November to April, depending on snow conditions.

Some like to ski the old logging roads of Mount Taylor in **Cíbola National Forest** near Grants. Contact the Ranger Station in Grants at ✆ **505/287-8833** for more information. If you need to rent ski equipment, try **Chama Ski Service** (✆ **575/756-2492**), which also offers snow reports and trail information.

SWIMMING Good swimming is available at **Navajo Lake State Park** (✆ **505/632-2278**). Before diving in at other lakes in state parks, make sure swimming is permitted.

2 ACOMA & LAGUNA PUEBLOS & GRANTS

Your best base for exploring the Acoma and Laguna pueblos, as well as the El Malpais and El Morro National Monuments (see "El Malpais & El Morro National Monuments," below), is the town of Grants, 1¼ hours west of Albuquerque on I-40 west.

ACOMA PUEBLO ★★★

The spectacular Acoma Sky City, a walled adobe village perched high atop a sheer rock mesa 367 feet above the 6,600-foot valley floor, is said to have been inhabited at least since the 11th century—it's the longest continuously occupied community in the United States. Native history says it has been inhabited since before the time of Christ. Both the pueblo and its mission church of **San Esteban del Rey** are National Historic Landmarks.

When Coronado visited in 1540, he suggested that Acoma was "the greatest stronghold in the world"; those who attempt to follow the cliffside footpath down after their guided tour, rather than take the bus back down, may agree.

About 50 to 75 Keresan-speaking Acoma (pronounced *Ack*-oo-mah) reside year-round on the 70-acre mesa top. Many others maintain ancestral homes and occupy them during ceremonial periods. The terraced three-story buildings face south for maximum exposure to the winter sun. Most of Sky City's permanent residents make their living off the throngs of tourists who flock here to see the magnificent church, built in 1639 and containing numerous masterpieces of Spanish colonial art, and to purchase the thin-walled white pottery with brown-and-black designs for which the pueblo is famous.

Many Acomas work in Grants, 15 miles west of the pueblo; in Albuquerque; or for one of Acoma's business enterprises, such as Sky City Casino. Others are cattle ranchers and farm individual family gardens.

Essentials

GETTING THERE To reach Acoma from Grants, drive east 15 miles on I-40 to McCartys, and then south 13 miles on paved tribal roads to the visitor center. From Albuquerque, drive west 65 miles to the Acoma–Sky City exit (102), and then 15 miles southwest.

VISITOR INFORMATION For additional information before you leave home, contact the Sky City Cultural Center and Pueblo of Acoma (✆ **800/747-0181;** www.acomaskycity.org).

ADMISSION FEES & HOURS Admission is $12 for adults, $11 for seniors 60 and over, $9 for children 6 to 17, and free for children 5 and under. There's a discount for Native American visitors. The photography charge is $10; tripods are prohibited, telephoto lenses are restricted, and no video cameras are allowed. No cellphones, binoculars, sketching, or painting is allowed except by special permission. The pueblo is open daily in the summer from 8am to 6:30pm; daily in the spring, fall, and winter 8am to 5pm. One-hour tours begin every 30 minutes, depending on the demand; the last tour is scheduled 1 hour before closing. The pueblo is closed June 24 and 29; July 10 through 13 and 25; the first or second weekends in October; and the first Saturday in December. It's best to call ahead to make sure that the tour is available when you're visiting.

Seeing the Highlights

You absolutely cannot wander freely around Acoma Pueblo, but you can start your tour there at the 40,000-square-foot museum and peruse their gallery, offering art and crafts for sale, and have a meal at the Yaak'a Café. One-hour tours begin every 30 minutes, depending on the demand; the last tour is scheduled 1 hour before closing. The pueblo is closed to visitors on Easter weekend (some years), June 24 and 29, July 10 to 13, and the first or second weekend in October. It's best to call ahead to make sure that the tour is available when you're visiting.

You'll board the tour bus, which climbs through a rock garden of 50-foot sandstone monoliths and past precipitously dangling outhouses to the mesa's summit. With no running water or electricity in this medieval-looking village, it's a truly unique place. A small reservoir collects rainwater for most uses, and drinking water is transported up from below. Wood-hole ladders and mica windows are prevalent among the 300-odd adobe structures. As you tour the village, you'll have many opportunities to buy pottery and other pueblo treasures. Pottery is expensive here, but you're not going to find it any cheaper anywhere else, and you'll be guaranteed that it's authentic if you buy it directly from the craftsperson. Along the way, be sure to sample some Indian fry bread topped with honey.

Dances & Ceremonies

The annual San Esteban del Rey feast day is September 2, when the pueblo's patron saint is honored with a morning Mass, a procession, an afternoon corn dance, and an arts-and-crafts fair. The Governor's Feast is held annually in February; and 4 days of Christmas festivals run from December 25 to 28. Guided tours do not operate on the mesa during feast days, and cameras are not permitted on the pueblo on feast days.

Other celebrations are held in low-lying pueblo villages at Easter (in Acomita), the first weekend in May (Santa Maria feast at McCartys), and August 10 (San Lorenzo Day in Acomita).

Where to Stay & Dine

The **Sky City Hotel & Casino,** off I-40 at exit 102, (© **888/759-2489;** www.skycity.com) offers good basic accommodations with prices ranging from $79 to $129 double. The hotel has a restaurant, snack bar, night club, casino, and RV park.

An Attraction near Laguna

Seboyeta, the oldest Hispanic community in western New Mexico, is 3½ miles north of Paguate, outside Laguna Pueblo. Still in view are ruins of adobe fortress walls built in the 1830s to protect the village from Navajo attack. The Mission of Our Lady of Sorrows was built in the 1830s, as was the nearby Shrine of Los Portales, built in a cave north of town.

GRANTS

If you've ever wondered what a "boom-and-bust town" looks like, come to Grants and find out. Grants first boomed with the coming of the railroad in the late 19th century, when 4,000 workers descended on the tiny farm town. When the railroad was completed, the workers left, and the town was bust. Next, Grants saw high times in the 1940s, growing carrots and sending them to the East Coast, but when packaging became more advanced, Grants lost its foothold in the market and busted again. Then came the 1950s, when a Navajo sheep rancher named Paddy Martinez discovered some strange yellow rocks near Haystack Mountain, northwest of town. The United States was in need of uranium, and his find led to the biggest boom in the area. By the early 1980s, demand for uranium had dropped, and so went the big wages and big spenders that the ore's popularity had produced. However, recent demand may just revive that industry once again. Today, the city on a segment of Route 66 is a jumping-off point for outdoor adventures.

The city is the seat of expansive Cíbola County, which stretches from the Arizona border nearly to Albuquerque. For more information, contact the **Grants/Cíbola County Chamber of Commerce** at 100 N. Iron Ave. (P.O. Box 297), Grants, NM 87020 (© **800/748-2142** or 505/287-4802; www.grants.org). It's in the same building as the New Mexico Mining Museum.

An Attraction in Grants

New Mexico Mining Museum ★ Kids This enormously interesting little museum primes you for the underground adventure of traveling into a re-creation of a mine shaft by showing you, on ground level, some geology, such as a fossilized dinosaur leg bone and a piece of Malpais lava. The world's only underground uranium-mining museum also gives you a sense of the context within which uranium was mined, through photos of the uranium-mining pioneers. Thus, the stage is set for your walk into a mine-shaft-like doorway adorned with rusty metal hats. An elevator takes you down into a spooky, low-lit place with stone walls. You begin in the station where uranium was loaded and unloaded and travel through the earth to places defined on wall plaques. While exploring, you get a sense of the dark and dirty work that mining can be. Those with claustrophobia may have to content themselves with visiting the exhibits *above* ground.

100 N. Iron Ave., at Santa Fe Ave. ✆ **800/748-2142** or 505/287-4802. www.grants.org. Admission $3 adults, $2 seniors 60 and over and children 7–18; free for children 6 and under. Mon–Sat 9am–4pm.

Northwest New Mexico Visitor Center ★ East of Grants, this center sits within an expansive Pueblo-style building with a broad atrium showing off views of the Malpais. It offers fliers and films on the region's parks, forests, and Indian country. A real treat here is a series of suggested driving tours displayed with large color photos and free cards describing the routes. One tour takes visitors along the volcanoes of the Malpais, another through the abandoned logging communities of the Zuni Mountains Historical Loop, and another to the stunning geologic formations of the Cabezon and Rio Puerco area. A fun shelf of Southwest book titles is worth perusing.

1900 Santa Fe Ave. ✆ **505/876-2783.** Free admission. Daily 9am–6pm during daylight saving time; 8am–5pm during Mountain Standard Time.

Where to Stay in Grants

Grants hotels are all on or near Route 66, with major properties near I-40 interchanges, and smaller or older motels nearer downtown. Lodger's tax is 5%, which is added to the gross receipts tax of 7.50%, for a total room tax of 12.5%. Parking is usually free.

Best Western Inn & Suites Built in 1976 with remodeling ongoing, this hotel provides spacious rooms and good amenities, though you have to like to walk. Rooms are built around a huge quadrangle with an indoor pool in a sunny, plant-filled courtyard at the center. Request a room at one of the four corner entrances to avoid trudging down the long hallways. Also, request a room that is facing outside rather than in toward the courtyard, where noise from the pool carries. Though not as up-to-date as the Holiday Inn Express (see below), more amenities are provided here. Rooms are bright, with comfortable beds, and decorated in floral prints with Aztec trim. Bathrooms are medium-size and clean.

1501 E. Santa Fe Ave. (I-40 exit 85), Grants, NM 87020. ✆ **800/528-1234** or 505/287-7901. Fax 505/285-5751. www.bestwestern.com. 126 units. $75–$89 double. Rates include full breakfast. AE, DC, DISC, MC, V. Pets welcome. **Amenities:** Indoor pool; exercise room; Jacuzzi; men's and women's saunas; coin-op laundry. *In room:* A/C, TV, Wi-Fi, coffeemaker, hair dryer, iron.

Holiday Inn Express This two-story motel, just off the interstate, provides large, well-conceived rooms with a comfortable atmosphere. Ground-floor rooms open both off an inner corridor and from an outside door where your car is parked. Rooms are spacious, with high ceilings, comfortable beds, and large bathrooms.

1496 E. Santa Fe Ave., Grants, NM 87020. ✆ **800/HOLIDAY** or 505/285-4676. Fax 505/285-6998. www.hiexpress.com. 58 units. $119 double. Rates include hot breakfast. AE, DC, DISC, MC, V. Pets welcome. **Amenities:** Small indoor pool; Jacuzzi. *In room:* A/C, TV, Wi-Fi, coffeemaker, hair dryer, iron.

Camping

Grants has three decent campgrounds with both tent and RV facilities. All range in price from $12 to $15 for tent camping and $15 to $20 for full hookups. **Blue Spruce RV Park** (✆ **505/287-2560**) has 25 sites and 16 full hookups and is open year-round. It has enough trees to block the wind, some grass, and the roads and parking spaces are gravel, so dust is minimized. Cable television hookups are available, as are laundry facilities and

Route 66 Gallery Stop

To see local and regional art, stop by the Cíbola Arts Council's **Double Six Gallery,** 1001 W. Santa Fe Ave. (✆ **505/287-7311**), a community space featuring photos, sculpture, and paintings. As well, the gallery houses the **Cíbola Art and Artifacts Museum,** which mounts shows related to regional history and invites artists to display related works. Recent exhibitions include a homestead show and railroading show.

a recreation room. To reach the park, take I-40 to exit 81 and then go a quarter mile south on NM 53.

Lavaland RV Park (✆ **505/287-8665;** www.lavalandrvpark.com), the closest site to Grants, has 51 sites and 39 full hookups. Near a lava outcropping, the site is clean, though a little desolate and dusty, with a few pine trees to block the wind. Air-conditioning and heating hookups are available, as are some free cable and telephone hookups. In addition, you'll find cabins, laundry, limited grocery facilities, picnic tables and grills, and recreation facilities. Lavaland is open year-round. From I-40, get off at exit 85 and continue 100 yards south on Access Road.

Where to Dine in Grants

In general, you won't find much to eat at pueblos or national monuments, so you're best off looking for a restaurant in Grants.

El Cafecito (Value) (Kids) AMERICAN/MEXICAN This real locals' spot serves up tasty food in a relaxed atmosphere. At mealtime, the brightly lit space with Saltillo tile floors bustles with families eating huevos rancheros (eggs over tortillas, smothered in chile) for breakfast, and enchiladas, stuffed *sopaipillas,* and burgers for lunch and dinner. All meals are large and inexpensive. Kids enjoy their own menu selections.

820 E. Santa Fe Ave. ✆ **505/285-6229.** Main courses $4–$8 breakfast, $6–$12 lunch or dinner. AE, DISC, MC, V. Mon–Fri 7am–9pm; Sat 7am–8pm.

La Ventana NEW MEXICAN/STEAKS Grants locals come here for a special lunch or dinner out. With one large room that seats about 50 people, the restaurant has a Southwestern decor, with a two-horse sculpture and some dancing katsinas (kachinas). Ironically, the place is dark, with windows blinded, despite its name, which means "the window," referring to the natural arch south of town. If you can catch Grants on a non-windy day, opt for the patio. Service is friendly and varies in its efficiency. Recommended dishes include chicken fajita salad and prime rib. You'll also find sandwiches such as turkey and guacamole served on seven-grain bread. You can order from a full bar.

110½ Geis St., Hillcrest Center. ✆ **505/287-9393.** Reservations recommended. Main courses $5–$12 lunch, $8–$20 dinner. AE, DC, DISC, MC, V. Mon–Sat 11am–11pm.

Wow Diner ★ (Kids) DINER/NEW MEXICAN This new cafe offers tasty food in a flashy stainless steel and tile building on the west side of town. Comfortable booths lining the walls and a soda fountain with stools create a classic Route 66 diner ambiance. You might start your day with French toast stuffed with cream cheese and strawberries. For lunch you could try pork carnitas—pulled pork that you fold into corn tortillas—with Spanish rice and beans on the side. A good dinner offering is pan fried trout, with buerre blanc and almond sauce and a potato, rice, or fries. Finish with a hot chocolate brownie with ice cream. The restaurant also serves some Asian dishes, steaks, and salads. Chase it all down with beer or wine. Kids have their own menu options. The diner is located across the street from the Petro Truck Stop.

1300 Motel Dr., in Milan. ✆ **505/287-3801.** Main courses $6–$22. AE, DISC, MC, V. Tues–Sun 6am–midnight.

3 EL MALPAIS & EL MORRO NATIONAL MONUMENTS

Northwestern New Mexico has two national monuments that are must-sees for anyone touring this region: El Malpais and El Morro. The region is also home to the Cíbola National Forest, with its stately Mount Taylor, visible from miles away and an excellent place to hike and backcountry ski.

EL MALPAIS: EXPLORING THE BADLANDS ★

Designated a national monument in 1987, El Malpais (Spanish for "badlands") is an outstanding example of the volcanic landscapes in the United States. El Malpais contains 115,000 acres of cinder cones, vast lava flows, hundreds of lava tubes, ice caves, sandstone cliffs, natural bridges and arches, Anasazi ruins, ancient Native American trails, and Spanish and Anglo homesteads.

Essentials

GETTING THERE You can take one of two approaches to El Malpais, via NM 117 or NM 53. NM 117 exits I-40 7 miles east of Grants.

VISITOR INFORMATION Admission to El Malpais is free (unless you're visiting the privately owned Ice Caves), and it's open to visitors year-round. The **visitor center,** off Route 53 between mile markers 63 and 64, is open daily from 8:30am to 4:30pm. Here you can pick up maps of the park, leaflets on specific trails, and other details about exploring the monument. For more information, contact **El Malpais National Monument,** NPS, P.O. Box 939, Grants, NM 87020 (✆ **505/285-4641;** www.nps.gov/elma).

Seeing the Highlights

From **Sandstone Bluffs Overlook** (10 miles south of I-40 off NM 117), many craters are visible in the lava flow, which extends for miles along the eastern flank of the Continental Divide. The most recent flows are only 1,000 years old; Native American legends tell of rivers of "fire rock." Seventeen miles south of I-40 is **La Ventana Natural Arch,** the largest accessible natural arch in New Mexico.

From NM 53, which exits I-40 just west of Grants, visitors have access to the **Zuni–Acoma Trail,** an ancient Pueblo trade route that crosses four major lava flows in a 7½-mile (one-way) hike. A printed trail guide is available. **El Calderon,** a forested area 20 miles south of I-40, is a trail head for exploring a cinder cone, lava tubes, and a bat cave. (***Warning:*** Hikers should not enter the bat cave or otherwise disturb the bats.)

The largest of all Malpais cinder cones, **Bandera Crater** is on private property 25 miles south of I-40. The National Park Service has laid plans to absorb this commercial operation, known as **Ice Caves Resort** (✆ **888/ICE-CAVE** or 505/783-4303; www.icecaves.com). For a fee ($9 for adults and $4 for children 5–12), visitors hike up the crater or walk to the edge of an ice cave. It's open daily from 8am to 7pm in summer and from 8am to 4pm in winter (generally closing 1 hr. before sunset).

Perhaps the most fascinating phenomenon of El Malpais is the lava tubes, formed when the outer surface of a lava flow cooled and solidified. When the lava river drained, tunnel-like caves were left. Ice caves within some of the tubes have delicate ice-crystal ceilings, ice stalactites, and floors like ice rinks.

Hiking & Camping

El Malpais has several hiking trails, including the above-mentioned Zuni–Acoma Trail. Most are marked with rock cairns; some are dirt trails. The best times to hike this area are during spring and fall, when it's not too hot. You're pretty much on your own when you explore this area, so prepare accordingly. Carry plenty of water with you; do not drink surface water. Carrying first-aid gear is always a good idea; the lava rocks can be extremely sharp and inflict nasty cuts. Never go into a cave alone. The park service advises wearing hard hats, boots, protective clothing, and gloves, and carrying three sources of light when entering lava tubes. The weather can change suddenly, so be prepared; if lightning is around, move off the lava as quickly as possible.

Primitive camping is allowed in the park, but you must first obtain a free backcountry permit from the visitor center.

EL MORRO NATIONAL MONUMENT ★★

Travelers who like to look history straight in the eye are fascinated by "Inscription Rock," 43 miles west of Grants along NM 53. Looming up out of the sand and sagebrush is a bluff 200 feet high, holding some of the most captivating messages in North America. Its sandstone face displays a written record of the many who inhabited and traveled through this land, beginning with the ancestral Puebloans, who lived atop the formation around 1200. Carved with steel points are the signatures and comments of almost every explorer, conquistador, missionary, army officer, surveyor, and pioneer emigrant who passed this way between 1605, when Gov. Don Juan de Oñate carved the first inscription, and 1906, when it was preserved by the National Park Service. Oñate's inscription, dated April 16, 1605, was perhaps the first graffiti any European left in America.

A paved walkway makes it easy to walk to the writings, and a stone stairway leads up to other treasures. One entry reads: "Year of 1716 on the 26th of August passed by here Don Feliz Martinez, Governor and Captain General of this realm to the reduction and conquest of the Moqui." Confident of success as he was, Martinez actually got nowhere with any "conquest of the Moqui," or Hopi, peoples. After a 2-month battle, they chased him back to Santa Fe.

Another special group to pass by this way was the U.S. Camel Corps, trekking past on their way from Texas to California in 1857. The camels worked out fine in mountains and deserts, outlasting horses and mules 10 to 1, but the Civil War ended the experiment. When Peachy Breckinridge, fresh out of the Virginia Military Academy, came by with 25 camels, he noted the fact on the stone here.

El Morro was at one time as famous as the Blarney Stone of Ireland: Everybody had to stop by and make a mark. But when the Santa Fe Railroad was laid 25 miles to the north, El Morro was no longer on the main route to California, and from the 1870s, the tradition began to die out.

If you like to hike, be sure to take the full loop to the top of Inscription Rock. It's a spectacular trip that takes you along the rim of this mesa—offering 360 degree views—culminating in an up-close look at Anasazi ruins, which occupy an area 200 by 300 feet.

 Inscription Rock's name, Atsinna, suggests that carving one's name here is a very old custom indeed: The word, in Zuni, means "writing on rock."

Essentials

GETTING THERE El Morro is 43 miles west of Grants on NM 53.

VISITOR INFORMATION For information, contact **El Morro National Monument,** HC61, Box 43, Ramah, NM 87321-9603 (✆ **505/783-4226;** www.nps.gov/elmo). Admission to El Morro is $3 per person 16 and older. Self-guided trail booklets are available at the visitor center (turn off NM 53 at the El Morro sign and travel approximately a half mile), open year-round from 9am to 5pm. Trails are also open year-round; check with the **visitor center** for hours. A **museum** at the visitor center features exhibits on the 700 years of human activity at El Morro. A 15-minute video gives a good introduction to the park. Also within the visitor center is a **bookstore** where you can pick up souvenirs and informational books. It takes approximately 2 hours to visit the museum and hike the trails. The park is closed on Christmas and New Year's Day.

Camping & Lodging

Though it isn't necessary to camp here in order to see most of the park, a nine-site campground at El Morro is open year-round, with a fee of $5 per night charged from approximately April to November. No supplies are available within the park, so if you're planning on spending a night or two, be sure to arrive well equipped.

One nearby private enterprise, **El Morro RV Park, Cabins & Cafe,** HC 61, Box 44, Ramah, NM 87321 (✆ **505/783-4612;** www.elmorro-nm.com), has cabins, RV and tent camping, and a cafe (see below). The cabins are well appointed, and the baths clean.

For a completely unique place to stay, check out **Cimarron Rose Bed & Breakfast ★★**, 30 miles southwest of Grants on NM 53 (✆ **800/856-5776;** www.cimarronrose.com). This ecofriendly inn offers three suites, a great place for families or a romantic getaway. The atmospheric country lodgings range in size from their Cimarron, with a 1930s mountain cabin feel, to the Zuni Mountain, with two cozy bedrooms and a living room with a wood-burning stove. All have full kitchens, with Mexican tile and generous food supplies in case you don't want to eat out. The suites also offer living and dining areas, and are decorated with antiques and colorful local art. Each has a comfortable bed or beds, a patio, and medium size bath. The windows look out on ponderosa pine forest and native gardens certified as Backyard Wildlife Habitat, hosting more than 80 species of birds, including many zooming hummingbirds. Prices range from $125 to $195 per night. The inn also houses the **Tierra Madre Arts Gallery ★**, displaying regional art, with an excellent collection of Zuni fetishes and katsinas.

Dining

A fun stop while exploring this part of New Mexico is the **Ancient Way Café ★**, near mile marker 46 on NM 53 (✆ **505/783-4612**). Amidst knotty pine walls, comfortable booths, and local art, this place serves imaginative food using such treats as free-range chicken and eggs, hormone-free beef, and seasonal vegetables. For breakfast you might have huevos rancheros (eggs over tortillas smothered in chile), along with housemade muffins. Lunch or dinner might bring a burger or salad or a grilled veggie wrap with Anasazi beans. On a recent visit I had their special: chicken and vegetable pesto over chile/tomato linguine, which was excellent. Follow it up with a piece of apple piñon nut chile pie. Prices range from $5 to $20. It's open Monday to Friday 9am to 5pm. As well, dinner is served Friday and Saturday 5 to 8pm by reservation only.

EXPLORING THE AREA: CIBOLA NATIONAL FOREST

Cíbola National Forest is actually a combination of parcels of land throughout the state that total more than 1.6 million acres. Elevation varies from 5,000 to 11,301 feet, and the forest includes the Datil, Gallinas, Bear, Manzano, Sandia, San Mateo, and Zuni mountains.

Two major pieces of the forest flank I-40 on either side of Grants, near the pueblos and monuments described above. To the northeast of Grants, NM 547 leads some 20 miles into the San Mateo Mountains. The range's high point, and the highest point in the forest, 11,301-foot Mount Taylor, is home of the annual Mount Taylor Winter Quadrathlon in February. The route passes two campgrounds: Lobo Canyon and Coal Mine Canyon. Hiking and enjoying magnificent scenery are popular in summer, cross-country skiing in winter.

JUST THE FACTS For more information about this section of Cíbola National Forest, contact the **Mount Taylor Ranger District,** 1800 Lobo Canyon Rd., Grants, NM 87020 (✆ **505/287-8833**). For general information about all six districts of the National Forest, contact **Cíbola National Forest,** 2113 Osuna Rd. NE, Suite A, Albuquerque, NM 87113-1001 (✆ **505/346-2650;** www.fs.fed.us/r3/cibola).

A modern road stop on I-40 heading west, 17 miles before Gallup, is the **Pilot Travel Center** (✆ **505/722-6655**). This is my idea of what a space station would be like. Not only can you get gas here, you also can also fill up at a Subway. There's also a full restaurant with a salad bar and hot food bar. The center has plenty of pay phones, clean bathrooms, a post office, and a video arcade.

4 GALLUP: GATEWAY TO INDIAN COUNTRY ★

For me, **Gallup** has always been a mysterious place, home to many Native Americans, with dust left from its Wild West days, and with an unmistakable Route 66 architectural presence; it just doesn't seem to exist in this era. The best way to get a sense of the place is by walking around downtown, wandering through the trading posts and pawnshops and by the historic buildings. In doing so, you'll probably encounter many locals and get a real feel for this "Heart of Indian Country."

Gallup began as a town when the railroad from Arizona reached this spot in 1881. At that time, the town consisted of a stagecoach stop and a saloon, the Blue Goose. Within 2 years, coal mining had made the town boom, and some 22 saloons (including the Bucket of Blood) and an opera house filled the town, most of which was inhabited by immigrants from mining areas in eastern Europe, England, Wales, Germany, and Italy.

When the popularity of the railroads declined, Gallup turned briefly to the movie business as its boom ticket. The area's red-rock canyons and lonely deserts were perfect for Westerns of the era, such as *Big Carnival,* with Kirk Douglas; *Four Faces West,* with Joel McCrea; and *The Bad Man,* starring Wallace Beery, Lionel Barrymore, and Ronald Reagan. These stars and many others stayed in a Route 66 hotel built by R. E. Griffith in 1937. Today, the El Rancho Hotel and Motel is one of Gallup's most notable landmarks and worth strolling through (see "Where to Stay in Gallup," and "Where to Dine in Gallup," below). Gallup now relies on trade and tourism, due to its central location within the Navajo Reservation and the Zuni lands, as well as its proximity to the ancient ruins at Chaco.

Gallup's most notable special event is the **Inter-Tribal Indian Ceremonial** held every August. Native Americans converge on the town for a parade, dances, and an all-Indian rodeo east of town, at Red Rock State Park. It's a busy time in Gallup, so make reservations far in advance. If you're not in town for the Ceremonial, try visiting on a Saturday, when many Native Americans come to town to trade. Best of all on this day is the **flea market,** north of town just off US 491. Here you can sample fry bread, Zuni bread, and Acoma bread, eat real mutton stew, and shop for anything from jewelry to underwear. After the flea market, most Gallup-area residents, native and nonnative alike, go to Earl's (see "Where to Dine in Gallup," below) to eat.

ESSENTIALS

GETTING THERE From Albuquerque, take I-40 west (2½ hr.). From Farmington, take US 64 west to Shiprock, and then US 491 south (2½ hr.). From Flagstaff, Arizona, take I-40 east (3 hr.). Gallup is not served by any commercial airlines at this time.

VISITOR INFORMATION The **Gallup–McKinley County Chamber of Commerce,** 103 W. US 66, Gallup, NM 87301 (✆ **800/242-4282** or 505/722-2228; www.thegallupchamber.com), is just south of the main I-40 interchange for downtown Gallup.

WHAT TO SEE & DO

Exploring Gallup

Gallup has 20 buildings that are either listed on or have been nominated to the National Register of Historic Places. Some hold trading posts worth visiting. A good place to start is at the **Santa Fe Railroad Depot,** which also houses the **Gallup Cultural Center ★**, at East 66 Avenue and Strong Street (✆ **505/863-4131**). Built in 1923 in modified Mission style, it has been renovated into a community transportation and cultural center, with a museum worth visiting, as well as a gift shop and diner. Note especially the exhibits on regional history and the Master's Exhibit of paintings, pottery, and basketry from area Native Americans (for more activities see "Sunset Dances," below). The center is open weekdays from 9am to 5pm, often with extended hours in the summer. Across the street, the **Drake Hotel** (later the Turquoise Club but now abandoned), built of blond brick in 1919, had the Prohibition-era reputation of being controlled by bootleggers, with wine running in the faucets in place of water.

The 1928 **White Cafe,** 100 W. 66 Ave., is an elaborate decorative brick structure that catered to the early auto tourist traffic. Now it's a jewelry store. Down the street, the **Eagle Café,** 220 W. 66 Ave. (✆ **505/722-3220**), open since 1920, serves diner food in an authentic atmosphere. A few doors down, **Richardson's Trading Company,** 222 W. 66 Ave. (✆ **505/722-4762;** www.richardsontrading.com), has been selling good Native American arts and crafts since 1913.

The **Rex Hotel,** 300 W. 66 Ave., constructed of locally quarried sandstone, was once known for its "ladies of the night." It's now the **Rex Museum** (✆ **505/863-1363**), a somewhat random display of items from the Gallup Historical Society Collection, but fun for history buffs. It's open daily but with unpredictable hours. Call before setting out.

Gallup's architectural gems include the **Chief Theater,** 228 W. Coal Ave. This structure was built in 1920; in 1936, it was completely redesigned in Pueblo-Deco style, with zigzag relief and geometric form, by R. E. "Griff" Griffith (who also built the El Rancho Hotel), brother of Hollywood producer D. W. Griffith. Now this is **City Electric Shoe Shop** (✆ **505/863-5252;** www.cityelectricshoe.com), where Native Americans go to buy feathers, leather, and other goods to make ceremonial clothing. It's known to locals simply as City Electric, so called because it was the first shop in town to have an automated shoe-repair machine. It also has a good selection of moccasins and hats. Also visit the 1928 **El Morro Theater,** 207 W. Coal Ave., built in Spanish colonial revival style with Spanish baroque plaster carving and bright polychromatic painting; it's where locals come to see movies and dance performances.

Getting Outside: A Nearby Park

Six miles east of downtown Gallup, **Red Rock Park,** NM 566 (P.O. Box 10), Church Rock, NM 87311 (✆ **505/722-3839;** 505/722-3839 for campground), is not part of the New Mexico State Park system, so it doesn't have the fine services you'd expect in those parks. It does have a natural amphitheater set against elegantly shaped red sandstone buttes. It includes an auditorium/convention center, a historical museum, a post office, a trading post, stables, and modern campgrounds.

The 8,000-seat arena is the site of numerous annual events, including the Intertribal Indian Ceremonial in mid-August. Red Rock Convention Center accommodates 600 for trade shows or concert performances.

A nature trail leads up into these stone monuments and makes for a nice break after hours on the road. See "Where to Stay in Gallup," below, for camping information. The park also has a playground, horseback riding trails, and a sports field.

The **Red Rock Museum** has displays on prehistoric Anasazi and modern Zuni, Hopi, and Navajo cultures, including an interesting collection of very intricate katsinas. A gallery features changing exhibits, often locally made crafts such as prayer and dancing fans, pottery, or weavings. It's open year-round 8am to 4:30pm Monday through Friday. There's a suggested donation of $2 for adults, $1 for seniors, and 50¢ for children.

Also at this site, in early December, is the **Red Rock Balloon Rally,** a high point on the sporting balloonist's calendar. For information, call the Gallup–McKinley County Chamber of Commerce (see "Visitor Information," above).

Shopping

Nowhere are the jewelry and crafts of Navajo, Zuni, and Hopi tribes less expensive than in Gallup. The most intriguing places to shop are the trading posts and pawnshops, which provide a surprising range of services for their largely Native American clientele and have little in common with the pawnshops of large U.S. cities.

Navajoland **pawnbrokers** in essence are bankers, at least from the Navajo and Zuni viewpoint. Pawnshops provide safekeeping of valuable personal goods and make small-collateral loans. The trader will hold on to an item for months or even years before deeming it "dead" and putting it up for sale. Fewer than 5% of items ever go unredeemed, but over the years traders do accumulate a selection, so the shops are worth perusing.

Most shops are open Monday through Saturday from 9am to 5pm. For a look at everything from pawn jewelry to Pendleton robes and shawls to enamel and cast-iron kitchenware, visit **Ellis Tanner Trading Company** (✆ **505/863-4434;** www.etanner.com), Hwy. 602 Bypass, south from I-40 on Hwy. 602 about 2 miles; it's at the corner of Nizhoni Boulevard. Also try **Perry Null-Tobe Turpen's Indian Trading Company,** 1710 S. Second St. (✆ **505/722-3806**), farther out on Second Street; it's a big free-standing brick building full of jewelry, rugs, katsinas, and pottery.

Sunset Dances

Every evening Memorial Day to Labor Day, dancers from a variety of area tribes sing, drum, and twirl in a stunning display of ritual from 7 to 8pm. The dances take place at the **Gallup Cultural Center** on East 66 Avenue and Strong Street (✆ **505/863-4131**). Admission to the center and dances is free.

WHERE TO STAY IN GALLUP

Virtually every accommodation in Gallup is somewhere along Route 66, either near the I-40 interchanges or on the highway through downtown.

El Rancho Hotel and Motel ★ This historic hotel owes as much to Hollywood as to Gallup. Built in 1937 by R. E. "Griff" Griffith, brother of movie mogul D. W. Griffith, it became the place for film companies to set up headquarters when filming here. Between the 1940s and 1960s, a who's who of Hollywood stayed here. Their autographed photos line the walls of the hotel's cafe. Spencer Tracy and Katharine Hepburn stayed here during production of *The Sea of Grass;* Burt Lancaster and Lee Remick were guests when they made *The Hallelujah Trail.* The list goes on and on: Gene Autry, Lucille Ball, Jack Benny, Humphrey Bogart, James Cagney, Errol Flynn, Henry Fonda, the Marx Brothers, Ronald Reagan, Rosalind Russell, James Stewart, John Wayne, and Mae West all stayed here.

In 1986, Gallup businessman Armand Ortega, a longtime jewelry merchant, bought the then run-down El Rancho and restored it to its earlier elegance. The lobby staircase rises to the mezzanine on either side of an enormous stone fireplace, while heavy ceiling beams and railings made of tree limbs give the room a hunting-lodge ambience. The hotel is on the National Register of Historic Places.

Rooms in El Rancho differ from one to the next and are named for the stars that stayed in them. Most are long and medium-size, with wagon-wheel headboards and good, heavy pine furniture stained dark. The beds are comfortable. The bathrooms can be small, some with showers, others with tub/shower combos. All have lovely white hexagonal tiles. Many rooms have balconies. Two suites with kitchenettes are also available. My favorite rooms are on the ground floor, which is the quietest part of the hotel. Light sleepers should be aware that the train can be heard from rooms in the upper stories. Wireless Internet and a courtesy computer are available in the lobby.

1000 E. 66 Ave., Gallup, NM 87301. ✆ **800/543-6351** or 505/863-9311. Fax 505/722-5917. www.elranchohotel.com. 99 units. $84–$92 double; $130 suite. AE, DISC, MC, V. Pets welcome. **Amenities:** Restaurant (p. 260); lounge; outdoor pool (in summer); coin-op laundry. *In room:* A/C, TV.

La Quinta ★ The challenge in Gallup is to find a quiet place to sleep. With busy train tracks running right through town, most accommodations stay noisy through the night. Sitting east of town, this is one of the quietest places I've found, but you'll have to reserve carefully. The trick here is to ask for a room on the side of the hotel that faces *away* from the tracks and you'll get a good night's sleep. Rooms are medium-size, with high ceilings and the calming green decor for which this chain is known. The rooms are new and have comfortable beds and fairly spacious bathrooms. A hot breakfast adds to the appeal. On a recent visit I met a couple of professionals who work each month in Gallup and they said this is their choice of lodgings.

675 Scott Ave., Gallup, NM 87401. ✆ **800/531-5900** or 505/327-4706. Fax 505/325-6583. www.laquinta.com. 66 units. $102 double; $138 suite. Rates include hot breakfast. AE, DC, DISC, MC, V. **Amenities:** Outdoor pool; Jacuzzi; guest laundry. *In room:* A/C, TV, fridge, coffeemaker, hair dryer, iron, microwave, high-speed Internet.

Camping

As in the rest of the state, the Gallup area offers plenty of places to pitch a tent or hook up your RV. **USA RV Park** (✆ **505/863-5021;** www.usarvpark.com) has 145 sites, 50 full hookups (cable TV costs extra), and cabins, as well as grocery and laundry facilities. Recreation facilities include arcade games, a seasonal heated swimming pool, and a playground. An outdoor breakfast and dinner are served at an extra cost. Sites range from $21 for tents to $28 for full hookups. Cabins are $37. To reach the campground, take I-40 to the US 66/Business I-40 junction (exit 16); go 1 mile east on US 66/Business I-40.

Red Rock Park campground (✆ **505/722-3839**) has 106 sites—50 with no hookups and 56 with water and electricity. Tent sites are available. Sites range from $20 for tents to $25 for full hookups. The sites are right against the buttes, though in the spring they will surely be dusty because of little protection from the wind. Also accessible are a convenience store, picnic tables, and grills. For more information on Red Rock Park, see "Getting Outside: A Nearby Park," above.

WHERE TO DINE IN GALLUP

Camille's Sidewalk Café SANDWICHES/SALADS New to Gallup, this bright little cafe offers tasty smoothies, sandwiches, and salads that are a bit overpriced. Still, locals seem to enjoy it. Amid lozenge green and orange walls and with formica tables, diners order at a counter and then food is brought to their table. Service is friendly. Be aware that this is semi-fast food, with little cooking going on. Breakfast might bring a wrap with scrambled eggs, bacon or ham, and provolone in a jalapeno-cheddar tortilla. A good lunch option is one of the grilled paninnis, such as the Italian roast beef on focaccia with provolone and pesto-mayo, or a salad such as the apple-walnut tuna with veggies and pepperjack cheese. Soups are available as well.

306 S. 2nd St. ✆ **505/722-5017.** www.camillescafe.com. Main courses $4–$9. AE, DISC, MC, V. Mon–Fri 8am–9pm; Sat–Sun 8–9pm.

Coal Street Pub ★ AMERICAN In the center of downtown, this restaurant serves tasty food in a fun atmosphere full of Gallup memorabilia. Though the owners don't brew their own beer, they do a good job of creating a brewpub atmosphere. Hardwood floors and booths set the tone here along with ceiling fans and a curved bar at the back. Service is good. The big draw is the appetizers and sandwiches. You might start with fried zucchini strips or buffalo chicken wings. For a main course, half-pound burgers are popular, but the big winner is the Monte Cristo—ham, turkey, Swiss, and American on bread lightly battered and fried golden, served with raspberry preserves. At dinner, try the grilled chicken with a salad, sautéed veggies, and baked potato or fries. The pizzas are also good. For dessert, try the cheesecake. Beer and wine accompany the menu.

303 W. Coal Ave. ✆ **505/722-0117.** www.coalstreetpub.com Reservations accepted. Main courses $8–$17. AE, DISC, MC, V. Mon–Sat 11am–10pm.

The Coffee House ★ BAKED GOODS/SANDWICHES This cafe in a historic building in the center of town offers a little big-city flair. Sparse decor with wood tables under an old copper ceiling is accented by local art shows. The espresso and cappuccino are delicious, as are the homemade cookies and muffins. For lunch or dinner, try the turkey and Swiss sandwich, the Waldorf chicken salad, or the homemade red chile chicken *posole* (hominy). Wireless Internet is available.

203 W. Coal Ave. ✆ **505/726-0291.** Reservations not accepted. All menu items under $8. No credit cards. Mon–Thurs 7am–9:30pm; Fri 7am–11pm; Sat 8am–11pm; Sun 10am–4pm.

Earl's ★ Kids AMERICAN/NEW MEXICAN This is where the locals come to eat, particularly on weekends, en route to and from trading in Gallup. The place fills up with a variety of clientele, from college students to Navajo grandmothers. A Denny's-style diner, with comfortable booths and chairs, the restaurant allows Native Americans to sell their wares to you while you eat; however, you have the option of putting up a sign asking not to be disturbed. Often on weekends, vendors set up tables out front, so the whole place takes on a bustling bazaar atmosphere. And the food is good. I recommend the New Mexican dishes such as huevos rancheros, the enchilada plate, or the smothered grande burrito. Earl's offers a kids' menu and half-portion items for smaller appetites, as well as some salads and a "baked potato meal." Open since 1947, Earl's continues to please.

1400 E. 66 Ave. ✆ **505/863-4201.** Reservations accepted except Fri–Sat. Most menu items under $10. AE, MC, V. Mon–Sat 6am–9pm; Sun 7am–9pm.

El Rancho ★ (Moments) (Kids) AMERICAN/NEW MEXICAN Set in the historic El Rancho Hotel (see above), this restaurant has fans all across the Southwest. They come to experience the Old West decor—with well-spaced, heavy wooden furniture and movie memorabilia on the walls—and the sense of the many movie stars who once ate here. The food is fine-diner-style, with dishes such as steak and eggs or hot cakes for breakfast, as well as regional delights, such as *atole* (hot blue-corn cereal) or a breakfast taco. At lunch you can always count on a good burger here or select from a cast of sandwiches, such as the Doris Day (sirloin steak on French bread), or salads. At dinner, steaks are a big hit, as is the grilled salmon, both served with soup or salad, vegetable, and your choice of potato or rice. The New Mexican food is also good. Kids can select from the "little buckaroos" menu. A full bar is available.

In the El Rancho Hotel and Motel, 1000 E. 66 Ave. ✆ **800/543-6351** or 505/863-9311. www.historicelranchohotel.com. Reservations not accepted. Main courses $5–$12 breakfast, $8–$13 lunch, $9–$20 dinner. AE, DISC, MC, V. Daily 6:30am–10pm.

Jerry's Cafe (Value) (Kids) AMERICAN/NEW MEXICAN This is where the locals go to eat New Mexican food. It's a narrow and cozy space with booths on both walls and dark-wood paneling. Usually it's packed with all manner of people, especially Native Americans, filling up on big plates of food smothered in chile sauces. You can't go wrong with any of the New Mexican dishes; I like the scrambled eggs with chile for breakfast. For lunch or dinner, try the flat enchiladas topped with an egg and served with a flour tortilla and *sopaipilla,* or the stuffed *sopaipilla,* with guacamole, beans, and beef, smothered in chile. Jerry's has a children's menu as well as burgers and basic sandwiches. Alcohol isn't served.

406 W. Coal Ave. ✆ **505/722-6775.** Reservations not accepted. Main courses $4–$8 breakfast, $7–$12 lunch and dinner. MC, V. Mon–Sat 8am–9pm.

5 ZUNI PUEBLO & THE NAVAJO RESERVATION

ZUNI PUEBLO

The largest of New Mexico's 19 pueblos, encompassing more than 600 square miles and home to over 11,000 people, Zuni still clings to its traditional language and culture, a great part of which includes art. It's estimated that 80% of its families are involved in creating arts, most notably intricate stone inlay jewelry, carved stone animal fetishes, and katsina figures. Visitors to Zuni will encounter a place that's just beginning to welcome travelers, so don't yet expect to find a great deal to do. The Zuni Arts and Visitor Center (see below) has begun offering tours, so your best bet is to check in there and ask what's available. They range from visits to the Mission, to directions to places to buy traditional oven bread, to archaeological tours.

Zuni has a rich history. When the Spanish first arrived in the area, approximately 3,000 Zunis lived in six different villages, and they had occupied the region since at least the year 700. One of the main villages amid the high pink-and-gold sandstone formations of the area was **Hawikuh.** It was the first Southwestern village to encounter Europeans. In 1539, Fray Marcos de Niza, guided by the Moor Esteban (who had accompanied Cabeza de Baca in his earlier roaming of the area), came to New Mexico in search of the Seven Cities of Cíbola, cities that Baca had said were made of gold, silver, and precious stones. Esteban antagonized the inhabitants and was killed. De Niza was forced to retreat without really seeing the pueblo, although he described it in exaggerated terms on his return to Mexico, and the legend of the golden city was fueled.

The following year Coronado arrived at the village. Though the Zunis took up arms against him, he conquered the village easily, and the Zunis fled to **Towayalane** (Corn Mountain), a noble mile-long sandstone mesa near the present-day pueblo, as they would later do during the 1680 Pueblo Revolt.

At the time, the Zunis had a sophisticated civilization, with a relationship to the land and to each other that had sustained them for years. Today, the tribe continues efforts to preserve its cultural heritage. It has recovered valuable seed strains once used for dryland farming, it's teaching the Zuni language in schools, and it's taking measures to preserve area wildlife that's critical to the Zuni faith.

The Zunis didn't fully accept the Christianity thrust upon them. Occasionally, they burned mission churches and killed priests. Though the Catholic mission, dedicated to Our Lady of Guadalupe, sits in the center of their village, clearly their primary religion is their own ancient one, and it's practiced most notably during the days of **Shalako,** an elaborate ceremony that takes place in late November or early December, reenacting the creation and migration of the Zuni people to Heptina, or the "Middle Place," which was destined to be their home.

Essentials

GETTING THERE Zuni Pueblo is about 38 miles south of Gallup via NM 602 and NM 53.

VISITOR INFORMATION For information, contact the **Zuni Arts and Visitor Center,** P.O. Box 339, Zuni, NM 87327 (✆ **505/782-7238;** www.zunitourism.com). This is the place to buy photography permits and inquire about pueblo tours and directions to sites. As at all Indian reservations, visitors are asked to respect tribal customs and individuals' privacy. No sketching or painting is allowed, but photography ($10 fee) and filming ($20 fee) are permitted. Although the pueblo is never completely closed to outside visitors, certain areas may be off-limits during ceremonies, and photography may be prohibited at times.

ADMISSION FEES & HOURS Admission is free, and visitors are welcome daily from dawn to dusk.

Seeing the Highlights

As you make your way around, you'll find a mix of buildings—modern ones, along with traditional adobes, and 100-year-old structures made from red carved sandstone. The

Old Zuni Mission (Our Lady of Guadalupe Mission), on Old Mission Drive (✆ **505/782-7238**), was first built in 1629, then destroyed during the Pueblo Revolt, and rebuilt in 1699. It was renovated in 1966, but currently is in need of a major restoration. It's most famed for life-size murals of Katsinas by Zuni Alex Seowtewa, which are now at the center of controversy over how to restore them. It's fronted by a picturesque cemetery. Contact the number above to see if a tour of the interior is available.

In addition, some Native American archaeological ruins on Zuni land date from the early 1200s, but you must obtain permission from the Visitor Center to see them. The **A:shiwi A:wan Museum and Heritage Center,** 1222 NM 53 (✆ **505/782-4403**), offers a glimpse into traditional Zuni culture. An exhibit under the auspices of the museum, "Echoes from the Past," set in a building in the heart of Zuni, presents artifacts from Hawikuh (on loan from the Smithsonian Institute). The main museum is open weekdays, year-round, from 9am to 5:30pm (same hours on Sat during the summer). Admission is free. Call first to be sure it is open and to ask for directions.

Today, Zuni tribal members are widely acclaimed for their jewelry, made from turquoise, shell, and jet, set in silver in intricate patterns called "needlepoint." The tribe also does fine beadwork, carving in shell and stone, and some pottery. Jewelry and other crafts are sold at the tribally owned **Pueblo of Zuni Arts and Crafts,** 1222 NM 53 (✆ **505/782-5531**). Look especially for the hand-carved fetishes as well as the acclaimed needlepoint jewelry. At this writing, it is open only weekdays from 9am to 5pm.

If you're planning your visit for late August, call ahead and find out if you're going to be around during the pueblo's annual fair and rodeo.

Where to Stay in Zuni

Inn at Halona *Finds* Situated in the center of Zuni, this inn provides a peek into Zuni life. The inn itself fills two homes—one built in 1920, the other in 1940. I recommend the main house (built in 1920) as it's the brighter of the two and was remodeled in 1998. Both are filled with local art and decorated with handcrafted furniture. Most rooms are fairly small, and some rooms share bathrooms, so you'll want to reserve accordingly. All rooms have good linens and comfortably firm beds. My favorite, the Penthouse Room, is small but very sunny and quaint. Over a full and delicious breakfast served family-style in the dining room or out on the lovely patio, innkeepers Roger Thomas and Elaine Dodson Thomas will delight you with stories of living at Zuni, where Elaine's Dutch family started the first trading post in 1903. Basic food is available in the trading post store.

23B Pia Mesa Rd. (P.O. Box 446), Zuni, NM 87327-0446. ✆ **800/752-3278** or 505/782-4547. Fax 505/782-2155. www.halona.com. 8 units. $84 double. $10 for each extra person. Rates include full breakfast. MC, V.

NAVAJO INDIAN RESERVATION

Navajos comprise the largest Native American tribe in the United States, with more than 200,000 members. Their reservation, known to them as Navajoland, spreads across 26,000 square miles of Arizona, Utah, and New Mexico. The New Mexico portion, extending in a band 45 miles wide from just north of Gallup to the Colorado border, comprises only about 15% of the total area.

Until the 1920s, the Navajo Nation governed itself with a complex clan system. When oil was discovered on reservation land, the Navajos established a tribal government to handle the complexities of the 20th century. Today, the Navajo Tribal Council has 88 council delegates representing 110 regional chapters, some two dozen of which are in New

Mexico. They meet at least four times a year as a full body in Window Rock, Arizona, capital of the Navajo Nation, near the New Mexico border, 24 miles northwest of Gallup.

Natural resources and tourism are the mainstays of the Navajo economy. Coal, oil, gas, and uranium earn much of the Navajo Nation's money, as does tourism, especially on the Arizona side of the border, which contains or abuts Grand Canyon National Park, Petrified Forest National Park, Canyon de Chelly National Monuments, Wupatki National Monuments, Navajo National Monument, and Monument Valley Navajo Tribal Park; and in Utah, Glen Canyon National Recreation Area, Rainbow Bridge National Monuments, Hovenweep National Monument, and Four Corners Monument.

The Navajos, like their linguistic cousins the Apaches, belong to the large family of Athapaskan Indians found across Alaska and northwestern Canada and in parts of the Northern California coast. They are believed to have migrated to the Southwest around the 14th century. In 1864, after nearly 2 decades of conflict with the U.S. Army, the entire tribe was rounded up and forced into internment at an agricultural colony near Fort Sumner, New Mexico—an event still recalled as "the Long March." Four years of near starvation later, the experiment was declared a failure, and the Navajos returned to their homeland.

During World War II, 320 Navajo young men served in the U.S. Marine Corps as communications specialists in the Pacific. The code they created, 437 terms based on the extremely complex Navajo language, was never cracked by the Japanese. Among those heroes was artist Carl Gorman, coordinator of the Navajo Medicine Man Organization and father of internationally famed painter R. C. Gorman. The 2002 movie *Windtalkers,* starring Nicholas Cage, was based on their story.

Although Navajos express themselves artistically in all media, they are best known for their work in silversmithing, sand painting, basketry, and weaving. Distinctive styles of hand-woven rugs from Two Grey Hills, Ganado, and Crystal are known worldwide.

Essentials

GETTING THERE From Gallup, US 491 goes directly through the Navajo Indian Reservation up to Shiprock. From there you can head over to Farmington (see "Farmington & Environs," below) on US 64. ***Warning:*** US 491, previously labeled US 666, running between Gallup and Shiprock, has been called America's "most dangerous highway" by *USA Today.* In hopes of changing the fate of what many called the "Devil's Highway," the name was changed to a more benign set of numbers. Even with the new designation, you'll want to drive carefully!

VISITOR INFORMATION For information before your trip, contact the **Navajo Tourism Department,** P.O. Box 663, Window Rock, AZ 86515 (✆ **928/871-6436;** www.discovernavajo.com).

What to See & Do

Attractions in Window Rock, Arizona, include the Navajo Nation Council Chambers; the Navajo Nation Arts and Crafts Enterprise; the Navajo Museum, Library, and Visitors Center; and Window Rock Tribal Park, containing the natural red-rock arch after which the community is named.

Nearby attractions include **Hubbell Trading Post National Historic Site** (✆ **928/755-3254;** www.nps.gov/hutr), on Arizona 264, a half mile west of AZ 191, at Ganado, 30 miles west of Window Rock, and **Canyon de Chelly National Monument** (✆ **928/674-5500**), 39 miles north of Ganado on U.S. 191, at Chinle.

Five Hunnerd, Six Hunnerd, Sold!

The **Crownpoint Rug Weavers Association** ★ holds 12 public auctions a year, normally on Friday evening, about 5 weeks apart. Travelers come from all over the world to sit in the stuffy Crownpoint Elementary School gymnasium (drive 20 miles north of I-40 on NM 371, turn west on Indian Rte. 9, and drive a half mile) and bid on lovely rugs made throughout the Southwest. Prices are good, and the bidding can get exciting. Indian tacos and sodas are offered for sale outside. For more information, call ✆ **505/786-7386;** www.crownpointrugauction.com.

In early September, the annual 5-day **Navajo Nation Fair** (✆ **928/871-6478;** www.navajonationfair.com) attracts more than 100,000 people to Window Rock for a huge rodeo, parade, carnival, Miss Navajo Nation contest, arts-and-crafts shows, intertribal powwow, concerts, country dancing, and agricultural exhibits. It's the country's largest Native American fair. A smaller but older and more traditional annual tribal fair is the early October **Northern Navajo Nation Fair** (✆ **505/368-1315**), held 90 miles north of Gallup in the town of Shiprock.

Where to Stay & Dine on the Navajo Indian Reservation

The place to stay on the reservation is the **Quality Inn Navajo Nation Capital,** 48 W. Hwy. 264 (P.O. Box 2340), Window Rock, AZ 86515 (✆ **928/871-4108**). The modern guest rooms are comfortable and moderately priced (a double costs $88), and the restaurant offers Navajo specialties.

6 CHACO CULTURE NATIONAL HISTORICAL PARK ★★★

A combination of a stunning setting and well-preserved ruins makes the long drive to **Chaco Culture National Historic Park,** often referred to as Chaco Canyon, worth the trip. Whether you come from the north or south, you drive in on a dusty (and sometimes muddy) road that seems to add to the authenticity and adventure of this remote New Mexico experience.

When you finally arrive, you walk through stark desert country that seems perhaps ill suited as a center of culture. However, the ancestral Puebloan (Anasazi) people successfully farmed the lowlands and built great masonry towns, which connected with other towns over a wide-ranging network of roads crossing this desolate place.

What's most interesting here is how changes in architecture—beginning in the mid-800s, when the Anasazi started building on a larger scale than they had previously—chart the area's cultural progress. The Anasazi used the same masonry techniques that tribes had used in smaller villages in the region (walls one stone thick, with generous use of mud mortar), but they built stone villages of multiple stories with rooms several times larger than in the previous stage of their culture. Within a century, six large pueblos were underway. This pattern of a single large pueblo with oversize rooms, surrounded by conventional villages, caught on throughout the region. New communities built along these lines sprang up. Old villages built similarly large pueblos. Eventually there were more than 75 such towns, most of them closely tied to Chaco by an extensive system of roads. Aerial photos show hundreds of miles of roads connecting these towns with the Chaco pueblos, one of the longest running 42 miles straight north to Salmon Ruins and the Aztec Ruins. It is this road network that leads some scholars to believe that Chaco was the center of a unified Anasazi society.

This progress led to Chaco becoming the economic center of the San Juan Basin by A.D. 1000. As many as 5,000 people may have lived in some 400 settlements in and around Chaco. As masonry techniques advanced through the years, walls rose more than four stories in height. Some of these are still visible today.

Chaco's decline after 1½ centuries of success coincided with a drought in the San Juan Basin between A.D. 1130 and 1180. Scientists still argue vehemently over why the site was abandoned and where the Chacoans went. Many believe that an influx of outsiders may have brought new rituals to the region, causing a schism among tribal members. Most agree, however, that the people drifted away to more hospitable places in the region and that their descendants are today's Pueblo people.

This is an isolated area, and there are **no services** available within or close to the park—no food, gas, auto repairs, firewood, lodging (besides the campground), or drinking water (other than at the visitor center) are available. Overnight camping is permitted year-round. If you're headed toward Santa Fe after a day at the park and looking for a place to spend the night, one nice option is the **Cañon del Rio–A Riverside Inn,** 16445 Scenic Hwy. 4, Jemez Springs, NM 87025 (✆ **505/829-4377;** www.canondelrio.com; p. 118).

ESSENTIALS

GETTING THERE To get to Chaco from Santa Fe, take I-25 south to Bernalillo and then US 550 northwest. Turn off US 550 at CR 7900 (3 miles southeast of Nageezi and about 50 miles west of Cuba at mile 112.5). Follow the signs from US 550 to the park boundary (21 miles). This route includes 8 miles of paved road (CR 7900) and 13 miles of rough dirt road (CR 7950). This is the recommended route. NM 57 from Blanco Trading Post is closed. The trip takes about 3½ to 4 hours. Farmington is the nearest population center, a 1½-hour drive away. The park can also be reached from Grants via I-40 west to NM 371, which you follow north to Indian Route 9, east, and north again on NM 57 (IR 14), with the final 19 miles ungraded dirt. This route is rough to impassable and is not recommended for RVs.

Whichever way you come, call ahead to inquire about **road conditions** (✆ **505/786-7014**) before leaving the paved highways. The dirt roads can get extremely muddy and dangerous after rain or snow, and afternoon thunderstorms are common in late summer. Roads often flood when it rains.

VISITOR INFORMATION Ranger-guided walks and campfire talks are available in the summer at the visitor center where you can get self-guiding trail brochures and permits for the overnight campground (see "Camping," below). If you want information before you leave home, contact the Superintendent, Chaco Culture National Historical Park, 1808 County Rd. 7950, Nageezi, NM 87037 (✆ **505/786-7014;** www.nps.gov/chcu).

ADMISSION FEES & HOURS Admission is $8 per car; a campsite is $10 extra. The visitor center is open daily from 8am to 5pm. Trails are open from sunrise to sunset.

SEEING THE HIGHLIGHTS

Exploring the ruins and hiking are the most popular activities here. A series of pueblo ruins stands within 5 or 6 miles of each other on the broad, flat, treeless canyon floor.

Plan to spend at least 3 to 4 hours here driving to and exploring the different pueblos. A one-way road from the visitor center loops up one side of the canyon and down the other. Parking lots are scattered along the road near the various pueblos; from most, it's only a short walk to the ruins.

You may want to focus your energy on seeing **Pueblo Bonito,** the largest prehistoric Southwest Native American dwelling ever excavated. It contains giant kivas and 800 rooms covering more than 3 acres. Also, the **Pueblo Alto Trail** is a nice hike that takes you up on the canyon rim so that you can see the ruins from above—in the afternoon, with thunderheads building, the views are spectacular. If you're a cyclist, stop at the visitor center to pick up a map outlining ridable trails.

WHERE TO STAY & DINE

If you're driving from the northwest, your best bet is to stay in the Farmington/Aztec area. However, if you're driving on US 550 from Albuquerque, you have limited options. The town of Cuba (pop. 600) offers good dining and okay accommodations. You may want to plan your drive to stop for lunch at **El Bruno's Restaurante y Cantina,** 6453 Main St. (US 550), in the center of Cuba (✆ **575/289-9429**). Within an adobe building with ceiling vigas and Mexican leather furniture, and with a lovely patio, this place serves good New Mexican food and steaks. It's open daily 11am to 10pm. Diners can order from a full bar. Meanwhile, the lodging situation in this little town isn't quite so bright. Your only option here, really, is the **Frontier Motel,** on US 550 (✆ **505/289-3474**). This place straddling both sides of the highway offers clean rooms to travelers. Be sure to get one on the south side of the highway, which is more upscale. Rooms have decent furnishings, fairly comfortable beds, and small baths. Most have a fridge and microwave. Prices range from $45 to $60.

CAMPING

Gallo Campground, within the park, is quite popular with hikers. It's about 1 mile east of the visitor center; fees are $10 per night. The campground has 48 sites (group sites are also available), with fire grates (bring your own wood or charcoal), central toilets, and nonpotable water. Drinking water is available only at the visitor center. The campground cannot accommodate trailers over 30 feet.

As I said above, there's no place to stock up on supplies once you start the arduous drive to the canyon, so if you're camping, make sure you're well supplied, especially with water, before you head out.

7 FARMINGTON & ENVIRONS

Farmington has historic and outdoor finds that can keep you occupied for at least a day or two. It sits at the junction of the San Juan, Animas, and La Plata rivers. Adorned with arched globe willow trees, it's a lush place by New Mexico standards. A system of five parks along the San Juan River and its tributaries is its pride and joy. What's most notable for me, however, is the quaint downtown area, where century-old buildings still house thriving businesses and some trading posts with great prices. It's also an industrial center (coal, oil, natural gas, and hydroelectricity) and a shopping center for people within a 100-mile radius.

For visitors, Farmington is a takeoff point for explorations of the Navajo Reservation and Chaco Culture National Historical Park. For outdoors lovers, it's the spot to head to the Bisti/De-Na-Zin Wilderness; world-class fly-fishing on the San Juan River; lovely scenery at the Angel Peak Recreation Area; and even a trip up to Durango to enjoy some rafting, kayaking, skiing, and mountain biking. The nearby towns of Aztec and Bloomfield offer a variety of attractions as well.

ESSENTIALS

GETTING THERE From Albuquerque, take US 550 (through Cuba) from the I-25 Bernalillo exit, and then head west on US 64 at Bloomfield (45 min.). From Gallup, take US 491 north to Shiprock, and then head east on US 64 (2¼ hr.). From Taos, follow US 64 all the way (4½ hr.). From Durango, Colorado, take US 500 south (1 hr.).

All commercial flights arrive at busy **Four Corners Regional Airport** on West Navajo Drive (✆ **505/599-1395**). The principal carrier is **Great Lakes Airlines** (✆ **800/554-5111;** www.flygreatlakes.com).

Car-rental agencies at Four Corners Regional Airport include **Avis** (✆ **800/331-1212** or 505/327-9864), **Budget** (✆ **505/327-7304**), and **Hertz** (✆ **800/654-3131** or 505/327-6093).

VISITOR INFORMATION The **Farmington Convention and Visitors Bureau,** 3041 E. Main St. (✆ **800/448-1240** or 505/326-7602; www.farmingtonnm.org), is the clearinghouse for tourist information for the Four Corners region. For more information, contact the **Farmington Chamber of Commerce,** 100 W. Broadway (✆ **505/325-0279;** www.gofarmington.com).

SEEING THE SIGHTS IN THE AREA

In Farmington

Farmington Museum and Gateway Center (Kids) Small-town museums can be completely precious, and this one and its neighbor in Aztec (see below) typify a tiny part of the world, but the truths they reveal span continents. Here you get to see the everyday struggle of a people to support themselves within a fairly inhospitable part of the world, spanning boom and bust years of agriculture, oil and gas production, and tourism. Located in the slick Gateway Visitor Center, exhibits vary, utilizing over 7,000 objects. You may walk through displays of a 1930s trading post, with an old enameled scale, cloth bolts, and vintage saddles. Next, you can tour the Dinosaurs to Drill Bits exhibit, exploring the region's rich oil and gas history of the area, including a 7-minute ride in the **Geovator,** which simulates a trip 7,285 feet into an oil well. Kids enjoy this! Excellent changing exhibits rotate through as well. A gift shop sells fun local art and some nice New Mexico–made crafts.

3041 E. Main St. ✆ **505/599-1174.** Fax 505/326-7572. www.farmingtonmuseum.org. Free admission. Mon–Sat 8am–5pm.

In Nearby Aztec

VISITOR INFORMATION The **Aztec Chamber of Commerce,** 110 N. Ash St. (✆ **505/334-9551;** www.aztecchamber.com), is a friendly place with a wealth of information about the area.

Aztec Museum and Pioneer Village (Kids) A real treat for kids, this museum and village transport visitors back over a century to a place populated by strangely ubiquitous mannequins. The museum is crammed with memorabilia, but the outer **Pioneer Village**

of replicas and real buildings, with all the trimmings, is what will hold interest. You'll walk through the actual 1912 Aztec jail—nowhere you'd want to live—into the sheriff's office, where a stuffed Andy of Mayberry look-alike is strangely lethargic. The blacksmith shop has an anvil and lots of dusty, uncomfortable-looking saddles, even some oddly shaped burro shoes. The Citizens Bank has a lovely oak cage and counter, and it's run by attentive mannequin women. You'll see an authentic 1906 church and a schoolhouse where mannequins Dick and Jane lead a possibly heated discussion. New additions include a farmhouse and historic drilling rigs. The second Saturday in September the museum celebrates Founders' Day, with living exhibits, food, and games.

125 N. Main Ave., Aztec. ✆ **505/334-9829.** www.aztecmuseum.org. Admission $3 adults, $1 children 11–17, free for children 10 and under. Summer Wed–Sat 10am–4pm; winter variable hours, see website.

In Nearby Bloomfield

Salmon Ruins ★ Kids What really marks the 150 rooms of these ruins 11 miles west of Farmington near Bloomfield is their setting on a hillside, surrounded by lush San Juan River bosque. You'll begin in the museum, though, where a number of informative displays range from one showing the variety of types of ancestral Puebloan vessels, from pitchers to canteens, to wild plants. Like the ruins at Aztec, two strong architectural influences are visible here. First the Chacoan, who built the village around the 11th century, with walls of an intricate rubble-filled core with sandstone veneer. The more simple Mesa Verde masonry was added in the 13th century. A trail guide will lead you to each site.

Built in 1990, **Heritage Park,** on an adjoining plot of land, comprises a series of reconstructed ancient and historic dwellings representing the area's cultures, from a paleoarchaic sand-dune site to an Anasazi pit house, from Apache wickiups and tepees to Navajo hogans, and an original pioneer homestead. Visitors are encouraged to enter the re-creations.

In the visitor center, you'll find a gift shop and a scholarly research library.

6131 US 64 (P.O. Box 125), Bloomfield, NM 87413. ✆ **505/632-2013.** Fax 505/632-8633. www.salmonruins.com. Admission $3 adults, $1 children 6–16, $2 seniors, free for children 5 and under. Summer Mon–Fri 8am–5pm, Sat–Sun 9am–5pm; winter Mon–Fri 8am–5pm, Sat 9am–5pm, and Sun noon–5pm.

AZTEC RUINS NATIONAL MONUMENT ★

These ruins offer an exciting and rare glimpse of a restored kiva, which visitors can enter and sit within, sensing the site's ancient history. The ruins of this 450-room Native American pueblo, left by the ancestral Puebloans 7 centuries ago, are 14 miles northeast of Farmington, in the town of Aztec on the Animas River. Early Anglo settlers, convinced that the ruins were of Aztec origin, misnamed the site. Despite the fact that this pueblo was built long before the Aztecs of central Mexico lived, the name persisted.

The influence of the Chaco culture is strong at Aztec, as evidenced in the preplanned architecture, the open plaza, and the fine stone masonry in the old walls. But a later occupation shows the influence of Mesa Verde (which flourished 1200–75). This second group of settlers remodeled the old pueblo and built others nearby, using techniques less elaborate and decorative than those of the Chacoans. Aztec Ruins is best known for its Great Kiva, the only completely reconstructed Anasazi great kiva in existence. Visiting Aztec Ruins National Monument will take you approximately 1 hour, even if you take the .25-mile self-guided trail and spend some time in the visitor center, which displays some outstanding examples of Anasazi ceramics and basketry. Add another half-hour if you plan to watch the video that imaginatively documents the history of native cultures in the area.

Essentials

GETTING THERE Aztec Ruins is approximately a half mile north of US 550 on Ruins Road (C.R. 2900) on the north edge of the city of Aztec. Ruins Road is the first street immediately west of the Animas River Bridge on Hwy. 516 in Aztec.

VISITOR INFORMATION For more information, contact **Aztec Ruins National Monument,** 84 C.R. 2900, Aztec, NM 87410-0640 (✆ **505/334-6174,** ext. 30; www.nps.gov/azru).

ADMISSION FEES & HOURS Admission is $5 for adults; children under 17 are admitted free. The monument is open daily from 8am to 6pm Memorial Day through Labor Day and 8am to 5pm the rest of the year; it's closed Thanksgiving, Christmas, and New Year's Day.

Camping

Camping is not permitted at the monument. Nearby, **Bloomfield KOA,** on Blanco Boulevard (✆ **800/562-8513** or 505/632-8339; www.koa.com), offers 83 sites, 73 full hookups, tenting, cabins, laundry and grocery facilities, picnic tables, grills, and firewood. The recreation room/area has arcade games, a heated swimming pool, a basketball hoop, a playground, horseshoes, volleyball, and a hot tub.

Camping is also available at **Navajo Lake State Park** (✆ **505/632-2278**).

Shopping

Downtown Farmington shops are generally open from 10am to 6pm Monday through Saturday. Native American arts and crafts are best purchased at trading posts, either downtown on Main or Broadway streets, or west of Farmington on US 64 toward Shiprock. You may want to check out the following stores: One of the best in the city is

Historic Art Stroll

Northwestern New Mexico's lush green fields and mild (mostly) climate are attracting more and more artists. A great place to sample some of the lively work is **Artifacts Gallery,** 302 E. Main St. (✆ **505/327-2907;** www.artifacts-gallery.com) in Farmington. Set in a Victorian-style lumber building is a collection of art studios whose artists are often on hand to discuss their work. Just down the street, step into **Andrea Kristina's Bookstore & Kafé,** 218 W. Main St. (✆ **505/327-3313;** www.andreakristinas.com). This lively place, in a historic building with tables set amid bookshelves, has a great selection of books and offers live music, poetry, and films on Friday and Saturday nights from 7 to 9pm. A range of coffee drinks and soups, salads, sandwiches, and pizza dress the menu. It's open Monday to Friday 7am to 9pm and Saturday 8am to 10pm. In nearby Aztec, stop in at **Feat of Clay,** 107 S. Main St. (✆ **505/334-4335**). A cooperative gallery, it holds the work of 14 local artists and has great prices. Look for "Molten Treasures," glass jewelry by Jinx Bolli. While in Aztec be sure to take some time to stroll through the town's newly renovated 19th-century **historic district.**

 Fifth Generation Trading Company ★, 232 W. Broadway (✆ **505/326-3211;** www.tannertrading.com). Trading since 1875, the Tanner family offers jewelry, Navajo rugs, pottery, alabaster sculptures, old pawn, and katsinas (kachinas). **Bob French Navajo Rugs,** on US 64 18 miles west of Farmington (✆ **505/598-5621;** www.bobfrenchnavajorugs.com), sells silver and turquoise jewelry and a range of antique and new rugs. **Hogback Trading Company,** 3221 US 64, Waterflow, 17 miles west of Farmington (✆ **505/598-5154**), has large displays of Indian jewelry, rugs, and folk art. And **Navajo Trading Company,** 126 E. Main St. (✆ **505/325-1685**), is an actual pawnshop, with lots of exquisite old jewelry; you can peruse bracelets and necklaces while listening to clerks speaking Navajo.

GETTING OUTSIDE: NEARBY PARKS & RECREATION AREAS

Shiprock Peak

This distinctive landmark, on the Navajo Indian Reservation southwest of Shiprock, 29 miles west of Farmington via US 64, is known to the Navajo as *Tse bidá hi,* "Rock with wings." Composed of igneous rock flanked by long upright walls of solidified lava, it rises 1,700 feet off the desert floor to an elevation of 7,178 feet. There are scenic viewing points off US 491, 6 to 7 miles south of the town of Shiprock. You can get closer by taking the tribal road to the community of Red Rock, but you must have permission to get any nearer to this sacred Navajo rock. Climbing is not permitted.

The town named after the rock is a gateway to the Navajo reservation and the Four Corners region. There's a tribal visitor center here.

From Shiprock, you may want to make the 32-mile drive west on US 64 to Teec Nos Pos, Arizona, and then north on US 160, to the **Four Corners Monument** (✆ **928/871-6647;** www.navajonationsparks.org). A concrete slab here sits astride the only point in the United States where four states meet: New Mexico, Colorado, Utah, and Arizona. Kids especially like the idea of standing at the center and occupying four states at once. There's no view here, but vendors sell crafts and food. Some people find a visit here not worth the trip or cost. The monument is open daily 7am to 8pm Memorial Day to Labor Day and 8am to 5pm the rest of the year. The cost is $3 per person for all ages.

Navajo Lake State Park

The **San Juan River, Pine River,** and **Sims Mesa recreation sites,** all with camping, fishing, and boating, make this the most popular watersports destination for residents of northwestern New Mexico. Trout, northern pike, largemouth bass, and catfish are caught in lake and river waters, and the surrounding hills attract hunters seeking deer and elk. A visitor center at Pine River Recreation Area has interpretive displays on natural history and on the construction and use of the dam.

Navajo Lake, with an area of 15,000 acres, extends from the confluence of the San Juan and Los Pinos rivers 25 miles north into Colorado. Navajo Dam, an earthen embankment, is three-quarters of a mile long and 400 feet high. It provides Farmington-area cities, industries, and farms with their principal water supply. It's also the main storage reservoir for the Navajo Indian Irrigation Project, designed to irrigate 110,000 acres.

Anglers come from all over the world to fish the San Juan below the dam, a pastoral spot bordered by green hills, where golden light reflects off the water. Much of the water is designated "catch and release" and is teeming with rainbow, brown, and cutthroat

Kids Wet & Wild

If tromping through ruins and across desert sand has left you parched, head to the **Farmington Aquatic Center,** 1151 N. Sullivan (✆ **505/599-1167;** www.fmtn.org). Serious swimmers can do laps in an Olympic-size pool, while the kids play in their own large one, with slides and jungle-gym type games. It's open daily 1 to 4pm and Monday to Saturday 4:30 to 7:30pm in summer; Monday, Wednesday, and Friday 4:30 to 7:30pm and Wednesday 1 to 4pm in winter. Admission costs $5 for adults, $4.50 for teens 13 to 18, $3.25 for kids 3 to 12, and free for those under 3.

trout. Experts will be heartily challenged by these fish that are attuned to the best tricks, while amateurs may want to hire a guide. For more information, see "Northwestern New Mexico's Great Outdoors," earlier in this chapter. The park is 40 miles east of Farmington on NM 511. For more information, call ✆ **505/632-2278.**

Not far from the park, **Wines of the San Juan,** 233 NM 511 at Turley (✆ **505/632-0879;** www.winesofthesanjuan.com), offers wine tastings and sells bottles of wines ranging from merlot to malvasia bianca. Call ahead to find out about the Sunday programs offered spring through fall, which might include flamenco guitar. The last weekend in September, the winery holds a festival featuring several bands and arts-and-crafts booths. The tasting room is open Monday to Saturday 10am to 6pm and Sunday noon to 6pm. Closed Tuesday.

Angel Peak Recreation Area

The distinctive pinnacle of 6,991-foot Angel Peak can often be spotted from the hillsides around Farmington. The area offers a short nature trail and a variety of unusual, colorful geological formations and canyons to explore on foot. The Bureau of Land Management has developed a primitive campground with nine campsites and provided picnic tables in a few spots, but no drinking water is available here. The park is about 35 miles south of Farmington on US 550; the last 6 miles of access, after turning off US 550, are over a graded dirt road. For more information on the park, call ✆ **505/599-8900.**

Bisti/De-Na-Zin Wilderness

Often referred to as Bisti Badlands (pronounced Bist-*eye*), this barren region may merit that name today, but it was once very different. Around 70 million years ago, large dinosaurs lived near what was then a coastal swamp, bordering a retreating inland sea. Today, their bones, and those of fish, turtles, lizards, and small mammals, are eroding slowly from the low shale hills.

Kirtland Shale, containing several bands of color, dominates the eastern part of the wilderness and caps the mushroom-shaped formations found there. Along with the spires and fanciful shapes of rock, hikers may find petrified wood sprinkled in small chips throughout the area, or even an occasional log. Removing petrified wood, fossils, or anything else from the wilderness is prohibited.

Hiking in the Bisti is fairly easy; from the small parking lot, follow an arroyo east 2 or 3 miles into the heart of the formations, which you'll see on your right (aim for the two red hills). The De-Na-Zin Wilderness to the east requires more climbing and navigational skills. It has no designated trails, bikes and motorized vehicles are prohibited, and it has no water or significant shade. The hour just after sunset or, especially, just before sunrise is a pleasant and quite magical time to see this starkly beautiful landscape. Primitive camping is allowed, but bring plenty of water and other supplies.

Bisti/De-Na-Zin Wilderness is just off NM 371, 37 miles south of Farmington. For more information, call the **Bureau of Land Management** at ✆ **505/599-8900.**

WHERE TO STAY IN FARMINGTON & AZTEC

Courtyard by Marriott ★ (Kids) This newer hotel provides elegant rooms and all the amenities of a full-service inn, with the consistency you'd expect from Marriott. The expansive lobby looking out over Riverwalk Park is decorated in a Southwestern style. Just off it is a quiet lounge and a restaurant. The style carries into the rooms. They are spacious with comfortable beds and medium-size bathrooms with outer vanities. Southwestern landscape paintings adorn the walls. The suites are large and contain one bedroom and a living room with a foldout couch, wet bar, and microwave—a good choice for small families.

560 Scott Ave., Farmington, NM 87401. ✆ **800/228-9290** or 505/325-5111. Fax 505/325-5588. www.marriott.com. 125 units. $89–$105 double; $125–$130 suite. AE, DC, DISC, MC, V. **Amenities:** Restaurant; bar; indoor pool w/sun deck; exercise room; Jacuzzi; room service; coin-op laundry; same-day dry cleaning. *In room:* A/C, TV, high-speed Internet, Wi-Fi, coffeemaker, hair dryer, iron.

Soaring Eagle Lodge ★ (Finds) This lodge offers basic and clean cabins on a poetic bend of the San Juan River. It's mostly a place for fishing enthusiasts, who come to ply these world-renowned waters, but those seeking to escape to the quiet of a lovely river would like it too. Each cabin has a kitchenette, partitioned-off bedroom space, and a front room with two easy chairs. Beds are comfortable and bathrooms very clean. A restaurant on-site serves tasty breakfasts and dinners. Be sure to reserve a cabin on the river edge where the views couldn't be finer. The lodge can set you up with a guide, and you may fish for free from shore on the lodge's private waters. Wireless Internet is available in the conference room.

48 C.R. 4370, off NM 511, Navajo Dam, NM, 87419. ✆ **800/866-2719** or 505/632-5621. www.soaringeaglelodge.net. 11 units. $156 per person, double. Price includes a full breakfast and fishing privileges. MC, V. **Amenities:** Restaurant; conference room; guide service. *In room:* A/C, TV, fridge, microwave, coffeemaker.

Step Back Inn ★ This inn imparts a bit of Victorian charm to its fairly standard rooms. It's a friendly place offering iced tea and lemonade in their parlor throughout the day. Rooms are well planned and functional, with comfortable beds and medium-size bathrooms, as well as plenty of quiet. They also have pretty touches such as wallpaper, a recliner, and early American antique replica armoires, which hold the televisions. Each is named after a pioneer family of the area, some of whom are the ancestors of the hotel's owner, and each room includes a small booklet that tells their stories. Breakfast brings a warm, delicious cinnamon roll as large as a plate, served in a tearoom. Wireless Internet is available in some rooms and a dataport is available in the parlor.

123 W. Aztec Blvd., Aztec, NM 87410. ✆ **800/334-1255** or 505/334-1200. 39 units. May 15–Nov 1 $98 double; Nov 2–May 14 $78 double. Rates include cinnamon roll, juice, and coffee. AE, MC, V. *In room:* A/C, TV, hair dryer.

Bed & Breakfasts

Casa Blanca ★★★ (Finds) (Kids) This B&B offers such nice rooms, it's a travel destination. In a quiet residential neighborhood just a few blocks from the shops and restaurants of Main Street, this inn, built in the 1940s, was once the home of a wealthy family that traded with the Navajos. In 2004, new owners expanded it, adding patios and fountains, creating a lovely oasis. The large rooms, decorated in an elegant Southwestern style, have original artwork and plenty of amenities. My favorite room is the Chaco, with red-brick floors, authentic Navajo rugs, and antique furnishings. Also of note is the Vista Grande, a large upstairs room with views in every direction. Travelers with disabilities are treated especially well here (there are two large suites especially for them), as are business travelers (there's high-speed and wireless Internet, a courtesy computer, and a meeting room). The full breakfast is always gourmet. Ask about their lovely two-bedroom, two-bath cottage, with a full kitchen, a great place for families, marked by the same elegance as the rest of the inn.

505 E. La Plata St., Farmington, NM 87401. ✆ **800/550-6503** or 505/327-6503. Fax 505/326-5680. www.casablancanm.com. 8 units. $125–$215 double; $20 single-traveler discount. Rates include full breakfast. AE, MC, V. *In room:* A/C, TV, high-speed Internet, Wi-Fi, fridge, coffeemaker, hair dryer, iron, microwave.

Kokopelli's Cave ★★ Retired geologist Bruce Black wanted to build a cave, so he gave some laid-off Grants miners $20,000 to bore as deeply as they could into the side of a cliff face. This luxury apartment was the result. Built in a semicircle, both the entry hall and the bedroom have wide sliding glass doors leading to little balconies beyond which the cliff face drops hundreds of feet below. This really is a cliff dwelling, and you must hike a bit down to it, though good guardrails guide you. The apartment is laid out around a broad central pillar, and the ceilings and walls are thick, undulating stone. A grill is outside, as are chairs where you can relax in the mornings and evenings. Fruit, juice, coffee, and pastries make up a self-serve breakfast.

3204 Crestridge Dr., Farmington, NM 87401. ✆ **505/326-2461.** Fax 505/325-9671. www.bbonline.com/nm/kokopelli. 1 unit. $240 double; $280 for 3–4 people. Closed Dec–Feb. AE, MC, V. **Amenities:** Jacuzzi. *In room:* TV/VCR, kitchen, hair dryer, iron.

Camping

Mom and Pop RV Park (✆ **505/327-3200**) has 36 sites, 35 of them with full hookups, tenting, a bathhouse, and a toy soldier shop. The sites are a bit desolate, around an asphalt central area, but a little grassy spot at the office has an incredible electric train set that Pop runs at certain times during the day. Mom and Pop RV Park is at 901 Illinois Ave., in Farmington (just off US 64).

WHERE TO DINE IN FARMINGTON & AZTEC

Expensive

The Bluffs ★★ *(Finds)* SANDWICHES/SEAFOOD/STEAKS Ten minutes east of town center, the Bluffs serves inventive food with attention to detail. A large room is sectioned off by wooden partitions crowned with elegantly glazed glass shaped like the bluffs prominent in the surrounding area. It's a comfortable atmosphere with roomy booths and stacked sandstone accents. Service is efficient. The outdoor patio is a nice spot on not-so-hot days. For lunch, my pick is the turkey-bacon club, served on ciabatta bread. The Thai beef salad is also tasty. At dinner, try your favorite steak cut of Angus beef or sesame-crusted ahi tuna. Dinners come with salad and a choice of vegetable or potato. A full bar accompanies the menu.

3450 E. Main St. ✆ **505/325-8155.** Reservations recommended on weekend nights. Main courses $8–$12 lunch, $15–$39 dinner. AE, DISC, MC, V. Mon–Fri 11am–2pm, Mon–Sat 5–9pm; lounge daily 4–9 or 10pm.

Moderate

Rubio's ★ NEW MEXICAN Set in the center of Aztec, this restaurant and bar offers a festive dining experience. Amid brightly painted walls, with comfy booths, the restaurant portion provides a relaxing atmosphere for families. Meanwhile, the bar next door, with ceiling fans and a beach mural, gets livelier. Service is friendly and eager to please. Meals start with chips and salsa, followed by such tasty fare as breakfast burritos or French toast in the morning. Lunch and dinner might start with nachos or guacamole and move on to their "Sopaipilla el Grande," a favorite—*sopaipilla* topped with taco meat, cheese, guac, and sour cream. Grilled burgers, chicken, and steak also dress the menu here, as do a variety of combo plates. Kids have their own menu and adults a full bar. Live music, ranging from rock to country, plays on most Saturday nights.

116 S. Main St., Aztec. ✆ **505/334-0599.** Main courses $4–8 breakfast; $5–$20 lunch and dinner. AE, DISC, MC, V. Mon–Thurs 8am–9pm; Fri–Sat 8am–10pm.

3 Rivers Eatery & Brewhouse ★ Kids AMERICAN This brewpub on an elegant corner in the center of downtown serves some of the region's best food and beer. After my first sip of their Arroyo Amber Ale, I was sold. The restaurant is set in a big two-story brick building that once housed the Farmington Drug Store and the Farmington *Times-Hustler* newspaper. Hardwood floors and vintage items, such as period bottles and posters found in the renovation, complete the experience. It's a comfortable place where the owner might just sit down in one of the comfy booths with you and chat about his passion, beer brewing. I recommend the burgers, which come in a variety of flavors, from grilled onion and Swiss to jack and green chile. You'll also find barbecue pork ribs, steaks, and seafood. Families enjoy the spacious booths in the back and a kid's menu.

101 E. Main St., Farmington. ✆ **505/324-2187.** www.threeriversbrewery.com. Main courses $6–$25. AE, DISC, MC, V. Mon–Thurs 11am–10pm; Fri–Sat 11am–11pm; Sun 11am–9pm.

Inexpensive

Main Street Bistro ★ BAKERY/CAFE This imaginative little cafe in Aztec, with brightly colored floors and walls, offers tasty housemade breakfasts, sandwiches, soups, and salads. Order at the counter and the friendly waitstaff will bring your food to the table. Be aware that the place bustles during peak hours; so if you want quiet time, go midmorning or later in the afternoon. At breakfast, you might order the egg-centric—two eggs, hash browns, English muffin, and fruit. For lunch, you can't go wrong with the daily soup special, a salad, or sandwich (try the Ultimate—turkey, bacon, avocado, and sprouts), or the quiche, made fresh daily. Wash it all down with a full range of coffee drinks or their delicious raspberry iced tea.

122 N. Main St., Aztec. ✆ **505/334-0109.** All menu items under $9. DISC, MC, V. Mon–Fri 7am–4pm; Sat 7am–noon.

FARMINGTON AFTER DARK

Sandstone Production's **Summer Outdoor Theater** ★ stages two fun shows each year. Presented in the Lions Wilderness Park Amphitheater (off College Blvd.) against a sandstone backdrop, the offerings are usually a dramatic piece and a musical. For information and advance ticket sales, contact ✆ **505/599-1148;** www.fmtn.org/sandstone. Shows are Wednesday through Saturday from mid-June through July, with dinner at 6:30pm and the performance at 8pm.

If you're looking for a pub, **3 Rivers Tap & Game Room,** 113 E. Main St. (✆ **505/325-6605;** www.threeriversbrewery.com), is a big hit with locals. This brewpub/game room has the feel of the bar from the television show *Cheers,* with wood floors, high ceilings, and lots of laughter and brew flowing. Pool tables, foosball, and shuffleboard fill patrons' time while they munch on popcorn and peanuts, and, some nights, listen to live music jam. Patrons can order food from the next-door brewpub/restaurant of the same name (see above).

8 THE JICARILLA APACHE RESERVATION

About 3,200 Apaches live on the Jicarilla Apache Indian Reservation along US 64 and NM 537. Its 768,000 acres stretch from the Colorado border south 65 miles to US 550 near Cuba, New Mexico.

The word *jicarilla* (pronounced hick-ah-*ree*-ah) means "little basket," so it's no surprise that tribal craftspeople are noted for their basket weaving and beadwork. See their work, both contemporary and of museum quality, at the **Jicarilla Apache Arts and Crafts Shop and Museum,** a green building along US 64 west of the central village on the reservation (✆ **575/759-4274;** www.jicarillaonline.com). In the back rooms here, I found women listening to 1950s rock while they wove baskets and strung beads. Two isolated pueblo ruins, open to the public, are found on the reservation: **Cordova Canyon** ruins on tribal Road 13 and **Honolulu** ruins on Road 63.

Though the area is lovely, there's not much else to do unless you're interested in hunting and fishing. Tribe members guide fishers and trophy hunters, most of whom seek elk, mule deer, or bear, into the reservation's rugged wilderness backcountry. Highlights of the Jicarilla calendar are the **Little Beaver Celebration** (mid-July), which features a rodeo, a 5-mile run, a draft-horse pull, and a powwow. The **Stone Lake Fiesta** (Sept 14–15 annually) includes a rodeo, ceremonial dances, and a footrace.

Admission to Jicarilla Apache Reservation is free, and visitors are welcome year-round. For information on outdoor activities and for general information, contact the Tribal Office at P.O. Box 507 (✆ **575/759-3242**).

The **Best Western Jicarilla Inn and Casino** on US 64 (P.O. Box 233), Dulce, NM 87528 (✆ **800/742-1938** or 575/759-3663; www.bestwestern.com/jicarillainn), offers decent rooms and slot-machine play, though you'll find better accommodations in Chama (see below).

9 CHAMA & ITS SCENIC RAILROAD

Some of my best outdoor adventuring has taken place in the area surrounding this pioneer village of 1,250 people at the base of the 10,000-foot Cumbres Pass. With backpacks on, we cross-country skied high into the mountains and stayed the night in a *yurt* (Russian hut), the next day waking to hundreds of acres of snowy fields to explore. Another time, we headed down **Rio Chama,** an official wild and scenic river, on rafts and in kayaks following the course that Navajos, Utes, and Comanches once traveled to raid the Pueblo Indians down river. The campsites along the way were pristine, with mule deer threading through the trees beyond our tents. In a more recent visit to the village, it was summertime, and I'd just come from Durango, which was packed with tourists, to hike, raft, and ride the train. Chama was still quiet, and I realized Chama is New Mexico's undiscovered Durango, without the masses. And now, with some new additions, the town is really looking up. A park, clock-tower, and, drum-roll please . . . sidewalks! give it a more friendly tone.

Bordered by three wilderness areas, the Carson, Rio Grande, and Santa Fe national forests, the area is indeed prime for hunting, fishing, cross-country skiing, snowmobiling, snowshoeing, and hiking.

Another highlight here is America's longest and highest narrow-gauge coal-fired steam line, the **Cumbres & Toltec Scenic Railroad,** which winds through valleys and mountain meadows 64 miles between Chama and Antonito, Colorado. The village of Chama boomed when the railroad arrived in 1881. A rough-and-ready frontier town, the place still maintains that flavor, with lumber and ranching making up a big part of the economy.

Landmarks to watch for are the **Brazos Cliffs** and waterfall and **Heron and El Vado lakes.** Tierra Amarilla, the Rio Arriba County seat, is 14 miles south, and is at the center—along with Los Ojos and Los Brazos—of a wool-raising and weaving tradition where local craftspeople still weave masterpieces. Dulce, governmental seat of the Jicarilla Apache Indian Reservation, is 27 miles west.

ESSENTIALS

GETTING THERE From Santa Fe, take US 84 north (2 hr.). From Taos, take US 64 west (2½ hr.). From Farmington, take US 64 east (2¼ hr.).

VISITOR INFORMATION The **New Mexico Visitor Information Center,** P.O. Box 697, Chama, NM 87520 (© **575/756-2235**), is at 2372 US 17. It's open daily from 8am to 6pm in the summer, from 8am to 5pm in the winter. At the same address is the **Chama Valley Chamber of Commerce** (© **800/477-0149** or 575/756-2306; www.chamavalley.com).

ALL ABOARD THE HISTORIC C&T RAILROAD

Cumbres & Toltec Scenic Railroad ★★ Moments If you have a passion for the past and for incredible scenery, climb aboard America's longest and highest narrow-gauge steam railroad, the historic C&T. It operates on a 64-mile track between Chama and Antonito, Colorado. Built in 1880 as an extension of the Denver and Rio Grande line to serve the mining camps of the San Juan Mountains, it is perhaps the finest surviving example of what once was a vast network of remote Rocky Mountain railways.

The C&T passes through forests of pine and aspen, past striking rock formations, and over the magnificent Toltec Gorge of the Rio de los Pinos. It crests at the 10,015-foot Cumbres Pass, the highest in the United States used by scheduled passenger trains.

Halfway through the route, at Osier, Colorado, the *New Mexico Express* from Chama meets the *Colorado Limited* from Antonito. They stop to exchange greetings, engines, and through passengers. A lunch of roast turkey, mashed potatoes, gravy, and other offerings is served in a big, barn-like dining hall in Osier. From there, through passengers continue on to Antonito and return by van, while round-trip passengers return to their starting point. Be aware that both trips are nearly full-day events. Those who find it uncomfortable to sit for long periods may instead want to opt for hiking or skiing in the area. Ask about their Parlor Car, a more luxurious alternative to coach seating.

Steam Power Shopping

After sitting on the steam train, you may want to stroll for a while, hitting a few of the shops in Chama. One of note is the **Local Color Gallery,** 567 Terrace Ave. (✆ **888/756-2604** or 575/756-2604), in the center of town. Here you'll find all kinds of locally made arts and crafts, from pottery to moody candles painted with petroglyph symbols to picturesque watercolors of the Chama area. Nearby, the **Trackside Emporium,** 611 Terrace Ave. (✆ **575/756-1848**), offers train books and videos and model cars.

A walking-tour brochure, describing 23 points of interest in the Chama railroad yards, can be picked up at the 1899 depot in Chama. These yards are a living, working museum, which fascinates history buffs. A registered National Historic Site, the C&T is owned by the states of Colorado and New Mexico. Special cars with lifts for people with disabilities are available with a 7-day advance reservation.

500 Terrace Ave., Chama, NM 87520. ✆ **888/CUMBRES** or 575/756-2151. Fax 575/756-2694. www.cumbrestoltec.com. Lunch is included with all fares. Round-trip to Osier: adults $70, children 11 and under $35. Through trip to Antonito, return by van (or to Antonito by van, return by train): adults $80, children $40. Reservations highly recommended. Memorial Day to mid-Oct trains leave Chama daily at 10am; vans depart for Antonito at 8:30am.

WHERE TO STAY IN CHAMA

Most accommodations in this area are found on NM 17 or south of the US 64/84 junction, known as the "Y."

Hotels/Lodges

Chama Station Inn ★ Set in downtown Chama, right across the street from the Cumbres & Toltec Scenic Railroad station, this inn offers clean, atmospheric rooms in a 1920s building. Wood floors, high ceilings, and quilts on the comfortable beds create a cozy atmosphere. Bathrooms are small, with only a shower, but functional. A portal on the two-story building allows a nice place to lounge next to an elaborate garden. Best of all, you can climb out of bed and walk to the train. The only drawback here is that the inn is only open from late May to mid-October, when the train is running. Two of the rooms have kiva fireplaces. Next door, a coffee shop offers breakfast. I'd give its name but it seems to change hands every year, so your guess is as good as mine.

423 Terrace Ave., Chama, NM 87520. ✆ **888/726-8150** or 505/756-2315. www.chamastationinn.com. 9 units. $75–$85 double. AE, DISC, MC, V. *In room:* TV, hair dryer and iron upon request.

River Bend Lodge Set on a bend of the Chama River, this lodging offers the best cabins in town and clean motel rooms. Though they're prefab cabins, they're better than some of the more authentic and overly rustic ones at nearby lodgings. If you can reserve cabin no. 40, 50, or 60 at the back of the property, you'll have a sweet riverside stay. Some of these are split level, with a queen-size sleeping loft and a bedroom—not great for privacy, but good for a family that doesn't mind sharing space. Others are similar, but without the loft. Every cabin has a fold-out futon in the living room, an efficient little kitchen, and a small bathroom. The motel rooms are medium-size, with basic furnishing and a long portal to relax under in the afternoons. Guests may fish and wade in the river flowing through the property.

2625 US 84/64, Chama, NM 87520. ✆ **800/288-1371** or 505/756-2264. Fax 505/756-2664. www.chamariverbendlodge.com. 21 units. Motel rooms $68–$89 double; cabins $115–$135 double. Children 12 and under stay free in parent's room. AE, DC, DISC, MC, V. Pets accepted with $10 fee. **Amenities:** Jacuzzi; coffee and microwave in lobby. *In room:* A/C, TV, fridge.

Camping

At **Rio Chama RV Campground** (✆ **575/756-2303**), you're within easy walking distance of the Cumbres & Toltec Scenic Railroad depot. This shady campground with 94 sites along the Rio Chama is ideal for RVers and tenters who plan to take train rides. The campground also offers great photo opportunities of the old steam trains leaving the depot. Hot showers, a dump station, and complete hookups are available. It's open from May to mid-October only. The campground is 2¼ miles north of the US 84/64 junction on NM 17.

Twin Rivers Trailer Park (✆ **575/756-2218;** www.twinriversonline.net) has 50 sites and 40 full hookups; phone hookups are offered. Tenting is available, as are laundry facilities and ice and picnic tables. River swimming and fishing are popular activities; other sports facilities include basketball, volleyball, badminton, and horseshoes. Twin Rivers is open from April 15 to November 15 and is 100 yards west of the junction of NM 17 and US 84/64.

WHERE TO DINE IN CHAMA

Cookin' Books ★★ Finds DELI/AMERICAN This is Chama's gem, a fun community-style cafe serving creative, delectable food. The main room has a vaulted ceiling with bookshelves on one side and lots of windows. Diners order at a counter and serve themselves water and coffee, while the food is made fresh and brought to them. The menu ranges broadly. You might start with shrimp ceviche or a chicken quesadilla. For an entree, the tastiest sandwich is the roast turkey, goat cheese, and pesto served on a fresh ciabatta roll. The Reuben on rye is also delicious. Lighter appetites may select from a few salad options such as a grilled salmon steak on organic greens. During my most recent visit, I had the daily special: a stellar chicken putanesca (chicken cooked with olives, tomatoes, and onions), served with a salad. While you wait for your food, be sure to peruse the community room/gallery in back, displaying local art including "found" pieces by Bruce McIntosh. Beer and wine accompany the menu.

2449 US 84/64, at the Y, Chama. ✆ **505/756-1717.** All menu items under $9. MC, V. Thurs–Mon 10am–4pm, with longer hours in summer.

High Country Restaurant and Saloon ★ STEAKS/SEAFOOD/NEW MEXICAN This is definitely a country place, with functional furniture, orange vinyl chairs, brown carpet, and a big stone fireplace. But it's *the* place innkeepers recommend, and one traveling couple I spoke to had eaten lunch and dinner here every day of their weeklong stay. The steaks are a big draw here. More sophisticated appetites may like the *trucha con piñon,* trout dusted in flour and cooked with pine nuts, garlic, and shallots. Meals are served with a salad and choice of potato. The New Mexican food is also good. The attached saloon has a full bar and bustles with people eating peanuts and throwing the shells on the floor. Breakfast on Sunday is country-style, with offerings such as steak and eggs and biscuits and gravy topping the menu, as well as omelets, pancakes, and huevos rancheros (eggs atop tortillas smothered in chile sauce).

Main St. (1/10 mile north of the Y), Chama. ✆ **575/756-2384.** Breakfast $4–$10; lunch $6–$12; dinner $5–$20; Sun breakfast buffet $8.95. AE, DISC, MC, V. Mon–Sat 11am–10pm; Sun 8am–10pm. Closed Easter, Thanksgiving, Christmas.

CHAMA AFTER DARK

Summer evenings in Chama now include entertainment beyond watching the river flow in its banks or the beer flow in the local tavern. The Elkhorn Lodge, 2663 S. US 84 (✆ **800/532-8874** or 575/756-2105; www.elkhornlodge.net), sponsors a **Chuckwagon Cowboy Dinner** Saturday evenings. Guests chow down on beef brisket, beans, and corn bread while watching a historical western narrative told through guitar music and singing. Kids like the food and the fun story. Reservations required; contact Elkhorn Lodge. Performances start at 7pm, and prices run $20 for adults and $9 for children 12 and under; children under 2 eat free (no plate).

ON THE ROAD: WHAT TO SEE & DO ON US 84 SOUTH

Distinctive yellow earth provided a name for the town of **Tierra Amarilla,** 14 miles south of Chama at the junction of US 84 and US 64. Throughout New Mexico, this name is synonymous with a continuing controversy over the land-grant rights of the descendants of the original Hispanic settlers. But the economy of this community of 1,000 is dyed in the wool—literally.

The organization *Ganados del Valle* (Livestock Growers of the Valley) is at work to save the longhaired Spanish churro sheep from extinction, to introduce other unusual wool breeds to the valley, and to perpetuate a 200-year-old tradition of shepherding, spinning, weaving, and dyeing. Many of the craftspeople work in conjunction with **Tierra Wools ★**, P.O. Box 229, Los Ojos, NM 87551 (✆ **505/588-7231;** www.handweavers.com), which has a showroom and workshop in a century-old mercantile building just north of Tierra Amarilla. One-of-a-kind blankets and men's and women's apparel are among the products displayed and sold.

Just down the street, across from the Los Ojos General Store, is an interesting little art studio worth checking out. **Yellow Earth Studio** (✆ **575/588-7807**), the passion of Paul Trachtman, the resident artist, is a great place to see and purchase enchanting scenes of the Los Ojos area in the form of paintings and monotype, woodcut, and metal engraving prints. His work is part of the permanent collection of the New Mexico State Capitol. Paul will likely be working away in his studio in back, and if you're fortunate, he'll guide you through some of his techniques.

Two state parks are a short drive west from Tierra Amarilla. **El Vado Lake State Park,** 14 miles southwest on NM 112 (✆ **575/588-7247;** www.nmparks.com), offers boating and water-skiing, fishing, and camping in summer; cross-country skiing and ice fishing in winter. **Heron Lake State Park,** 11 miles west on US 64 and NM 95 (✆ **575/588-7470;** www.nmparks.com), has a no-wake speed limit for motor vessels, adding to its appeal for fishing, sailing, windsurfing, canoeing, and swimming. The park has an interpretive center, plus camping, picnic sites, hiking trails, and cross-country skiing in the winter. The 5.5-mile Rio Chama trail connects the two lakes.

East of Tierra Amarilla, the Rio Brazos cuts a canyon through the Tusas Mountains and around 11,403-foot Brazos Peak. Just north of Los Ojos, NM 512 heads east 7½ miles up the **Brazos Box Canyon.** High cliffs that rise straight from the valley floor give it a Yosemite-like appearance—which is even more apparent from an overlook on US 64, 18 miles east of Tierra Amarilla en route to Taos. **El Chorro,** an impressive waterfall at the mouth of the canyon, usually flows only from early May to mid-June. Several resort lodges are in the area.

About 37 miles south of Tierra Amarilla on US 84, and 3 miles north of Ghost Ranch, is **Echo Canyon Amphitheater** (✆ **575/684-2486**), a U.S. Forest Service campground and picnic area. The natural "theater," hollowed out of sandstone by thousands of years of erosion, is a natural work of art with layers of stone ranging from pearl-color to blood red. The walls send back eerie echoes and even clips of conversations. It's just a 10-minute walk from the parking area. The fee is $2 per car. Some 13 miles west of here, via the dirt Forest Service road 151 into the Chama River Canyon Wilderness, is the isolated **Monastery of Christ in the Desert** (www.christdesert.org), built in 1964 by Benedictine monks. The brothers produce crafts, sold at a small gift shop, and operate a guesthouse.

Along the same road (FS 151) is access to the Chama River, a good place to hike, mountain bike, kayak, and camp. The **Rim Vista Trail** will take you to the top of the rim, with vast views out across Abiquiu Lake and Ghost Ranch. Primitive campsites can be found all along the river.

A 3-mile drive from there is **Ghost Ranch,** a collection of adobe buildings that make up an adult study center maintained by the United Presbyterian Church. A number of hauntingly memorable hikes originate from this place, which gets its name from the *brujas,* or witches, said to inhabit the canyons. Most popular among the hikes is spectacular **Chimney Rock,** but even more notable in my opinion is **Kitchen Mesa.** Directions for the hikes can be obtained at the visitor center. World-renowned painter Georgia O'Keeffe spent time at Ghost Ranch painting these canyons and other land formations. Eventually she bought a portion of the ranch and lived in a humble adobe house there. The ranch now offers seminars on a variety of topics, ranging from art to literature to religion, that are open to all. For information, contact **Ghost Ranch,** 401 Old Taos Hwy., Santa Fe (✆ **505/982-8539;** www.ghostranch.org).

The **Florence Hawley Ellis Museum of Anthropology** has interpretative exhibits of a Spanish ranch house and Native American anthropology, and the **Ruth Hall Paleontology Museum** (both museums ✆ **505/685-4333;** www.ghostranch.org) displays fossils of the early dinosaur named coelophysis found on the ranch. A lightly built creature, it was very fast when chasing prey. It roamed the area 250 million years ago, making it the oldest dinosaur found in New Mexico.

Many dinosaur skeletons have been found in rocks along the base of cliffs near **Abiquiu Reservoir** (✆ **505/685-4371**), a popular boating and fishing spot formed by the Abiquiu Dam.

A good place to stay and dine in the area is the **Abiquiu Inn** ★, a small country inn, restaurant, art gallery, and gift shop, 1/2 mile north of the village of Abiquiu (✆ **505/685-4378**). The casitas are especially nice. Rates are $139 to $199.

Heading south from Abiquiu, watch for **Dar al Islam** (✆ **505/685-4515**), a spiritual center with a circular Middle Eastern–style mosque made of adobe; the small community of **Mendanales,** is the home of renowned weaver Cordelia Coronado; and **Hernandez,** the village immortalized in Ansel Adams's famous 1941 photograph *Moonrise, Hernandez, New Mexico.* **Rancho de San Juan** (p. 198) is a wonderful nearby place to stay and dine.

If you're in the area and need gas for your car or a snack for yourself (or goodies for a picnic), stop in at **Bode's,** on US 84 in Abiquiu (✆ **505/685-4422**). The general store for the area, this place has shovels and irrigation boots, and better yet, cold drinks, gourmet sandwiches, and other deli items—even a hearty green chile chicken stew.

10

Northeastern New Mexico

The long distances along the mountains from Las Vegas to Cimarron, or across the plains from Raton to Clayton, are worth the driving time. History is everywhere, from evidence of Coronado's passage during his 16th-century search of Cíbola, to the Santa Fe Trail ruts on the prairie made some 300 years later. In **Cimarron,** you'll see evidence of the holdings of cattle baron Lucien Maxwell, who controlled most of these prairies as his private empire in the latter half of the 19th century. During his era, this was truly the Wild West. Cimarron attracted nearly every gunslinger of the era, from Butch Cassidy to Clay Allison, Black Jack Ketchum to Jesse James. Bullet holes still decorate the ceiling of the St. James Hotel.

Established long before its Nevada namesake, **Las Vegas** was the largest city in New Mexico at the turn of the 20th century, with a fast-growing, cosmopolitan population. Doc Holliday, Bat Masterson, and Wyatt Earp walked its wild streets in the 1880s. A decade later, it was the headquarters of Teddy Roosevelt's Rough Riders, and early in the 20th century, it was a silent film capital and the site of a world heavyweight boxing match. Today, with a population of approximately 17,000, it is the region's largest city and the proud home of 900 historic properties. **Raton** (pop. 7,000), on I-25 in the Sangre de Cristo foothills, is the gateway to New Mexico from the north. **Clayton** (pop. 2,100), **Tucumcari** (pop. 5,200), and **Santa Rosa** (pop. 2,500) are all transportation hubs and ranching centers.

Two national monuments are particular points of interest. **Fort Union,** 24 miles north of Las Vegas, was the largest military installation in the Southwest in the 1860s and 1870s. **Capulin Volcano,** 33 miles east of Raton, last erupted 60,000 years ago; visitors can now walk inside the crater. Also of note are the **Kiowa and Rita Blanca National Grasslands** preserves: 136,000 acres of pure prairie.

Drained by the Pecos and Canadian rivers, northeastern New Mexico is otherwise notable for the number of small lakes that afford opportunities for fishing, hunting, boating, camping, and even scuba diving. Eleven state parks and about a half-dozen designated wildlife areas are within the region. **Philmont Scout Ranch,** south of Cimarron, is known by Boy Scouts throughout the world.

1 NORTHEASTERN NEW MEXICO'S GREAT OUTDOORS

Northeastern New Mexico encompasses a variety of Southwestern landscapes. The undulating grasslands of the eastern portion of the region eventually give way to the cliffs, canyons, and forests of the mighty Sangre de Cristo Mountains, which offer some of the best hiking and camping in the state. The area is drained by the Pecos and Canadian rivers and has many small streams and lakes, including Ute Lake, the second-largest in the state, that afford opportunities for bait fishing, fly-fishing, boating, swimming, and sailing in this seemingly arid region.

BIRD-WATCHING **Las Vegas National Wildlife Refuge** (✆ **505/425-3581**), 5 miles southeast of Las Vegas, is a great place for bird-watching. Species spotted year-round include prairie falcons and hawks; during late fall and early winter, migratory birds such as sandhill cranes, snow geese, Canada geese, and bald and golden eagles frequent the refuge. In all, more than 240 species can be sighted in the area. The **Maxwell National Wildlife Refuge** (✆ **575/375-2331**), near Raton, also boasts a rich population of resident and migratory birds, including raptors and bald eagles.

BOATING You'll find opportunities for boating, windsurfing, and swimming throughout this region. Two of the most popular boating areas are **Storrie Lake State Park** (✆ **505/425-7278**), 6 miles north of Las Vegas, and **Conchas Lake State Park** (✆ **575/868-2270**), near Tucumcari. Storrie Lake is especially popular among **windsurfers,** who favor its consistent winds. To find information on New Mexico state parks, go to **www.nmparks.com**.

FISHING Isolated and primitive **Morphy Lake State Park** is a favorite destination for serious anglers. The lake is regularly stocked with rainbow trout. **Cimarron Canyon State Park** is also popular with fishers. Lake Alice in **Sugarite Canyon State Park,** just north of Raton at the Colorado border, is a good spot for fly-fishing. For more information on the best fishing opportunities in the area, see chapters 7 and 8.

GOLF Duffers can get in a few holes in or near virtually every town covered in this section. I recommend the following courses: **Raton Municipal Golf Course,** 510 Country Club Rd., Raton NM 87740 (✆ **575/445-8113**); **Pendaries Village Mountain Resort,** in Rociada (✆ **505/425-3561;** www.pendaries.net), 13 miles south of Mora and 27 miles northwest of Las Vegas; and **Tucumcari Municipal Golf Course,** Route 66 Boulevard, Tucumcari, NM 88401 (✆ **575/461-1849**).

HIKING Northeastern New Mexico abounds in great places to hike, including the trails at Capulin Volcano; however, the best places are in the mountains to the north of Las Vegas and west of Santa Fe and Taos. The region's premier hike takes you to the top of **Hermit's Peak,** a lovely but strenuous 8-mile round-trip foray onto a stunning precipice. Take NM 65 about 15 miles northwest of Las Vegas to the El Porvenir Campground. It's probably best to acquire equipment and supplies in Albuquerque before you set out.

HORSEBACK RIDING If you'd like to try your spurs at some real ranch riding, moving cattle, and spitting on the plains and such, contact the **Hartley Guest Ranch,** 50 Guest Ranch Lane, Roy (✆ **800/OUR-DUDE** or 575/673-2244). The ranch offers 3- and 5-night packages from April through September.

HOT SPRINGS In this region, look for **Montezuma Hot Springs,** located on the campus of the Armand Hammer United World College of the American West, near Las Vegas (see "Exploring Las Vegas," below). Open daily from 8am to midnight.

SCUBA DIVING There couldn't possibly be scuba diving in this dry, landlocked state, could there? Yes, there is, with the best at Santa Rosa, where you'll find the **Blue Hole,** an 81-foot-deep artesian well that's a favorite of divers from around the world. The best place to rent equipment is at the **Santa Rosa Dive Center** on Blue Hole Road, open only on weekends (✆ **575/472-3370**).

SWIMMING Swimming is best (although chilly) at **Clayton, Conchas, Morphy, Storrie,** and **Ute lakes.** (You can find directions to and specifics about these lakes at

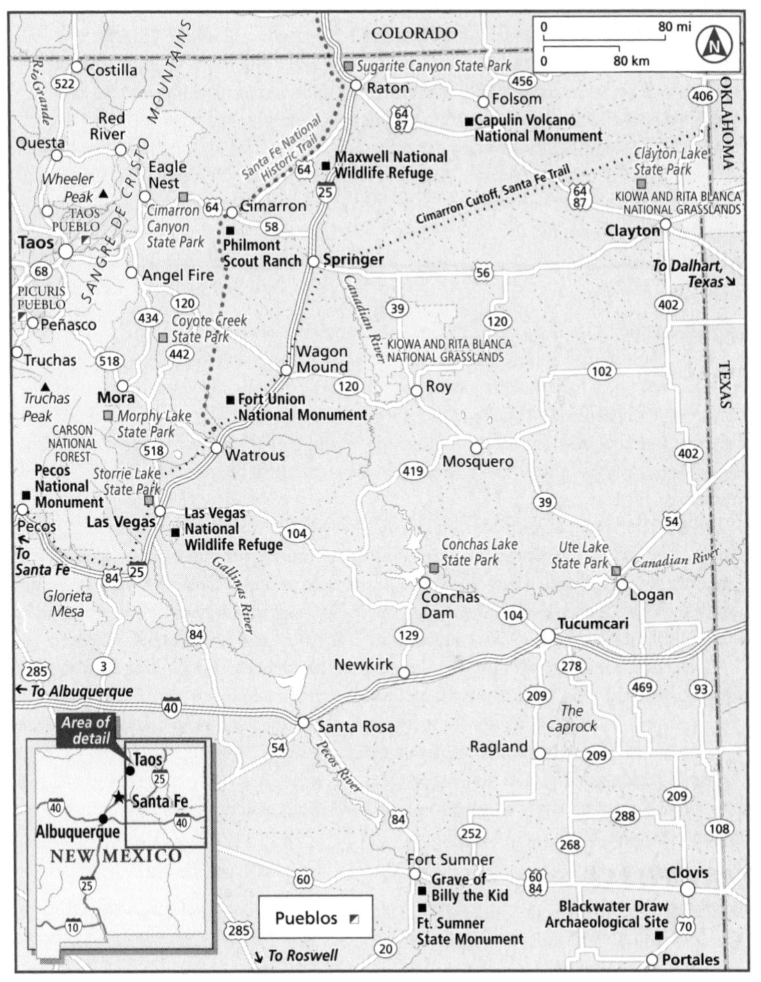

various points in the rest of this chapter.) In addition, though it's an indoor rather than outdoor experience, the **Las Vegas Recreation Center**'s (✆ **505/426-1739**) swimming pool, at 1751 N. Grand Ave., is an especially good place to take kids. It's Olympic-size and has a fun slide that will keep kids busy for hours. Call for more information.

2 LAS VEGAS & ENVIRONS ★★

Once known as the "gateway to New Mexico," **Las Vegas,** a pleasant town in the foothills of the Sangre de Cristo Mountains, was founded with a land grant from the Mexican

Finds **Smiling Food**

En route to Las Vegas from Santa Fe, along I-25, stop in at **La Risa Café★**, **© 575/421-3883**) on NM 3 in Ribera. In a cozy old house with brightly painted walls and on a fun patio, "the Smile" offers imaginative food made with fresh ingredients. For breakfast, their "Hangover stew" (green chile stew topped with eggs) is delicious. Lunch and dinner bring sandwiches, salads, and New Mexican dishes, as well as daily specials. Beer and wine accompany the menu. La Risa is open Wednesday to Saturday 10am to 8pm and Sunday 8am to 6pm, with abbreviated hours in winter.

government in 1835. A group of 29 Spanish colonists planted crops in the area and built a central plaza, which started out as a meeting place and a defense against Indian attack but soon became a main trading center on the Santa Fe Trail. Las Vegas boomed with the advent of the Atchison, Topeka, and Santa Fe Railway in 1879; almost overnight the town became the most important trading center and gathering place in the state and one of the largest towns in the Rocky Mountain West, rivaling Denver, Tucson, and El Paso in size.

Town settlers who arrived by train in the late 19th century shunned the indigenous adobe architecture, favoring instead building styles more typical of the Midwest or New England. They put up scores of fancy Queen Anne– and Victorian-style houses and hotels, and the town is noted to this day for its dazzling diversity of architectural styles. Some 900 buildings in Las Vegas are on the National Register of Historic Places.

Meanwhile, the town saw visits from many notable characters, including Billy the Kid, Wyatt Earp, and Doc Holliday (who practiced dentistry here). It continues to play its Old West part in movies: Scenes from *Wyatt Earp, The HiLo Country,* and *All the Pretty Horses* were shot here, as were Tom Mix's vintage westerns. Strolling the streets, you'll get a sense of those past times as you peruse Western wear shops, bookstores, and old soda fountains that seem caught in a time warp, with their period architecture and friendly business owners.

ESSENTIALS

GETTING THERE From Santa Fe, take I-25 northeast 60 miles (1¼ hr.); from Raton, take I-25 south 105 miles (1¾ hr.); from Taos, follow NM 518 southeast 78 miles through Mora (2 hr.); from Tucumcari, follow NM 104 west 112 miles (2 hr.). **Las Vegas Municipal Airport** handles private flights and charters but has no regularly scheduled commercial service.

VISITOR INFORMATION The **Las Vegas & San Miguel County Chamber of Commerce** is at 503 Sixth St. (P.O. Box 128), Las Vegas, NM 87701 (**© 800/832-5947** or 505/425-8631; www.lvsmchamber.org). It's open weekdays from 9am to 5pm.

EXPLORING LAS VEGAS

The Railroad District

When you first enter Las Vegas, you may want to take a brief driving tour through the railroad district and "east Las Vegas" to get a sense of how the railroad's arrival in the 1870s shaped that side of the city. Turn east on Douglas Avenue, which will take you to

Railroad Avenue. In this district are turn-of-the-20th-century brick buildings housing such businesses as Moonlite Welding and Blue Dart Upholstery Shop. The center of the railroad district is the old Fred Harvey **Castañeda Hotel** at 510 Railroad. Built in 1898, it is one of the early Harvey Houses to be built in the Mission Revival style. It no longer operates as a hotel; however, you'll want to stop and take a peek into the lobby, which is still elegant, with a molded tin ceiling and arched windows.

The Historic District

The chamber of commerce on Grand Avenue (see "Essentials," above) has a map of a self-guided tour of this area. What's most notable is the town's early Spanish history; adobe buildings going back to the first Spanish visits in the 16th century are still standing alongside the ornate structures of the late 1800s. In addition, it's hard to find such a well-preserved collection of Territorial-style buildings. Most of the interesting structures can be found in the Plaza–Bridge Street area.

In particular, don't miss the **Plaza Hotel,** 230 Old Town Plaza, the finest hotel in the New Mexico Territory back in 1881. Its three-story facade, topped with a fancy broken pediment decoration, was the town's pride and joy, and it has been happily restored. (See "Where to Stay in Las Vegas," below.)

Another highlight is the **Dice Apartments,** 210 Old Town Plaza. Although the low adobe building is unimpressive, its history is distinguished—it is the sole building on the plaza that predates the U.S.–Mexican War of 1846. In that year, Gen. Stephen Kearny, commander of the Army of the West, stood on a one-story building on the north side of the plaza (probably this one) to address the town's population, claiming New Mexico for the United States.

For shopping, be sure to browse through **Rough Rider Antiques,** at 501 Railroad St. (✆ **505/454-8063**). You'll find Southwestern furniture, eclectic Western art, and quilts here. Another good shopping stop is **Plaza Antiques,** 1805 Old Town Plaza (✆ **505/454-9447**), a fun place to browse for antique clothing and kitchen tables. A great place to browse for books on regional history is **Tome on the Range,** 158 Bridge St. (✆ **505/454-9944**).

Housed in a 1940s-era Work Projects Administration (WPA) building, the **Las Vegas City Museum and Rough Riders Memorial Collection,** 727 Grand Ave. (✆ **505/454-1401,** ext. 283), is a fun spot to spend about an hour. The largest contingent of Rough Riders was recruited from New Mexico to fight in the 1898 Spanish–American War. This museum chronicles their contribution to U.S. history and also contains artifacts relating to the history of the city. Another exhibit documents the history of Las Vegas. Admission is free. The museum is open Tuesday to Sunday 10am to 4pm, and by appointment.

In the plaza area, the **Santa Fe Trail Interpretive Center,** 127 Bridge St. (✆ **505/425-8803;** www.lvsmchamber.org), offers a glimpse into efforts to restore the town's 918 historic buildings as well as information about the Santa Fe Trail. Set in the 1890s Winternitz Building, it's a fun stop, if you find it open. Hours vary greatly, as it is staffed by volunteers.

Other Attractions near Town

Las Vegas has two colleges. **New Mexico Highlands University** (✆ **505/425-7511;** www.nmhu.edu), a 4-year liberal arts school of almost 3,000 students, was established in 1893. The **Armand Hammer United World College,** 5 miles west of Las Vegas via NM 65 (✆ **505/454-4200;** www.uwc.org), is an international school with students from more than 70 countries. It is housed in the former **Montezuma Hotel,** a luxury resort

(Value) Weaving Magic

You can watch weavers at work at **Tapetes de Lana** on the Las Vegas Plaza. Appropriately set in a late-1800s textile shop, this fun import shop, weavers' studio, and cafe offers a peek into the art as well as lovely works to buy. Hanging from antique stone walls are scarves, shawls, and Rio Grande–style rugs woven as part of a job-training program for people with low income, many of whom have mastered the art beautifully. Now the shop has a cafe selling organic free trade coffee, baked goods, salads, sandwiches, and pizza. It's located at 1814 Plaza (✆ **505/426-8638;** www.tapetesdelana.com) and is open Monday through Friday 7am to 6:30pm, Saturday 8am to 6:30pm, and Sunday 10am to 4pm. Prices are uncommonly reasonable. You may also visit **Tapetes de Lana in Mora,** open Monday to Saturday 10am to 5pm.

built by the Santa Fe Railroad in the 1880s and now a historic landmark. Three U.S. presidents, Germany's Kaiser Wilhelm II, and Japan's Meiji Emperor Mutsuhito stayed in the multistoried, turreted, 270-room "Montezuma Castle," as it came to be known. One-hour tours of the Castle are offered on select Saturdays at 1pm. Call ✆ **505/454-4221** for a schedule.

EXPLORING THE AREA

Mora, a small village 31 miles north of Las Vegas via NM 518, is the main center between Las Vegas and Taos, and it's the seat of sparsely populated Mora County. The 15-mile-long Mora Valley is one of New Mexico's prettiest but most economically depressed regions, where families have for centuries lived by subsistence farming and are only recently having to adapt to other means of earning income. An interesting stop here is the **Tapetes de Lana** (see "Weaving Magic," above) shop in the middle of town.

Cleveland Roller Mill ★ One vestige of a more prosperous past is this two-story adobe mill, which ground out 50 barrels of wheat flour a day, virtually every day, from 1901 to 1947. It was the last flour mill to be built in New Mexico and the last to stop running, and it is the only roller mill in the state to have its original milling works intact. Today, it's been converted into a museum with exhibits on local regional history and culture. The Millfest, on Labor Day weekend, features the mill in operation, dances, arts and crafts, music, and more. It's advisable to call ahead because the mill is closed from time to time. Plan to spend 1 to 2 hours exploring.

NM 518, about 2 miles west of Mora, Cleveland, NM 87715. ✆ **505/387-2645.** Admission $2 adults, $1 children 7–17, free for ages 6 and under. Weekends only Memorial Day–Labor Day 9am–3pm (closed 12–12:30 for lunch), or by appointment.

La Cueva National Historic Site and Salman Ranch ★ (Finds) Each fall, I make a bit of a pilgrimage to this spot in a lush valley along the Mora River. Its history is rich, dating from the early 1800s, when a man named Vicente Romero began farming and raising sheep here. He completed an elegant two-story northern New Mexico home that still stands, as well as a mill that ground flour and supplied electricity for the area (the real draw). Just north of these historic sites is the San Rafael Mission Church, with exquisite French Gothic windows. Recently restored by local people, it's now painted blue and white. The trip through these sites is worth the time during any season, but in the fall, the raspberries ripen and turn this into a must-do trip to sample berries by the basket or crate, as well as in jams and over soft vanilla ice cream. Delicious.

NM 518, 6 miles east of Mora, Buena Vista, NM 87712. ✆ **505/387-2900.** Free admission. Summer Mon–Sat 9am–5pm, Sun 10am–5pm; winter hours limited (call first).

Victory Ranch (Kids) Few things surprise me in this strange part of the state, where images of Jesus are known to appear on stucco walls and ghosts are said to inhabit the old haciendas, but I must say that my head turned when I saw alpacas grazing in a meadow here. I stopped immediately and stepped out of my car just in time for a tour. With a small cup of feed I purchased, I followed a young boy out to some lush pens where the odd South American Andean creatures greeted us with a harmonica-like hum. Very friendly, they ate from our hands while the babies roamed about, heads held high, marble-clear brown eyes looking quizzical. Also on-site is a store that sells sweaters and shawls made from alpaca wool, as well as a loom where visitors can try weaving. Weaving and spinning demonstrations are available on request. Group tours are also available.

1 mile north of Mora on NM 434, Mora, NM 87732. ✆ **505/387-2254.** Fax 505/387-9005. www.victoryranch.com. Admission for feeding tour $3 adults, $2 children 11 and under. Daily 10am–4pm, with tours at 11am, 1pm, and 3pm.

Getting Outside: Off-the-Beaten-Path State Parks & Other Scenic Highlights

Storrie Lake State Park (✆ **505/425-7278**), 4 miles north via NM 518, open daily during daylight hours year-round, offers fishing, swimming, windsurfing, water-skiing, camping, a visitor center with historic exhibits, and a playground.

Villanueva State Park (✆ **575/421-2957**), 31 miles southwest via I-25 and NM 3 and open daily from 7am to 9pm (until 7pm in winter), offers excellent hiking, camping, and picnicking between red sandstone bluffs in the Pecos River Valley. Nearby are the Spanish colonial villages **Villanueva** and **San Miguel del Vado;** the latter is a national historic district built around an impressive 1805 church.

Fourteen miles north of Mora via NM 434 is an out-of-the-way beauty, **Coyote Creek State Park** (✆ **505/387-2328**), with fully developed and primitive campsites beside a stream. The fishing is good, and a few well-marked hiking trails head into the mountains.

If you prefer your nature a little less primitive, head for the **Pendaries Village Mountain Resort,** P.O. Box 820, Rociada, NM 87742 (✆ **505/425-3561;** www.pendaries.net), located 13 miles south of Mora and 27 miles northwest of Las Vegas, on NM 105 off NM 94. This lovely foothills lodge boasts the region's finest 18-hole golf course and fishing. It also has overnight accommodations and a restaurant/lounge, open May to October.

Fort Union National Monument ★

Established in 1851 to defend the Santa Fe Trail against attacks from Plains Indians, Fort Union was expanded in 1861 in anticipation of a Confederate invasion, which was subsequently thwarted at Glorieta Pass, 20 miles southeast of Santa Fe. Fort Union's location on the Santa Fe Trail made it a welcome way station for travelers, but when the railroad replaced the trail in 1879, the fort was on its way out. It was abandoned in 1891. Today, Fort Union, the largest military installation in the 19th-century Southwest, is in ruins. Though it offers little to see but adobe walls and chimneys, the very scope of the fort is impressive. Santa Fe Trail wagon ruts can still be seen nearby. Follow the 1.5-mile self-guided interpretive trail that wanders through the ruins and imagine yourself a weary 19th-century wagon traveler stopping for rest and supplies.

The national monument has a small visitor center and museum with exhibits and booklets on the fort's history. Visitors should allow 2 hours to tour the ruins.

JUST THE FACTS To reach the site from Las Vegas, drive 18 miles north on I-25 to the Watrous exit, and then another 8 miles northwest on NM 161. Admission is $3 per person. Fort Union National Monument is open Memorial Day to Labor Day daily from 8am to 6pm; during the rest of the year, it is open daily from 8am to 4pm. It's closed Thanksgiving, Christmas, and New Year's Day.

A gift shop carries a wide selection of books on New Mexico history and women's history, and frontier military books. Camping is not available at the monument, but facilities are available in nearby Las Vegas.

For more information on the monument, contact Fort Union National Monument, P.O. Box 127, Watrous, NM 87753 (✆ **505/425-8025;** www.nps.gov/foun).

WHERE TO STAY IN LAS VEGAS

Most motels are on US 85 (Grand Ave.), the main north–south highway through downtown Las Vegas. (An exception is the Plaza Hotel, below.)

Inn on the Santa Fe Trail ★ Built in the 1920s as a court motel, this inn has been remodeled in a hacienda style, with all rooms looking out onto the central courtyard, creating a quiet retreat just off busy Grand Avenue. Although it's not as historical as the Plaza Hotel (see below), the rooms are a bit more up-to-date and functional, and you can park your car right outside. Rooms are medium-size with nice accents, such as handcrafted iron light fixtures and hand-carved pine furniture—including *trasteros* (armoires) to conceal the televisions. The beds are comfortably firm, and each room has a table with two chairs and a desk. The bathrooms are small but very clean. Suites have sofa beds and minifridges. Be sure to read about the motel's restaurant, Blackjack's Grill (p. 289). The heated outdoor pool, open seasonally, is lovely.

1133 Grand Ave., Las Vegas, NM 87701. ✆ **888/448-8438** or 505/425-6791. www.innonthesantafetrail.com. 42 units. $82 double. Rates include continental breakfast. Extra person $5. AE, DISC, MC, V. Pets permitted for $5 fee. **Amenities:** Restaurant (p. 289); outdoor heated pool. *In room:* A/C, TV, Wi-Fi, coffeemaker.

Plaza Hotel ★ A stay in this hotel offers a romantic peek into the past, with a view of the plaza. The inn was built in Italianate bracketed style in 1882, in the days when Western towns, newly connected with the East by train, vied with one another in constructing fancy "railroad hotels," as they were known. Considered the finest hotel in the New Mexico Territory when it was built, it underwent a $2-million renovation exactly 100 years later. Stately walnut staircases frame the lobby and conservatory (with its piano); throughout the hotel, the architecture is true to its era.

As with most renovations in northern New Mexico, don't expect to see the elegance of the Ritz. Instead, expect a more frontier style, with Old West antiques. Rooms vary in size, but most are average size, with elegantly high ceilings, antique furnishings, comfortably firm beds, and armoires concealing the televisions. The bathrooms also range in size; most are small, with lots of original tile but up-to-date fixtures. The rooms either have windows facing outward toward the plaza and surrounding streets or inward toward an atrium. The inward-facing rooms are quieter but a bit claustrophobic. All rooms open onto spacious hallways with casual seating areas.

The hotel offers three meals daily and limited room service from its Landmark Grill (see below). Byron T's 19th-century saloon often features live music on Friday evenings.

230 Plaza, Las Vegas, NM 87701. ✆ **800/328-1882** or 505/425-3591. Fax 505/425-9659. www.plazahotel-nm.com. 36 units. $109–$130 double; $154–$180 suite. Rates include cooked-to-order breakfast. AE, DC, DISC, MC, V. **Amenities:** Restaurant; bar. *In room:* A/C, TV, Wi-Fi, coffeemaker.

Camping

There's plenty of camping available in and around Las Vegas. I recommend the **Las Vegas KOA** (✆ **800/562-3423** or 505/454-0180; www.koa.com), which has 65 sites, 15 with full hookups, 26 with water and electricity. Laundry, grocery, ice, and recreational facilities (including a pool) are available, as is a large gift shop. Seasonal cookouts are offered. From I-25, go 1 block southeast on US 84, and then half a mile southwest on Frontage Road (also called Sheridan Rd.).

Also in Las Vegas is **Vegas RV Park** (✆ **505/425-5640**), which offers 40 sites, 33 with full hookups, and cable TV availability. It's located at 504 Harris Rd. in Las Vegas.

If you'd rather camp at a state park, try **Storrie Lake State Park** (✆ **505/425-7278**), which offers 20 sites with electricity, 23 sites without it, and primitive camping in an open area close to the lake. Developed sites have water, picnic tables, and grills, and a visitor center is nearby.

WHERE TO DINE IN LAS VEGAS

Blackjack's Grill ★★ SEAFOOD/STEAKS Set in the Inn on the Santa Fe Trail, this restaurant serves tasty food with a bit of flair. The main dining room is small and cozy, done in bright colors with moody lighting. In the warmer months, diners can sit on a patio under white cloth umbrellas. As befits the area, it's a fairly informal restaurant that does fill up, so try to make reservations. Each night the chef serves some special dishes. Most are fairly traditional. I've enjoyed beef medallions in wine sauce served with garlic mashed potatoes. The pasta dishes, such as fettuccine Alfredo, can also be good. Most meals come with bread, a choice of salad or soup, and a vegetable. A variety of dessert specials are available. Beer and wine are served.

At the Inn on the Santa Fe Trail, 1133 Grand Ave. ✆ **888/448-8438** or 505/425-6791. Reservations recommended. Main courses $15–$22. AE, MC, V. Daily 5:30–9pm.

Plaza Hotel's Landmark Grill ★★ (Finds) AMERICAN/NEW MEXICAN Lately this has become my favorite place to dine while looking out upon the graceful Las Vegas plaza, with its towering elm trees. The restaurant, set in the historic 1882 Plaza Hotel, has good food, especially the New Mexican and the grilled dishes. It has a sunny dining room, with tables well spaced, adorned by the original 19th-century stenciling along the walls. Service is good. At breakfast you might have egg and pancake dishes, and on Sunday for brunch eggs florentine (poached eggs, spinach, grilled tomato, and hollandaise sauce on an English muffin), served with hash browns. Lunch brings salads, sandwiches, burgers, pasta, and New Mexican food. I've enjoyed a grilled turkey with Swiss cheese and green chile on rye. At dinner, you might enjoy a filet with bleu cheese mushroom sauce, or grilled pecan crusted trout with pecan butter, each served with salad, vegetable, and choice of starch. Beer and wine accompany the menu. Byron T's 19th-century saloon next door offers food daily from 2 to 5pm.

230 Plaza. ✆ **800/328-1882** or 505/425-3591. www.plazahotel-nm.com. Reservations recommended on weekend nights. Main courses breakfast/brunch and lunch $5–$15; dinner $8–$25. AE, DC, DISC, MC, V. Daily 7am–2pm and 5–9pm.

3 ON THE SANTA FE TRAIL: CIMARRON & RATON

CIMARRON ★

Few towns in the American West have as much lore or legend attached to them as Cimarron, 41 miles southwest of Raton via US 64. Nestled against the eastern slope of the Sangre de Cristo Mountains, the town (its name is Spanish for "wild" or "untamed") achieved its greatest fame as a "wild and woolly" outpost on the Santa Fe Trail between the 1850s and 1880s and a gathering place for area ranchers, traders, gamblers, gunslingers, and other characters.

Essentials

GETTING THERE From Fort Union National Monument, head north on I-25, and then west on US 58 to Cimarron.

VISITOR INFORMATION The **Cimarron Chamber of Commerce,** 104 N. Lincoln Ave. (P.O. Box 604), Cimarron, NM 87714 (✆ **575/376-2417;** www.cimarronnm.com), has complete information on the region. It is open June to August daily 9am to 5pm, and November to April Monday through Saturday 10am to 3pm; the rest of the year 10am to 4pm.

Exploring the Wild West Town

Frontier personalities such as Kit Carson and Wyatt Earp, Buffalo Bill Cody and Annie Oakley, Bat Masterson and Doc Holliday, Butch Cassidy and Jesse James, painter Frederic Remington and novelist Zane Grey all passed through and stayed in Cimarron—most of them at the **St. James Hotel** (p. 292). Even if you're not planning an overnight stay here, it's a fun place to visit for an hour or two.

Land baron Lucien Maxwell founded the town in 1848 as the base of operations for his 1.7-million-acre empire. In 1857, he built a mansion at his **Maxwell Ranch,** furnishing it opulently with heavy draperies, gold-framed paintings, and two grand pianos. The ranch isn't open for viewing today, but Maxwell's 1864 stone gristmill, built to supply flour to Fort Union, is. The **Old Mill Museum** (✆ **575/376-2417**), a grand, three-story stone structure that's well worth visiting, houses an interesting collection of early photos, as well as memorabilia including a saddle that belonged to Kit Carson. It's open in May and September, Saturday from 10am to noon and 1 to 5pm, and Sunday from 1 to 5pm; Memorial Day to Labor Day, Friday through Wednesday from 10am to noon and 1 to 5pm. It's closed October through April. Admission is by donation. Ask for a historic walking-tour map at the Old Mill Museum.

A block north of US 64, look for a few historic buildings housing shops. In particular check out the **Cimarron Art Gallery,** 337 E. 9th St. (✆ **575/376-2614**), which has a 1937 soda fountain, and offers ice cream, flavored coffees, as well as jewelry, sculptures, and a huge selection of Boy Scout badges. Another good stop is **Blue Moon Eclectics,** 333 E. 9th St. (✆ **575/376-9040**), selling artful pottery, jewelry, books, and knives. Down the street, stop in at the studio of L. Martin Pavletich, 428 E. 9th St. (✆ **575/376-2871;** www.lmartinpavletich.com), to see colorful landscape paintings of the region.

Nearby Attractions

Cimarron is the gateway to the **Philmont Scout Ranch** (✆ **575/376-2281;** www.philmont.com), a 137,500-acre property donated in pieces, beginning in 1938, to the Boy Scouts of America by Texas oilman Waite Phillips. Scouts from all over the world use the ranch for backcountry camping and leadership training in the summer and for conferences the remainder of the year. Even if you have no interest in scouting you'll want to visit the elegant Villa. It and two other museums on the ranch are open to the public.

Getting Outside: Cimarron Canyon State Park

US 64 from Cimarron leads west 24 miles to Eagle Nest, passing en route the popular and often crowded **Cimarron Canyon State Park** (✆ **575/377-6271**). A 32,000-acre designated state wildlife area, it sits at the foot of crenelated granite cliffs, 800 feet high in some areas, known as the Palisades. Rock climbing is allowed throughout the park except in the Palisades area. The river and the two park lakes attract anglers; for the best fishing, move away from the heavily populated campgrounds.

Just east of Cimarron, County Road 204 offers access to the Carson National Forest's **Valle Vidal** recreation area (see chapter 8), a scenic and remote place to hike, backpack, and see hundreds of elk.

Where to Stay & Dine in Cimarron

Casa del Gavilan ★ *Finds* Built in 1910 on a broad hill overlooking Philmont and the mountains beyond, this sprawling adobe villa provides a quiet Southwestern ranch-style experience. The common areas have high ceilings with thick vigas (beams) and wooden floors. The rooms surround a central courtyard, a nice place to sit and relax in the cool evenings. The rooms are spacious, with comfortably firm beds and plenty of antiques. The bathrooms are medium-size and maintain an old-style charm. The two-bedroom suite, which is housed in what's called the Guest House, is good for families, though lower ceilings give it a slightly newer feel. There isn't a television on the premises, but a hiking trail just off the courtyard leads to amazing vistas. Breakfast is served in a big, sunny dining room; you'll find such specialties as baked French toast with ham-and-fruit salad and a baked apple pancake served with sausage. Dial-up computer connection is available in the library.

6 miles south of Cimarron on NM 21 (P.O. Box 518), Cimarron, NM 87714. ✆ **800/GAVILAN** or 575/376-2246. Fax 575/376-2247. www.casadelgavilan.com. 5 units. $85–$145 per unit. Rates include full breakfast. Extra person $20, extra child between the ages of 5–10 $10. DISC, MC, V. *In room:* Coffeemaker, no phone.

Finds Cold Beer

For a funky break between Raton and Cimarron, stop in at the **Colfax Tavern.** A bar since 1929, this lone building on the prairie is so popular that people call it Cold Beer, New Mexico, as though it were a town in itself. The owner says that Cold Beer is a "state of mind." Many ingredients go into creating that state, including a pool table, photos on the walls of locals imbibing, decent pizza and burgers, and few tail-wagging mutts to welcome you. It's at the corner of US 64 and NM 505 (✆ **575/376-2229**).

St. James Hotel ★ If a romantically historic stay in an Old West town appeals to you, consider spending a night at this landmark hotel. It looks much the same today as it did in 1873, when it was built by Henri Lambert, previously a chef for Napoleon, Abraham Lincoln, and Ulysses S. Grant. In its early years, it was a rare luxury hotel on the Santa Fe Trail, with a dining room, a saloon, gambling rooms, and lavish guest rooms outfitted with Victorian furniture. Today, you'll find lace and cherrywood in the bedrooms, though the feel is frontier elegance rather than lavishness. Rooms don't have televisions or phones—the better to evoke the days when famous guests such as Zane Grey, who wrote *Fighting Caravans* at the hotel, were residents. Annie Oakley's bed is here, and a glass case holds a register with the signatures of Buffalo Bill Cody and the notorious Jesse James. The beds are comfortably soft, and the bathrooms small and basic. One room just off the lobby stays open so that those not spending the night can have a peek. The most authentic and atmospheric rooms are next to this one, all on the ground floor.

The St. James was a place of some lawlessness: 26 men were said to have been killed within the 2-foot-thick adobe walls, and bullet holes can be seen in the pressed-tin ceiling of the dining room. The ghosts of some are believed to inhabit the hotel still.

Next door are 12 more rooms in a motel. These basic accommodations offer clean bathrooms, TVs, and telephones for those who prefer the 21st century.

Lambert's at the St. James serves good food in semi Old West ambiance, with a molded tin ceiling and Western murals. The menu is short, but good, with dishes such as fettuccine primavera and prime rib, priced from $15 to $30. It's open in summer for dinner daily and in winter Wednesday to Sunday. A separate coffee shop serves three meals daily, purveying sandwiches and large portions of tasty New Mexican food. On a large patio outside, bands sometimes play in summer.

617 S. Collinson, Cimarron, NM 87714. ✆ **866/472-5019** or 505/376-2664. Fax 505/376-2623. 22 units. Hotel $70–$95 double, $130 suite; motel $70 double. AE, DISC, MC, V. **Amenities:** Restaurant; bar; coffee shop; billiards room. *In room:* No phone in some rooms.

RATON

Raton was founded in 1879 at the site of Willow Springs, a watering stop on the Santa Fe Trail. Mountain man "Uncle Dick" Wooton, a closet entrepreneur, had blasted a pass through the Rocky Mountains just north of the spring and began charging tolls. When the railroad bought Wooton's road, Raton developed as the railroad, mining, and ranching center for this part of the New Mexico Territory. Today it has a well-preserved historic district and the finest shooting facility in the United States.

East of Raton is Capulin Mountain, home to Capulin Volcano National Monument. The volcanic crater of the majestic 8,182-foot peak, inactive for 60,000 years, is open to visitors. See below for more about Capulin Volcano National Monument.

Essentials

GETTING THERE From Santa Fe, take I-25 north; from Taos, take US 64 east.

VISITOR INFORMATION The tourist information center is at the **Raton Chamber and Economic Development Council,** 100 Clayton Rd., at the corner of 2nd Street (P.O. Box 1211), Raton, NM 87740 (✆ **800/638-6161** or 575/445-3689; www.raton.info). Memorial Day to Labor Day, the center is open daily from 8am to 6pm; hours are 8am to 5pm during the rest of the year.

Finds Hat Cemetery

While strolling Raton's main drag, step into **Solano's Boot & Western Wear,** 101 S. 2nd St. (✆ **575/445-2632**). As well as selling the latest in cowboy/cowgirl chic, the place has a "hat cemetery" where northern New Mexico and southern Colorado ranchers have retired their bent and sweaty favorites.

Strolling Historic Raton

Five blocks of Raton's original town site are listed on the National Register of Historic Places, with some 70 significant buildings. It's best to explore the historic district by foot, allowing 1 to 2 hours. Start at the **Raton Museum,** 108 S. 1st St. (✆ **575/445-8979**), where you can pick up a walking-tour map. The museum, open Tuesday through Saturday from 9am to 5pm, displays a wide variety of mining, railroad, and ranching items from the early days of the town. If you're not up for the full tour, at least take a stroll down 1st Street to see the **Mission Santa Fe Depot,** 1st St. and Cook Ave., a 1903 Spanish Mission Revival structure, where Amtrak still stops. Also of note is the **Wells Fargo Express Building,** 145 S. 1st St., erected in 1910, also in Spanish Mission Revival style. Now it houses the **Old Pass Gallery,** (✆ **575/445-2052**), which features regional art well worth perusing. Across the street is the **Abourezk Building,** 132 S. 1st St., which over time has been a drugstore, dry-good and grocery store, and is now home of the **Heirloom Shop** (✆ **575/445-8876**), a fun antiques shop. My mother likes to buy vintage handkerchiefs here.

A few blocks west on 2nd Street, be sure to take note of the **Shuler Theater,** 131 N. 2nd St. (✆ **575/445-4746**), which brings a variety of productions to Raton, including concerts of Music from Angel Fire. Across the street, shoppers will enjoy **Santa Fe Trail Traders,** 100 S. 2nd St. (✆ **575/445-2888**), which carries turquoise jewelry, Native American pottery, and weavings.

Nearby Attractions

The **NRA Whittington Center** (✆ **575/445-3615;** www.nrawc.org), off US 64 about 10 miles south of Raton, is considered the most complete nonmilitary shooting and training facility in the world. Operated by the National Rifle Association, it spans 50 square miles of rolling hills.

In the little town of **Springer** (pop. 1,300), 39 miles south of Raton via I-25, the **Santa Fe Trail Museum,** in the center of town on Maxwell Avenue (✆ **575/483-5554**), is housed in the old three-story 1881 Colfax County Courthouse. It contains pioneer artifacts and memorabilia from travelers along the Santa Fe Trail and early residents of the area. Hours are Tuesday through Saturday from 10am to noon and 1 to 3pm. Admission is $4 for adults, $2 for seniors, and $2 for students; free for children 8 and under with an adult, free on Saturday. The **Colfax County Fair** takes place in Springer annually in mid-August, with a rodeo and 4-H fair. Call ✆ **575/445-8071** for more information.

If you want to stay or dine in Springer, stop in at the **Brown Hotel & Café,** 302 Maxwell Ave. (✆ **575/483-2269**). This old-time place has photos of area ranchers on the walls and sweet country-style rooms upstairs. The food is diner-style, with plenty of pancakes, burritos, and, of course, chicken-fried steak.

Sugarite Canyon State Park (✆ **575/445-5607**), 10 miles northeast of Raton via NM 72 and NM 526, offers historic exhibits, camping, boating, and excellent fishing at two trout-stocked lakes. Lake Alice is the best place in the park for fly-fishing. Numerous hiking trails meander through the park, and a museum at the visitor center traces the canyon's mining history.

South of US 56 via NM 39 is the westernmost of the two parcels that comprise the **Kiowa and Rita Blanca National Grasslands** (✆ **575/374-9652**). The 263,954-acre area is a project to reclaim once-barren prairie land, the result of over-farming in the late 19th and early 20th centuries, and the Great Plains Dustbowl of the 1930s. Today the plains are irrigated and green, and the area provides food, cover, and water for a wide variety of wildlife.

Where to Stay in Raton

Best Western Sands ★ Kids Rooms in this hotel, equidistant between downtown and the interstate, are so clean and roomy that reservations are a must during summer months. Built in 1959, the hotel updates its furnishings and decor periodically. All rooms are decorated with Southwestern prints, with nice touches such as ceramic or iron lamps and finely made oak or pine furniture. In the luxury wing, rooms have minifridges and recliners. All rooms have comfortable beds and medium-size baths. The standard rooms are more than adequate and provide plenty of space and parking right outside your door.

300 Clayton Hwy., Raton, NM 87740. ✆ **800/518-2581,** 800/528-1234, or 575/445-2737. Fax 575/445-4053. www.bestwestern.com/sandsraton. 50 units. $66–$120 double. Extra person $3. AE, DC, DISC, MC, V. **Amenities:** Outdoor heated pool in summer; Jacuzzi; business center. *In room:* A/C, TV, Wi-Fi, coffeemaker, hair dryer, iron.

Heart's Desire Bed & Breakfast ★ Finds Set in the Raton Historic District, this little crystal of history was built in 1885 to serve as a boardinghouse during Raton's railroad heyday. In 1997, Barbara Riley restored it, bringing splendor to the Victorian building. Guest rooms are medium-size, all decorated with Victorian touches, all with a shared bathroom. Each room has a sink and a comfortable bed. There's also a suite with a full kitchen and its own bathroom. Over a tasty breakfast such as eggs Benedict with fresh fruit, Barbara will regale you with tales of the area, where she grew up out on the plains. A courtesy computer with wireless Internet is available in the dining area.

301 S. 3rd St., Raton, NM 87740. ✆ **866/488-1028** or 575/445-1000. www.heartsdesireraton.com. 3 units, 1 suite. $75–$90 double with shared bathroom, $98–$130 double suite. Rates include full breakfast. AE, DISC, MC, V. **Amenities:** Access to health club. *In room:* Hair dryer, iron upon request.

Holiday Inn Express ★★ Kids This hotel on the south end of Raton offers comfortable rooms and excellent service. Three times running, it's earned the Torchbearer award from Holiday Inn Express, which puts it in their top 20 properties in the Americas. Rooms come with a king or two queens, some with sleeper sofas as well. Each is medium size, with comfortable beds with good linens. Baths are small with an outer vanity. As well, this hotel offers a variety of "specialty suites," one for business travelers, which includes a large desk, 2 TVs, and a wet bar; another "spa suite," has a hot tub for two; and a "family suite" offers a dining area, and two separate bedrooms, one with bunk beds, so the space can sleep six or more. Service here is excellent.

101 Card Ave., Raton, NM 87440. ✆ **800/HOLIDAY** or 575/445-1500. Fax 575/445-7650. www.hiexpress.com/ratonnm. 80 units. $110 double; $140–$310 suite. Rates include full breakfast. AE, DISC, MC, V. Pets

$10 per night. **Amenities:** Indoor pool; Jacuzzi; business center; exercise room; shuttle to airport and town. *In room:* A/C, TV, Wi-Fi, coffeemaker, hair dryer, iron.

Camping

Quite a few campgrounds are in the Raton area, including the **Raton KOA,** in town at 1330 S. 2nd St. (✆ **800/562-9033** or 575/445-3488; www.koa.com), with 54 sites, grocery and laundry facilities, and picnic tables and grills.

Summerland RV Park, at 1900 S. Cedar/I-25 and US 87 (✆ **575/445-9536**), which is convenient to the interstate, has 44 sites (plus 16 monthly sites), laundry and grocery facilities, and picnic tables.

Where to Dine in Raton

Oasis Restaurant ★ Kids At mealtime, area residents crowd this bright, open cafe on the south end of town, which serves quality diner-style food. With comfortable American decor and tables and booths adequately spaced, the restaurant provides a good setting for locals to chat and gossip. "You gettin' old?" one man asked another. "Naw," his neighbor said. "I'm *already* old." All ages fill this place, though—they seem to enjoy the burgers (hand-patted) and fries (hand-cut). Soups are homemade, as are rolls, tortillas, and *sopaipillas.* Each day brings a special such as green chile chicken casserole. Breakfasts are hearty, with lots of egg and pancake options.

1445 S. 2nd St. (from Clayton Hwy., turn south). ✆ **575/445-2221.** Reservations not needed. $4–$8 breakfast; $5–$16 lunch or dinner. AE, DISC, MC, V. Winter daily 6am–8pm; summer daily 6am–8:30pm.

Pappas' Sweet Shop Restaurant ★ SEAFOOD/STEAKS Founded almost 78 years ago, this restaurant still seems to draw praise from most locals. It's an interesting place, with counters full of chocolate candies and fudge upfront. The big dining room has a comfortable tearoom feel, but only one window. And though the food isn't sophisticated, it's carefully prepared and tasty. Best known are the beef dishes; prime rib is a big seller here. I've enjoyed a filet that was perfectly prepared and served with tender vegetables. Meals come with homemade bread, a salad, and your choice of a potato dish or pasta. A full-service lounge adjoins the restaurant, and there's also a gift shop.

1201 S. 2nd St. ✆ **575/445-9811.** Reservations suggested at dinner in summer. Main courses $6–$12 lunch, $9–$35 dinner. AE, DISC, MC, V. Mon–Sat 11am–2pm and 5–9pm.

4 CAPULIN VOLCANO NATIONAL MONUMENT ★★

Capulin Volcano National Monument offers visitors the rare opportunity to walk inside a volcanic crater. A 2-mile road spirals up from the visitor center more than 600 feet to the crater of the 8,182-foot peak, where two self-guided trails leave from the parking area: an energetic and spectacular 1-mile hike around the crater rim and a 100-foot descent into the crater to the ancient volcanic vent. One of the most interesting features here is the symmetry of the main cinder cone. The volcano was last active about 60,000 years ago, when it sent out the last of four lava flows. Scientists consider it dormant, with a potential for future activity, rather than extinct.

Because of the elevation, wear light jackets in the summer and layers during the rest of the year. Be aware that the road up to the crater rim is frequently closed due to weather conditions. Plan on spending 1 to 3 hours at the volcano; a more in-depth exploration could take several days, but camping is not permitted.

 A short nature trail behind the center introduces plant and animal life of the area and is great for kids and accessible to people with disabilities. A longer hike starts at park headquarters up to the parking lot at the crater rim. The crater rim offers magnificent panoramic views of the surrounding landscape, the Sangre de Cristo Mountains, and, on clear days, portions of four contiguous states: Kansas, Texas, Colorado, and Oklahoma. During the summer, the volcano attracts swarms of ladybird beetles (ladybugs).

ESSENTIALS

GETTING THERE The monument is located 30 miles east of Raton via US 64/87 and north 3 miles on NM 325.

VISITOR INFORMATION The visitor center, at the base of the western side of the volcano, is open daily Memorial Day to Labor Day from 7:30am to 6:30pm, the rest of the year daily from 8am to 4pm. An audiovisual program discusses volcanism, and park personnel will answer questions. Admission is $5 per car. For more information, contact **Capulin Volcano National Monument,** P.O. Box 40, Capulin, NM 88414 (✆ **575/278-2201;** www.nps.gov/cavo).

DINING

Capulin Country Store, US 64/87 and NM 325 (✆ **575/278-3900**) offers up excellent chicken-fried steak and volcano burgers (smothered in chili and cheese) to area ranchers daily from 11am to 3pm from May through October. You'll rub elbows with area ranchers here, the only dining spot within many miles.

CAMPING

Camping is not permitted inside the monument; however, camping facilities are available only 3 miles away, in Capulin (try the **Capulin RV Park,** at ✆ **575/278-2921;** www.capulinrvpark.com), as well as in the neighboring towns of Raton and Clayton.

5 ALONG THE CLAYTON HIGHWAY

FOLSOM

Near here, cowboy George McJunkin discovered the 10,000-year-old remains of "Folsom Man." The find, excavated by the Denver Museum of Natural History in 1926, represented the first association of the artifacts of prehistoric people (spear points) with the fossil bones of extinct animals (a species of bison). The site is on private property and is closed to the public, but some artifacts (prehistoric as well as from the 19th c.) are displayed at the **Folsom Museum,** Main Street, Folsom (✆ **575/278-2122** in summer, 575/278-3616 in winter; http://folsommuseum.netfirms.com). The museum does not, however, contain any authentic Folsom prints, only copies. The museum has limited exhibits on prehistoric and historic Native Americans of the area, as well as Folsom's settlement by whites. Hours are daily 10am to 5pm from Memorial Day to Labor Day, winter by appointment. The museum is open weekends only in May and September. Admission is $1.50 for adults, 50¢ for children 6 to 12, and free for children under age 6. To get to Folsom, take NM 325 off the Clayton Highway (US 64/87, running 83 miles east-southeast from Raton to Clayton) for 7 miles.

CLAYTON

Clayton (pop. 2,100) is a ranching center just 9 miles west of the Texas and Oklahoma panhandle borders. Rich prairie grasses, typical of nearby **Kiowa and Rita Blanca National Grasslands** (✆ **575/374-9652**), led to its founding in 1887 at the site of a longtime cowboy resting spot and watering hole. In the early 19th century, the Cimarron Cutoff of the Santa Fe Trail passed through here. This area was also the site of numerous bloody battles between Plains Indians and Anglo settlers and traders. Clayton is most known as the town where the notorious train robber Thomas "Black Jack" Ketchum was inadvertently decapitated while being hanged in 1901 (a doctor carefully reunited head and body before Ketchum was buried here).

Tracks from eight species of dinosaurs can be clearly seen on the **Dinosaur Trackway at Clayton Lake State Park** ★, 12 miles north of town off NM 370, near the distinctive Rabbit Ears Mountains (✆ **575/374-8808;** www.claytonlakestatepark.com). The lake is crystalline blue and is strange to come upon after driving across these pale prairies. It offers fishing, swimming, boating, hiking, and camping. A half-mile trail on the southeast side of the lake leads across the dam to an exhibit describing the types of dinosaurs that roamed this area. From there, you can wander along a boardwalk to the amazingly intact dinosaur tracks. In 2006, the park gained an $85,000 observatory, where stargazers can take advantage of the region's especially dark skies to see to the edge of the universe.

Lay your head for the night at the **Eklund Hotel Dining Room and Saloon** ★, 15 Main St. (✆ **575/374-2551;** www.theeklund.com). Recently remodeled, this hotel offers late-1800s-style rooms updated with contemporary amenities. And if you're hungry and thirsty, head for its restaurant and bar, where you'll dine on New Mexican food, steaks, and seafood in an Old West atmosphere. You can also get a good night's rest at the **Best Western Kokopelli Lodge,** 702 S. 1st St., Clayton, NM 88415 (✆ **800/528-1234** or 575/374-2589; www.bestwestern.com).

VISITOR INFORMATION For information on other area attractions, as well as more lodging and dining options, contact the **Clayton–Union County Chamber of Commerce,** 1103 S. 1st St. (P.O. Box 476), Clayton, NM 88415 (✆ **575/374-9253;** www.claytonnewmexico.org).

6 THE I-40 CORRIDOR

The 216 freeway miles on I-40 from Albuquerque to the Texas border cross featureless prairie and very few towns. But the valleys of the Pecos River (site of Santa Rosa) and the Canadian River (Tucumcari is on its banks) have several attractions, including natural lakes. In recent years, both towns have revitalized their historic districts, creating little art centers, with a few galleries, shops, and restaurants. Start your tour of Santa Rosa along Historic Route 66, which is also a great place to peruse the Mother Road's neon signage. The historic district is just south of there. Tucumcari also has a great display of Route 66 neon and architecture along its main route, with the historic district a few blocks north. Both are well worth driving.

ESSENTIALS

GETTING THERE Travel time from Albuquerque to Tucumcari via I-40 is 2 hours, 40 minutes; to Santa Rosa, 1 hour, 45 minutes. There's no regularly scheduled commercial service into either Tucumcari or Santa Rosa. Private planes can land at **Tucumcari Municipal Airport** (© **575/461-3229**).

VISITOR INFORMATION Contact the **Tucumcari–Quay County Chamber of Commerce,** 404 W. Rte. 66 Blvd. (P.O. Drawer E), Tucumcari, NM 88401 (© **575/461-1694;** www.tucumcarinm.com), or the **Santa Rosa City Information Center,** 244 S. Fourth St., Santa Rosa, NM 88435 (© **575/472-3763;** www.santarosanm.org).

SEEING THE SIGHTS

The **Mesalands Community College's Dinosaur Museum** ★, 222 E. Laughlin (© **575/461-3466;** www.mesalands.edu/museum/museum.htm), half a block east off 1st Street, is home to the largest collection of life-size bronze prehistoric skeletons in the world. It's open from March 1 to Labor Day, Tuesday through Saturday 10am to 6pm (noon–5pm the rest of the year). Admission is $6 for adults, $3.50 for children 5 to 11, free for children 4 and under, and $5 for seniors 65 and older.

A fun small-town stop is **Tucumcari Historical Museum,** 416 S. Adams (© **575/461-4201**), 1 block east of 1st Street. Renovated in 1999, the museum showcases Route 66 and other regional memorabilia. It's open from 8am to 5pm Monday through Saturday in summer and from 8am to 5pm Monday through Friday in winter. Admission is $2.50 for adults and 75¢ for children 6 to 15; it's free for kids under age 5. The moonlike **Mesa Redondo,** a round mesa rising 11 miles south of town via NM 209, was once train robber "Black Jack" Ketchum's hideout—he was eventually captured and executed in Clayton in 1901.

To the northwest, 34 miles distant from Tucumcari over NM 104, is **Conchas Lake State Park** (© **575/868-2270**), with a reservoir 25 miles long. Though the water is a beautiful aqua, it sits within a desert environment, with lots of sand and little shade. A marina on the northern side provides facilities for boating, fishing, and water-skiing, while nearby you'll find a store, cafe, RV park with hookups, and trailers available to rent. If you'd like to spend a few days here, contact the **Adobe Belle** ★, P.O. Box 131, Conchas Dam, NM 88416 (© **575/868-3351;** www.geocities.com/adobebelle), an inn just above the lake's shore that offers adobe cabins. The decor is a little dated, but the cabins provide plenty of space.

Ute Lake State Park (© **575/487-2284**) is 22 miles northeast of Tucumcari on US 54, near the town of Logan. It has a full-service marina, docking facilities, picnic tables, campsites, and rental boats.

Quay County around Tucumcari is noted for its blue-quail hunting, said to be the best anywhere in the United States.

Santa Rosa calls itself "the city of natural lakes." Those bodies of water include **Blue Hole** ★, Blue Hole Road (turn south off Rte. 66 onto Lake Dr. then left onto Blue Hole Rd.; © **575/472-3763**), a crystal-clear, 81-foot-deep artesian well just east of downtown. Fed by a subterranean river that flows 3,000 gallons per minute at a constant 61°F (16°C), it's a favorite of scuba divers and is deep enough to merit open-water certification. Divers must either be certified or be with a certified instructor. Equipment can be rented at the nearby **Santa Rosa Dive Center** (© **575/472-3370**), open on weekends only. Swimming and snorkeling are also fun here, with a bathhouse on-site. This is a great place to cool off on a hot summer day. **Park Lake** (© **575/472-3763**), in the middle of town, serves as the town's municipal pool. It's a natural lake so the water is fresh, and visitors can rent paddleboats and canoes. The kids can swim with the geese while you cool off under the elm trees. The lake offers free swimming, picnicking, and fishing, as well as a softball field and playground. **Santa Rosa Lake State Park,** P.O. Box 384, Santa Rosa, NM 88435 (✆ **575/472-3110**), on a dammed portion of the Pecos River, has camping, hiking, boating, and excellent fishing. Ten miles south of town via NM 91, the village of **Puerto de Luna** is a 19th-century county seat with a mid-1800s courthouse and church, Nuestra Señora del Refugio. Francisco Vásquez de Coronado was believed to have camped here as he traveled en route to Kansas. For insight into village life here, read Rudolfo Anaya's *Bless Me, Ultima,* a tale of growing up on the *llano* (plains) of the area.

WHERE TO STAY

Major chain hotels are at I-40 interchanges in both Tucumcari and Santa Rosa. Smaller ma-and-pa motels can be found along the main streets through town that were once segments of legendary Route 66—still bearing that historic name.

In Tucumcari

Hampton Inn With the consistency of its brand name, this hotel provides a bit of an oasis in this part of the state. It's located near I-40, but has some very quiet rooms. Each is medium size with earth tone decor and comfortable beds with luxury bedding. Some have microwaves and fridges. The baths are standard size with floor tiles. The west side rooms offer the most quiet and a bit of a view out across meadows and ponds.

3409 E. Rte. 66. (at I-40 exit 335), Tucumcari, NM 88401. ✆ **800/HAMPTON** or 575/461-1111. Fax 575/461-0000. www.hamptoninn.hilton.com. 58 units. $99–$115. Price includes hot breakfast. AE, DC, DISC, MC, V. **Amenities:** Indoor pool; Jacuzzi; sauna; business center; coin-op laundry. *In room:* A/C, TV, Wi-Fi, coffeemaker, hair dryer, iron.

Camping near Tucumcari

There are three good campgrounds around Tucumcari. **Tucumcari KOA** (✆ **800/562-1871** or 575/461-1841; www.koa.com) has 111 sites, laundry and grocery facilities, RV supplies, picnic tables, and grills. It also offers a recreation hall with video games, a heated swimming pool, a basketball hoop, a playground, horseshoes, and shuffleboard, along with lots of elm trees for shade. To get there from I-40, get off the interstate at exit 335, and then go a quarter mile east on South Frontage Road.

Mt. Road RV Park (✆ **575/461-9628**) has 60 sites with full hookups, tenting, laundry facilities, and picnic tables. From I-40, take exit 333 to Mountain Road; the park is on the US 54 bypass.

The campground in **Conchas Lake State Park** (✆ **575/868-2270**) has 104 sites, 40 full hookups, lake swimming, boating, and fishing.

In Santa Rosa

La Quinta ★ Perched on a hill above Santa Rosa, this newer whitewashed chain hotel offers clean and very functional rooms. All are medium-size, decorated in tasteful earth tones. Each has an extremely small bathroom with an outer sink/vanity. Beds are comfy and are accompanied by a table and chairs. The place is inventively landscaped with a rock grotto patio where the hot tub sits.

1701 Will Rogers Dr., Santa Rosa, NM 88435. ✆ **800/531-5900** or 575/472-4800. Fax 575/472-4809. www.laquinta.com. 60 units. $75–$95 double. Rates include continental breakfast. AE, DC, DISC, MC, V. **Amenities:** Indoor pool; outdoor Jacuzzi. *In room:* A/C, TV, high-speed Internet, Wi-Fi, coffeemaker, hair dryer, safe.

Camping near Santa Rosa

The **Santa Rosa Campground** (✆ **575/472-3126**) offers 94 sites, 33 full hookups, laundry and grocery facilities, fire rings, grills, a heated swimming pool, and a playground

Moments Route 66 Revisited: Rediscovering New Mexico's Stretch of the Mother Road

As the old Bobby Troupe hit suggests: Get your kicks on Route 66. The highway that once stretched from Chicago to California was hailed as the road to freedom. During the Great Depression, it was the way west for farmers escaping Dust Bowl poverty out on the plains. If you found yourself in a rut in the late 1940s and 1950s, all you had to do was hop in the car and head west on Route 66.

Of course, the road existed long before it gained such widespread fascination. Built in the late 1920s and paved in 1937, it was the lifeblood of communities in eight states. Nowadays, however, US 66 is as elusive as the fantasies that once carried hundreds of thousands west in search of a better life. Replaced by other roads, covered up by interstates (mostly I-40), and just plain out of use, Route 66 still exists in New Mexico, but you'll have to do a little searching and take some extra time to find it.

Motorists driving west from Texas can take a spin (make that a slow spin) on a 20-mile gravel stretch of the original highway running from Glenrio (Texas) to San Jon. From San Jon to Tucumcari, you can enjoy nearly 24 continuous paved miles of vintage 66. In Tucumcari, the historic route sliced through the center of town along what is now Route 66 Boulevard. Santa Rosa's Historic Route 66 is that city's 4-mile claim to the Mother Road. In Albuquerque, US 66 follows Central Avenue for 18 miles, from the 1936 State Fairgrounds, past original 1930s motels and the historic Nob Hill district, on west through downtown.

One of the best spots to pretend you are a 1950s road warrior crossing the desert—whizzing past rattlesnakes, tepees, and tumbleweeds—is along NM 124, which winds 25 miles from Mesita to Acoma in northwestern New Mexico. You can next pick up old Route 66 in Grants, along the 6-mile Santa Fe Avenue. In Gallup, a 9-mile segment of US 66 is lined with restaurants and hotels reminiscent of the city's days as a Western film capital from 1929 to 1964. Just outside Gallup, the historic route continues west to the Arizona border as NM 118.

For more information about Route 66, contact the **Grants/Cíbola County Chamber of Commerce** (✆ **800/748-2142**) or the **New Mexico Department of Tourism** (✆ **800/545-2040**).

for the kids. Situated in a piñon and juniper forest near town, the campground has a few small elm trees on the grounds. Coming from the east on I-40, take exit 277 and go 1 mile west on Business Loop; coming from the west on I-40, take exit 275 and go 1/4 mile east on Business Loop.

Also in the area is **Santa Rosa Lake State Park** (✆ **575/472-3110**), with year-round camping featuring 75 sites (about a third with electric hookups) as well as grills, boating, fishing, and hiking trails. Swimming in the lake is permitted but not encouraged because of the lake's uneven bottom and lack of beaches; children would be safer swimming in Park Lake in Santa Rosa.

TWO GOOD PLACES TO EAT IN THE AREA

Del's Family Restaurant AMERICAN/NEW MEXICAN The big cow atop Del's neon sign is not only a Route 66 landmark, but it also points to the fine steaks inside. The restaurant has big windows along most every wall, letting in plenty of daylight or neon light at night. It's a casual, diner-style eatery with lots of plants. Breakfast brings big plates of dishes such as scrambled eggs and pancakes. At lunch, sample sandwiches and salads. The roast beef is a big seller here at dinnertime, served with a scoop of mashed potatoes and a trip to the salad bar. You can also order a grilled chicken breast. The New Mexican food is good but not great. Del's is not licensed for alcoholic beverages.

1202 E. Rte. 66, Tucumcari. ✆ **575/461-1740.** Reservations not accepted. Main courses $5–$8 breakfast, $5–$10 lunch, $8–$16 dinner. MC, V. Mon–Sat 7am–9pm.

Joseph's Restaurant & Cantina ★ AMERICAN/NEW MEXICAN You may want to plan your drive so that you can eat a meal at "Joe's." In business since 1956, it's a real Route 66 diner, with linoleum tables, comfortable booths, and plenty of memorabilia, from license plates to vintage RC Cola posters. The locals all eat here: You'll see Hispanic grandmothers, skinny cowboys in straw hats, and dusty farmhands just in from the fields. The varied menu offers excellent fare. Breakfast brings eggs and bacon or omelets. At lunch, I've enjoyed a salad topped with tender grilled chicken. The New Mexican dishes are large and chile-smothered, and the burgers juicy, with a variety of toppings, from the Rio Pecos topped with green chile to the Acapulco, with guacamole. Steaks are a big seller, also at a good price. For dessert, try a piece of pie or a shake. Also on the premises are a bakery, a full-service bar, and a gift shop.

865 Historic Rte. 66, Santa Rosa. ✆ **575/472-3361.** Reservations not accepted. Main courses $4–$8 breakfast, $6–$9 lunch, $7–$15 dinner. AE, DC, DISC, MC, V. Summer daily 7am–10pm; winter daily 7am–9pm.

11

Southwestern New Mexico

This region, defined by the border with Mexico and cloaked by the 3.3-million-acre **Gila National Forest,** offers ruggedness and remoteness, and always an echo of history. It's the region that wealthy Zacatecan mine owner Juan de Oñate passed through in 1598 to take possession of the territory for the Spanish King.

It was and still is a good place to hide out. Billy the Kid lived here; so did Geronimo. You'll stumble upon relics of their past at many junctures. You'll see thousands of snow geese taking flight at the **Bosque del Apache National Wildlife Refuge.** You can even contemplate the vastness of space at the **Very Large Array (VLA),** the world's most powerful radio telescope.

The most settled part of the area is down the center of the state, where the Rio Grande marks a distinct riparian line. Throughout history, this river has nourished the Native American, Hispanic, and Anglo settlers who have built their homes beside its banks. The river land was especially fertile around modern Las Cruces; the settlement of La Mesilla was southern New Mexico's major center for 3 centuries.

West of the river, the Black Range and Mogollon Mountains rise in the area now cloaked by Gila National Forest. This was the homeland of the Mogollon Indians 1,000 years ago. **Gila Cliff Dwellings National Monument** preserves one of their great legacies. This was also the homeland of the fiercely independent Chiricahua Apaches in the 19th century. Considered the last North American Indians to succumb to the whites, they counted Cochise and Geronimo among their leaders.

Mining and outdoor recreation, centered in historic **Silver City** (pop. 12,500), are now the economic stanchions of the region. But dozens of mining towns have boomed and busted in the past 140 years, as a smattering of ghost towns throughout the region attest, some such as Silver City and Hillsboro now home to artists who have opened galleries along the Old West streets.

Las Cruces, at the foot of the Organ Mountains, is New Mexico's second largest city, with 86,268 people. It's a busy agricultural and education center. North up the valley are **Truth or Consequences** (pop. 7,500), a spa town named for the 1950s radio and TV game show, and **Socorro** (pop. 9,000), a historic city with Spanish roots. West, on the I-10 corridor to Arizona, are the ranching centers of **Deming** (pop. 14,500) and **Lordsburg** (pop. 3,379).

1 SOUTHWESTERN NEW MEXICO'S GREAT OUTDOORS

Rugged, remote, forested, and fascinating all describe southwestern New Mexico, where few tourists venture—lucky for you if you're looking for backcountry adventure.

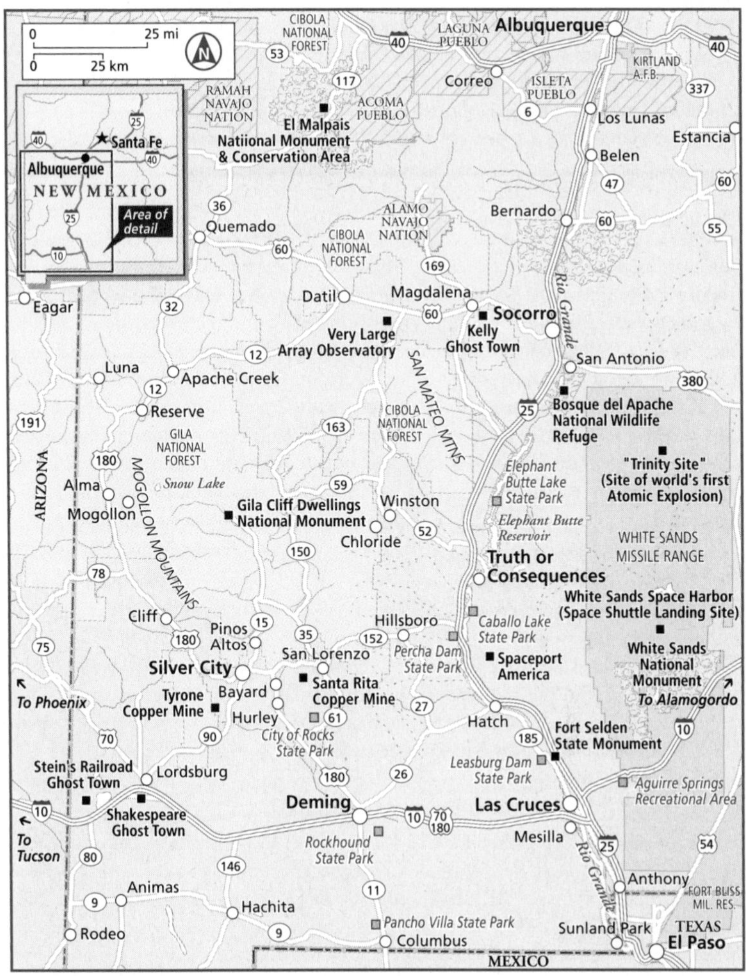

BIKING Bikes are not allowed in the Gila Wilderness, but they are permitted on trails in other parts of **Gila National Forest** (✆ **575/388-8201;** www.fs.fed.us/r3/gila). Refer to "Other Adventures in Gila National Forest," later in this chapter, for some specific ride suggestions and contact **Gila Hike and Bike** (✆ **575/388-3222**) in Silver City for rentals and guidebooks to riding in the Gila National Forest.

BIRD-WATCHING **Bosque del Apache National Wildlife Refuge** (✆ **575/835-1828**) is a refuge for migratory waterfowl such as snow geese and cranes. It's 16 miles south of Socorro. **North Monticello Point** (✆ **575/744-5421**), on Elephant Butte Lake, is a great place to see pelicans, bald eagles, and a variety of waterfowl, while **Water Canyon** (✆ **575/854-2281**), 14 miles west of Socorro in the **Cíbola National Forest,**

Hummingbird Safari at Lake Roberts

At the **Annual Hummingbirds of New Mexico Festival** (✆ **888/536-4266;** www.hbnm.org) in the village of Lake Roberts, the third week in July, bird lovers can watch as little cuffs are placed on hummingbird ankles, a remarkable process called "banding" to help identify them and learn about their lives. The weekend includes talks, guided walks, arts-and-crafts booths, and baked goods for sale.

is home to golden eagles. The **Sevilleta National Wildlife Refuge** (✆ **575/864-4021**), north of Socorro between La Joya and Chamizal, is a long-term ecological research site under the direction of the National Science Foundation. Its visitor center is open 7:30am to 4pm weekdays, and 9am to 3pm Saturday (closed Sun, Christmas, and New Year's Day) and has exhibits about the refuge. The refuge offers free tours during its open house, the second Saturday in October. In recent years, the **Gila National Forest** (✆ **575/388-8201**) has become quite popular with birders. Guests at the **Bear Mountain Lodge** (✆ **877/620-BEAR** [2327] or 575/538-2538; www.bearmountainlodge.com) benefit from an on-site naturalist and occasional birding tours. In the Gila, my favorite birding spot is **Lake Roberts,** where hummingbirds abound.

BOATING In the Gila National Forest, both **Lake Roberts** (✆ **575/536-2250**), about 40 miles north of Silver City on NM 15, and **Snow Lake** (✆ **575/533-6231**), north on US 180 from Silver City and then east on NM 159, allow boating. Lake Roberts features motorboat rentals, whereas Snow Lake only permits canoes, rowboats, and other boats without gas motors.

Elephant Butte Lake State Park (✆ **575/744-5923**) boasts the largest body of water in New Mexico. The lake is 43 miles long and popular with boating enthusiasts. Three ramps provide boating access to the lake, and there are launching areas for smaller vessels. (To find information on New Mexico state parks, go to www.nmparks.com.)

FISHING **Caballo Lake State Park** (✆ **575/743-3942**), about 18 miles south of Truth or Consequences, offers smallmouth and largemouth bass, stripers, bluegill, crappie, catfish, and walleye fishing in its 11,500-acre lake. **Elephant Butte Lake State Park** (✆ **575/744-5923**), also near Truth or Consequences, is another great fishing location. Look to catch white bass, black bass, catfish, walleye, crappie, and stripers here. **Lake Roberts** (✆ **575/536-2250**), about 40 miles north of Silver City in the Gila National Forest, is prime rainbow trout fishing waters. A fishing license and habitat stamp are both required. You'll find fly-fishing in the **Gila River** year-round, but the best seasons are spring and fall. Mainly rainbow trout swim these waters, with catfish on the lower Gila. For more information, contact the **New Mexico Game and Fish Department** (✆ **505/476-8000;** www.wildlife.state.nm.us).

GOLF In Socorro, the 18-hole **New Mexico Tech Golf Course** (✆ **575/835-5335;** www.nmt.edu) offers tree-lined fairways and water on more than half of its holes. The **Truth or Consequences Golf Course** (✆ **575/894-2603**) offers 9 fairly traditional holes in a desert setting. But the new **Sierra del Rio Golf Course** at Turtleback Mountain Resort (✆ **575/744-4653;** www.sierradelrio.com), opened in 2007, offers 18 holes that area golfers are talking about. Another contemporary course is in Las Cruces, at the 18-hole **Sonoma Ranch Golf Course** (✆ **575/521-1818;** www.sonomaranchgolf.com), which opened in 2000. Las Cruces also has the **New Mexico State University Golf Course** (✆ **575/646-3219;** www.nmsu.edu/golf), built with collegiate golf in mind. With wide-spanning views and undulating terrain, this Cal Olsen–designed course has much to offer. Deming has the 18-hole **Rio Mimbres Country Club** (✆ **575/546-9481**), while Silver City golfers go to the 18-hole **Silver City Golf Course** (✆ **575/538-5041;** www.silvercity.org), home to the annual Billy Casper Golf Tournament.

HIKING It goes without saying that there's great hiking available in the **Gila National Forest** (✆ **575/388-8201**), which has approximately 1,500 miles of trails, ranging in length and difficulty. Your best bet for hiking in the area is to purchase a guidebook devoted entirely to hiking the Gila National Forest, but popular areas include the Crest Trail, the West Fork Trail, and the Aldo Leopold Wilderness. One favorite day hike in the forest is the Catwalk, a moderately strenuous hike along a series of steel bridges and walkways suspended over Whitewater Canyon. See "Other Adventures in Gila National Forest," later in this chapter, for more hiking suggestions. Whenever and wherever you go hiking, be sure to carry plenty of water.

HORSEBACK RIDING If you want to go horseback riding, the **Double E Guest Ranch** (✆ **575/535-2048;** www.doubleeranch.com) offers authentic ranch riding in the southwestern New Mexico desert and forest lands. Because the ranch is also a working cattle ranch, it has an authentic feel, and a guest capacity of only 12 adds to the experience. About a half-hour from Silver City, the ranch sits on a shady bend of Bear Creek, a place that draws plenty of wildlife. The accommodations are in old ranch buildings, which range from cozy to expansive. These are not luxury rooms; instead, they're real ranch lodgings. The ranch does not have a separate children's program but does accept kids.

HOT SPRINGS This is hot springs country. For locations in Truth or Consequences, call ✆ **800/831-9487** or 575/894-3536, or see "Truth or Consequences," later in this chapter for my choices of bathhouses. **Lightfeather Hot Spring** is a spring near the Gila Cliff Dwellings National Monument visitor center.

SWIMMING Swimming is permitted at **Elephant Butte Lake State Park** (✆ **575/744-5923**) and **Caballo Lake State Park** (✆ **575/743-3942**), but not at some others. Be sure to ask first.

2 SOCORRO & THE VLA

Socorro, a quiet, pleasant town of about 9,000, is an unusual mix of the 19th, 20th, and 21st centuries. Established as a mining settlement and ranching center, its downtown area is dominated by numerous mid-1800s buildings and the 17th-century San Miguel Mission. **The New Mexico Institute of Mining and Technology** (New Mexico Tech) is a major research center. Socorro is also the gateway to a vast and varied two-county region that includes the **Bosque del Apache National Wildlife Refuge,** the **Very Large Array National Radio Astronomy Observatory (VLA),** and three national forests.

ESSENTIALS

GETTING THERE From Albuquerque, take I-25 south (1¼ hr.). From Las Cruces, take I-25 north (2¾ hr.).

Cruising the Royal Road

As you skim across the open desert on Interstate 25, take heart in knowing that you're following an ancient route: El Camino Real, or the Royal Road that ran from Mexico to San Juan Pueblo north of Santa Fe. It's older than recorded history, traveled first by indigenous people. Later the Spaniards, beginning with Juan de Oñate in 1598, made their way north on it, seeking adventure and prosperity. They brought herds of horses and cattle, flocks of sheep and goats, and, most transformative, Catholicism. In subsequent centuries it continued to be the main road for travelers and traders carrying goods and ideas. Eventually it connected up with the Santa Fe Trail, which was the east-west route from Missouri. To find out more about this route, visit the **El Camino Real International Heritage Center.** See below for details.

VISITOR INFORMATION The **Socorro County Chamber of Commerce,** which is also the visitor information headquarters, is at 101 Plaza (P.O. Box 743), Socorro, NM 87801 (✆ **575/835-0424;** www.socorro-nm.com).

EXPLORING SOCORRO

The best introduction to Socorro is a walking tour of the historic district. A brochure with a map and guidebook, available at the chamber of commerce on the **plaza,** where the tour begins, points out several historic buildings, many on the National Register of Historic Places.

You'll definitely want to check out the old **Val Verde Hotel.** The horseshoe-shaped Val Verde, a National Historic Landmark, was built in 1919 in California Mission style. It's been converted to apartments. Another interesting spot is the **Fullingim-Isenhour-Leard Gallery,** 113-C W. Abeyta St., just off the plaza, (✆ **575/835-4487;** www.fi galleries.com). In a historic building, four artists share their bronze-work, paintings, and etchings. If you're craving a cappuccino or latte while in Socorro, head to the **Manzanares Coffee House** ★, 110 Manzanares St. (✆ **575/838-0809**). As well as coffee drinks, the shop offers good sandwiches on foccacia bread, salads, and house-made gelato and sorbet. It's also a wireless Internet zone.

OTHER ATTRACTIONS

El Camino Real International Heritage Center ★ This museum, opened in 2005, tells the story of El Camino Real, the 1,500-mile international trade route from Mexico to San Juan Pueblo, near Santa Fe. The impressive $5-million, 20,000-square-foot structure, set in the middle of the desert, is an award-winning building perched like a ship above Sheep Canyon between Socorro and Truth or Consequences. In fact, the center is designed with ship elements, including a bowsprit on the helm. "The journey across the Jornada del Muerto reminded travelers of crossing the sea, with its tufts of grass, mirages, and overwhelming silence," says Monument Ranger Dave Wunker. The real fun starts in the exhibit hall, where visitors get to travel the trail themselves, beginning at Zacatecas Plaza in Mexico, one of many stops along the road. Artifacts from the Camino days—*a caja fuerte* (strong box) and an Apache water jug—help tell the story, though my one complaint about the museum is that it's a bit short on artifacts, which may be remedied as it matures. Excellent period photos and some high-tech displays help fill the gap.

C.R. 1598, 30 miles south of Socorro. From I-25 take exit 115 and follow the signs. ✆ **575/854-3600.** www.caminorealheritage.org. Admission $5 adult; free for children 15 and under. Daily 8:30am–5pm.

Mineral Museum Run by the New Mexico Bureau of Geology and Mineral Resources, this museum has the largest geological collection in the state. Its more than 10,000 specimens include mineral samples from all over the world, fossils, mining artifacts, and photographs.

Campus Rd., New Mexico Tech campus. ✆ **575/835-5420.** Free admission. Mon–Fri 8am–5pm; Sat–Sun 10am–3pm.

Old San Miguel Mission ★★ Built during the period from 1615 to 1626 but abandoned during the Pueblo Revolt of 1680, this graceful church was subsequently restored, and a new wing was built in 1853. It boasts thick adobe walls, large carved vigas (rafters), and supporting corbel arches. English-language Masses are Saturday at 6pm and Sunday at 9:30 and 11am.

403 El Camino Real NW, 2 blocks north of the plaza. ✆ **575/835-1620.** Free admission. Summer Mon–Fri 8am–7:30pm; winter Mon–Fri 8am–6:30pm.

SEEING THE SIGHTS NEAR SOCORRO

SOUTH OF SOCORRO The village of **San Antonio,** the boyhood home of Conrad Hilton, is 10 miles from Socorro via I-25. During the financial panic of 1907, his merchant father, Augustus Hilton, converted part of his store into a rooming house. This gave Conrad his first exposure to the hospitality industry, and he went on to worldwide fame as a hotelier. Only ruins of the store/boardinghouse remain.

WEST OF SOCORRO US 60, running west to Arizona, is the avenue to several points of interest. **Magdalena,** 27 miles from Socorro, is a mining and ranching town that preserves an 1880s Old West spirit. In mid-November, this little town holds its Fall Festival, which includes a variety of studio tours, artist demonstrations, and a silent auction. If you want to stay in Magdalena, I recommend the **Western Bed and Breakfast & RV Park,** 404 First St. (✆ **575/854-2417** or 575/854-2412; www.thewesternmotel.com), a rustic and quaint motel, with pine walls decorating most rooms. Be sure to stop in at **Evett's Cafe** on US 60 (✆ **575/854-2449**) for one of the best milkshakes in New Mexico; order yours made from hand-packed ice cream.

Three miles south, the ghost town of **Kelly** produced more than $40 million worth of lead, zinc, copper, silver, and gold in the late 19th and early 20th centuries. Today, unfortunately, the ghost town is closed to visitors.

The Pie Way

The long stretch of highway on U.S. 60 between Socorro and Quemado offers few islands on its vast sea of grass. One of them is Pie Town. In the 1920s, a Texan named Clyde Norman settled here, started baking and selling pies, and his talent won the town a name. It has even been written up in *Smithsonian Magazine.* Set along the Continental Divide, today the **Pie-O-Neer** cafe, on U.S. 60 (✆ **575/772-2711;** www.pie-o-neer.com) offers up a treat worth clocking the miles for. The cafe bakes a variety of types—with their specialty apple—daily. Simple meals, such as burgers and green chile stew, are offered as well. The town's **Pie Festival** takes place in mid-September.

Fifty-four miles west of Socorro via US 60 is the **Very Large Array National Radio Astronomy Observatory (VLA)** ★★. (The Socorro office is at 1003 Lopezville Rd. NW; ✆ **575/835-7000;** www.nrao.edu.) Here, 27 dish-shaped antennas, each 82 feet in diameter, are spread across the plains of San Agustin, forming a single gigantic radio telescope. Many recognize the site from the 1997 movie *Contact,* starring Jodie Foster. Photographs taken with this apparatus are similar to those taken with the largest optical telescopes, except that radio telescopes are sensitive to low-frequency radio waves. All types of celestial objects are photographed, including the sun and its planets, stars, quasars, galaxies, and even the faint remains of the "big bang" that scientists believe occurred some 10 billion years ago. On the outdoor, self-guided walking tour, you'll have a chance to get a closer look at the massive antennas. Admission is free, and visitors are welcomed daily from 8:30am to sunset.

WHERE TO STAY IN THE SOCORRO AREA

Most accommodations are along California Street, the main highway through town, or the adjacent I-25 frontage road. Most lodgings provide free parking.

Casa Blanca ★ The ideal situation in this part of the world is to be just a few minutes away from the Bosque del Apache. That way, you only have to get out of bed a half-hour or so before sunup in order to get to the wildlife refuge and see the morning flight (see "Oasis in the Desert: Bosque del Apache National Wildlife Refuge," below). Casa Blanca is the place to stay for this reason. It's a cozy Victorian farmhouse and home to proprietor Phoebe Wood, a former schoolteacher. The place has a genuine homelike quality—comfortable and well maintained. The best room is the Heron with a queen-size bed and private bathroom with a whirlpool tub. An early morning snack and coffee are offered for those leaving early to the Bosque, and later, upon your return a full breakfast is available. Fruit, cereals, eggs and home-baked muffins are served in a homey kitchen. Smoking is not permitted.

13 Montoya St. (P.O. Box 31), San Antonio, NM 87832. ✆ **575/835-3027.** www.casablancabedandbreakfast.com. 3 units. $80–$100 double. Rates include generous breakfast. MC, V. Closed June–Sept. Children and pets welcome.

Holiday Inn Express ★ (Kids) Opened in 2007, this new hotel right within town with good access to I-25 offers the region's best lodgings. Rooms come in kings, two queens, and suites. All are medium size, with a lounge chair and/or desk and/or two chairs and a table. The rooms, decorated in earth tones, have comfortable beds and nice linens. The suites have fold-out couches, a good option for those traveling with children. Baths are medium size, with granite countertops. Service here is courteous and efficient. A hot breakfast is served in the sunny breakfast room or on the patio.

1040 California St. NE, Socorro, NM 87801. ✆ **800/HOLIDAY** or 575/838-4600. Fax 575/838-4700. www.hiexpress.com/socorronm. 77 units. $105 double; $135 suite. Rates include breakfast. AE, DISC, MC, V. **Amenities:** Indoor pool; exercise room; indoor Jacuzzi. *In room:* A/C, TV, Wi-Fi, fridge, microwave, coffeemaker, hair dryer, iron, safe.

Camping

Casey's Socorro RV Park (✆ **800/674-2234** or 575/835-2234) offers mountain and valley views and plenty of shade, as well as 100 sites and 30 full hookups. Tenting is available, as are picnic tables, grills, and ice. A playground and swimming pool are open year-round. To reach Casey's, take I-25 to exit 147, go 1 block west on Business I-25 and then 1 block south on West Frontage Road.

WHERE TO DINE IN THE SOCORRO AREA

El Sombrero ★ NEW MEXICAN This is a real locals' place. My Socorran friends call it "the Hat" and always request the garden room, where tables surround a small fountain. This is some of the best New Mexican food around. I especially enjoy the chicken enchiladas, though my friends in town often order the spinach ones. They come rolled, with beans, rice, and a *sopaipilla.* Most popular on the menu are the fajitas, beef or chicken, served with rice, beans, tortillas, and guacamole. The restaurant is known for its trademark sauces, especially the poblano chile and mole sauces, which are served over enchiladas or meats such as chicken. For dessert, try the churro, a cinnamon sugared stick, with vanilla ice cream. Beer and wine are available.

210 Mesquite NE, Socorro. ✆ **575/835-3945.** Main courses $6–$12. AE, DC, DISC, MC, V. Daily 11am–9pm.

Manny's Buckhorn Tavern ★★ AMERICAN For years, the cafe across the street from this place in San Antonio (10 miles south of town), the Owl Bar, held the state's title for the best green chile cheeseburger. More recently this spry contender has come to dominate the ring. With the title has come a slew of press, including *GQ* magazine naming its burgers on their national top-20 burger list. *Travel + Leisure* and the *New York Times* have also written about this charming place that's full of local color. It has hardwood floors, beer neons, and memorabilia on the walls—a Christ crucifix, antelope antlers—set above cozy booths. Order their specialty, a Buckhorn Burger, made with hand-patted 80% lean beef topped with green chile and cheese. On the side, choose fries or onion rings, both good and crispy. If you're not a burger fan, try the tacos or tamales. Wash your meal down with a beer or margarita from the full bar.

Building 68, NM 380, San Antonio (10 miles south of Socorro). ✆ **575/835-4423.** All menu items under $8. MC, V. Mon–Sat 11am–8pm.

Socorro Springs Brewing Company ★★ AMERICAN/PIZZA This little pocket of sophistication is a nice addition to small-town Socorro. On most any day, the place is full of happy diners sampling the brew and eating tasty wood-oven and grilled cuisine. It's a casual place with a refined brewpub atmosphere, with wooden tables and colorful walls. The service is congenial though not quick. You may choose from salads and sandwiches, calzones and pizzas, and more upscale dishes. A good pizza choice is the Bandido, with pepperoni, Italian sausage, prosciutto, and jalapeños, or the Vigilante, with artichoke hearts, chicken, and kalamata olives. Most recently, I enjoyed the baked penne carbonara—penne pasta with a cheddar/bacon sauce baked in the wood-fired oven. The grilled salmon served with a red-pepper sauce is also delicious.The beer is nice, with a bit of a smoky taste.

1012 W. California St., Socorro. ✆ **575/838-0650.** www.socorrosprings.com. Reservations accepted. Main courses $8–$23. AE, DISC, MC, V. Daily 10:30am–10pm.

Stage Door Grill ★★ STEAKS/SEAFOOD/CAJUN Set in the historic 1850 Elfego Baca building, with adobe walls, a viga ceiling, and bright paintings, this new restaurant serves tasty steaks, seafood, burgers, pasta, and Cajun dishes. A little dark inside, the restaurant rambles through three rooms and is anchored by a classic wooden bar in the back. Service is good. For lunch, locals seem to prefer burgers in a variety of types or salads such as the Asian chicken, with mandarin oranges, chow mein noodles, and sesame vinaigrette. At dinner, the steaks are a good choice, served with soup or salad, vegetable, and potato or rice, as are the Cajun dishes (the restaurant owner's relations cook at many venues in Louisiana, so he's pulled recipes from them). The shrimp etoufee is quite nice.

 A brief but international wine list and a selection of brew pub beers accompany the menu. Thursday through Saturday nights, live music—ranging from folk to country to blues to jazz—plays.

Bernard and Abeyta (just north of Plaza). ✆ **575/835-2403.** www.stagedoorgrill.net. Reservations accepted. Main courses $7–$20. AE, DISC, MC, V. Daily 11am–10pm.

3 BOSQUE DEL APACHE NATIONAL WILDLIFE REFUGE

By Ian Wilker

The barren lands to either side of I-25 south of Albuquerque seem hardly fit for rattlesnakes, much less one of the Southwest's greatest concentrations of wildlife. The plants that do find purchase in the parched washes and small canyons along the road—forbiddingly named hardies such as creosote bush, tarbush, and white thorn—serve notice that you are indeed within the northernmost finger of the great Chihuahuan Desert, which covers southern New Mexico and southwestern Texas, and runs deep into Mexico.

However, to the east of the interstate is the green-margined Rio Grande. In the midst of such a blasted landscape, the river stands out as an inviting beacon to wildlife, and nowhere does it shine more brightly than at Bosque del Apache's 7,000 acres of carefully managed riparian habitat, which includes marshlands, meadows, agricultural fields, arrow-weed thickets on the riverbanks, and big old-growth cottonwoods lining what were once the oxbows of the river. The refuge supports a riot of wildlife, including all the characteristic mammals and reptiles of the Southwest (mule deer, jackrabbits, and coyotes are common) and about 377 species of birds.

A visit here during the peak winter season—from November to March—is one of the most consistently thrilling wildlife spectacles you can see anywhere in the lower 48 states, especially if you're an avid bird-watcher. Bosque del Apache is, you might say, the LAX of the Central Flyway, one of four paths that migratory birds follow every year between their summer breeding grounds in the tundral north and wintering grounds in the southern United States, Mexico, even as far away as South America—and many of these birds either stop over here to recharge their batteries or settle down for the winter.

It's not enough to say that hundreds of species of birds are on hand. The wonder is in the sheer numbers of them. In early December the refuge may harbor as many as 45,000 snow geese, 57,000 ducks of many different species, and 18,000 sandhill cranes—huge, ungainly birds that nonetheless have a special majesty in flight, pinkish in the sun at dawn or dusk. Plenty of raptors are also about—numerous red-tailed hawks and northern harriers (sometimes called marsh hawks), Cooper's hawks and kestrels, and even bald and golden eagles—as well as Bosque del Apache's many year-round avian residents: pheasants and quail, wild turkeys, and much mythologized roadrunners (*El Paisano,* in Mexican folklore). Everyone will be mesmerized by the huge societies of sandhills, ducks, and geese, going about their daily business of feeding, gabbling, quarreling, honking, and otherwise making an immense racket.

The refuge has a 12-mile auto tour loop, which you should drive very slowly; the south half of the loop travels past numerous water impoundments, where the majority of the ducks and geese hang out, and the north half has the meadows and farmland, where you'll see the roadrunners and other land birds, and where the cranes and geese feed from midmorning through the afternoon.

A few special experiences bear further explanation. Dawn is definitely the best time to be here—songbirds are far more active in the first hours of the day, and the cranes and geese take flight en masse. This last is not to be missed. Dusk, when the birds return to the water, is also a good time. At either dawn or dusk, find your way to one of the observation decks and wait for what birders call the "fly out" (off the water to the fields) or "fly in" (from the fields to the water).

Don't despair if you can't be at the Bosque del Apache during the prime winter months, for it's a special place any time of year. By April, the geese and ducks have flown north, and the refuge drains the water impoundments to allow the marsh plants to regenerate; the resulting mud flats are an ideal feeding ground for the migrating shorebirds that arrive in April and May.

If you'd like to stretch your legs a bit, check out the **Chupadera Peak Trail,** which follows a 2.5-mile loop or a 10-mile loop to a high point overlooking the refuge. Ask for directions at the visitor center.

JUST THE FACTS The Bosque del Apache National Wildlife Refuge is about a 1½-hour drive from Albuquerque. Follow I-25 for 9 miles south of Socorro, and then take the San Antonio exit. At the main intersection of San Antonio, turn south onto NM 1. In 3 miles, you'll be on refuge lands, and another 4 miles will bring you to the excellent visitor center, which has a small museum with interpretive displays and a large shelf of field guides, natural histories, and other books of interest for visitors to New Mexico. The visitor center is open from 7:30am to 4pm weekdays, and from 8am to 4:30pm weekends. The refuge itself is open daily year-round from 1 hour before sunrise to 1 hour after sunset. Admission is $3 per vehicle. For more information, contact **Bosque del Apache National Wildlife Refuge,** P.O. Box 1246, Socorro, NM 87801 (✆ **575/835-1828;** www.fws.gov/southwest/refuges/newmex/bosque).

4 TRUTH OR CONSEQUENCES

Originally known as Hot Springs, after the therapeutic mineral springs bubbling up near the river, the town took the name Truth or Consequences—usually shortened to "T or C"—in 1950. That was the year that Ralph Edwards, producer of the popular radio and television program *Truth or Consequences,* began his weekly broadcast with these words: "I wish that some town in the United States liked and respected our show so much that it would like to change its name to Truth or Consequences." The reward to any city willing to do so was to become the site of the 10th-anniversary broadcast of the program, which would put it on the national map in a big way. The locals voted for the name change, which has survived three protest elections over the years.

Although the TV program was canceled decades ago, Ralph Edwards continued to return for the annual **Truth or Consequences Fiesta,** the first weekend of May. He died in 2005. Another popular annual festival is **Geronimo Days,** the second weekend of October. Despite its festive roots, T or C seems to have an identity crisis—perhaps a consequence of giving up your name for the fame and fortune of television. The city displays a forlorn quality, possibly due to the struggling economy. However, in recent years, a few of the bathhouses have undergone renovation, and a number of galleries and restaurants have opened up, bringing new life to the town.

Fun Facts Next Stop—Space

Fasten your seat belt and settle back for an orbit or two of Earth—that's what space-minded folks, such as New Mexico Governor Bill Richardson and British tycoon Richard Branson foresee as a reality soon. Space tourists would take off from the proposed $225-million Airport America near Truth or Consequences. In its embryonic stages now, the spaceport will include one or more runways, hangars, a control building, and launch pads. The first test flights took place in 2007, while the completion date for the spaceport is 2010.

When it's complete, Branson plans to headquarter Virgin Galactic here. Currently Virgin is selling tickets for $200,000 apiece for a 2½-hour flight, including 5 minutes of weightlessness. The first of these flights will likely fly out of the Mojave Airport in California, where SpaceShipOne became the first privately manned rocket to reach space in 2004. Virgin Galactic has contracted to build a fleet of rockets called SpaceShipTwo, with hopes of initiating tourist flights in 2009. For updates, log onto www.virgingalactic.com or www.edd.state.nm.us.

ESSENTIALS

GETTING THERE From Albuquerque, take I-25 south (2½ hr.). From Las Cruces, take I-25 north (1¼ hr.). Though no commercial flight service exists, those who fly themselves may contact the **Truth or Consequences Municipal Airport,** Old North Hwy. 85 (✆ **575/894-6199**).

VISITOR INFORMATION The **visitor information center** is at the corner of Main (Business Loop 25) and Foch streets in downtown Truth or Consequences. Also there is the **Truth or Consequences & Sierra County Chamber of Commerce,** P.O. Box 31, Truth or Consequences, NM 87901 (✆ **575/894-3536;** www.truthorconsequencesnm.net).

CITY LAYOUT This year-round resort town and retirement community of 7,500 is spread along the Rio Grande between the Elephant Butte and Caballo reservoirs, two of the three largest bodies of water in the state. Business Loop 25 branches off from I-25 to wind through the city, splitting into Main Street (one-way west) and South Broadway (one-way east) in the downtown area. Third Avenue connects T or C with the Elephant Butte resort community, 5 miles east.

TAKING THE WATERS AT THE HISTORIC HOT SPRINGS

The town's "original" attraction is its hot springs. The entire downtown area is located over a table of odorless hot mineral water, 98° to 115°F (37°–46°C), that bubbles to the surface through wells or pools. The first bathhouse was built in the 1880s; most of the half-dozen historic spas operating today date from the 1930s. Generally open from morning to early evening, these spas welcome visitors for soaks and massages. Baths of 20 minutes or longer start at $7 per person.

The chamber of commerce has information on all the local spas (see "Essentials," above). Among them is **Sierra Grande Lodge & Spa ★★**, 501 McAdoo St. (✆ **575/894-6976;** www.sierragrandelodge.com), where Geronimo himself is rumored to have taken a break. (See "Where to Stay in & Around Truth or Consequences," below.) **Artesian Bath House,** 312 Marr St. (✆ **575/894-2684**), is quite clean and has an RV park on the premises.

I highly recommend the **Hay-Yo-Kay Hot Springs** ★, 300 Austin St. (✆ **575/894-2228;** www.hay-yo-kay.com). It has natural-flow pools (versus tubs filled with spring water). The tub rooms are private and gracefully tiled. The Long House, a cooler tub, is the largest in town and can hold up to 20 people. Hay-Yo-Kay is open Wednesday through Sunday 11am to 7pm. Massages and reflexology are also available.

A MUSEUM IN T OR C

Geronimo Springs Museum Outside this museum is Geronimo's Spring, where the great Apache shaman is said to have taken his warriors to bathe their battle wounds. Turtleback Mountain, looming over the Rio Grande east of the city, is believed to have been sacred to Native Americans.

Exhibits include prehistoric Mimbres pottery (A.D. 950–1250); the Spanish Heritage Room, updated and renovated, featuring artifacts of the first families of Sierra County; and artists' work, including historical murals and sculptured bronzes. An authentic miner's cabin has been moved here from the nearby mountains. The Ralph Edwards Wing contains the history and highlights of the annual fiestas and celebrates the city's name change, including television footage from the shows filmed in T or C.

211 Main St. ✆ **575/894-6600.** Admission $4 adults, $2 students; family rates available. DISC, MC, V. Mon–Sat 9am–5pm; Sun 11am–4pm.

GETTING OUTSIDE

Elephant Butte Lake State Park encompasses New Mexico's largest body of water, with 36,500 lake surface acres. It's one of the most popular state parks in New Mexico, attracting watersports enthusiasts and fishers from throughout the south and central regions of the state. Fishing for white bass, black bass, catfish, walleye, crappie, and stripers goes on year-round. Trout are stocked in the Rio Grande below Elephant Butte Dam. The park has sandy beaches for tanning and swimming (though don't expect the white sands of the Cayman Islands here). You can also find boating, sailing, water-skiing, windsurfing, jet-skiing, scuba diving, nature trails, and camping. Beware of going to the lake on summer weekends—Fourth of July and Labor Day weekend in particular—when the crowds are overwhelming. However, in the other seasons and during the week in summer, it's a quiet place.

Bird-watchers also enjoy the park, spotting hundreds of species, including bald eagles, great blue herons, and more than 20 species of duck during migrations in spring and fall. The lake was named for a huge rock formation that makes an island; before the inundation that created the lake, it clearly looked like an elephant. Today, it's partially submerged.

The park is about 5 miles north of Truth or Consequences via I-25. For more information, call ✆ **575/744-5923.**

About 18 miles south of Truth or Consequences via I-25 is another recreation area, **Caballo Lake State Park** (✆ **575/743-3942**), which, like Elephant Butte, has year-round watersports, fishing, swimming, and campsites. The lofty ridge of the Caballo Mountains just to the east of the lake makes a handsome backdrop. Park facilities include a full-service marina with a shop for boaters and full hookups for recreational vehicles.

Reached from the same exit off I-25 is yet another recreation area, **Percha Dam State Park** (✆ **575/743-3942**), a lovely shaded spot under great cottonwood trees, part of the ancient bosque, or woods, the Spanish found bordering the Rio Grande when they first arrived in this area in the 1530s. The dam here diverts river water for irrigation. The park offers campsites, restrooms and showers, hiking trails, and access to fishing.

EXPLORING THE GHOST TOWNS IN THE AREA

NORTH OF TRUTH OR CONSEQUENCES About 40 miles from Truth or Consequences are the precarious remains of Winston and Chloride, two so-called ghost towns—abandoned mining centers that nevertheless do have a few residents. Exploring these towns makes for a nice side trip off I-25. You may want to include a visit to the Very Large Array and the old mining town of Magdalena in the trip (see "Socorro & the VLA," earlier in this chapter). However, be aware that if you do, much of the journey from Winston to the VLA is on graded dirt road.

Winston, 37 miles northwest of Truth or Consequences on NM 52, was abandoned in the early 1900s when silver prices dropped and local mining became unprofitable. Some of the original structures from that era are still standing. A similar fate befell **Chloride,** 5 miles west of Winston on a side road off NM 52, where famed silver mines had such names as Nana, Wall Street, and Unknown. Chloride also figured in many battles in the turn-of-the-20th-century war between cattle-ranching and sheep-ranching interests. In the very center of town is the "hanging tree," where the town used to tie drunks to "dry" in the sun.

SOUTH OF TRUTH OR CONSEQUENCES Thirty-two miles from Truth or Consequences, via I-25 south to NM 152, then west, is **Hillsboro** ★, another ghost town that's fast losing its ghosts to a small invasion of artists and craftspeople, antiques shops, and galleries. This town boomed after an 1877 gold strike nearby, and during its heyday it produced $6 million in silver and gold. It was the county seat from 1884 to 1938. Hillsboro's Labor Day weekend **Apple Festival** is famous throughout the state. You may want to plan your drive to include breakfast or lunch at **Hillsboro General Store & Country Café** ★, on NM 152 in the center of town, (✆ **575/895-5306**). Serving excellent burgers and burritos in a historic general store ambiance, this spot also has some of the best pie in the region; it's called bumbleberry and combines many berries in a flaky crust. Open daily for breakfast and lunch.

The **Black Range Historical Museum** (✆ **575/895-5233** or 575/895-5685) contains exhibits and artifacts from Hillsboro's mining boom. In the former Ocean Grove Hotel, a turn-of-the-20th-century brothel operated by Sadie Orchard, the museum collection includes some of the madam's effects. This volunteer-staffed museum is supposed to be open Wednesday through Saturday from 11am to 4pm, Sunday from 1 to 5pm, but it isn't always. It's closed most major holidays. Suggested donation is $2 for adults, $1 for children, and $5 for a family.

The **Enchanted Villa** bed-and-breakfast inn, a quarter mile west of Hillsboro on NM 152 (no street address), P.O. Box 456, Hillsboro, NM 88042 (✆ **575/895-5686**), is a 1941 adobe structure that offers decent accommodations. The rates, $84 for a double and $55 for a single, include full hot breakfasts.

Nine miles west of Hillsboro on NM 152, just after you've entered the Gila National Forest, is **Kingston,** born with a rich silver strike in 1880 and reputed to have been among the wildest mining towns in the region, with 7,000 people, 22 saloons, a notorious red-light district (conveniently located on Virtue Ave.), and an opera house. Kingston was also once the home of Albert Fall, a U.S. secretary of state who gained notoriety for his role in the Teapot Dome Scandal.

Your headquarters in Kingston should be the **Black Range Lodge,** 119 Main St., Kingston, NM 88042 (✆ **575/895-5652;** www.blackrangelodge.com), a rustic stone lodge that dates from the 1880s, and over the years has housed miners and soldiers, as well as Pretty Sam's Casino and the Monarch Saloon. The lodge has seven rooms—all with private bathrooms and some with private balconies—a large game room with a pool table and video games, and family suites, as well as a new luxury guesthouse. Rates are $89 for a double, with multiple-night discounts; the guesthouse is $139 per night. Well-behaved pets are welcome for a $5 per day fee.

Among historic buildings in Kingston are the brick assay office, the **Victorio Hotel,** and the **Percha Bank,** now a museum open by appointment—ask at Black Range Lodge. The town bell in front of the Volunteer Fire Department was once used to warn residents of Native American attacks.

WHERE TO STAY IN & AROUND TRUTH OR CONSEQUENCES

Elephant Butte Inn ★ For a comfortable stay and a unique experience, try Elephant Butte Inn. It sits above Elephant Butte Lake and has panoramic views as well as a relaxing resortlike feel. Recent years have brought a face-lift to many of the rooms. It caters to boaters, fishers, and other relaxation lovers. Rooms are standard size, furnished with medium-firm king- or queen-size beds. Bathrooms are small but functional, with an outer sink vanity. I recommend the lakeside view, where a big grassy lawn stretches down to tennis courts. These rooms are a bit more upscale, with unique decor in each, and equipped with plasma TVs, fridges, and microwaves. For golfers, packages are available that include greens fees at the new Sierra del Rio Golf Course at Turtleback Mountain Resort (p. 304). The new Ivory Spa here offers a full range of treatments, including reasonably priced spa packages. A courtesy computer with Internet is available in the lobby.

401 NM 195 (P.O. Box 996), Elephant Butte, NM 87935. © **575/744-5431.** Fax 575/744-5044. www.elephantbutteinn.com. 45 units. Mid-Sept to Apr $90–$129 double; May to early Sept $80–$100 double. Golf and spa packages available. AE, DC, DISC, MC, V. Pets welcome $15–$20 per visit. **Amenities:** Restaurant; lounge w/outdoor patio; outdoor pool; tennis courts; spa; salon; room service. *In room:* A/C, TV, Wi-Fi, coffeemaker, hair dryer, iron.

Sierra Grande Lodge & Spa ★★ Prepare yourself for a sensual oasis at this resort in southern New Mexico. The biggest draw is the springs. Nowhere else in the state can you stay in luxury while partaking of warm, healing waters rich in minerals. The medium-size rooms in this renovated 1920s lodge have handcrafted furnishings, and many have balconies. All have comfortable beds with good linens. Bathrooms are small but functional. Suites have in-room Jacuzzis. A special casita with its own outdoor tub is so popular it's reserved months in advance. The spa offers a full range of treatments. Wireless Internet is available on the guest room balconies, in the hotel lobby, and on the patio. The Sierra Grande Restaurant opened to wide acclaim but since then has only remained open sporadically.

501 McAdoo St., Truth or Consequences, NM 87901. © **575/894-6976.** www.sierragrandelodge.com. 18 units. $99–$129 double Sun–Thurs; $129–$159 double Fri–Sat; $259 suite. AE, DISC, MC, V. **Amenities:** Restaurant; spa; massage. *In room:* A/C, TV, DVD player upon request, hair dryer.

Camping

Elephant Butte Lake State Park (© **575/744-5923**) welcomes backpackers and RVs alike, with 200 developed campsites, 150 RV hookups, picnic tables, and access points for swimming, hiking, boating, and fishing. Kids love the playground.

Not far from Elephant Butte Lake is **Monticello Point RV Park** (© **575/894-6468**), which offers tenting and 69 sites with full hookups. Laundry and grocery facilities are also on the premises, as are restrooms with showers. To reach Monticello Point, take I-25 to exit 89, and proceed 5½ miles east on the paved road—follow the signs.

Lakeside RV Park and Lodging (✆ **575/744-5996**), also near Elephant Butte, has 50 sites, two overflow sites (all 52 are full hookups), as well as a recreation room with cable and laundry facilities. When you are headed south on I-25, the RV park is 4 miles southeast of the I-25 and NM 195 junction (exit 83) on NM 195. To reach the RV park when you're headed north on I-25, take exit 79, go half a mile east on the paved road, 1½ miles north on NM 181, then 1½ miles east on NM 171, and finally a quarter mile south on NM 195.

Camping is also available at **Caballo Lake State Park** and **Percha Dam State Park.** For information on either park, call ✆ **575/743-3942** or visit **www.nmparks.com**.

WHERE TO DINE IN & AROUND TRUTH OR CONSEQUENCES

Café Bella Luca ★★ TUSCAN/ITALIAN Set in a historic building, renovated to have a clean look, with high ceilings, stained concrete floors, and warm earth tones, this new restaurant serves some of the best food in the region. Chef Byron Harrel hand-makes all the sauces and breads here, and the seafood is flown-in fresh. For breakfast, locals fill the place to drink espresso, eat pastries, and check e-mail on the wireless Internet. Lunch or dinner might start with crispy fried calamari or a crab cake. At lunch, one of the many sandwiches is a good bet. I've enjoyed the turkey pancetta on foccacia with house-made fries or a salad. The pasta alfredo with grilled shrimp is also nice. At dinner, the seafood *puttanesca* has a nice bite, and the roasted grouper is delectable. An extensive wine and beer list with organic options accompanies the menu, as do a variety of house-made desserts.

303 Jones St. ✆ **575/894-9866.** Reservations recommended on weekends. Main courses $6–10 lunch; $10–23 dinner. AE, DISC, MC, V. Wed–Mon 11am–4pm; Wed–Thurs and Sun–Mon 5–9pm; Fri–Sat 5–10pm.

La Cocina Kids AMERICAN/NEW MEXICAN A real locals' place, this restaurant serves decent New Mexican food in a festive atmosphere. The *tostadas* (crispy tortillas covered with beans and meat) and chile rellenos are tasty, but my favorite is the cheese enchiladas. For dessert, try the *sopaipillas.* Kids like the big booths and their own quesadillas and tacos.

Wandering in T or C

Truth or Consequences has become a bit of an art hot spot recently, with many artists moving here to enjoy the temperate climate and low cost of living. As a result, many galleries have opened up. Unfortunately, they seem to close just as quickly. So rather than give you a list that will surely change by press time, I recommend you check out **www.torcart.com**, the website for the **Downtown Gallery District Association.** The site provides a map of its members' locations and dates for their monthly art hop, when they hold receptions into the evening.

While you're out wandering, if you need a little energy, head to **Little Sprout** ★, 400 N. Broadway (✆ **575/894-4114**) to get a health fix. This cafe serves coffee, a broad range of freshly squeezed juices and smoothies, as well as sandwiches and baked goods. A favorite is the roast chicken paninni, with mozzarella, roasted red peppers, basil leaves, and pesto on a ciabatta bun. The cafe is open Monday to Saturday 8am to 6pm, and Sunday 8am to 4:30pm.

1 Lakeview Dr. (at Date St.). ✆ **575/894-6499.** Reservations recommended on weekends. Main courses $8–$20 lunch and dinner. DISC, MC, V. Mon–Thurs 10:30am–9pm; Fri–Sun 10:30am–10pm.

Los Arcos Steak & Lobster ★ AMERICAN A favorite of my father's, this spacious hacienda-style restaurant fronted by a lovely desert garden is intimate and friendly in atmosphere, as if you're at an old friend's home. Its steaks are regionally famous; my choice is always the filet mignon, served with salad and your choice of potato or rice. The fish dishes are also good. You may want to try a fresh catch, such as walleye pike or catfish, served on the weekends. The restaurant also has a fine dessert list and cordial selection. During warmer months, diners enjoy the outdoor patio.

1400 Date St. ✆ **575/894-6200.** Main courses $11–$40. AE, DC, DISC, MC, V. Sun–Thurs 5–9:30pm; Fri–Sat 5–10:30pm.

Pacific Grill *Finds* SEAFOOD With salmon-colored walls and palm tree art, this restaurant serves decent fish prepared inventively. It's a good family spot or a fun place for a night out with friends. Service is friendly but it can be overworked. Though the fish is brought to the restaurant frozen, the preparations make it seem fresh. I've enjoyed the lemon-pepper salmon and the island-style sweet-and-sour chicken (the menu has some chicken, beef, and pork selections).

304 S. Pershing St. (behind the State National Bank). ✆ **575/894-7687.** Main courses $6–$21. AE, DISC, MC, V. Mon–Sat 11am–2pm and Thurs–Sat 5–8pm.

5 LAS CRUCES

Picture a valley full of weathered wooden crosses marking graves of settlers brutally murdered by Apaches, behind them mountains with peaks so jagged they resemble organ pipes. Such was the scene that caused people to begin calling this city Las Cruces, meaning "the crosses." Even today, the place has a mysterious presence, its rich history haunting it still. Reminders of characters such as Billy the Kid, who was sentenced to death in this area, and Pancho Villa, who spent time here, are present throughout the region.

Established in 1849 on El Camino Real, the "royal highway" between Santa Fe and Mexico City, Las Cruces became a supply center for miners prospecting the Organ Mountains and soldiers stationed at nearby Fort Selden. Today, it's New Mexico's second-largest urban area, with 86,268 people. It's noted as an agricultural center, especially for its cotton, pecans, and chiles; as a regional transportation hub; and as the gateway to the White Sands Missile Range and other defense installations.

Las Cruces manages to survive within a desert landscape that gets only 8 inches of moisture a year, pulling enough moisture from the Rio Grande, which runs through, to irrigate a broad swath of valley.

ESSENTIALS

GETTING THERE From Albuquerque, take I-25 south (4 hr.). From El Paso, take I-10 north (3/4 hr.). From Tucson, take I-25 east (5 hr.).

Las Cruces International Airport (✆ **575/541-2471;** www.las-cruces.org/facilities/airport), 8 miles west of the city, offers no commercial flights at this time. **El Paso International Airport** (✆ **915/772-4271;** www.elpasointernationalairport.com), 47 miles south, has daily flights to Albuquerque, Phoenix, Dallas, and Houston, among other cities. The **Las Cruces Shuttle Service,** P.O. Box 3172, Las Cruces, NM 88003 (✆ **800/288-1784** or 575/525-1784; www.lascrucesshuttle.com), provides service between the El

Paso airport and Las Cruces. It leaves Las Cruces 12 times daily between 5am and 9:30pm for a charge of $40 one-way or $70 round-trip per person, with large discounts for additional passengers traveling together. A $9 charge is added for pickup or drop-off at places other than its regular stops at major hotels. Connections can also be made three times a day from Las Cruces to Deming and Silver City.

VISITOR INFORMATION The **Las Cruces Convention and Visitors Bureau** is at 211 N. Water St., Las Cruces, NM 88001 (✆ **877/266-8252** or 575/541-2444; www.lascrucescvb.org). The **Greater Las Cruces Chamber of Commerce,** 760 W. Picacho Ave., can be reached at P.O. Drawer 519, Las Cruces, NM 88005 (✆ **575/524-1968;** www.lascruces.org).

WHAT TO SEE & DO IN LAS CRUCES

On a hot day, when the church bells are ringing and you're wandering the brick streets of **Mesilla ★★**, you may for a moment slip back into the late 16th century—or certainly feel as though you have. This village on Las Cruces's southwestern flank was established in the late 1500s by Mexican colonists. It became the crossroads of El Camino Real and the Butterfield Overland Mail route. The Gadsden Purchase, which annexed Mesilla to the United States and fixed the current international boundaries of New Mexico and Arizona, was signed here in 1854.

Mesilla's most notorious resident, William Bonney, otherwise known as Billy the Kid, was sentenced to death at the county courthouse here. He was sent back to Lincoln, New Mexico, to be hanged, but escaped before the sentence was carried out. Legendary hero Pat Garrett eventually tracked down and killed the Kid at Fort Sumner; later, Garrett was mysteriously murdered in an arroyo just outside Las Cruces. He is buried in the local Masonic cemetery.

Thick-walled adobe buildings, which once protected residents against Apache attacks, now house art galleries, restaurants, museums, and gift shops. Throughout Mesilla, colorful red chile *ristras* decorate homes and businesses. On Thursday and Sunday afternoons year-round locals sell crafts and baked goods.

Touring Mesilla

For a fun and easy jaunt that will familiarize you with the history and architecture of this interesting village, purchase the booklet *A Walking Tour of Mesilla, NM,* sold at shops around the plaza and at the **J. Paul Taylor Visitor Center** in the Mesilla Town Hall, 2231 Avenida de Mesilla (✆ **575/524-3262,** ext. 117), where you'll find period photos and plenty of brochures on the area, as well as clean public restrooms. A good source for Mesilla events is **www.oldmesilla.org**.

Some places of note on the area include the **San Albino Church** (see "Other Attractions," below), from which you can get a view of the plaza and even peek down the side streets, where some of the old adobe houses have been restored and painted bold pinks and greens. East on Calle de Santiago is **Silver Assets ★** (✆ **575/523-8747**). Set in the old Valles Gallegos building (1850s), it was once a carpentry shop and now sells jewelry, native crafts, and hats to block the harsh Southwestern sun. On Calle de Parian look for the **Purple Lizard** (✆ **575/523-1419**), which sells ethnic clothing and accessories to dress your wild side. Across the street is the **William Bonney Gallery** (✆ **575/526-8275**). Here you'll find some nice local paintings as well as lovely pottery and katsinas. On the plaza, the **Nambe Showroom** (✆ **575/527-4623;** www.nambe.com) displays handcrafted tableware by Nambe Mills in Santa Fe. It's a great place to shop for gifts. On the southwest corner of the plaza is the oldest documented brick building in New

Mexico, built by Augustin Maurin in 1860. It has a sad history of its proprietors being murdered by robbers.

If you'd like a treat, head to **Stahmann's on the Plaza** (✆ **575/527-0667**), which shares a space with a jewelry store. A retail outlet for the notable Stahmann Farms, Stahmann's sells cookies, pecan candy, and just plain, but delicious, pecans. Chocolate lovers will find chocolate-dipped frozen strawberries and homemade ice cream at the **Chocolate Lady,** 2379 Calle de Guadalupe (✆ **575/526-2744**). If you get thirsty for a caffeine fix, head to the **Bean,** 2011 Ave. de Mesilla (✆ **575/523-0560**). As well as a full array of coffees, the cafe offers scones and muffins. Breakfast brings such delicacies as French toast made with homemade bread; and lunch, a turkey, Swiss cheese, and avocado sandwich.

This is a good place to meet locals. It's open Sunday to Wednesday 7:30am to 6pm, and Thursday to Saturday 7:30am to 9pm. Live music plays on weekends.

If you prefer a guided historic walking tour, contact **Preciliana Sandoval,** 2488 Calle Principal, P.O. Box 981, Mesilla, NM 88046 (behind El Patio Bar; ✆ **575/647-2639**). This bold artist/historian, a fifth-generation Mesilla Valley native, will regale you with stories of ghosts and historic battles in the area. Tours cost $10 per person and take about an hour, and group discounts are available.

Places of Note in Historic Las Cruces

Though it has a much less romantic atmosphere than Mesilla, downtown Las Cruces has a few historical buildings, which make visiting it worthwhile. If you'd like to do a walking tour of the area, pick up a map at the **Las Cruces Convention and Visitors Bureau** at 211 N. Water St.

Central to the area is **Downtown Mall** (✆ **575/541-2155**), an open-air arcade which hosts the **Las Cruces Farmers' & Crafts Market** ★, which specializes in locally handcrafted items and seasonal local produce, on Wednesday and Saturday from 8am to noon. Established in 1888, **New Mexico State University,** University Avenue and Locust Street (✆ **575/646-0111;** www.nmsu.edu), has an enrollment of 24,000 students and is especially noted for its schools of engineering and agriculture. It has a museum and two galleries.

Other Attractions

Branigan Cultural Center If you'd like to learn about Las Cruces history, this museum will inform you of the region's prehistory to its settlement as a city, with an excellent array of period photos, and military, ranching, railroad, and rocket memorabilia. Another gallery houses changing shows of local and regional art and traveling exhibitions. The center also presents performing arts, educational programs, and special events. It's set in an elegant historic 1935 Branigan Library and still has its original desk, skylight, and mural.

500 N. Water St. ✆ **575/541-2155.** http://museums.las-cruces.org. Free admission. Mon–Fri 10am–4pm; Sat 9am–1pm.

Las Cruces Museum of Art This museum houses galleries, art studios, and classrooms, with frequently changing exhibitions of contemporary art in a variety of media. It offers art classes year-round. Two recent exhibitions included traveling shows by Salvador Dali and Auguste Rodin.

490 N. Water St. ✆ **575/541-2137.** http://museums.las-cruces.org. Free admission. Mon–Fri 9am–4pm; Sat 9am–1pm.

Las Cruces Museum of Natural History Kids This small city-funded museum offers a variety of exhibits, changed quarterly, that emphasize science and natural history. The museum features live animals of the Chihuahuan Desert, hands-on science activities, and a small native plant garden. The Cenozoic Shop offers scientific toys and books about the region. Exhibits, such as "Insects and Bugs" and "Every Body Eats," change every few months. This museum has plans to move to a new venue in the downtown mall, though an opening date is not yet set.

Mesilla Valley Mall, 700 S. Telshor Blvd. ✆ **575/522-3120.** http://museums.las-cruces.org. Free admission. Mon–Thurs and Sat 10am–5pm; Fri 10am–8pm; Sun 1–5pm.

Las Cruces Railroad Museum Located in the historic Santa Fe Depot, which is on the National Registry of Historic Buildings, this museum offers exhibits of Las Cruces railroad history from the train's arrival in 1881 to the present. Exhibits include period photos, antique equipment and tools, and model trains. Driving through residential neighborhoods en route to the museum you'll get a feel for the many styles of architecture that the train's arrival sparked, including Queen Anne, Mission Revival, and Gothic Revival. My favorite part of the display is a photo of Theodore Roosevelt on a train during his 1912 visit to Las Cruces.

Corner of Mesilla St. and Las Cruces Ave. ✆ **575/647-4480.** http://museums.las-cruces.org. Free admission. Thurs–Sat 10am–4pm.

New Mexico Farm and Ranch Heritage Museum ★★ This 47-acre interactive museum brings to life the 3,000-year history of farming, ranching, and rural living in New Mexico. It's housed within a huge structure that's designed to look like a hacienda-style barn, with a U-shaped courtyard in back and exhibits surrounding it on expansive grounds. The museum displays such relics as a 1937 John Deere tractor and a number of examples of how ranchers "make do," ingeniously combining tools such as a tractor seat with a milk barrel to come up with a chair. Visitors can watch a cow being milked, stroll along corrals filled with livestock, enjoy several gardens, and drop by the blacksmith shop. Annual events at the museum are the La Fiesta de San Ysidro in May and Cowboy Days the third weekend in October.

4100 Dripping Springs Rd. (follow University Ave. east beyond the edge of town). ✆ **575/522-4100.** www.frhm.org. Admission $5 adults, $3 seniors 60 and over, $2 children 5–17; free for children 4 and under. Mon–Sat 9am–5pm; Sun noon–5pm.

San Albino Church ★★ This is one of the oldest churches in the Mesilla valley. The present structure was built in 1906 on the foundation of the original church, constructed in 1851. It was named for St. Albin, a medieval English bishop of North Africa, on whose day an important irrigation ditch from the Rio Grande was completed. The church bells date from the early 1870s; the pews were made in Taos of Philippine mahogany.

North side of Old Mesilla Plaza. ✆ **575/526-9349.** Free admission; donations appreciated. Usually Mon–Sat 1–3pm (call ahead). English-language Mass Sat 5:30pm and Sun 11am; Spanish Mass Sun 8am, weekdays 7am.

Spectator Sports

New Mexico State University football, basketball, baseball, softball, and volleyball teams play intercollegiate schedules in the Big West Conference, against schools from California, Nevada, and Utah. The Aggies play their home games on the NMSU campus, south of University Avenue on Locust Street. Football is played in the Aggie Memorial Stadium, and basketball games are held in the Pan American Center arena. For information about the games, call the **Pan Am Ticket Office** (✆ **575/646-1420;** www.nmsu.edu/tickets.html).

New Mexico's longest horse-racing season takes place 45 miles south of Las Cruces at **Sunland Park Racetrack and Casino** (✆ **575/874-5200;** www.sunland-park.com). Live races run Friday, Saturday, Sunday, and Tuesday, from December to April. The casino, which features 700 slot machines, is open Sunday through Thursday from 9:30am to 1am, Friday and Saturday until 2am.

Shopping

Shoppers should be aware that in Las Cruces, Monday is a notoriously quiet day. Some stores close for the day, so it's best to call ahead before traveling to a specific store.

For art, visit **Lundeen's Inn of the Arts** ★, 618 S. Alameda Blvd. (✆ **575/526-3326;** www.innofthearts.com), displaying the works of about 30 Southwest painters, sculptors, and potters; **Rising Sky Artworks,** 415 E. Foster (✆ **575/525-8454;** www.risingskypottery.com), which features works in clay by local and Western artists; and the **William Bonney Gallery,** 2060 Calle de Parian, just off the southeast corner of Old Mesilla Plaza (✆ **575/526-8275**), with a variety of Southwestern art.

For books, try **Mesilla Book Center,** in an 1856 mercantile building on the west side of Old Mesilla Plaza (✆ **575/526-6220**).

For native crafts and jewelry, check out **Silver Assets** ★, 1948 Calle de Santiago (✆ **575/523-8747;** www.silverassetsonline.com), 1½ blocks east of San Albino Church in Mesilla. Set back from the plaza itself, look for **Galeri Azul,** Mesilla Plaza (✆ **575/523-8783**), where you'll find colorful handmade altars by Ernie Bean, whimsical T-shirts and sun hats, and kitschy jewelry.

Mesilla Valley Mall is a full-service shopping center at 700 S. Telshor Blvd., just off the I-25 interchange with Lohman Avenue (✆ **575/522-1001;** www.mesillavalleymall.com), with well over 100 stores. The mall is open Monday through Saturday from 10am to 9pm and Sunday from noon to 6pm.

The Las Cruces area has two wineries. **Blue Teal Vineyards** (✆ **877/669-4637** or 575/524-0390; www.blueteal.com) has a tasting room next to the historic Fountain Theater, 2461 Calle de Guadalupe, south of Old Mesilla Plaza. It's open Monday through Thursday 11am to 6pm, Friday and Saturday 11am to 8pm, and Sunday noon to 6pm. The tasting room at **La Viña Winery** (✆ **575/882-7632;** www.lavinawinery.com), south of Las Cruces off NM 28, is open daily from noon to 5pm, and by appointment.

LAS CRUCES AFTER DARK

National recording artists frequently perform at NMSU's **Pan Am Center** (✆ **575/646-1420;** www.nmsu.edu). The **NMSU Music Department** (✆ **575/646-2421**) offers free jazz, classical, and pop concerts from August to May, and the **Las Cruces Symphony Orchestra** (✆ **575/646-3709;** www.lascrucessymphony.com) often performs here as well.

Hershel Zohn Theater (✆ **575/646-4515**), at NMSU, presents plays of the professional/student **American Southwest Theatre Company** from September to May, featuring

Rambling Downtown

The first Friday of each month all the galleries on the Downtown Mall stay open until 7pm for the **Downtown Ramble.** Most serve refreshments and have artists on-hand to visit with patrons. While wandering in the area stop in the **Rio Grande Theatre,** 211 N. Downtown Mall, (✆ **575/523-7403;** www.daarts.org). Built in 1926 as a movie palace, it has been restored to an elegant performing arts center. With Art Deco touches inside and out, including a restored neon sign and elaborate tile work, it's worth seeing in its own right. But plenty happens in the theater as well. Recent shows include Eliza Gilkyson in concert and a rendition of *Prairie Home Companion.* The theater sits along Main Street in downtown, also restored, offering a great place to stroll, though at this writing few shops had as yet opened up. One gallery worth checking out is **M. Phillip's,** 300 N. Downtown Mall (✆ **575/525-1367**) which carries Russian and European fine art.

dramas, comedies, musicals, and original works. Visit **http://theatre.nmsu.edu/astc** for information. The **No Strings Theatre Company** at the Black Box Theatre, 430 N. Downtown Mall (✆ **575/523-1223;** www.no-strings.org), presents an eclectic selection of plays in a relaxed atmosphere, including some excellent local works.

The **Las Cruces Community Theatre** (✆ **575/523-1200;** www.lcctnm.org) mounts six productions a year at its own facility on the downtown mall.

The **Mesilla Valley Film Society** (✆ **575/524-8287**) runs a good selection of contemporary and vintage art films at the Fountain Theatre (www.fountaintheatre.org), 2469 Calle de Guadalupe, a half-block south of the plaza in Mesilla, nightly at 7:30pm and sometimes 9:45pm, and Sunday at 2:30pm and sometimes 5pm.

If you'd like a cocktail in a fun atmosphere, a new option has opened up. **Azul Nightclub** ★ in the Hotel Encanto, 705 S. Telshor Blvd., (✆ **866/383-0443** or 575/522-4300; www.hhandr.com). In a contemporary setting reminiscent of a Spanish nightclub, the city's youngish business set has drinks and hors 'd oeuvres.

EXPLORING THE AREA

NORTH OF LAS CRUCES The town of **Hatch,** 39 miles north via I-25 or 34 miles north via NM 185, calls itself the "chile capital of the world." It's the center of a 22,000-acre agricultural belt that grows and processes more chile than anywhere else in the world. The annual Hatch Chile Festival over Labor Day weekend celebrates the harvest. For information, call the **Hatch Chamber of Commerce** (✆ **575/267-5050**).

Fort Selden State Monument is 15 miles north of Las Cruces between I-25 (exit 19) and NM 185. Founded in 1865, Fort Selden housed the famous Black Cavalry, the "Buffalo Soldiers" who protected settlers from marauding natives. It was subsequently the boyhood home of Gen. Douglas MacArthur, whose father, Arthur, was in charge of troops patrolling the U.S.–Mexico border in the 1880s. The fort closed permanently in 1891. Today, elegantly eroded ruins remain and are worth. Displays in the visitor center tell Fort Selden's story, including photos of young Douglas and his family. The monument is open from 8:30am to 5pm Wednesday to Monday; admission is $3 for adults and free for children age 16 and under. For more information, call ✆ **575/526-8911** or visit **www.nmmonuments.org**. Adjacent to the state monument, **Leasburg Dam State Park** (✆ **575/524-4068**) offers picnicking, camping, canoeing, and fishing.

SOUTH OF LAS CRUCES **Stahmann Farms,** 10 miles south of La Mesilla on NM 28, is one of the world's largest single producers of pecans. Several million pounds are harvested, mostly during November, from orchards in the bed of an ancient lake. **Stahmann's Country Store** ★ (✆ **800/654-6887** or 575/525-3470; www.stahmanns.com) sells pecans, pecan candy, ice cream, and other specialty foods, and it has a small cafe. It's open Monday through Saturday from 9am to 6pm, Sunday from 11am to 5pm. If you'd like to stay south of Las Cruces, book a night or two at **Casa de Sueños** ★, 405 Mountain Vista Rd., La Union, NM 88021 (✆ **575/874-9166;** www.casaofdreams.com). Set high on a plain overlooking the Rio Grande River Valley, with the Franklin Mountains in the distance, it offers atmospheric Southwest-style rooms about a half-hour south of Las Cruces, with good access to El Paso.

War Eagles Air Museum ★ (✆ **575/589-2000;** www.war-eagles-air-museum.com), at the Santa Teresa Airport, about 35 miles south of Las Cruces via I-10 (call or check the website for directions), has an extensive collection of historic aircraft from World War II and the Korean War, plus automobiles and a tank. The museum is open Tuesday

Finds **Weaving Dreams**

One day after enchiladas at Chope's Café in La Mesa, I wandered down a dirt road nearby and found a little adobe garden house, the studio of weaver Rosie Chavarria-Jones. "I use whatever I have around and let the yarn solar dye," she says. That might include marigolds, prickly pear cactus, purple cabbage, or pomegranates. Once the wool is dyed, she spins it and weaves it into scarves and shawls, which she sells from her shop. Her "A Mano Weaving Workshop" is at 216 E. Bellman in La Mesa, (✆ **575/233-4363**). Call to be sure she's in.

through Sunday from 10am to 4pm; admission is $5 for adults, $4 for senior citizens age 65 and over; free for children age 11 and under.

EAST OF LAS CRUCES The **Organ Mountains,** so-called because they resemble the pipes of a church organ, draw inevitable comparisons to Wyoming's Grand Tetons. Organ Peak, at 9,119 feet, is the highest point in Doña Ana County.

The **Aguirre Springs Recreation Area** (✆ **575/525-4300;** www.blm.gov.nm), off US 70 on the western slope of the Organ Mountains, is one of the most spectacular places I've ever camped. Operated by the Bureau of Land Management, the camping and picnic sites sit at the base of the jagged Organ Mountains. Visitors to the area can hike, camp, picnic, or ride horseback (no horse rentals on-site). If you'd like to hike, don't miss the **Baylor Pass** trail, which crosses along the base of the Organ peaks, up through a pass, and over to the Las Cruces side. Though the hike is 6 miles one-way, just over 2 miles will get you to the pass, where there's a meadow with amazing views.

WHERE TO STAY IN & AROUND LAS CRUCES

Hotel Encanto de Las Cruces ★★★ Spanish Colonial elegance defines this seven-story hotel on the east side of town, about a 15-minute drive from Mesilla, with an incredible view of the city and the Organ Mountains. The hotel was built in 1986, and implemented a major remodel in 2006, including new bedding and furnishings, all with a lovely Old World Mexican/Colonial motif. The lobby has a tiered fountain, colorful tile, and museum-quality furnishings. Rooms are spacious and outfitted with handcrafted furniture and comfortable beds with good linens. Photography by the noted artist Miguel Gandert dresses the walls. Baths are medium-size with granite countertops and Aveda bath products. Some rooms flank the pool and have little patios. The service here is excellent. The Café España serves breakfast, lunch, and dinner, in an elegant Spanish Colonial ambiance, and the Azul Nightclub offers drinks with a contemporary Southwest flair.

705 S. Telshor Blvd., Las Cruces, NM 88011. ✆ **866/383-0443** or 575/522-4300. Fax 575/521-4707. www.hhandr.com. 203 units. $109–$159 double; $179–$199 suite. AE, DC, DISC, MC, V. Pets welcome. **Amenities:** Restaurant; lounge; heated outdoor pool; exercise room; Jacuzzi; car rental; courtesy van; business center; salon; room service; laundry service. *In room:* A/C, TV, Wi-Fi, coffeemaker, hair dryer, iron.

La Quinta ★ Five minutes from Old Mesilla, this chain hotel provides relatively quiet and very comfortable rooms with plenty of amenities. The clean and well-designed rooms range from medium to large, all with desks and medium-size bathrooms. An outdoor pool sits within a comfortable courtyard, an important addition in this warm climate. Guests eat their continental breakfast in a bright garden room off the lobby.

When you reserve here ask for one of the "annex" rooms, which are the largest and newest. Also, be aware that trains pass near this area at night. A few new casual dining restaurants have opened across the street.

790 Av. de Mesilla, Las Cruces, NM 88005. ✆ **800/531-5900** or 575/524-0331. Fax 575/525-8360. www.laquinta.com. $78–$97 double. Rates include continental breakfast. AE, DISC, MC, V. Pets welcome. **Amenities:** Outdoor pool; small fitness room. *In room:* A/C, TV, Wi-Fi, coffeemaker, hair dryer, iron.

Bed & Breakfasts

The Lundeen Inn of the Arts ★★ This inn is a late-1890s adobe home, with whitewashed walls, narrow alleys, and arched doorways. It's a composite of rooms stretching across 10,000 square feet of floor space. There's a wide range of rooms, each named for an artist. My favorites are in the main part of the house, set around a two-story garden room, with elegant antiques and arched windows. Most rooms are medium-size with comfortably firm beds dressed in good linens. Bathrooms are generally small and simple but clean. The inn is also an art gallery, displaying the works of about 30 Southwestern painters, sculptors, and potters. Breakfast includes fresh fruit and such specialties as pumpkin pancakes and huevos rancheros.

618 S. Alameda Blvd., Las Cruces, NM 88005. ✆ **888/526-3326** or 575/526-3326. Fax 575/647-1334. www.innofthearts.com. 7 units. $85–$99 double; $85–$105 suite. Rates include full breakfast. AE, DC, DISC, MC, V. Pets welcome. **Amenities:** Secretarial service. *In room:* A/C, TV, Wi-Fi, hair dryer, iron.

Camping

Quite a few campgrounds are within or near Las Cruces. All the ones listed here include full hookups for RVs, tenting areas, and recreation areas. **Best View RV Park** (✆ **575/526-6555**) also offers cabins and laundry and grocery facilities. From the junction of I-10 and US 70 (exit 135), go 1½ miles east on US 70, and then half a block south on Weinrich Road.

Another option is **Dalmont's RV Park** (✆ **575/523-2992**). If you're coming from the west, when you reach the junction of I-25 and I-10, go 2½ miles northwest on I-10 to the Main Street exit, and then go 2 blocks west on Valley Drive. If you're coming from the east, at the junction of I-10 and Main Street, go a quarter mile north on Main Street and then 1 block west on Valley Drive. To reach **Siesta RV Park** (✆ **575/523-6816**), at the junction of I-10 and NM 28, take exit 140 and go half a mile south on NM 28. **Leasburg Dam State Park** (✆ **575/524-4068**) is a smaller park that also offers RV and tent camping, but it has no laundry or grocery facilities. A general country store is about 1 mile down the road, and hiking and fishing are available.

WHERE TO DINE IN & AROUND LAS CRUCES

Expensive

Double Eagle ★★ CONTINENTAL When I was a kid, whenever we went to Las Cruces, we always made a special trip to this elegant restaurant imbued with Old West style. I'm pleased to say that it's still a quality place to dine. This 150-year-old Territorial-style hacienda that was once the governor's mansion is on the National Register of Historic Places. Built around a central courtyard, it has numerous rooms, one of which is said to be frequented by a woman's ghost. Another room has a 30-foot-long bar with Corinthian columns in gold leaf, Gay Nineties oil paintings, and 18-armed brass chandeliers hung with Baccarat crystals. The menu is quite varied and includes pasta, chicken, fish, and steak dishes. My favorite is the filet mignon bordelaise, served on a French rusk with a rich red-wine sauce. The Columbia River salmon, served with a triple citrus-chipotle chile sauce, is also delicious. All entrees come with salad, vegetable, and choice of potato or pasta. There's a full bar, from which you might want to order a mango margarita, and for dessert you can end it all with the Death by Chocolate Cake.

2355 Calle de Guadalupe, on the east side of Mesilla Plaza. ✆ **575/523-6700.** www.double-eagle-messilla.com. Reservations recommended. Main courses $8–$15 lunch, $14–$36 dinner. AE, DC, DISC, MC, V. Mon–Sat 11am–10pm; Sun 11am–9pm.

Moderate

Lemongrass ★★ *Finds* THAI This addition to the Las Cruces dining scene offers delicious flavors in a comfortably elegant atmosphere. It's set in an open room accented with Thai tapestries on the tables and Thai village scenes on the walls. Service is congenial, though be prepared to wait a bit for the food. Chef Kimberly Miag uses very fresh ingredients and brings her own touch to traditional Thai dishes such as pad Thai—rice noodles with egg, bean sprouts, tofu, tamarind sauce, and shrimp or chicken. I've also enjoyed a delicious pad pong kari—broccoli, bell pepper, straw mushrooms, and chicken or shrimp in a yellow curry and coconut milk sauce. Unique to this Thai restaurant, the chef is open to dialing the spice way down so even tender stomachs can enjoy eating here. Enjoy beer and wine with your meal.

2540 El Paseo Rd. ✆ **575/523-8778.** Reservations recommended on weekends in summer. Main courses $7–$15 lunch, $16–$25 dinner. AE, DISC, DC, MC, V. Mon–Fri 11am–2pm; Sat–Sun 5–9pm.

Mix Pacific Rim Cuisine ★★ ASIAN/SUSHI With moody lighting and lots of fine details, this intimate new restaurant serves artful Pacific Rim cuisine. Chinese paper lamps seem to float on the ceiling, while the wood tables are topped with inlaid Asian knickknacks, and a sushi bar lines one wall. Service is good. You might start with one of their fun drinks such as a Pacific Pleasure—silver saki with mango, orange, and apple juice. Next, move onto to some Polynesian spring rolls, with mango salsa. A number of salads dress the menu, as do a full range of sushi offerings. For lunch, the "bento" combinations are a good buy; such entrees as grilled salmon come with soup, salad, and steamed or fried rice. Dinner offerings are more upscale. You might try the steak wrap—fresh asparagus wrapped with grilled New York steak, or the spicy miso sea bass. Both come with wasabi mashed potatoes and stir-fried vegetables. A fun choice for dessert is the banana spring rolls with ice cream. Beer and wine accompany the menu. Next door, the same restaurateur serves quality fast Asian food at Mix Express.

1001 University Ave. D4. ✆ **575/532-2042.** www.mixpacificrim.com. Reservations accepted. Main courses lunch $7–$10, dinner $13–$20. AE, DISC, MC, V. Mon–Fri 11am–2pm and 5–9pm; Sat noon–2pm and 5–9pm.

Inexpensive

Chope's Bar & Cafe ★ *Kids* NEW MEXICAN This is one of those legendary spots, a requisite weekly pilgrimage for many. Drive 15 minutes south of Old Mesilla through pecan orchards to its door, and you'll encounter a real locals' scene. The dining rooms are plain. Set in an old house, they have tile floors, faux wood paneling, and closely set tables, usually full of families, business people, and college students. You'll feast on chile rellenos, enchiladas, and burritos. Whatever you order, make sure it's smothered with red or green chile, if you can handle the heat. If not, opt for tacos or a hamburger. Kids like the place because it's casual and they have their own menu. Service is friendly but very overworked. With your meal, order up margaritas or a Mexican beer, or, if you really wish to partake, head next door to the cantina, a dark and raucous place reminiscent of a border-town bar.

NM 28 (in the center of town in La Mesa; no street address). ✆ **575/233-3420** or 575/233-9976. Main courses $5–$10. MC, V. Tues–Sat 11:30am–1:30pm and 5:30–8:30pm; cantina Tues–Sat 11:30am–9:30pm.

Farley's ★ Kids BURGERS/SANDWICHES This big barnlike redbrick place offers pub food in a festive ambiance. Part of a chain throughout southern New Mexico, it offers entertainment along with food. While awaiting their meals kids and adults enjoy foosball, air hockey, and video games in the game room. The main part of the restaurant is a bar with tall tables for mixing with the scene or booths for more privacy. The third room is quieter and more family-oriented. Food here is rib-sticking, with such offerings as chicken alfredo, pork ribs, fajitas, soups, salads, and burgers.

3499 Foothills Rd. ✆ **575/522-0466.** Main courses $7–$13. AE, DISC, MC, V. Daily 11am–11pm.

La Posta de Mesilla Kids NEW MEXICAN/STEAKS If you're on the Mesilla Plaza and want to eat New Mexican food for not much money, walk in here. The restaurant occupies a mid-18th-century adobe building that is the only surviving stagecoach station of the Butterfield Overland Mail route from Tipton, Missouri, to San Francisco. Kit Carson, Pancho Villa, General Douglas MacArthur, and Billy the Kid were all here at one time. The entrance leads through a jungle of tall plants beneath a Plexiglas roof, past a tank of piranhas and a noisy aviary of macaws and Amazon parrots, to nine dining rooms with bright, festive decor. (Kids love this and their own menu selections.) The tables are basic, with vinyl and metal chairs. Try the enchiladas, which come with a nice chile sauce. Avoid the dry rellenos and the soggy tacos. The tostadas (tortilla cups filled with beans and topped with chile and cheese) are a house specialty. There's a full-service bar.

2410 Calle de San Albino (southeast corner of Old Mesilla Plaza). ✆ **575/524-3524.** Reservations recommended. Main courses $6–$17. AE, DC, DISC, MC, V. Sun and Tues–Thurs 11am–9pm; Fri–Sat 11am–9:30pm.

Lorenzo's Restaurante Italiano de Old Messilla ★★ SICILIAN In a spirited building with lots of brick and with murals depicting rural scenes on the walls, the restaurant offers the feel of a Sicilian village cafe, a good indication of the quality of the food here. Rather than fancy Italian food like you find in many cities, this restaurant serves traditional Sicilian meals, with lots of red sauces and homemade pasta. It's big with locals, and it fills up, so you may want to make reservations. The atmosphere is jovial and the service is good, though it can be a bit slow because the food is cooked in-house. You can't go wrong with standards such as spaghetti marinara or lasagna, or for something more adventurous, try the linguini and clams. Meals are served with bread so good you'll have a tough time stopping yourself from eating it all, and a salad of freshly tossed greens. Wash it down with a carafe of Chianti or your favorite beer.

1750 Calle de Mercado #4 (Onate Plaza, a block from Old Mesilla Plaza). ✆ **575/525-3174.** Reservations recommended. Main courses $8–$16. AE, DISC, MC, V. Mon–Thurs 11am–9pm; Fri–Sat 11am–9:30pm; Sun 11–8:30pm.

Tiffany's Pizza & Greek American Cuisine ★★ Kids GREEK FOOD/PIZZA Between sky blue walls decorated with photos of Greece, this cafe serves flavorful pizza, sandwiches, and entrees to the tune of festive music. It's a casual place with faux wood tables and tile floors and a TV with the sound off, but the food is authentic. One favorite is the Tiffany's Pizza, which comes with sausage, pepperoni, pastrami, bell peppers, onion, and mushrooms, a good dish to take back to your hotel room after a long day. Or you could have a lamb gyro sandwich. My favorite here is the mousaka or the baked chicken; the latter comes with potatoes, vegetables, and salad at a great price. In fact, the portions are so large here, a couple could easily split a meal. Kids have their own menu, and the relaxed attitude here will make them comfortable. Though no alcohol is served, there is Greek coffee, and baklava or Greek wedding cookies for dessert.

Telshor Tower Plaza G-1. (two buildings behind the Hotel Encanto). ✆ **575/532-5002.** Main courses lunch or dinner $8–$14. AE, DISC, MC, V. Tues–Thurs 9am–8pm; Fri 9am–9pm; Sat 11am–11pm.

6 DEMING & LORDSBURG

New Mexico's least populated corner is this one, which includes the "boot heel" of the Gadsden Purchase, poking 40 miles down toward Mexico (a great place for backpacking). These two railroad towns, an hour apart on I-10, see a lot of traffic; but whereas **Deming** (pop. 14,500) is thriving as a ranching and retirement center, **Lordsburg** has had a steady population of about 3,379 for years. This is a popular area for rockhounds, aficionados of ghost towns, and history buffs: **Columbus,** 32 miles south of Deming, was attacked by the Mexican bandit-revolutionary Pancho Villa in 1916. The U.S. military retaliated by sending 10,000 troops into Mexico to find him, to no avail.

ESSENTIALS

GETTING THERE From Las Cruces, take I-10 west (1 hr. to Deming, 2 hr. to Lordsburg). From Tucson, take I-10 east (3 hr. to Lordsburg, 4 hr. to Deming).

Great Lakes Airlines (✆ **575/388-4115**) flies daily to **Grant County Airport** (✆ **575/388-4554**), 15 miles south of Silver City near Hurley. The **Las Cruces Shuttle Service,** P.O. Box 3172, Las Cruces, NM 88003 (✆ **800/288-1784** or 575/525-1784; www.lascrucesshuttle.com), runs several times daily between Deming and the El Paso airport by way of Las Cruces.

VISITOR INFORMATION The **Deming–Luna County Chamber of Commerce** is at 800 E. Pine St., Deming (✆ **800/848-4955** or 575/546-2674; www.demingchamber.com). The **Greater Hidalgo Area Chamber of Commerce** is at 117 E. 2nd St., Lordsburg, NM 88045 (✆ **575/542-9864**).

WHAT TO SEE & DO NEAR DEMING

Deming Luna Mimbres Museum ★ Deming was the meeting place of the second east-west railroad to connect the Pacific and Atlantic coasts, and that heritage is recalled in this museum, run by the Luna County Historical Society. It has a military room that contains exhibits from the Indian wars, Pancho Villa's raid, WWI and WWII, and the Korean and Vietnam wars; a room featuring the John and Mary Alice King Collection of Mimbres pottery; and a doll room with more than 800 dolls. A 5,000-square-foot adjacent space displays transportation-related exhibits, including a replica of a railroad depot, a Harvey House, and vintage firetrucks. Across the street is the Custom House, a turn-of-the-20th-century adobe home that has been turned into a walk-through exhibit.

301 S. Silver Ave., Deming. ✆ **575/546-2382.** Fax 575/544-0121. Free admission; donations encouraged. Mon–Sat 9am–4pm; Sun 1:30–4pm.

Getting Outside

At **Rockhound State Park ★**, 14 miles southeast of Deming via NM 11, visitors are encouraged to pick up and take home with them as much as 15 pounds of minerals—jasper, agate, quartz crystal, flow-banded rhyolite, and others. At the base of the Little Florida Mountains, the park is a lovely, arid, cactus-covered land with paths leading down into dry gullies and canyons. (You may have to walk a bit, as the more accessible minerals have been largely picked out.)

The campground ($10 for nonelectric hookup; $14 with electric hookup), which has shelters, restrooms, and showers, offers a distant view of mountain ranges all the way to the Mexican border. The park also has one marked hiking trail and a playground. Admission is $5 per vehicle, and the park is open year-round from dawn to dusk. For more information, call ✆ **575/546-6182.**

Some 35 miles south of Deming is the tiny border town of **Columbus,** which looks across at Mexico. The **Pancho Villa State Park** ★ here marks the last foreign invasion of American soil. A temporary fort, where a tiny garrison was housed in tents, was attacked in 1916 by 600 Mexican revolutionaries, who cut through the boundary fence at Columbus. Eighteen Americans were killed, 12 wounded; an estimated 200 Mexicans died. The Mexicans immediately retreated across their border. An American punitive expedition, headed by Gen. John J. Pershing, was launched into Mexico but got nowhere. Villa restricted his banditry to Mexico after that, until his assassination in 1923.

The state park includes ruins of the old fort and a new visitor center and 7,000-square-foot museum offering exhibits and a film. The park also has a strikingly beautiful desert botanical garden (worth the trip alone), plus campsites, restrooms, showers, an RV dump station, and a playground. There's a $5-per-vehicle entrance fee; the park is staffed from 8am to 5pm daily. For more information, call ✆ **575/531-2711.**

Across the street from the state park is the old Southern Pacific Railroad Depot, which has been restored by the Columbus Historical Society and now houses the **Columbus Historical Museum** (✆ **575/531-2620**), which contains railroad memorabilia and exhibits on local history. Call for hours, which vary.

If you'd like to stay in Columbus, call **Martha's Place Bed & Breakfast,** Main and Lima streets (✆ **575/531-2467**). It's a two-story stucco Pueblo-style adobe painted cream and green, with Victorian touches inside. The medium-size rooms have comfortable beds and French doors leading to a balcony. Prices are $70 double. Rates include breakfast. Pets are welcome.

Three miles south across the border in Mexico is **Las Palomas, Chihuahua** (pop. 1,500). The port of entry is open 24 hours. A few desirable restaurants and tourist-oriented businesses are in Las Palomas. Mostly, though, it's a drug-trafficking town. Beware of barhopping in Palomas at night, as it can be dangerous.

WHAT TO SEE & DO NEAR LORDSBURG

Visitors to Lordsburg can go **rockhounding** in this area rich in minerals of many kinds. Desert roses can be found near Summit, and agate is known to exist in many abandoned mines locally. Mine dumps, southwest of Hachita, contain lead, zinc, and gold; the Animas Mountains have manganese. Volcanic glass can be picked up in Coronado National Forest, and you can pan for gold in Gold Gulch.

Rodeo, 30 miles southwest via I-10 and NM 80, is the home of the **Chiricahua Gallery** (✆ **575/557-2225;** www.rodeonewmexico.com), open Monday through Saturday from 10am to 4pm. Regional artists have joined in a nonprofit, cooperative venture to exhibit works and offer classes in a variety of media. Many choose to live on the high-desert slopes of the Chiricahua Range. Look especially for the inspirational bird-filled landscapes of Jean Bohlender. The gallery is on NM 80 en route to Douglas, Arizona.

Shakespeare Ghost Town (Kids) A national historic site, Shakespeare was once the home of 3,000 miners, promoters, and dealers of various kinds. Under the name Ralston, it enjoyed a silver boom in 1870. This was followed by a notorious diamond fraud in 1872, in which a mine was salted with diamonds in order to raise prices on mining stock; many notables were sucked in, particularly William Ralston, founder of the Bank of California. It enjoyed a mining revival in 1879 under its new name, Shakespeare. It was a town with no church, no newspaper, and no local law. Some serious fights resulted in hangings from the roof timbers in the Stage Station. Since 1935, it's been privately owned by the Hill family, which has kept it uncommercialized, with no souvenir hype or gift shops. Six original buildings and two reconstructed buildings survive in various stages of repair. Two-hour guided tours are offered on a limited basis, and reenactments and living history are staged on the fourth weekends of April, June, August, and October, if performers are available. Phone to confirm the performances.

2$^1/_2$ miles south of Lordsburg (no street address), P.O. Box 253, Lordsburg, NM 88045. ✆ **575/542-9034.** www.shakespeareghostown.com. Admission $4 adults, $3 children 6–12; for shoot-outs and special events $5 adults, $4 children. 10am–2pm on the 2nd Sun and preceding Sat of each month. Special tours by appointment. To reach Shakespeare, drive 1$^1/_2$ miles south from I-10 on Main St. Just before the town cemetery, turn right, proceed $^1/_2$ mile, and turn right again. Follow the dirt road another $^1/_2$ mile into Shakespeare.

WHERE TO STAY IN DEMING & LORDSBURG

In Deming

Holiday Inn ★ Just off I-10, the Holiday Inn brings a bit of style to dusty Deming. Though from the outside the 1974 two-story white brick structure appears basic, the rooms—with renovations ongoing—tell another story. Each is medium-size with light pine furniture and decorated in Aztec prints, with bold expressionist paintings on the walls. Bathrooms are small but each has a vanity and dressing area. Some of the suites come with Jacuzzis. The large pool is surrounded by lush grass; request a poolside room and you'll have a bit of a resort feel. The hotel's restaurant is open for breakfast, lunch, and dinner, serving New Mexican and American cuisine.

Off I-10, exit 85 (P.O. Box 1138), Deming, NM 88031. ✆ **800/HOLIDAY** or 575/546-2661. Fax 575/546-6308. www.ichotels.com. 116 units. $67–$85 double. AE, DC, DISC, MC, V. Pets welcome. **Amenities:** Restaurant; outdoor heated pool (summer); exercise room; Jacuzzi; room service; coin-op laundry; laundry service; dry cleaning. *In room:* A/C, TV, Wi-Fi, fridge, coffeemaker, hair dryer, iron.

La Quinta Inn ★ True to its origins, this new whitewashed hotel provides consistent and comfortable rooms at a decent price. Each is medium-size with high ceilings, redwood furniture, and earth-tone decor. The beds are comfortable and the bathrooms spacious enough and with granite countertops. This is a good option if you like a newer style hotel than the Holiday Inn next door.

4300 E. Pine St., Deming, NM 88030. ✆ **800/531-5900** or 575/546-0600. Fax 575/544-8207. www.laquinta.com. 58 units. $79–$105 double. Rates include continental breakfast. AE, DC, DISC, MC, V. **Amenities:** Outdoor heated pool (summer); exercise room; business center. *In room:* A/C, TV, Wi-Fi, fridge, coffeemaker, hair dryer, iron, microwave.

In Lordsburg

Holiday Inn Express ★ This hotel remains true to the Holiday Inn Express name, providing clean and comfortable rooms at a reasonable price. This is a motel-style property, allowing you to park right outside your room. All accommodations are medium-size with earth-tone-colored decor and comfortable beds. The bathrooms are small but have an outer sink vanity. A newer property than the Best Western, it provides more up-to-date accommodations in a quiet location in the center of town. Four of the rooms offer a fridge and microwave.

1408 S. Main St., Lordsburg, NM 88045. ✆ **800/HOLIDAY** or 575/542-3666. Fax 575/542-3665. www.hiexpress.com. 40 units. $89 double. Rates include continental breakfast. AE, DC, DISC, MC, V. Pets $20 fee. **Amenities:** Outdoor pool; business center. *In room:* A/C, TV, Wi-Fi, coffeemaker, hair dryer, iron.

Camping in & Around Deming & Lordsburg

City of Rocks State Park, in Deming (✆ **575/536-2800**), has 52 campsites, 10 with electric hookups; tenting is available, and picnic tables and a hiking trail are nearby. **Dreamcatcher RV Park** (✆ **575/544-4004**), also in Deming (take exit 85, Motel Dr., off I-10 and go 1 block south on Business I-10), has 92 sites, all with full hookups. It also offers free access to a nearby swimming pool and on-site laundry facilities. **Little Vineyard RV Park** (✆ **575/546-3560**) in Deming (from I-10 take exit 85 and go 1 mile southwest on Business I-10 toward Deming) is larger than those already mentioned. It offers the same facilities as Dreamcatcher RV Park, with the addition of limited groceries, an indoor pool and hot tub, cable TV hookups, e-mail access, and a small RV parts store. The campground at **Rockhound State Park** (✆ **575/546-6182**) is picturesque and great for rockhounds who can't get enough of their hobby. RV sites with hookups and tenting are both available, as are shelters, restrooms, and showers.

If you'd rather camp near Lordsburg, try **Lordsburg KOA** (✆ **800/562-5772** or 575/542-8003; www.koa.com). It's in a desert setting but with shade trees, and tenting is permitted. Grocery and laundry facilities are available, in addition to a recreation room/area, a swimming pool, a playground, and horseshoes. To reach the campground, take I-10 to exit 22 and then go 1 block south; next, turn right at the Chevron station and follow the signs to the campground.

WHERE TO DINE IN DEMING & LORDSBURG

In Deming

Palma's Italian Grill ★ Kids ITALIAN Set in an old bank building still equipped with its late 1800s vault, this fun restaurant serves traditional Italian dishes in a festive atmosphere. With checkered tablecloths and high ceilings, the place is airy and the service friendly. A big seller here is the spaghetti and meatballs with sausage, as is the lasagna, both served with a salad and fresh-baked bread. The steaks are also good, served with soup or salad, and baked potato or pasta. Lighter dishes such as a Caesar salad with grilled chicken, shrimp, or salmon, are available as well. A kids' menu, including some American offerings, makes them feel at home. Finish with a piece of homemade pies, cannoli, or spumoni ice cream. A beer and wine list accompanies the menu.

110 S. Silver Ave., Deming. ✆ **575/544-3100.** Main courses lunch or dinner $7–$24. MC, DISC, V. Tues–Thurs 11am–8:30pm; Fri–Sat 11am–9pm; Sun 11am–3pm.

Si Señor ★ NEW MEXICAN Locals crowd this downtown cafe to eat platters full of tasty New Mexican food. The interior has functional furniture and a lovely tile floor. At breakfast, try the huevos rancheros (eggs over corn tortillas, smothered in chile). The big seller here for lunch and dinner is the deluxe combination, with a chile relleno, a tamale, a cheese enchilada, a taco, refried beans, Spanish rice, and red or green chile. The menu also sports salads, hamburgers, and chicken and fish dishes. All come with chips and salsa, and wine and beer are served.

200 E. Pine, Deming. ✆ **575/546-3938.** Main courses $6–$10 breakfast, $5–$12 lunch and dinner. DISC, MC, V. Mon–Sat 9am–8 pm; Sun 1–10pm.

In Lordsburg

Kranberry's Family Restaurant AMERICAN/MEXICAN A friendly, casual Denny's-style family restaurant decorated with Southwestern art, Kranberry's offers American favorites, including eggs and pancakes for breakfast; and burgers, chicken, beef, and salads, as well as Mexican selections for lunch and dinner. Baked goods are made on the premises daily. My favorite is the corn bread, served with the soup special.

1405 S. Main St., Lordsburg. ✆ **575/542-9400.** Main courses $4–$7 breakfast, $6–$17 lunch and dinner. AE, DC, DISC, MC, V. Daily 6am–10pm.

Triple J Café ★ *Finds* NEW MEXICAN/AMERICAN Spend your meal surrounded by the sweet scent of red and green chile in the Triple J Café, the central meeting spot in town, where "railroaders" and travelers come to eat homemade enchiladas, chicken tacos (the best in New Mexico), and hand-patted burgers. It's a clean, friendly spot in a building built around 1900 with big windows letting in lots of light and offering a view of the action on the railroad tracks across the street. The combination plate (not on the menu) has a chile relleno, taco, and enchilada. Be sure to strike up a conversation with owners Leroy and Lucina Jones, and pick up their son Arliss' CD, a great accompaniment to the many miles between stops in this part of the world.

228 E. Motel Dr., Lordsburg. ✆ **575/542-3073.** www.triplejsalsa.com. Main courses $5–$16. DISC, MC, V. Mon–Thurs 6am–1pm.

7 SILVER CITY ★★

Silver City (pop. 12,500) is an old mining town, in the foothills of the Pinos Altos Range of the Mogollon Mountains, and gateway to the Gila Wilderness and the Gila Cliff Dwellings. Early Native Americans mined turquoise from these hills, and by 1804, Spanish settlers were digging for copper. In 1870, a group of prospectors discovered silver, and the rush was on. In 10 short months, the newly christened Silver City grew from a single cabin to more than 80 buildings. Early visitors included Billy the Kid, Judge Roy Bean, and William Randolph Hearst.

This comparatively isolated community kept pace with every modern convenience: telephones in 1883, electric lights in 1884 (only 2 years after New York City installed its lighting), and a water system in 1887. The town should have busted with the crash of silver prices in 1893. But unlike many Western towns, Silver City did not become a picturesque memory. It capitalized on its high dry climate to become today's county seat and trade center. Copper mining and processing are still the major industry. But Silver City also can boast a famous son: The late Harrison (Jack) Schmitt, the first civilian geologist to visit the moon, and later a U.S. senator, was born and raised in nearby Santa Rita.

ESSENTIALS

GETTING THERE From Albuquerque, take I-25 south, 15 miles past Truth or Consequences; then west on NM 152 and US 180 (5 hr.). From Las Cruces, take I-10 west to Deming, and then north on US 180 (2 hr.).

Great Lakes Airlines (✆ **575/388-4115**) flies daily to **Grant County Airport** (✆ **575/388-4554**), 15 miles south of Silver City near Hurley. **Silver Stage Lines** (✆ **800/522-0162**) offers daily shuttle service to the El Paso airport, and charter service to Tucson.

The **Las Cruces Shuttle Service** (✆ **800/288-1784** or 575/525-1784; www.lascruces shuttle.com) runs several times daily from Silver City to the El Paso airport, by way of Las Cruces.

VISITOR INFORMATION The **Murray Ryan Visitor Center** at 201 N. Hudson St., Silver City, NM 88061 (✆ **800/548-9378** or 575/538-3785; www.silvercity.org), also houses the Silver City Grant County Chamber of Commerce and is a good source of information. The chamber produces extremely useful tourist publications. Also of note at this site is a replica 1870s log cabin donated to the city by movie producer Ron Howard. It was built for the filming of the 2005 movie *The Missing.* A plaque on it says that Billy the Kid likely lived in one similar to it when he was a young resident of this town.

WHAT TO SEE & DO IN SILVER CITY

Silver City's downtown **Historic District** ★, the first such district to receive National Register recognition, is a must for visitors. The downtown core is marked by the extensive use of brick in construction: Brick clay was discovered in the area soon after the town's founding in 1870, and an 1880 ordinance prohibited frame construction within the town limits. Mansard-roofed Victorian houses, Queen Anne and Italianate residences, and commercial buildings show off the cast-iron architecture of the period. Some are still undergoing restoration.

An 1895 flood washed out Main Street and turned it into a gaping chasm, which was eventually bridged over; finally, the **Big Ditch,** as it's called, was made into a green park in the center of town. Facing downtown, in the 500 block of North Hudson Street, was a famous red-light district from the turn-of-the-century until the late 1960s.

Billy the Kid lived in Silver City as a youth. You can see his cabin site a block north of the Broadway Bridge, on the east side of the Big Ditch. The Kid (William Bonney) waited tables at the Star Hotel, at Hudson Street and Broadway. He was jailed (at 304 N. Hudson St.) in 1875 at the age of 15, after being convicted of stealing from a Chinese laundry, but he escaped—a first for the Kid. The grave of Bonney's mother, Catherine McCarty, is in Silver City Cemetery, east of town on Memory Lane, off US 180. She died of tuberculosis about a year after the family moved here in 1873.

Silver City Museum ★ This very well-presented museum of city and regional history contains collections relating to southwestern New Mexico history, mining, Native American pottery, and early photographs. Exhibits include a southwestern New Mexico history timeline, a parlor displaying Victorian decorative arts, and a chronicle of commerce in early Silver City. A local history research library is available to visitors also. The main gallery features changing exhibits. The museum is lodged in the 1881 H. B. Ailman House, a former city hall and fire station, remarkable for its cupola and Victorian mansard roof. Ailman came to Silver City penniless in 1871, made a fortune in mining, and went on to start the Meredith and Ailman Bank. Guided historic district walking tours are offered on Memorial Day and Labor Day. There's also a museum store. Take a fun trip up into the cupola for a nice view of the city.

312 W. Broadway. ✆ **575/538-5921.** Fax 575/388-1096. Free admission. Tues–Fri 9am–4:30pm; Sat–Sun 10am–4pm. Closed Mon except Memorial Day and Labor Day.

Western New Mexico University Museum Spread across 80 acres on the west side of Silver City, WNMU celebrated its centennial in 1993. The university boasts a 2,500-student enrollment and 24 major buildings. Among them is historic Fleming Hall, which houses this interesting museum. The WNMU museum has the largest permanent exhibit of prehistoric Mimbres pottery in the United States. Also displayed are Casas Grandes Indian pottery, stone tools, ancient jewelry, historic photographs, and mining and military artifacts. Displays change regularly, so there's always something new to see, such as vanishing Americana, riparian fossils, Nigerian folk art, or a collection of 18th- to 20th-century timepieces. There is a gift shop here.

1000 W. College, Fleming Hall, WNMU. ✆ **575/538-6386.** www.wnmu.edu/univ/museum.htm. Free admission. Mon–Fri 9am–4:30pm; Sat–Sun 10am–4pm.

SILVER CITY AFTER DARK

Some of southwestern New Mexico's most passionate performances are held at the **Pinos Altos Melodrama Theater,** 30 Main St., Pinos Altos (in the Pinos Altos Opera House, next to the Buckhorn Saloon; ✆ **575/388-3848;** www.pinosaltos.org). Local actors fight the forces of good and evil in such productions as *The Legend of Billy the Kid* or *It's Just a Little Gun Play.* Productions are on Friday and Saturday nights from February to November. **Silver City Brewing Co.** ★ 101 E. College (✆ **575/534-2739;** www.swnmbeer.com), the town's new brewpub, offers tasty beer and a brewpub menu including pizza, pasta, sandwiches, and salads. Best of all here, during warm months, live music plays on the patio on weekends. It's open Tuesday to Friday 11am to 8pm and Saturday noon to 8pm. **Isaac's Bar & Grill** ★ offers live entertainment on Saturday nights. See "Where to Dine in & Around Silver City," below.

EXPLORING THE AREA

NORTH OF SILVER CITY The virtual ghost town of **Pinos Altos** ★, straddling the Continental Divide, is 6 miles north of Silver City on NM 15. Dubbed "Tall Pines" when it was founded in the gold- and silver-rush era, Apache attacks and mine failures took their toll.

Way Beyond Silver

Silver City has become an artists' mecca, as creative people retreat to the small town for the peace it offers. You can spend a fun day wandering the streets. Some of my favorite shops and galleries include **Silver City Trading Company's Antique Mall,** 205 W. Broadway (✆ **575/388-8989**), which is packed with a range of items, from fun junk to Western antiques. **Copper Quail Gallery,** 211-A N. Texas St. (✆ **575/388-2646**), offers wonderful regional art; look for artful landscape photos by Allen Sanders. Imaginative fiber art adorns the walls at **Yello on Yankee,** 108 W. Yankie St. (✆ **575/534-4968;** www.susanszajer.com). Meanwhile **Elemental Arts,** 106 W. Yankie St. (✆ **575/590-7554;** www.gourdweb.com), offers fabulous folk art, much of it made out of gourds by Valerie M. Milner. Also look for oil paintings here by Chris Alvarez. A fun stop for coffee and a look at period photos of Silver City's "Big Ditch" is **Yankie Creek Coffee House,** 112 W. Yankie (✆ **575/534-9025**), open Monday to Saturday 7am to 6pm, and Sunday 7am to 4pm. If you're craving a cold treat, head to **Alotta Gelato,** 619 N. Bullard St. ✆ **575/534-4995;** www.alottagelato.com), serving a broad range of gelato flavors, including Romeo and Juliet, their primo chocolate chip. Open Sunday to Thursday noon to 9pm, Friday and Saturday noon to 10pm.

Thar's Copper in Them Thar Hills

Southern New Mexico has carried on its mining legacy into the present, with two fully operating mines. South of Silver City 12 miles on NM 90 is the Freeport-McMoRan **Tyrone Inc. Open Pit Copper Mine** (✆ **575/538-5331**). Some 60 million tons of rock are taken out every year. Former mine owner Phelps Dodge consolidated its Tyrone holdings in 1909 and hired famous architect Bertram Goodhue to design a "Mediterranean-style" company town. Tyrone, later referred to as the Million Dollar Ghost Town, was constructed between 1914 and 1918. A drop in copper prices caused it to be abandoned virtually overnight. After a pre–World War II incarnation as a luxurious dude ranch, Tyrone lay dormant for years until the late 1960s, when the town made way for the present-day open pit mine and mill.

The oldest active mine in the Southwest, and among the largest in America, is the Freeport-McMoRan **Chino Mines Co. Open Pit Copper Mine** (commonly called the Santa Rita Copper Mine; ✆ **575/537-3381**) at Santa Rita, 15 miles east of Silver City via US 180 and NM 152. The multicolored open pit is a mile wide and 1,000 feet deep, and can be viewed from an observation point. Even if you scorn such catastrophic gashes in the earth, it's worth stopping to look out over the mine. Unfortunately, no tours are available at this writing.

The adobe **Methodist-Episcopal Church** was built with William Randolph Hearst's money in 1898 and now houses the Grant County Art Guild. The town also has the **Log Cabin Curio Shop and Museum,** set in an 1866 cabin (✆ **575/388-1882**), and the **Buckhorn Saloon and Opera House** (p. 337).

SOUTH OF SILVER CITY **City of Rocks State Park** ★ (✆ **575/536-2800**), 25 miles from Silver City via US 180 and NM 61, is an area of fantastically shaped volcanic rock formations, formed in ancient times from thick blankets of ash that hardened into tuff. This soft stone, eroded by wind and rain, was shaped into monolithic blocks reminiscent of Stonehenge. For some, the park resembles a medieval village; for others, it's a collection of misshapen, albeit benign, giants. Complete with a desert garden, the park offers excellent camping and picnic sites. It's also a renowned spot for *bouldering,* a type of rock climbing in which participants don't use ropes. Day use is allowed from 6am to 9pm for $5 per vehicle; a campsite costs $8 to $18. The visitor center is typically open from 10am to 4pm, but its hours vary, depending on volunteer staffing.

WEST OF SILVER CITY US 180, heading northwest from Silver City, is the gateway to Catron County and most of the Gila National Forest, including the villages of Glenwood, Reserve, and Quemado. For details on this area, see "Other Adventures in Gila National Forest," later in this chapter.

WHERE TO STAY IN & AROUND SILVER CITY

Silver City now offers a full range of chain hotels, many with reasonable prices, so if you have a favorite, call their 800 number to see if it's represented. Most lodgings in town provide free parking.

Holiday Inn Express ★ Kids East of downtown, this hotel offers clean and quiet rooms with standards you expect from the brand name. Rooms are medium-size, decorated with earth tones, and have high ceilings and large windows letting in lots of sunlight. Beds are comfortable. The medium-size bathrooms are very clean. Be sure *not* to book room no. 121, which has noisy pipes playing tunes through the night. Wireless Internet is available in the lobby and breakfast bar.

1103 Superior St., Silver City, NM 88061. ✆ **800/HOLIDAY** or 575/538-2525. Fax 575/538-2525. 60 units. $110 double. AE, DC, DISC, MC, V. Pets allowed in some rooms. **Amenities:** Jacuzzi; exercise room; business center; coin-op laundry; dry cleaning. *In room:* A/C, TV, high-speed Internet, coffeemaker, hair dryer, iron.

The Palace Hotel If you like the feel of an Old West downtown hotel in the center of the historic district, this is your spot. First established in 1882 as a bank, then opened as a hotel in 1900, it closed for many years but was reopened in 1990 as a small European-style hotel. Each of the rooms on the second floor is shaped and decorated differently. All are eclectic, some with antiques. The beds are medium firm, and the standard-size bathrooms are very clean with old fixtures, some with new toilets. Suites have a microwave and fridge. The rooms closest to the upstairs sitting room and breakfast area are the nicest. If you're not accustomed to city noise, you'll want to avoid this place, as traffic noise can be loud into the night. Wireless Internet access is available in some parts of the hotel.

106 W. Broadway (P.O. Box 5093), Silver City, NM 88061. ✆ **575/388-1811.** www.zianet.com/palacehotel. 18 units. $48–$63 double; $79 suite. Rates include continental breakfast. AE, DC, DISC, MC, V. **Amenities:** Access to nearby health club.

Smaller Inns

Bear Mountain Lodge ★★★ Set on 160 acres just 3½ miles northwest of downtown Silver City, this lodge, owned and operated by the Nature Conservancy, is ideal for outdoors enthusiasts, from birders to bicyclers. The 1920s inn offers large rooms with Old World charm, accented by maple floors, high ceilings, and with such details as authentic Navajo rugs and original art on the walls. Beds are very comfortable, and baths are medium-size with elegant tile work. Four rooms have private balconies. This is a nature lover's delight. On-site naturalist staff members are on hand to inform visitors about the flora and fauna of the area, and they also conduct guided trips. Breakfasts are hearty and healthy, with treats such as muffins and quiche. Dinner is served for guests nightly for an extra fee. It's a gourmet buffet-style affair that changes seasonally with such offerings as poached salmon and a Thai dinner. A guest computer provides Internet access. What's best here is that you can count on complete quiet.

2251 Cottage San Rd., Silver City, NM 88061. (P.O. Box 1163, Silver City, NM 88062). ✆ **877/620-BEAR** (2327) or 575/538-2538. www.bearmountainlodge.com. 11 units. $125–$185 double. 2-night minimum stay. Rates include full breakfast. Box lunches available for an extra charge. Horse boarding $15/night. AE, MC, V. Turn north off US 180 on Alabama St. (½ mile west of NM 90 intersection). Proceed 3 miles (Alabama becomes Cottage San Rd.) to dirt road turnoff to left; the lodge is another ½ mile. No children 9 or under. **Amenities:** Mountain bikes; library; hiking trails. *In room:* A/C, Wi-Fi, hair dryer.

Casitas de Gila ★★ If you're looking for a remote and peaceful stay in the quintessential southern New Mexico terrain, this inn is for you. Set on a little bluff above Bear Creek, about a half-hour from Silver City, these five casitas offer the epitome of Southwestern style. The adobe-style dwellings are decorated with Spanish-style furniture and Mexican rugs. The medium-size bedrooms and bathrooms come well equipped with comfortable beds, bath supplies, and bathrobes. Each also has a kiva fireplace and a small porch with a *chiminea* (Mexican ceramic fireplace) and a grill. On hand is a hot tub with a view of the creek, canyon, and sky. The area is great for birding and hiking, and horseback riding can be arranged. Also on the property are 226 acres with hiking trails, an art gallery, and a courtyard.

Relax in History

Set in a Queen Anne–style home dating from 1906, the **Ciénega Spa & Salon,** 101 N. Cooper St. (✆ **575/534-1600;** www.cienegaspasalon.com), offers a full range of treatments between bisque- and azure-colored walls. The place also serves as an art gallery, representing many local artists as well as pottery from the villagers of Mata Ortiz, Mexico.

50 Casita Flats Rd. (P.O. Box 325), Gila, NM 88038. ✆ **877/923-4827** or 575/535-4455. Fax 575/535-4456. www.casitasdegila.com. 5 casitas. $130–$210 double. Rates include continental breakfast. AE, DISC, MC, V. **Amenities:** Jacuzzi; activities desk. *In room:* Wi-Fi, kitchen, hair dryer, iron.

Camping

Silver City KOA (✆ **800/562-7623** or 575/388-3351; www.koa.com) has 82 sites and 42 full hookups, and it offers groceries, laundry facilities, and a pool. The campground is 5 miles east of the NM 90/US 180 junction on US 180. **Silver City RV Park** (✆ **575/538-2239;** www.silvercityrv.com) has 48 sites (45 with full hookups), showers, laundry facilities, and picnic tables. It's downtown on Bennett Street, behind Food Basket supermarket. Camping is also available at the Gila Cliff Dwellings (see "Gila Cliff Dwellings National Monument," below).

WHERE TO DINE IN & AROUND SILVER CITY

Buckhorn Saloon and Opera House ★ BURGERS/SEAFOOD/STEAKS Seven miles north of Silver City in Pinos Altos, the Buckhorn offers fine dining in 1860s decor. It's completely authentic, with vigas on the ceiling and thick adobe walls, but be aware that the dining room has very low light. The restaurant is noted for its Western-style steaks, seafood, homemade desserts, and excellent wine list. If you've got a big appetite, try the New York strip with green chile and cheese. I like the shrimp and chicken kabobs. Entrees are served with a salad (try the blue-cheese dressing) or soup and choice of potatoes or rice. Live entertainment is offered nightly. The high-personality saloon offers big round tables and a great wooden bar. Many come to this saloon to have excellent burgers and hear live music on selected nights. While waiting for your food, take a moment to peruse the attached opera house, where good melodrama theater is presented seasonally. Enjoy a drink from the full bar.

32 Main St., Pinos Altos. ✆ **575/538-9911.** Reservations highly recommended. Main courses $10–$46. MC, V. Mon–Sat 6–10pm; saloon Mon–Sat 3–10pm.

Diane's Bakery & Cafe ★★ NEW AMERICAN This is a wonderful find in such a small town. Diane Barrett, who was once a pastry chef at La Traviata and Eldorado in Santa Fe, has brought refined city food to this small town. At lunch, the atmosphere is bustling, usually with a slight wait for a table. At dinner, the tone is more romantic and low key, with more nouveau specialties. The service is friendly and adequate. You can't go wrong with any of the baked goods here. At brunch, try the hatch Benedict, a version of eggs Benedict made with home-baked chile cheddar toast. At lunch I suggest the spanokopita, a baked spinach pastry, served with a salad; the quiche of the day is also delicious. At dinner, you may want to order the pork loin, with apricot brandy demi-glaze, served with red potatoes and seasonal vegetables, or the seafood Thai coconut curry. Diane's also serves great steaks. There's a small but creative wine and beer menu. Don't leave without sampling one of the desserts, such as the four-layer chocolate cake.

510 N. Bullard St., Silver City. ✆ **575/538-8722.** Reservations recommended for dinner. Main courses $6–$9 breakfast and lunch, $15–$25 dinner. MC, V. Tues–Sat 11am–2pm and 5:30–9pm; brunch Sat–Sun 9am–2pm.

Isaac's Bar & Grill ★ PUB FOOD/AMERICAN With the charm of an 1881 historic building, once housing Isaac N. Cohen's mercantile business, this new restaurant and bar serves good sandwiches, burgers, salads, and grilled meat and fish dishes. The main room is a pub, with tall tables and lots of locals talking among them. The second room is large with tables spread about. Both rooms have hardwood floors, aged brick walls, and high ceilings. The service here can be somewhat evasive, though friendly. Brunch is served Saturday and Sunday, with standards such as eggs Benedict and French toast. A big seller here at lunch and dinner is the buffalo burger, with a choice of salad, soup, or the restaurant's special duck fat french fries. Lighter appetites might like the Greek salad, with veggies, kalamata olives, and feta, served with pita bread. Local live music, ranging from rock to Western to folk to blues, plays on Saturday nights.

200 N. Bullard. ✆ **575/388-4090.** Main courses $8–$19. MC, V. Wed–Sat and Mon 11:30am–9pm; Sun noon–9pm. Bar closing variable; Sat night to midnight or later.

Jalisco's ★ **Kids** NEW MEXICAN Set within an enchanting brick building in the historic district, this festive, nonsmoking restaurant serves big portions of good food. Three dining rooms fill the old structure, which has been Latinized with arched doorways and bold Mexican street-scene calendars on the walls. The combination plates are large and popular, as are the enchiladas. There are also burgers and a children's menu. Whatever you do, be sure to order a *sopaipilla* for dessert. They're delicious and huge. Beer and wine are served.

103 S. Bullard St., Silver City. ✆ **575/388-2060.** Reservations not accepted. Main courses $6–$12. DISC, MC, V. Mon–Sat 11am–8:30pm.

Shevek & Mi ★ **Finds** ECLECTIC You can travel to many places at this sweet restaurant in the center of town. Chef Shevek Barnhart has spent much of his life absorbing culinary magic from relatives and friends with backgrounds ranging from Italian to Moroccan. That, combined with training at the Culinary Institute of America, makes for a journey of delicious flavors. The ambience is clean bistro in the main room, a little more formal in a connecting dining room, and more casual on the patio. Sunday brunch brings bagels made from dough shipped in from New York, an example of the authentic New York deli food that pervades the menu, as is the challah French toast and, at lunch, the kosher pastrami Reuben, made nice and thick. Dinner brings such delights as chicken ashke, a chicken breast rubbed with curry and topped with smoked salmon and béarnaise sauce, served with herb-roasted potatoes. Shevek & Mi boasts the largest selection of wines and microbrews in the region.

602 N. Bullard St. ✆ **575/534-9168.** www.silver-eats.com. Reservations recommended on weekends. Main courses $3–$12 brunch, $5–$10 lunch, $10–$33 dinner. DISC, MC, V. Mon–Tues and Thurs 4:30–9pm; Fri 4:30–10pm; Sat–Sun 11am–2pm and 4–9pm (hours may be abbreviated in winter; call to confirm).

Vicki's Eatery ★ SALADS/SANDWICHES Set off a side street in the historic district, this little gem serves artfully prepared and healthy comfort food using fresh ingredients. In four small rooms with high ceilings and squash-colored walls, the place specializes in soups, salads, and sandwiches ranging from purely healthful to decadent. Service can be forgetful, and even, at times, rude, so beware. For brunch, you might have blueberry pancakes or biscuits and gravy. At lunch, the chicken fajita salad has lots of veggies and is topped with guacamole, while the Reuben sandwich is thick and served on robust pumpernickel, with German potato salad on the side. Quesadillas are also popular. Their German chocolate cake is so moist it seems to be imploding. On warmer days, the fenced-in patio offers nice outdoor dining.

107 Yankie St. ✆ **575/388-5430.** Reservations recommended in summer. Main courses $5–$9. AE, DC, DISC, MC, V. Mon–Sat 11am–3pm; Sun 9am–2pm.

8 GILA CLIFF DWELLINGS NATIONAL MONUMENT ★★

It takes 1½ to 2 hours to reach the **Gila Cliff Dwellings** from Silver City, but it's definitely worth the trip. First-time visitors are inevitably awed by the remains of an ancient civilization set in the mouths of caves, abandoned for 7 centuries. You reach the dwellings on a 1-mile moderate hike along which you catch glimpses of the ruins. This walk is an elaborate journey into the past. It winds its way into a narrow canyon, from which you first spot the poetic ruins perched in six caves 180 feet up on the canyon wall, stone shiny and hard as porcelain. Then the ascent begins up innumerable steps and rocks until you're standing face-to-face with these ancient relics, which offer a glimpse into the lives of Native Americans who lived here from the late 1270s through the early 1300s. Tree-ring dating indicates their residence didn't last longer than 30 to 40 years.

What's remarkable about the journey through the cliff dwellings is the depth of some of the caves. At one point, you'll climb a ladder and pass from one cave into the next, viewing the intricate little rooms (42 total) and walls that once made up a community dwelling. Probably not more than 10 to 15 families (about 40–50 people) lived in the cliff dwellings at any one time. The inhabitants were excellent weavers and skilled potters.

The cliff dwellings were discovered by Anglo settlers in the early 1870s, near where the three forks of the Gila River rise. Once you leave the last cave, you'll head down again traversing some steep steps to the canyon floor. Pets are not allowed within the monument, but they can be taken on trails within the Gila Wilderness. Be sure to pick up a trail guide at the visitor center.

ESSENTIALS

GETTING THERE From Silver City, take NM 15 north 44 miles to the Gila Cliff Dwellings. Travel time from Silver City is approximately 2 hours. You won't find any gas stations between Silver City and Gila Cliff Dwellings, so plan accordingly. Also know that at the monument, vehicles are permitted on paved roads only.

VISITOR INFORMATION For more information, contact **Gila Cliff Dwellings National Monument,** HC 68, Box 100, Silver City, NM 88061 (✆ **575/536-9461;** www.nps.gov/gicl).

ADMISSION FEES & HOURS Admission to the monument is $3 per person, with children age 12 and under admitted free. The visitor center, where you can pick up detailed brochures, is open from 8am to 5pm Memorial Day to Labor Day and from 8am to 4:30pm the rest of the year. The cliff dwellings are open from 8am to 6pm in the summer and from 9am to 4pm the rest of the year.

SEEING THE HIGHLIGHTS

Today, the dwellings allow a rare glimpse inside the homes and lives of prehistoric Native Americans. About 75% of what is seen is original, although the walls have been capped and the foundations strengthened to prevent further deterioration. It took a great deal of effort to build these homes: The stones were held in place by mortar, and all the clay and water for the mortar had to be carried by hand up from the stream, as the Mogollon did not have any pack animals. The vigas for the roof were cut and shaped with stone axes or fire.

The people who lived here were farmers, as shown by the remains of beans, squash, and corn in their homes. The fields were along the valley of the west fork of the Gila River and on the mesa across the canyon. No signs of irrigation have been found.

Near the visitor center, about a mile away, the remains of an earlier pit house (A.D. 100–400), built below ground level, and later pit houses (up to A.D. 1000), aboveground structures of adobe or wattle, have been found.

CAMPING

Camping and picnicking are encouraged in the national monument, with four developed campgrounds. Camping is free and some sites are RV accessible, though there are no hookups. Overnight lodging can be found in Silver City and in the nearby town of Gila Hot Springs, which also has a grocery store, horse rentals, and guided pack trips. For information, contact the visitor center (✆ **575/536-9461**).

9 OTHER ADVENTURES IN GILA NATIONAL FOREST

Gila National Forest, which offers some of the most spectacular mountain scenery in the Southwest, comprises 3.3 million acres in four counties. Nearly one-fourth of that acreage (790,000 acres) comprises the **Gila, Aldo Leopold,** and **Blue Range wildernesses.** Its highest peak is Whitewater Baldy, at 10,892 feet. Within the forest, six out of seven life zones can be found, so the range of plant and wildlife is broad. You may see mule deer, elk, antelope, black bear, mountain lion, and bighorn sheep. Nearly 400 miles of streams and a few small lakes sustain healthy populations of trout as well as bass, bluegill, and catfish. Anglers can head to Lake Roberts, Snow Lake, and Quemado Lake.

JUST THE FACTS For more information on the national forest, contact the **U.S. Forest Service,** Forest Supervisor's Office, 3005 E. Camino del Bosque, Silver City, NM 88061 (✆ **575/388-8201;** www.fs.fed.us).

The national forest has 29 campgrounds, all with toilets and six with drinking water. Car and backpack camping are also permitted throughout the forest.

HIKING & OTHER ACTIVITIES

Within the forest are 1,490 miles of trails for hiking and horseback riding, and in winter, cross-country skiing. Outside the wilderness areas, trail bikes and off-road vehicles are also permitted. Hiking trails in the Gila Wilderness, especially the 41-mile Middle Fork Trail, with its east end near Gila Cliff Dwellings, are among the most popular in the state and can sometimes be crowded. If you are more interested in communing with nature than with fellow hikers, however, you will find plenty of trails to suit you, both in and out of the officially designated wilderness areas.

Most of the trails are maintained and easy to follow. Trails along river bottoms, however, have many stream crossings (so be prepared for hiking with wet feet) and may be washed out by summer flash floods. It's best to inquire about trail conditions before you set out. More than 50 trail heads provide roadside parking.

A Shocking Experience

If you'd like to have an electrifying moment or two, plan a visit to the **Lightning Field,** near Quemado (✆ **575/773-4560** or 575/898-3335; www.lightningfield.org). An enormous sculpture by American artist Walter De Maria, it consists of 400 stainless-steel poles arranged in a rectangular grid. Its purpose? To attract those most picturesque and deadly bolts. Visitors are welcome May through October but must reserve months in advance.

Some of the best hikes in the area are the Frisco Box, Pueblo Creek, Whitewater Baldy, the Catwalk and Beyond, the Middle Fork/Little Bear Loop, and the Black Range Crest Trail. The Gila National Forest contains several wilderness areas that are off-limits to mountain bikes, including the Gila, Aldo Leopold, and the Blue Range Primitive Area. However, cyclists can access quite a few trails. Some to look for are the Cleveland Mine trail, Silver City Loop, Continental Divide, Signal Peak, Pinos Altos Loop, Fort Bayard Historical Trails, and Forest Trail 100.

The Catwalk National Recreation Trail ★ (✆ **575/539-2481**), 68 miles north of Silver City on US 180, then 5 miles east of Glenwood via NM 174, is a great break after a long drive. Kids are especially thrilled with this hike. It follows the route of a pipeline built in 1897 to carry water to the now-defunct town of Graham and its electric generator. About a quarter mile above the parking area is the beginning of a striking 250-foot metal causeway clinging to the sides of the boulder-choked Whitewater Canyon, which in spots is 20 feet wide and 250 feet deep. Along the way, you'll find water pouring through caves and waterfalls spitting off the cliff side. Farther up the canyon, a suspension bridge spans the chasm. Picnic facilities are near the parking area. There's a $3 fee per car.

OTHER HIGHLIGHTS

The scenic ghost town of **Mogollon** is 3½ miles north of Glenwood on US 180, and then 9 miles east on NM 159, a narrow mountain road that takes a good 25 minutes to negotiate. The village bears witness to silver and gold mining booms beginning in the late 19th century, and to the disastrous effects of floods and fire in later years. Remains of its last operating mine, the Little Fanny (which ceased operation in the 1950s), are still visible, along with dozens of other old buildings, miners' shacks, and mining paraphernalia. An art gallery and museum are found along Mogollon's main street. The movie *My Name Is Nobody,* starring Henry Fonda, was filmed here.

Cochise, Geronimo, and other Apache war chiefs held forth in these mountains in the late 19th century. **Reserve** (pop. 482), 100 miles northwest of Silver City, has a few homes, a store, and a bar. As Catron County's seat, it's noted as the place where, in 1882, Deputy Sheriff **Elfego Baca** made an epic stand in a 33-hour gun battle with 80 cowboys. In spring 2008, Reserve unveiled a statue of the hero at the center of town. It's an excellent artwork, well worth stopping to see. A good stop in town is **Henry's Corner,** 109 Main St. (✆ **575/533-6488**), where you'll find gas, ice cream, and books, including ones on Elfego Baca, and my own *King of the Road.* If you're fortunate, owner Henry Martinez will be there to regale you with tales of Elfego.

12

Southeastern New Mexico

Whether you're an adult or a child, the wonder of nature in this part of the world will inspire you. Here you'll find Carlsbad Caverns National Park and White Sands National Monument, whose immensity and intricate beauty speak in unique ways to each.

Running east of the Rio Grande (the I-25 corridor) and south of I-40, southeastern New Mexico has other sites as well. Along with the natural wonders, this is the home of the fierce Mescalero Apaches and the world's richest quarter-horse race. Billy the Kid lived and died in southeastern New Mexico in the 19th century, and the world's first atomic bomb was exploded here in the 20th. From west to east, barren desert gives way to high, forested peaks, snow-covered in winter; to the fertile valley of the Pecos River; and to plains beloved by ranchers along the Texas border.

The main population center in this section of the state is **Roswell** (pop. 45,500), famous as the purported landing place of an unidentified flying object (UFO). **Ruidoso** (pop. 10,000), in the mountains between Alamogordo and Roswell, is a booming resort town. **Carlsbad** (pop. 25,500), 76 miles south of Roswell, and **Alamogordo** (pop. 36,000), 117 miles west of Roswell, are of more immediate interest to tourists. Other sizable towns are **Clovis** (pop. 33,000) and **Hobbs** (pop. 32,000), both on the Texas border, and **Artesia** (pop. 10,500), between Roswell and Carlsbad, has a pretty restored historic district.

1 SOUTHEASTERN NEW MEXICO'S GREAT OUTDOORS

BIKING Several forest roads and single-track trails in this region are favorites with mountain bikers. In the Ruidoso area, near Cloudcroft, the **Rim Trail,** a 17-mile intermediate trail that offers views of the White Sands, is considered one of the top 10 trails in the nation. To reach the trail, take NM 130 from Cloudcroft to NM 6563, turn right, and look for the Rim Trail signs. The Cloudcroft area offers three other good trails: La Luz Canyon, Silver Springs Loop, and Pumphouse Canyon. For directions, contact the Cloudcroft Ranger Station (✆ **575/682-2551**). The paved road up to **Carlsbad Caverns National Park** is scenic, and the auto traffic drives slowly, but it's very hot in the summer.

BIRD-WATCHING **Bitter Lake National Wildlife Refuge** (✆ **575/622-6755**), northeast of Roswell, is particularly good for watching migratory waterfowl, and **Bluff Springs** (✆ **575/682-2551**), south of Cloudcroft, is popular with turkeys and hummingbirds. If you find turkey vultures particularly fascinating, **Rattlesnake Springs** (✆ **575/785-2232**), south of Carlsbad, is the place to go.

BOATING Boating, water-skiing, jet-skiing, and sailing are permitted at **Carlsbad Municipal Park,** which runs through town for just over a mile along the west bank of Lake Carlsbad. The lake also has a beach that's open to swimmers. **Brantley Lake State**

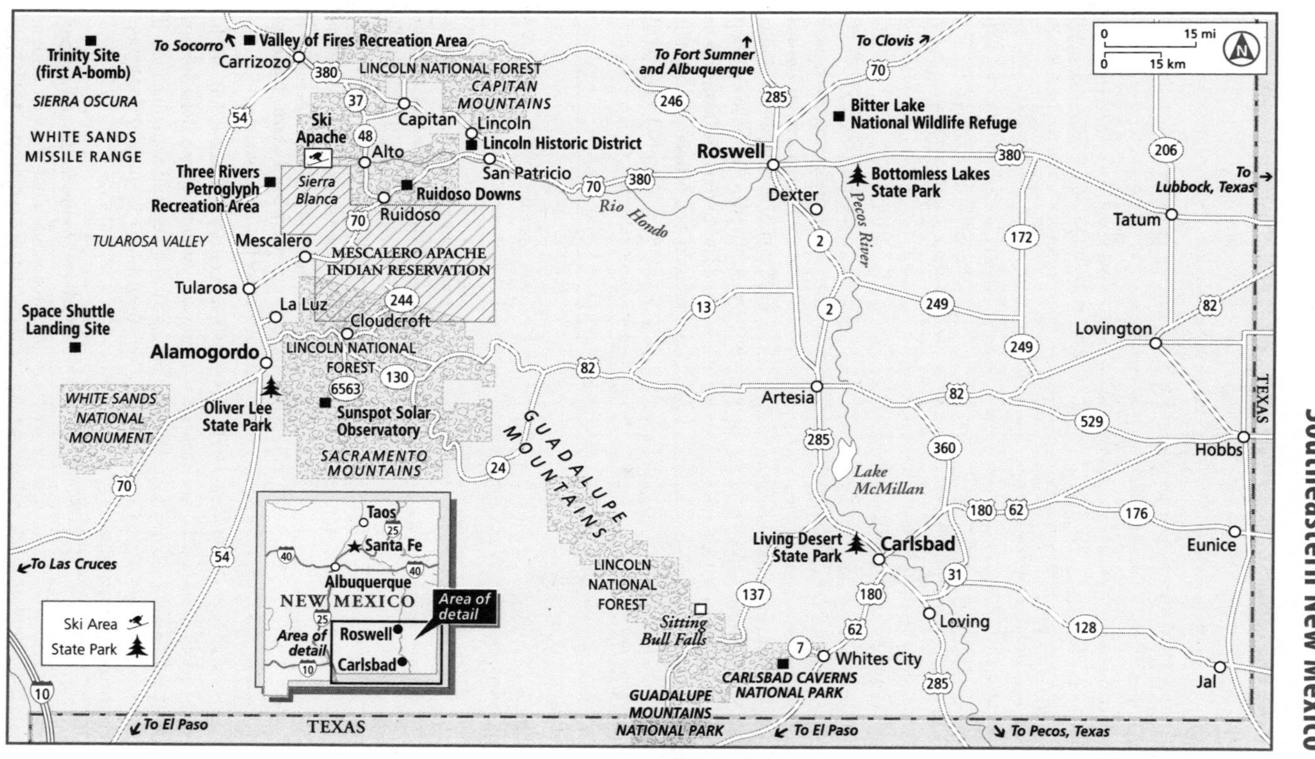

Trinity Site (first A-bomb)
To Socorro
Valley of Fires Recreation Area
Carrizozo
LINCOLN NATIONAL FOREST
CAPITAN MOUNTAINS
SIERRA OSCURA
WHITE SANDS MISSILE RANGE
Ski Apache
Capitan
Lincoln
Lincoln Historic District
Alto
San Patricio
Three Rivers Petroglyph Recreation Area
Sierra Blanca
Ruidoso Downs
Ruidoso
Rio Hondo
TULAROSA VALLEY
Mescalero
MESCALERO APACHE INDIAN RESERVATION
Tularosa
La Luz
Cloudcroft
Space Shuttle Landing Site
Alamogordo
LINCOLN NATIONAL FOREST
WHITE SANDS NATIONAL MONUMENT
Oliver Lee State Park
Sunspot Solar Observatory
SACRAMENTO MOUNTAINS
GUADALUPE MOUNTAINS
To Fort Sumner and Albuquerque
To Clovis
Bitter Lake National Wildlife Refuge
Roswell
Dexter
Bottomless Lakes State Park
Pecos River
Artesia
Lake McMillan
Living Desert State Park
Carlsbad
Loving
Whites City
CARLSBAD CAVERNS NATIONAL PARK
LINCOLN NATIONAL FOREST
Sitting Bull Falls
GUADALUPE MOUNTAINS NATIONAL PARK
0 15 mi
0 15 km
To Lubbock, Texas
Tatum
Lovington
Hobbs
Eunice
Jal
TEXAS
To Las Cruces
Taos
Santa Fe
Albuquerque
NEW MEXICO
Area of detail
Roswell
Carlsbad
Ski Area
State Park
To El Paso
TEXAS
To El Paso
To Pecos, Texas

Park (✆ **575/457-2384**), 15 miles north of Carlsbad, is popular with windsurfers who favor its consistent desert winds. (To find information on New Mexico state parks, go to **www.nmparks.com**.)

FISHING **Bonito Lake** and **Rio Ruidoso** are popular destinations for trout fishing. The scenic **Oasis State Park** (✆ **575/356-5331**) just north of Portales, also offers fishing.

GOLF This region has plenty of golfing opportunities. In Ruidoso, **Cree Meadows Country Club,** Country Club Drive off Sudderth Drive (✆ **575/257-5815;** www.playcreemeadows.com), is an 18-hole public course. Also public in the Ruidoso area are the 18-hole courses at the **Inn of the Mountain Gods Resort & Casino,** 287 Carrizo Canyon Rd. (✆ **800/545-6040** or 575/464-4100; www.innofthemountaingods.com); and the **Links at Sierra Blanca,** 105 Sierra Blanca Dr. (✆ **575/258-5330;** www.thelodgeatsierrablanca.com). In Cloudcroft, the 9-hole **Lodge at Cloudcroft Golf Course** (✆ **800/395-6343** or 575/682-2566; www.thelodgeresort.com) boasts an elevation of 9,200 feet; it's one of the highest courses in the world and one of the oldest in the United States. Alamogordo's **Desert Lakes Golf Course** (✆ **575/437-0290;** www.desertlakesgolf.com) has views of Sierra Blanca and the Sacramento Mountains.

HIKING More than 225 miles of trails weave a web through the Smokey Bear Ranger District of the **Lincoln National Forest.** From Ruidoso, a favorite destination of hikers is the White Mountain Wilderness, with nine trails, and the Capitan Mountains Wilderness, with 11 trails. **Smokey Bear Ranger District office,** 901 Mechem Dr., Ruidoso (✆ **575/257-4095**), has excellent and inexpensive maps of each wilderness area. Monjeau Lookout is a popular destination off Ski Run Road (NM 532). **Carlsbad Caverns National Park** has an extensive trail system as well (outside the caves, of course).

HORSEBACK RIDING Horseback riding is popular in Ruidoso. Try the **Inn of the Mountain Gods Resort & Casino** (✆ **800/545-6040** or 575/464-4100; www.innofthemountaingods.com) or **Cowboys Riding Stables** (✆ **575/378-8217;** www.cowboysridingstables.com).

SKIING Southern New Mexico's premier ski resort is **Ski Apache** (✆ **575/257-9001** for snow reports, 575/336-4356 for information; www.skiapache.com), only 20 miles northwest of Ruidoso in the Mescalero Apache Indian Reservation. Situated on an 11,500-foot ridge of the 12,003-foot Sierra Blanca, the resort boasts a gondola, two quad chairs, five triple chairs, one double chair, a day lodge, a sport shop, a rental shop, a ski school, a first-aid center, four snack bars, and a lounge. Ski Apache has 55 trails and slopes (20% beginner, 35% intermediate, and 45% advanced), with a vertical drop of 1,900 feet and a total skier capacity of 16,500 an hour. Though its location seems remote, a lot of skiers fill this mountain during weekends and holidays. Because the mountain is owned and run by the Apaches, you can experience another culture while skiing. All-day lift tickets cost $51 for adults, $45 for seniors, $43 for teens (13–17), $25 for children 12 and under. The mountain is open Thanksgiving to Easter daily from 8:45am to 4pm. Lift-and-lodging packages can be booked through the **Inn of the Mountain Gods Resort & Casino** (✆ **800/545-6040** or 575/464-4100; www.innofthemountaingods.com).

2 ALAMOGORDO

Famous for its leading role in America's space research and military technology industries, **Alamogordo** (pop. 35,582) achieved worldwide fame on July 16, 1945, when the first atomic bomb was exploded at nearby Trinity Site. Today, it is home of the New Mexico Museum of Space History, White Sands National Monument, and Holloman Air Force Base. Twenty miles east and twice as high, the resort village of **Cloudcroft** (elevation 8,650 ft.) attracts vacationers to the forested heights of the Sacramento Mountains.

ESSENTIALS

GETTING THERE From Albuquerque, take I-25 south 87 miles to San Antonio; turn east on US 380, go 66 miles to Carrizozo; then turn south on US 54 for 58 miles (4 hr.). From Las Cruces, take US 70 northeast (1½ hr.). (Note that US 70 may be closed for up to 2 hr. during tests on White Sands Missile Range.) From El Paso, take US 54 north (1½ hr.).

The nearest major airport is **El Paso International.** The local airport, **Alamogordo–White Sands Regional Airport** (✆ **575/439-4110**) does not offer commercial service.

VISITOR INFORMATION The **Alamogordo Chamber of Commerce** and visitor center is at 1301 N. White Sands Blvd., Alamogordo, NM 88311 (✆ **800/826-0294** or 575/437-6120; www.alamogordo.com).

CITY LAYOUT Alamogordo is on the eastern edge of the Tularosa Valley, at the foot of the Sacramento Mountains. US 54 (White Sands Blvd.) is the main street, extending several miles north and south. The downtown district is actually a few blocks east of White Sands Boulevard, off 10th Street.

WHAT TO SEE & DO IN ALAMOGORDO

In addition to the attractions in Alamogordo itself, also enjoyable is the small, historic village of **La Luz,** just 3 miles north of Alamogordo. It has attracted a number of resident artists and craftspeople who live, work, and display some of their products for sale. Worth seeing are the cactus-filled park and the small Our Lady of Light Church.

New Mexico Museum of Space History ★ The New Mexico Museum of Space History comes in two parts: the International Space Hall of Fame and the Clyde W. Tombaugh IMAX Dome Theater. Both are on the lower slopes of the Sacramento Mountains, 2 miles east of US 54, and just above New Mexico State University's Alamogordo branch campus.

The Space Hall of Fame occupies the "Golden Cube," a five-story building with walls of golden glass. Visitors are encouraged to start on the top floor and work their way down. En route, they recall the accomplishments of the first astronauts and cosmonauts, including America's Mercury, Gemini, and Apollo programs, and the early Soviet orbital flights. Spacecraft and a lunar exploration module are exhibited. Displays tell the history and purposes of rocketry, missiles, and satellites and provide an orientation to astronomy and other planets.

At Tombaugh Theater, IMAX projection and Spitz 512 Planetarium Systems create earthly and cosmic experiences on a 2,700-square-foot dome screen.

Located at the top of NM 2001. ✆ **877/333-6589** outside New Mexico, or 575/437-2840. Fax 575/434-2245. www.spacefame.org. Admission to International Space Hall of Fame $6 adults, $5 seniors (age 60 and older) and military, $4 children age 4–12, free for children 3 and under. IMAX Theater $6 adults, $5.50 seniors, $4.50 children age 4–12, free for children 3 and under; additional charge for double feature. Daily 9am–5pm.

Toy Train Depot (Kids) The brainchild of John Koval (whom you're likely to meet at the door), this is an interesting attraction for train fanatics and laypeople. Koval started the nonprofit museum, housed in a genuine 1898 railroad depot, as a means to celebrate the railroad's important presence in the area. The museum meanders back through three

The Nut House

While traveling this area, you'll likely see signs pointing into thick groves of pecan trees directing you to the **Nut House,** 32 Ivy Lane, in La Luz (✆ **575/437-NUTY**). When you step inside, you'll be greeted by the scent of pecan pie with a hint of chocolate. As well, the place—an airy space with a long, aged-wood bar—is packed with local art, much of it made by the artists of the legendary La Luz art colony from the 1960s and some of their children. As well as perusing art, you can sip a latte, and eat homemade soups and sandwiches on a lovely patio within the pecan trees. Don't leave without sampling a piece of apple, peach, or chocolate pie, all laced with pecans.

rooms, each filled with tracks laid along colorful miniature cityscapes and countryside—1,200 feet of track altogether. The highlight is a re-creation of the Alamogordo, Carrizozo, and Cloudcroft train system. Rides through the grounds on 12-inch and 16-inch gauge trains are offered. There's also a railroad hobby shop.

1991 N. White Sands Blvd. ✆ **888/207-3564** or 575/437-2855. Admission $4. Train rides $4. Wed–Sun noon–4pm.

Something Unusual

Eagle Ranch Pistachio Groves This is a tasty and fun step into the nutty world of pistachio farming. New Mexico's first and largest pistachio groves, Eagle Ranch offers free 45-minute tours weekdays at 10am and 1:30pm in summer and at 1:30pm in winter. The tour offers a brief history of the pistachio groves and a tour of the shipping and receiving facility, salting and roasting department, and out through the groves. A visitor center with an art gallery displays the work of local artists, and at the gift shop, you can buy pistachio nuts, custom baskets, and a variety of other items. Try the pistachio-nut brittle!

7288 US 54/70 (5 miles north of Alamogordo). ✆ **800/432-0999** or 575/434-0035. Fax 575/434-2132. www.eagleranchpistachios.com. Free admission. Gift shop and gallery Mon–Sat 8am–6pm; Sun 9am–6pm.

Trinity Site

The world's first atomic bomb was exploded in this desert never-never land on July 16, 1945. It is strictly off-limits to civilians—except twice a year, on the first Saturday of April and October. A small lava monument commemorates the explosion, which left a crater a quarter mile across and 8 feet deep, and transformed the desert sand into a jade green glaze called "Trinitite" that remains today. The McDonald House, where the bomb's plutonium core was assembled 2 miles from ground zero, has been restored to its 1945 condition. The site is on the west slope of Sierra Oscura, 90 air miles northwest of Alamogordo. For more information, call the public affairs office of **White Sands Missile Range** (✆ **575/678-1134;** www.wsmr.army.mil).

GETTING OUTSIDE

Fifteen miles southeast of Alamogordo via US 54 and Dog Canyon Road, you'll find **Oliver Lee Memorial State Park.** Nestled at the mouth of Dog Canyon, a stunning break in the steep escarpment of the Sacramento Mountains, the site has drawn human visitors for thousands of years. Springs and seeps support a variety of rare and endangered plant species, as well as a rich animal life. Hiking trails into the foothills are well marked;

the park also offers a visitor center with excellent exhibits on local history, and picnic and camping grounds, with showers, electricity, and a dump station.

Dog Canyon was one of the last strongholds of the Mescalero Apache, and it was the site of battles between Native Americans and the U.S. Cavalry in the 19th century. Around the turn of the 20th century, rancher Oliver Lee built a home near here and raised cattle. Guided tours from the visitor center to Lee's restored house give a taste of early ranch life in southern New Mexico.

The park is open 24 hours a day; admission is $5 per car. The visitor center is open daily from 9am to 4pm. Guided tours are offered Saturday and Sunday at 3pm, weather permitting. For more information, call ✆ **575/437-8284.**

EXPLORING THE SURROUNDING AREA

Cloudcroft ★ is a picturesque mountain village of 765 people high in the Sacramento Mountains, surrounded by Lincoln National Forest. Though only about 20 miles east of Alamogordo via US 82, it is twice as high, overlooking the Tularosa Valley from a dizzying elevation of almost 9,000 feet. It was founded in 1899 when railroad surveyors reached the mountain summit and built a lodge for Southern Pacific Railroad workers. Today, the Lodge is Cloudcroft's biggest attraction and biggest employer (see "Nearby Places to Stay & Dine," below). Other accommodations are also available in town, as are lots of recreational opportunities and community festivals. For information, contact the **Cloudcroft Chamber of Commerce,** P.O. Box 1290, Cloudcroft, NM 88317 (✆ **866/874-4447** or 575/682-2733; www.cloudcroft.net). It's in a log cabin in the center of town, on the south side of US 82.

The **Sacramento Mountains Historical Museum and Pioneer Village,** US 82 east of downtown Cloudcroft (✆ **575/682-2932**), recalls the community's early days, with several pioneer buildings, historic photos, and exhibits of turn-of-the-20th-century railroad memorabilia, clothing, and other artifacts. Call for hours. Nearby, **Lincoln National Forest** (✆ **575/682-2551**) maintains the unique **La Pasada Encantada Nature Trail,** a short footpath from Sleepygrass Campground, off NM 130 south of town, with signs in Braille inviting walkers to touch the various plants, leaves, and trees. A new trail is a several-mile moderate hike to the historic **Mexican Canyon Railroad Trestle.** The trail head is in a U.S. Forest Service picnic area, west of the junction of US 82 and NM 130, where you'll also find a short walk to an observation point offering spectacular views across White Sands Missile Range and the Tularosa Basin. The picnic area also has tables, grills, drinking water, and restrooms.

National Solar Observatory–Sacramento Peak (✆ **575/434-7000;** www.nso.edu), 18 miles south of Cloudcroft via NM 6563, a National Scenic Byway, attracts astronomers from around the world to study the sun and its effects on our planet. Actually, three observatories are here, with two open to the public for self-guided tours (allow at least 1 hr.), open daily from 8am to 6pm. Free guided tours are offered Saturday at 2pm from June to October. The visitor center, which is open daily from 9am to 5pm, has a gift shop and scientific exhibits geared toward children.

If you'd like a tasty meal in this mountain town, head to where the locals eat, **Dave's Café,** 300 Burro Ave. (✆ **575/682-2127**). You can order from an array of sandwiches and salads. Try the Coney-style burger with grilled onions or the grilled chicken salad with lots of veggies and bacon. For dessert, pick up truffles or ice cream from the attached sweets shop. Dave's is open Sunday to Thursday 10:30am to 5pm and Friday and Saturday 10:30am to 7pm.

If you like outdoor gear and items such as scented candles and tie-dyed clothes, stop next door at **High Altitude,** 310 Burro Ave. (✆ **575/682-1229**).

WHERE TO STAY IN ALAMOGORDO

All accommodations in Alamogordo are along White Sands Boulevard, the north-south highway through town, and parking is free.

Best Western Desert Aire ★ Value Kids This motel, remodeled in 2007, has a new roof and new stucco, with upgrading to the rooms as well. It provides a quiet night's rest, which is likely why this place fills up most every night during Alamogordo's busier months of the year. The medium-size rooms have contemporary furnishings and comfortable new beds. The bathrooms are small, with an outer sink vanity. Also available are kitchenettes, which contain stoves, ovens, and microwaves. The suites are inexpensive and have 3-foot-deep Jacuzzi tubs. The central point of this motel is the pool, a great place to cool off on hot days, though it can fill up with kids.

1021 S. White Sands Blvd., Alamogordo, NM 88310. ✆ **800/565-1988** or 575/437-2110. Fax 575/437-1898. www.bestwestern.com. 99 units. $60–$72 double; $65–$82 suite. Rates include continental breakfast. AE, DISC, MC, V. Pets welcome with $50 deposit. **Amenities:** Outdoor pool; Jacuzzi; sauna; game room; coin-op laundry; same-day dry cleaning. *In room:* A/C, TV, Wi-Fi, fridge, coffeemaker, hair dryer, iron, microwave.

Holiday Inn Express ★ This newer hotel on the south end of town provides what you'd expect from this chain—clean, comfortable rooms with a bit of flair. The hotel is steps above the Best Western, though it doesn't offer even near the competitive price. Rooms are medium size, with high ceilings and come in standards and suites. All are spacious, decorated in natural hues, with comfortable beds, while the bathrooms are medium size with granite countertops. A full, hot breakfast comes with the room.

100 Kerry Ave. ✆ **800/465-4329** or 575/434-9773. Fax 575/434-3279. www.hiexpress.com. 80 units. $105 double; $119–$149 suite. Rates include breakfast. AE, DC, DISC, MC, V. **Amenities:** Indoor pool; exercise room. *In room:* A/C, TV, high-speed Internet, fridge, coffeemaker, hair dryer, iron, microwave.

Camping

I strongly recommend camping at **White Sands National Monument,** (see "Camping," under "White Sands National Monument," below).

If you'd rather have amenities, try **Alamogordo Roadrunner** (✆ **877/437-3003** or 575/437-3003; www.roadrunnercampground.com). It has laundry and grocery facilities as well as a recreation room/area, swimming pool, playground, shuffleboard, and planned group activities in winter. The campground is on 24th Street in Alamogordo, just east of the US 54/70/82 junction. If you're looking for something in between, **Oliver Lee State Park,** 15 miles southeast of Alamogordo via US 54 and Dog Canyon Road (✆ **575/437-8284**), is a good choice, with 44 sites, 10 full hookups, picnic tables, grills, tenting availability, a playground, and hiking trails.

WHERE TO DINE IN ALAMOGORDO

Margo's Kids MEXICAN Since 1976, the Sandoval family has been feeding New Mexicans and travelers hearty, flavorful food at a decent price. Set in a windowless building with two main dining rooms, the restaurant isn't much for atmosphere, though colorful Mexican blankets provide a festive touch, and the casualness makes it comfortable for families. Now Margo's serves breakfast, the most popular dish, huevos rancheros (eggs over tortillas, smothered in chile). Lunch and dinner start with complimentary chips and salsa; with it, you may order from a variety of domestic and imported beers and a few wines. Service is good, though this place can get busy (and noisy), which can slow things down a bit. The Margo's Special is a big seller here, a combo plate with guacamole salad, beef taco, enchilada, chile relleno, Spanish rice, and refried beans.

504 E. 1st St. (1 block east of White Sands Blvd.). ✆ **575/434-0689.** Main courses $4.25–$12. AE, DISC, MC, V. Mon–Sun 6:30am–9pm.

Memories Restaurant ★ Finds AMERICAN Set in a 1907 Victorian home in a residential neighborhood right on the edge of historic downtown, this restaurant serves excellent food in an old-world setting. Functional tables sit on Brazilian-oak floors within what was once the living room and den, creating a casual, comfortable atmosphere, which is a good thing because the service can be overworked. Diners come to sample salads and croissant sandwiches for lunch and grilled steaks and seafood for dinner. Basically, the place is packed nonstop while it's open. I recommend the crab salad served over avocado, or the turkey and avocado croissant sandwich. For dinner, a big seller is the prime rib, which comes with salad or soup, bread, a side dish, and vegetable. The grilled shrimp is also good. Beer and wine are available.

1223 New York Ave. (corner of 13th St.). ✆ **575/437-0077.** Reservations recommended. Main courses $6–$13 lunch, $13–$21 dinner. AE, DISC, MC, V. Mon–Sat 11am–9pm.

Nature's Pantry ★ Finds DELI/HEALTH FOOD If many days on the road have left your stomach weary, step into this downtown oasis of healthiness. Brian and Linda Jungling sell all manner of vitamins and tonics, but they also have a few tables and a juice bar, where locals come to eat baked goods, sandwiches, and salads. At lunchtime, try the chicken salad sandwich with avocado and sprouts served on whole grain bread, or any number of salads, all made with fresh vegetables.

2909 N. White Sands Blvd. ✆ **575/437-3037.** AE, DISC, MC, V. All menu items under $10. Mon–Tues and Thurs–Sat 8am–8pm; Wed 8am–6pm.

Nearby Places to Stay & Dine

Casa de Sueños ★ Kids NEW MEXICAN For tasty New Mexican fare, with a good dose of the whimsy of Mexico, check out this fun restaurant about 15 miles north of Alamogordo, outside Tularosa. Decorated with Mexican folk paintings and a country home mural, it exudes a fiesta atmosphere. Outside, the broad patio is lit with little Christmas lights and has chile peppers printed on the tablecloths. For breakfast, try the huevos rancheros. A lunch buffet provides a good sampling of enchiladas and beans. To start your meal, try the guacamole, made with red onions. For an entree, order anything with the green chile sauce, made with fresh chiles and well seasoned. Vegetarian and children's selections round out the menu. You can order from a variety of beers and wines.

35 St. Francis Dr., Tularosa, NM. ✆ **575/585-3494.** Reservations recommended on weekends. Main courses $5–$8 breakfast, $7–$15 lunch and dinner. AE, DISC, MC, V. Mon–Fri and Sat–Sun 11am–8pm.

The Lodge at Cloudcroft ★★ This lodge is an antique jewel, a well-preserved relic of another era. From the grand fireplace in the lobby to the homey Victorian decor in the guest rooms, it exudes gentility and class. Its 9-hole golf course, one of the nation's highest, challenges golfers across rolling hills between 8,600 and 9,200 feet elevation. Most rooms in the Lodge have views and all are filled with antiques, from sideboards and lamps to mirrors and steam radiators. The standard rooms are small so you may want to reserve one of their suites, which have a bedroom and a sitting room with a fold-out couch. Some suites have Jacuzzi tubs. Guests are greeted by a stuffed bear sitting on their bed with a sampler of homemade fudge from the Lodge Mercantile. In 1991, more rooms were added in the form of the Pavilion and the Retreat, which were built adjacent to the Lodge. These are most often rented out in blocks and are less desirable than those in the main hotel. The hotel's new Spirit of the Mountain Spa offers a variety of massage treatments.

Rebecca's (✆ **575/682-2566**), the lodge's restaurant, is named for the resident ghost, believed to have been a chambermaid in the 1930s who was killed by her lumberjack lover. Three meals, plus a midday snack menu, are served daily. Service is friendly and very efficient, and the atmosphere is elegant, with bright sunshine during the day and romantic lighting at night. I recommend the roasted duck with Madeira wine sauce and rice. For dessert, try one of their tableside flambé desserts. The champagne Sunday brunch is a must here, offering a prime rib serving station and an array of side selections.

1 Corona Place (P.O. Box 497), Cloudcroft, NM 88317. ✆ **800/395-6343** or 575/682-2566. Fax 575/682-2715. www.thelodgeresort.com. 59 units. $109–$159 double; $169–$329 suite. AE, DC, DISC, MC, V. Free parking. **Amenities:** Restaurant; bar; outdoor heated pool; golf course; access to nearby tennis courts; exercise room; spa; Jacuzzi; sauna; fax and photocopying services; babysitting. *In room:* A/C, TV, Wi-Fi, coffeemaker; hair dryer and iron upon request.

Tulie Oasis ★★ Red brick floors, a tree-size bougainvillea, and pressed tin lamps set the tone for a creative meal in this historic building in Tularosa. It's the creation of Bob and Karen Hembree, former owners of the Roslyn Café seen in the classic TV series *Northern Exposure.* A broad menu is highlighted by freshly baked breads and seasonal vegetables. Bring patience with you, though, as on my last visit the place was still ironing out the kinks in their service. Breakfast omelets are excellent here, while my favorite meal for lunch is any of their sandwiches made on their sourdough bread, or a salad with bread as an accompaniment—it's that good! I've enjoyed a turkey and avocado with Swiss cheese sandwich and a grilled chicken salad. Heartier appetites might like their top sirloin, which comes with soup or salad, a vegetable, and a choice of potatoes (choose the grilled red potatoes, which are excellent). Finish with coconut cream pie.

512 St. Francis. ✆ **575/585-2102.** Main courses $4–$7 breakfast, $5–$9 lunch, $8–$23 dinner. MC, V. Mon–Thurs 8am–8pm; Fri–Sat 8am–8:30pm; Sun 8am–2pm.

3 WHITE SANDS NATIONAL MONUMENT ★★★

Arguably the most memorable natural area in this part of the Southwest, **White Sands National Monument** preserves the best part of the world's largest gypsum dune field, an area of 275 square miles of pure white gypsum sand reaching out over the floor of the Tularosa Basin in wavelike dunes. Plants and animals have evolved in special ways to adapt to the bright white environment here. Some creatures have a bleached coloration to match the whiteness all around them, and some plants have evolved means for surviving against the smothering pressures of the blowing sands.

The surrounding mountains—the Sacramentos to the east, with their forested slopes, and the serene San Andres to the west—are composed of sandstone, limestone, sedimentary rocks, and pockets of gypsum. Over millions of years, rains and melting snows dissolved the gypsum and carried it down into Lake Lucero. Here the hot sun and dry winds evaporate the water, leaving the pure white gypsum to crystallize. Then the persistent winds blow these crystals, in the form of minuscule bits of sand, in a northeastern direction, adding

Warning! Safety Tips

The National Park Service emphasizes that (1) tunneling in this sand can be dangerous because it collapses easily and could suffocate a person; (2) sand-surfing down the dune slopes, although permitted, can also be hazardous, so it should be undertaken with care, and never near an auto road; and (3) hikers can get lost in a sudden sandstorm if they stray from marked trails or areas.

them to growing dunes. As each dune grows and moves farther from the lake, new ones form, rank after rank, in what seems an endless procession.

The dunes are especially enchanting at sunrise and under the light of a full moon, but you'll have to camp here to experience this extraordinary sight (see "Camping," below). If you're not camping, you'll probably want to spend only a couple of hours here. Refreshments and snacks can be purchased at the visitor center, along with books, maps, posters, and other souvenirs; however, no dining or grocery facilities are available here.

ESSENTIALS

GETTING THERE The visitor center is 15 miles southwest of Alamogordo on US 70/82. (***Note:*** Due to missile testing on the adjacent White Sands Missile Range, this road is sometimes closed for up to 2 hr. at a time.) The nearest major airport is **El Paso International,** 90 miles away (see "Essentials," under "Alamogordo," earlier in this chapter).

VISITOR INFORMATION For more information, contact **White Sands National Monument,** P.O. Box 1086, Holloman AFB, NM 88330-1086 (✆ **575/479-6124;** www.nps.gov/whsa). When driving near or in the monument, tune your radio to 1610 AM for information on what's happening.

ADMISSION FEES & HOURS Admission is $3 (free for children 15 and under). Memorial Day to Labor Day, the visitor center is open daily from 8am to 7pm, and Dunes Drive is open daily from 7am to 9pm. Ranger talks and sunset strolls are given nightly at 7 and 8:30pm during summer. During the rest of the year, the visitor center is open daily from 8am to 5pm, and Dunes Drive is open daily from 7am to sunset.

SEEING THE HIGHLIGHTS

The 16-mile **Dunes Drive** loops through the "heart of sands" from the visitor center. Information available at the center tells you what to look for on your drive. Sometimes the winds blow the dunes over the road, which must then be rerouted. All the dunes are in fact moving slowly to the northeast, pushed by prevailing southwest winds, some at the rate of as much as 20 feet per year.

In the center of the monument, the road itself is made of hard-packed gypsum. (***Note:*** It can be especially slick after an afternoon thunderstorm, so drive cautiously!) Visitors are invited to get out of their cars at established parking areas and explore a bit; some like to climb a dune for a better view of the endless sea of sand. If you'd rather experience the park by hiking than on the long drive, try the Big Dune Trail, a good trail right near the entrance. It takes you on a 45-minute loop along the edges of the dunes and then into their whiteness, ending atop a 60-foot-tall one. In summer, ranger-guided nature walks and evening programs take place in the dunes.

CAMPING

I recommend camping here, especially to see the dunes at sunrise or under a full moon. The park closes at dusk, and you'll have to leave if you're not camping. It doesn't reopen until after dawn, so you'll have no way to see the sunrise unless you camp. White Sands has no facilities, however, so this is strictly a backcountry adventure. Only tent camping is allowed, and you'll hike three-quarters of a mile to the campsite where you can pitch a tent. On a full moon, the campsites go quickly; you may want to arrive early in the morning. At other times, availability shouldn't be a problem. You must register at the visitor center, get clearance, and pay a small fee. Call ✆ **575/479-6124** for information.

If backcountry camping isn't your speed, try one of the other campgrounds in nearby Alamogordo and Las Cruces (see the "Where to Stay" sections under "Alamogordo," earlier in this chapter, and "Las Cruces" in chapter 11).

4 RUIDOSO ★ & ENVIRONS

Ruidoso (most New Mexicans pronounce it "Ree-uh-*do*-so") is situated at 6,900 feet in the timbered Sacramento Mountains, the southernmost finger of the Rockies. It is a mountain resort town most famous for the nearby Ruidoso Downs racetrack, where the world's richest quarter-horse race is run for a $2.5-million purse. Outdoors lovers, hikers, horseback riders, fishers, and hunters are drawn to the surrounding Lincoln National Forest. Southern New Mexico's most important ski resort, Ski Apache, is just out of town. The nearby **Mescalero Apache Indian Reservation** includes the Inn of the Mountain Gods Resort & Casino. Not far away, the historic village of **Lincoln** recalls the Wild West days of Billy the Kid. Be aware that during those busiest of months, Ruidoso seems to live up to its Spanish name—which translates as "noisy," although the name originally referred to the sound of the river running through town.

ESSENTIALS

GETTING THERE From Albuquerque, take I-25 south 87 miles to San Antonio; turn east on US 380 and travel 74 miles; then head south on NM 37/48 (4 hr.). From Alamogordo, take US 70 northeast via Tularosa (1 hr.). From Roswell, take US 70 west (1½ hr.). No commercial service is available to **Sierra Blanca Regional Airport** (✆ **575/336-8111**), 17 miles north, near Alto.

VISITOR INFORMATION The **Ruidoso Valley Chamber of Commerce** and visitor center is at 720 Sudderth Dr. (✆ **800/253-2255** or 575/257-7395; www.ruidosonow.com).

EXPLORING RUIDOSO

Gallery Hopping

Many noted artists—among them Peter Hurd, Henriette Wyeth, and Gordon Snidow—made their homes in Ruidoso and the surrounding Lincoln County. Dozens of other art-world hopefuls have followed them here, resulting in a proliferation of galleries in town. Most are open Monday to Saturday from 10am to 5pm, except where noted. Among my favorites are **De Carol Designs,** 2616 Sudderth Dr. (✆ **575/257-5024**); **McGary Studios,** a bronze foundry at 2002 Sudderth Dr. (✆ **575/257-1000**); and **Hurd–La Rinconada** (✆ **575/653-4331**), in San Patricio, 20 miles east of Ruidoso on

Savoring New Mexico

If you're enchanted with New Mexico and want to take some of the state home with you, head to **Viva New Mexico,** 2811 Sudderth Dr. (✆ **575/257-VIVA**), to choose from a range of New Mexico products. You'll find New Mexico Piñon Coffee from Albuquerque, and Indian Summer Salsa from Laguna Pueblo. Most notably, the shop sells 13 different wine labels. If you want to take home treats for loved ones, pick up one of the elaborate gift baskets, offering a sampling of many products.

US 70 (see "A Scenic Drive Around the Lincoln Loop," later in this chapter), open Monday through Saturday from 9am to 5pm.

Ruidoso's best shopping is at 2801 Sudderth Dr., where a cluster of shops fulfill many desires. Slip on sassy sandals and other contemporary shoes at **Steppin' Out** (✆ **575/257-5924**). Next door, tots and teens can find upscale duds at **Klassy Kids** (✆ **575/257-3857**). Meanwhile, wine lovers may want to sample the grape and artisanal cheeses at **End of the Vine** (✆ **575/630-WINE**). And finally, foodies will like the kitchen selection at **House of Kelham** (✆ **575/257-2492**).

Ruidoso Downs

In a stunning setting surrounded by green grass and pine trees, the famous **Ruidoso Downs racetrack** and **Billy the Kid Casino** (✆ **575/378-4431;** www.ruidosodowns racing.com), 2 miles east of Ruidoso on US 70, is home to the world's richest quarter-horse race, the $2 million **All American Futurity,** run each year on Labor Day. Many other days of quarter-horse and thoroughbred racing lead up to the big one, beginning in May and running to Labor Day. Post time is 1pm Thursday through Sunday. Grandstand admission is free; call about reserved seating prices, which range from $5 to $42.

The on-site casino has all the neon, noise, and smoke gamblers love. Though you'll find only slots at this casino (for more variety, head to Inn of the Mountain Gods Resort & Casino, p. 357), bonuses here include simulcast racing on big-screen TVs in the bar and a well-priced buffet with tables overlooking the track. It's open Saturday through Thursday from 11am to 11pm, and Friday from noon to midnight.

An Interesting Museum

The Hubbard Museum of the American West ★ This museum contains a collection of thousands of horse-related items, including saddles from all over the world, a Russian sleigh, a horse-drawn "fire engine," and an 1860 stagecoach. Several great American artists, including Frederic Remington and Charles M. Russell, are represented in the museum's permanent collection. A gift shop has some interesting books and curios.

841 W. US 70, Ruidoso Downs, NM 88346. ✆ **575/378-4142.** Fax 575/378-4166. www.hubbardmuseum.org. Admission $8 adults, $6 seniors and military, $3 children 6–16, free for children 5 and under. Mon–Fri 10am–5pm. Closed Thanksgiving and Christmas.

Spencer Theater for the Performing Arts ★★

The dream of Alto, New Mexico, residents Dr. A. N. and Jackie Spencer, the 514-seat Spencer Theater, on Sierra Blanca Airport Hwy. 220, 4½ miles east of NM 48 (✆ **888/818-7872**

 **Family Fun**

Families enjoy the excitement at **Funtrackers Family Fun Center,** 101 Carrizo Canyon Rd. (✆ **575/257-3275**), which offers go-kart courses, bumper boats, bull riding, and miniature golf. ***Beware:*** It can be crammed with people midsummer. It's open Memorial Day to Labor Day from 10am to 10pm; from September to May it's open weekends only, with limited hours.

or 575/336-4800; www.spencertheater.com), is a model performance space that cost more than $20 million to construct. Opened in 1997, the theater has drawn such talents as Ottmar Liebert and Chuck Mangione. Free tours are offered at 10am Tuesday and Thursday. Performances take place weekends and weekdays. The theater runs two seasons year-round, and tickets cost from $30 to $70.

MESCALERO APACHE INDIAN RESERVATION

Immediately south and west of Ruidoso, the Mescalero Apache Indian Reservation covers over 460,000 acres (719 sq. miles) and is home to about 2,800 members of the Mescalero, Chiricahua, and Lipan bands of Apaches. Established by order of President Ulysses S. Grant in 1873, it sustains a profitable cattle-ranching industry and the Apache-run logging firm of Mescalero Forest Products.

Seeing the Highlights

Even if you're not staying or dining here, be sure to visit the **Inn of the Mountain Gods Resort & Casino,** a luxury resort owned and operated by the tribe (p. 357); it's the crowning achievement of Wendell Chino, former president of the Mescalero Apache tribe.

Also on the reservation, on US 70 about 17 miles southwest of Ruidoso, is the **Mescalero Cultural Center** (✆ **575/671-4494**), open weekdays from 8am to 4:30pm. Photos, artifacts, clothing, crafts, and other exhibits demonstrate the history and culture of the tribe.

St. Joseph's Apache Mission ★ (✆ **575/464-4473**), just off US 70 in Mescalero, on a hill overlooking the reservation, is a grand, stone Romanesque-style structure that stands 103 feet tall and has walls 4 feet thick. Built between 1920 and 1939, the mission church also contains an icon of the Apache Christ, with Christ depicted as a Mescalero holy man, as well as other Apache religious art. Local arts and crafts and religious items are for sale at the parish office. The church is open daily during daylight hours.

Ruidoso at Night

If you'd like a rollicking night out, check out **Mountain Annie's Dinner Theater** ★, 2710 Sudderth Dr. (✆ **575/257-7982**). Set in a 7,000 square-foot building with chandeliers and red velvet drapes, the dinner theater features a variety of types of performances but most are music variety shows, with tunes ranging from rock to country. The cost for a beef brisket or chicken dinner is $35 adults and $15 for children. Doors open at 6:30pm; dinner is served at 7pm, and the show begins at 8pm. Children can either watch the show or hang out in the supervised playhouse, free of charge. In a similar but Old West vein, the **Flying J Ranch,** on NM 48, 1 mile north of Alto (✆ **888/458-3595** or 575/336-4330), offers fun family entertainment and chuck-wagon fare. This ranch is like a Western village, complete with staged gunfights and pony rides for the kids. Gates open at 6pm; a hearty chuck-wagon dinner of barbecue beef or chicken is served promptly at 7:30. Then, at 8:20pm, the Flying J Wranglers present a fast-paced stage show with Western music and a world-champion yodeler. Reservations highly recommended. It costs $22 for ages 13 and up, $12 for ages 4 to 12, and is free for ages 3 and under. It's open May to Labor Day Monday to Saturday (Labor Day to mid-Oct Sat only).

Dances & Ceremonies

Throughout the year, the Mescalero Cultural Center hosts powwows of colorful dancing and traditional drumming, open to the public and with unrestricted photography. The most accessible to visitors are dances and a rodeo on July 4.

For more information about the reservation, write to the Tribal Office at P.O. Box 227, Mescalero, NM 88340 or call ✆ **575/671-4494.**

Lincoln Historic District: A Walk in the Footsteps of Billy the Kid ★★

One of the last historic yet uncommercialized 19th-century towns remaining in the American West, the tiny community of Lincoln lies 37 miles northeast of Ruidoso on US 380, in the valley of the Rio Bonito. Few people live here today, but it was once the seat of the largest county in the United States, and the focal point of the notorious Lincoln County War of 1878–79. Though the town contains a number of museums today, a single ticket will get you entry into all of them.

The bloody Lincoln County War was fought between various ranching and merchant factions over the issue of beef contracts for nearby Fort Stanton. A sharpshooting teenager named William Bonney—soon to be known as "Billy the Kid"—took sides in this issue with "the good guys," escaping from the burning McSween House after his employer and colleague were shot and killed. Three years later, after shooting down a sheriff, he was captured in Lincoln and sentenced to be hanged. But he shot his way out of his cell in what is now the **Lincoln County Courthouse Museum,** which still has a hole made by a bullet from the Kid's gun. Of special note here is a letter handwritten by Billy defending himself to Governor Lew Wallace.

Many of the original structures from that era have been preserved and restored by the Museum of New Mexico, the Lincoln County Historical Society, and an organization called **Historic Lincoln** (✆ **575/653-4025;** www.nmmonuments.org), a subsidiary of the Lincoln State Monument.

JUST THE FACTS At the **Visitor Center,** on NM 380 on the east side of town (✆ **575/653-4025**), exhibits explain the role in Lincoln's history of Apaches, Hispanics, Anglo cowboys, and the black Buffalo Soldiers, and detail the Lincoln County War. A 12-minute film on Lincoln history is presented in an old-fashioned theater. Start your visit here and join a tour given every hour by docents in period costumes, included in the admission cost. Across the courtyard is the **Luna Museum Store.** Also of note in the town is the short, round **Torreon** fortress, which served as protection from Apache raids; the **Montaño Store,** once a saloon and boarding house; **Dr. Wood's House,** filled with pre-1920s furnishings, books, and instruments; and the **Tunstall Store Museum,** with late 19th- and early 20th-century clothes, hardware, and butter churns.

An annual **folk pageant,** *The Last Escape of Billy the Kid,* has been presented outdoors since 1949 as a highly romanticized version of the Lincoln County War. It's staged Friday and Saturday night and Sunday afternoon during the first full weekend in August as part of the **Old Lincoln Days** celebration. The festival also includes living-history demonstrations of traditional crafts, musical programs, and food booths throughout the village.

The historic district is open year-round daily from 8:30am to 4:30pm. Admission is $5 for adults (includes entry to six buildings during summer and four in winter). It's free for children 16 and under. For more information, write to P.O. Box 36, Lincoln, NM 88338, or call ✆ **575/653-4025.**

WHERE TO STAY IN & AROUND RUIDOSO

If you're looking for a budget stay in Ruidoso, the **Motel 6** (✆ **800/466-8356;** www.motel6.com), on the outskirts of town has reliably clean rooms. In recent years Ruidoso has landed many other major chains including Ramada, La Quinta, Comfort Inn, and Days Inn. Decide on your favorite and find their number in the Appendix.

In Alto

Scarborough House ★★ (Finds) On a ridge top 15 minutes northeast of Ruidoso, this B&B offers rustic elegance and spectacular views. The creation of a couple from Austin, Texas, the inn has a bit of city flair. It is timber-frame construction, with high Douglas fir beams above a stacked flagstone fireplace in the great room. Guest rooms offer tasteful, imaginative sojourns, with an eye for detail. My favorite is the East Meets West room, which has Old West rusticity and old East Coast elegance. All rooms have pillow-top mattresses, fine linens, and signature soaps, as well as robes, spa towels, and slippers, handy when you're heading out to the hut tub, which occupies part of the 2,000 square feet of deck space. Those decks offer views of Sierra Blanca Peak and the Capitan Mountains.

110 Great View Court, Alto, NM 88312. ✆ **866/875-2592** or 575/336-4500. www.scarboroughhousebandb.com. 4 units. $149–$109 double. Rates include full breakfast and afternoon snacks. AE, DISC, MC, V. **Amenities:** Jacuzzi, courtesy computer. *In room:* A/C, TV/CD player, Wi-Fi, hair dryer.

In Town

Best Western at Pine Springs Nestled within ponderosa pines well above Ruidoso Downs, this inn offers the consistency of a Best Western, with a few extras. Rooms are fairly spacious, set either motel-style so you can park nearby, or in a grassy courtyard, which I recommend, all only minutes from town and a stone's throw from the racetrack and casino. Rooms are decorated in soft colors and have comfortable beds and medium-size, clean bathrooms. Though they could use some updating, as could the cracked sidewalks, the setting and price still recommend this place. The inn's two best points: It's located away from the town of Ruidoso, which during busy months is unbearably noisy, and it has a lovely outdoor pool with a view of the mountains. Wireless Internet access is available in the lobby and in the downstairs rooms.

1420 US 70, Ruidoso Downs, NM 88346. ✆ **800/237-3607** or 575/378-8100. Fax 575/378-8215. www.bestwestern.com. 100 units. $75–$139 double. Rates include continental breakfast. AE, DC, DISC, MC, V. Pets welcome. **Amenities:** Outdoor pool (summer only); Jacuzzi. *In room:* A/C, TV, fridge, coffeemaker, hair dryer, iron, microwave.

Escape Resort ★★★ (Finds) Finally! For years Ruidoso has needed a really upscale lodging, one with elegance and functionality. Now it has one. This cluster of five casitas, set within town a little off the main road and surrounded by pine trees, offers accommodations of a level one would find in Santa Fe. They come in 1-bedroom and 2-bedroom sizes and have large rooms with high ceilings, comfortable beds with fine linens, contemporary furnishings in muted earth tones, and gas fireplaces fashioned from stacked sandstone. The bathrooms are large, with a Jacuzzi tub, tile, and steam-shower. All have fully equipped kitchens with stainless steel appliances. Calling this a "resort" is a bit of a stretch, since it has few amenities, but all else here is stellar.

1016 Mechem Rd., Ruidoso, NM 88345. ✆ **888/762-8551** or 575/258-1234. www.theescaperesort.com. 5 units. $229 1-bedroom casita; $279 2-bedroom casita. Rates include complimentary wine. AE, DISC, MC, V. **Amenities:** Outdoor pool seasonally; guest laundry. *In room:* A/C, TV, Wi-Fi, kitchen, hair dryer, iron, safe.

Hotel Ruidoso ★★ (Value This new hotel, set in the center of town, but a little back from the main street and surrounded by pines, offers clean contemporary rooms with a bit of flair. Currently, it's one of the town's best values. It's a big, blocky looking 3-story building, but it has well-appointed accommodations. Rooms are medium size and come in standards or minisuites. All have comfortable beds and are decorated in earth tones, with medium-size bathrooms with granite sinks and tilework in the baths. Minisuites have a fold-out couch, a good option for small families. Service is good. The breakfast room is a comfortably airy place to spend the morning.

110 Chase St. ✆ **866/734-5197** or 575/257-2007. Fax 575/257-2008. www.hotelruidos.net. 55 units. $79–$99 weekdays; $119–$169 weekends. Rates include continental breakfast. AE, DISC, MC, V. **Amenities:** Medium-size indoor pool; Jacuzzi; exercise room; business center. *In room:* A/C, TV, Wi-Fi, fridge, coffeemaker, hair dryer, iron, microwave.

Inn of the Mountain Gods Resort & Casino ★★ What's most impressive about this resort is its location, set on a grassy slope above a mountain lake on the Mescalero Apache Indian Reservation, 3½ miles southwest of Ruidoso. In 2004, the original resort was leveled and a new one built, much in the style of a Lake Tahoe casino, with glossy gaming rooms, a variety of restaurants, and a golf course. Though the architecture has a cold modernity, the rooms are comfortable with luxurious touches. You're greeted outside by an impressive Crown Dancer fountain, and inside by banks of windows looking out on the lake. The rooms come in a few sizes, though standard ones are pretty spacious, all with quality bedding, very comfortable beds, and medium-size bathrooms. I recommend paying a little more for a lakeside view. Wendell's, with a mountain and lake view, features steak and seafood, with extensive wine offerings. The resort also has a sports bar, a nightclub with live music Friday and Saturday nights, and a casino with more than 1,000 slot machines and 34 table games.

287 Carrizo Canyon Rd., Mescalero, NM 88340. ✆ **800/545-9011** or 575/464-7777. www.innofthemountaingods.com. 273 units. $129–$209 forest-view double, $169–$289 lake-view double; $269–$349 suite, depending on the season and type of room. Golf and ski packages available. AE, DC, DISC, MC, V. **Amenities:** 3 restaurants; 2 bars; indoor pool; golf course; Jacuzzi; watersports equipment/rentals; tour/activities desk; room service. *In room:* A/C, TV, Wi-Fi, coffeemaker, hair dryer, iron, safe.

The Lodge at Sierra Blanca ★★ Surrounded by a golf course and plenty of quiet, this hotel offers clean, reliable rooms in a picturesque setting. However, if you find convention traffic daunting, you'll want to ask what's scheduled at the next-door convention center before reserving. When I visited, the hotel was quiet and serene. The lobby centers around an Anasazi-style stacked sandstone fireplace, creating an elegance that carries into the rooms. The rooms are medium-size, decorated in a contemporary Southwestern style, with comfortable beds and medium-size baths. The suites, which are large, have sofa beds, fireplaces, and balconies. Many of the rooms have two-person Jacuzzi tubs. The hotel offers golf packages.

107 Sierra Blanca Dr., Ruidoso, NM 88345. ✆ **866/211-7727** or 575/258-5500. Fax 575/258-2419. www.thelodgeatsierrablanca.com. 120 units. $149–$169 double; $169–$189 suite. Rates include full breakfast, AE, DISC, MC, V. Take Mechem Dr. 5 min. north of Sudderth. Pets allowed. **Amenities:** Indoor pool; golf

course; exercise room; Jacuzzi; massage; courtesy computer. *In room:* A/C, TV, Wi-Fi, fridge, coffeemaker, iron, microwave.

Ruidoso Lodge Cabins ★ This 1950s cabin complex ranks as one of the quaintest accommodations in the Ruidoso area. Set on the banks of the Ruidoso River, these cabins have knotty-pine walls and small rooms decorated with quilts and some antiques. All cabins are very clean, with full kitchens, small bathrooms, and porches with gas grills. My favorite, newly remodeled, is #6, right on the river and with a fireplace and Jacuzzi tub. Newer units adjacent to these, the **Riverside Cottages** ★★, where kids aren't welcome, are more upscale, decorated in a country inn style, with vaulted ceilings and in-room Jacuzzis. Though the road passing close to the cabins can prove noisy, it quiets down at night. During the day, the river is a nice spot to fish (for trout) or simply watch the minnows swim by. The lodge restricts outside visitors in order to keep the grounds quiet for all guests. If you're looking for complete quiet, ask about their new **Hidden Canyon** ★★, three cabins on 50 acres of forested land.

300 Main Rd., Ruidoso, NM 88345. ✆ **800/950-2510** or 575/257-2510. www.ruidosolodge.com. 23 cabins. Sept–June $99–$189 double; July–Aug, and major holidays $139–$209 double. Ask about midweek specials. DISC, MC, V. Children not permitted in Riverside Cottages or Hidden Canyon. *In room:* TV, Wi-Fi, kitchenette, coffeemaker, hair dryer, iron.

In Lincoln: A Historic B&B

Ellis Store and Co. Country Inn ★ With part of this house dating from 1850, this is believed to be the oldest existing residence in Lincoln County, and as a B&B, it gives visitors a real taste of 19th-century living but with most of today's luxuries. The house has plenty of history. Billy the Kid spent several weeks here, although somewhat unwillingly, according to court records that show payment of $64 for 2 weeks' food and lodging for the Kid and a companion held under house arrest.

Three rooms in the main house are a step back into the 1800s, with wood-burning fireplaces or stoves providing heat, antique furnishings, and handmade quilts. The separate Mill House, built of adobe and hand-hewn lumber in the 1880s, isn't quite as cozy as the main house, but it definitely offers an Old West feel. Two suites are good for families and those seeking solitude. Be aware that service here has become less consistent in recent years.

US 380 (mile marker 98, P.O. Box 15), Lincoln, NM 88338. ✆ **800/653-6460** or 575/653-4609. 8 units, 4 with private bathrooms. $89–$119 double. Rates include gourmet breakfast. AE, DISC, MC, V. Pets not allowed inside, but kennels are available. **Amenities:** Restaurant by reservation only. *In room:* No phone.

In San Patricio

Hurd Ranch Guest Homes ★★ (Kids) About 20 miles east of Ruidoso on the 2,500-acre Sentinel Ranch, these attractive casitas are part of the Hurd–La Rinconada Gallery, which displays the work of well-known artists Peter and Michael Hurd, Henriette Wyeth Hurd, N. C. Wyeth, and Andrew Wyeth.

Units available are two older one-bedroom casitas, built in the early part of the 20th century, and three new and much larger units. Of the casitas, Orchard House is my favorite; it sits on the edge of an apple orchard and is furnished in weathered Southwestern antiques. Both of the larger units are elegant, especially the newer La Helenita, a pitched-roofed adobe house that's large enough for two families. All also have fireplaces and comfortable living areas and are decorated with antiques, primitives, and art by the Hurd-Wyeth family. These casitas serve as good bases for families that enjoy having a kitchen.

A Silver Dollar Dinner

One of the region's most cherished relics has been restored. **Tinnie Silver Dollar Steakhouse and Saloon,** on US 70, 43 miles west of Roswell and 28 miles east of Ruidoso (✆ **575/653-4177;** http://tinniesilverdollar.com), offers excellent food and fine accommodations. The elegant 1870s Victorian structure provides a perfect backdrop for frontier-style dining. A meal here might start with coconut shrimp and move on to a filet mignon with green chile au gratin potatoes or roasted chicken with mashed potatoes and a light gravy. Tinnie also serves Sunday champagne brunch, including such traditional favorites as eggs Benedict and prime rib. The steakhouse is open Monday to Thursday from 5 to 9pm, and Friday and Saturday from 5 to 10pm, with the saloon opening at 4pm. While eating, enjoy the view of the gardens and water fountain from the veranda and the original Peter Hurd paintings that hang in each room of the restaurant.

The same location has a deli (Mon–Sat 10am–9pm and Sun 10am–8pm) offering packaged liquor sales, a gift shop, and two suites for overnight guests. The suites range in price from $89 to $175 depending on the season.

NM 70 (mile marker 281), San Patricio, NM 88348. ✆ **800/658-6912** or 575/653-4331. Fax 575/653-4218. www.wyethartists.com. 5 units. $140–$410 per casita. AE, DISC, MC, V. Pets welcome, with limitations and $20 per day fee. **Amenities:** Laundry facilities; access to e-mail and fax at gallery. *In room:* A/C, TV/VCR w/ pay movies, kitchen, iron.

Camping

Lincoln National Forest has more than a dozen campgrounds in the region; four of them are within the immediate area. The **Smokey Bear Ranger Station,** 901 Mechem Dr., Ruidoso (✆ **575/257-4095**), is open Memorial Day to Labor Day from 7:30am to 4:30pm Monday through Saturday, and the same hours Monday through Friday the rest of the year.

WHERE TO DINE IN & AROUND RUIDOSO

In Town

Expensive

Willmon's Prime Grille ★ SEAFOOD/STEAK This new restaurant offers a relaxing retreat from the bustle of the main drag. In a cozy atmosphere of earth tones accented with comfy bancos along the walls, Willmon's serves decent contemporary American cuisine. Unfortunately, at this writing, the place isn't yet living up to its billing as the city's best, but maybe the owners will iron out the kinks soon. For a starter, you might try the jumbo lump crab cakes served with key lime mustard sauce. For an entree I'd recommend a steak, though be sure to inquire about the meat's freshness. They come with a variety of topping options including a porcini mushroom or au poivre sauce. The grilled free range chicken in Mediterranean seasonings is also nice. All entrees come with only one side, which for the price in this part of the state is a little skimpy. Choices include baked potato, mac 'n Gruyere cheese, and butternut squash polenta. A select beer and wine list accompanies the menu.

2523 Sudderth Dr. ✆ **575/257-2954.** Reservations recommended. Main courses $18–$38. AE, DC, DISC, MC, V. Mon–Sat 5–9pm.

Moderate

Cattle Baron Steak House ★ SEAFOOD/STEAK This is the place to go if you really have an appetite. It's a casually elegant restaurant, part of a chain with six locations around the Southwest, that may not serve the best steaks and seafood you've tasted, but still provides good-quality food. It's a casual restaurant decorated in an opulent Western style with lots of burgundy upholstery and brass. Often the place is busy and festive, so it's not ideal for a romantic getaway. Service is efficient and friendly. For lunch, try the turkey and avocado sandwich or the teriyaki kabob. For dinner, I usually order the filet mignon or the shrimp scampi. An extensive salad bar dominates the main dining room, and a comfortable lounge sits near the entryway.

657 Sudderth Dr. ✆ **575/257-9355.** Reservations recommended for 6 or more. Main courses $8–$12 lunch, $12–$22 dinner. AE, DC, DISC, MC, V. Mon–Thurs and Sun 11am–10pm; Fri–Sat 11am–10:30pm.

Le Bistro ★★ FRENCH In some kind of alchemistic feat, chef Richard Girot has transformed casual into elegant in this downtown cafe set in an oddly round building. Decorated with French posters, the place is laid back enough for folks walking in off the street. But the food is more refined—bistro-style fare like what you might find at a streetside cafe in France. Still, it's usually a quiet place, and it's a good spot for a romantic dinner. The service is friendly, though at times overworked. Try the pork tenderloin with rosemary and whipped potatoes, or one of the daily specials, such as seafood-stuffed sea bass. All dinners come with baguette-style bread and a salad. Finish with a chocolate or strawberry crepe. Wine and beer accompany the menu. The patio offers a front-row view of the busy downtown Ruidoso scene.

2800 Sudderth Dr. ✆ **575/257-0132.** Reservations recommended for dinner. Main courses $6–$10 lunch, $9–$18 dinner. AE, MC, V. Mon–Sat 11am–2pm and 5–9pm.

Texas Club Grill & Bar ★ SEAFOOD/STEAK Hidden away and somewhat hush-hush, this steakhouse isn't really a club, but because it advertises only by word of mouth, it has an exclusive quality, accented by plenty of Texas twang in the air and longhorns hanging on the walls. The place's secrets are a hometown friendliness and steaks hand-rubbed with signature seasonings. The dining room, which overlooks a small lake, has comfy booths and sturdy chairs. It's a lively place with a broad menu, including many cuts of beef and other dishes, such as chicken, shrimp, pasta, and salads. My favorite dish is the filet, and my mom's is the jumbo charbroiled shrimp, both served with a choice of potato, pasta, or vegetable, and hot rolls. Service is efficient. Also on-site is a lounge with a dance floor, where a DJ spins music every night the place is open.

212 Metz Dr. ✆ **575/258-3325.** Reservations recommended. Main courses $12–$35. AE, DC, DISC, MC, V. Wed–Thurs and Sun 5–9pm; Fri–Sat 5–10pm. From Mechem Dr., turn east on Cree Meadows Dr.

Inexpensive

Casa Blanca ★ Kids NEW MEXICAN This is a real locals' favorite for the margaritas and fun Tex/Mex and New Mexican food. You can count on a good meal here, the food made with fresh ingredients. The decor is casual—four rooms in a sprawling house on a hill within town, each with brick or tile floors and colorful art on the walls. The garden room and patio are my choices. All of them can get a little noisy from the many kids who like the menu selections here. Your efficient and friendly server will start you out with complimentary chips and salsa. The best bet here is the chicken enchiladas with sour cream, or the beef or chicken fajitas. Recently I enjoyed some excellent chicken tacos as well. For dessert? Try the chocolate flan cake.

501 Mechem Dr. ✆ **575/257-2495.** Main courses $5–$10. AE, MC, V. Mon–Sat 11am–9pm; Sun 11am–8pm. Closed Thanksgiving and Christmas.

Cornerstone Bakery and Café ★ BAKERY/CAFE In this café on the east side of town, amid comfortable garden-style decor, diners relish rich slabs of chocolate cream pie while sipping espresso and cappuccino. During breakfast, this place is packed, serving omelets and eggs Benedict to locals and travelers. Lunch is equally bustling, with offerings such as quiche, an almond–chicken salad croissant, or one of their daily specials. This might include any variety of dishes made with organic beef, which is served once a week, or a salad niçoise, or seared mahi mahi.

359 Sudderth Dr. (3 miles east of downtown). ✆ **575/257-1842.** Most menu items under $8. AE, DISC, MC, V. Daily 7:30am–2pm.

Hummingbird Tearoom ★ Kids AMERICAN If you're looking for a light lunch, head to this little room pinched into a corner of a small strip mall in the center of town. Though you won't find anything extravagant on the menu, everything is well prepared and tasty. I had a tuna salad sandwich made with sweet pickles the way my mother makes them. You can also order their daily frittata, made with cheese and various types of vegetables. A kid's menu features such favorites as a PB&J and macaroni and cheese.

2306 Sudderth Dr., Village Plaza. ✆ **575/257-5100.** Main courses $5–$9. AE, DISC, MC, V. Mon–Sat 11am–3pm.

North of Town

Greenhouse Café ★★ Moments NEW AMERICAN A complete novelty, this little gem in Capitan, about 25 minutes from Ruidoso, serves fresh dishes highlighted by vegetables grown in Tom Histen's own greenhouse just up the hill. Veggies always vary, with heirloom lettuces the top stars. The setting is eclectic, a gallery displaying lovely jewelry and other art, accented by tile-topped tables and lots of plants, with a patio out back. Food ranges from vegan offerings to meatier options. My favorite is a sun-dried tomato–spinach cream sauce with shrimp over angel hair pasta. The breaded chicken with apple, pear, and cranberry compote is also nice. Soups, sandwiches, and salads are also delicious, as are desserts such as the carrot cake. Sunday brunch might bring a salmon omelet with cream cheese and caper filling. The menu is enhanced by select wines and beers.

103 S. Lincoln, Capitan. ✆ **575/354-0373.** Reservations recommended. Main courses $8–$13 lunch, $16–$32 dinner. MC, V. Wed–Sat 11am–2pm and 5–9pm; Sun 10am–2pm. Hours may be abbreviated in winter, so call first.

5 A SCENIC DRIVE AROUND THE LINCOLN LOOP

An enjoyable way to see many of the sights of the area while staying in Ruidoso is on a 1- or 2-day 162-mile loop tour. Heading east from Ruidoso on US 70, about 18 miles past Ruidoso Downs, is the small community of **San Patricio,** where you'll find (watch for signs) the **Hurd–La Rinconada Gallery** (✆ **575/653-4331;** www.wyethartists.com). Late artist Peter Hurd, a Roswell native, flunked out of West Point before studying with artist N. C. Wyeth and marrying Wyeth's daughter, Henriette, eventually returning with her to New Mexico. This gallery shows and sells works by Peter Hurd, Henriette Wyeth, their son Michael Hurd, Andrew Wyeth, and N. C. Wyeth. Many of the works capture

Finds No Scum Allowed

In the "ghost town" of White Oaks, the **No Scum Allowed Saloon** (© **505/648-5583**) sits in an atmospheric 1880s brick building, with signed dollar bills plastered to the ceiling and vintage license plates nailed all over the walls. While there, ask the owner, Tony Marsh, how he got the place. You're in for many laughs. On NM 349 near Carrizozo, it's well worth a stop to have refreshments and see the art town of White Oaks. Open most weekends.

the ambience of the landscape in the San Patricio area. In addition to original works, signed reproductions are available. The gallery is open Monday through Saturday from 9am to 5pm and Sunday from 10am to 4pm. Several rooms and guesthouses are also available by the night or for longer periods (see "Where to Stay in & Around Ruidoso," under "Ruidoso & the Mescalero Apache Indian Reservation," earlier in this chapter).

From San Patricio, continue east on US 70 for 4 miles to the community of Hondo, at the confluence of the Rio Hondo and Rio Bonito, and turn west onto US 380. From here, it's about 10 miles to **Lincoln,** a fascinating little town that is also a National Historic Landmark (see "Lincoln Historic District: A Walk in the Footsteps of Billy the Kid," earlier in this chapter). From Lincoln, continue west on US 380 about a dozen miles to **Capitan** and **Smokey Bear Historical Park,** 118 Smokey Bear Blvd. (© **575/354-2748;** www.smokeybearpark.com), open daily from 9am to 5pm. Smokey, the national symbol of forest fire prevention, was born near here and found as an orphaned cub by firefighters in the early 1950s. Admission to this park is $2 for adults, $1 for children age 7 to 12, and free for children 6 and under. The park has exhibits on Smokey's rescue and life at the National Zoo in Washington, D.C.; fire prevention; and forest health. Visitors can also stop at Smokey's grave and explore a nature path that represents six vegetation zones of the area. If you'd like to stay in Capitan, check out **Capitan Cabins,** 321 3rd St. (© **575/354-6010;** www.capitancabins.com), which has well-appointed cabins on one of the town's back streets.

Heading west from Capitan about 20 miles takes you to **Carrizozo,** the Lincoln County seat since 1912. One of the best green chile cheeseburgers in the Southwest can be found at the **Outpost** (© **575/648-9994**), 415 Central Ave. They're served in a basket, with fries if you'd like. Inside this dark, cool bar/restaurant, you'll find cowboys and farmers chowing under the gaze of bison and deer heads. From there, take 2nd Street east to 12th Street, where a few galleries have opened up. Also of note is the **Carrizozo Heritage Museum,** 103 12th St. (© **575/648-1105**). It features displays on the history of this small railroad town and Lincoln County. The museum is open Wednesday to Saturday 10am to 2pm.

Continue west on US 380 for 4 miles to **Valley of Fires Recreation Area** (© **575/648-2241**), where you'll find what is considered one of the youngest and best-preserved lava fields in the United States. Among the black lava formations is a .8-mile self-guided nature trail, which is well worth the walk. Part of it is wheelchair accessible. You'll discover a strange new landscape that at first glance appears inhospitable but really is rich with plant life and wildlife. Be sure to walk far enough to see the 400-year-old juniper wringing itself from the black stone. A small visitor center and bookstore is in the park campground. Admission is $3 per person or $5 per car for day use, and camping costs $7 to $18. The park is open year-round.

To continue the loop tour, return 4 miles to Carrizozo, turn south onto US 54, and go about 28 miles to the turnoff to **Three Rivers Petroglyph National Recreation Area** (✆ **575/525-4300**), about 5 miles east on a paved road. Some 20,000 individual rock art images are here, carved by Mogollon peoples who lived in the area centuries ago. A trail about .8 mile long links many of the most interesting petroglyphs; and the view surrounding the area, with mountains to the east and White Sands to the southwest, is outstanding. The park also includes the partially excavated ruins of an ancient Native American village, including a multiroom adobe building, pit house, and masonry house that have been partially reconstructed. Administered by the U.S. Bureau of Land Management, the park has facilities for picnicking and camping. The day use fee is $2 per vehicle. Overnight camping is $10. The U.S. Forest Service also has a campground in the area, about 5 miles east via a gravel road.

From the recreation area, return 5 miles to US 54 and continue south about 15 miles to **Tularosa Vineyards** (✆ **575/585-2260;** www.tularosavineyards.com), which offers tours daily from noon until 5pm. Tastings by appointment. Using all New Mexico grapes, the winery is especially known for its award-winning reds. Wines can be purchased by the bottle, with prices ranging from $8 to $25. (***Note:*** A fun pastime while traveling in this area is to read *Tularosa* by Michael McGarrity. Set in the Tularosa Basin, it's a thrilling mystery about the White Sands Missile Range and Spanish gold.)

Continuing south from the winery, drive about 2 miles to Tularosa and turn east onto US 70, which you take for about 16 miles to the village of **Mescalero** on the Mescalero Apache Indian Reservation. From US 70, take the exit for the Bureau of Indian Affairs and follow the signs to the imposing **St. Joseph's Apache Mission** (see "Mescalero Apache Indian Reservation," earlier in this chapter). After you return to US 70, it's about 19 miles back to Ruidoso.

6 ROSWELL

Best known as a destination for UFO enthusiasts and conspiracy theorists, Roswell has become a household name thanks to old Mulder and Scully. And even if you're not glued to your set for reruns of *The X-Files,* you may remember Roswell as the setting for major scenes from the 1996 blockbuster *Independence Day.* Government cover-ups, alien autopsies, and cigarette-smoking feds . . . come along as we venture into the UFO capital of the world.

ESSENTIALS

GETTING THERE From Albuquerque, take I-40 east 59 miles to Clines Corners; turn south on US 285, and travel 140 miles to Roswell (4 hr.). From Las Cruces, take US 70 east (4 hr.). From Carlsbad, take US 285 north (1½ hr.).

Roswell Airport, at Roswell Industrial Air Center on South Main Street (✆ **575/347-5703**), is served commercially by **American Eagle Airlines** (✆ **800/433-7300;** www.aa.com), directly from Dallas, Texas, twice daily.

VISITOR INFORMATION The **Roswell Chamber of Commerce** is at 131 W. 2nd St. (P.O. Box 70), Roswell, NM 88202 (✆ **575/623-5695;** www.roswellnm.org). The Roswell Convention and Visitors Center is at 912 N. Main (✆ **575/624-6860**).

Fun Facts The Incident at Roswell

In July 1947, something "happened" in Roswell. What was it? Debate still rages. On July 8, 1947, a local rancher named MacBrazel found unusual debris scattered across his property. The U.S. military released a statement saying the debris was wreckage from a spaceship crash. Four hours later, however, the military retracted the statement, claiming what fell from the sky was "only a weather balloon." Most of the community didn't believe the story, although some did suspect that the military was somehow involved—Robert Goddard had been working on rockets in this area since the 1930s, and the Roswell Air Base was nearby. Eyewitnesses to the account, however, maintain the debris "was not of this world."

Theorists believe that the crash actually involved two spacecraft. One disintegrated, hence the debris across the MacBrazel ranch, and the other crash-landed, hence the four alien bodies that were also claimed to have been discovered.

UFO believers have remained dissatisfied with the U.S. Air Force's weather balloon story and have insisted on an explanation for the "alien bodies." The most recent comment from the Air Force came in 1997, 2 weeks before the 50th anniversary of the "crash." The Air Force said that the most likely explanation for the unverified alien reports was that people were simply remembering and misplacing in time a number of life-size dummies dropped from the sky during a series of experiments in the 1950s.

The main place to go in Roswell to learn more about the incident is the **International UFO Museum and Research Center** (✆ **575/625-9495;** www.roswellufomuseum.com), in the old Plains Theater on Main Street. Staffers will be more than happy to discuss the crash and the alleged military cover-up. As well as displaying an hour-by-hour timeline of the "incident," the museum has photographs of bizarre and elaborate crop circles, and a videotape in which an alleged witness tells his account. The museum is open daily from 9am to 5pm; admission is $5 for adults, $2 for those 5 to 15, and free for kids 4 and under.

Roswell hosts a **UFO Festival** every year during the first week in July. Some of the events include guest speakers, celebrity appearances, an Alien Village, and parade. For details on the event, call ✆ **575/625-8607;** www.roswellufofestival.com.

—Su Hudson

SEEING THE SIGHTS

Historical Society for Southeast New Mexico The handsome mansion that houses this historical collection is as much a part of the museum as the collection itself. A three-story, yellow-brick structure, it was built between 1910 and 1912 by rancher J. P. White. Its gently sweeping rooflines and large porches reflect the prairie style of architecture made popular by Frank Lloyd Wright. The White family lived here until 1972; today, this home, on the National Register of Historic Places, is a monument to early-20th-century lifestyles. First- and second-floor rooms, including the parlor, bedrooms, dining room, and kitchen, have been restored and furnished with early-20th-century antiques. The second floor has a gallery of changing historic exhibits, from fashions to children's toys. The third floor, once White's private library, now houses the Pecos Valley Collection and the center's archives. A gift shop sells books and other gift items.

200 N. Lea Ave. (at W. 2nd St.), Roswell, NM 88201. ✆ **575/622-8333.** Fax 575/623-8746. www.hssnm.net. Admission by donation. Daily 1–4pm.

Roswell Museum and Art Center ★ This highly acclaimed small museum is a good place to stop in order to get a sense of this area before heading out to explore. The art center contains an excellent collection of works by Peter Hurd and his wife, Henriette Wyeth, many of which depict the gentry-ranching lifestyle in this area. You'll also find works by Georgia O'Keeffe, Ernest Blumenschein, Joseph Sharp, and others famed from the early-20th-century Taos and Santa Fe art colonies. The museum has an early historical section, but its pride and joy is the **Robert Goddard Collection,** which presents actual engines, rocket assemblies, and specialized parts developed by Goddard in the 1930s, when he lived and worked in Roswell. Goddard's workshop has been re-created for the exhibit.

100 W. 11th St., Roswell, NM 88201. ✆ **575/624-6744.** Fax 575/624-6765. www.roswellmuseum.org. Free admission. Mon–Sat 9am–5pm; Sun and holidays 1–5pm. Closed Thanksgiving, Christmas Eve, Christmas Day, and New Year's Day.

Spring River Park and Zoo (Kids) This lovely park, covering 36 acres on either side of a stream a mile east of New Mexico Military Institute, incorporates a miniature train, an antique carousel, a large prairie-dog town, a children's fishing pond, a picnic area, and playgrounds. The zoo features 150 native and exotic animals, as well as some Texas longhorns.

1306 E. College Blvd. (at Atkinson Ave.), Roswell, NM 88203. ✆ **575/624-6760.** Fax 575/624-6941. Free admission. Summer daily 10am–8pm; winter daily 10am–5:30pm. Gift shop summer Wed–Sun 1–5pm.

GETTING OUTSIDE

Fifteen miles northeast of Roswell, on the Pecos River, at the **Bitter Lake National Wildlife Refuge ★**, a great variety of waterfowl—including cormorants, herons, and pelicans—find a winter home. The refuge, reached via US 380 and NM 265 from Roswell, comprises 24,000 acres of river bottomland, marsh, stands of salt cedar, and open range. All told, more than 300 species of birds have been sighted here. You can get information at the headquarters building at the entrance, or call ✆ **575/622-6755.** Fall and early winter are the best times to visit.

Bottomless Lakes State Park is a chain of seven lakes surrounded by rock bluffs 16 miles east of Roswell via NM 409, off US 380. It got its name from early cowboys, who tried to fathom the lakes' depth by plumbing them with lariats. No matter how many ropes they tied together and lowered into the limpid water, they never touched bottom. In truth, though, none of the lakes are deeper than 100 feet. The park offers fishing for rainbow trout, swimming and windsurfing, campsites for trailers or tents, shelters, showers, a dump station, and a concession area with vending machines and paddleboat rentals (open 9am–6pm Memorial Day–Labor Day). The park is open year-round from 6am to 9pm daily, and admission is $5 per vehicle. For more information, call ✆ **575/624-6058.**

Originally built to raise bass and catfish, the **Dexter National Fish Hatchery,** 1 1/2 miles east of Dexter on NM 190, about 16 miles southeast of Roswell via NM 2, is now a center for the study and raising of 15 threatened and endangered fish species, such as the razorback sucker, Colorado squawfish, and Chihuahuan chub. Year-round, visitors can take self-guided tours among the hatchery's ponds; from late March to October, the visitor center is open, with exhibits and an aquarium containing endangered fish. The hatchery (✆ **575/734-5910**) is open weekdays from 7am to 3:30pm, and admission is free.

WHERE TO STAY IN ROSWELL

In recent years most major motel chains have opened in Roswell, including Hampton Inn, Holiday Inn Express, Motel 6, and Comfort Suites. If you have a favorite, you can find their contact information in the Appendix.

Best Western Sally Port Inn & Suites ★ Built in 1976, and under new ownership in 2007, this hotel provides bright, spacious rooms with comfortable beds and good amenities. The new owners are making their way through, updating rooms with new mahogany style furniture, new carpet, and comfortable beds. The baths are receiving granite countertops. However, at this writing, not all rooms had been completed, so be sure to request an updated one. A huge plant-filled indoor courtyard with a pool provides a centerpiece around which the rooms are built. It's a big place, so you may want to ask for a room at one of the four corner entrances; that way, you won't have to trudge down the long hallways. The rooms with windows facing outside are quieter than those facing in toward the often-kid-filled pool. This is your best bet for full-service lodging. It's at the center of town, adjacent to the New Mexico Military Institute.

2000 N. Main St., Roswell, NM 88201. ✆ **800/WESTERN** or 575/622-6430. Fax 575/623-7631. www.bestwestern.com. 124 units. $70–$100 double. Rates include full breakfast. AE, DC, DISC, MC, V. Pets welcome in smoking rooms, with $10 fee. **Amenities:** Restaurant; sports bar; indoor pool; nearby golf course; exercise room; Jacuzzi; sauna; room service; coin-op laundry; laundry service. *In room:* A/C, TV, high-speed Internet, coffeemaker, hair dryer, iron.

Fairfield Inn & Suites by Marriott ★ This inn at the center of town offers bright rooms with plenty of amenities. The lobby and breakfast area have a living room feel, and the whole place offers the convenience and good prices one can expect from a Fairfield. Elements such as marble and tile in the bathrooms and a nice pool further enhance the place. The suites offer an interesting angled two-room configuration, with a big TV and a CD player, and the standard rooms are medium size, each with a desk. All rooms have comfortable beds. Wireless Internet is available in the lobby.

1201 N. Main St., Roswell, NM 88201. ✆ **800/228-2800** or 575/624-1300. www.marriott.com. 67 units. $90–$139 double. Rates include continental breakfast. AE, DC, DISC, MC, V. **Amenities:** Outdoor pool; exercise room; business center; guest laundry. *In room:* A/C, TV, high-speed Internet, coffeemaker, hair dryer, iron, microwave.

Camping

Town and Country RV Park (✆ **800/499-4364** or 575/624-1833; www.roswell-usa.com/tandcrv), south of Roswell, is your best bet for camping, with some grass and cottonwood and elm trees for shade. The campground has 75 sites, most with full hookups. Prices range from $33 to $39. Tent campers can set up here as well. Bathrooms are clean and convenient, as is the large pool. The campground is at 331 W. Brasher Rd. Head south on Main Street for 3 miles; turn west on West Brasher Road.

WHERE TO DINE IN ROSWELL

Cattle Baron ★ SEAFOOD/STEAK This popular restaurant is always busy during mealtimes. You can usually get a table, however, and they are nicely spaced so that the noise level is minimal. It's an informal place with a wealthy ranch feel—lots of burgundy and brass. Service is fast and friendly. Many come here just to feast at the salad bar, which is one of the best I've seen and includes many potato and pasta dishes, as well as a choice of two soups. Everything is made fresh here—the bread baked in-house, the beef even hand-cut by the manager. You can't go wrong with the steaks, such as the tender filet mignon wrapped in bacon. You can also get dishes such as shrimp scampi at a price that will make you glad for Roswell's provincialism. The lounge is a comfortable place to come for evening drinks, and there's a full bar here.

1113 N. Main St. ✆ **575/622-2465.** Reservations recommended. Main courses $6–$13 lunch, $12–$25 dinner. AE, DISC, MC, V. Mon–Thurs 11am–9:30pm; Fri–Sat 11am–10pm; Sun 11am–9pm.

Farley's (Kids) AMERICAN This raucous place can really draw crowds. Folks come for the barnlike atmosphere, where they can throw peanut shells on the floor and scream at TVs. Lots of booths inside and a patio outside please kids and their parents, as does the menu variety. Soups and salads, pizza, sandwiches, and burgers are the big sellers. Entrees such as chicken alfredo and baby back ribs will fill you up if you want a real meal. ***Beware:*** On weekend nights and holidays, you'll have to wait for a table. A full bar is available.

1315 N. Main St. ✆ **575/627-1100.** Main courses $8–$20. AE, DC, DISC, MC, V. Daily 11am–midnight or so, depending on the crowd.

Tia Juana's Mexican Grille & Cantina ★★ (Kids) NEW MEXICAN On the north end of town, this spot serves tasty New Mexican fare in a festive Mexican cantina ambience. Red chile lights and photos of Oaxaca accent the large dining area, which is made intimate with booths and tables nicely spaced. Service is friendly and on the mark. The food is prepared with fresh ingredients and good chile—the restaurant even makes its own tortillas daily. You can't go wrong with the enchiladas, served rolled or stacked, or the tacos, served soft or crisp. Finish your meal with the Kahlúa sombrero cake, made with liqueur and topped with toffee whipped cream. Kids have plenty of menu options, as well as crayons to draw with, and adults can enjoy a full bar.

3601 N. Main St. ✆ **575/627-6113.** http://tiajuanas.net. Main courses $6–$20. AE, DC, DISC, MC, V. Mon–Thurs 11am–9:30pm; Fri–Sat 11am–10pm; Sun 11am–9pm.

7 ALSO WORTH A LOOK: FORT SUMNER & ENVIRONS

The little town of **Fort Sumner,** home to 1,300 people, 84 miles north of Roswell via US 285 and NM 20, is important in New Mexico history because it's the site of Fort Sumner State Monument and the burial place of the notorious Billy the Kid. Stop by if you're in the vicinity and have some time to spare.

Fort Sumner State Monument ★ (✆ **575/355-2573;** www.nmmonuments.org) recalls a tragic U.S. Army experiment (1864–68) to create a self-sustaining agricultural colony for captive Navajos and Mescalero Apaches. Many still recall the "Long March," during which some Navajos walked a distance of more than 400 miles. By fall 1864, some 9,000 people were held captive here, site of the Bosque Redondo Reservation. Disaster followed: disease, blighted crops, alkaline water, Comanche raids, and the Navajos' devastating alienation from their homelands. Some 3,000 Native Americans died here. Part of the fort where the military lived and worked has been reconstructed at the site. A short walking tour takes you to various signposts that explain what was once on the land, illustrated with sad photographs of the dismal conditions. The visitor center (open daily 8:30am–5pm) gives you a good background before you head out to the site. The monument is 7 miles southeast of the modern town, via US 60/84 and NM 272. Admission is $5 for adults, free for children age 17 and under.

Nearby, the **Old Fort Sumner Museum** (✆ **575/355-2942**) displays artifacts, pictures, and documents. It's a private enterprise that may not quite be worth the $3.50 admission.

Behind the museum (you don't have to go through the museum) is the **Grave of Billy the Kid,** its 6-foot tombstone engraved to "William H. Bonney, alias 'Billy the Kid,' died July 16, 1881," and to two previously slain comrades with whom he was buried. Also in the graveyard is the tomb of Lucien Maxwell, the land czar from the Cimarron area, who purchased Fort Sumner after the military abandoned it.

If you're curious about the notorious Kid, you can learn more at the **Billy the Kid Museum** (✆ **575/355-2380**), 1 mile east of downtown Fort Sumner on US 60/84. In operation for over half a century, it contains more than 60,000 relics of the Old West, including some that recall the life of young Bonney himself, such as his rifle. Admission is $5 for adults, $4 for seniors 62 and older, $3 for ages 7–15, free age 6 and under.

The **Old Fort Days** celebration, the second week of June, is Fort Sumner's big annual event. It includes the World's Richest Tombstone Race (inspired by the actual theft of Billy's tombstone, since recovered), 2 nights of rodeo, a country music show, a barbecue, and a parade.

Sumner Lake State Park (✆ **575/355-2541**), 16 miles northwest of Fort Sumner via US 84 and NM 203, is a 1,000-acre property with a campground (with electric and water hookups). Boating, fishing, swimming, and water-skiing are popular recreations.

For more information on the town, contact the **Fort Sumner Chamber of Commerce,** P.O. Box 28, Fort Sumner, NM 88119 (✆ **575/355-7705;** www.ftsumnerchamber.com).

CLOVIS/PORTALES

Clovis, 110 miles northeast of Roswell via US 70, is a major market center on the Texas border. Founded in 1906 as a railway town, it is now the focus of an active ranching and farming region. The **Lyceum Theatre,** 409 Main St. (✆ **575/763-6085**), is a significant restoration of a former vaudeville theater; it's now the city's center for performing arts. A major rodeo on the national circuit is held the first weekend in June. "Clovis Man," who hunted mammoths in this region about 10,000 B.C., was first discovered at a site near the city. For more information, contact the **Clovis/Curry County Chamber of Commerce** (✆ **575/763-3435;** www.clovisnm.org).

Nineteen miles south of Clovis is **Portales,** a town of 12,500 people that is the home of the main campus of **Eastern New Mexico University.** On campus are the **Roosevelt County Historical Museum** (✆ **575/562-2592**) of regional ranching history and the **Natural History Museum** (✆ **575/562-2723**), with wildlife exhibits, including a bee colony. Anthropology and paleontology exhibits are at the **Blackwater Draw Archaeological Site and Museum** ★ (✆ **575/562-2202**), 7 miles northeast of Portales on US 70 toward Clovis. The museum isn't much, but the archaeological site draws bone buffs from around the world. Especially notable is the Interpretive Center, where visitors can watch an excavation in progress. The site is on NM 467, 5 miles north of US 70. For more information, contact the **Roosevelt County Chamber of Commerce** at ✆ **575/356-8541** or www.portales.com.

For lodging in the Clovis/Portales area, try the **La Quinta Inn,** 4521 N. Prince, Clovis, NM 88101 (✆ **800/531-5900** or 575/763-8777; www.lq.com). Clovis is the site of the original restaurant of the **K-Bob's Steakhouse** chain. The restaurant is at 1600 Mabry Dr. (✆ **575/763-4443**).

In Portales, stay at the **Super 8 Motel,** 1805 W. 2nd St. (✆ **800/800-8000** or 575/356-8518; www.super8.com). The **Cattle Baron,** 1600 S. Avenue D (✆ **575/356-5587**), has good steaks and a nice salad bar.

8 CARLSBAD & ENVIRONS

Carlsbad, named for a spa in Bohemia, offers almost 3 miles of beaches and paths along the tree-shaded Pecos River. Founded in the late 1800s, its back streets have many elegant homes, and its town square encircles a Pueblo-style courthouse designed by New Mexico architect John Gaw Meem. Besides getting a good tourist business from Carlsbad Caverns, the town thrives on farming, with irrigated crops of cotton, hay, and pecans.

The caverns (see "Carlsbad Caverns National Park," later in this chapter) are the big attraction, having drawn more than 33 million visitors since opening in 1923. A satellite community, White's City (www.whitescity.com), was created 20 miles south of Carlsbad at the park entrance junction. The family of Jack White, Jr., owns all its motels, restaurants, gift shops, and other attractions.

ESSENTIALS

GETTING THERE From Albuquerque, take 1-40 east 59 miles to Clines Corners; turn south on US 285, and travel 216 miles to Carlsbad via Roswell (6 hr.). From El Paso, take US 62/180 east (3 hr.).

New Mexico Airlines (✆ **888/564-6119;** www.pacificwings.com/nma) provides commercial service, with daily flights between Albuquerque and **Cavern City Air Terminal** (✆ **575/887-3060**), 4 miles south of the city via National Parks Highway (US 62/180). You can rent a car from **Enterprise,** 609 N. Canal St. (✆ **575/887-3039**); with an advance reservation they will pick you up at the airport.

VISITOR INFORMATION The **Carlsbad Chamber of Commerce** and the **Carlsbad Convention and Visitors Bureau,** both at 302 S. Canal St. (US 285), P.O. Box 910, Carlsbad, NM 88220 (✆ **800/221-1224** or 575/887-6516; www.carlsbadchamber.com), are open Monday from 9am to 5pm and Tuesday through Friday from 8am to 5pm.

SEEING THE SIGHTS

Carlsbad's pride and joy is the broad Pecos River, with a 3½-mile **riverwalk** along the tree-shaded banks, beginning near the north end of Riverside Drive. This is a lovely place for a picnic, and if you'd like to cool off, a municipal beach at the north end has changing rooms and showers. Annual **Christmas on the Pecos** ★★ pontoon boat rides take place each evening from Thanksgiving to New Year's Eve (except Christmas Eve), past a fascinating display of Christmas lights on riverside homes and businesses. Advance reservations, available from the chamber of commerce, are required.

The **Carlsbad Museum and Art Center,** 418 W. Fox St., 1 block west of Canal Street (✆ **575/887-0276**), contains Apache relics, pioneer artifacts, and an impressive art collection. The museum's store has a small but fine selection of jewelry and books at reasonable prices. The museum is open Monday through Saturday from 10am to 5pm; admission is free, although donations are welcome. If you're looking to shop, check out the **Artist Gallery,** 120 S. Canyon St. (© **575/887-1210**), selling local and regional art. Look especially for Helen Gwinn's mixed-media pieces.

GETTING OUTSIDE

Recreational facilities in the Carlsbad area include some two dozen parks, several golf courses, numerous tennis courts and swimming pools, a municipal beach, and a shooting and archery range. Contact the **City of Carlsbad Recreation Department** (© **575/887-1191**).

Living Desert Zoo & Gardens State Park ★ (Kids) Situated within 1,200 acres of authentic Chihuahuan Desert, this park contains more than 50 species of desert mammals, birds, and reptiles, and almost 500 varieties of plants. Even for someone like me, who cringes at the thought of zoos, this is a pleasant 1.3-mile walk. You pass through displays with plaques pointing out vegetation such as mountain mahogany, and geologic formations such as gypsum sinkholes. In addition to a nocturnal exhibit, you're likely to see lizards and other wild creatures, as well as captive ones.

Rehabilitation programs provide for the park's animals, which have been sick or injured and are no longer able to survive in the wild. You'll see golden eagles and great horned owls among the birds of prey in the aviary, and large animals such as deer and elk in outdoor pastures. The view from the park, high atop the Ocotillo Hills on the northwest side of Carlsbad, is superb.

1504 Miehls Dr. (P.O. Box 100), Carlsbad, NM 88221-0100. © **575/887-5516.** www.emnrd.state.nm.us/prd/livingdesert.htm. Admission $5 adults, $3 children 7–12, free for children 6 and under. Group rates are available. Memorial Day weekend to Labor Day 8am–8pm, last park entry by 6:30pm; rest of year 9am–5pm, last park entry by 3:30pm. Gift shop closes 45 min. prior to zoo. Closed Christmas. Take Miehls Dr. off US 285 west of town and proceed just over a mile.

WHERE TO STAY IN & AROUND CARLSBAD

Most properties are along the highway south toward Carlsbad Caverns National Park (see "Carlsbad Caverns National Park," below). Only the Best Western Cavern Inn is near the National Park. The downside to staying there is that your restaurant and activity options are limited.

Best Western Cavern Inn If you'd like to be close to the caverns, this hotel is there, but it's not my choice. This whole complex could use updating, but seems to survive because it's the only lodging near the caverns. The lobby is within an Old West storefront, and the accommodations are across the street. The staff here seems to be overworked, so you may not get the service you would in Carlsbad. The motel has two main sections. The best is the Cavern Inn. This section is built around a courtyard, and rooms have an updated feel, with vigas on the ceilings and Southwestern pine furniture. Bathrooms are roomy enough, and the beds are comfortably firm. Next door, the two-story Walnut Canyon Inn provides 1970s rooms that are large, though the small bathrooms with jetted tubs could use sprucing up.

The White's City Arcade contains a post office, a grocery store, a gift shop, and the Million Dollar Museum of various antiques and paraphernalia. The hotel's two restaurants serve three meals in an ambiance that could also use updating.

17 Carlsbad Cavern Hwy. at NM 7 (P.O. Box 128), White's City, NM 88268. © **800/CAVERNS** or 575/785-2291. Fax 575/785-2283. www.bestwestern.com. 63 units. May 15–Sept 15 $104 double; Sept 16–May 14 $85 double. Rates include breakfast. AE, DC, DISC, MC, V. Pets welcome with $10 fee. **Amenities:** 2 restaurants; outdoor pool; game room; shopping arcade; courtesy computer. *In room:* A/C, TV, Wi-Fi, coffeemaker, hair dryer, iron.

Best Western Stevens Inn ★ This is a comfortable and welcoming place after the rigor of traveling in this part of the state, where there are miles between stops. The grounds are carefully landscaped, and the inn offers numerous types of rooms built in different eras. Some need to be upgraded, so be sure to request a remodeled one or, better yet, request one of the newest rooms at the south end of the property, which are large and have large bathrooms; each has a fridge and microwave, and some have full kitchens. The rooms in the 400 and 600 numbered buildings are also updated. All the rooms are medium size, decorated in a Southwestern print, and have firm beds. Bathrooms are small but have outer double-sink vanities. The Flume (p. 372) is one of the better restaurants in town.

1829 S. Canal St., Carlsbad, NM 88220. ✆ **800/730-2851,** 800/528-1234, or 575/887-2851. Fax 575/887-6338. www.bestwestern.com. 221 units. $62–$89 double; $70–$99 suite. Rates include breakfast buffet. AE, DISC, MC, V. Small pets allowed, with $25 deposit. **Amenities:** 2 restaurants; bar; large outdoor pool; exercise room; playground; airport shuttle; business center; room service; coin-op laundry; laundry service; same-day dry cleaning; executive-level rooms available; courtesy computer. *In room:* A/C, TV, Wi-Fi, fridge, coffeemaker, hair dryer, iron, microwave.

Holiday Inn Express ★★ **Kids** One of Carlsbad's newest lodgings, this hotel, opened in 2007, provides well-planned, comfortable rooms on the north side of town. Rooms are medium-size, with comfortable beds dressed in earthy colors, and a desk, and with lots of amenities. The medium-size bathrooms have granite countertops and tile baths. As well, the hotel has king and queen suites, which include two TVs and a fold-out couch, a good option for families. Service here is courteous and on-the-mark.

2210 W. Pierce St., Carlsbad, NM 88220. ✆ **800/HOLIDAY** or 575/234-1252. Fax 575/234-1253. www.hiexpress.com. 80 units. $99–105 double; $133–$143 suite. Rates include full hot breakfast. AE, DISC, MC, V. **Amenities:** Indoor pool; Jacuzzi; exercise room; business center. *In room:* A/C, TV, Wi-Fi, fridge, coffeemaker, hair dryer, iron, microwave.

Camping

Brantley Lake State Park (✆ **575/457-2384;** www.nmparks.com) in Carlsbad has RV hookups as well as tent campsites. Picnic tables, grills, and recreational facilities are available. Boating and lake fishing are popular here. **Carlsbad RV Park and Campground,** on the south end of town at 4301 National Parks Hwy. (✆ **888/878-7275** or 575/885-6333; www.carlsbadrvpark.com), is a large, full-service campground with a swimming pool and playground. In Artesia, try **Artesia RV Park** (✆ **575/746-6184;** www.artesiarvpark.com), a more moderately sized campground, on Hermosa Drive just south of the junction of US 82/285. Laundry facilities and a game room are available.

WHERE TO DINE IN & AROUND CARLSBAD

Blue House ★ **Finds** BAKERY/CAFE In a quest to find good coffee in even the smallest of New Mexico towns, I now rate Carlsbad high. On a quiet residential street just north of historic downtown is this gem, set in a Queen Anne–style blue house with morning-glory vines adorning the front fence. Inside, Parisian colors warm the walls, contrasting with brightly painted chairs and small round tables. The fare is simple, fresh, and imaginative, with espresso, lattes, and Italian sodas the biggest draws, along with special sandwiches and soups daily. Excellent baked goods top the breakfast menu, including homemade cinnamon rolls. For lunch, try any of the fresh organic salads such as the grilled chicken or Oriental. For something sweeter, order the cream cheese–raspberry coffee cake.

609 N. Canyon Rd. ✆ **575/628-0555.** All menu items under $8. DISC, MC, V. Mon–Fri 6am–2pm; Sat 6am–noon (lunch served Tues–Fri 11am–1pm). Take Canal St. to Church St. east, and then south on Canyon Rd.

The Flume ★ AMERICAN Named for the irrigation ditch that brings water to the region's farmers, the Flume serves reliable beef, pork, and chicken dishes in a comfortable atmosphere. This is where Carlsbad locals come for their special nights out. The decor in the two-room dining area, separated by arches, has a bit of a 1970s feel, but includes comfortable chairs. Service is good. Breakfast brings standard egg and pancake offerings. For lunch you might try one of their sandwiches such as the smoked turkey with Swiss cheese and avocado. The salads and burgers are also tasty. At dinner, I've enjoyed a nice grilled chicken here, and my mother liked her fettuccine alfredo with shrimp. Others seem to order the rib-eye or prime rib, which is served on Friday and Saturday nights. Entrees come with a trip to the salad bar, a vegetable, and choice of a starch. Diners can order from a full bar. A senior menu is available.

1829 S. Canal St., ✆ **575/887-2851.** www.bestwestern.com. Breakfast and lunch $5–$12; dinner $13–$23. AE, DISC, MC, V. Daily 6am–10pm.

Lucy's ★ Kids MEXICAN When you walk in the door of this busy restaurant with festive Mexican decor, Lucy is likely to wave you toward the dining room and tell you to find a seat. Such is the casual nature of the place—and a sign of the good home-style food to come. Since 1974, Lucy and Justo Yanez's restaurant has been dedicated to the words of a Mexican proverb printed on the menu: *El hambre es un fuego, y la comida es fresca* (Hunger is a burning, and eating is a coolness). You'll probably want to start with a margarita or Mexican beer. The food is tasty, with Lucy's personal adaptations of old favorites, often invented by requests from regulars. I recommend the chicken fajita burrito or the combination plate. Finish with a dessert of *buñelos* (fritters), sprinkled with cinnamon sugar. Children's plates are available; diners can choose mild or hot chile. A second Lucy's restaurant is in Hobbs, at 4428 Lovington Hwy.

701 S. Canal St. ✆ **575/887-7714.** Reservations recommended on weekends. Main courses $6–$15. AE, DC, DISC, MC, V. Mon–Sat 11am–9pm.

CARLSBAD AFTER DARK

Fairly recently Carlsbad has sprung a night scene. You have two options. The **Silver Spur,** 1829 S. Canal St. (✆ **575/887-2851**), offers live country-and-western music most nights and free hors d'oeuvres during happy hour, as well as a big-screen TV. The **Post Time Saloon,** 313 W. Fox St. (✆ **575/628-1977**), is a huge place with pool tables, three bars, and a dance floor. The club offers a range of DJ mixes, including country, Tejano, and karaoke.

EXPLORING THE ENVIRONS

A Side Trip to Texas: Guadalupe Mountains National Park ★★

Some 250 million years ago, the Guadalupe Mountains were an immense reef poking up through a tropical ocean. Marine organisms fossilized this 400-mile-long Capitan Reef as limestone; later, as the sea evaporated, a blanket of sediments and mineral salts buried the reef. Then, just 10 to 12 million years ago, a mountain-building uplift exposed a part of the fossil reef. This has given modern scientists a unique opportunity to explore earth's geologic history, and outdoor lovers a playground for wilderness experience.

The steep southern end of the range makes up **Guadalupe Mountains National Park** and includes Guadalupe Peak, at 8,749 feet the highest in Texas, while the northern part lies within Lincoln National Forest and Carlsbad Caverns National Park. Deer, elk, mountain lion, and bear are found in the forests, which contrast strikingly with the desert around them.

JUST THE FACTS To reach the park, take US 62/180, 55 miles southwest of Carlsbad. Admission to the park is $5, and the visitor center is open June through August daily from 8am to 6pm; September through May from 8am to 4:30pm. For more information, contact **Park Ranger,** HC-60, Box 400, Salt Flat, TX 79847 (✆ **915/828-3251;** www.nps.gov/gumo). The park has more than 80 miles of trails; most are steep, rugged, and rocky. No lodging, restaurants, stores, or gas exist within 35 miles of the park. Leashed pets are permitted only in the campground parking area.

SEEING THE HIGHLIGHTS The visitor center offers a variety of exhibits and slide programs that tell the story of the Guadalupe Mountains, as well as ranger-guided walks and lectures. Information, maps, and backcountry permits can also be obtained at **McKittrick Canyon Visitor Center** (10 miles northeast via US 62/180 and a side road; ✆ **915/828-3381**) and the **Dog Canyon Ranger Station** (reached through Carlsbad via NM 137 and C.R. 414, about 70 miles; ✆ **575/981-2418**).

One of the most spectacular hikes in Texas is to the top of **Guadalupe Peak,** an 8.5-mile round-trip trek accessed from the Pine Springs Campground. **McKittrick Canyon,** protected by its high sheer walls, with a green swath of trees growing along the banks of its spring-fed stream, is a beautiful location. It is a great spot for hiking, bird-watching, and viewing other wildlife, and it's an especially lovely sight during fall foliage season, from late October to mid-November.

CAMPING Pine Springs and Dog Canyon both have developed camping areas, with restrooms and water, but no hookups or showers. Fires, including charcoal, are not permitted.

Artesia

A downtown rejuvenation project has brought a sparkle to **Artesia,** a town of 10,692 people, 36 miles north of Carlsbad on US 285. The **Artesia Historical Museum and Art Center,** housed in a Victorian home at 505 W. Richardson Ave. (✆ **575/748-2390**), is worth visiting just to see the Queen Anne–style home with the outside covered with round river stones. Open Tuesday through Friday from 9am to 5pm and Saturday from 1 to 5pm, the museum exhibits Native American and pioneer artifacts, traveling exhibits, and art shows. Admission is free.

If you want to stop over in Artesia, consider the **Best Western Pecos Inn,** 2209 W. Main St. (US 82), Artesia, NM 88211 (✆ **575/748-3324;** www.bestwestern.com). A great place to eat is the **Wellhead** ★, 332 W. Main St. (✆ **575/746-0640**), a brewpub designed around the notion of oil wells. It's open Sunday through Thursday from 11am to 11pm and Friday and Saturday from 11am to midnight. Reservations are recommended on weekends and holidays. Main courses range from $8 to $24, and most major credit cards are accepted. Further information can be obtained from the **Artesia Chamber of Commerce,** P.O. Box 99, Artesia, NM 88211 (✆ **575/746-2744;** www.artesiachamber.com).

Hobbs

Located 69 miles east of Carlsbad on US 62/180, on the edge of the Llano Estacado tableland, Hobbs is at the center of New Mexico's richest oil field. Many oil companies base their headquarters here.

The **Lea County Cowboy Hall of Fame and Western Heritage Center** near New Mexico Junior College, on the Lovington Highway (✆ **575/492-2676**), honors the area's ranchers (both men and women) and rodeo performers and is open Monday through Saturday from 10am to 5pm (closed college holidays).

Twenty-two miles northwest of Hobbs via NM 18, at the junction with US 82, is the town of **Lovington** (pop. 9,500), another ranching and oil center. The **Lea County Historical Museum,** 103 S. Love St. (✆ **575/396-4805**), presents memorabilia of the region's unique history in a World War I–era hotel (ca. 1918).

If you plan to stay in Hobbs, try the **Holiday Inn Express,** 3610 N. Lovington Hwy. (✆ **800/377-8660** or 575/392-8777; www.hiexpress.com). **Harry McAdams Park,** 4 miles north of Hobbs on NM 18 (✆ **575/397-9291**), has campsites and a visitor center set on acres of lovely grass. You can get a good square meal at the **Cattle Baron Steak and Seafood Restaurant,** 1930 N. Grimes St. (✆ **575/393-2800**). Gamblers and horse-racing fans enjoy the **Black Gold Casino at Zia Park,** 3901 W. Millen Dr. (✆ **888/ZIAPARK** or 575/492-7000; www.blackgoldcasino.net), with over 700 slot machines. Live horse racing takes place September to December. For more information on the area, contact the **Hobbs Chamber of Commerce,** 400 N. Marland Blvd. (✆ **800/658-6291** or 575/397-3202; www.hobbschamber.org), or the **Lovington Chamber of Commerce,** 201 S. Main St. (✆ **575/396-5311**).

9 CARLSBAD CAVERNS NATIONAL PARK ★★★

One of the largest and most spectacular cave systems in the world, **Carlsbad Caverns** comprise some 100 known caves that snake through the porous limestone reef of the Guadalupe Mountains. Fantastic and grotesque formations fascinate visitors, who find every shape imaginable (and unimaginable) naturally sculpted in the underground world—from frozen waterfalls to strands of pearls, from soda straws to miniature castles, from draperies to ice-cream cones.

Although Native Americans had known of the caverns for centuries, they were not discovered by Anglos until about a century ago, when settlers were attracted by sunset flights of bats from the cave. Jim White, a guano miner, began to explore the main cave in the early 1900s and to share its wonders with tourists. By 1923, the caverns had become a national monument, upgraded to national park status in 1930.

ESSENTIALS

GETTING THERE Take US 62/180 from either Carlsbad (see "Essentials," under "Carlsbad & Environs," earlier in this chapter), which is 23 miles to the northeast, or El Paso, Texas, which is 150 miles to the west. The scenic entrance road to the park is 7 miles long and originates at the park gate at White's City. Van service to Carlsbad Caverns National Park from White's City, south of Carlsbad, is provided by **Sun Country Tours/White's City Services** (✆ **575/785-2291**).

Carlsbad Cavern Tour Tips

Wear flat shoes with rubber soles and heels because of the slippery paths. A light sweater or jacket feels good in the constant temperature of 56°F (13°C), especially when it's 100°F (38°C) outside in the sun. The cavern is well lit, but you may want to bring along a flashlight as well. Rangers are stationed in the cave to answer questions.

VISITOR INFORMATION For more information about the park, contact **Carlsbad Caverns National Park,** 3225 National Parks Hwy., Carlsbad, NM 88220 (✆ **800/967-CAVE** for tour reservations, 575/785-2232 for information about guided tours, and 575/785-3012 for bat flight information; www.nps.gov/cave).

ADMISSION FEES & HOURS General admission to the park is $6 for adults, free for children under age 15. Admission is good for 3 days and includes entry to the two self-guided walking tours. Guided tours range in price from $7 to $20, depending on the type of tour, and reservations are required. The visitor center and park are open daily from Memorial Day to mid-August from 8am to 7pm; the rest of the year they're open from 8am to 5pm. They're closed Christmas.

TOURING THE CAVES

Two caves, **Carlsbad Cavern** and **Slaughter Canyon Cave,** are open to the public. The National Park Service has provided facilities, including elevators, to make it easy for everyone to visit the cavern, and a kennel for pets is available. Visitors in wheelchairs are common.

In addition to the tours described below, inquire at the visitor center information desk about other ranger-guided tours, including climbing and crawling "wild" cave tours. Be sure to call days in advance because some tours are offered only 1 day per week. Spelunkers who seek access to the park's undeveloped caves require special permission from the park superintendent.

Carlsbad Cavern Tours

You can tour Carlsbad Cavern in one of three ways, depending on your time, interest, and level of ability. The first, and least difficult, option is to take the elevator from the visitor center down 750 feet to the start of the self-guided tour of the Big Room. More difficult and time-consuming, but vastly more rewarding, is the 1-mile self-guided tour along the Natural Entrance route, which follows the traditional explorer's route, entering the cavern through the large historic natural entrance. The paved walkway through the natural entrance winds into the depths of the cavern and leads through a series of underground rooms; this tour takes about an hour. Parts of it are steep. At its lowest point, the trail reaches 750 feet below the surface, ending finally at an underground rest area.

Visitors who take either the elevator or the Natural Entrance route begin the self-guided tour of the spectacular Big Room near the rest area. The floor of this room covers 14 acres; the tour, over a relatively level path, is 1.25 miles long and takes about an hour.

The third option is the 1½-hour ranger-guided Kings Palace tour, which also departs from the underground rest area. This tour descends 830 feet beneath the surface of the desert to the deepest portion of the cavern open to the public. Reservations are required, and an additional fee is charged.

Other Guided Tours

Be sure to ask about the Slaughter Canyon Cave, Left Hand Tunnel, Lower Cave, Hall of the White Giant, and Spider Cave tours. These vary in degree of difficulty and adventure, from Left Hand, which is an easy half-mile lantern tour, to Spider Cave, where you can expect tight crawlways and canyonlike passages, to Hall of the White Giant, a strenuous tour in which you're required to crawl long distances, squeeze through tight crevices, and climb up slippery flow-stone-lined passages. Call in advance for times of each tour. All these tours depart from the visitor center.

BAT FLIGHTS

Every sunset from May to October, a crowd gathers at the natural entrance of the cave to watch a quarter-million bats take flight for a night of insect feasting. (The bats winter in Mexico.) All day long, the Mexican free-tailed bats sleep in the cavern; at night, they strike out on an insect hunt. A ranger program is offered around 7:30pm (verify the time at the visitor center) at the outdoor Bat Flight Amphitheater. Midsummer, the park sponsors a **Bat Flight Breakfast** beginning at 5am, during which visitors watch the bats return to the cavern. The cost is $7 for adults and $3 for children 12 and under. For information and specific date, call ✆ **575/785-2232,** ext. 0 or check www.nps.gov/cave.

OTHER PARK ACTIVITIES

Aside from the caves, the park offers a 10-mile one-way scenic loop drive through the Chihuahuan Desert to view Rattlesnake and Upper Walnut canyons. Picnickers can head for Rattlesnake Springs Picnic Area, on C.R. 418 near Slaughter Canyon Cave, a water source for hundreds of years for the Native Americans, and a primo birding spot. Backcountry hikers must register at the visitor center before going out on any of the trails in the park's 46,766 acres.

DINING

A cafe at the base of the caverns serves refreshments. Otherwise, your best bet is to eat in Carlsbad. If you are hungry while in the area, head to the **Velvet Garter Saloon & Restaurant** and **Jack's,** 26 Carlsbad Cavern Hwy., White's City. (✆ **575/785-2291**). Both are part of White's City. The food is decent, the Velvet Garter serving steaks and pasta in the evenings, and Jack's serving basic breakfasts and lunches. Dinner reservations are recommended in summer. The saloon is unmistakable, with longhorns mounted over the door. Main courses are $10 to $21 (Velvet Garter); $5.50 to $10 breakfast or lunch (Jack's). Velvet Garter is open daily 4 to 9pm (8:30pm in winter); Jack's daily 7am to 4pm.

Appendix: Fast Facts, Toll-Free Numbers & Websites

1 FAST FACTS: NEW MEXICO

AREA CODES The telephone area code for northwestern New Mexico, including Albuquerque and Santa Fe, is **505.** For the rest of the state, including Taos, the code is **575.**

ATM NETWORKS/CASHPOINTS See "Money & Costs," p. 50.

AUTOMOBILE ORGANIZATIONS Motor clubs will supply maps, suggested routes, guidebooks, accident and bail-bond insurance, and emergency road service. The **American Automobile Association (AAA)** is the major auto club in the United States. If you belong to a motor club in your home country, inquire about AAA reciprocity before you leave. You may be able to join AAA even if you're not a member of a reciprocal club; to inquire, call AAA (✆ **800/222-4357;** www.aaa.com). AAA is actually an organization of regional motor clubs, so look under "AAA Automobile Club" in the White Pages of the telephone directory. AAA has a nationwide emergency road service telephone number (✆ 800/AAA-HELP).

BUSINESS HOURS **Offices** and **stores** are generally open Monday to Friday, 9am to 5pm, with many stores also open Friday night, Saturday, and Sunday in the summer season. Most **banks** are open Monday to Thursday, 9am to 5pm, and Friday, 9am to 6pm. Some may also be open Saturday morning. Most branches have ATMs available 24 hours. Call establishments for specific hours.

CAR RENTALS See "Toll-Free Numbers & Websites," p. 383.

DRINKING LAWS The legal age for purchase and consumption of alcoholic beverages is 21; proof of age is required and often requested at bars, nightclubs, and restaurants, so it's always a good idea to bring ID when you go out. In New Mexico, major supermarkets and liquor stores sell beer, wine, and liquor.

Do not carry open containers of alcohol in your car or any public area that isn't zoned for alcohol consumption. The police can fine you on the spot. And nothing will ruin your trip faster than getting a citation for DUI ("driving under the influence"), so don't even think about driving while intoxicated.

DRIVING RULES See "Getting There & Getting Around," p. 46, in chapter 3.

ELECTRICITY Like Canada, the United States uses 110 to 120 volts AC (60 cycles), compared to 220 to 240 volts AC (50 cycles) in most of Europe, Australia, and New Zealand. Downward converters that change 220–240 volts to 110–120 volts are difficult to find in the United States, so bring one with you.

EMBASSIES & CONSULATES All embassies are located in the nation's capital, Washington, D.C. Some consulates are located in major U.S. cities, and most nations have a mission to the United Nations in New York City. If your country isn't listed below, call for directory information in Washington, D.C. (✆ **202/555-1212**) or check **www.embassy.org/embassies**.

The embassy of **Australia** is at 1601 Massachusetts Ave. NW, Washington, DC 20036 (✆ **202/797-3000**).

The embassy of **Canada** is at 501 Pennsylvania Ave. NW, Washington, DC 20001 (✆ **202/682-1740;** www.canadianembassy.org). Other Canadian consulates are in Buffalo (New York), Detroit, Los Angeles, New York, and Seattle.

The embassy of **Ireland** is at 2234 Massachusetts Ave. NW, Washington, DC 20008 (✆ **202/462-3939;** www.irelandemb.org). Irish consulates are in Boston, Chicago, New York, San Francisco, and other cities. See website for complete listing.

The embassy of **New Zealand** is at 37 Observatory Circle NW, Washington, DC 20008 (✆ **202/328-4800;** www.nzembassy.com). New Zealand consulates are in Los Angeles, Salt Lake City, San Francisco, and Seattle.

The embassy of the **United Kingdom** is at 3100 Massachusetts Ave. NW, Washington, DC 20008 (✆ **202/588-7800;** www.britainusa.com). Other British consulates are in Atlanta, Boston, Chicago, Cleveland, Houston, Los Angeles, New York, San Francisco, and Seattle.

EMERGENCIES In case of emergency, dial 911.

GASOLINE (PETROL) At press time, in the U.S., the cost of gasoline (also known as gas, but never petrol), is abnormally high. In New Mexico, prices run a little above the national average. Taxes are already included in the printed price. One U.S. gallon equals 3.8 liters or .85 imperial gallons. Fill-up locations are known as gas or service stations.

HOLIDAYS Banks, government offices, post offices, and many stores, restaurants, and museums are closed on the following legal national holidays: January 1 (New Year's Day), the third Monday in January (Martin Luther King, Jr., Day), the third Monday in February (Presidents' Day), the last Monday in May (Memorial Day), July 4 (Independence Day), the first Monday in September (Labor Day), the second Monday in October (Columbus Day), November 11 (Veterans' Day/Armistice Day), the fourth Thursday in November (Thanksgiving Day), and December 25 (Christmas). The Tuesday after the first Monday in November is Election Day, a federal government holiday in presidential-election years (held every 4 years, and next in 2012).

For more information on holidays see "New Mexico Calendar of Events," in chapter 3.

HOSPITALS See the "Fast Facts" section in the major city chapters for the closest one to you.

HOT LINES See the "Fast Facts" section in the major city chapters for the closest one to you.

INSURANCE **Medical Insurance** Although it's not required of travelers, health insurance is highly recommended. Most health insurance policies cover you if you get sick away from home—but check your coverage before you leave.

International visitors to the U.S. should note that unlike many European countries, the United States does not usually offer free or low-cost medical care to its citizens or visitors. Doctors and hospitals are expensive, and in most cases will require advance payment or proof of coverage before they render their services. Good policies will cover the costs of an accident, repatriation, or death. Packages such as **Europ Assistance's "Worldwide**

Healthcare Plan" are sold by European automobile clubs and travel agencies at attractive rates. **Worldwide Assistance Services, Inc.** (✆ **800/777-8710;** www.worldwideassistance.com) is the agent for Europ Assistance in the United States. Though lack of health insurance may prevent you from being admitted to a hospital in nonemergencies, don't worry about being left on a street corner to die: The American way is to fix you now and bill the daylights out of you later.

If you're ever hospitalized more than 150 miles from home, **MedjetAssist** (✆ **800/527-7478;** www.medjetassistance.com) will pick you up and fly you to the hospital of your choice in a medically equipped and staffed aircraft 24 hours a day, 7 days a week. Annual memberships are $225 individual, $350 family; you can also purchase short-term memberships.

Canadians should check with their provincial health plan offices or call **Health Canada** (✆ **866/225-0709;** www.hc-sc.gc.ca) to find out the extent of their coverage and what documentation and receipts they must take home in case they are treated in the United States.

Travelers from the U.K. should carry their European Health Insurance Card (EHIC), which replaced the E111 form as proof of entitlement to free/reduced cost medical treatment abroad (✆ **0845/606-2030;** www.ehic.org.uk). Note, however, that the EHIC only covers "necessary medical treatment," and for repatriation costs, lost money, baggage, or cancellation, travel insurance from a reputable company should always be sought (www.travelinsuranceweb.com).

Travel Insurance The cost of travel insurance varies widely, depending on the destination, the cost and length of your trip, your age and health, and the type of trip you're taking, but expect to pay between 5% and 8% of the vacation itself. You can get estimates from various providers through **InsureMyTrip.com.** Enter your trip cost and dates, your age, and other information, for prices from more than a dozen companies.

U.K. citizens and their families who make more than one trip abroad per year may find an annual travel insurance policy works out cheaper. Check **www.moneysupermarket.com**, which compares prices across a wide range of providers for single- and multi-trip policies.

Most big travel agents offer their own insurance and will probably try to sell you their package when you book a holiday. Think before you sign. **Britain's Consumers' Association** recommends that you insist on seeing the policy and reading the fine print before buying travel insurance. **The Association of British Insurers** (✆ **020/7600-3333;** www.abi.org.uk) gives advice by phone and publishes *Holiday Insurance,* a free guide to policy provisions and prices. You might also shop around for better deals: Try **Columbus Direct** (✆ 0870/033-9988; www.columbusdirect.net).

Trip Cancellation Insurance Trip-cancellation insurance will help retrieve your money if you have to back out of a trip or depart early, or if your travel supplier goes bankrupt. Trip cancellation traditionally covers such events as sickness, natural disasters, and State Department advisories. The latest news in trip-cancellation insurance is the availability of **expanded hurricane coverage** and the **"any-reason"** cancellation coverage—which costs more but covers cancellations made for any reason. You won't get back 100% of your prepaid trip cost, but you'll be refunded a substantial portion. **TravelSafe** (✆ **888/885-7233;** www.travelsafe.com) offers both types of coverage. Expedia also offers any-reason cancellation coverage for its air-hotel packages. For details, contact one of the following recommended insurers: **Access America** (✆ 866/807-3982; www.accessamerica.com); **Travel Guard International** (✆ 800/826-4919; www.travelguard.com); **Travel Insured International**

(✆ 800/243-3174; www.travelinsured.com); and **Travelex Insurance Services** (✆ 888/457-4602; www.travelex-insurance.com).

INTERNET ACCESS See the "Fast Facts" section in the major city chapters for the closest one to you. As well, you can try **www.cybercafe.com**.

LEGAL AID If you are "pulled over" for a minor infraction (such as speeding), never attempt to pay the fine directly to a police officer; this could be construed as attempted bribery, a much more serious crime. Pay fines by mail, or directly into the hands of the clerk of the court. If accused of a more serious offense, say and do nothing before consulting a lawyer. Here the burden is on the state to prove a person's guilt beyond a reasonable doubt, and everyone has the right to remain silent, whether he or she is suspected of a crime or actually arrested. Once arrested, a person can make one telephone call to a party of his or her choice. International visitors should call their embassy or consulate.

LOST & FOUND Be sure to tell all of your credit card companies the minute you discover your wallet has been lost or stolen and file a report at the nearest police precinct. Your credit card company or insurer may require a police report number or record of the loss. Most credit card companies have an emergency toll-free number to call if your card is lost or stolen; they may be able to wire you a cash advance immediately or deliver an emergency credit card in a day or two. Visa's U.S. emergency number is ✆ **800/847-2911** or 410/581-9994. American Express cardholders and traveler's check holders should call ✆ **800/221-7282.** MasterCard holders should call ✆ **800/307-7309** or 636/722-7111. For other credit cards, call the toll-free number directory at ✆ **800/555-1212.**

If you need emergency cash over the weekend when all banks and American Express offices are closed, you can have money wired to you via **Western Union** (✆ **800/325-6000;** www.westernunion.com).

MAIL At press time, domestic postage rates were 27¢ for a postcard and 42¢ for a letter. For international mail, a first-class letter of up to 1 ounce costs 94¢ (72¢ to Canada and Mexico); a first-class postcard costs the same as a letter. For more information go to **www.usps.com** and click on "Calculate Postage."

If you aren't sure what your address will be in the United States, mail can be sent to you, in your name, c/o General Delivery at the main post office of the city or region where you expect to be. (Call ✆ **800/275-8777** for information on the nearest post office.) The addressee must pick up mail in person and must produce proof of identity (driver's license, passport, and so on). Most post offices will hold your mail for up to 1 month and are open Monday to Friday from 8am to 6pm, and Saturday from 9am to 3pm.

Always include zip codes when mailing items in the U.S. If you don't know your zip code, visit www.usps.com/zip4.

MAPS The New Mexico Department of Tourism will send you a free state map. Call **800/545-2070** or 505/827-7400.

MEASUREMENTS See the chart on the inside front cover of this book for details on converting metric measurements to nonmetric equivalents.

MEDICAL CONDITIONS If you have a medical condition that requires **syringe-administered medications,** carry a valid signed prescription from your physician; syringes in carry-on baggage will be inspected. Insulin in any form should have the proper pharmaceutical documentation. If you have a disease that requires treatment with **narcotics,** you should also carry documented proof with you—smuggling narcotics aboard a plane carries severe penalties in the U.S.

For **HIV-positive visitors,** requirements for entering the United States are somewhat vague and change frequently. For up-to-the-minute information, contact **AIDSinfo** (✆ **800/448-0440** or 301/519-6616 outside the U.S.; www.aidsinfo.nih.gov) or the **Gay Men's Health Crisis** (✆ **212/367-1000;** www.gmhc.org).

NEWSPAPERS & MAGAZINES National newspapers include the *New York Times, USA Today,* and the *Wall Street Journal.* National news weeklies include *Newsweek, Time,* and *U.S. News & World Report.* In large cities, most newsstands offer a small selection of the most popular foreign periodicals and newspapers, such as *The Economist* and *Le Monde.* For information on local publications, see the "Fast Facts" sections in chapters 6, 7, and 8.

PASSPORTS The websites listed provide downloadable passport applications as well as the current fees for processing applications. For an up-to-date, country-by-country listing of passport requirements around the world, go to the "International Travel" tab of the U.S. State Department at **http://travel.state.gov**. International visitors to the U.S. can obtain a visa application at the same website. ***Note:*** Children are required to present a passport when entering the United States at airports. More information on obtaining a passport for a minor can be found at http://travel.state.gov. Allow plenty of time before your trip to apply for a passport; processing normally takes 4 to 6 weeks (3 weeks for expedited service) but can take longer during busy periods (especially spring). And keep in mind that if you need a passport in a hurry, you'll pay a higher processing fee.

For Residents of Australia You can pick up an application from your local post office or any branch of Passports Australia, but you must schedule an interview at the passport office to present your application materials. Call the **Australian Passport Information Service** at ✆ **131-232,** or visit the government website at www.passports.gov.au.

For Residents of Canada Passport applications are available at travel agencies throughout Canada or from the central **Passport Office,** Department of Foreign Affairs and International Trade, Ottawa, ON K1A 0G3 (✆ **800/567-6868;** www.ppt.gc.ca). ***Note:*** Canadian children who travel must have their own passports. However, if you hold a valid Canadian passport issued before December 11, 2001, that bears the name of your child, the passport remains valid for you and your child until it expires.

For Residents of Ireland You can apply for a 10-year passport at the **Passport Office,** Setanta Centre, Molesworth Street, Dublin 2 (✆ **01/671-1633;** www.irlgov.ie/iveagh). Those under age 18 and over 65 must apply for a 3-year passport. You can also apply at 1A South Mall, Cork (✆ **21/494-4700**) or at most main post offices.

For Residents of New Zealand You can pick up a passport application at any New Zealand Passports Office or download it from the website. Contact the **Passports Office** at ✆ **0800/225-050** in New Zealand or 04/474-8100, or log on to www.passports.govt.nz.

For Residents of the United Kingdom To pick up an application for a standard 10-year passport (5-yr. passport for children under 16), visit your nearest passport office, major post office, or travel agency or contact the **United Kingdom Passport Service** at ✆ **0870/521-0410** or search its website at www.ukpa.gov.uk.

For Residents of the United States: Whether you're applying in person or by mail, you can download passport applications from the U.S. State Department website at **http://travel.state.gov**. To find your regional passport office, either check the U.S. State Department website or call the **National Passport Information Center** toll-free number (✆ **877/487-2778**) for automated information.

POLICE In case of emergencies, dial ✆ **911.** For local police stations, see chapters 6, 7, and 8.

SMOKING New Mexico recently outlawed smoking at indoor public places, including restaurants and nightclubs. Some hotels offer rooms which allow smoking, though the number of these is dwindling.

TAXES Please see chapters 6, 7, and 8 for specifics about city taxes. The United States has no value-added tax (VAT) or other indirect tax at the national level. Every state, county, and city may levy its own local tax on all purchases, including hotel and restaurant checks and airline tickets. These taxes will not appear on price tags.

TELEGRAPH, TELEX & FAX **Telegraph and telex services** are provided primarily by **Western Union** (✆ **800/325-6000;** www.westernunion.com). You can telegraph (wire) money, or have it telegraphed to you, very quickly over the Western Union system, but this service can cost as much as 15% to 20% of the amount sent.

Most hotels have **fax machines** available for guest use (be sure to ask about the charge to use them). Many hotel rooms are wired for guests' fax machines. A less expensive way to send and receive faxes may be at stores such as the **UPS Store.**

TELEPHONES Many convenience groceries and packaging services sell **prepaid calling cards** in denominations up to $50; for international visitors these can be the least expensive way to call home. Many public pay phones at airports now accept American Express, MasterCard, and Visa credit cards. **Local calls** made from pay phones in most locales cost either 25¢ or 35¢ (no pennies, please). Most long-distance and international calls can be dialed directly from any phone. **For calls within the United States and to Canada,** dial 1 followed by the area code and the seven-digit number. **For other international calls,** dial 011 followed by the country code, city code, and the number you are calling.

Calls to area codes **800, 888, 877,** and **866** are toll-free. However, calls to area codes **700** and **900** (chat lines, bulletin boards, "dating" services, and so on) can be very expensive—usually a charge of 95¢ to $3 or more per minute, and they sometimes have minimum charges that can run as high as $15 or more.

For **reversed-charge or collect calls,** and for person-to-person calls, dial the number 0 then the area code and number; an operator will come on the line, and you should specify whether you are calling collect, person-to-person, or both. If your operator-assisted call is international, ask for the overseas operator.

For **local directory assistance** ("information"), dial 411; for long-distance information, dial 1, then the appropriate area code, and 555-1212.

TIME The continental United States is divided into **four time zones:** Eastern Standard Time (EST), Central Standard Time (CST), Mountain Standard Time (MST), and Pacific Standard Time (PST). Alaska and Hawaii have their own zones. For example, when it's 9am in Los Angeles (PST), it's 7am in Honolulu (HST), 10am in Denver (MST), 11am in Chicago (CST), noon in New York City (EST), 5pm in London (GMT), and 2am the next day in Sydney.

New Mexico is on Mountain Standard Time (MST), 7 hours behind Greenwich Mean Time. **Daylight saving time** is in effect from 1am on the second Sunday in March to 1am on the first Sunday in November, except in Arizona, Hawaii, the U.S. Virgin Islands, and Puerto Rico. Daylight saving time moves the clock 1 hour ahead of standard time.

TIPPING Tips are a very important part of certain workers' income, and gratuities are the standard way of showing appreciation for services provided. (Tipping is certainly not compulsory if the service is poor!) In hotels, tip **bellhops** at least $1 per bag ($2–$3 if you have a lot of luggage) and tip the **chamber staff** $1 to $2 per day (more if you've left a disaster area for him or her to clean up). Tip the **doorman** or **concierge** only if he or she has provided you with some specific service (for example, calling a cab for you or obtaining difficult-to-get theater tickets). Tip the **valet-parking attendant** $1 every time you get your car.

In restaurants, bars, and nightclubs, tip **service staff** 15% to 20% of the check, tip **bartenders** 10% to 15%, tip **checkroom attendants** $1 per garment, and tip **valet-parking attendants** $1 per vehicle.

As for other service personnel, tip **cab drivers** 15% of the fare; tip **skycaps** at airports at least $1 per bag ($2–$3 if you have a lot of luggage); and tip **hairdressers** and **barbers** 15% to 20%.

TOILETS You won't find public toilets or "restrooms" on the streets in most U.S. cities but they can be found in hotel lobbies, bars, restaurants, museums, department stores, railway and bus stations, and service stations. Large hotels and fast-food restaurants are often the best bet for clean facilities. Restaurants and bars in resorts or heavily visited areas may reserve their restrooms for patrons.

USEFUL PHONE NUMBERS **U.S. Dept. of State Travel Advisory:** ✆ 202/647-5225 (manned 24 hr.). **U.S. Passport Agency:** ✆ 202/647-0518. **U.S. Centers for Disease Control International Traveler's Hotline:** ✆ 404/332-4559.

VISAS For information about U.S. Visas go to **http://travel.state.gov** and click on "Visas." Or go to one of the following websites:

Australian citizens can obtain up-to-date visa information from the **U.S. Embassy Canberra,** Moonah Place, Yarralumla, ACT 2600 (✆ **02/6214-5600**) or by checking the U.S. Diplomatic Mission's website at **http://usembassy-australia.state.gov/consular**.

British subjects can obtain up-to-date visa information by calling the **U.S. Embassy Visa Information Line** (✆ **0891/200-290**) or by visiting the "Visas to the U.S." section of the American Embassy London's website at **www.usembassy.org.uk**.

Irish citizens can obtain up-to-date visa information through the **Embassy of the USA Dublin,** 42 Elgin Rd., Dublin 4, Ireland (✆ **353/1-668-8777**) or by checking the "Consular Services" section of the website at **http://dublin.usembassy.gov**.

Citizens of **New Zealand** can obtain up-to-date visa information by contacting the **U.S. Embassy New Zealand,** 29 Fitzherbert Terrace, Thorndon, Wellington (✆ **644/472-2068**), or get the information directly from the website at **http://wellington.usembassy.gov**.

2 TOLL-FREE NUMBERS & WEBSITES

MAJOR U.S. AIRLINES

An asterisk (*) below indicates an airline that flies internationally as well.

American Airlines*
✆ 800/433-7300 (in U.S. or Canada)
✆ 020/7365-0777 (in U.K.)
www.aa.com

Continental Airlines*
✆ 800/523-3273 (in U.S. or Canada)
✆ 084/5607-6760 (in U.K.)
www.continental.com

Delta Air Lines*
✆ 800/221-1212 (in U.S. or Canada)
✆ 084/5600-0950 (in U.K.)
www.delta.com

Frontier Airlines
✆ 800/432-1359
www.frontierairlines.com

Northwest Airlines
✆ 800/225-2525 (in U.S.)
✆ 870/0507-4074 (in U.K.)
www.flynaa.com

United Airlines*
✆ 800/864-8331 (in U.S. or Canada)
✆ 084/5844-4777 (in U.K.)
www.united.com

US Airways*
✆ 800/428-4322 (in U.S. or Canada)
✆ 084/5600-3300 (in U.K.)
www.usairways.com

MAJOR INTERNATIONAL AIRLINES

American Airlines
✆ 800/433-7300 (in U.S. or Canada)
✆ 020/7365-0777 (in U.K.)
www.aa.com

Continental Airlines
✆ 800/523-3273 (in U.S. or Canada)
✆ 084/5607-6760 (in U.K.)
www.continental.com

Delta Air Lines
✆ 800/221-1212 (in U.S. or Canada)
✆ 084/5600-0950 (in U.K.)
www.delta.com

Frontier Airlines
✆ 800/432-1359
www.frontierairlines.com

Southwest Airlines
✆ 800/435-9792 (in U.S., U.K., or Canada)
www.southwest.com

United Airlines*
✆ 800/864-8331 (in U.S. or Canada)
✆ 084/5844-4777 (in U.K.)
www.united.com

US Airways*
✆ 800/428-4322 (in U.S. or Canada)
✆ 084/5600-3300 (in U.K.)
www.usairways.com

CAR RENTAL AGENCIES

Advantage
✆ 800/777-5500 (in U.S.)
✆ 021/0344-4712 (outside of U.S.)
www.advantagerentacar.com

Alamo
✆ 800/GO-ALAMO (800/462-5266)
www.alamo.com

Avis
✆ 800/331-1212 (in U.S. or Canada)
✆ 084/4581-8181 (in U.K.)
www.avis.com

Budget
✆ 800/527-0700 (in U.S.)
✆ 087/0156-5656 (in U.K.)
✆ 800/268-8900 (in Canada)
www.budget.com

Dollar
✆ 800/800-4000 (in U.S.)
✆ 800/848-8268 (in Canada)
✆ 080/8234-7524 (in U.K.)
www.dollar.com

Enterprise
✆ 800/261-7331 (in U.S.)
✆ 514/355-4028 (in Canada)
✆ 012/9360-9090 (in U.K.)
www.enterprise.com

Hertz
✆ 800/645-3131
✆ 800/654-3001 (for international reservations)
www.hertz.com

National
✆ 800/CAR-RENT (800/227-7368)
www.nationalcar.com

Rent-A-Wreck
✆ 800/535-1391
www.rentawreck.com

Thrifty
✆ 800/367-2277
✆ 918/669-2168 (international)
www.thrifty.com

MAJOR HOTEL & MOTEL CHAINS

Best Western International
✆ 800/780-7234 (in U.S. or Canada)
✆ 0800/393-130 (in U.K.)
www.bestwestern.com

Clarion Hotels
✆ 800/CLARION or 877/424-6423 (in U.S. or Canada)
✆ 0800/444-444 (in U.K.)
www.choicehotels.com

Comfort Inns
✆ 800/228-5150
✆ 0800/444-444 (in U.K.)
www.comfortinnchoicehotels.com

Courtyard by Marriott
✆ 888/236-2427 (in U.S.)
✆ 0800/221-222 (in U.K.)
www.marriott.com/courtyard

Crowne Plaza Hotels
✆ 888/303-1746
www.ichotelsgroup.com/crowneplaza

Days Inn
✆ 800/329-7466 (in U.S.)
✆ 0800/280-400 (in U.K.)
www.daysinn.com

Doubletree Hotels
✆ 800/222-TREE (800/222-8733; in U.S. or Canada)
✆ 087/0590-9090 (in U.K.)
www.doubletree.com

Econo Lodges
✆ 800/55-ECONO (800/552-3666)
www.choicehotels.com

Embassy Suites
✆ 800/EMBASSY (800/362-2779)
www.embassysuites.hilton.com

Fairfield Inn by Marriott
✆ 800/228-2800 (in U.S. or Canada)
✆ 0800/221-222 (in U.K.)
www.marriott.com/fairfieldinn

Four Seasons
✆ 800/819-5053 (in U.S. or Canada)
✆ 0800/6488-6488 (in U.K.)
www.fourseasons.com

Hampton Inn
✆ 800/HAMPTON (800/426-4766)
www.hamptoninn.hilton.com

Hilton Hotels
✆ 800/HILTONS (800/445-8667; in U.S. or Canada)
✆ 087/0590-9090 (in U.K.)
www.hilton.com

Holiday Inn
✆ 800/315-2621 (in U.S. or Canada)
✆ 0800/405-060 (in U.K.)
www.holidayinn.com

Howard Johnson
✆ 800/446-4656 (in U.S. or Canada)
www.hojo.com

Hyatt
✆ 888/591-1234 (in U.S. or Canada)
✆ 084/5888-1234 (in U.K.)
www.hyatt.com

InterContinental Hotels & Resorts
✆ 800/424-6835 (in U.S. or Canada)
✆ 0800/1800-1800 (in U.K.)
www.ichotelsgroup.com

La Quinta Inns and Suites
✆ 800/642-4271 (in U.S. or Canada)
www.lq.com

Marriott
© 877/236-2427 (in U.S. or Canada)
© 0800/221-222 (in U.K.)
www.marriott.com

Motel 6
© 800/4MOTEL6 (800/466-8356)
www.motel6.com

Quality
© 877/424-6423 (in U.S. or Canada)
© 0800/444-444 (in U.K.)
www.qualityinn.choicehotels.com

Radisson Hotels & Resorts
© 888/201-1718 (in U.S. or Canada)
© 0800/374-411 (in U.K.)
www.radisson.com

Ramada Worldwide
© 888/2-RAMADA (888/272-6232; in U.S. or Canada)
© 080/8100-0783 (in U.K.)
www.ramada.com

Red Roof Inns
© 866/686-4335 (in U.S. or Canada)
© 614/601-4075 (international)
www.redroof.com

Residence Inn by Marriott
© 800/331-3131
© 800/221-222 (in U.K.)
www.marriott.com/residenceinn

Rodeway Inns
© 877/424-6423
www.rodewayinn.choicehotels.com

Sheraton Hotels & Resorts
© 800/325-3535 (in U.S.)
© 800/543-4300 (in Canada)
© 0800/3253-5353 (in U.K.)
www.starwoodhotels.com/sheraton

Super 8 Motels
© 800/800-8000
www.super8.com

Travelodge
© 1-800-578-7878
www.travelodge.com

Vagabond Inns
© 800/522-1555
www.vagabondinn.com

Westin Hotels & Resorts
© 800-937-8461 (in U.S. or Canada)
© 0800/3259-5959 (in U.K.)
www.starwoodhotels.com/westin

Wyndham Hotels & Resorts
© 877/999-3223 (in U.S. or Canada)
© 050/6638-4899 (in U.K.)
www.wyndham.com

INDEX

A Guide for Every Type of Travel

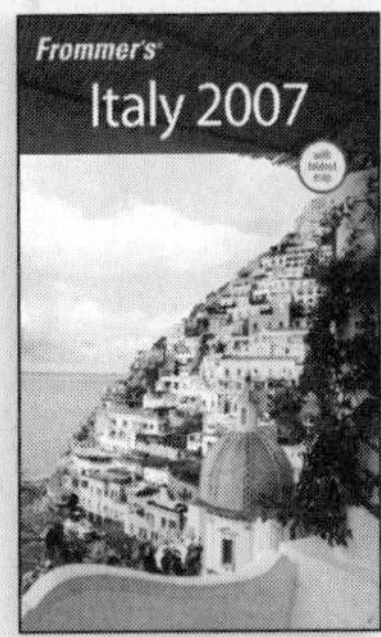

Frommer's Complete Guides
For those who value complete coverage, candid advice, and lots of choices in all price ranges.

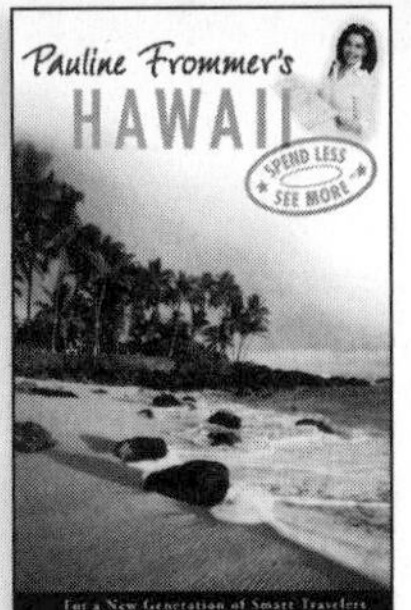

Pauline Frommer's Guides
For those who want to experience a culture, meet locals, and save money along the way.

MTV Guides
For hip, youthful travelers who want a fresh perspective on today's hottest cities and destinations.

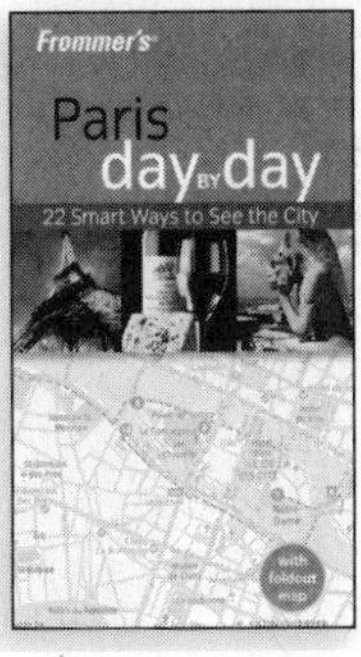

Day by Day Guides
For leisure or business travelers who want to organize their time to get the most out of a trip.

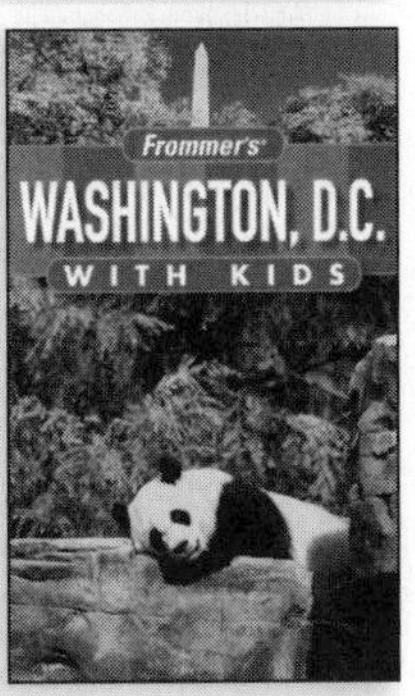

Frommer's With Kids Guides
For families traveling with children ages 2 to 14 seeking kid-friendly hotels, restaurants, and activities.

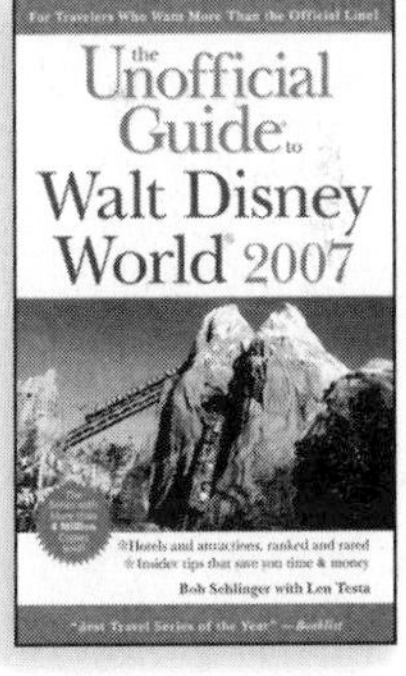

Unofficial Guides
For honeymooners, families, business travelers, and others who value no-nonsense, *Consumer Reports*–style advice.

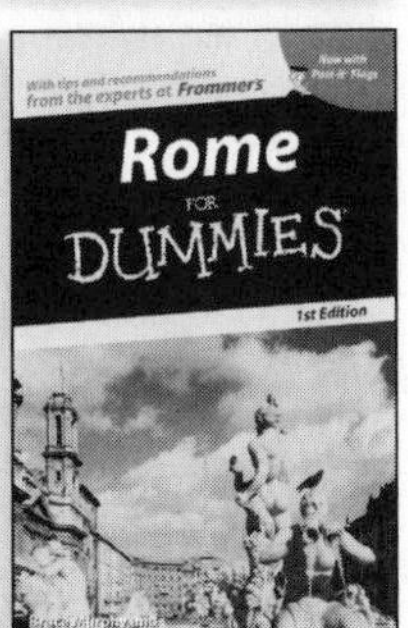

For Dummies Travel Guides
For curious, independent travelers looking for a fun and easy way to plan a trip.

Visit Frommers.com

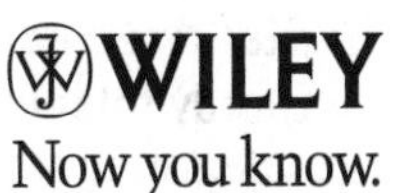

Frommer's® Complete Travel Guides

Alaska
Amalfi Coast
American Southwest
Amsterdam
Argentina
Arizona
Atlanta
Australia
Austria
Bahamas
Barcelona
Beijing
Belgium, Holland & Luxembourg
Belize
Bermuda
Boston
Brazil
British Columbia & the Canadian Rockies
Brussels & Bruges
Budapest & the Best of Hungary
Buenos Aires
Calgary
California
Canada
Cancún, Cozumel & the Yucatán
Cape Cod, Nantucket & Martha's Vineyard
Caribbean
Caribbean Ports of Call
Carolinas & Georgia
Chicago
Chile & Easter Island
China
Colorado
Costa Rica
Croatia
Cuba
Denmark
Denver, Boulder & Colorado Springs
Eastern Europe
Ecuador & the Galapagos Islands
Edinburgh & Glasgow
England
Europe
Europe by Rail
Florence, Tuscany & Umbria
Florida
France
Germany
Greece
Greek Islands
Guatemala
Hawaii
Hong Kong
Honolulu, Waikiki & Oahu
India
Ireland
Israel
Italy
Jamaica
Japan
Kauai
Las Vegas
London
Los Angeles
Los Cabos & Baja
Madrid
Maine Coast
Maryland & Delaware
Maui
Mexico
Montana & Wyoming
Montréal & Québec City
Morocco
Moscow & St. Petersburg
Munich & the Bavarian Alps
Nashville & Memphis
New England
Newfoundland & Labrador
New Mexico
New Orleans
New York City
New York State
New Zealand
Northern Italy
Norway
Nova Scotia, New Brunswick & Prince Edward Island
Oregon
Paris
Peru
Philadelphia & the Amish Country
Portugal
Prague & the Best of the Czech Republic
Provence & the Riviera
Puerto Rico
Rome
San Antonio & Austin
San Diego
San Francisco
Santa Fe, Taos & Albuquerque
Scandinavia
Scotland
Seattle
Seville, Granada & the Best of Andalusia
Shanghai
Sicily
Singapore & Malaysia
South Africa
South America
South Florida
South Korea
South Pacific
Southeast Asia
Spain
Sweden
Switzerland
Tahiti & French Polynesia
Texas
Thailand
Tokyo
Toronto
Turkey
USA
Utah
Vancouver & Victoria
Vermont, New Hampshire & Maine
Vienna & the Danube Valley
Vietnam
Virgin Islands
Virginia
Walt Disney World® & Orlando
Washington, D.C.
Washington State

Frommer's® Day by Day Guides

Amsterdam
Barcelona
Beijing
Boston
Cancun & the Yucatan
Chicago
Florence & Tuscany
Hong Kong
Honolulu & Oahu
London
Maui
Montréal
Napa & Sonoma
New York City
Paris
Provence & the Riviera
Rome
San Francisco
Venice
Washington D.C.

Pauline Frommer's Guides: See More. Spend Less.

Alaska
Hawaii
Italy
Las Vegas
London
New York City
Paris
Walt Disney World®
Washington D.C.

Frommer's® Portable Guides

Acapulco, Ixtapa & Zihuatanejo
Amsterdam
Aruba, Bonaire & Curacao
Australia's Great Barrier Reef
Bahamas
Big Island of Hawaii
Boston
California Wine Country
Cancún
Cayman Islands
Charleston
Chicago
Dominican Republic
Florence
Las Vegas
Las Vegas for Non-Gamblers
London
Maui
Nantucket & Martha's Vineyard
New Orleans
New York City
Paris
Portland
Puerto Rico
Puerto Vallarta, Manzanillo & Guadalajara
Rio de Janeiro
San Diego
San Francisco
Savannah
St. Martin, Sint Maarten, Anguila & St. Bart's
Turks & Caicos
Vancouver
Venice
Virgin Islands
Washington, D.C.
Whistler

Frommer's® Cruise Guides

Alaska Cruises & Ports of Call
Cruises & Ports of Call
European Cruises & Ports of Call

Frommer's® National Park Guides

Algonquin Provincial Park
Banff & Jasper
Grand Canyon
National Parks of the American West
Rocky Mountain
Yellowstone & Grand Teton
Yosemite and Sequoia & Kings Canyon
Zion & Bryce Canyon

Frommer's® With Kids Guides

Chicago
Hawaii
Las Vegas
London
National Parks
New York City
San Francisco
Toronto
Walt Disney World® & Orlando
Washington, D.C.

Frommer's® PhraseFinder Dictionary Guides

Chinese
French
German
Italian
Japanese
Spanish

Suzy Gershman's Born to Shop Guides

France
Hong Kong, Shanghai & Beijing
Italy
London
New York
Paris
San Francisco
Where to Buy the Best of Everything.

Frommer's® Best-Loved Driving Tours

Britain
California
France
Germany
Ireland
Italy
New England
Northern Italy
Scotland
Spain
Tuscany & Umbria

The Unofficial Guides®

Adventure Travel in Alaska
Beyond Disney
California with Kids
Central Italy
Chicago
Cruises
Disneyland®
England
Hawaii
Ireland
Las Vegas
London
Maui
Mexico's Best Beach Resorts
Mini Mickey
New Orleans
New York City
Paris
San Francisco
South Florida including Miami & the Keys
Walt Disney World®
Walt Disney World® for Grown-ups
Walt Disney World® with Kids
Washington, D.C.

Special-Interest Titles

Athens Past & Present
Best Places to Raise Your Family
Cities Ranked & Rated
500 Places to Take Your Kids Before They Grow Up
Frommer's Best Day Trips from London
Frommer's Best RV & Tent Campgrounds in the U.S.A.
Frommer's Exploring America by RV
Frommer's NYC Free & Dirt Cheap
Frommer's Road Atlas Europe
Frommer's Road Atlas Ireland
Retirement Places Rated